10 0788910 7

KU-794-046

Simply Psychology

Simply Psychology, fourth edition, is an engaging and reader-friendly introduction to the key principles of psychology. Organized around the major
approaches to the subject, it covers biological, developmental, social, and cognitive psychology, as well as individual differences.

Supported by a wealth of colour illustrations, it provides students new to
the subject with straightforward and clear explanations of all the key topics
within contemporary psychology. The features spread throughout the book are
designed to help readers to engage with the material and include:

- highlighted key terms and comprehensive glossary
- chapter introductions and summaries
- further reading and evaluation boxes
- structured essay and self-assessment questions
- case-studies and examples illustrating the application of key theories

It also concludes with a practical chapter that offers students tips and advice
to help them improve their study skills and get the most out of the book and
their studies.

New for the fourth edition

- expanded coverage of abnormal psychology
- coverage of developments in neuroscience
- new 'In the real world' feature showing how psychology can be used in a
  range of professional contexts

Simply Psychology is ideal for students studying psychology for the first time,
as well as those in related fields such as nursing, social work and the social
sciences.

Michael W. Eysenck is one of the best-known psychologists in Europe. He is
Emeritus Professor of Psychology in the psychology department at Royal Holloway University of London and Professorial Fellow at Roehampton University.
He is especially interested in cognitive psychology (about which he has written
several books) and most of his research focuses on the role of cognitive factors
in anxiety within normal and clinical populations.

Simply Psychology

Fourth Edition

Michael W. Eysenck

GEORGE GREEN LIBRARY OF
SCIENCE AND ENGINEERING

Routledge
Taylor & Francis Group

LONDON AND NEW YORK

Fourth edition published 2018
by Routledge
2 Park Square, Milton Park, Abingdon, Oxon, OX14 4RN

and by Routledge
711 Third Avenue, New York, NY 10017

Routledge is an imprint of the Taylor & Francis Group, an informa business

© 2018 Michael W. Eysenck

The right of Michael W. Eysenck to be identified as author of this work has been asserted by him in accordance with sections 77 and 78 of the Copyright, Designs and Patents Act 1988.

All rights reserved. No part of this book may be reprinted or reproduced or utilised in any form or by any electronic, mechanical, or other means, now known or hereafter invented, including photocopying and recording, or in any information storage or retrieval system, without permission in writing from the publishers.

Trademark notice: Product or corporate names may be trademarks or registered trademarks, and are used only for identification and explanation without intent to infringe.

First edition published by Psychology Press 1996
Third edition published by Routledge 2013

British Library Cataloguing-in-Publication Data
A catalogue record for this book is available from the British Library

10078891o7

Library of Congress Cataloging-in-Publication Data
A catalog record for this book has been requested

ISBN: 978-1-138-69895-6 (hbk)
ISBN: 978-1-138-69896-3 (pbk)
ISBN: 978-1-315-51793-3 (ebk)

Typeset in Sabon
by Apex CoVantage, LLC

Printed and bound in Great Britain
by Bell and Bain Ltd, Glasgow

Visit the companion website: www.routledge.com/cw/eysenck

Contents

About the author   *vii*
Preface   *ix*

1   Introduction   3
2   History of psychology   17
3   Methods of investigation   41

Part 1   **Biological approach**   **57**
4   Biological bases of behaviour   59
5   Stress   75
6   Emotion   93
7   Aggression   105

Part 2   **Developmental approach**   **121**
8   Cognitive development   123
9   Language development   137
10   Moral development   149
11   Sex and gender   163

Part 3   **Social approach**   **177**
12   Attachment and deprivation   179
13   Prejudice and discrimination   195
14   Prosocial behaviour   211
15   Social influence   227
16   Social perception and attraction   245

Part 4   **Individual differences**   **261**
17   Intelligence   263
18   Personality   279
19   The self-concept   293

Part 5   **Cognitive approach**   **307**
20 Abnormal psychology   309
21 Visual perception   325
22 Memory   341
23 Problem solving, expertise, and creativity   361

Part 6   **Effective learning**   **379**
24 Effective studying and learning   381

Glossary   397
References   407
Index   443
Illustrations credits   455

About the author

Michael W. Eysenck is one of the best-known psychologists in Europe. He is Professorial Fellow at Roehampton University and Emeritus Professor at Royal Holloway, University of London. He is especially interested in cognitive psychology (about which he has written several books), and most of his research focuses on the role of cognitive factors in anxiety within normal and clinical populations.

He has published 52 books. His previous textbooks published by Psychology Press include *Psychology for AS Level (5th Edn)* (2012), *Psychology for A2 Level* (2009), *A2 Psychology: Key Topics (2nd Edn)* (2006), *Psychology: An International Perspective* (2004), *Psychology: A Student's Handbook (6th Edn)* (with Mark Keane) (2010), *Fundamentals of Psychology* (2009), *Fundamentals of Cognition (2nd Edn)* (2012), *Perspectives on Psychology* (1994), and *Individual Differences: Normal and Abnormal* (1994). He has also written several articles on topics within the AS Psychology specification for the journal *Psychology Review*, and has given talks at numerous A-level conferences.

In his spare time, Michael Eysenck enjoys travelling, croquet, walking, bridge, and an occasional game of golf. He is (unusually) a keen supporter of Crystal Palace and (less unusually) Manchester United Football Clubs.

Preface

There has been a dramatic increase in the number of students of psychology in recent years. This increase has happened at all levels, and includes GCSE, AS level, A level, and university degree courses. In addition, there are many more students of nursing, education, business studies, and so on, who study psychology as part of their courses. It is my hope that this book will be of use to all students who are starting to study psychology.

There are two main approaches to writing a simple introduction to psychology. One is to leave out everything that is hard or challenging; this is what might be called the "filleted" approach. The other is to present a more rounded account of modern psychology in a simple and accessible way. I have done my best to follow the second approach. Whether I have succeeded is for the readers of this book to decide.

This is the fourth edition of *Simply Psychology*. I have mostly retained the structure of previous editions. However, there are now new chapters focusing on abnormal psychology and the history of psychology. In addition, all the chapters have been extensively updated and some are very different from the previous edition.

In my opinion (I may be biased!), psychology is the most interesting subject you can study. An important part of my intention in this book is to try to convince you of that. Media coverage often makes it look as if psychologists have only succeeded in discovering things everyone has always known. I feel very strongly that this state of affairs tells us more about the media than about psychology. Hopefully, as you read this book, you will find yourself agreeing with me that psychological research goes considerably beyond the obvious. In fact, such research is full of important insights into human behaviour that can (and already have) benefited society greatly.

What could be more interesting or important than achieving a better understanding of our fellow human beings? Enjoy psychology!!!

Introduction

1

What is psychology?

Psychology is amazingly wide ranging – indeed, it is relevant to almost every-thing in our everyday lives as Sigmund Freud was the first to recognise. Here are just a few examples.

What is the science of psychology actually about?

Some psychologists are involved in treating mental disorders in increasingly effective ways. Forensic psychologists are engaged in offender profiling and tracking down serial killers and other criminals. Other psychologists use brain scanners to understand the workings of the human mind. Still other psychologists (healthy psychologists) are hard at work trying to persuade us to adopt healthier lifestyles with less smoking and drinking and more physical exercise.

What are the common elements in the very diverse activities of psychologists? Perhaps the most common definition of "psychology" is that it is the scientific study of behaviour. However, this definition is too limited because most psychologists try to understand *why* people behave in certain ways. This requires that they consider *internal* processes and motives. Thus, we arrive at the following definition:

> Psychology is a science in which behavioural and other evidence (e.g., individuals' reports of their thoughts and feelings, patterns of brain activation) is used to understand the internal processes leading people (and members of other species) to behave as they do.

As you read this book, you may find yourself bewildered (hopefully not *too* bewildered!) by the numerous approaches psychologists have adopted in their attempts to understand human behaviour. The main reason for these different approaches is because our behaviour is jointly determined by several factors, including the following:

- The specific stimuli presented to us
- Our recent experiences (e.g., being stuck in a traffic jam)
- Our genetic endowment
- Our physiological system
- Our cognitive system (our perceptions, thoughts, and memories)

- The social environment
- The cultural environment
- Our previous life experiences (including those of childhood)
- Our personal characteristics (including intelligence, personality, and mental health)

We can see the importance of the above factors by considering "road rage" (an angry motorist threatening physical violence to another motorist). His behaviour may depend partly on the genes he has inherited that led him to develop a very aggressive personality. It may depend in part on his childhood experiences, for example, the presence of violence in the family. It may depend in part on his clinical history (e.g., a history of psychopathic or antisocial behaviour).

Still other factors may be involved in causing a man to exhibit road rage. It may depend on his thoughts and feelings (e.g., the other motorist reminds him of someone he despises). It may depend on the man's physiological state. For example, his internal bodily state may be highly aroused and agitated because he is late for an important appointment or has a very stressful job. Finally, his behaviour may depend on cultural factors – expressing one's anger by physically attacking someone is less unacceptable in some cultures than others.

The take-home message is that there is no *single* "correct" interpretation of the man's road rage. Probably several factors just discussed contributed to his behaviour. Thus, the scope of psychology must be very broad to understand human behaviour. More generally, psychology is a multidisciplinary science that has been enriched by physiologists, neuroscientists, sociologists, biologists, biochemists, anthropologists, and others.

How useful is psychology?

Why is common sense of limited usefulness?

Most people think psychology is a fascinating subject (which it is!). We all want to understand ourselves and other people, and that is the central goal of psychology. However, there is much controversy concerning the usefulness of psychology. Sceptics argue that psychology tells us things we already know (the science of the bleeding obvious?). They also argue that laboratory findings often fail to generalise to everyday life because laboratory research is so artificial. Finally, sceptics claim most psychological research is trivial (e.g., rats running through mazes).

One of the most common criticisms of psychology is that it is "just common sense". There are three major problems with that criticism. First, common sense is based only on drawing conclusions that are based only on observations whereas psychology involves experimental testing and attempts to distinguish among alternative explanations of phenomena (Rutter & Solantaus, 2014). As is discussed in Chapter 3, laboratory research allows us to study behaviour under well-controlled conditions. As a result, we can identify the determinants of behaviour more clearly than is possible through simply observing people in everyday life. The advantages of experimental control (i.e., our ability to manipulate variables to see how they influence behaviour) typically outweigh any disadvantages of artificiality.

Note that it is not always possible to use the experimental method fully. More specifically, the experimental method can most easily be used when we want to study the effects of the *immediate situation* on behaviour. In addition to the immediate situation, however, our behaviour is also influenced by several other factors that cannot be manipulated. These factors include recent events (e.g., row with partner) or physical health, our personality, childhood events, genetic factors, cultural expectations, and so on.

Second, common sense does not form a coherent set of assumptions about behaviour. Consider the commonsensical views contained in proverbs. Several pairs of proverbs express opposite meanings to each other. For example, "Absence makes the heart grow fonder" can be contrasted with "Out of sight, out of mind", and "Many hands make light work" is the opposite of "Too many cooks spoil the broth". Since common sense involves such incompatible views, it cannot be used as a sound basis for understanding human behaviour.

Third, the notion that psychology is just common sense can be disproved by considering psychological research in which the findings differed greatly from what most people would have predicted. Here are two such findings. A well-known example is Milgram's (1974) research on obedience to authority. Participants were instructed to administer increasingly strong electric shocks to a middle-aged man with a heart condition (see Chapter 15). A psychiatrist predicted only one person in a thousand would administer the maximum and potentially lethal electric shock. In fact, 65% of Milgram's participants did do so – 650 times as many people as the expert had predicted!

Below is a short quiz so you can see for yourself whether the findings in psychology are obvious (many items are based on those used by Furnham, 1988). For each item, decide whether it is true or false:

Psychology quiz	
1. Flashbulb memories (i.e., vivid memories of dramatic world events like 9/11) are exceptionally accurate and long-lived.	TRUE/FALSE
2. In making decisions, committees tend to be more conservative than individuals.	TRUE/FALSE
3. In small amounts, alcohol is a stimulant.	TRUE/FALSE
4. Physically attractive adults have better social skills and physical health than unattractive ones.	TRUE/FALSE
5. Very intelligent children tend to be less strong physically than those of average intelligence.	TRUE/FALSE

6. Patients with amnesia have very poor long-term memory but can still acquire many skills such as learning the piano.	TRUE/FALSE
7. People's behaviour in most situations depends far more on their personality than the situation itself.	TRUE/FALSE
8. A schizophrenic is someone with a split personality.	TRUE/FALSE

The correct answer is "False" to most of the questions. However, the correct answer is "True" to questions 4 and 6. Unless you already know a lot about psychology, you probably had several wrong answers – thus, psychology is *not* simply common sense!

Hindsight bias

When is hindsight bias involved?

We have seen that many findings in psychology do *not* correspond to common sense. Why, then, do so many people claim such findings are unsurprising or obvious? In other words, why do they argue, "I knew it all along"? The answer lies in a phenomenon known as **hindsight bias**. When you know some outcome (e.g., Leicester City winning the Premiership in 2016), you believe you regarded that outcome as much more likely beforehand than was actually the case. Even warning people in advance about hindsight bias generally does not reduce it (Pohl & Hell, 1996).

What causes hindsight bias? One reason is that information about what has actually happened alters the memory for what had been *expected* ahead of the event itself (Hardt et al., 2010). This helps to explain why it is very hard to prevent hindsight bias. Pohl and Hell (1996) found that warning people in advance about hindsight bias did not reduce the bias at all. There are also motivational reasons – most people prefer order and predictability in their lives, and hindsight bias satisfies those preferences (Roese & Vohs, 2012).

The prevalence of hindsight bias is a problem for teachers of psychology. What it does is to produce students who are unimpressed by most findings in psychology!

Findings: simple and complex

In spite of the existence of hindsight bias, I must admit some findings in psychology are actually obvious. For example, you will not be surprised to hear that practice has beneficial effects on long-term memory.

So far I have only provided you with a *simple* finding relating to the effects of practice. The findings are much less obvious when we consider more *complex* issues. Suppose you need to remember material from a textbook for a test next week. Is it better to spend nearly all your time studying the material or to spend some time studying the material but most of it testing how much you can remember? Most people think the former strategy is better. However, the evidence indicates the latter is typically superior (Karpicke et al., 2009; see Chapter 24).

In sum, simple findings in psychology are often fairly obvious. However, that is rarely the case with more complex findings, which are generally hard for non-psychologists to predict or to explain.

KEY TERM

Hindsight bias: the tendency to be wise after the event using the benefit of hindsight

Cross-cultural psychology

Planet Earth is home to over seven billion people living in a huge range of cultures and conditions. However, this richness and diversity is not reflected in psychological research, the overwhelming majority of which has been on people from Western, Educated, Industrialised, Rich, and Democratic (WEIRD) societies (Henrich et al., 2010). WEIRD societies account for only 12% of the world's population, but 96% of the participants in research published in leading psychology journals are from these societies (Arnett, 2008). The United States alone has 5% of the world's population but 68% of the research participants.

Why is it is important to study cross-cultural differences?

Cross-cultural psychology is concerned with the major differences across the world's cultures. What is a **culture**? It is "a way of life, often equated with shared knowledge or what one needs to know to live successfully in a community" (Ojalehto & Medin, 2015, p. 250). Next, we consider some major aspects of cross-cultural psychology. Note that a culture is by no means the same as a country. Indeed, there are several cultures *within* countries such as the United Kingdom or United States.

As people and cultures are so diverse, psychologists must take care not to overgeneralise their findings to everyone without sufficient evidence.

There are large differences in attitudes and behaviour across cultures and countries (see Henrich et al., 2010, for a review). As Westen (1996, p. 679) pointed out, "By twentieth century Western standards, nearly every human who has ever lived outside the contemporary West is lazy, passive, and lacking in industriousness. In contrast, by the standards of most cultures in human history, most Westerners are self-centred and frenetic." Since those living in WEIRD societies are not remotely representative of the world's population as a whole, it is ill-advised to generalise from them to the rest of mankind.

How do cultures differ?

There is an important distinction between individualistic and collectivistic cultures. **Individualistic cultures** emphasise independence, personal responsibility, and each person's uniqueness. In contrast, **collectivistic cultures** emphasise interdependence, sharing of responsibility, and group membership.

There are various limitations with the distinction between individualistic and collectivistic cultures. First, the concepts of individualism and collectivism are very broad. For example, as Fiske (2002, p. 83) pointed out, "IND [individualism] amalgamates Thomas Paine, Vincent van Gogh, Mahatma Gandhi, Michael Jordan, Hugh Hefner, and Adolf Hitler into one category!" Second, what is true at the cultural level is not necessarily the case at the level of individuals within that culture. Triandis et al. (2001) found only 60% of those living in individualistic cultures had individualistic beliefs, and only 60% of those in collectivistic cultures had collectivistic beliefs.

Recent research by Saucier et al. (2015) covering 33 countries suggests other cross-cultural differences are more important. Cultural differences in

KEY TERMS

Cross-cultural psychology: the systematic study of similarities in (and differences among) cultures around the world.

Culture: the values, beliefs, and practices shared by members of a given society.

Individualistic cultures: cultures (mainly in Western societies) in which the focus is on personal responsibility rather than group needs.

Collectivistic cultures: cultures (such as many in the Far East) in which the focus is on group solidarity rather than individual responsibility.

religious beliefs and practices were much greater than those in individualism-collectivism. Why might that be? Religious beliefs play a major role in individuals' moral judgments, how they treat members of other groups, and how they perceive themselves (Cohen, 2015).

Cultural influences: fixed or flexible?

As Hong et al. (2000, p. 709) pointed out, "Cultural knowledge is [typically] conceptualised to be like a contact lens that affects the individual's perceptions of visual stimuli all the time." In other words, it is generally assumed that our culture has a fixed and constant impact on us. That assumption is incorrect. Cultural influences affect us most when we are in situations making culture-relevant information easily accessible. For example, you may identify more with your own culture when you hear the national anthem than at other times.

Brannon et al. (2015) used a game (the Prisoner's Dilemma) in which participants decided whether to behave cooperatively or in a self-interested way. The participants (African Americans) were presented with images related to American (e.g., image of classic American food) or African American (e.g., image of African American soul food) culture. They were much less likely to make cooperative decisions when primed with American images. These findings showed the predicted flexibility in cultural influences – images related to American culture produced more self-interested behaviour whereas those related to African American culture produced more cooperative behaviour.

Conclusions

Since people's behaviour is strongly influenced by their culture, we must be cautious about assuming that findings obtained in American or European studies are applicable elsewhere. It is also important not to assume that some cultures are superior to others (e.g., Western cultures are "developed" whereas non-Western ones are "undeveloped"). It is arguable that there is "a materially advanced but spiritually bankrupt culture in the West, a spiritually developed and relatively socially stagnant culture in the East, and a developed social consciousness, but relatively undeveloped material culture in Africa" (Owusu-Bempah & Hewitt, 1994, p. 165).

Why is psychology important?

Psychology is important because it addresses issues of enormous significance to us such as how to understand ourselves and others better so as to enrich and enhance our lives. Another major reason why psychology is important is because it has numerous applications to everyday life. Applications of special importance can be found in clinical and health psychology. We will consider both briefly.

Clinical psychology

Mental disorders cause untold human misery to tens of millions of people around the world every year. For many centuries, it was believed that mental disorders were caused by demons or other supernatural forces. Popular "cures" for mental illness involved making things as unpleasant as possible for the demons. The techniques used included immersing the patient in boiling hot water, flogging, starvation, and torture. It was (erroneously) believed these "cures" would persuade the demons to leave the patient's body and so remove their disorder.

The turning point in treatment of mental disorders came in the early years of the twentieth century when Sigmund Freud developed psychoanalysis as a form of therapy (see Chapters 2 and 20). His great insight was that the best way to treat mental disorders was by using psychological techniques. In the century or so since then, clinical psychology has contributed enormously to the treatment of mental disorders. Of the numerous forms of psychological therapy developed during the twentieth century, cognitive behavioural therapy is of particular importance (see Chapter 20). Unsurprisingly, this form of therapy focuses on cognitive factors (i.e., changing patients' negative views about themselves and their lives). It also focuses on behavioural factors (i.e., changing patients' undesirable patterns of behaviour into desirable ones).

Are all psychological forms of therapy effective? The most common way of answering that question involves the use of **meta-analysis** based on the findings from numerous studies. Matt and Navarro (1997) considered 63 meta-analyses in which different forms of therapy had been compared. Overall, 75% of patients receiving therapy based on psychological principles improved more than the average untreated control patient, and there were only modest differences in the effectiveness of different therapies.

Most studies have concluded that all forms of psychological therapy are comparably effective in the treatment of mental disorders. This has been called the "Dodo Bird verdict" – in *Alice in Wonderland*, the Dodo Bird declared after a race that "Everyone has won, and all must have prizes". However, a recent meta-analysis by Marcus et al. (2014) came to a somewhat different conclusion. They found that all major forms of therapy were effective, but in general, cognitive behavioural therapy was the most effective.

Depression and anxiety

The most common mental disorders worldwide are depression and anxiety disorders. Between 5% and 8% of the European population suffer from clinical depression during any given year (Andlin-Sobocki et al., 2005), and the figure

Sigmund Freud.

KEY TERM

Meta-analysis: an analysis in which the findings from many studies are combined statistically to obtain an overall picture

is 12% for anxiety disorders (Andlin-Sobocki & Wittchen, 2005). Overall, 75 million Europeans currently suffer from anxiety and/or depression.

Apart from the cost in human misery, there are also very large financial costs. The total annual cost of mental disorders within Europe is 240 billion euros (about £190 or $289 billion) when account is taken of lost workdays and productivity loss.

What would happen if all Europeans suffering from anxiety or depression received effective psychological therapy? We cannot provide a precise answer. However, it is indisputable that tens of millions of patients would benefit from such therapy every year. In addition, the cost savings would run into tens of billions of pounds.

Summary

Many different forms of psychological therapy have proved to be consistently effective in treating mental disorders. There is reasonable evidence that cognitive behavioural therapy is more effective than any other form of therapy in the treatment of many mental disorders. Since 75 million Europeans suffer from anxiety and/or depression at any given time, there is enormous scope for psychological therapies to enhance psychological well-being across Europe. This enhanced psychological well-being could increase the Gross National Product of European countries by enabling millions of individuals to work more effectively.

Health psychology

In England and Wales, there were 68,000 fewer deaths from heart disease in 2000 than 1981 (Ünal et al., 2005). This reduction has produced a total gain of about 925,415 life years. There are two major possible explanations for this reduced mortality. First, there have been many important advances in medicine (e.g., use of statins; more precise and effective surgical interventions). Second, there have been many changes in lifestyle. Most are clearly beneficial (e.g., reductions in smoking), but others have adverse effects (e.g., increased obesity).

What percentage of the reduced mortality from heart disease reported by Ünal et al. (2005) is due to medical advances and what percentage to lifestyle changes influencing the risk of heart disease? The answer may surprise you – only 21% of the gain in life years was due to improved medical interventions compared to 79% due to lifestyle changes (Ünal et al., 2005).

What is the relevance of the above study to psychology? Lifestyle changes involve altering behaviour and so fall within psychology. Many health psychologists specialise in designing interventions to promote healthy lifestyles. The lifestyle change having by far the greatest impact on reduced mortality from heart disease (almost 45% of the total gain in life years) was a reduction in the number of people smoking.

Viswesvaran and Schmidt (1992) reviewed 633 smoking cessation studies. The annual success rate achieved by health psychologists was 30% with multi-component packages (e.g., basic counselling; information on the health effects of smoking; social skills training). This compared to only 6% for smokers receiving no treatment. If all 10 million smokers in the UK received multi-component smoking cessation packages from health psychologists, this could produce a gain of 24 *million* life years!

Most interventions used by health psychologists are labour-intensive and so relatively expensive. An effective but much less costly intervention was used by

Simmons et al. (2013). In essence, smokers produced a short video emphasising negative aspects of smoking. This intervention was designed to produce conflict between the views they expressed (which were made publicly available on the Internet) and their smoking behaviour. This inexpensive intervention was very effective: 33% of daily smokers were non-smokers 6 months later compared to only 12% of smokers in the control condition. It would be feasible in the future to use this Internet-based approach with large numbers of smokers.

Healthy diet

An area in which health psychologists have an increasing role to play is that of healthy eating. There has been a dramatic increase in obesity through most of the Western world in recent times, and it is predicted that 50% of the British male population will be obese in 2030. Indeed, we might say that obesity is a huge problem. Since obesity increases the likelihood of many serious diseases (e.g., diabetes; heart disease), it is important to persuade people to have a healthy diet.

Researchers have used implementation intentions to encourage individuals to eat more healthily. Implementation intentions are action plans that specify where, when, and how someone is going to achieve a certain goal (see Chapter 24). Here is an implementation intention relating to healthy eating: "If I am at home and I want to have some dessert after dinner, then I will make myself a fruit salad" (Adriaanse et al., 2011b, p. 184).

Many researchers have compared the effectiveness in promoting a healthy diet of implementation intentions against vague intentions such as "I want to eat more fruit". Adriaanse et al. (2011b) reviewed the relevant studies. Implementation intentions were much more effective than vague intentions in increasing healthy eating and decreasing unhealthy eating.

Why are implementation intentions so effective? They create "instant habits" in which the desired behaviour is produced fairly effortlessly when the individual finds himself/herself in the appropriate situation or situations. As a result, those using implementation intentions can eat healthily without requiring high motivation or thinking about their eating behaviour.

Health psychologists have an increasing role to play, helping people change their lifestyle e.g., to eat more healthily.

The important role of habits in influencing eating behaviour was confirmed by Adriaanse et al. (2014). They studied eating of unhealthy snacks in individuals high or low in self-control. The main reason those high in self-control ate fewer unhealthy snacks was because they had weaker unhealthy snacking habits.

In sum, health psychologists are having an increasing influence on eating behaviour. More specifically, they have developed techniques whereby individuals develop habits that promote healthy eating.

Organisation of this book

The organisation of this book is based on several major approaches to psychology. For example, social psychologists focus on our interactions with others, biological psychologists study how brain activity and physiological processes relate to behaviour, and developmental psychologists consider changes in children's behaviour over time.

There are five main approaches discussed in this book: biological approach, developmental approach, social approach, individual differences' approach, and cognitive approach. In addition, there is the behaviourist approach (discussed in Chapter 2). Note, however, that most topics covered are of relevance to more than one approach. I have assigned such topics to the approach of most direct relevance. The last chapter of the book moves beyond the above six approaches to discuss practical ways of achieving effective learning.

Finally, there is a chapter on effective learning. It provides a practical account of what you can do to improve your study skills and ensure you benefit fully from reading this book.

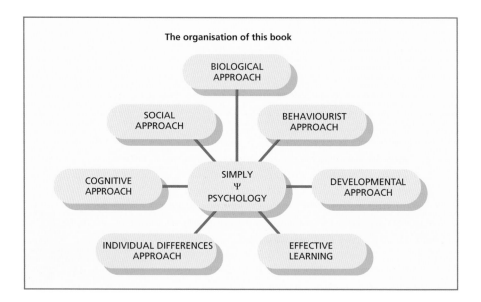

The organisation of this book

Useful features
Five features of this book are designed to make it maximally useful:

1. Psychologists often use words differently from their everyday usage, which can be confusing. Accordingly, key terms are highlighted with their definitions given in the margin alongside.
2. A glossary at the end of the book lists all these key terms in alphabetical order.
3. The text is punctuated with Evaluation boxes consisting of positive (+) and negative (–) points.
4. There are structured essay questions at the end of nearly every chapter to focus your mind on important issues.
5. The practical relevance to everyday life of the material covered in each chapter is indicated clearly by 'In real life' boxes.

Chapter summary

- Psychology is a science that involves trying to understand people's behaviour.
- Behaviour is jointly determined by numerous factors. These include the current stimuli; recent and childhood experiences; personality; intelligence; and genetic, physiological, cognitive, social, and cultural factors.
- Critics argue that laboratory research is artificial. However, observing behaviour in experiments conducted under well-controlled conditions is the best way of identifying the main determinants of behaviour.
- The criticism that psychological findings are merely common sense is wrong. There is no coherent commonsensical account of human behaviour, and many (or even most) findings in psychology are *not* obvious.
- People often mistakenly believe findings in psychology are obvious because of a tendency to be wise after the event (hindsight bias).
- Most psychological research has been on individuals living in Western societies, which are markedly different from other cultures in the world.
- There is an important (but oversimplified) distinction between individualistic and collectivistic cultures.
- Cultural influences are not fixed but instead depend on the accessibility of culture-relevant information (e.g., national anthem).
- Most psychological therapies for mental illnesses are comparably effective, but cognitive behavioural therapy is often the most effective.
- Psychological therapies greatly enhance psychological well-being and increase productivity at work.
- Most of the reduction in deaths from heart disease in recent years is due to lifestyle changes. These lifestyle changes (e.g., quitting smoking) owe much to the interventions of health psychologists.
- This book is organised into five main approaches (biological, developmental, social, individual differences, and cognitive) with additional coverage of the behaviourist approach.

Further reading

- Colman, A. (1999). *What is psychology?* (3rd ed.). London: Routledge. Andrew Colman's book provides a very readable introduction to psychology for those with little background knowledge of the subject.

- Eysenck, M.W. (2009). *Fundamentals of psychology*. Hove, UK: Psychology Press. Chapter 1 of this textbook contains a longer introduction to psychology than the one presented in this chapter.

- Furnham, A. (1988). *Lay theories: Everyday understanding of problems in the social sciences*. Oxford, UK: Pergamon. Adrian Furnham discusses a formidable amount of evidence on the limitations of commonsensical views of psychology.

- Henrich, J., Heine, S.J., & Norenzayan, A. (2010). The weirdest people in the world. *Behavioral and Brain Sciences*, *33*, 61–83. This article contains convincing evidence that the cultures studied in most psychological research are very unrepresentative of the world's cultures.

Essay questions

1. Discuss possible definitions of "psychology". What are the main factors studied by psychologists in their attempts to understand human behaviour?

2. "Psychology is just common sense." Discuss.

3. What is cross-cultural research? Why is it important for psychologists to study many different cultures?

4. "Psychology has contributed little to well-being in society." Discuss.

The history of psychology spans over 2,000 years from the ancient Greeks (especially Plato and Aristotle) through to the present day. However, most advances in psychology have occurred over the past 150 years, and so I will focus on that time period. There are two remarkable aspects to the recent history of psychology. First, many different approaches have been taken in the attempt to understand human behaviour. Second, psychology has made dramatic progress over what is (compared to most other sciences) a relatively short time.

Behaviourism (an approach to psychology starting approximately 100 years ago) was incredibly influential. Its main goal was to identify the main kinds of basic learning found in the human and other species. In view of its historical importance, the second part of this chapter is devoted to behaviourism.

History of psychology

2

■ ■ ■ ■ ■ ■ ■ ■ ■ ◻

As Cronbach (1957) pointed out, we can identify "two disciplines of scientific psychology". First, most psychologists carry out laboratory experiments and try to identify general laws that determine our behaviour. Second, other psychologists seek to understand individual differences (e.g., in intelligence or personality) and often use correlational methods. In the latter group are clinical psychologists who study (and provide treatment for) individuals suffering from mental disorders.

Historically, these two groups tended to be entirely separate, but there have been welcome moves in recent times towards combining the two approaches. I will start with the general approach. After that, I will briefly discuss some of the main subdivisions within psychology (e.g., social psychology; developmental psychology). Finally, I will discuss approaches based on individual differences.

One of the most important events in the entire history of psychology was the approach known as behaviourism, which started in the early twentieth century. The central assumption of the behaviourists was that psychology should strive to be a science which, they argued, had not previously been the case. This assumption led them to investigate animal and human learning by focusing on what they called conditioning. Their research on conditioning was the first systematic attempt to study behaviour in a scientific fashion. In view of its importance, much of this chapter is devoted to conditioning.

Wilhelm Wundt

Wilhelm Wundt (1832–1920) established the world's first laboratory of psychology in Leipzig in 1879. This was important because it helped to identify psychology as a scientific discipline separate from its origins in philosophy. The setting up of this laboratory led many people to describe Wundt as the "father of experimental psychology".

Wundt attached much importance to **introspection** (reporting one's conscious thoughts) as a way of studying the mind. More specifically, he favoured experimental introspection, in which individuals provided immediate reports of conscious experience under carefully controlled conditions.

> **KEY TERM**
>
> **Introspection:** a careful examination and description of one's own conscious mental thoughts and states.

How did Wilhelm Wundt contribute to the development of psychology?

Introspection often provides useful information. However, it is limited in scope. We are generally aware of the outcome of our cognitive processes rather than those processes themselves (Valentine, 1992). For example, what is the name of the first African American President of the United States? I imagine you rapidly thought of Barack Obama without any clear idea of how you produced the right answer.

In sum, Wundt was a very influential figure historically in the development of psychology. He was also exceptionally prolific, producing over 50,000 pages in his various books and articles. However, his reputation has not lasted well. As William James (cited in Boring, 1950, p. 346) wrote of him, Wundt "aims at being a Napoleon of the intellectual world. Unfortunately, he will have a Waterloo, for he is Napoleon without genius and with no central idea".

John Watson (1878–1958) believed that psychology should study behaviour rather than thoughts and feelings (behaviourism).

Behaviourism

John Watson (1878–1958) was a very influential psychologist who played a major role in the development of **behaviourism**. According to him, "Psychology as the behaviourist views it is a purely objective, experimental branch of natural science. Its theoretical goal is the prediction and control of behaviour. Introspection forms no essential part of its method" (Watson, 1913, p. 176).

Why did Watson argue that psychologists should focus on behaviour rather than introspection? Introspection is limited because we are unaware of most internal processes influencing our behaviour. It is also limited because our reports of our conscious experience are sometimes distorted (deliberately or otherwise). In contrast, Watson claimed that behaviour provides us with observable and objective information. There is another reason. Watson argued that "The behaviourist . . . recognises no dividing line between man and brute" (Watson, 1913, p. 158). You cannot use introspection with other species and so have no choice but to study their behaviour.

Watson's (1913) notion that behaviour is objective and observable is an exaggeration as was pointed out by Popper (1968). He said to his students during lectures, "Observe!", to which they replied, "Observe what?" The point is that no-one ever observes without some idea of what they are looking for.

There were two rather separate strands to behaviourism. First, as discussed already, it was concerned with the methods psychology should use. Second, it involved a theoretical approach with an emphasis on simple forms of learning such as classical and operant conditioning (discussed in detail later). Of major importance was the assumption that our behaviour is determined almost entirely by environmental factors rather than by heredity. As we will see, a key figure was the Russian physiologist Ivan Pavlov. His famous research on salivating dogs had a massive influence on the development of behaviourism.

KEY TERM

Behaviourism: an approach to psychology started in the United States by John Watson, according to which psychologists should focus on observable stimuli and responses and learning can be accounted for in terms of conditioning principles.

EVALUATION

➕ The notion that psychology should be a properly scientific discipline remains extremely important.

➕ The careful observation of behaviour is of fundamental importance to psychology.

➕ Understanding of the processes involved in human learning was greatly enhanced by research on classical and operant conditioning based on the behaviourist approach.

➖ Environmental factors are *not* all-important in determining our behaviour – genetic factors often play a significant role (see Chapters 3, 17, and 18).

➖ The behaviourists de-emphasised *internal* factors (e.g., goals; personality; intelligence) in influencing our behaviour.

➖ The rise of behaviourism was less of a revolution than is generally assumed. In fact, psychology was already moving in the direction of experimental research based on careful observation of behaviour under controlled conditions. (Leahey, 1992).

Cognitive approach

What is **cognitive psychology**? It is an approach focusing on numerous processes related to the acquiring, processing, and transforming of information. Examples of such processes include attention, perception, language comprehension and production, learning, memory, problem solving, decision making, and reasoning.

Cognitive psychology developed during the 1950s because of a growing dissatisfaction with the behaviourist approach. It is very hard to understand cognitive abilities such as language or problem solving from the behaviourist approach because of its emphasis on observable behaviour. For example, what someone is thinking is generally not obvious from their behaviour. What is needed is a focus on *internal* mental processes, which is exactly what cognitive psychologists do.

The previous paragraph is somewhat of an oversimplification. Some behaviourists (especially Tolman) argued that theorists should consider internal processes intervening between stimuli and responses. For example, he emphasised the notion of "cognitive map" (Tolman, 1948), according to which even rats learn spatial representations of their environment.

Cognitive psychology has mostly involved carrying out experiments on healthy individuals under laboratory conditions. However, from the 1970s onwards, there was a dramatic increase in **cognitive neuropsychology**. This approach differs from

KEY TERMS

Cognitive psychology: is concerned with internal mental processes (e.g., attention; perception; learning; thinking) and how these processes influence our behaviour.

Cognitive neuropsychology: research on brain-damaged patients designed to increase our understanding of cognition in healthy individuals.

most research in cognitive psychology because the participants are brain-damaged patients. However, the aim of cognitive neuropsychology is to enhance our knowledge of cognition in healthy individuals.

Here is a concrete example of cognitive neuropsychology in action (see Chapter 22). The hypothesis that there is an important distinction between short-term memory (remembering information for a few seconds) and long-term memory was put forward over a hundred years ago. Cognitive neuropsychologists discovered that many brain-damaged patients (suffering from a condition known as amnesia) had severely impaired long-term memory but intact short-term memory. That strongly suggested the hypothesis is essentially correct.

How can we assess the internal (and thus unobservable) processes involved in human cognition? It is not straightforward. An approach that has become markedly more popular within the past decade is that of **cognitive neuroscience** – evidence from brain activity as well as from behaviour is obtained while individuals perform cognitive tasks under experimental conditions (see Chapter 4). The single most important technique used by cognitive neuroscientists is **functional magnetic resonance imaging (fMRI),** which involves the use of an MRI scanner containing a very heavy magnet. fMRI allows us to work out activation levels in various brain areas during performance of a task.

Here is a concrete example of successful research in cognitive neuroscience. Kosslyn (1994) put forward the hypothesis that visual imagery involves mostly the same processes as visual perception. However, it could be argued that visual imagery depends on stored knowledge of what objects look like and so involves different processes from visual perception. Experimental research within cognitive psychology failed to provide definitive evidence for either point of view.

Suppose we use fMRI to assess activation in brain areas at the back of the brain associated with the early stages of visual processing. If visual imagery resembles visual perception, we would expect these areas to be activated during a visual imagery task just as they are during visual perception. However, if visual imagery relies on stored knowledge, there is no reason why these areas would be activated during visual imagery.

Kosslyn and Thompson (2003) carried out a meta-analysis based on numerous fMRI studies. Brain areas involved in early visual processing were generally activated during visual imagery. These findings provided some of the strongest evidence for Kosslyn's (1994) theoretical position.

KEY TERMS

Cognitive neuroscience: an approach designed to understand human cognition by combining information from behaviour and brain activity.

Functional magnetic resonance imaging (fMRI): a technique providing detailed and accurate information concerning activation in brain areas while a cognitive task is being performed.

EVALUATION

➕ The cognitive approach is extremely flexible and can be applied to almost any aspect of human cognition.

➕ The cognitive approach (especially since the arrival of cognitive neuroscience) has greatly increased our understanding of human cognition.

➕ The cognitive approach has become very influential within other areas of psychology including developmental, social, and abnormal psychology.

- The cognitive approach depends mostly on laboratory research and its findings may lack **ecological validity** (relevance to everyday life).

- Most research in cognitive neuroscience reveals associations between brain activity and behaviour. Such evidence does not *prove* the brain activity is necessary to produce the behaviour.

Developmental psychology

Everyone accepts nowadays that it is important to study the psychology of childhood for its own sake and also because it helps us to understand adult thinking and behaviour. Sigmund Freud's (1856–1939) psychoanalytic theories in the early 1900s were a major milestone in the history of developmental psychology. He argued we could only understand the origins of mental disorders in adults by considering their childhood experiences.

However, the greatest impetus to developmental psychology came from Jean Piaget (1896–1980). He spent several decades studying the development of thinking and intelligence through the years of childhood. In essence, he argued that cognitive development involves a shift from the irrational and illogical to the rational and logical. Piaget revolutionised our understanding of the development of cognitive abilities in children. However, his experimental methods were not well controlled, and he systematically underestimated the cognitive abilities of children of different ages (see Chapter 8)

Jean Piaget.

One of the most remarkable achievements of young children is their rapid development of language. How can this be explained? Noam Chomsky (e.g., 1965) argued we are all born with a language acquisition device, which provides children with an innate ability to master language. This theory has been disproved (see Chapter 9). However, it was very important in the history of developmental psychology because it was the first systematic attempt to explain language development.

The scope of developmental psychology has increased greatly since the pioneering efforts of Freud, Piaget, and Chomsky. Examples include moral development (Chapter 10) and gender development (Chapter 11). More generally, the links between developmental and cognitive psychology have become much stronger over time. Many of the most influential theories of language development, moral development, and gender development have a very cognitive flavour about them.

Social psychology

The early history of social psychology was largely dominated by American psychologists. The American, Floyd Allport, published a very influential book *Social Psychology* in 1924. From our current perspective, what is intriguing about this book is that it is actually not very social in its approach! Much of the book concerns the issue of how an individual's behaviour differs when he/she

KEY TERM

Ecological validity: the extent to which research findings are applicable to everyday settings and generalise to other locations, times, and measures.

is alone compared to in the presence of others. For example, he reported that many simple tasks were completed faster when performed in a group situation, and he claimed this was due to social facilitation. Thus, he did not focus on distinctively social processes such as group dynamics in small groups.

We can see echoes of this approach in subsequent American research. For example, the American, Solomon Asch (1951), carried out some of the most famous studies in the history of social psychology. In essence, individuals were often prepared to conform to the judgments of other group members even when they knew they were wrong. Of relevance here is that none of the participants had ever met before and so many of the processes found in groups of friends were missing.

European social psychologists reacted against the excessive focus on the individual within social psychology. As Hogg and Vaughan (2005, p. 33) pointed out, "Europeans pushed for a more *social* social psychology." This manifested itself in various ways. First, there was increased interest in the relationships between groups (seen in research on prejudice and discrimination: see Chapter 13). Second, research on social influence began to compare the extent of social influence on an individual as a function of whether he/she perceived group members to belong to his/her ingroup (see Chapter 15).

One of the greatest changes in social psychology in recent decades has been an increasing focus on the cognitive processes at work in social situations. This cognitive focus can be seen in research on prosocial behaviour (Chapter 14), social influence (Chapter 15), and social perception and attraction (Chapter 16).

In sum, the horizons of social psychology have expanded over the years in that it has become more genuinely social in approach and includes more of a focus on cognitive processes. Vaughan and Hogg (2014) provide good coverage of the history of social psychology if you would like to know about it.

Individual differences

The distinction between approaches designed to produce general laws and those designed to understand individual differences is of value but should not be regarded as absolute. In practice, several approaches attempt to achieve both goals. In addition, as we are about to see, several distinct approaches can all be categorised as focusing on individual differences. For example, psychologists who study abnormal psychology, intelligence, or personality all focus on individual differences. However, we start with the biological approach, which has had a major influence on the areas of abnormal psychology, intelligence, and personality.

Individual differences: biological approach

It is generally accepted that psychology is linked to biology (including related disciplines such as physiology, biochemistry, and genetics). However, it was only after the publication of the book *The Origin of Species* by Charles Darwin that the relevance of biology to psychology became accepted. Before its publication in 1859, most people had assumed only humans had minds, thus making us radically different from other species. The notion that human beings evolved from other species meant this inflated view of the importance of the human species had to be reassessed.

Darwin was a biologist rather than a psychologist. However, his theory of evolution has had four major effects on psychology. First, psychologists started to develop theories of human psychology from the biological perspective. The most famous psychologist to do so was Sigmund Freud (discussed in the next section). His emphasis on the sex drive in humans would have been almost unthinkable in the days before Darwin.

Second, an implication of Darwin's theory of evolution was that the study of *nonhuman* species could greatly enhance our understanding of human behaviour. This led to the development of comparative psychology. It is called comparative psychology because it involves comparing human behaviour with that of other species. Darwin's influence helps to explain why the behaviourists argued that carrying out research on dogs, rats, and pigeons could shed important light on human behaviour.

Third, Darwin argued that heredity is important in the development of a species and that offspring tend to be like their parents. These ideas led psychologists to investigate the relative importance of heredity and environment (the nature-nurture debate) in influencing human behaviour. Twin studies have shed much light on this important issue (see Chapter 4).

Fourth, Darwin focused on *variation* among the members of any given species. According to his notion of survival of the fittest, evolution favours those individuals best equipped to live in a given environment. These ideas led to an interest in individual differences and to the study of intelligence (Chapter 17) and personality (Chapter 18). It also led to research on the different mating strategies of men and women. In essence, Darwin's theoretical approach suggested men could best achieve the goal of maximising the number of their surviving children by focusing on *quantity* of mates, whereas women could achieve the same goal by focusing on *quality* of mates (Stewart-Williams & Thomas, 2013; see Chapter 16).

In sum, the biological approach has strongly influenced the development of psychology in numerous ways. For example, evolutionary psychology (which focuses on the impact of evolutionary processes on human behaviour) is based directly on Darwinian ideas. The influence of the biological approach is so wide ranging that many ways in which it has been influential have been omitted here. For example, consider cognitive neuroscience (discussed earlier), in which human cognition is studied by obtaining information about brain activity as well as behaviour. Cognitive neuroscience combines the cognitive and biological approaches.

Charles Darwin (1809–1882). Darwin's theory of evolution led psychologists to focus on individual differences, genetic influences on behaviour, and the relevance of biology to psychology.

Individual differences: psychoanalysis and abnormal psychology

Sigmund Freud (1856–1939) is the most famous psychologist of all time. Darwin's theory of evolution had a significant influence on his general approach: "The theories of Darwin . . . strongly attracted me, for they held hopes of extraordinary advance in our understanding of the world" (cited in Jones, 1981, p. 211). The influence of Darwin can be seen in Freud's emphasis on biological forces such as the life instinct (sex drive) and death instinct.

Freud's psychoanalytic approach was based on the assumption that mental disorders have their origins in psychological factors rather than physical ones. More specifically, unresolved unconscious conflicts are of central importance in triggering metal disorders. It follows that treatment for mental disorders should be psychological – this led Freud to develop psychoanalysis as a method of treatment.

Freud's development of psychoanalysis paved the way for numerous other psychologically-based forms of therapy for mental disorders (see Chapter 20). As a result, he transformed the treatment of mental disorders and created the field of abnormal psychology.

More generally, Freud hugely expanded the scope of psychology. He argued that psychology is relevant to virtually all human behaviour, whereas before him the focus was on limited topics such as simple learning and the association of ideas.

Individual differences: intelligence and personality

As mentioned earlier, major areas in which the emphasis is on individual differences are intelligence (see Chapter 17) and personality (see Chapter 18). Here we will briefly consider the historical origins of research in these two areas.

Intelligence

The systematic investigation of individual differences in intelligence started with Sir Francis Galton (1822–1911). The publication of his book *Hereditary Genius* in 1869 was a major landmark in the study of individual differences. In this book, he argued that the tendency for certain families to produce several eminent scientists, lawyers, authors, or whatever meant genius is mostly inherited. In fact, it could plausibly be argued that children born into a distinguished family are likely to have environmental advantages and opportunities denied to most other children.

Galton (1876) carried out the first proper twin study: his discovery that identical twins were more similar in intelligence than fraternal twins strengthened his conviction that inheritance is of crucial importance in determining individual differences in intelligence. Galton also devised the first-ever intelligence test. However, his test focused on simple tasks such as reaction time and did not provide a proper assessment of intelligence.

In the early twentieth century, psychologists started to focus on the issue of how many different types of intelligence there are. The pioneer here was the English psychologist Charles Spearman (1863–1945). He used a statistical technique known as factor analysis to address this issue (Spearman, 1904). Some individuals generally scored highly across all the tests he used whereas others generally obtained low scores. This suggested there was a general factor of intelligence resembling IQ. Subsequent research confirmed the importance of the general factor but also indicated the existence of somewhat more specific factors (e.g., crystallised ability: stored knowledge and experience; short-term memory).

Personality

The history of research in personality parallels that of research in intelligence in many ways. For example, twin studies starting with Newman et al. (1937) have

Francis Galton.

played a major role in understanding individual differences in personality (see Chapter 18). The evidence from numerous studies over the years indicates that individual differences in intelligence and personality both depend very much on genetic factors.

Another similarity between personality and intelligence research is in the use of factor analysis to establish the number and nature of factors involved. Early research was carried out by Burt (1915, 1940), who identified general emotionality (similar to neuroticism) and a factor resembling introversion-extraversion as major factors. Subsequent research by Eysenck (1975) and by Costa and McCrae (1992) confirmed the importance of these factors and provided a more comprehensive account by including additional factors.

What are the similarities in the ways in which intelligence and personality have been studied?

Summary

It has not been possible to do justice to approaches based on individual differences in the above brief account. A unifying theme across such approaches is the importance of genetic factors. That includes abnormal psychology – there is convincing evidence that most mental disorders (especially schizophrenia) depend in part on genetic factors (see Chapter 20). Another unifying theme is that it is increasingly recognised that the study of individual differences can best be understood by considering the contributions made by the cognitive, social, and developmental approaches.

Conditioning and learning

There are many kinds of learning. For example, you probably spend much of your time learning information that will allow you to pass examinations. You also learn how to solve difficult problems, how to think about issues, and so on. The behaviourists argued that *all* learning (even complex forms of learning) could be understood in terms of fairly simple principles. More specifically, they focused on classical conditioning and operant conditioning. After discussing classical and operant conditioning, I will turn to other kinds of learning ignored by the behaviourists. Of special importance is observational learning, which involves learning by observing and then imitating the actions of others in social situations.

Classical conditioning

Imagine going to the dentist. As you lie down on the reclining chair, you start to feel frightened. Why are you frightened before the dentist has caused you any pain? The sights and sounds of the dentist's surgery lead you to *expect* that you are shortly going to be in pain. In other words, you have formed an association between the neutral stimuli of the surgery and the painful stimuli involved in drilling. Such associations are of crucial importance in **classical conditioning**. In essence, the fear created by drilling in the past is now triggered by the neutral stimuli of the surgery.

Textbook writers nearly always focus on unpleasant everyday examples of classical conditioning (I have just been guilty of that myself!). However, there are also pleasant examples. Most middle-aged people have especially positive feelings for music popular when they were teenagers. Associations are formed between the music and various exciting kinds of stimuli encountered during adolescence.

KEY TERM

Classical conditioning: a basic form of learning in which simple responses (e.g., salivation) are associated with a new or conditioned stimulus (e.g., tone).

Ivan Pavlov.

Findings

The best-known example of classical conditioning comes from Ivan Pavlov's (1849–1936) research on dogs. He started his research in Russia towards the end of the nineteenth century (Pavlov, 1897), and it had a large impact on the development of behaviourism in America.

Dogs (and other animals) salivate when food is put in their mouths. In technical terms, what we have here is an **unconditioned reflex** – this consists of an unlearned reaction (**unconditioned response**) to a stimulus (**unconditioned stimulus**). In Pavlov's work, food in the mouth was the unconditioned stimulus and salivation was the unconditioned response.

Pavlov trained dogs to salivate to other stimuli not naturally associated with salivation. In some of his studies, he presented a tone (the training stimulus) just before food on several occasions so the tone signalled that food would be arriving shortly. Finally, he presented the same tone (the test stimulus) on its own without any food following. The dog salivated to the tone.

This example illustrates a type of learning known as a **conditioned reflex**. A previously neutral stimulus (**conditioned stimulus**) is associated with the unconditioned stimulus and the **conditioned response** (learned response to the conditioned stimulus). In the example, the tone is the conditioned stimulus, the sight of food is the unconditioned stimulus, and salivation is the conditioned response.

Pavlov discovered various features of classical conditioning. One example is generalisation. Generalisation refers to the finding that the strength of the conditioned response (e.g., amount of salivation) depends on the *similarity* between the test stimulus and the previous training stimulus.

Another example is discrimination. Suppose a given tone is paired several times with the sight of food. The dog learns to salivate to the tone. Then another tone is presented on its own. This tone produces a smaller amount of salivation than the first one through generalisation. After that, the first tone is paired with food several more times, but the second tone is never

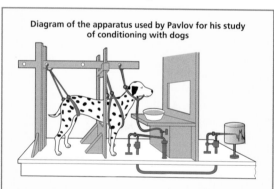

Diagram of the apparatus used by Pavlov for his study of conditioning with dogs

The three stages of classical conditioning

Stage 1: Before conditioning

Conditioned stimulus → No response

Unconditioned stimulus → Unconditioned response

Stage 2: During conditioning

Conditioned stimulus ↘

Unconditioned stimulus → Unconditioned response

Stage 3: After conditioning

Conditioned stimulus → Conditioned response

KEY TERMS

Unconditioned reflex: a well-established association between an unconditioned stimulus and an unconditioned response.

Unconditioned response: a well-established reaction (e.g., salivation) to a given unconditioned stimulus (e.g., food) in an unconditioned reflex.

Unconditioned stimulus: a stimulus that produces a well-established unconditioned response in an unconditioned reflex.

Conditioned reflex: a new association between a conditioned stimulus and an unconditioned stimulus that produces a conditioned response.

Conditioned stimulus: a neutral stimulus paired with an unconditioned stimulus to produce classical conditioning.

Conditioned response: a new response produced as a result of classical conditioning.

paired with food. Salivation to the first tone increases whereas that to the second tone decreases. Thus, the dog learns to *discriminate* between the two tones.

When Pavlov presented the tone on its own several times, there was less and less salivation. Thus, the repeated presentation of the unconditioned stimulus in the absence of the unconditioned stimulus stops the conditioned response. This is known as **extinction**.

However, the dog or other animal has *not* lost the relevant conditioned reflex. Animals brought back into the experimental situation after extinction produce some salivation in response to the tone. This is known as **spontaneous recovery**. It shows the salivary response to the tone was *inhibited* (rather than lost) during extinction.

Explanation: prediction

Conditioning occurs because the conditioned stimulus (e.g., a tone) allows the dog or other animal to *predict* the unconditioned stimulus (e.g., food) is about to be presented. As a result, the conditioned stimulus produces an effect (i.e., salivation) similar to that produced by the food itself. Extinction occurs when the tone no longer predicts the arrival of food.

Suppose we reverse the order of the two stimuli, with the conditioned stimulus *following* the unconditioned one (i.e., backward conditioning). In these circumstances, the conditioned stimulus cannot predict the arrival of the unconditioned stimulus. As expected, there is little or no backward conditioning.

Kamin (1969) showed conditioning depends on expectation. Rats in the experimental group received light paired with electric shock and learned to react with fear and avoidance when the light came on. Rats in the control group had no training. Then both groups received a series of trials with a light-tone combination followed by shock. Finally, both groups of animals received only the tone. The control group responded with fear to the tone on its own but the experimental animals did not.

What was going on? The experimental animals learned initially that light predicted shock. As a result, they subsequently ignored the fact that the tone also predicted shock. This is the **blocking effect** – conditioning to one stimulus (i.e., tone) was blocked by prior conditioning to a different stimulus (i.e., light). In contrast, the control animals learned tone predicted shock because they had not previously learned something different. Attentional processes are crucial in the blocking effect: animals pay little attention to any given conditioned stimulus if another conditioned stimulus already predicts the arrival of the unconditioned stimulus (Shanks, 2010).

Explanation: evolutionary perspective

In most research, the relationship between the conditioned and unconditioned stimuli is *arbitrary* (e.g., a tone paired with the sight of food). Indeed, according to the typical approach, any neutral stimulus can be associated with any unconditioned stimulus. What are the chances an animal in the wild will often encounter the same arbitrary conditioned stimulus immediately before a given unconditioned stimulus? The answer is slim or none.

What is going on? According to the evolutionary perspective (Krause, 2015), conditioning is fastest when learning is highly beneficial to animals in their natural environment. For example, animals should rapidly learn to avoid poisonous foods as was found by Garcia et al. (1966). Rats were given saccharine-flavoured water followed by a drug causing intestinal illness several hours

KEY TERMS

Extinction: the elimination of a response when it is not followed by reward (operant conditioning) or by the unconditioned stimulus (classical conditioning).

Spontaneous recovery: the re-emergence of responses over time in classical conditioning after extinction.

Blocking effect: the absence of a conditioned response to a conditioned stimulus if another conditioned stimulus already predicts onset of the unconditioned stimulus.

How does classical conditioning in the natural environment differ from classical conditioning in the laboratory?

later. The rats only needed to be sick *once* to learn to avoid drinking the water. This shows the effectiveness of classical conditioning when relevant to survival.

How does classical conditioning occur in the natural environment? Domjan (2005) argued that the conditioned and unconditioned stimuli are typically different features of the *same* object. He discussed findings from experiments on male Japanese quail in which the conditioned stimulus was the stuffed head of a female quail and the unconditioned stimulus was access to a live female. In these circumstances, classical conditioning was very strong. Indeed, it was so strong the male quail often grabbed the stuffed head and tried to copulate with it!

Classical conditioning can be useful because the presentation of the conditioned stimulus gives the animal time to prepare to cope effectively with the unconditioned stimulus. We can see this in Pavlov's research. Conditioning causing the animal to salivate before the arrival of food enhanced digestion by secreting digestive hormones and enzymes before the food reached the gut.

There are many other examples. For example, male blue gourami fish that copulated after exposure to a sexually conditioned stimulus produced 10 times as many offspring as occurred in the absence of the conditioned stimulus (Hollis et al., 1997). The finding that classical conditioning can enhance reproductive success indicates its importance.

Exposure therapy

Conditioning principles have been applied to patients suffering from mental disorders. Many individuals suffer from **phobias** (extreme fears of certain objects or stimuli). Common examples include snake phobia, spider phobia, and **social phobia** (great fear of social situations; see Chapter 20). The fear can be so great it leads the individual to avoid the phobic objects or situations. According to the behaviourist account, phobias develop when the conditioned or phobic stimulus (e.g., a social situation) is associated with a painful or aversive stimulus, causing fear.

If phobias are acquired through classical conditioning, then presumably they can be eliminated through extinction. In other words, if the phobic or conditioned stimulus is presented repeatedly *without* aversive consequences, the fear associated with that stimulus should gradually diminish. As a result, exposure therapy was developed. In **exposure therapy**, phobic individuals are exposed to the feared object or situation (often gradually increasing in threateningness) for lengthy periods of time until their anxiety levels reduces.

Exposure therapy has proved very effective in the treatment of most phobias (Choy et al. 2007). It is also effective in the treatment of other anxiety disorder such as posttraumatic stress disorder (PTSD; Eftekhari et al., 2013). However, the explanation of exposure therapy's effectiveness is less clear. Theoretically, it is supposed to be due to the extinction of the fear response, which is undoubtedly part of what is involved. In addition, however, cognitive beliefs are also important. For example, Vögele et al. (2010) found much of the beneficial effect of exposure therapy in treating social phobia occurred because patients perceived themselves as having more control over themselves and their emotions.

KEY TERMS

Phobias: excessive fears of certain objects or places leading to avoidance of those objects or places.

Social phobia: a mental disorder in which the patient experiences very high levels of anxiety in social situations which often causes him/her to avoid such situations.

Exposure therapy: a form of treatment in which phobic patients are exposed to stimuli or situations they fear greatly.

EVALUATION

⊕ All the main phenomena of classical conditioning have been demonstrated numerous times.

⊕ Classical conditioning often has important biological value (e.g., taste aversion). It allows animals (and humans) to prepare themselves for the imminent arrival of the unconditioned stimulus.

⊕ Exposure therapy (successful in the treatment of phobias) apparently involves the process of extinction.

⊖ Classical conditioning is only relevant to a very small part of human learning. Most human learning involves cognitive processes much more complex than the basic mechanisms involved in classical conditioning. For example, we can produce immediate extinction in humans by telling them the unconditioned stimulus will not be presented again.

⊖ As we will see shortly, operant conditioning and observational learning are both important in human learning.

⊖ The effectiveness of exposure therapy in treating phobias often depends on processes (e.g., cognitive ones) ignored by conditioning theorists.

KEY TERMS

Operant conditioning: a form of learning in which an individual's responses are controlled by their consequences (reward or punishment).

Law of reinforcement: the probability of a response being produced is increased if it is followed by a reward but decreased if followed by punishment.

Operant conditioning

We often behave in certain ways to obtain reward. For example, young children are well behaved in return for sweets, and students try hard to obtain good marks. **Operant conditioning** is a form of learning in which behaviour is controlled by rewards (also called positive reinforcers) and by unpleasant or aversive stimuli. Much of operant conditioning is based on the **law of reinforcement**. According to this law, the probability of a given response occurring increases if it is followed by a reward or reinforcer. However, the probability decreases if it is followed by negative or aversive consequences.

Skinner (1904–1990) contributed more than anyone else to our understanding of operant conditioning. He carried out his famous research on rats during the 1930s and reported the findings in his 1938 book, *The behaviour of organisms*. He placed a hungry rat in a small box (called a Skinner box) containing a lever. When the rat pressed the lever, a food pellet appeared. The rat learned that food could be obtained by lever pressing, and so pressed the lever increasingly often. This provides a clear example of the law of reinforcement. Not surprisingly, reward's effects were greater when provided shortly after the response rather than when delayed.

This photo from 1964 shows B. F. Skinner.

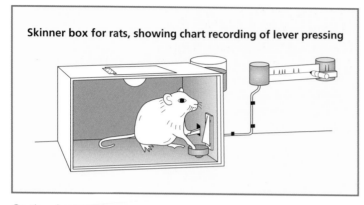

Skinner box for rats, showing chart recording of lever pressing

On the chart, each vertical line represents a single press on the lever.

There are two types of positive reinforcers or rewards: primary reinforcers and secondary reinforcers. **Primary reinforcers** are stimuli needed for survival (e.g., food, water, sleep, air). **Secondary reinforcers** are stimuli that are rewarding because we have learned to associate them with primary reinforcers (e.g., money, praise, attention).

In operant conditioning, the required response must be produced *before* it can be reinforced or rewarded. How can we train an animal to produce a complex response it would not produce naturally? The answer is **shaping** – the animal's behaviour moves progressively towards the desired response. For example, suppose we wanted to teach a pigeon to play table tennis. It might initially be rewarded for touching a table-tennis ball. Over time, its actions would need increasingly to resemble those involved in playing table tennis to be rewarded.

Schedules of reinforcement

It seems reasonable that we continue to do things that are rewarding and stop doing things that are not rewarding. In real life, however, continuous reinforcement (in which the reinforcer or reward is given after every response) is rare. This led Skinner to consider what happens with partial reinforcement, in which only some responses are rewarded. He identified four main schedules of reinforcement:

- *Fixed ratio*: every *n*th (e.g., fifth) response is rewarded. Workers receiving extra money for achieving certain targets are on this schedule.
- *Variable ratio*: on average, every *n*th response is rewarded but the actual gap between rewards may be very small or fairly large. This schedule is found in fishing and gambling.
- *Fixed interval*: the first response produced after a given interval of time (e.g., 60 seconds) is rewarded. Workers paid regularly every week are on this schedule – they receive reward after a given interval of time but do not need to produce a specific response.
- *Variable interval*: on average, the first response produced after a given interval of time is rewarded. However, the actual interval is mostly shorter or longer than this. Self-employed workers whose customers make payments at irregular times are rewarded at variable intervals. However, they do not have to produce a specific response.

The variable schedules (especially variable ratio) lead to the fastest rates of responding because they create high levels of motivation. This helps to explain why gamblers find it hard to stop their addiction. In contrast, continuous

KEY TERMS

Primary reinforcers: rewarding stimuli that are essential for survival (e.g., food; water).

Secondary reinforcers: stimuli that are rewarding because they have repeatedly been associated with primary reinforcers; examples include money and praise.

Shaping: a form of operant conditioning in which behaviour is changed slowly in the desired direction by requiring responses to resemble increasingly the desired response for reward to be given.

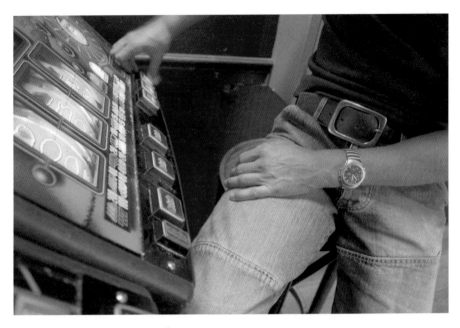

Although gamblers have no idea when or if they will receive a payout, they continue to play. This is an example of the most successful reinforcement schedule—variable ratio reinforcement.

reinforcement leads to the lowest rate of response because only a single response is needed to produce each reward.

What about **extinction** (the cessation of responding in the absence of reward)? Schedules of reinforcement associated with the best conditioning also show the most resistance to extinction. Why is extinction very slow in animals trained on the variable ratio schedule? The animals are used to reward being provided infrequently and irregularly and so it takes them a long time to realise they are no longer going to be rewarded. Why is extinction rapid in animals trained with continuous reinforcement? There is a very obvious shift from reward being provided on every trial to reward not being provided at all.

Instinctive influences

Skinner assumed that virtually *any* response could be conditioned in *any* stimulus situation. This assumption is known as **equipotentiality**, but it is incorrect. In fact, animals' behaviour mostly resembles their natural or instinctive behaviour. For example, it might well be impossible to train an animal to run away from food to obtain a food reward.

Breland and Breland (1961) trained pigs to insert wooden coins into a piggy bank for reward. The pigs rapidly learned to do this. Much more interestingly, the pigs performed slower and slower over time until eventually they were not getting enough food to eat. The pigs would "root the coin [turn it up with its snout], drop it again, root it along the way, pick it up, toss it in the air, drop it, root it some more, and so on" (Breland & Breland, 1961, p. 683). In other words, the pigs' behaviour increasingly reflected their natural food-getting behaviours. This "instinctive drift" cannot easily be explained in conditioning terms.

> **KEY TERM**
>
> **Equipotentiality:** the notion that any response can be conditioned in any stimulus situation.

What are the strengths and limitations of the token economy?

IN THE REAL WORLD: token economy

Operant conditioning has been used successfully in the real world to train circus animals, to persuade individuals to work long hours for payment, and to raise academic standards by praising students who perform well. Here we will focus on the token economy.

The essence of the **token economy** is that individuals are given tokens (e.g., poker chips) for desirable behaviour. These tokens can then be exchanged for rewards. Alternatively, individuals who exhibit desirable behaviour can simply be rewarded or reinforced with money.

Impressive findings were reported by Silverman and colleagues (2004) in a study in which the token economy was used with cocaine users who had proved extremely hard to treat. Some patients were offered up to $3,480 (about £2,000) in vouchers for remaining cocaine-free over a 39-week period. Of those given a high incentive, 45% managed to remain abstinent for at least four weeks compared to 0% of those with no incentive.

Silverman et al. (2012) reviewed several studies in which positive reinforcers or rewards for abstinence were used to treat individuals addicted to drugs such as cocaine or alcohol. Such token economies were generally successful, but there was evidence of relapse when rewards were no longer available. It may be necessary to provide rewards over very long periods of time to minimise the risk of relapse.

Token economies have also proved very useful in assisting individuals to stop smoking. In one study (Halpern et al., 2015), some smokers were exposed to a token economy in which they could gain an $800 (£500) reward if they stopped smoking for 6 months. Other smokers received usual care, which in many cases including nicotine-replacement therapy. The findings were clear-cut: 16% of those receiving the reward stopped smoking for six months compared to only 7% of those receiving usual care.

In sum, token economies are very effective at treating severe problems such as cocaine or alcohol addiction. A major advantage is that they can be used in numerous different situations. For example, Mazureck and van Hattem (2006) studied the effects on drivers' speed of providing an intervention (feedback and rewards for good driving). The percentage of kilometres driven within the speed limit increased from 68% in the control condition to 86% with the intervention.

What are the limitations of token economies? First, individuals whose behaviour is influenced by the presence of reward may change their behaviour (e.g., start drinking again) when reward is no longer present. Second, token economies can be very expensive. However, they are often cheaper than other interventions. In addition, the costs of token economies can be reduced by rewarding the desired behaviour (e.g., smoking abstinence) on a variable-ratio schedule rather than continuously (Gupta, 2015).

KEY TERM

Token economy: a form of therapy based on operant conditioning in which tokens are given to patients for producing desirable behaviour; these tokens can then be exchanged for rewards.

Theoretical perspectives

Skinner argued that reinforcement strengthens the association between the stimulus (e.g., the inside of a Skinner box) and the reinforced response (e.g., lever press). This viewpoint is too simple. Tolman (1959) argued that animals learn much more than was assumed by Skinner. According to Tolman, animals learn a **means-ends relationship** – the knowledge that a given response will produce a given outcome. This is a much more cognitive approach.

Support for Tolman's approach over Skinner's was reported by Dickinson and Dawson (1987). Rats learned to press a lever to receive a reward: some received sugar water and the others dry food pellets. Rats deprived of water produced far more lever presses in extinction when they had previously been reinforced with sugar water than with dry food. Thus, their behaviour was influenced by their knowledge of the expected reinforcer.

Gaffan et al. (1983) also found that animals do not simply produce previously reinforced responses. Rats in a T-shaped maze chose to turn left or right. Suppose a rat turns left and finds food at the end of that arm of the maze. According to conditioning principles, the rat has been rewarded for turning left and so should turn left on the next trial. In the rat's natural environment, however, it is generally *not* sensible to return to a place from which food has just been removed. Early in training, rats *avoided* the arm of the T-shaped maze in which they had previously found food.

In sum, animals do not simply learn mechanically that certain responses are rewarded as implied by Skinner.

Punishment

Operant conditioning can involve unpleasant or aversive stimuli (e.g., electric shocks) as well as positive reinforcers or rewards. Humans (and other species) learn to decrease their exposure to aversive stimuli just as they learn to increase their exposure to rewards.

Operant conditioning in which a response is followed by an aversive or unpleasant stimulus is **positive punishment**. If the aversive stimulus occurs shortly after the response, it reduces the likelihood that response will be produced thereafter. The aversive stimulus is much less if there is a long delay between the response and the aversive stimulus.

There is also **negative punishment**, in which a positive reinforcer or reward is removed following a given response. For example, a child who starts throwing food on the floor may have the food removed. The typical effect of negative punishment is to reduce the probability that the punished response will be produced. Another form of negative punishment is the **time-out technique** in which a child is removed from a situation in which he/she has behaved badly (see Chapter 7).

Findings

Positive punishment has various unwanted effects. In a review, Gershoff (2002) found punishment typically produced immediate compliance with the parent's wishes. However, it was associated with subsequent aggressive behaviour and with impaired mental health (e.g., depression) (see Chapter 7). It was also associated with a tendency for punished children to abuse their own children or spouse in adulthood.

What is the form of conditioning in which a response is followed by an aversive stimulus?

KEY TERMS

Means-ends relationship: the knowledge that a given action in a given situation will produce a certain outcome.

Positive punishment: a form of operant conditioning in which the probability of a response is reduced by following it with an unpleasant or aversive stimulus.

Negative punishment: a form of operant conditioning in which the probability of a response is reduced by following it with the removal of a positive reinforcer.

Time-out technique: a form of negative punishment in which undesirable behaviour (e.g., aggression) is reduced by removing the individual from the situation in which they have been aggressive.

Gershoff et al. (2010) considered the effects of punishment administered by mothers in six countries (China, India, Italy, Kenya, Philippines, and Thailand). In all six countries, physical punishment and yelling were associated with greater child aggression, and physical punishment and the time-out technique were associated with greater child anxiety.

Avoidance learning

Nearly all drivers stop at traffic lights because of the possibility of aversive consequences (e.g., having an accident) if they do not. This is a situation in which no aversive stimulus is presented if suitable action is taken, and is an example of **avoidance learning**. Many aversive stimuli (**negative reinforcers**) strengthen any response that stops the aversive stimulus being presented.

In experiments on avoidance learning, there is typically an initial warning stimulus. This is followed by an aversive stimulus unless the participant makes a given avoidance response. For example, consider a study by Solomon and Wynne (1953). Dogs were placed in a two-compartment apparatus. A change in the lighting was the warning signal that an aversive stimulus (a strong electric shock) was about to be presented. This stimulus could be avoided by jumping into the other compartment. Most dogs received a few shocks early in the experiment but then generally avoided shocks for the remaining hundreds of trials.

How can we account for avoidance learning? The avoidance response is rewarded or reinforced by fear reduction (Mowrer, 1947). In addition, participants acquire two beliefs (Lovibond, 2006):

1. After the warning stimulus, the unconditioned stimulus will be presented.
2. After performing a given response, the unconditioned stimulus will be omitted.

Declercq and Houwer (2011) carried out an experiment on avoidance learning with human participants. Questioning of the participants revealed they had acquired those two beliefs.

KEY TERMS

Avoidance learning:
a form of operant conditioning in which an appropriate avoidance response prevents presentation of an unpleasant or aversive stimulus.

Negative reinforcers:
unpleasant or aversive stimuli that strengthen responses preventing those stimuli from being presented.

EVALUATION

➕ Operant conditioning is often very effective.

➕ Positive and negative punishment are also effective (e.g., in improving children's behaviour).

➕ Token economies have successfully reduced undesirable forms of behaviour (e.g., drug addiction).

➖ Skinner minimised the role of *internal* factors (e.g., goals; beliefs). As Bandura (1977, p. 27) pointed out, "If actions were determined solely by external rewards and punishments, people would behave like weather vanes, constantly shifting in radically different directions to conform to the whims of others." In fact, we often pursue our long-term goals rather than allowing ourselves to be influenced by the immediate situation.

- Operant conditioning is more about influencing people's *behaviour* than about *learning*. Suppose I offered you £1 every time you said, "The Earth is flat." You might (especially if short of money!) say it hundreds of times, so the reward would have influenced your behaviour. However, I doubt whether it would make you believe the Earth is flat.

- In real life, we learn far more by observing others' behaviour than by learning to perform rewarded responses as claimed by Skinner (discussed in the next section).

- Skinner's notion of equipotentiality is incorrect because it de-emphasises the importance of instinctive behaviour.

Observational learning

Albert Bandura (1925–) agreed with Skinner that learning typically involves rewards. However, he argued convincingly that much everyday human learning does *not* involve operant conditioning. We learn a huge amount by observing someone else's behaviour (the other person is the model) – this is **observational learning**.

Why is observational learning so important? According to Bandura (1977, p. 12), "Psychological theories have traditionally assumed that learning can occur only by performing responses and experiencing their effects. In actuality, virtually all learning phenomena resulting from direct experience occur on a vicarious [second-hand] basis by observing other people's behaviour and its consequences for them." Note that observational learning is *not* the same as imitation learning. You might well imitate the behaviour of someone whose behaviour was followed by reward, but you would be much less likely to imitate punished behaviour.

There is plentiful evidence of observational learning. Examples can be found with respect to aggression (Chapter 7), moral development (Chapter 10), and acquisition of gender roles (Chapter 11).

Bandura's approach is much more cognitive than Skinner's. Successful observational learning requires the individual to attend to the model's behaviour, to store away information about that behaviour in long-term memory, and to be motivated to perform the learned behaviour (e.g., by expecting to be rewarded).

Findings

Is observational learning as effective as learning based on actually performing the behaviour in question? Blandin and Proteau (2000) found that performance on a timing task was comparable following observational learning and prior physical practice. In addition, participants in the observational learning condition developed error-correction mechanisms at least as effective as those of participants receiving physical practice.

KEY TERM

Observational learning: learning based on watching the behaviour of others and copying behaviour that is rewarded and not copying punished behaviour.

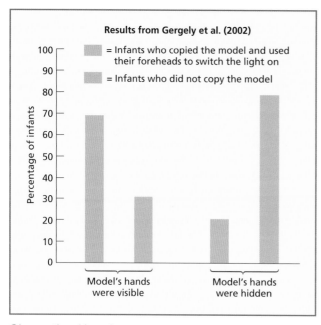

Results from Gergely et al. (2002)

= Infants who copied the model and used their foreheads to switch the light on

= Infants who did not copy the model

Percentage of infants

Model's hands were visible

Model's hands were hidden

Observational learning in infants is strongly influenced by the context.

Observational learning can be more subtle than assumed by Bandura. Gergely et al. (2002) and Király et al. (2013) trained 14-month-old infants to turn on a light having observed an adult model use her forehead to touch the light and turn it on. When the model's hands were free, 69% of the infants copied her behaviour by using their forehead. When the model's hands were under the table wrapped in a blanket (and so were not free), only 21% copied her behaviour, choosing instead to use their hands. Thus, infants take account of the reasons for the model's behaviour and so do not always imitate his/her successful or rewarded actions.

Why do some children exhibit more observational learning than others? Bandura assumed that children's particular experiences were all-important. However, Fenstermacher and Saudino (2007) found that identical twins were much more similar in observational learning than fraternal twins. This finding indicates that genetic factors are also important.

EVALUATION

➕ Observational learning occurs very often in children and adults. Indeed, it probably occurs more often than operant conditioning.

➕ Observational learning can have powerful effects on subsequent behaviour comparable to learning based on actual performance (e.g., Blandin & Proteau, 2000).

➖ Observational learning can be more complex than assumed by Bandura. Even infants can take account of factors such as the model's intention and situational constraints on her/his behaviour (Gergely et al., 2002).

➖ Observational learning depends more on the individual's interpretation of the situation than assumed by Bandura. Suppose you observe a fellow student receiving a prize for winning a race in athletics. If you are not interested in athletics, you might decide the other student has been wasting their time and so not feel tempted to imitate them.

➖ Individual differences in observational learning depend on genetic factors as well as the environmental factors emphasised by Bandura.

Chapter summary

- There is an important distinction between the experimental approach with its focus on general laws and the approach emphasising individual differences.
- Behaviourism transformed psychology with its emphasis on studying behaviour rather than introspection. It also had a major theoretical impact on the psychology of learning with research on classical and operant conditioning.
- The cognitive approach differed from behaviourism by focusing on internal mental processes as well as on behaviour. Cognitive neuroscience, which uses evidence from brain activity as well as behaviour to understand internal mental processes, represents a major development of the cognitive approach.
- The developmental approach was hugely influenced by Freud and by Piaget, both of whom emphasised that adult behaviour depends importantly on childhood learning and experiences.
- Social psychology initially focused excessively on the individual but subsequently expanded to consider group processes in detail. It increasingly focuses on cognitive processes influencing behaviour in social situations.
- A focus on individual differences is apparent in biological psychology, abnormal psychology, and research on intelligence and personality. A unifying theme across these approaches is that individual differences depend in part on genetic factors. This theme was introduced into psychology by Charles Darwin. Darwin also had an important influence by arguing that human behaviour depends on evolutionary pressures faced by our ancestors.
- Classical conditioning involves learning to predict that a neutral stimulus will be followed shortly by a pleasant (or unpleasant) stimulus.
- Classical conditioning has great survival value (e.g., taste aversion).
- Exposure therapy (based on classical conditioning) is an effective treatment for various phobias.
- A variable ratio schedule of reinforcement (as found in gambling and fishing) is associated with the fastest rate of responding and the greatest resistance to extinction.
- Token economies have proved effective in treating many severe problems (e.g., alcohol and cocaine addiction).
- Positive and negative punishment are both effective. However, the former produces more unwanted side effects.
- Skinner's approach is much better suited to situations where we respond to immediate rewards and punishments than to situations where we pursue long-term goals.
- Observational learning is very common in everyday life. It is typically more efficient than operant conditioning.
- Observational learning can be more subtle than assumed by Bandura.

Further reading

- Brennan, J. (2013). *History and systems of psychology*. New York: Pearson. The history of psychology is discussed fully in an accessible fashion.

- Domjan, M. (2015). *The principles of learning and behavior* (7th ed.). Stamford, CT: Cengage Learning. This textbook contains very thorough and up-to-date information on all the approaches to learning discussed in this chapter.

- Eysenck, M.W., & Brysbaert, M. (2017). *Fundamentals of cognition* (3rd ed.). Abingdon, Oxford: Psychology Press. Chapter 1 of this textbook provides an account of the history of cognitive psychology.

- Leahey, T.H. (1992). The mythical revolutions of American psychology. *American Psychologist*, 47, 308–318. Thomas Leahey argues persuasively that the changes occurring at the start of the so-called behaviourist and cognitive "revolutions" were much less dramatic than is usually assumed.

Essay questions

1. Compare and contrast the behaviourist and cognitive approaches to understanding human behaviour.

2. Discuss the major approaches within psychology that emphasise individual differences. What are some of the main similarities among these approaches?

3. What is classical conditioning? In what ways does laboratory research on classical conditioning differ from classical conditioning in real life?

4. How did Skinner explain operant conditioning? What are the main limitations with his explanation?

Suppose you wanted to carry out a piece of research to increase your understanding of human behaviour. For example, you might be interested in the issue of whether watching violence on television makes individuals more aggressive. How would you go about studying that issue? How many different approaches could you use? Which approach do you think would be most useful? Why do you think that?

Methods of investigation

3

In this chapter we consider how psychologists carry out research into human behaviour. Most of this research has its origins in some theory. Theories provide general explanations or accounts of various findings or data. They also generate **hypotheses** (predictions or expectations about factors influencing certain forms of behaviour). For example, someone might propose a theory claiming some people are generally more sociable or friendly than others. Here are some hypotheses this theory might generate: sociable people smile more at other people; sociable people talk more than unsociable ones; sociable people agree with the views of others more than unsociable ones.

Psychologists collect data (especially behavioural data). Data is collected to test various hypotheses. Most people assume this data collection involves proper laboratory experiments, and there have been literally millions of laboratory experiments in psychology. However, as we will see, psychologists use several methods of investigation, each providing useful information about human behaviour.

As you read about the various methods of investigation in psychology, you may find yourself wondering which method or methods are best. In fact, it is more useful to compare psychologists' methods to the clubs used by golf players. The driver is not a better or worse club than the putter, it is simply used for a different purpose. In similar fashion, each method of investigation used by psychologists is very useful for testing some hypotheses but of little use when testing other hypotheses.

Experimental method

The experimental method is used more often than any other method in psychological research. Use of the **experimental method** involves a generally high level of *control* over the experimental situation. Whichever aspect of the situation is of primary interest is manipulated systematically to observe the effects on behaviour. The experimental method can be used for laboratory experiments in controlled conditions or for field experiments in more naturalistic conditions.

Most laboratory research starts with the experimenter thinking of an **experimental hypothesis**. This is simply a prediction or expectation concerning what

> **KEY TERMS**
>
> **Hypotheses:** predictions concerning the effects of some factor(s) on behaviour based on a given theory.
>
> **Experimental method:** a method involving a generally high level of control over the experimental situation (especially the independent variable).
>
> **Experimental hypothesis:** prediction as to what will happen in a given experiment; it typically involves predicting the effect of an independent variable on a dependent variable and is often theory-based.

What variables does an experimental hypothesis usually refer to?

will happen in a given situation. An example of an experimental hypothesis is that loud noise disrupts people's ability to carry out a task such as learning the information in a chapter of an introductory psychology textbook.

As with most experimental hypotheses, the one just mentioned predicts that some aspect of the situation (the presence of loud noise) affects the participants' behaviour (learning of the information). We can express this more technically. The experimental hypothesis refers to an **independent variable** manipulated or altered by the experimenter. In our example, the presence or absence of loud noise is the independent variable.

The experimental hypothesis also refers to a **dependent variable** (some aspect of the participants' behaviour). In our example, a measure of learning (e.g., a comprehension test) would be used to assess the dependent variable. In a nutshell, most experimental hypotheses predict that a given independent variable will have a specified effect on the dependent variable.

Psychologists using the experimental method hope to show the independent variable *causes* certain effects on behaviour. There is some validity in the notion that we can establish cause-and-effect relationships using the experimental method. However, matters are not always straightforward. For example, consider a thought experiment on malaria in a hot country. Half the participants sleep in bedrooms with the windows open and the other half in bedrooms with the windows closed. Those sleeping in rooms with the windows open are found to be more likely to catch malaria. The independent variable (i.e., windows open or closed) is relevant to catching malaria, but our findings tell us nothing directly about the major causal factor in malaria (i.e., infected mosquitoes).

The experimental hypothesis consists of the predicted effect of the independent variable on the dependent variable. There is also the null hypothesis. The **null hypothesis** states the independent variable will have no effect on the dependent variable. In our example, the null hypothesis would be that loud noise has no effect on learning the information in a chapter of an introductory psychology textbook. The goal of most laboratory studies is to decide whether the obtained findings fit better with the experimental hypothesis or the null hypothesis.

It might seem easy to carry out a study to test the experimental hypothesis that loud noise disrupts learning. However, various problems need to be avoided. First, we must decide how to manipulate the independent variable. In our example, we have to decide how loud the noise should be. If it is extremely loud, it might damage the hearing of our participants and so be totally unacceptable. If it is fairly soft, it is unlikely to have any effect. It is also likely to make a difference whether the noise is meaningful (e.g., music or speech) or meaningless (e.g., the noise of a road drill).

Second, we must decide how to measure the dependent variable. We could ask our participants various questions to measure their understanding of the material in the chapter. However, we need to select questions so they are neither too easy nor too hard.

Limitations

The experimental method is limited in application. Consider the factors influencing our current behaviour (see Chapter 1). The immediate situation is one such factor, and its effects can easily be studied using the experimental method.

KEY TERMS

Independent variable: some aspect of the experimental situation that the experimenter manipulates in order to test a given experimental hypothesis.

Dependent variable: some aspect of the participants' behaviour that is measured in an experiment.

Null hypothesis: prediction that the independent variable (manipulated by the experimenter) will have no effect on the dependent variable (some measure of behaviour).

However, our behaviour is also influenced by our personality, our intelligence, our childhood experiences, whether we have recently had an argument with a close friend, whether or not we have a headache, and so on. Alas, none of these factors can be turned into an independent variable for the purposes of a laboratory experiment.

Confounding variables

It is crucially important when using the experimental method to avoid confounding variables. **Confounding variables** are factors mistakenly manipulated along with the independent variable. Consider, for example, a study by Jenkins and Dallenbach (1924) involving two groups. One group received a learning task in the morning and were given a memory test later in the day. The other group received the same learning task in the evening and were given the memory test the following morning after a night's sleep. Memory performance was much better for the second group. Jenkins and Dallenbach concluded that sleep is beneficial for memory because it reduces interference from environmental stimulation.

Can you see what is wrong with this study? The two groups learned the material at different times of day, and so this was a confounding variable. Hockey et al. (1972) found the time of day at which learning takes place is much more important than whether participants sleep between learning and the memory test.

In sum, the presence of confounding variables means we cannot interpret the findings from an experiment. The reason is that we do not know whether the findings are due to the independent variable manipulated by the experimenter (e.g., sleep vs. no sleep between learning and memory test) or the confounding variable (e.g., time of day at which learning occurred).

How can we avoid having any confounding variables? One approach is to turn confounding variables into controlled variables by holding their value constant. Suppose we want to study the effects of noise on learning and are concerned that time of day may influence our findings. We could make time of day a controlled variable by testing all our participants at a given time of day (e.g., late morning). That would prevent time of day from distorting our findings. Alternatively, we could simply test our participants at random times of day while checking there were no systematic time-of-day differences between the noise and no-noise conditions.

When selecting participants for an experimental study, what should we do?

Selecting participants

Most psychological experiments use fewer than 100 participants. The participants used in any given experiment are typically a **sample** drawn from some larger **population** (e.g., college students). Since experimenters want the sample findings to apply to the population, those included in the sample must be a **representative sample** of the population.

How can we obtain a representative sample? The best way is generally to use **random sampling**.

KEY TERMS

Confounding variables: variables that are not of interest to the experimenter that are mistakenly manipulated along with the independent variable.

Sample: the participants actually used in a study drawn from some larger population.

Population: a large collection of individuals (e.g., female musicians) from whom the sample used in a study is drawn.

Representative sample: a sample of participants that is chosen to be typical or representative of the population from which it is drawn.

Random sampling: selecting the individuals for a sample from a population using some random process.

For example, if we knew the names of every member of the relevant population, we would select members of the sample by some random procedure such as picking names out of a hat. Alas, the use of random sampling does not guarantee that we will obtain a truly representative sample because several of those invited to take part are likely to refuse. Marcus and Schulz (2005) found volunteers differed from non-volunteers in various ways: they were more agreeable, open to experience, and extraverted than non-volunteers.

Another way to obtain a representative sample is to use **quota sampling**. Suppose our population of college students is 55% female with 80% aged between 18 and 21 and the remaining 20% over 21. We could select our sample to ensure 55% were female and 80% between the ages of 18 and 21. If we take account of several features of the population, quota sampling can be an effective way of producing a representative sample.

Random and quota sampling are often expensive and time-consuming. As a result, many experimenters use **opportunity sampling** in which participants are selected purely on the basis of their availability. For example, you could ask all students leaving the college restaurant whether they would take part in a study. This approach is simple but has the disadvantage that your participants may be nothing like a representative sample.

Experimental designs

Suppose we want to compare two groups exposed to different levels of an independent variable (e.g., loud noise vs. no noise) to observe the effects on learning. We would need to ensure the groups do not differ any other important way. If, for example, all the least intelligent participants received loud noise and all the most intelligent ones no noise, we would not know whether it was the loud noise or the participants' intelligence level that caused poor learning in that group.

There are three main types of experimental design:

* **Independent design**: each participant is included in only one group.
* **Matched participants design**: each participant is included in only one group but each participant in one group is matched with one in the other group on some relevant factor (e.g., ability; sex).
* **Repeated measures design**: each participant is included in both groups so the two groups have exactly the same participants.

With the independent design, the most common way of allocating participants to groups is by **randomisation**. In our example, this could involve a random process such as coin tossing to decide whether any given participant is exposed to loud noise or no noise. What typically happens is that the participants in the two groups are similar in intelligence, age, sex, and so on. However, occasionally you will be unlucky!

With the matched participants design, we use information about the participants to decide the group into which each participant should be put. In our example, we might have information about the participants' intelligence levels. We could then use that information to ensure each person in one group is matched with someone in the other group on intelligence.

What is an experiment in which each participant is selected for only one group known as?

KEY TERMS

Quota sampling: selecting a sample from a population in such a way that those selected are similar to it in certain respects (e.g., proportion of females).

Opportunity sampling: selecting a sample of participants simply because they happen to be available.

Independent design: an experimental design in which each participant is included in only one group.

Matched participants design: an experimental design in which the participants in each of two groups are matched in terms of some relevant factor(s).

Repeated measures design: an experimental design in which each participant appears in both groups.

Randomisation: placing participants into groups on some random basis (e.g., by tossing a coin).

With the repeated participants design, every participant is in both groups. In our example, each participant would learn the chapter in loud noise and also learn it in no noise. This design means we do not have to worry about the participants in one group being more clever or better at learning than those in the other group.

Issues with repeated measures design

The main problem with the repeated measures design is that there may well be order effects. Participants' experiences during the experiment may change them in various ways. For example, they may perform *better* when tested on the second occasion because they have previously gained useful knowledge about the experiment or task. However, they may perform *worse* on the second occasion because they are tired or bored.

It would be difficult to use a repeated measures design in our example. Participants are bound to show better learning of the chapter the second time they read it, regardless of whether or not they are exposed to loud noise.

Suppose we use a repeated measures design in which all participants first learn the chapter in loud noise and then in no noise. The participants would show better learning in no noise simply because of order effects. A better procedure would be to have half the participants learn the chapter first in loud noise and then no noise, while the other half learn the chapter in no noise and then again in loud noise. In that way, any order effects would be balanced out. This is **counterbalancing**, and it helps to prevent order effects from distorting the findings.

Standardised procedures

It is very important the experimenter ensures every participant in a given condition is treated in the same way. Thus, standardised procedures must be used. For example, the instructions can be written down to ensure all participants receive exactly the same instructions.

What are field experiments?

We also need to use standardised procedures when collecting data from the participants. Suppose we want to assess the effects of loud noise on learning from a book chapter. We could ask participants to write down everything they can remember. However, it would be very hard to compare the memory performance of different participants with any precision. A standardised procedure would be to ask all participants the same 20 questions relating to the chapter. Each participant then obtains a score between 0 and 20. This would make it easy to compare memory performance across groups or conditions.

One reason it is hard to ensure all procedures are standardised in laboratory research is that most experiments can be regarded as social encounters between the experimenter and the participant. Unsurprisingly, male experimenters are more pleasant, friendly, honest, encouraging and relaxed when participants are female than when they are male (Rosenthal, 1966).

Rosenthal's (1966) research is an example of an experimenter effect. An **experimenter effect** consists of unintended effects experimenters have on participants' behaviour (Ambady & Rosenthal, 1996). The most famous example of an experimenter effect involved a horse known as Clever Hans. In the early twentieth century, he apparently showed he could count by tapping his hoof

KEY TERMS

Counterbalancing: this is used with the repeated measures design; each condition is equally likely to be used first or second.

Experimenter effect: the various ways in which the experimenter's expectations, personal characteristics, misrecordings of data, and so on can influence the findings of a study.

the correct number of times when asked mathematical questions (e.g., "If the eighth day of the month comes on a Tuesday, what is the date of the following Friday?") by his owner and teacher Wilhelm von Osten.

The psychologist Oskar Pfungst was sceptical of Clever Hans' talent. He discovered Clever Hans was responding to von Osten's subtle movements when the horse had tapped out the correct answer. All Clever Hans was doing was using these movements as the cue to stop tapping!

Artificiality of the experiment

A potential limitation with laboratory research based on the experimental method is artificiality. Of particular concern is **ecological validity** (the extent to which research findings can be applied to the real world). Here we consider two ways experiments can lack ecological validity.

First, the fact that participants in experiments know they are being observed by the experimenter can influence their behaviour. For example, they may try to work out the experimenter's hypothesis. As a result, participants are influenced by **demand characteristics**, which are "the totality of cues which convey an experimental hypothesis to the subjects" (Orne, 1962).

Young et al. (2007) used a questionnaire to assess motion sickness in a virtual environment designed to create motion sickness. Participants who completed the questionnaire before as well as after the virtual environment reported much more motion sickness (e.g., nausea) than those only given it afterwards. These participants were alerted to the demand characteristic that the study concerned motion sickness – it was almost as if taking the questionnaire beforehand made them sick!

Second, the experimenter's behaviour influences the participant's behaviour, but the participant's behaviour rarely influences that of the experimenter. Wachtel (1973) used the term **implacable experimenter** to refer to this state of affairs. He pointed out that it is very different from everyday life, in which we often try to persuade other people to behave in certain ways. Psychological research is in danger of providing an oversimplified view focusing on the individual's *response* to situations but not allowing him/her to change the situation or the experimenter's behaviour.

Replication

When psychologists report the findings from an experiment, they hope other psychologists will obtain similar findings. This is known as **replication**, meaning the experimental findings can be repeated by others. How can researchers maximise the chances of replication? First, the way in which the experiment was carried out should be reported in detail so others can understand exactly what happened. Second, standardised procedures need to be used. Third, it is important to avoid confounding variables.

Field experiments

Laboratory and field experiments both involve the experimental method. However, field experiments take place in more natural settings, and the participants typically do not realise they are taking part in an experiment. This gives field experiments the advantage of being less artificial than laboratory experiments and reduces problems such as experimenter effects and demand characteristics.

What are longitudinal studies?

KEY TERMS

Ecological validity: the extent to which research findings are applicable to everyday settings and generalise to other locations, times, and measures.

Demand characteristics: cues that are used by participants to try to guess the nature of the study or to work out what the experiment is about.

Implacable experimenter: the typical laboratory situation in which the experimenter's behaviour is uninfluenced by the participant's behaviour.

Replication: repeating the findings of a previous study using the same design and procedures.

We can see the value of field experiments by considering two examples. First, Shotland and Straw (1976) staged an argument and fight between a man and a woman close to several bystanders. The woman screamed, "I don't know you", or "I don't know why I married you". The bystanders were much less inclined to intervene when they thought it was a "lovers' quarrel": 19% did so when they thought it involved a married couple compared to 65% when it involved strangers.

Second, Gueguen et al. (2010) showed field experiments can have practical value. They wanted to find ways of increasing patients' adherence to the medication prescribed by doctors. Some patients were touched briefly on the forearm by the doctor whereas others were not. Those who were touched took more of their pills. One week later, patients who had been touched rated their doctor as more competent and concerned about them. Thus, a very simple gesture by the doctor can have beneficial effects on patients.

Limitations

Field experiments have various limitations. First, good experimental control can be hard to achieve in the real world. Second, it is hard to obtain detailed information from participants without them becoming aware they are in an experiment. Note that in our examples the dependent variable was very simple (intervention: yes or no?; number of pills taken). Third, ethical research typically requires obtaining voluntary informed consent from participants beforehand. This is rarely possible with field experiments.

OVERALL EVALUATION

⊕ Laboratory studies permit good experimental control and so may allow us to identify some of the causes of certain forms of behaviour. However, such control is often less with field experiments.

⊕ The findings from laboratory and field experiments can usually be replicated or repeated by other experimenters.

⊕ All the main types of experimental design (independent design; matched participants design; repeated measures design) are suitable when used appropriately.

⊖ The experimental method cannot be used to assess the impact of several major factors influencing our behaviour (e.g., our personality; our childhood; our genes).

⊖ It is important not to be carried away with the notion that psychology involves the experimental approach to the exclusion of almost everything else (David Scott, personal communication). As we will see shortly, there are other important approaches within psychology.

⊖ Participants in laboratory studies often do not behave naturally because they are being observed by strangers in an artificial situation.

There are also potential problems from demand characteristics and the implacable experimenter. However, experimenter effects and demand characteristics are usually less (or absent) in field experiments.

 The findings from laboratory studies often differ from what is found in everyday life; this is the issue of ecological validity. However, ecological validity is often high with field experiments.

Other methods

The experimental method is used more often than any other in psychology. However, researchers also use many other methods, and we will consider some of them in this section.

Observational studies

Observational studies resemble field experiments in that behaviour is observed in the real world. However, there is an important difference – with observational studies, the experimenter exerts no control over the situation but simply observes people's behaviour as they go about their daily business. This typically makes it hard to interpret the findings from observational studies.

Watching children interact in a playground is an example of an observational study. It might be predicted that girls would interact more cooperatively than boys, whereas boys would interact more aggressively than girls.

Two or more observers could record the number of cooperative and aggressive actions by boys and girls to test these hypotheses. It could be very demanding to do this non-stop. Accordingly, researchers often use time-sampling in which they record observations only part of the time. For example, they might observe the children's behaviour for 10 minutes, have a 5-minute break, observe for 10 more minutes, and so on.

Two related problems can arise in observational studies. First, different observers may have different ideas about the meaning of the different categories of behaviour they are looking for. One observer may regard a gentle tap as aggressive behaviour whereas another observer may not. Therefore, very clear definitions of the forms of behaviour to be measured need to be provided.

Second, the existence of clear definitions of the various categories of behaviour to be recorded may not prevent all problems. For example, some observers may fail to spot certain actions through inattention. We can see whether two observers produce similar judgments by calculating **inter-observer reliability**. The closer the agreement between the observers, the greater is the inter-observer reliability.

Cross-sectional and longitudinal studies

Suppose we wanted to explore the effects of age on two types of long-term memory (see Chapter 22):

1. *Episodic memory* (memory for events occurring at a given time in a given place)
2. *Semantic memory* (knowledge about the world)

KEY TERM

Inter-observer reliability: the extent of agreement between two observers rating the behaviour of participants.

The easiest approach would be to use the **cross-sectional method** in which different age groups are all tested at the same point in time. Another approach is the **longitudinal method** in which the same group of individuals is tested at two or more points in time.

You might imagine the apparent effects of age on memory would be the same with both methods. In fact, that is *not* the case. Rönnlund et al. (2005) found there was a substantial decrease in episodic memory between the ages of 35 and 60 using the cross-sectional approach. In contrast, episodic memory was stable across those years using the longitudinal approach. Semantic memory was stable from 35 to 60 years using the cross-sectional approach but increased over the years with the longitudinal approach.

Why did the two approaches produce different findings? A potential problem with the cross-sectional approach is that younger people have a higher level of educational attainment than older ones and so there is a confounding of age and educational attainment. When Rönnlund et al. (2005) removed this confounding effect statistically, the cross-sectional findings much more closely resembled those obtained with the longitudinal approach. Thus, aging (at least up to the age of 60) has very few negative effects on episodic or semantic memory.

The longitudinal method is generally preferable because the *same* individuals are studied throughout. That eliminates effects stemming from age-related changes in educational attainment. In view of the superiority of longitudinal studies, you might wonder why there are far more cross-sectional studies. The main reason is that such studies are much less time-consuming and expensive to carry out. Note, however, a limitation with some longitudinal studies is that performance is artificially inflated at later ages because participants show a practice effect with repeated testing (Salthouse, 2014).

Correlational studies

Suppose we formed the hypothesis that watching violence on television leads to aggressive behaviour in children (see Chapter 7). If this hypothesis is correct, we would expect children who have seen the most violence on television to be the most aggressive. This hypothesis could be tested by looking for a positive **correlation** or association between watching violent programmes and being aggressive. The closer the link between these two dependent variables, the higher is the correlation or association.

The main limitation with correlational studies is that it is hard to interpret the findings. A positive correlation or association between television violence watched and aggressive behaviour would be consistent with the hypothesis. However, another possible explanation is that aggressive children choose to watch more violent programmes than unaggressive children. A third explanation is that disadvantaged children may watch more television of all kinds than non-disadvantaged children, and their deprived circumstances may also make them aggressive.

In view of the limitations of correlational studies, why do researchers carry them out? First, many hypotheses cannot be tested directly using the experimental method. For example, the hypothesis that smoking causes several physical diseases cannot be tested by forcing some people to smoke and forcing others not to smoke! However, we can examine associations or

KEY TERMS

Cross-sectional method: different groups (e.g., varying in age) are all studied at the same time.

Longitudinal method: this is a method in which one group of participants is studied repeatedly over a relatively long period of time.

Correlation: an association (positive or negative) between two dependent variables or responses produced by the participants.

correlations between the number of cigarettes and the probability of suffering from various diseases.

Second, we can obtain large amounts of data on several variables in a correlational study much more rapidly than could be done with experimental designs. For example, use of questionnaires would allow an experimenter to study the associations or correlations between aggressive behaviour and numerous activities (e.g., watching violent movies; reading violent books; being frustrated at work or at home).

Case studies

There are often good reasons why it is not possible to use a large number of participants in a study. For example, there are patients who have a rare form of brain damage or who exhibit very unusual symptoms. In such circumstances, it can be very useful to carry out a **case study** in which one or two individuals are studied in great detail.

A famous case study was carried out by Sigmund Freud on Little Hans, a boy with an extreme fear of horses. According to Freud, Little Hans was sexually attracted to his mother. However, he was very frightened his father would punish him for this. Horses resembled his father in that their black muzzles and blinkers looked like his moustache and glasses. As a result, Little Hans transferred or displaced his fear of his father onto horses.

Freud's analysis was incorrect. On Freud's account, Hans should have had a strong fear reaction every time he saw a horse. In fact, he only showed strong fear when he saw a horse pulling a cart at high speed. Little Hans' fear of horses started after he saw a serious accident involving a horse and cart moving at high speed. It was probably this that made him fearful of horses (Rolls, 2010).

Other case studies have proved much more revealing. For example, there is Henry Molaison (HM). He was a patient with amnesia causing severe memory problems (see Chapter 22). It would be easy (but wrong!) to conclude HM simply had very impaired long-term memory. Surprisingly, his ability to learn (and remember) motor skills was essentially intact.

Research on HM indicated that the notion there is only a single long-term memory system is wrong (see Chapter 22). More specifically, we must distinguish between memory involving conscious recollection (e.g., where do you live?) and memory not requiring conscious recollection (e.g., performing motor skills).

EVALUATION

➕ Case studies provide rich information that can increase our theoretical understanding.

➕ Case studies can show a given theory is wrong. For example, HM showed previous views on long-term memory were oversimplified.

➖ What is true of a particular individual may not be true of other people. Thus, it can be dangerous to draw general conclusions from

KEY TERM

Case study: the intensive study of one or two individuals.

case studies. In the case of HM, however, other amnesic patients have similar patterns of memory impairment.

● Case studies (e.g., those of Freud) often involve the use of lengthy, fairly unstructured interviews. The evidence from such interviews can be excessively influenced by the interviewer's views.

Ethical issues

There are more major ethical issues associated with research in psychology than other scientific disciplines. There are various reasons for this. First, all psychological studies involve living creatures (human or nonhuman), and their right to be treated caringly can easily be infringed by an unprincipled or careless researcher.

Second, psychological findings may reveal unpleasant or unacceptable facts about human nature or certain groups within society. This is especially true of socially sensitive research. Such research was defined by Sieber and Stanley (1988, p. 49) as "studies in which there are potential social consequences or implications either directly for the participants in research or the class of individuals represented by the research".

Socially sensitive research can pose risks for many people in addition to those directly involved as participants. Consider, for example, a researcher who asks the question, "Are there racial differences in intelligence?", and decides to answer it by carrying out a study. This can produce risks for members of the racial groups to which the participants belong.

Simply asking the question about racial differences in intelligence immediately raises ethical issues. It is likely the researcher assumes there are racial differences in intelligence and that these differences are important. These assumptions are ethically dubious (and almost certainly incorrect). Studying racial differences in intelligence is unhelpful and can be very damaging.

Third, psychological research may lead to the discovery of powerful techniques of social control. It would obviously be dangerous if such techniques were exploited by dictators or others seeking to exert undue influence on society.

General principles

The British Psychological Society (BPS) is the major organisation for professional psychologists in the United Kingdom. It has produced several versions of ethical guidelines (most recently in 2009 and 2014) that should be adhered to by all researchers. Some of the most important features of these guidelines are shown in the figure.

An overarching requirement of ethical research is the following: "Psychologists should consider all research from the standpoint of the research participants and any other persons, groups, or communities who may be potentially affected

For ethical experimentation, what is it necessary to make sure of?

Ethical guidelines that should be addressed by psychologists and students of psychology.

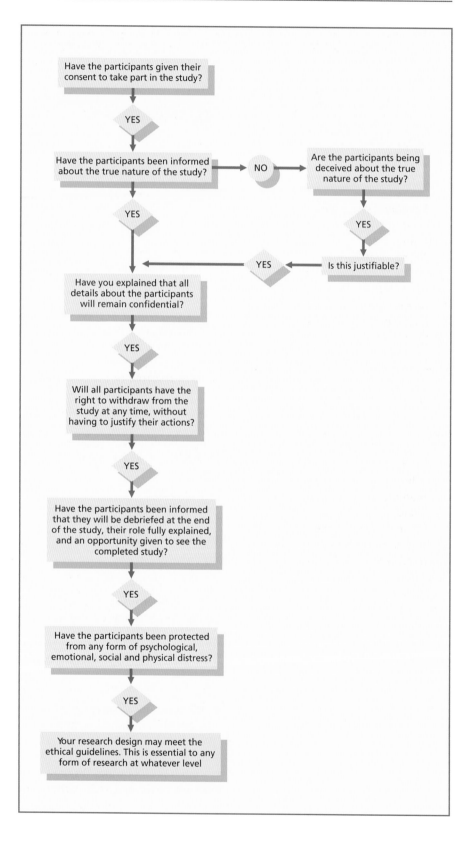

by the research, with the aim of avoiding potential risks to psychological well-being, mental health, personal values, the invasion of privacy or dignity" (British Psychological Society, 2014, p. 11). More specifically, the 2014 version of the BPS guidelines emphasises four major ethical principles:

1. *Respect*: Researchers should respect individual, cultural, and role differences. Of crucial importance is the need for researchers to obtain voluntary informed consent from participants having told them in detail what the experiment involves.
2. *Competence*: Researchers should recognise the limits of their knowledge and experience when planning and carrying out research.
3. *Responsibility*: Researchers should consider all research from the standpoint of research participants. Participants should be told clearly they can withdraw from the experiment at any time without providing a reason. There should also be a debriefing at the end of the experiment. At this debriefing, participants should be given fairly detailed information about the nature of the research.
4. *Integrity*: Researchers should strive to be honest, fair, and accurate in their interactions with participants. For example, they should not exaggerate their professional qualifications.

There are two further issues. First, ethical research involves a balance between means and ends. This requires a cost-benefit analysis in which attention is paid to the value of research when deciding whether it is ethically acceptable. For example, causing suffering to animals is easier to justify ethically if the goal is to find a cure for a serious human illness rather than merely to develop a new cosmetic. However, it can be hard to predict costs and benefits *before* an experiment has been carried out (Diener & Crandall, 1978). Even after a study has been completed, it can still be hard to assess costs and benefits – for example, sometimes the value of a study only becomes clear many years afterwards.

Second, there is the acceptability of deceiving participants. It is generally important to avoid deception because participants cannot give voluntary informed consent if key aspects of the experiment are not revealed. However, deception is common – Menges (1973) found that full information about what was going to happen was provided to participants in only 3% of American studies. Deception is sometimes justifiable and is clearly more acceptable if the effects are not damaging. It is also more justifiable if there are no other, deception-free ways of studying an issue.

Finally, there has been a trend over the years towards the adoption of increasingly ethical standards in the conduct of research. For example, consider research on social influence. It would be difficult (or impossible) in many countries to carry out studies such as Milgram's research on obedience to authority or Zimbardo's Stanford prison experiment (see Chapter 15).

Chapter summary

- An experimental hypothesis is a prediction of what will happen in a given experiment. More specifically, it refers to the predicted effect of an independent variable on a dependent variable.
- Confounding variables should be avoided when using the experimental method. This can be done by controlling as many variables as possible.
- Participants should form a representative sample from some population. This can be done by random or quota sampling.
- Within the experimental method, there are independent designs, repeated measures designs, and matched participants designs.
- Repeated measures designs produce unwanted order effects. These can be handled by counterbalancing.
- When using the experimental method, we should use standardised procedures, avoid experimenter effects, and try to achieve ecological validity.
- Field experiments have the advantage that behaviour can be assessed without participants' knowledge. However, such experiments often have poor experimental control.
- Observational studies can be very informative. However, there is a lack of experimental control and there can be issues about measurement reliability.
- Cross-sectional studies involve various groups studied at a single point in time, whereas longitudinal studies involve one group studied several times. Longitudinal studies are preferable because all findings are based on the same individuals.
- Correlational studies involve comparing two measures of behaviour from the same participants. The findings are hard to interpret because correlations do not indicate what has caused any given behaviour.
- Case studies involve investigating one or two individuals in detail. It is often hard to generalise from such studies.
- Socially sensitive research raises ethical issues because of its potentially damaging effects on many people not directly tested.
- Ethical research is based on respect, competence, responsibility, and integrity.
- When deciding whether a proposed piece of research is ethically acceptable, a cost-benefit analysis should be carried out.

Further reading

- Coolican, H. (2014). *Research methods and statistics in psychology* (6th ed.). Hove, UK: Psychology Press. Most of the topics in this chapter are discussed in a clear fashion by Hugh Coolican.

- Eysenck, M.W. (2015). *AQA psychology: AS and A-level year 1* (6th ed.). Hove, UK: Psychology Press. Chapter 8 in this textbook has detailed coverage of research methods and also shows how to calculate several statistical tests.

- Howitt, D., & Cramer, D. (2014). *Introduction to research methods in psychology* (4th ed.). London: Pearson. This textbook provides a readable introduction to research methods.

Essay questions

1. What are the key features of the experimental method? What are its strengths and limitations?

2. What are the main methods of investigation (other than the experimental method) available to researchers in psychology? What are the advantages and disadvantages of these methods?

3. What are the main aspects of ethical research? Why is it important for research to be ethical?

Part 1

Biological approach

Biological psychology (often shortened to biopsychology) is an important approach. It has been defined as "the study of behaviour and experience in terms of genetics, evolution, and physiology, especially the physiology of the nervous system" (Kalat, 1998, p. 1). More generally, the biological approach to psychology focuses on the ways in which our behaviour is influenced by the body and the brain. Of major importance, much of our behaviour is influenced by the genes we have inherited from our parents.

Chapter 4 • Biological bases of behaviour

We will consider key issues in biopsychology such as the role of genetic factors in explaining behaviour and the organisation of the brain.

Chapter 5 • Stress

We will discuss the causes of stress and the nature of stress including a focus on its physiological aspects with which we are all familiar.

Chapter 6 • Emotion

The nature of emotion is discussed, including a consideration of the physiological effects associated with emotional experience.

Chapter 7 • Aggression

The causes of aggression (including the role of genetic factors) are considered, as are ways in which aggression can be reduced.

Everyone agrees that our behaviour is strongly influenced by our body and brain. That is the starting point for the biological approach to psychology. This approach also involves addressing the issue of whether our behaviour is determined more by environmental factors (e.g., our friends; our experiences; our culture) or by genetic factors (e.g., the genetic make-up we have inherited). Do you think genetic factors have a major influence on our behaviour?

Centuries ago, phrenologists claimed that it is possible to understand individual differences in how the brain works by feeling the bumps on the skull. That approach was unsuccessful (to put it mildly!). What techniques do you think we could use to shed true light on the mysteries of how the brain works? The phrenologists assumed each part of the brain had its own special function. Do you think this assumption is correct? How could we decide?

Biological bases of behaviour

4

As we saw in Chapter 2, Darwin's (1859) theory of evolution has had a dramatic impact on psychology. For example, a major reason why the behaviourists (e.g., Watson; Skinner) tried to understand human behaviour via experiments on other species (e.g., rats) is because of Darwin's emphasis on similarities across species. Sigmund Freud was also strongly influenced by Darwin's ideas. In essence, Darwin played a major role in showing psychologists the value of considering the contribution that biology could make to our understanding of human behaviour.

In this chapter, we focus on contemporary theory and research in psychology based on the biological approach. That part of the biological approach currently most directly influenced by Darwinian ideas is evolutionary psychology (discussed shortly). A major development that will be discussed in detail is the huge increase in our understanding of the role of genetic factors in human behaviour. Finally, we discuss how the invention of sophisticated techniques for studying the brain in action is transforming our understanding of how the brain works.

Evolutionary psychology

Evolutionary psychology is based on the assumption that the process of evolution has shaped human minds and behaviour as well as their bodies. More specifically, evolutionary pressures have produced **adaptations** (inherited characteristics enhancing the likelihood of survival and reproduction). As a result, most of our behaviour is adaptive, meaning it is well suited to the environment in which we find ourselves. However, some adaptations that had great functional value in our distant ancestral past no longer do so. For example, eating food whenever it was available made sense when food was scarce and considerable energy was expended in hunting for it. Nowadays it is no longer adaptive in Western societies and may help to explain the dramatic increase in obesity.

Findings

One obvious adaptation in humans is that the size of our brains has increased considerably over the millennia. According to Stewart (1997), seven million years ago our ancestors' brains were only 400 cubic centimetres (cc). This

KEY TERMS

Evolutionary psychology: an approach to psychology based on the assumption that much human behaviour can be understood on the basis of Darwin's theory of evolution.

Adaptations: inherited mechanisms that evolved to solve problems encountered in our ancestral past.

increased to 1000cc in *Homo erectus* and is now 1350cc. This huge increase has enormous adaptive value because it allows us to think and reason far more effectively than any other species. Oddly, however, the frontal area of the brain (involved in complex cognitive processes relating to thinking) is *not* proportionately greater in humans than in gorillas (Kaufman, 2013). Our superior mental powers compared to gorillas probably occur because there are more efficient interconnections between areas in our brains.

Patients with obsessive-compulsive disorder (OCD) have recurrent intrusive thoughts (obsessions) and repetitive behaviours (compulsions). What is somewhat mystifying is that many patients with OCD have compulsions about washing and wash their hands dozens of times a day. A plausible answer is that millions of our ancestors died because of unhygienic conditions and so humans evolved to be very sensitive to possible contamination. Szechtman and Woody (2004) argued that we have a security motivation system designed to detect possible contamination. This system has an "easy-to-turn-on-hard-to-turn off" quality because a single failure to be vigilant to contamination can prove fatal. OCD patients differ from healthy individuals in that they find it much harder to turn this system off.

Further support for the evolutionary approach is discussed in other chapters. For example, it provides an explanation for unselfish or altruistic behaviour (Chapter 14) and for differences in dating and mating strategies between men and women (Chapter 16).

EVALUATION

➕ Evolutionary psychologists often have an advantage over other psychologists in that they focus on *why* humans behave in the ways they do rather than simply on *how* they behave.

➕ Our understanding of many phenomena (e.g., handwashing in OCD; unselfish or altruistic behaviour) has been enhanced by the insights of evolutionary psychologists.

➖ Evolutionary psychology has been much more successful at explaining adaptations found in the great majority of members of a species than accounting for individual differences *within* a species. (Confer et al., 2010).

➖ We cannot explain *all* human behaviour on the basis that it is (or was) adaptive and promotes survival of the individual's genes. Examples include homosexuality and suicide.

➖ Evolutionary explanations are often rather speculative given that we typically lack detailed knowledge of the environmental pressures to which our ancestors were subject.

Heredity vs. environment

Human beings differ from each other in endless ways. Some are tall and thin whereas others are short and fat. Some are intelligent and hard-working, whereas others are unintelligent and poorly motivated.

At the most general level, there are only *two* possible sources of individual differences in behaviour: heredity (nature) and environment (nurture). Thus, individuals may differ because of differences in what they have inherited or because of differences in the environment or experiences they have had. Realistically, most individual differences in behaviour are likely to depend on heredity *and* environment.

The nature-nurture issue is concerned with the relative importance of heredity and environment and is dealt with at various places in this book. Examples include individual differences in aggression (Chapter 7), intelligence (Chapter 17), and personality (Chapter 18).

Twin studies

The best method for addressing the nature-nurture issue involves twin studies. **Monozygotic twins** or identical twins derive from the same fertilised ovum or egg and so share 100% of their genes. **Dizygotic twins** or fraternal twins derive from two different fertilised ova or eggs and share on average 50% of their genes.

If individual differences in some behaviour or personal characteristic (e.g., intelligence) depend partly on genetic factors, identical twins should be more alike than fraternal twins with respect to that behaviour or personal characteristic. In contrast, if environmental factors are all-important, identical twins should be no more alike than fraternal twins.

The evidence indicates strongly that heredity and environment are both important in producing individual differences in numerous characteristics and forms of behaviour. What is surprising is the very wide range of individual differences influenced by genetic factors. For example, Verhulst and Hatemi (2013) carried out a twin study focusing on two kinds of political attitudes: (1) social ideology (e.g., attitudes towards abortion and divorce) and (2) religious attitudes (e.g., towards evolution and observance of the Sabbath). The views of identical twins with respect to both kinds of political attitudes were much more similar than those of fraternal twins thus indicating that individual differences in political attitudes owe much to genetic factors.

Common misunderstandings

There are three common misunderstandings about twin research. First, it is sometimes assumed twin studies provide information only about the impact of genetic factors. That is incorrect. Twin studies also provide an estimate of the importance of environmental factors. More specifically, they permit an assessment of the importance of two types of environmental influence:

1. Shared environmental influences are those within families that make children resemble each other.
2. Non-shared environmental influences are those unique to any given individual.

KEY TERMS

Monozygotic twins: twins that are formed from the same fertilised ovum or egg that splits and leads to the development of two individuals sharing 100% of their genes; also known as identical twins.

Dizygotic twins: twins derived from the fertilisation of two ova or eggs by two spermatozoa at approximately the same time; they share 50% of their genes and are also known as fraternal twins.

Consider twin studies on personality (see Chapter 18). According to Sigmund Freud (and many other theorists), children's personality is determined in large measure by the family environment provided by their parents. For example, if the family environment is stressful, we might expect children to develop anxious personalities. If Freud were correct, adolescents' and adults' personality should depend substantially on shared environmental influences.

What is actually the case? About 40% of individual differences in major personality factors are due to genetic factors, almost 60% are due to non-shared environmental influences, and very little is due to shared environmental influences (Plomin & Daniels, 2011). Thus, children's specific experiences (e.g., with friends; at school) have dramatically more impact on their personality development than any other environmental influences. In addition, another important source of non-shared environmental influences is the way in which children within a family are treated differently by their parents (Plomin & Daniels, 2011).

Second, it is often assumed the effects of heredity and environment on behaviour are entirely separate. However, that is *not* the case. Kendler and Baker (2007) considered several environmental factors including stressful life events, parenting, and family environment. Identical twins showed more similarity than fraternal twins with respect to these environmental factors – thus, there are genetic influences on environmental measures.

How can we explain these findings? In general terms, they indicate we have a significant impact on our environment. More specifically, Plomin (1990) identified *three* ways individuals' genetic endowment influences their environment. Below, these three ways are discussed with reference to individual differences in intelligence:

1. *Active covariation*: This occurs when children of differing genetic ability look for situations reinforcing their genetic differences. For example, children of high genetic ability read far more books than those of lower genetic ability and also receive several more years of education.
2. *Passive covariation*: This occurs when parents of high genetic ability provide a more stimulating environment than parents of lower genetic ability.
3. *Reactive covariation*: This occurs when an individual's genetically influenced behaviour influences how he/she is treated by other people. For example, adults are more likely to discuss complex issues with children of high genetic ability.

What can we conclude from Plomin's analysis? In essence, genetic factors can influence individual differences in intelligence in two ways. First, there is a *direct* genetic influence on intelligence. Second, there is an *indirect* genetic influence on intelligence – genetic factors help to determine the environment in which individuals find themselves, and this environment then influences their intelligence.

Third, many people assume the impact of genetic factors on individual differences (e.g., in intelligence) is fixed and unchanging. That is totally wrong. The impact of genetic factors is assessed within a given population and can vary dramatically from one population to another. Here are two examples (see Chapter 17). First, genetic factors account for approximately 80% of individual differences in intelligence in adulthood but for only 20% in childhood (Plomin & Deary, 2014). This happens because adults select their own environment to a much greater extent than children (i.e., active covariation discussed earlier).

The second example concerns the impact of genetic factors on children's intelligence in American families very high or low in socio-economic status.

Turkheimer et al. (2003) found genetic factors were SEVEN times more important in accounting for individual differences in intelligence in families of low socio-economic status than those of high status (72% vs. 10%, respectively). Within families of high socio-economic status, the great majority of children enjoyed favourable environmental conditions and so there was little scope for environmental influences to influence intelligence.

Nervous system

The nervous system contains all the nerve cells in the body. As we will see, the various parts of the nervous system are specialised for different functions. The nervous system is made up of between 15 and 20 billion neurons (nerve cells) and a much larger number of glia (small cells fulfilling various functions). The nervous system is divided into two main sub-systems:

Does the nervous system comprise one, two, or several smaller systems?

- **Central nervous system:** This consists of the brain and the spinal cord; it is protected by bone and fluid circulating around it.
- **Peripheral nervous system:** This consists of all the other nerve cells in the body. It is divided into the somatic nervous system (concerned with voluntary movements of skeletal muscles) and the autonomic nervous system (concerned with involuntary movements of non-skeletal muscles such as those of the heart).

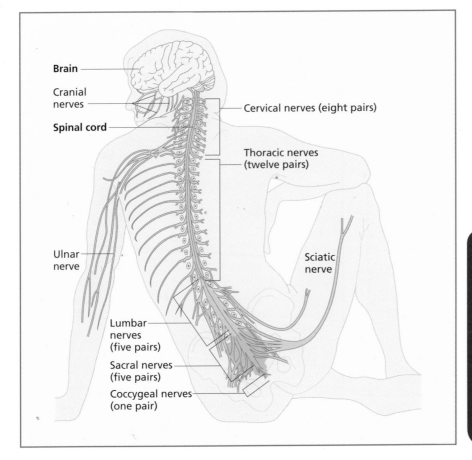

Brain
Cranial nerves
Spinal cord
Cervical nerves (eight pairs)
Thoracic nerves (twelve pairs)
Ulnar nerve
Sciatic nerve
Lumbar nerves (five pairs)
Sacral nerves (five pairs)
Coccygeal nerves (one pair)

> **KEY TERMS**
>
> **Central nervous system:** the brain and spinal cord; it is protected by bone and cerebrospinal fluid.
>
> **Peripheral nervous system:** it consists of all the nerve cells in the body not located within the central nervous system; it is divided into the somatic nervous system and the autonomic nervous system.

KEY TERMS

Somatic nervous system: the part of the peripheral nervous system that controls voluntary movements of skeletal muscles and hence the limbs.

Autonomic nervous system: the part of the peripheral nervous system that controls involuntary movements of non-skeletal muscles; it is divided into the sympathetic and parasympathetic nervous system.

Sympathetic nervous system: the part of the autonomic nervous system that produces arousal and energy (e.g., via increased heart rate).

Parasympathetic nervous system: the part of the autonomic nervous system involved in reducing arousal and conserving energy (e.g., by reducing heart rate).

Peripheral nervous system

Since there is detailed coverage of the brain shortly, we focus here on the peripheral nervous system. It consists of all the nerve cells in the body outside the central nervous system.

The peripheral nervous system divides into two parts: the somatic nervous system and the autonomic nervous system. The somatic nervous system is concerned with interactions with the external environment, whereas the autonomic nervous system is concerned with the body's internal environment.

The **somatic nervous system** consists in part of nerves carrying signals from the eyes, ears, skeletal muscles and the skin to the central nervous system. It also consists of nerves carrying signals from the central nervous system to the skeletal muscles, skin, and so on.

As mentioned already, the **autonomic nervous system** controls the movement of non-skeletal muscles. The organs within the control of the autonomic nervous system include the heart, lungs, eyes, stomach, and the blood vessels of internal organs. The autonomic nervous system is divided into the sympathetic nervous system and the parasympathetic nervous system.

The **sympathetic nervous system** is called into play in situations needing arousal and energy. It produces increased heart rate, reduced activity within the stomach, pupil dilation or expansion, and relaxation of the bronchi of the lungs. These changes prepare us for fight or flight.

The **parasympathetic nervous system** is involved when the body tries to save energy. The effects of activity in the parasympathetic nervous system are the opposite of those of activity in the sympathetic nervous system. The parasympathetic nervous system produces decreased heart rate, increased activity within the stomach, pupil contraction, and constriction of the bronchi of the lungs.

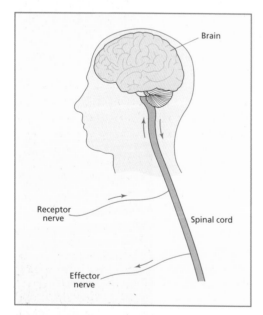

Receptor nerves transmit information to the brain via the spinal cord. Instructions from the brain are sent via the effector nerves.

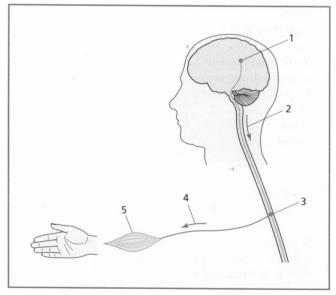

The somatic nervous system: What happens when you decide to move your fingers. (1) The decision arises in the brain; (2) is transmitted via the spinal cord; (3) transfers to another nerve (or series of nerves); (4) the instruction is transmitted to the skeletal muscles; (5) the muscles contract or relax, moving the fingers.

The sympathetic nervous system and the parasympathetic nervous system are both important. For example, consider the case of someone having excessive activity of the sympathetic nervous system but very little activity of the parasympathetic nervous system. He/she would probably be a highly stressed individual who found life very demanding.

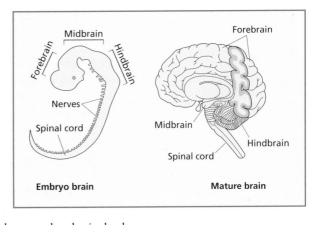

Embryo brain   **Mature brain**

Brain organisation

The first point to be emphasised about the brain is its complexity. It is much easier to study the brain's structure than to understand the functions or purposes of its various parts. However, as we will see later, technological advances have allowed researchers to assess brain functions by watching it in action.

At the most general level, the brain is divided into three main regions: forebrain, midbrain, and hindbrain. These terms refer to locations in an embryo's brain and do not indicate clearly the relative positions of the different brain regions in adults. Note that the forebrain and the hindbrain can each be divided into two somewhat separate regions (Pinel, 1998).

Forebrain

This is easily the most important division of the brain. It is located towards the top and the front of the brain and consists of four main parts:

- **Cerebrum**: this contains 70% of the neurons in the central nervous system. It plays a major role in thinking, use of language, and other cognitive abilities (discussed later).
- **Limbic system**: one major part of this system (the amygdala) is involved in several emotional states (see Chapter 6). Another major part (the hippocampus) is of importance in learning and memory.
- **Thalamus**: its main function is as a relay station that passes information on to higher brain centres. It is also involved in wakefulness and sleep.
- **Hypothalamus**: this structure serves various purposes including the control of autonomic functions such as body temperature, hunger, and thirst. It is also involved in the control of sexual behaviour and reactions to stress (see Chapter 5).

Midbrain

The **midbrain** has several important functions. First, parts of it are involved in vision and hearing, although most perceptual processes occur in the forebrain. Second, parts of the midbrain are used in movement control. Third, the midbrain contains the reticular activating system, although parts of this system extend into the hindbrain. The reticular activating system is involved in sleep regulation, arousal, and wakefulness, in part through its influence on heart rate and breathing rate.

Hindbrain

In evolutionary terms, the **hindbrain** is a very old part of the brain. Its brain structures resemble those of reptiles, leading the hindbrain to be called

KEY TERMS

Cerebrum: a part of the forebrain crucially involved in thinking and language.

Limbic system: a brain system consisting of the amygdala, hippocampus, and septal areas, all of which are involved in emotional processing.

Thalamus: a part of the forebrain involved in wakefulness and sleep.

Hypothalamus: a part of the forebrain involved in controlling body temperature, hunger, thirst, and sexual behaviour.

Midbrain: the middle part of the brain; it is involved in vision, hearing, and the control of movement.

Hindbrain: the "reptilian brain", concerned with breathing, digestion, swallowing, the fine control of balance, and the control of consciousness.

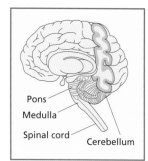

Pons
Medulla
Spinal cord
Cerebellum

the "reptilian brain". It consists of three parts, each serving one or more functions:

- *Medulla*: this is part of the reticular activating system and is involved in controlling breathing, digestion, and swallowing. Damage to this structure can cause death.
- *Pons*: this is also part of the reticular activating system; it is involved in the control of consciousness; it acts as a relay station passing messages between different parts of the brain.
- *Cerebellum*: its main functions are the fine control of balance and bodily coordination; information about overlearned skills such as riding a bicycle or touch typing is stored here.

Cerebral cortex

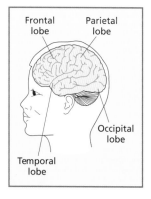

Frontal lobe
Parietal lobe
Occipital lobe
Temporal lobe

The **cerebral cortex** is the outer layer of the cerebrum. It is only 2 millimetres deep but is absolutely crucial for our ability to perceive, think, remember, and use language. We can divide the cerebral cortex up in two main ways:

1. The cerebral cortex within each hemisphere consists of four lobes or areas known as the frontal, parietal, temporal, and occipital. The frontal lobe is at the front of the brain and the occipital lobe at the back. The other two lobes are in the middle of the brain with the parietal lobe at the top and the temporal lobe below it.
2. The entire brain (including the cerebral cortex) is divided into two: the left and right cerebral hemispheres.

Localisation of function

What are the lobes of the cerebral cortex known as?

In spite of the enormous complexity of the cerebral cortex, it is possible to identify brain areas specialised for different kinds of processing. It is now time to consider in more detail the functions of the four lobes of the cerebral cortex.

The frontal lobe (especially the area towards the front known as the prefrontal cortex) is of central importance with respect to most complex forms of thinking. Consider brain-damaged patients who have suffered extensive damage to the frontal lobes. Such patients are said to have **dysexecutive syndrome** (Baddeley, 2007). This involves problems with planning behaviour, organising, monitoring their own behaviour, and sustaining attention or concentration.

We can obtain an approximate sense of the localisation of other brain functions with reference to the figure. It provides a useful summary. First, there is the visual centre based mostly in the occipital lobe at the back of the brain. More of the brain is devoted to visual processing than to processing in any other sense modality. Words flashed briefly activate the occipital area regardless of whether they are consciously perceived. However, only those consciously perceived (and so receiving extensive processing) cause significant activation in the frontal lobes (Gaillard et al., 2009).

Second, there is the auditory centre within the temporal lobes. It is involved in processing auditory stimuli such as speech and music. Conscious auditory processing typically involves activation in the prefrontal cortex as well as within the auditory centre.

KEY TERMS

Cerebral cortex: the outer layer of the cerebrum; it is involved in perception, learning, memory, thinking, and language.

Dysexecutive syndrome: a condition caused by brain damage (typically in the frontal lobes) in which there is severe impairment of complex cognitive functions (e.g., planning; decision making).

Third, there is the language centre. Numerous brain areas are involved in language and so there is no single language centre. For example, the visual centre is involved in reading and the auditory centre in speech comprehension. However, the areas most commonly associated with the language centre are Broca's area and Wernicke's area. Broca's area is involved in speech production, whereas Wernicke's area is involved in speech comprehension.

Fourth, there is the motor centre. It is located within the frontal lobes and is involved in the planning, control, and carrying out of voluntary movements. The brain is structured so that damage to parts of the motor cortex in one hemisphere often leads to movement problems on the other side of the body.

Fifth, there is the somatosensory centre. **Somatosensation** is "a cluster of perceptual processes that relate to the skin and body, and include touch, pain, thermal sensation and limb position" (Ward, 2010, p. 154). The somatosensory centre is complex in its organisation and processing. For example, consider touch. Our sense of touch depends on skin stretch, vibration, pressure, and temperature.

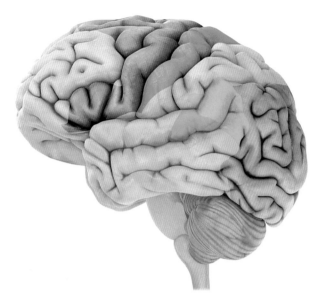

The human brain showing the motor centre (red), the somatosensory centre (orange), the visual centre (blue), the auditory centre (yellow), and the language centres (Broca's area: purple; Wernicke's area: green).

Note that brain activation is not limited to these specific centres. In practice, other brain areas (especially within the frontal lobes) are often involved in numerous kinds of processing. For example, language processing can involve at least six specific brain areas in addition to Broca's area and Wernicke's area (Berwick et al., 2013).

Hemispheric specialisation

So far I have discussed the cerebral cortex as if its two hemispheres or halves are very similar in their functioning. In fact, that is not correct. There is much **hemispheric lateralisation**, meaning the two hemispheres differ in their functions. As a consequence, there is some evidence of specialization within each hemisphere: this is hemispheric specialisation. There is cerebral dominance in many situations, with one hemisphere being mainly responsible for processing information in that situation. For example, language abilities are based mostly in the left hemisphere in 85%–90% of individuals. Approximately 10% of the world's population is left-handed with 80%–85% being right-handed (a few people are ambidextrous). In right-handed individuals, the motor centre in the left hemisphere is dominant because the right side of the body is controlled by the left hemisphere.

What about the right hemisphere? Increasing evidence suggests some aspects of visual and spatial attention are localised in the right hemisphere (Hervé et al., 2013). It has been claimed these functions are located in the right hemisphere because the left hemisphere is typically heavily involved in language and motor control and so has reduced capacity for other functions. However, spatial

What does hemispheric specialisation mean?

KEY TERMS

Somatosensation: several perceptual processes based on information received from the skin and body.

Hemispheric lateralisation: the notion that each hemisphere or half of the brain differs in its functioning to some extent even though both hemispheres coordinate their activities most of the time.

How are split-brain patients defined?

lateralisation is no greater in right-handed individuals than in left-handed ones, which suggests this is not the correct explanation.

Split-brain patients

Important (and interesting) evidence about hemispheric lateralisation has come from **split-brain patients**. In most of these patients, the corpus callosum (the major connection between the two hemispheres) has been cut surgically to contain severe epileptic seizures within one hemisphere.

It is sometimes thought that split-brain patients have great difficulty in functioning effectively in daily life. That is *not* the case. Split-brain patients ensure information about the environment reaches both hemispheres by moving their eyes around. To produce impaired performance in these patients, it is often necessary to present visual stimuli *briefly* to only one hemisphere to prevent it becoming available to the other hemisphere.

There is much controversy as to whether split-brain patients have two consciousnesses (one in each hemisphere) or only a single consciousness. Sperry (1968, p. 723) argued they have two consciousnesses: "The minor hemisphere [the right one] constitutes a second conscious entity that . . . runs along in parallel with the more dominant stream of consciousness in the major hemisphere [the left one]." He regarded the left hemisphere as dominant because language processing is typically centred there.

In contrast, Gazzaniga (e.g., 2013) emphasised the importance of a stream of consciousness centred in the dominant left hemisphere. This system is known as the interpreter. It "seeks explanations for internal and external events . . . to produce appropriate response behaviours" (Gazzaniga et al., 2008, p. 465). A major reason why the left hemisphere is likely to be dominant is that language abilities are typically centred in that hemisphere. Note, however, that Gazzaniga accepts that much processing also occurs in the right hemisphere.

What evidence supports Gazzaniga et al.'s viewpoint? The subjective experiences of split-brain patients are relevant. According to Colvin and Gazzaniga (2007, p. 189), "No split-brain patient has ever woken up following callostomy [cutting of the corpus callosum] and felt as though his/her experience of self had fundamentally changed or that two selves now inhabited the same body." Hellmann et al. (2013) assessed brain activity to visual stimuli in a split-brain patient (AC). He exhibited much more brain activity to stimuli presented to his left hemisphere than those presented to his right hemisphere. These findings suggested that AC had much greater conscious awareness of the former stimuli than the latter.

What evidence supports Sperry's view that split-brain patients have two streams of consciousness? On that view, we might expect *disagreements* between the two hemispheres. Such disagreements have occasionally been reported. Mark (1996, p. 191) discussed a patient having speech in both hemispheres: "She mentioned that she did not have feelings in her left hand. When I echoed the statement, she said that she was not numb, and then the torrent of alternating 'Yes!' and 'No!' replies ensued, followed by a despairing 'I don't know!'"

Baynes and Gazzaniga (2000) studied VJ, a split-brain patient whose writing is controlled by the right hemisphere whereas her speech is controlled by the

KEY TERM

Split-brain patients: individuals in whom the corpus callosum connecting the two halves of the brain has been severed; direct communication between the two hemispheres is not possible.

left hemisphere. According to Baynes and Gazzaniga (2000, p. 1362), "She [VJ] is the first split . . . who is frequently dismayed by the independent performance of her right and left hands. She is discomfited by the fluent writing of her left hand to unseen stimuli and distressed by the inability of her right hand to write out words she can read out loud and spell." Speculatively, these findings suggested limited dual consciousness.

In sum, both hemispheres in split-brain patients engage in many processing activities. However, the right hemisphere probably lacks its own consciousness. That makes sense because there could be numerous conflicts between the two hemispheres if both had their own consciousness.

Ways of studying the brain

Dramatic technological advances in recent years mean we now have many ways of obtaining detailed information about brain functioning. This has led to the development of cognitive neuroscience (see Chapter 2). Cognitive neuroscientists obtain information about patterns of brain activity and behavioural measures while individuals perform various cognitive tasks. Of crucial importance is the assumption that we can understand human cognitive processes better by considering information about brain activity and behaviour (i.e., task performance) than by considering only behavioural measures as was done by cognitive psychologists.

The available techniques for studying brain activity vary in terms of how precisely they identify *where* brain activity occurs (spatial resolution) and *when* it occurs (temporal resolution). Here we will focus on two major techniques: functional magnetic resonance imaging (fMRI) and event-related potentials (ERPs).

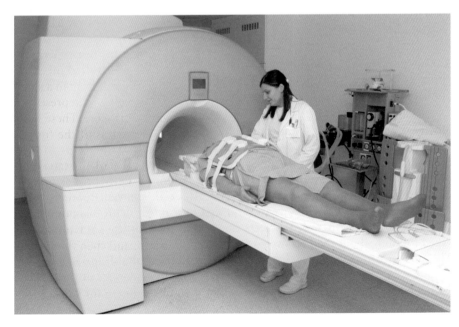

The magnetic resonance imaging (MRI) scanner has proved an extremely valuable source of data in psychology.

Does functional magnetic resonance imaging have poor or good spatial and/ or temporal resolution?

fMRI involves scanners containing a very large magnet weighing up to 11 tons. Brain areas with an accumulation of oxygenated red blood cells suggestive of activity in those areas are assessed. Technically, this is the BOLD (blood oxygen-level-dependent contrast) signal. Changes in the BOLD signal produced by increased neural activity take some time, so the temporal resolution of fMRI is about two or three seconds. However, its spatial resolution is very good (approximately 1 millimetre). An example of how fMRI can be used to resolve theoretical controversies is discussed in Chapter 2.

Event-related potentials (ERPs) provide a valuable way of measuring brain activity. A stimulus is presented several times, and scalp electrodes are used to obtain recordings of brain activity on each trial. Then information from all the recordings is averaged. Why is this done? There is so much brain activity going on all the time it can be hard to detect the effects of stimulus processing on brain-wave activity. Several trials are needed to distinguish genuine effects of stimulation from background brain activity.

ERPs provide extremely precise information about the time course of brain activity. Indeed, they often indicate when a given process occurred to within a few milliseconds. However, ERPs provide only a very approximate indication of the brain regions activated.

Here is an example of how ERPs helped to resolve a theoretical controversy relating to reading. It used to be thought that readers typically did not predict the word(s) that would be presented next because such predictions are often wrong and so lead to inefficient processing. However, some theorists disagreed with this viewpoint. This issue can be addressed using ERPs, specifically focusing on the N400 component (a negative wave peaking at about 400 ms after stimulus presentation). The N400 is smaller when what is presented matches the reader's expectation.

De Long et al. (2005) studied the N400 in a study in which readers received sentences such as the following:

The day was breezy so the boy went outside to fly [a kite/an airplane] in the park.

The key finding was that there was a larger N400 to the article *an* (preceding airplane) than to *a* (preceding kite). This finding occurred because readers were predicting the most likely noun would follow.

Neuroenchantment

Cognitive neuroscience has greatly enhanced our understanding of human cognition. However, we need to beware of what Ali et al. (2014) term "neuroenchantment" – the assumption that assessing brain activity provides direct information about psychological processes. Ali et al. showed the dangers of neuroenchantment. Participants were placed in a mock neuroimaging device constructed out of discarded objects including a hair dryer. They were then asked to think about their answers to various questions (e.g., name a country). The mock neuroimagaing device apparently "read their minds" and worked out exactly what they had been thinking. Amazingly, three-quarters of the student participants believed this was genuine rather than being due to the researcher's trickery!

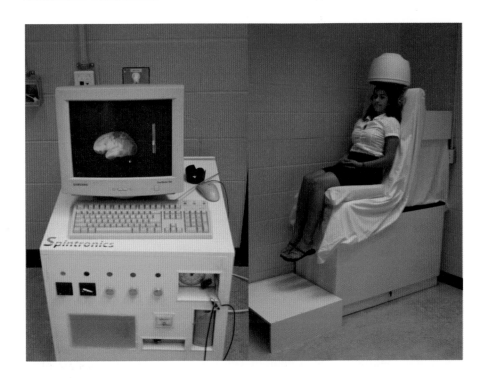

EVALUATION

⊕ Various techniques for studying the brain have shed much light on when (and where) cognitive processes occur.

⊕ Cognitive neuroscience has proved increasingly successful in clarifying major theoretical issues in cognitive psychology.

⊖ It has often been assumed that each brain region is *specialised* for a different function. That is a serious oversimplification – performance of any given task is typically associated with simultaneous activity in several different brain regions.

⊖ Findings in cognitive neuroscience are often over-interpreted because of "neuroenchantment".

⊖ Most cognitive neuroscience research reveals *associations* between patterns of brain activity and task performance. Such associations do not prove that all the brain areas activated are necessary or essential for task performance.

Chapter summary

- Evolutionary psychology has helped to explain why humans behave in the ways they do.
- Evolutionary explanations are often speculative and fail to account adequately for individual differences.
- Twin studies provide an effective way of addressing the nature-nurture issue. Such studies indicate that genetic factors often play an important role in influencing individual differences in behaviour.
- There are various ways an individual's genetic endowment influences his/her behaviour. These include active covariation, passive covariation, and reactive covariation.
- The nervous system consists of the central nervous system and peripheral nervous system. The latter is divided into the somatic nervous system and the autonomic nervous system.
- The autonomic nervous system controls the heart, lungs, eyes, stomach, and the blood vessels of the internal organs. It is divided into the sympathetic nervous system and the parasympathetic nervous system.
- The brain can be divided into three main regions: forebrain, midbrain, and hindbrain. The forebrain consists of the cerebrum (used in thinking), the limbic system (involved in aggression, fear, learning, and memory), the thalamus (a relay station), and the hypothalamus (used in the control of several autonomic functions). The midbrain is of relevance to the control of movement, sleep, arousal, and wakefulness. The hindbrain consists of the medulla oblongata, the pons, and the cerebellum.
- The cerebral cortex consists of the frontal lobe (front of the brain), the occipital lobe (back of the brain), the parietal lobe (top of the brain), and temporal lobe (lower part of the brain). The frontal lobes are especially involved in complex cognitive activities and motor processing, the occipital lobes in visual processing, the temporal lobes in auditory processing, and the parietal lobes in language processing and somatosensation.
- There is some hemispheric specialization with language abilities typically centred in the left hemisphere and spatial processing in the right hemisphere.
- Research on split-brain patients suggests there is a single consciousness based in the left hemisphere.
- fMRI provides precise evidence about *where* in the brain various processes occur, and ERPs indicate precisely *when* such processes occur.

Further reading

- Eysenck, M.W. (2015). *AQA psychology: AS and A-level year 1* (6th ed.). Hove, UK: Psychology Press. Chapter 6 in this textbook provides a detailed account of the biological approach to psychology.

- Pinel, J.P.J. (2015). *Biopsychology* (9th ed.). New York: Pearson. This successful textbook provides up-to-date coverage of all the main areas within biological psychology.

- Plomin, R., DeFries, J.C., Knopik, V.S., & Neiderhiser, J.M. (2016). Top 10 replicated findings from behavioural genetics. *Perspectives on Psychological Science, 11*, 3–23. Robert Plomin and his colleagues discuss the most important findings that have emerged from research on the impact of genetic factors on individual differences in behaviour.

- Stephen, I.D., Mahmut, M.K., Case, T.I., Fitness, J., & Stevenson, R.J. (2014). The uniquely predictive power of evolutionary approaches to mind and behaviour. *Frontiers in Psychology, 5* (Article 1372). The authors argue that evolutionary psychology is important because it explains why humans behave as they do.

Essay questions

1. In what ways has Darwin's theory of evolution influenced the development of psychology?

2. Describe and evaluate research on hemispheric specialisation.

3. Discuss some of the main complexities involved in making sense of the nature-nurture issue.

4. What are the main areas of the cerebral cortex? What are the main functions of each area?

We all know what it feels like to be stressed. Indeed, it is said that ours is the "age of stress" given the 24/7 nature of our lives. As a result, it is popularly believed that people today are more anxious and stressed than people in the past, and the number of newspaper articles on anxiety and depression has doubled in the past 30 years. Note, however, that our ancestors had to contend with major epidemics, short life expectancy, frequent wars, and poverty. Do you think we are more stressed and anxious than previous generations?

The term "stress" is often used rather vaguely. What do you think are the main signs of stress? In your everyday life, what factors cause you to feel stressed? How do you try to cope with the stress you experience? How successful are these attempts to cope with stress?

Stress

5

It is important to distinguish between "stressor" and "stress". A stressor refers to any situation that creates stress, and stress refers to our *reactions* to a stressor. More specifically, stress is "the psychological and physical strain or tension generated by physical, emotional, social, economic, or occupational circumstances, events, or experiences that are difficult to manage or endure" (Colman, 2009, p. 735).

What causes stress? A popular answer is that stress is what happens to us when we are exposed to a stressor (e.g., a forthcoming exam; rejection by one's partner). However, this answer is limited in two ways. First, it assumes we are *passive* and simply allow the environment to have an impact on us.

Second, it ignores the fact that our response to any given situation depends on our abilities and personalities as well as on the situation itself. For example, someone taking their first driving lesson typically finds driving very stressful and demanding, whereas experienced drivers generally do not.

A much better approach to stress is to regard it as the result of the *interaction* between an individual and his/her environment (Lazarus & Folkman, 1984). More specifically, stress occurs when perceived situational demands *exceed* the individual's ability to handle or cope with those demands. Driving is stressful for learner drivers because they have limited ability to meet the demands of handling a car in traffic. Driving is not stressful for experienced drivers because they are confident their ability will allow them to cope with most driving situations.

What effects are associated with stress? There are four major kinds of effects: physiological, emotional, cognitive, and behavioural. The physiological effects (which are the most complex ones) are discussed in the next section. The emotional effects can be assessed by self-questionnaires in which individuals answer questions about their mental and/or physical state (see Chapter 6).

With what effects is the stressed state associated?

There are several negative effects of stress and anxiety on the cognitive system. For example, stressed individuals performing a task find it hard to avoid being distracted by task-irrelevant stimuli (e.g., loud noises) and by their internal thoughts (e.g., about their current problems). Finally, the behavioural effects are related to the cognitive ones and include an inability to function effectively at work and a general reduction in motivation.

Emotional effects:
- Feelings of anxiety and depression
- Increased physical tension
- Increased psychological tension

Cognitive effects:
- Poor concentration
- Increased distractibility
- Reduced short-term memory capacity

Physiological effects:
- Release of adrenaline and noradrenaline
- Shut-down of digestive system
- Expansion of air passages in lungs
- Increased heart rate
- Constriction of blood vessels

Behavioural effects:
- Increased absenteeism
- Disrupted sleep patterns
- Reduced work performance

Are stress levels increasing?

Twenge (2000) wondered whether levels of trait anxiety (a personality dimension concerned with the experience of anxiety) had increased or decreased over time. She found the average score for trait anxiety in American children and college students was much higher in recent times than several decades ago suggesting we live in an increasingly stressed world. Booth et al. (2016) considered changes in trait anxiety between 1970 and 2010 in 57 countries and reported an increase over time in most of these countries. However, trait anxiety *declined* in the United Kingdom over that 40-year period, and the increase in trait anxiety in the United States was limited to students.

Twenge et al. (2010) compared the scores of American college students on the Minnesota Multiphasic Personality Inventory (MMPI) (which assesses psychiatric symptoms) between 1938 and 2007. There was a substantial increase in MMPI scores, leading Twenge et al. to conclude, "Five times as many now score above common cutoffs for psychopathology [mental illness]" (p. 145). Of direct relevance to stress, there were large increases in symptoms of depression, anxiety, and tension.

Similar findings from several countries were reported by Baxter et al. (2014). There was a general tendency for psychological distress (assessed by the General Health Questionnaire) to have increased in recent decades. In contrast, there were no changes in the incidence of anxiety disorders or clinical depression in several countries between 1990 and 2010. Lifestyle changes (including shorter sleep duration) may have increased psychological distress but insufficiently to impact on mental disorders.

Why are stress levels increasing in many countries? Materialism (which involves a focus on wealth and possessions) is an important factor. Many countries have seen a steady increase in materialism, which has been associated with poorer quality interpersonal relationships and reduced psychological well-being (Kasser, 2016). In other words, many young people nowadays belong to "Generation Me" – an increased focus on status and possessions but a reduced focus on social connectedness with others.

Physiology of stress

What does the general adaptation syndrome consist of?

How does our body respond to stressors? There is consensus that stress involves an immediate shock response followed by a countershock response. The first or shock response depends mainly on the sympathetic adrenal medullary

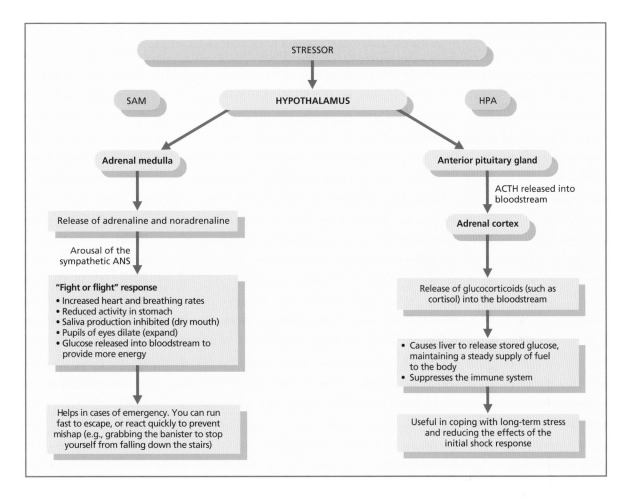

(SAM) system. In contrast, the second or countershock response involves the hypothalamic-pituitary-adrenocortical (HPA) axis.

One reason we know there are two systems is because stressors can have different effects on the two systems. Schommer et al. (2003) used the stressor of repeatedly requiring people to give a speech and perform a mental arithmetic task in front of an audience. With repetition, the SAM system continued to respond strongly, but there was a substantial reduction in HPA activation. Note, however, that the two systems typically influence each other rather than acting totally separately.

Sympathetic Adrenal Medullary (SAM) system

The initial response to shock involves the sympathetic adrenal medullary (SAM) system. Activity in the sympathetic branch of the autonomic nervous system (see Chapter 4) stimulates the adrenal medulla. This causes the release of the hormones **adrenaline** and **noradrenaline**. These hormones lead to increased arousal of the sympathetic nervous system and reduced activity in the parasympathetic nervous system.

Heightened SAM system activity prepares us for "fight or flight". More specifically, there are the following effects: increased alertness and energy, increased

KEY TERMS

Adrenaline: a hormone producing increased arousal within the sympathetic nervous system; it is very similar in structure and function to **noradrenaline**.

Noradrenaline: a hormone producing increased arousal within the sympathetic nervous system; it is very similar in structure and function to **adrenaline**.

blood flow to the muscles, increased heart and respiration rate, and reduced activity in the digestive system. There is also increased release of clotting factors into the bloodstream to reduce blood loss in the event of injury.

How can we explain individual differences in SAM system activity? Frigerio et al. (2009) found genetic factors partially accounted for infants' SAM system response when exposed to stress.

Finally, note that SAM activity is not *only* associated with stress. It is true that we often perceive heightened activity in the SAM as indicating we are stressed. However, we sometimes interpret such activity as meaning we are excited or stimulated.

How are adrenaline and noradrenaline related to stress?

Hypothalamic-Pituitary-Adrenocortical (HPA) axis

If we are exposed to a stressor for several hours, activity within the SAM system increasingly uses up bodily resources. This leads to a countershock response involving the hypothalamic-pituitary-adrenocortical (HPA) axis designed to minimise damage. The details of its functioning are discussed next.

The anterior pituitary gland releases several hormones of which the most important is **adrenocorticotrophic hormone (ACTH)**. ACTH stimulates the adrenal cortex, which produces cortisol. **Cortisol** is often called the "stress hormone" because large amounts are produced when someone is under prolonged stress.

Evidence of the importance of the HPA axis was shown by Hare et al. (2013) in a study on skydivers. They compared novice skydivers (no previous jumps) and experienced skydivers (average of 400 previous jumps). As we would expect, the experienced skydivers showed less stress than the novices in some ways (e.g., self-reported anxiety). However, HPA axis activity as indexed by cortisol levels was very similar in both groups. The fact that skydiving can potentially have fatal consequences explains why cortisol levels remain high in skydivers after extensive practice.

KEY TERMS

Adrenocorticotrophic hormone (ACTH): a hormone that leads to the release of the stress hormone cortisol.

Cortisol: the so-called "stress hormone" because elevated amounts are typically found in the bodies of highly stressed individuals.

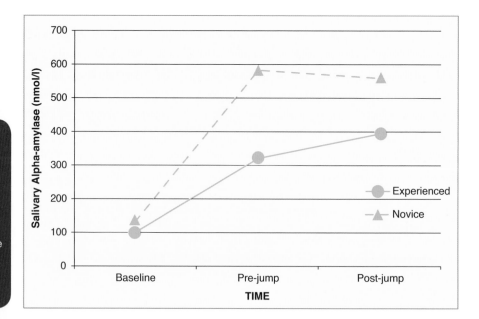

What stressors have the greatest effects on the HPA axis? Dickerson and Kemeny (2004) found in a large-scale review that uncontrollable tasks involving social evaluative threat produced the greatest ACTH changes, the highest levels of cortisol, and the longest recovery time.

Cortisol and other similar hormones are useful because they permit maintenance of a steady supply of fuel to the body. They also help to elevate blood glucose concentrations, to mobilise protein reserves, and to conserve salts and water. Individuals without adrenal glands cannot produce the normal amounts of glucocorticoids. As a result, they have to be given additional quantities of glucocorticoids to survive when stressed (Tyrell & Baxter, 1981).

The glucocorticoids also have negative effects. They suppress the immune system, which protects the body against intruders such as viruses and bacteria. They also have an anti-inflammatory action, slowing the rate at which wounds heal.

In sum, the beneficial effects of HPA activity are achieved at considerable cost, and the HPA cannot continue indefinitely at an elevated level of activity. If the adrenal cortex stops producing glucocorticoids, this eliminates the ability to maintain blood glucose concentrations at the appropriate level.

Causes of stress

There are many different causes of stress. First, severe negative life events and hassles often make us stressed. Second, workers are exposed to many workplace stressors. Third, some individuals are more susceptible than others to experiencing stress because of their personality. We will discuss these types of causes in turn.

Life events and hassles

We can distinguish between life events and hassles. **Life events** are often major negative events or occurrences (e.g., death of a loved one) causing high levels of stress. In contrast, hassles are the minor challenges and interruptions (e.g., arguing with a friend) of everyday life. On average, people experience at least one hassle on 40% of days.

Life events

Holmes and Rahe (1967) developed the Social Readjustment Rating Scale on which people indicate which out of 43 life events have happened to them over a period of time (usually 6 or 12 months). These life events are assigned a value based on their likely impact. Here are various life events taken from this scale with their associated life change units in parentheses:

Death of a spouse (100)
Divorce (73)
Marital separation (65)
Prison (63)
Death of a close family member (63)
Change in eating habits (15)

What types of life event does the Social Readjustment Rating Scale measure?

KEY TERM

Life events: these are major events (mostly have negative consequences) that create high levels of stress, often over a long period of time.

Findings

There is considerable evidence that the experience of life events is associated with many negative consequences. For example, Rahe and Arthur (1977) found individuals who had recently experienced several severe life events had an increased probability of various psychological illnesses, athletic injuries, physical illness, and even traffic accidents. More specifically, people experiencing more than 300 life change units (based on the number and severity of recent life events) are at increased risk for many physical and mental illnesses including heart attacks, diabetes, TB, asthma, anxiety, and depression (Martin, 1989).

Sbarra et al. (2011) reviewed the effects of divorce based on studies involving 6½ million people. Divorced individuals had a 20%–30% greater risk of early death than those who remained married due in part to changes in health behaviours and long-lasting psychological distress. However, most individuals coped well with divorce.

Sbarra et al. (2013) argued that a small minority of individuals lack the resilience to cope with the aftermath of divorce. People without a major depressive episode at first assessment (M1) only rarely had an episode following divorce or separation (M2). In contrast, those with a major depressive episode when first assessed had almost a 60% chance of having a depressive episode after divorce/separation.

The negative effects of negative life events depend in part on personality. Kendler et al. (2004) found that those high in neuroticism (a personality dimension associated with negative emotional states) were *four* times as likely as those low in neuroticism to develop major depression following severe life events.

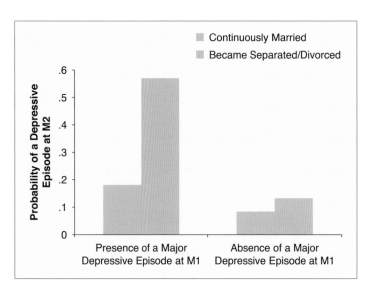

Probability of a major depressive episode at the second assessment (M2) as a function of their marital status and depression at first assessment (M1).

Hassles

DeLongis et al. (1988) considered the effects of hassles (e.g., losing things; concerns about weight) and uplifts (e.g., good weather; relations with friends). Hassles were associated with impaired overall health, but uplifts had little impact. Stone et al. (1987) considered the hassles and desirable events experienced by participants developing a respiratory illness during the 10 days before its onset. They experienced more hassles and fewer desirable events during that period than those not developing a respiratory illness.

Johnson and Sherman (1997) studied students experiencing major life events. Those who also had substantial numbers of daily hassles reported more psychiatric symptoms.

Summary

Severe life events and hassles both produce negative effects on physical health and psychological well-being. However, there are substantial individual differences in the response to life events and hassles. Many individuals (especially those low in neuroticism and/or high in resilience) manage to cope well even with very severe life events such as divorce.

Workplace stressors
More than 25 million people in the United Kingdom spend between 1,500–2,000 hours a year at work doing jobs that are often very demanding or boring. As a result, the workplace is a major source of stress. Several factors associated with the workplace environment can cause stress. However, three such factors are of special importance:

1. High job strain (low job control combined with high job demands).
2. Effort-reward imbalance (work rewards are low relative to the effort required).
3. Stress resulting from the huge increase in computer usage in the workplace.

Low job control
Low job control leads to several stress-related outcomes. Spector et al. (1988) found it was associated with frustration, anxiety, headaches, stomach upsets, and visits to the doctor. Marmot et al. (1997) found among 9,000 British civil servants that those on the lowest employment grades were *four* times more likely to die of a heart attack than those on the most senior grade. They were also more likely to suffer from cancer, strokes, and gastrointestinal disorders.

These differences probably occurred because those in the lower positions had much less control over their work than those in the higher positions. In addition, however, those resistant to the effects of stress may be more likely to rise to senior job positions.

Effort-reward imbalance
Kuper et al. (2002) studied over 10,000 civil servants followed up for 11 years. Effort-reward imbalance was associated with several outcomes suggestive of high stress: non-fatal heart attacks, fatal heart attacks, poor physical functioning, and poor mental functioning. Bohle et al. (2015) found among older Australian workers that high effort-reward imbalance was associated with reduced mental health.

Dramatic findings were reported by Klein et al. (2010). Surgeons with high effort-reward imbalance were *six* times more likely than other surgeons to report the symptoms of burnout. Smith et al. (2005) found that effort-reward imbalance caused high levels of anger, which in turn led to cardiovascular disease.

Conclusions
In sum, low job control and effort-reward imbalance are very stressful. However, two points need to be made. First, workplace stress can be created in other ways (e.g., job lacks variety; job is not valued by society; job does not provide the opportunity to socialise). Second, the existence of *associations* between poor job control and stress outcomes and between effort-reward imbalance and stress outcomes does not prove that the job factors actually *caused* the stress outcomes.

Technostress

The dramatic increase in the use of computers in the workplace over the past 20 years or so has had profound effects on the lives of millions of workers. Many of the changes stemming from this technological revolution have been very beneficial. However, there has been a cost in the form of **technostress**, "the mental stress that employees experience due to the use of ICT [information and communication technology] at work" (Fuglseth & Sorebo, 2014, p. 161).

Wang et al. (2008) wondered which kinds of organisation were associated with high levels of technostress. In a study on Chinese workers, they identified two major factors. First, there is power centralisation. Technostress was higher in very centralised companies. This happened because workers were excluded from involvement in major decisions (e.g., on possible technological changes). Second, technostress was higher in companies emphasising innovation.

In sum, technostress is an increasingly important source of work stress. There are several ways this trend could be reversed. For example, workers should feel involved in decisions requiring them to deal with complex technological changes. In addition, companies should ensure workers have adequate training in computer-based skills.

IN THE REAL WORLD: burnout

Burnout is "a syndrome combining emotional exhaustion, depersonalisation (cynical attitudes towards coworkers, students, and clients), and a reduced sense of personal accomplishment . . . with emotional exhaustion burnout's central component" (Schonfeld & Bianchi, 2016, p. 22). It occurs as a result of prolonged exposure to stressors (especially work-related ones).

The most commonly used measure of burnout is the Maslach Burnout Inventory. The original version was produced by Maslach and Jackson (1981) and the third edition was published by Maslach et al. (1996). Three dimensions relating to burnout are identified:

1. Emotional exhaustion: "feelings of being emotionally overextended and exhausted by one's work"
2. Depersonalisation: "an unfeeling and impersonal response towards recipients of one's care or service"
3. Personal achievement: "feelings of competence and successful achievement in one's work with people"

(Maslach & Jackson, 1981, p. 101).

Burnout depends on workers' personality as well as the nature of their work demands. Bakker et al. (2006) studied burnout in counsellors who had the stressful job of caring for terminally ill patients. They assessed the Big Five personality factors (extraversion, neuroticism, agreeableness, conscientiousness, and intellect; see Chapter 18).

KEY TERMS

Technostress: the anxiety and stress caused by difficulties in coping with technological advances (especially in computing).

Burnout: long-term emotional exhaustion, depersonalisation, and lack of personal achievement triggered by excessive work demands.

Emotional exhaustion, depersonalisation, and low personal achievement were all associated with high levels of neuroticism. Depersonalisation and low personal achievement were also associated with low extraversion, and depersonalisation was additionally associated with low intellect. Van der Wal et al. (2016) studied the relationship between the Big Five personality factors and burnout in anaesthesiologists. Workers suffering from burnout had much higher neuroticism scores than the other workers.

There is controversy concerning the relationship between burnout and depression. Burnout is often regarded as being specifically related to the work environment whereas depression affects every area of life. However, Schonfeld and Bianchi (2016) found the symptoms of burnout and of depression in teachers correlated highly with each other. Strikingly, 86% of teachers suffering from burnout satisfied the criteria for a diagnosis of depression.

What approaches can be used to prevent burnout? First, Maslach (2011, p. 45) argued that the best approach is to build engagement: "People who are engaged with their work are better able to cope with the challenges they encounter, and thus are more likely to recover from stress." Second, it is important to focus on the ways in which organisations function. For example, Leiter et al. (2012) used an intervention designed to increase civility within the workplace. This apparently modest organisational change decreased several symptoms of burnout (e.g., distress; poor work attitudes).

Personality

There are major individual differences in stress susceptibility. We can identify two major effects of stress: (1) *psychological* (e.g., reported distress; health complaints) and (2) *physical* (e.g., cardiovascular disease; early mortality). Individual differences in personality are much more strongly associated with psychological effects than physical ones. For example, consider the personality dimension of negative affectivity (susceptibility to anxiety, stress, and depression) which resembles neuroticism (see Chapter 18). Individuals high in negative affectivity report many more health complaints (e.g., headaches; racing heart) than low scorers and also claim to be considerably more stressed. However, there is practically no relationship between negative affectivity and more objective, physical measures of ill health (e.g., coronary heart disease; high blood pressure) (Watson & Pennebaker, 1989).

Disease and physical health

The best-known research attempting to link personality to physical disease was based on the **Type A personality** involving hostility, impatience, and time pressure. In contrast, individuals with **Type B personality** are more relaxed and less competitive. Rosenman et al. (1975) reported striking findings: over a period of 8½ years, Type A individuals were nearly twice as likely as Type Bs to develop coronary heart disease. Further analysis of their data suggested the hostility component of Type A was most responsible for heart disease (Matthews et al.,

KEY TERMS

Type A personality: a personality type characterised by impatience, competitiveness, time pressure, and hostility.

Type B personality: a personality type characterised by an easy-going approach to life and lacking the characteristics associated with Type A personality.

1977). In more recent research, however, the relationship between Type A personality and coronary heart disease has been very small (Myrtek, 2001).

Denollet (2005) argued that individuals having the Type D (distressed) personality are most susceptible to stress. The **Type D personality** has two aspects:

1. high negative affectivity or neuroticism (frequent experience of anxiety, depression, and other negative emotional states);
2. high social inhibition (inhibited behaviour in social situations).

Mols and Denollet (2010) found Type D individuals are highly stressed and have poor mental health (many symptoms of depression, anxiety, and posttraumatic stress disorder). There is also evidence that Type D individuals have impaired physical health. Denollet (2005) found only 19% of individuals in the general population have the Type D personality. However, the figure was 54% among those with hypertension (high blood pressure) and 27% among cardiac patients. In addition, 27% of cardiac patients with Type D personality died over a 10-year period compared to only 7% of those not having that personality type.

Grande et al. (2012) carried out a meta-analytic review of several studies. Overall, cardiac deaths and all-cause mortality were greater in Type D patients than other patients. However, the strength of these associations is less in more recent studies than earlier ones. These findings suggest there are only modest associations between Type D personality and health outcomes.

Conclusions

Type A individuals, Type D individuals, and those high in negative affectivity report high stress levels. However, they show relatively few physical symptoms of stress or increased susceptibility to disease. How can we reconcile these findings? Such individuals have an **interpretive bias** – they tend to interpret ambiguous information in a threatening fashion. Thus, for example, they are more likely than other people to interpret the minor aches and pains of everyday life as indicating that they have potentially serious health problems.

> **KEY TERMS**
>
> **Type D personality:** a personality type characterised by high negative affectivity and social inhibition.
>
> **Interpretive bias:** negatively biased or distorted interpretations of ambiguous stimuli and situations.
>
> **Immune system:** a system of biological structures and processes in the body that is involved in fighting disease

How does stress cause illness?

There are two main ways stress might cause illness:

1. *Directly* by reducing the body's ability to fight illness (e.g., by damaging the immune system).
2. *Indirectly* by leading the stressed individual to adopt an unhealthy lifestyle (e.g., smoking; excessive drinking).

Direct route

It is commonly thought that stress causes illness by impairing the **immune system** (a system of cells that fights disease). Cells in the immune system have receptors for various hormones and neurotransmitters involved in the stress response. These cells help to explain how stress influences the immune system's functioning.

We need to distinguish between natural immunity and specific immunity. Cells involved in natural immunity are all-purpose cells that have rapid effects. In contrast, cells involved in specific immunity are much more limited in their effects and take longer to work.

Segerstrom and Miller (2004) pointed out that it would be bad news for the survival of the human species if even short-term stress impaired the functioning of the immune system. They reviewed research on stress and immunity and came to the following conclusions:

- Short-lived stressors (e.g., public speaking) *increase* natural immunity.
- The stress produced by the death of a spouse reduces natural immunity.
- Stress caused by natural disasters produces a small increase in natural and specific immunity.
- Life events are associated with reduced natural and specific immunity only in individuals over 55 years of age.

Indirect route

Lifestyle has a major impact on illness and lifespan via the indirect route. Breslow and Enstrom (1980) considered the effects of seven health behaviours: not smoking, having breakfast every day, having no more than two alcoholic drinks a day, taking regular exercise, sleeping seven to eight hours a night, not eating between meals, and being no more than 10% overweight. Individuals practising all seven health behaviours had only 23% the mortality of those practising fewer than three in a follow-up 9½ years later.

Fortin et al. (2014) considered five lifestyle factors: smoking habit, high alcohol consumption, insufficient fruit and vegetable consumption, physical activity, underweight or overweight. Men with four or five unhealthy lifestyle factors were five times more likely than those with zero or one to suffer from multi-morbidity (three or more chronic diseases). Women with many unhealthy lifestyle factors were three times more likely to have multi-morbidity than those with no more than one unhealthy lifestyle factor.

Stressed individuals have somewhat less healthy lifestyles than non-stressed ones. They smoke more, drink more alcohol, take less exercise, and sleep less than non-stressed ones (Cohen & Williamson, 1991). Siegrist and Rodel (2006) reviewed the evidence from 46 studies. High levels of work stress were associated with being overweight and with heavy alcohol consumption by men.

Mainous et al. (2010) found life stress was associated with hardening of the arteries. This occurred in part because stressed individuals smoked more, had a higher caloric intake, and had a less active lifestyle.

In sum, the effects of stressors on the immune system depend on the nature and duration of the stressor. Two additional points need to be made. First, immune system functioning in most stressed individuals is within the normal range (Bachen et al., 1997) suggesting that stress often has small effects on physical health.

Second, the immune system is very complex. As a result, it is unwise to claim that stress impairs immune system functioning simply because it affects certain small parts of that system.

Methods for reducing stress

We have discussed stress and the factors that produce it. How do we handle and resolve stress in our everyday lives? Some of the main methods are considered next.

Stress inoculation training

What are the main phases in stress inoculation training?

One of the most-used interventions to reduce stress is stress inoculation training, which was developed by Meichenbaum (1985). It involves three main phases:

1. *Assessment*: the therapist discusses the individual's problem and asks his/her views on how to eliminate it.
2. *Stress reduction techniques*: the individual learns various techniques for reducing stress such as relaxation and self-instruction by using coping self-statements. Examples include "If I keep calm, I can handle this situation" and "Stop worrying because it's pointless."
3. *Application and follow-through*: the individual imagines using the stress reduction techniques learned in the second phase in difficult situations. After that, he/she uses the techniques in real-life situations.

Keogh et al. (2006) used an intervention closely resembling stress inoculation training on adolescents a few weeks before important examinations. The intervention significantly improved their examination performance. It also improved the students' mental health by reducing their negative thoughts and attitudes about their ability to cope successfully with the examinations.

Researchers have increasingly made use of computer-based interventions (cyber-interventions) to implement stress inoculation training. Sereno et al. (2014) concluded in a review of cyber-intervention studies that stress inoculation training is effective in reducing stress in several settings.

Most research has used self-report measures of stress. The potential limitation of such measures is that individuals may exaggerate training's beneficial effects. An alternative approach is to assess cortisol levels – remember it is the "stress hormone". Gaab et al. (2003) exposed participants to a stressful situation. Those who had received stress inoculation training beforehand had smaller cortisol responses to the stressful situation than did controls. They also interpreted the situation as less stressful and showed more competence in dealing with it.

EVALUATION

➕ Stress inoculation training reduces stress levels (assessed by self-report or cortisol responses) with both long-term and short-lasting stressors.

➕ Stress inoculation training can protect individuals from the negative effects of *future* stressors. This is valuable because "prevention is better than cure".

➖ Stress inoculation training consists of several components, and it is hard to identify *which* component is most responsible for beneficial effects.

➖ Not all the beneficial effects of stress inoculation training are due to *specific* components of training. General factors common to most interventions (e.g., therapist warmth; alliance between therapist and client) are also important.

Coping strategies

Much research on stress reduction has been devoted to coping. Coping can be defined as "efforts to prevent or diminish threat, harm, and loss, or to reduce associated distress" (Carver & Connor-Smith, 2010, p. 685). There is an important distinction between problem-focused and emotion-focused coping. **Problem-focused coping** involves using thoughts or actions to act directly on a stressful situation (e.g., purposeful action; decision making; planning). In contrast, **emotion-focused coping** involves attempting to reduce the emotional state experienced in a stressful situation (e.g., by distraction; avoidance of the situation; seeking social support).

Do you think problem-focused or emotion-focused coping is more effective? You probably chose problem-focused coping because it is thought desirable to *confront* stressful situation in Western societies. An alternative viewpoint emphasises **coping flexibility**, which is "intraindividual [within individual] variability in the deployment of coping strategies and . . . the capacity to exhibit such variability in a way that fosters adjustment" (Cheng et al., 2014, p. 1582).

Several theories based on the notion of coping flexibility have been proposed. For example, Zakowski et al. (2001) proposed the goodness-of-fit hypothesis. According to this hypothesis, it is preferable to use problem-focused coping when the stress is controllable, but emotion-focused coping is more effective when the stressor is uncontrollable.

Cheng et al. (2014) proposed a three-stage model:

1. *Planning*: selecting the strategies that are optimal for a given stressful situation.
2. *Execution*: evaluation coping (deciding to change the current coping strategy) and adaptive coping (identifying a preferable coping strategy).
3. *Feedback*: monitoring the success (or otherwise) of the chosen coping strategy.

Findings

There is some support for all these viewpoints. Penley et al. (2002) reviewed numerous studies concerned with coping strategies and health-related outcomes. Problem-focused coping was *positively* associated with physical and psychological health outcomes. In contrast, several forms of emotion-focused coping (e.g., avoidance; wishful thinking) were all *negatively* associated with the same outcomes.

Some support for the goodness-of-fit hypothesis was reported by Zakowski et al. (2001). Participants were more likely to use problem-focused coping when the stressor was perceived as controllable rather than uncontrollable. However, emotion-focused coping was used more often when the stressor was perceived as uncontrollable. The effects of emotion-focused coping on behavioural and self-report measures of stress were as predicted by the goodness-of-fit hypothesis – this form of coping was more effective with an uncontrollable stressor. However, the effects of problem-focused coping on stress did *not* vary as a function of stressor controllability, which is inconsistent with the hypothesis.

Forsythe and Compas (1987) studied the effectiveness of problem-focused and emotion-focused coping when dealing with major life events. The findings were as predicted by the goodness-of-fit hypothesis. Individuals had fewer psychological symptoms when problem-focused coping was used with controllable events and emotion-focused coping with uncontrollable events.

Kato (2015) studied individual differences in two aspects of coping flexibility (evaluation coping and adaptive coping). As predicted, both aspects were associated with better psychological health (low depression).

KEY TERMS

Problem-focused coping: a general strategy for dealing with stressful situations in which attempts are made to act directly on the source of the stress.

Emotion-focused coping: a general strategy for dealing with stressful situations in which the individual attempts to reduce his/her negative emotional state.

Coping flexibility: the notion that individuals who respond to stressful events flexibly via the use of various different coping strategies have better psychological adjustment than those who cope less flexibly.

Cheng et al. (2014) carried out a meta-analytic review based on findings from nearly 60,000 people. There was a consistent positive relationship between coping flexibility and psychological adjustment. The relationship was weaker in individualistic cultures (which emphasise personal responsibility) than collectivistic cultures (which emphasise group cohesion). Why is this? In individualistic cultures, it is regarded as more important to assert oneself and less important to change one's behaviour flexibly across situations than is the case in collectivistic cultures.

EVALUATION

➕ Problem-focused coping and emotion-focused coping are both generally applicable across numerous stressful situations.

➕ Several approaches emphasising coping flexibility (e.g., goodness-of-fit hypothesis; Cheng et al.'s model) have received much support.

➖ There is much evidence that the coping strategies people use influence their psychological adjustment. However, it is also likely that people's psychological adjustment also influences their choice of coping strategies. Thus, causality probably operates in both directions.

➖ Problem-focused and emotion-focused coping are not entirely separate. As Skinner et al. (2003, p. 227) pointed out, "Making a plan not only guides problem solving but also calms emotion."

➖ In spite of the importance of problem-focused and emotion-focused coping, individuals often use other coping strategies. Examples are rumination (e.g., self-blame; worry) and helplessness (e.g., inaction; passivity) (Skinner et al., 2003).

➖ It is often hard to assess the effectiveness of problem-focused coping because it can produce positive *and* negative outcomes. Wu et al. (1993) found doctors who accepted responsibility for their own mistakes made constructive changes to their work habits (a positive outcome). However, they also experienced more distress (a negative outcome).

Social support

How important is social support in reducing stress? First, we need to identify two different meanings of social support:

1. *Social network*: the number of people available to provide support (*quantity* of social support).
2. *Perceived support*: the strength of social support available from these individuals (*quality* of social support). This is how social support is typically defined.

Schaefer et al. (1981) found perceived support was positively related to health and well-being, but social network size was unrelated overall to well-being.

The latter is sometimes *negatively* related to well-being because it is very time-consuming and demanding to maintain a large social network.

Perceived support often reduces stress. Brown and Harris (1978) studied women who had recently experienced a serious life event. Of those who had an intimate friend, only 10% became depressed compared to 37% of those without an intimate friend. Becofsky et al. (2015) assessed the impact of social support on mortality over a 13-year period among participants whose average age was 53 at the start of the study. Receiving support from their spouse or partner reduced mortality risk by 19%, and regular social contact with several friends reduced mortality risk by 24% compared to social contact with zero or one friend.

How does social support reduce mortality? Uchino (2006) reviewed the relevant evidence. Social support is associated with positive changes in cardiovascular function (e.g., reducing blood pressure). It is also associated with positive effects on neuroendocrine function (e.g., reduced cortisol levels). In addition, social support is associated with enhanced functioning of the immune system.

Social support does not always have beneficial effects. Kirsch and Lehman (2015) studied female students performing the stressful task of giving a speech. Social support was provided in the form of helpful advice about how to deliver the speech. When this social support was provided *before* participants practised their speech, it reduced the stress response during the speech itself. When the social support was *given* after participants practised their speech, it could be perceived as indicating negative social evaluation – the participants' practice effort was so poor they needed advice. Social support in this condition failed to reduce the stress response during the speech.

Social support can make depressed individuals feel even more depressed. This happens when social support undermines the depressed person's basic psychological needs (Ibarra-Rouillard & Kuiper, 2011). For example, if friends adopt an over-controlling approach towards depressed individuals, these individuals may feel they are losing control of their lives.

Gender differences

Luckow et al. (1998) found women sought social support more than men in stressful situations in 25 out of 26 studies. Taylor et al. (2000) developed a theory based on this gender difference. She claimed men generally respond to stressful situations with a "fight-or-flight" response whereas women respond with a "tend-and-befriend" response. In other words, women respond to stressors by protecting and looking after their children (the tend response) and by actively seeking social support from others (the befriend response). Turton and Campbell (2005) found in a questionnaire-based study that females reported being more likely than males to use tend-and-befriend strategies in stressful situations.

Taylor et al. (2000) claimed that **oxytocin** (a hormone sometimes called the "cuddle hormone") plays an important role in the tend-and-befriend response. Of direct relevance to Taylor et al.'s theory, the effects of oxytocin are reduced by male sex hormones but increased by oestrogen (the female sex hormone). Cardoso et al. (2013) studied individuals who had the stressful experience of social rejection. The administration of oxytocin increased their trust in others, which would presumably have increased the likelihood they would have sought social support.

KEY TERM

Oxytocin: a hormone that promotes feelings of well-being by increasing sociability and reducing anxiety.

EVALUATION

➕ High levels of perceived support are associated with several beneficial effects on physical health, mental health, and mortality.

➕ The beneficial effects of perceived support occur in part because it produces positive changes in cardiovascular, neuroendocrine, and immune system functioning.

➕ Women are more likely than men to respond to stressful situations by producing the tend-and-befriend response whereas men often prefer the fight-or-flight response.

➖ Associations between social support and positive outcomes (e.g., low stress; good physical health) do not always mean that social support has produced those positive outcomes. The causal sequence may sometimes be in the opposite direction – individuals who are stressed and/or in poor physical health may find it harder to receive high levels of social support.

➖ The common assumption that social support always has beneficial effects is wrong. Social support can be perceived as being over-controlling or indicating negative social evaluation. (e.g., Ibarra-Rouillard & Kuiper, 2011; Kirsch & Lehman, 2015).

Chapter summary

- Stress results from interactions between an individual and their environment.
- The stress response consists of an initial shock response involving the sympathetic adrenal medullary (SAM) system followed by a countershock response involving the HPA axis. The hormone cortisol is of particular importance to activity within the HPA axis.
- Severe life events and hassles are both associated with various physical and psychological stress responses. However, some resilient individuals (e.g., those low in neuroticism) are relatively unaffected by life events and hassles.
- Two of the most damaging workplace stressors are low job control and effort-reward imbalance.
- Technostress is an increasingly common form of workplace stress.
- Burnout consists of emotional exhaustion, depersonalisation, and perceived lack of personal achievement. It is more common in individuals high in neuroticism and is related to depression.
- There are small effects of Type A personality and Type D personality on physical stress symptoms and impaired health.
- Stress can cause physical illness by impairing the immune system (direct route) or by leading to an unhealthy lifestyle (indirect route).
- Stress inoculation training reduces stress via techniques such as relaxation and coping self-statements.

- Problem-focused coping is often more effective than emotion-focused coping in reducing stress when stressors are controllable, with the opposite being the case when stressors are uncontrollable.
- Psychological adjustment in response to stressors is greater in individuals exhibiting coping flexibility.
- Social support is used more often by females than by males in response to stressors. It generally reduces stress but can have negative effects if it is perceived as undermining the individual's basic psychological needs.

Further reading

- Cheng, C., Lau, H.-P.B., & Chan, M.-P.S. (2014). Coping flexibility and psychological adjustment to stressful life changes: A meta-analytic review. *Psychological Bulletin, 140*, 1582–1607. The authors of this article provide a thorough discussion of theory and research on flexible coping with stressful events.
- Marks, D.F., Murray, M., Evans, B., & Estacio, E.V. (2015). *Health psychology: Theory, research and practice* (4th ed.). London: Sage. Chapter 12 in this textbook is concerned with issues relating to stress and coping.
- Rice, V.H. (Ed.) (2012). *Handbook of stress, coping, and health* (2nd ed.). London: Sage. There are chapters concerned with all major aspects of the interrelationships among stress, coping, and health in this book edited by Virginia Rice.
- Schaufeli, W.B., Leiter, M.P., & Maslach, C. (2009). Burnout: 35 years of research and practice. *Career Development International, 14*, 204–220. Developments in our understanding of burnout are discussed in this article.
- Segerstrom, S.C., & Miller, G.E. (2004). Psychological stress and the human immune system: A meta-analytic study of 30 years of inquiry. *Psychological Bulletin, 130*, 601–630. Hundreds of studies on the effects of stress on the immune system are reviewed in this thought-provoking article.

Essay questions

1. What are the effects of stressors on physiological processes? How do these effects change over time?

2. It is often claimed that stress can cause various physical illnesses by impairing the functioning of the immune system. Does the available evidence provide convincing support for this claim?

3. Suppose a friend of yours asked your advice on how to cope with stress. What advice would you give them based on the research evidence?

4. Which people are most susceptible to burnout? How can we try to prevent burnout?

5. What are the most important factors causing stress? Are some people more at risk of stress than others?

Sometimes you probably find it hard to know whether you are experiencing a weak emotion or no emotion at all. How could you decide which it is? There are many emotions including sadness, happiness, anxiety, and anger. Does it seem as if each of these emotions differs in terms of the physiological activity associated with it?

Most people feel anxious or depressed some of the time. If that is true of you, do you wish you could be free of these emotions? If not, in what ways do you think such negative emotions serve useful functions in your life?

Emotion

6

Most (or even all!) the really important and memorable events in our lives are associated with high levels of emotion. When we embark on a new relationship we feel excited, when we pass an important exam we feel elated, when we fail to achieve a major goal we feel depressed, and so on. Thus, emotions play a central role in our lives.

How can we define "emotion"? According to Colman (2009, p. 244), emotion is "any short-term evaluative, affective, intentional, psychological state". There are various ways of telling that someone is experiencing an emotional state:

1. Typical facial expressions are associated with most emotions (e.g., a smile is associated with happiness).
2. There are certain physiological patterns of activity involving the autonomic nervous system and the brain (see Chapter 4).
3. There are subjective feeling states.
4. An individual's behaviour often reveals their current emotional state.

We can consider the concrete example of fear to clarify matters. Someone who is fearful typically has the following facial expression: the eyebrows are raised and close together, the eyes are open wider than usual, the lips are pulled back, and there is tension in the lower lip. Fear is also associated with a substantial increase in the activity of the autonomic nervous system (e.g., faster heart rate + sweating). Fearful individuals use adjectives such as "nervous" or "frightened" to describe their feelings. Finally, a fearful person may run away from (or avoid) the source of their fear.

Emotions vs. moods

What are the main differences between emotions and moods? First, **moods** typically last much longer than emotions. Second, moods are less intense than emotions: we attend to our emotional states whereas moods generally provide a background to our everyday activities. Third, we typically know why we are experiencing a given emotion whereas the reasons for being in a given mood are often unclear.

> **KEY TERM**
>
> **Moods:** states resembling emotions but generally longer lasting, less intense, and of unknown cause.

Females vs. males

Are females more emotional than males?

Most of the evidence supports the common assumption that females are more emotional than males. Brody and Hall (2008) found across 37 cultures that women's emotions were more intense, longer lasting, and expressed more directly than men's. However, there was no gender difference in emotions such as contempt, loneliness, pride, excitement, or guilt.

It is also commonly assumed that females are more sensitive than males to others' emotional states. Supporting evidence was reported by Thompson and Voyer (2014), who reviewed findings from numerous studies. Females showed an advantage over males in recognising specific emotions (especially negative emotions such as anger, sadness, or fear). Note, however, that all the gender differences were relatively small in magnitude.

Why do males and females differ in the ways described earlier? In most cultures, males are expected to be independent whereas females are expected to be cooperative (see Chapter 11). Speculatively, the ability to express and recognise emotions may be more important for those trained to be cooperative than for those trained to be independent.

How useful are emotions?

Probably most individuals suffering from high levels of anxiety and/or depression regard these emotions as useless and undesirable. This viewpoint is understandable given that very few people actually *want* to become anxious or depressed. In addition, anxiety and depression can disrupt our current activities and behaviour. For example, there is much evidence that anxiety impairs concentration and attentional control (Eysenck et al., 2007).

In spite of these arguments, the dominant contemporary view is that all emotions are useful and serve valuable functions. For example, several theories have identified possible adaptive functions for depression or sadness. The major functions identified by these theories are as follows: "Biasing cognition to avoid losses, conserving energy, disengaging from unobtainable goals, signalling submission, soliciting resources, and promoting analytical thinking" (Durisko et al., 2015, p. 315). In essence, depression or sadness encourages us to abandon our current unachievable goal and to conserve energy so we can pursue a more realistic goal.

What are the functions of anxiety? Anxiety or fear is associated with selective attention to potential environmental threat, and rapid detection of danger can be life-saving in threatening environments (Eysenck, 1992). Another function of fear and anxiety is that it is associated with increased physiological activity that facilitates fight or flight.

Lee et al. (2006) discovered another advantage associated with anxiety. Individuals rated as highly anxious by their teachers at the age of 13 were 6 times less likely than those rated as non-anxious to die before the age of 25. The reason is that anxious individuals are more cautious and so less likely to take risks.

How can we bridge the gap between our feeling that negative emotions are disruptive and useless and the evidence that these emotions fulfil useful functions? Levenson (1999, p. 496) argued that it all depends on the perspective we adopt:

> Viewed from the perspective of what we were trying to accomplish prior to the emotion taking hold, the subsequent emotional behaviour may appear

chaotic and disorganised. But, viewed from the perspective of the survival of the organism, the emotional behaviour represents an elegant, adaptive, and highly organised state of affairs.

How many emotions are there?

The question, "How many emotions are there?", sounds easy. Alas, there is little agreement on the answer. One reason is that the question does not specify whether we are to consider only *basic* emotions (mostly shared with other species) or whether we should also include *complex* emotions (e.g., shame; guilt) derived from the basic ones. In addition, the boundary between emotions is often fuzzy – we sometimes find it hard to decide which emotion we are experiencing!

In what follows, we consider mostly the basic emotions. In so doing, we focus on evidence from (1) facial expressions and (2) self-reports.

Facial expressions

Everyone displays a wide range of facial expressions, and it seems likely that each basic emotion has its own distinctive expression. Ekman et al. (1972) reviewed the evidence from American studies and concluded that observers can reliably detect six emotions from faces: happiness, surprise, anger, sadness, fear, and disgust combined with contempt.

Most of the studies in Ekman et al.'s (1972) review involved American participants. Ekman et al. (1987) wondered whether similar findings would be obtained elsewhere in the world. In fact, they found a high level of agreement on the emotions shown by faces in 10 countries including Turkey, Greece, Sumatra, and Japan.

A note of caution about the use of facial expressions to assess emotional states is needed at this point. Individuals can have emotions in the absence of any obvious facial expressions (Matsumoto, 2009). In addition, individuals can produce "emotional" facial expressions without experiencing emotion (Matsumoto, 2009). More generally, most research on facial expressions has focused on emotion *recognition* rather than emotion *production*.

Facial expressions associated with emotion are generally recognised across cultures, suggesting that the expressive aspect of emotion is innate.

Self-report approach

We can assess people's emotional states by presenting them with adjectives (e.g., sad, happy, irritable) and asking them to indicate which ones describe their current feelings. The Positive and Negative Affect Schedule (PANAS-X; Watson & Clark, 1994) is an example of a self-report questionnaire. It assesses 11 emotions or moods (fear, sadness, hostility, guilt, shyness, fatigue, surprise, joviality, self-assurance, attentiveness, and serenity). An issue with this questionnaire

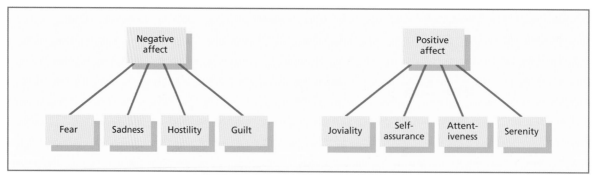

A two-level hierarchical model of emotion.

is that several of the mood states are rather similar to each other and so not clearly different.

Watson and Clark (1992) argued that the evidence favoured a hierarchical model. At the lower level, there are several related (but distinguishable) emotional states. At the upper level, there are two broad and unrelated factors called Negative Affect and Positive Affect. All emotional or mood states can be related to the two-dimensional structure formed by Negative and Positive Affect.

Support for this hierarchical model was reported by Lindquist et al. (2014). They studied brain-damaged patients with **semantic dementia** in which there are substantial impairments of concept and word knowledge. These patients were shown photographs of faces showing various emotions (anger, sadness, fear, disgust, and happiness). They distinguished clearly between positive and negative emotions but not among the negative emotions even though the task did not require the use of language. Thus, language is important at the lower level of the hierarchy but is not required for the crucial distinction between positive and negative affect.

According to the hierarchical model of emotions, what is measured by self-report assessments of any specific emotion?

Conclusions

Levenson (2011) argued that several criteria needed to be satisfied for an emotion to be regarded as basic:

1. Distinctness (clearly different from other emotions in physiology and what triggers the emotion).
2. Functionality (useful for solving survival-relevant challenges or opportunities).
3. Hard-wiredness (built into the nervous system; found cross-culturally).

Levenson (2011) reviewed the emotion literature and agreed with Ekman et al. (1972) that happiness, surprise, anger, sadness, fear, and disgust are all basic emotions. However, he also argued that there is fairly strong evidence for three other basic emotions: relief/contentment, interest, and love.

Psychological theories of emotion

There is a bewildering variety of theories of emotion. Here we will briefly consider two historically important theories followed by a major contemporary theoretical approach to emotion.

KEY TERM

Semantic dementia: a condition caused by brain damage in which the patient experiences considerable problems in accessing word meanings.

James-Lange theory

The first major theory of emotion was put forward independently by the American, William James, and the Dane, Carl Lange, towards the end of the nineteenth century. The essence of this approach was expressed by James (1890, p. 451): "If we fancy some strong emotion, and then try to abstract from our consciousness of it all the feelings of its bodily symptoms, we find we have nothing left behind." In other words, our awareness of our own bodily states plays a crucial role in our emotional experience.

This theory seems counterintuitive. For example, we generally assume that we smile because we are happy. According to the theory, in contrast, it is argued that we are happy because we smile. If the James-Lange theory is correct, each emotion must be associated with its own distinctive bodily state (e.g., pattern of physiological arousal; facial expression).

Findings

We saw earlier that several basic emotions are associated with distinctive facial expressions (Ekman et al., 1972). Nummenmaa et al. (2014) found evidence that 13 emotions differ in terms of their bodily state. For each emotion, people identified bodily regions whose activity becomes stronger or faster than

According to the James-Lange theory, how are bodily changes and emotions related?

Bodily topography of basic (Upper) and nonbasic (Lower) emotions associated with words. The body maps show regions whose activation increased (warm colours) or decreased (cool colours) when feeling each emotion. From Nummenmaa et al. (2014).

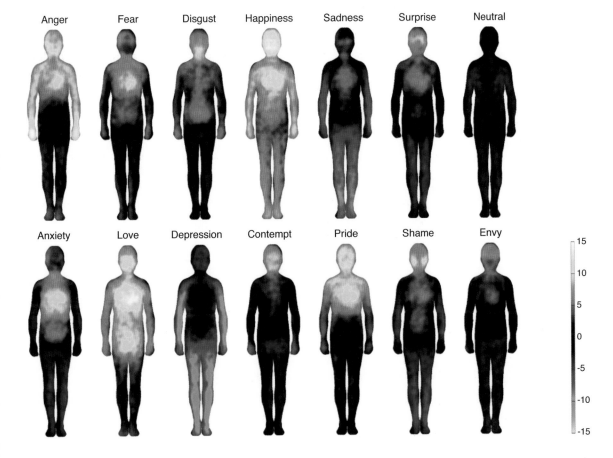

when in a neutral state; these regions are coloured red in the figure. They also identified regions whose activity becomes weaker or slower; these regions are coloured blue. Of importance, the findings were very similar in West European and East Asian samples.

Patients with spinal cord injuries have dramatically reduced awareness of their own bodily arousal. According to the James-Lange theory, we might expect such patients to have much less intense emotional experiences than healthy individuals. The findings are mixed. Deady et al. (2010) found that patients with spinal cord injury experienced as much emotion as healthy controls. However, Salter et al. (2013) found that such patients experienced less positive emotion than controls but comparable levels of negative emotion.

More supportive findings have been reported from studies in which facial expressions were manipulated. In a study by Strack et al. (1988), participants either held a pen between the teeth to facilitate smiling or between their lips to inhibit smiling. Those in the former condition found cartoons funnier than did those in the latter condition. Marzoli et al. (2013) found that frowning induced by looking in the direction of the sun increased feelings of anger and aggression.

Botox injections reduce facial wrinkles but also tend to paralyse the muscles involved in facial expression. According to the James-Lange theory (and its recent developments such as Niedenthal, 2007), people who have had Botox should have less intense emotional experiences than controls. Davis et al. (2010) presented their participants with positive and negative video clips and obtained support for this prediction.

There is increasing evidence that Botox has clinical relevance. Magid et al. (2015) reviewed studies in which depressed patients received Botox injections that reduced activity of the frown muscles. This led to a reduction in the symptoms of depression.

EVALUATION

➕ There is good evidence that several emotions are associated with distinctive facial expressions and bodily states.

➕ Manipulation of facial expressions typically influences emotional experience as predicted.

➖ It is often not clear *why* emotional bodily states occur. As is discussed later, it seems probable that emotional bodily states are often triggered by cognitive processes in which the current situation is appraised as supportive or threatening.

➖ Most studies in which facial expressions were manipulated focused on smiling-happiness and frowning-sadness and so the applicability of the theory to other emotions remains unclear.

➖ James (1890) claimed that some bodily changes give rise to emotional experience whereas other bodily changes do not. However, no-one has explained what features distinguish the two types of bodily changes.

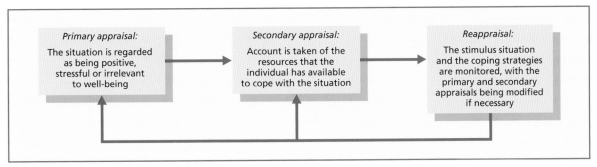

Cognitive appraisal.

Appraisal theory

Cognitive processes influence *when* we experience emotional states and *what* emotional state we experience in any given situation. Of special importance is **cognitive appraisal**, which is the evaluation of judgment we make about situations relevant to our goals, concerns, and well-being. It typically involves top-down processing based on our previous experience of similar situations. Note that we can distinguish among primary appraisal, secondary appraisal, and reappraisal.

What does cognitive appraisal consist of?

Appraisal theorists (e.g., Scherer & Ellsworth, 2009) claim that each emotion is elicited by its own specific pattern of appraisal. For example, you experience anger if you blame someone else for the current situation, and you appraise the situation as one offering you control and power.

Smith and Kirby (2001) argued that cognitive appraisal can occur below the level of conscious awareness based on activation of memories and involving automatic processes. It follows (implausibly?) that stimuli of which we are unaware might nevertheless trigger an emotional state.

Findings

People differ in their ability to distinguish among their emotional states (this is emotion differentiation). Erbas et al. (2015) argued from appraisal theory that emotion differentiation would be greater in individuals whose appraisal patterns showed little overlap across emotions than in those having considerable overlap. That is exactly what they found.

Kuppens et al. (2003) considered four appraisals (goal obstacle, other accountability: someone else is to blame, unfairness, and control) relevant to anger. No appraisal component was essential for the experience of anger in recently experienced unpleasant situations. For example, some participants felt angry *without* the appraisal of unfairness or the presence of a goal obstacle. Thus, there are complex relationships between cognitive appraisals and experienced emotion.

Winkielman et al. (2005) presented happy and angry faces subliminally (below the conscious level) to thirsty individuals. Those presented with subliminal happy faces poured and drank twice as much liquid as those presented with angry faces. These findings suggest that non-conscious processing of emotional stimuli can trigger emotional reactions.

> **KEY TERM**
>
> **Cognitive appraisal:** the individual's interpretation of the current situation; it helps to determine the nature and intensity of his/her emotional experience. It also helps the individual to decide whether he/she has the resources to cope with the situation.

Unconscious affective reactions to masked happy versus angry faces influence consumption behaviour and judgements of value. From Winkielman et al. (2005).

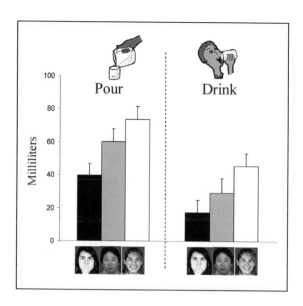

EVALUATION

➕ Appraisal processes influence *whether* we experience emotion and also *which* emotion is experienced.

➕ Individual differences in emotional experience in a given situation are determined in part by appraisals varying from person to person.

➕ The distinction between conscious appraisal processes and more automatic ones has proved useful.

➖ The links between appraisals and specific emotions are flexible and not very strong.

➖ It is generally assumed that patterns of appraisal cause certain emotions to be experienced. In practice, however, appraisals and emotional experiences often blur into each other (McEachrane, 2009) – there is no sharp distinction between cognition and emotion.

➖ Appraisal theory greatly underestimates the importance of bodily states in influencing our emotions.

KEY TERM

Emotion regulation: the management and control of emotional states by various processes (e.g., cognitive reappraisal; distraction).

IN THE REAL WORLD: emotion regulation and cognitive appraisal

Research on appraisal can be seen within the broader perspective of **emotion regulation** which is "a deliberate, effortful process that seeks to override people's spontaneous emotional responses" (Koole,

2009, p. 6). Emotion regulation is mostly used to reduce negative emotional states or turn them into positive ones and is very important in the real world.

Gross and Thompson's (2007) process model of emotion regulation (shown below) is very influential. We can try to change our emotional state by avoiding potentially stressful situations (situation selection) or by reducing the stressfulness of a situation by having a friend accompanying them (situation selection). However, most emotion-regulation strategies are used at the attentional deployment stage (e.g., **distraction** – disengaging attention from emotional processing) or the cognitive change stage (e.g., **reappraisal** – elaborating emotional information and then changing its meaning).

Webb et al. (2012) used meta-analysis (combining the findings from numerous studies) to assess the effectiveness of emotion regulation with respect to Gross and Thompson's (2007) model. Overall, strategies involving cognitive change had a moderate effect on emotion, strategies involving response modulation had a small effect, and strategies involving attentional deployment had a non-significant effect.

Patients with anxiety disorders or major depressive disorder typically have difficulties in emotion regulation, and so it is likely that their symptoms can be reduced through emotion-regulation strategies. Aldao et al. (2010) considered various such strategies. Across many studies, reappraisal, acceptance (accepting thoughts and feelings for what they are), and problem solving all reduced anxiety and depression. In contrast, rumination (obsessive thinking about emotional issues) and avoidance (deliberately not thinking about thoughts and feelings) both increased the symptoms of anxiety and depression.

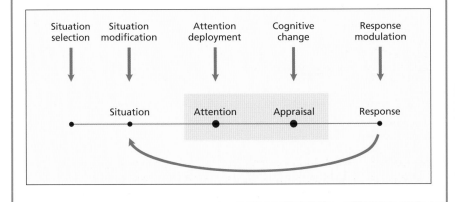

KEY TERMS

Distraction: an emotion-regulation strategy in which attention is switched from emotional processing to neutral information.

Reappraisal: an emotion-regulation strategy in which the emotional significance of an event is changed through additional cognitive processing.

Chapter summary

- Emotions are generally associated with certain facial expressions, patterns of activation in the body and brain, subjective feeling states, and forms of behaviour.
- Women tend to be more emotional than men and are more sensitive to others' emotional states.
- All emotional states (even negative ones) fulfil useful functions. For example anxiety focuses attention on potential threats.
- Approximately six emotions are associated with distinctive facial expressions.
- Self-report data indicate there are two independent emotion factors (positive and negative affect) plus several more specific emotional states.
- Three criteria for identifying basic emotions are as follows: distinctness; functionality; and hard-wiredness.
- The James-Lange theory emphasises how which our emotions reflect our experience of our bodily symptoms and de-emphasises the role of cognitive processes.
- According to appraisal theory, our interpretations of situations determine which emotion we experience. Such interpretations can occur rapidly in the absence of conscious awareness as well as more slowly based on conscious processes.
- We can account for our emotional experiences by combining the insights of the James-Lange and appraisal theories.
- There are numerous emotion-regulation strategies. Those focusing on producing cognitive change (e.g., reappraisal) are typically most effective.
- Patients with anxiety disorders or depression have ineffective emotion-regulation strategies and are inflexible in their use of such strategies.
- Emotion regulation therapy involving teaching effective emotion-regulation strategies has proved useful in treating anxiety and depression.

Further reading

- Sander, D., & Scherer, K.R. (Eds.) (2009) *The Oxford companion to emotion and the affective sciences*. Oxford: Oxford University Press. This volume edited by David Sander and Klaus Scherer contains numerous short articles on most of the major topics relating to emotion.
- Smith, R., & Lane, R.D. (2015). The neural basis of one's own conscious and unconscious emotional states. *Neuroscience and Biobehavioral Reviews*, 57, 1–29. This article presents a theoretical approach that combines elements of previous theories to provide a comprehensive account of emotion.

Essay questions

1. What is emotion? How can it be measured?

2. How many emotions are there? Discuss with reference to the relevant research.

3. Describe briefly *two* theories of emotion. What are the strengths and limitations of these theories?

4. What is "emotion regulation"? How have emotion regulation strategies been used to enhance individuals' psychological well-being?

Aggression takes many forms, ranging between physical violence and talking in hostile terms about others. You have probably had the misfortune to meet some people who were very aggressive and hard to handle. Mercifully, most people are not like that.

What do you think causes some individuals to be aggressive whereas others are gentle and unaggressive? Is it a question of personality or the experiences people have had? Are men generally more aggressive than women? Are the media to blame? What advice would you give to parents concerned about their aggressive child?

Aggression

7

■ ■ ■ ■ ■ ■ ■ ■ ■ □

What exactly is aggression? **Aggression** is "the intentional infliction of some type of harm on others" (Vaughan & Hogg, 2014, p. 450). Note that the harm has to be intentional or deliberate. If you slip on the ice and crash into someone by accident, you may cause them harm, but you are not behaving aggressively. It should also be pointed out that the victim must want to avoid harm. Whipping a masochist who derives sexual pleasure from the activity is not aggressive behaviour.

We need to distinguish among various types of aggression. **Reactive aggression** (or hostile aggression) is an angry response to a perceived provocation. In contrast, **proactive aggression** (or instrumental aggression) is an act planned deliberately beforehand to achieve a particular goal. Children and adolescents high in reactive aggression are more likely to be rejected by their peers (other children and adolescents) than those high in proactive aggression (Card & Little, 2006).

Note that levels of reactive and proactive aggression tend to be similar for any given individual. Kaat et al. (2015) reported a moderately high correlation of +.57 between measures of these two forms of aggression in a study on children. Thus, aggressive behaviour often involves both deliberate planning and anger.

There is also an important distinction between overt aggression and relational aggression. Overt aggression is intended to harm other people with physical actions or verbal threats, whereas relational aggression has the goal of harming others' relationships and/or reputation.

The distinction between overt and relational aggression closely resembles that between direct and indirect aggression. Direct aggression involves the use of physical force (e.g., punching). In contrast, indirect aggression involves more subtle techniques (e.g., gossiping; spreading false stories) and is used more often by women than men (Archer & Coyne, 2005). Why do these two forms of aggression exist? The main reason is that people make use of relational or indirect aggression when the costs of overt or direct aggression are high.

Historical and cultural factors

Human beings often behave aggressively and violently (e.g., there have been more than 15,000 wars in the past 6,000 years). It is often assumed that most human societies are becoming increasingly aggressive (e.g., the Holocaust,

KEY TERMS

Aggression: forms of behaviour deliberately intended to harm or injure someone else.

Reactive aggression: this is aggressive behaviour triggered by the anger created by a perceived provocation; this is hot-tempered aggression.

Proactive aggression: forms of aggressive behaviour that are planned in advance to achieve some goal; this is cold-tempered aggression.

genocide in Rwanda, and the First and Second World Wars). However, Pinker (2011) claims human violence has *declined* substantially (especially in Western societies). Suppose we consider the rate at which people were killed in typical tribal societies in the past. If that rate had been as great in the twentieth century, two billion people would have been killed rather than the actual figure of 100 million. According to Pinker, this reduction has occurred because human life is more valued than in the past and because of a "civilising process" influenced by the increasing power of the state.

It is true there have been fewer deaths on the battlefield in recent decades than in the period before that. However, this is more plausibly attributed to the existence of nuclear weapons rather than any civilising process. In addition, there has been an increase in the deaths of non-combatants. Of most importance, the recent absence of a rare event (a massively destructive war) does not indicate that no such wars will occur in the next few decades (Cirillo & Taleb, 2015). By analogy, we should not assume a volcanic mountain that has not had a large volcanic eruption for a long time will therefore not have one in the near future.

Cultural differences

There are large cultural differences in aggression and violence. For example, the murder rate is 46 per 100,000 people in South Africa, 5.6 in the United States, but only 2 in the United Kingdom (McGuire, 2008). Violence scarcely exists in some societies. For example, the Chewong people in the Malay Peninsula have no words for fighting, aggression, or warfare (Bonta, 1997). They believe that superhumans (spirits) will cause diseases if rules (including those relating to treating people with dignity) are not obeyed.

What is the main explanation for some societies being free of aggression and violence? Bonta (1997) found over 90% of such societies he studied believe strongly in cooperation and are opposed to competition. **Social norms** (cultural expectations concerning appropriate behaviour) are important. Such norms encourage Americans to be competitive and go-getting, and this may partly explain high levels of aggression in the United States.

Situational factors

Think of a situation that caused you to experience anger and feel aggressive. I would guess that the situation was one in which you felt thwarted or frustrated by someone or something. For me, discovering that my computer is not working properly and so I cannot get on with some urgent work often makes me angry. A Colorado man suffered such severe computer rage that he shot his computer eight times with a pistol!

According to the frustration-aggression hypothesis (Dollard et al., 1939, p. 1), "Aggression is always a consequence of frustration." This hypothesis has been very influential but is clearly an oversimplification. For example, Kuppens et al. (2003) asked people to recall recently experienced unpleasant situations. Three factors predicted the occurrence of anger: (1) goal obstacle: their current goal was thwarted, (2) other accountability: someone else was to blame, and (3) the situation was perceived as unfair. A crucial finding was that no single factor was essential for the experience of anger. Thus, anger (and aggression) can be triggered by various different combinations of factors.

According to the frustration-aggression hypothesis, what is the relationship between frustration and aggression?

KEY TERM

Social norms: agreed standards of behaviour within a group (e.g., family; organisations).

Roidl et al. (2014) studied the involvement of these factors in determining car drivers' reactions to traffic situations. The drivers had the goal of arriving rapidly at their destination or of driving safely. Their anger levels (and aggressive driving) were greatest when a traffic situation involved other-accountability and when it produced a goal obstacle. For example, a long wait at a construction site produced more of a goal obstacle (and more anger) when the goal was to arrive rapidly at the destination than when it was to drive safely.

In everyday life, several types of situations have been linked to anger and aggression. Examples include media violence, violent video games, and the family environment. Later on, we consider these situations. However, we start with the classic research on aggression by Bandura and his colleagues.

Social learning

Bandura (e.g., 1977; see Chapter 2) put forward social learning theory according to which much aggressive behaviour is influenced by observational learning – this involves watching the behaviour of others and then imitating it. More generally, "The specific forms that aggressive behaviour takes, the frequency with which it is expressed, the situations in which it is displayed, and the specific targets selected for attack are largely determined by social learning factors" (Bandura, 1977, p. 5).

Two major predictions follow from social learning theory. First, the behaviour produced by individuals who have watched someone behave aggressively will resemble the observed behaviour. Second, observers are more likely to imitate someone else's behaviour if it is rewarded than if it is punished.

Findings

Bandura et al. (1963) carried out classic research using a Bobo doll. The doll is inflatable and has a weighted base causing it to bounce back when punched. Young children saw a film of a female adult model behaving aggressively towards the Bobo doll or behaving non-aggressively towards it. Those children who saw the model behave aggressively were much more likely to attack the Bobo doll.

Bandura (1965) carried out a further study with the Bobo doll. As predicted, children were much more likely to copy the adult model's aggressive

Adult "model" and children attack the Bobo doll.

behaviour when it was rewarded than when it was punished (the model was warned not to be aggressive in future).

Coyne et al. (2004) presented children aged between 11 and 14 with videos showing direct or indirect aggression. Both forms of aggression led to aggressive behaviour in the children. However, viewing direct aggression led to more directly aggressive responses whereas viewing indirect aggression produced more indirectly aggressive responses.

EVALUATION

➕ There is strong evidence that aggressive behaviour often depends on observational learning.

➕ Aggressive behaviour is much more likely to be imitated if it is rewarded rather than punished.

➕ As predicted, the type of aggressive behaviour exhibited by children resembles the behaviour they have observed (Coyne et al., 2004).

➖ The fact that the Bobo doll bounces back up when knocked down gives it novelty value. Children unfamiliar with the Bobo doll were *five* times more likely to imitate aggressive behaviour against it than those who had played with it before (Cumberbatch, 1990).

➖ Bandura exaggerated children's imitation of the behaviour of models. For example, children are much less likely to imitate aggressive behaviour towards another child than towards a Bobo doll.

➖ The social learning approach de-emphasises the role of cognitive processes and biological factors in influencing aggressive behaviour (see the following sections).

Media violence

The average 16-year-old in Western society has seen thousands of violent murders on television. Children who have watched the most television violence tend to be the most aggressive. This finding is hard to interpret. Watching violent programmes may cause aggressive behaviour, or naturally aggressive children may watch more violent programmes than non-aggressive children: this is the causality issue. Of course, there may be some truth in both interpretations.

There is another point. Most research has focused on possible short-term effects (within 30 minutes of exposure to media violence). However, long-term effects are more important in terms of their impact on society and so we will consider such effects as well.

Findings

Leyens et al. (1975) addressed the causality issue directly. There was a special Movie Week at a school for juvenile delinquents in Belgium. During this week, some delinquents saw only violent films, whereas others saw only nonviolent films. Physical and verbal aggression increased among boys viewing the violent films but not among those viewing the nonviolent ones. However, the effects of the violent films were much stronger shortly after watching them than later on.

Williams (1986) studied the effects of the introduction of television on an isolated community in Canada on children aged 6–11 years. There were significant increases in aggressive behaviour among these children over the subsequent two years.

The effects of media violence on aggressive behaviour depend in part on individual differences in personality. Zillmann and Weaver (1997) showed films containing scenes of gratuitous violence to male participants. Only those high in psychoticism (a personality dimension involving coldness and hostility) showed greater acceptance of violence as an acceptable way of resolving conflicts after watching the films.

Huesmann et al. (2003) studied the long-term effects of exposure to television violence between the ages of 6 and 10. The amount of childhood exposure to television violence predicted adult aggressive behaviour 15 years later. However, aggression as a child did *not* predict exposure to media violence as a young adult. Together, these findings suggest media violence can lead to aggressive behaviour but not the other way around.

Does media violence have short- and/or long-term effects?

Coyne (2016) considered the effects of viewing relational and physical aggression on television among adolescents over a 3-year period. Watching relational aggression on television predicted future relational aggression. However, initial levels of relational aggression did not predict the amount of relational aggression watched subsequently. The findings were somewhat different with respect to physical aggression. Watching televised physical aggression predicted future physical aggression, *and* initial levels of physical aggression predicted subsequent exposure to televised physical aggression.

What do Coyne's (2016) findings mean? First, viewing relational and physical aggression produces long-term increases in aggressive behaviour even when taking account of participants' initial levels of aggression. Second, exposure to television violence is influenced by prior levels of physical aggression but not by prior levels of relational aggression. It remains unclear why there is this difference between the two types of aggression.

Comstock and Paik (1991) reviewed research on the effects of media violence. They identified five factors increasing its effects on aggression:

1. Violent behaviour is presented as an efficient way of getting what you want.
2. The violent person is portrayed as similar to the viewer.
3. Violent behaviour is presented naturalistically.
4. The victims' suffering is not shown.
5. The viewer is emotionally excited while watching the violent behaviour.

EVALUATION

➕ There is increasing evidence from long-term (longitudinal) studies that media violence (relational and physical aggression) can cause subsequent aggressive behaviour.

➕ Factors influencing the effects of media violence on aggression (e.g., similarity of violent person to the viewer; extent to which the victim's suffering is shown) have been identified.

➖ Many studies simply report associations between exposure to violence on television and aggressive behaviour. Such studies cannot establish causality.

➖ There is no comprehensive theory that accounts for the various factors influencing the impact of television violence on aggressive behaviour.

Violent video games

The amount of time young people (especially boys) spend playing violent video games has increased dramatically in the past 15 years. Anderson et al. (2010) carried out a meta-analysis (combining findings from many studies) and found greater exposure to video game violence was associated with more aggressive behaviour, aggressive thoughts, aggressive emotion, and physiological arousal. However, most of these effects were relatively modest. The findings were similar in Eastern and Western cultures, and were little affected by age or sex.

These findings only indicate an *association* between time spent playing violent video games and aggression. This association may occur because playing such games causes aggression or because individuals with aggressive personalities spend more time playing violent games. More convincing evidence was reported by Willoughby et al. (2012) in a study on adolescents studied over a 3-year period. Greater playing of violent video games predicted higher levels of aggression subsequently and did so even when the researchers controlled for previous levels of aggression. These findings suggest that playing violent video games can increase aggressive behaviour.

There has been some controversy about the strength of the relationship between playing violent video games and subsequent aggressive behaviour. Ferguson (2015) carried out a meta-analysis (combining findings from numerous studies). There was a significant but very small overall correlation of +.06 between the two factors, leading Ferguson to conclude that playing violent video games has "minimal deleterious effects on children's well-being" (p. 655). However, he reported a somewhat smaller relationship than in other meta-analyses (Boxer et al., 2015). Thus, there is a genuine (but rather small) association between playing violent video games and aggression.

Why is aggressive behaviour increased (even if only slightly) by playing violent video games? This issue is discussed in the next section. In essence, however, the evidence suggests the cognitions (e.g., violent thoughts) produced by violent video games play an important role.

According to the general aggression model, can situational cues and individual differences produce negative affect, arousal, and/or negative cognitions?

General aggression model

Anderson and Bushman (2002) proposed a general aggression model emphasising the role of situational factors in aggression. However, their theoretical approach was more comprehensive in scope than Bandura's social learning theory. Their model consists of four stages:

- *Stage 1*: The key variables are situational cues (e.g., weapons present) and individual differences (e.g., aggressive personality).
- *Stage 2*: What happens at Stage 1 causes various effects at Stage 2. These include affect (e.g., hostile feelings), arousal (e.g., activation of the autonomic nervous system), and cognitions (e.g., hostile thoughts).
- *Stage 3*: What happens at Stage 2 leads to *appraisal* processes (e.g., interpretation of the situation; possible coping strategies; consequences of behaving aggressively).
- *Stage 4*: Depending on the outcome of the appraisal processes at Stage 3, the individual decides to behave aggressively or non-aggressively.

Findings

Some findings discussed already are relevant to the model. For example, we have seen that playing violent video games has the predicted effects on affect, physiological arousal, and cognitions (Anderson et al., 2010).

It is assumed within the model that cognitive processes occurring at Stages 2 and 3 are of major importance in determining aggressive behaviour. Supporting evidence comes from research on the **weapons effect** – seeing one or more weapons increases the likelihood that an individual will behave aggressively (Berkowitz & LePage, 1967). Anderson et al. (1998) found that seeing a weapon increased the accessibility of aggression-related thoughts (e.g., assault; destroy; torture). Such thoughts can lead to aggressive behaviour. In the words of Berkowitz (1968, p. 22), "The finger pulls the trigger, but the trigger may also be pulling the finger."

According to the model, personality influences aggressive behaviour. Support for this prediction was reported by Schmidt and Jankowski (2014) in a study on

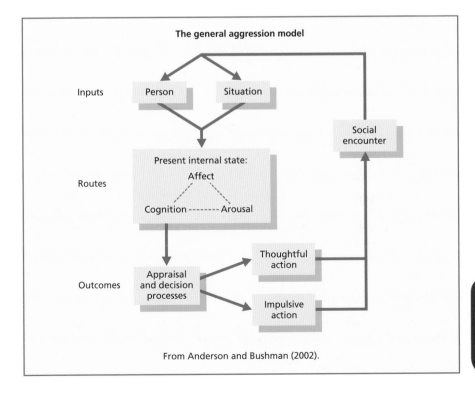

From Anderson and Bushman (2002).

> **KEY TERM**
>
> **Weapons effect:** an increase in aggressive behaviour produced by the sight of a weapon (e.g., gun).

Just seeing a weapon increases the accessibility of aggression-related thoughts, which can lead to aggressive behaviour.

relational or indirect aggression. Students high in neuroticism (tendency to experience much anxiety) and those low in agreeableness exhibited greater relational aggression than those low in neuroticism and high in agreeableness.

The model predicts that individuals' cognitions and interpretations of the situation influence whether they will behave aggressively. Hasan et al. (2012) studied the cognitions generated by playing a violent video game. They found it produced a **hostile expectation bias** (the assumption that others will behave aggressively in an ambiguous situation). This finding is consistent with the general aggression model, as is the further finding that individuals in whom the hostile expectation bias had been activated subsequently behaved more aggressively.

Bègue et al. (2010) asked participants to decide whether ambiguous behaviour (e.g., "She cut him off in traffic") was intentional or accidental. Participants who had consumed a lot of alcohol interpreted more behaviours as intentional than did those not having any alcohol. This helps to explain why people who are drunk are typically more aggressive.

Suppose we asked people to play a violent video game in which aggression was rewarded or punished. Suppose we found those in the reward condition behaved more aggressively than those in the punishment condition. According to the model, that would indicate that participants in the reward condition had more aggressive and hostile thoughts than those in the punishment condition. According to the model, that would mean the reward participants should then behave more aggressively than the punishment participants after the end of the game (post-game).

Sauer et al. (2015) carried out a study just like the hypothetical one described in the last paragraph. However, there was no difference in post-game aggression between the two groups. Why was the model's prediction not confirmed? The key reason is that our behaviour is strongly influenced by the immediate social situation – deciding that hostile thoughts should lead to aggressive behaviour in one situation does *not* necessarily mean that the same is true in another situation. Thus, the extent to which we behave aggressively depends more on subtleties of the current situation than is allowed for by the model.

EVALUATION

➕ The general aggression model is more comprehensive in scope than previous theories of aggression.

➕ As the model predicts, aggressive behaviour is determined in part by individual differences in personality and by cognitive interpretations and biases.

➖ Negative affect, arousal, and negative cognitions all have complex effects on behaviour. As a result, it is often hard to predict whether someone will behave aggressively.

KEY TERM

Hostile expectation bias: the bias to expect aggression from others in ambiguous situations.

- It is assumed within the model that aggressive behaviour depends primarily on learning. This minimises the role played by genetic factors in influencing aggressive behaviour (discussed by Ferguson & Dyck, 2012).

- The general aggression model provides more of a general framework than a detailed theoretical account.

- Aggressive behaviour in one situation (e.g., playing a violent video game) carries over less to other situations than predicted by the general aggression model (Sauer et al., 2015).

Family processes

Patterson (e.g., 2002) argued that children's aggressive behaviour depends very much on family processes. More specifically, he claimed that what matters is the functioning of the family as a whole rather than simply the behaviour of the child or its parents.

What is the name of the pattern within families in which aggressive behaviour by one family member is matched or exceeded by another family member?

The importance of the family was confirmed by Patterson et al. (1992), who observed the interaction patterns of families. There was a typical pattern of escalating aggression in the families of aggressive children:

1. The child behaves aggressively (e.g., refusing to do what his/her mother requested).
2. The mother responds aggressively (e.g., shouting angrily at her child).
3. The child reacts in a more aggressive and hostile way (e.g., shouting back loudly at his mother).
4. The mother responds more aggressively than before (e.g., hitting her son).

This pattern of behaviour forms a **coercive cycle** – a small increase in aggression by the parent or child is matched or exceeded by the other person's aggressive behaviour. According to Patterson et al. (1992), most aggressive behaviour displayed by parents and their children in aggressive families is an attempt to stop the other person being aggressive to them. However, these attempts often serve to provoke further aggression.

Smith et al. (2014) studied interactions between mothers and children aged between 2 and 5 years. Coercive (aggressive) behaviour by the mother increased non-compliance by the child and led the child to behave more aggressively afterwards. In contrast, aggressive behaviour by the child generally did *not* predict increased aggression by the mother. These findings suggest the role of the mother is crucial in preventing the development of a coercive cycle.

According to Patterson et al. (1992), the aggressive behaviour displayed by children trapped in a coercive cycle can cause problems *outside* the family such as rejection by their peers (children of the same age). This can lead to deviant behaviour and delinquency. Aggressive adolescents are more likely than non-aggressive ones to join a gang at 13 or 14 years of age. This is followed by deviant behaviour with friends at the age of 16 or 17 and then violence by the age of 18 or 19 (Dishion et al., 2010).

> **KEY TERM**
>
> **Coercive cycle:** a pattern of behaviour within families in which aggression by one family member produces an aggressive response leading to an escalation in aggression.

EVALUATION

➕ Family processes often play an important role in producing aggressive children.

➕ Coercive cycles are found in many aggressive families, and these cycles often have long-term negative consequences for children.

➕ Children often behave aggressively to attract attention from parents who would otherwise ignore them.

➖ The existence of coercive cycles in some families may reflect genetic factors more than is generally assumed – children may be aggressive in part because they have inherited genes for aggression from their parents rather than because of specific events within families. Genetic influences on aggression are discussed in the next section.

Biological approach

Does the evidence suggest that males are physically and/or psychologically more aggressive than females?

So far we have focused mostly on *external* or environmental influences on aggressive behaviour. However, *internal* influences are also important. According to the biological approach, some individuals inherit genes making them more likely than other individuals to be highly aggressive. It has also been argued that males engage in more overt aggression than females because of biological factors. For example, males have higher levels of the sex hormone **testosterone**, which may partly explain their greater physical aggressiveness.

Findings

Twin studies allow us to decide whether human aggression is influenced by genetic factors. If identical or monozygotic twins (who share 100% of their genes) are more similar in aggression than fraternal or dizygotic twins (who share 50% of their genes), then genetic factors probably play a role in determining aggression.

Tuvblad et al. (2009) carried out a twin study on children. At the age of 9 or 10, 26% of individual differences in reactive or hot-tempered aggression were due to genetic factors, and the figure for proactive aggression was 32%. These figures increased to 50% for both forms of aggression in twins aged 11–14. Kendler et al. (2015) investigated biological factors in crime using identical and fraternal male twins. Genetic factors accounted for 45% of individual differences in the incidence of violent crime (e.g., assault).

Gender differences

It is widely believed that males are more aggressive than females. Is this belief true? It certainly is if we focus on extreme violence. Brehm et al. (1999) considered figures produced by the US Department of Justice. In 1996, 90% of murderers in the United States were male. A similar gender imbalance was found in most other countries.

Much evidence indicates that gender differences in aggression depend on the type of aggressive behaviour. Men engage in overt aggression more often

KEY TERM

Testosterone: a hormone present in much greater quantities in males than females; it has been linked to aggressive and sexual behaviour.

than women and are also more often the target of such aggression (Archer & Coyne, 2005). In contrast, women make use of relational aggression more than men (Archer & Coyne, 2005). A partial explanation of these findings is probably that women are more concerned than men that overt aggression on their part might lead to physical retaliation.

Are males *always* more physically aggressive than females? Bettencourt and Miller (1996) combined the findings from numerous studies and argued the answer is, "No". Men typically behave more aggressively than women in neutral or ambiguous situations. However, sex differences in aggression were much smaller when people were frustrated, threatened, or insulted.

The role of the sex hormone testosterone in explaining gender differences in physical aggression was investigated by Cohen-Kettenis and van Goozen (1997). They studied transsexuals undergoing hormone treatment in order to change sex. Female-to-male transsexuals were given high dosages of testosterone, whereas male-to-female transsexuals were given female hormones and deprived of male hormones. As predicted by the biological approach, female-to-male transsexuals showed *increased* aggression during hormone treatment. In contrast, male-to-female transsexuals showed *lowered* levels of aggression.

Why does testosterone lead to increased aggression? Mehta and Beer (2010) addressed this issue in a study in which participants were exposed to social provocation. As expected, individuals with high levels of testosterone responded more aggressively to this provocation. Of most interest, testosterone led to reduced activity in brain areas associated with impulse control and self-regulation. Thus, testosterone reduces the tendency to inhibit aggressive behaviour when angry.

Much research has focused on baseline levels of testosterone in males and females. However, Carré and Olmstead (2015) reviewed research showing fluctuations in testosterone level in competitive situations were positively associated with aggression in males (but not females). Thus, we need to consider fluctuations in testosterone as well as baseline levels.

EVALUATION

➕ Twin studies indicate that genetic factors are important in explaining individual differences in aggressive behaviour.

➕ The male sex hormone testosterone is associated with increased levels of aggression.

➕ High levels of testosterone are associated with reduced impulsive control and self-regulation.

➖ Sex differences in aggression (especially indirect aggression) are smaller than expected by the biological approach.

➖ Much remains to be discovered about the ways biological factors *combine* with environmental factors to produce aggressive behaviour.

➖ More research is needed to establish the roles played by baseline testosterone and fluctuations in testosterone in leading to aggressive behaviour.

Reducing aggression

How can we reduce aggression in children and adolescents? One approach is to focus directly on changing children's behaviour (child-based interventions), although there is often some parental involvement. An alternative approach focuses more on the parents and on family dynamics (e.g., coercive cycles). We will briefly discuss both approaches.

Child-based interventions

Wilson et al. (2003) reviewed studies in which children had received intervention programmes to reduce aggression. Nearly all interventions had beneficial effects, but social competence training and behavioural interventions were especially effective.

Social competence training often involves communication skills, conflict resolution, self-statements (e.g., "I must remain calm"), and empathy (understanding others' feelings). Aggressive children and adolescents generally show little empathy (de Wied et al., 2010), which helps to explain why they attack other people. Zahavi and Asher (1978) told aggressive adolescents that aggression hurts other people, makes them unhappy, and causes resentment. This led to increased empathy and greatly reduced aggressive behaviour.

One of the most common behavioural interventions involves providing reward or reinforcement when children behave in helpful, non-aggressive ways (Parke & Slaby, 1983). There is also the time-out technique. Children who behave aggressively are prevented from continuing with a pleasurable activity such as playing with toys or by being sent to their room.

Another way of removing rewards is the incompatible-response technique. It is based on the assumption that children often behave aggressively to gain the reward of receiving adult attention. With this technique, children's aggressive behaviour is ignored (to remove attentional reward) but their helpful behaviour is rewarded. This technique produces substantial reductions in aggression (Slaby & Crowley, 1977).

In the time-out technique, what happens to children who behave aggressively?

IN THE REAL WORLD: coercive cycles and family check-ups

We saw earlier in the chapter that family dynamics often play a key role in increasing children's aggressive behaviour. Of special importance are coercive cycles in which there is a rapid escalation of aggression between mother and child when they both respond aggressively to aggression by the other person. It follows that an effective method for reducing aggression in children would be to focus on parent-based interventions to eliminate coercive cycles within families. Precisely this was done by Patterson et al. (1992). Some of the steps involved were as follows:

1. Describe the nature of the coercive cycle to parents and explain its disadvantages (e.g., escalation of aggression).
2. Emphasise to parents that they should not give in when their child behaves aggressively.
3. Instruct parents not to respond aggressively when their child is aggressive.

4. Set up a system in which the child is rewarded for reasonable behaviour but loses rewards for aggressive behaviour.
5. Display warmth and affection when the child exhibits signs of positive or desirable behaviour.

Lundahl et al. (2006) reviewed studies in which parent training (including techniques such as those used by Patterson et al., 1992) was used to reduce children's disruptive behaviour. There were typically beneficial effects, some of which lasted for months following training.

Most interventions have been designed to reduce existing high levels of child aggression. This resembles a disease model: wait for a disease to appear and then treat it. Recently, the emphasis has shifted to a dental model: interventions provided *before* problems manifest themselves may prevent their occurrence in the first place. This approach has been used in a recent large-scale study on 731 at-risk families (Sitnick et al., 2015; Smith et al., 2014).The Family Check-Up (FCU) intervention was used several times over a period of three years. This intervention focuses on the three main aspects of the caregiving environment: positive behaviour support (e.g., rewards for positive behaviour), limit setting and monitoring, and relationship quality. More generally, the FCU increases the family's motivation to change by using collaborative techniques to promote change talk and fostering motivation to address key issues.

What were the key findings? First, the FCU reduced children's aggressive behaviour at home and in school. Second, the emphasis in the FCU on increasing caregivers' positive engagement with children was particularly effective. The beneficial effects of this positive engagement on children's aggressive behaviour two years later occurred mainly because such engagement reduced the occurrence of the coercive cycle during the intervening period of time.

In sum, the evidence suggests that "prevention is better than cure". In other words, it makes much sense to stop children becoming aggressive in the first place rather than delaying interventions until children are repeatedly aggressive in their everyday lives.

Chapter summary

- It is important to distinguish between reactive aggression (triggered by anger) and proactive aggression (triggered by the prospect of some desired outcome).
- Another important distinction is between overt or direct aggression and relational or indirect aggression; the latter is preferred when the costs of overt or direct aggression are high.
- The apparent decline in human violence over the past century may be due to the existence of nuclear weapons rather than any civilising process. Cultures with very low levels of aggression and violence have social norms emphasising cooperation and the disadvantages of competition.

- Anger typically occurs when an individual's goal is thwarted, someone else is perceived as being to blame, and the situation is perceived as unfair.
- Media violence can cause subsequent aggressive behaviour; this depends in part on observational learning.
- Playing violent video games slightly increases aggressive behaviour; this effect depends in part on cognitive processes (especially hostile expectation bias).
- According to the general aggression model, aggressive behaviour is influenced by cognitive interpretations and biases and by personality. The model fails to provide a detailed theoretical account and de-emphasises genetic factors.
- Children's aggressive behaviour is determined in part by family processes (e.g., coercive cycles).
- Men exhibit more direct or overt aggression than women. Men have higher levels of testosterone, and this is associated with reduced impulse control. However, women use relational aggression more often than men.
- Child-based interventions involving communication skills, conflict resolution, and increasing empathy have proved effective in reducing aggression.
- Interventions based on changing family dynamics (e.g., The Family Check-Up) can be used to prevent children developing high levels of aggression.

Further reading

- Archer, J. (2009). Does sexual selection explain human sex differences in aggression? *Behavioral and Brain Sciences, 32,* 249–266. John Archer argues that sex differences in aggression depend mainly on biological factors in our evolutionary history.

- Ferguson, C.J., & Dyck, D. (2012). Paradigm change in aggression research: The time has come to retire the General Aggression Model. *Aggression and Violent Behavior, 17,* 220–228. The limitations and problems with the general aggression model are discussed fully in this article.

- Greitemeyer, T., & Mügge, D.O. (2014). Video games do affect social outcomes: A meta-analytic review of the effects of violent and prosocial video game play. *Personality and Social Psychology Bulletin, 40,* 578–589. This article provides an up-to-date review of research on the effects of violent video games on aggression.

- Vaughan, G.M., & Hogg, M.A. (2014). *Social psychology* (7th ed.). London: Prentice Hall. Theory and research on aggression are discussed in Chapter 12 of this excellent textbook.

Essay questions

1. Describe and evaluate the biological approach to understanding aggression.

2. What evidence supports the view that media violence and playing violent video games increases aggression? How can we best explain this evidence?

3. It is very important that children do not behave aggressively. What approaches would you recommend to produce non-aggressive children?

Part 2

Developmental approach

Developmental psychology is concerned with the psychological changes occurring during the time between birth and adulthood. However, our primary focus will be on infancy and childhood, because that is the period of time during which the most dramatic changes in development are to be found. Developmental psychology (as Sigmund Freud was one of the first psychologists to realise) is of crucial importance to an understanding of adult behaviour.

The study of children's development is fascinating. This book is dedicated to Sebastian, who was born in May 2012. His parents are my daughter Fleur and her husband Simon, and everyone in the family is looking forward excitedly to watching every stage of his development.

Chapter 8 • Cognitive development

We will consider how and why most young children show rapid development in their ability to think and reason.

Chapter 9 • Language development

The mysterious issue of how it is that most young children acquire language at astonishing speed is addressed at length.

Chapter 10 • Moral development

The processes that allow children to develop an increasingly sophisticated understanding of moral values are discussed.

Chapter 11 • Sex and gender

We will consider how children from a surprisingly young age have a clear sense of being male or female and of the cultural expectations associated with being male or female.

When you look at infants and young children, it is obvious that their ability to think and reason is much less than that of older children and adults. This is due in large measure to the fact that they have less knowledge at their disposal. In addition, it is likely that they see the world and think in ways that are very different to ours. For example, when my children were very young, they thought you could tell someone's age by seeing how tall they were! That is an understandable error given that most five-year-old children are taller than most four-year-old children, who in turn are taller than most three-year-olds. What do you think goes on in young children's minds?

Cognitive development

8

Children develop and change enormously in almost every conceivable way between infancy and adolescence. Some of the most dramatic changes involve their cognitive development. Easily the most influential psychologist to focus on cognitive development was the Swiss psychologist Jean Piaget. A Russian psychologist, Lev Vygotsky, has also been very influential, and so his views and those of Piaget are discussed at length. After that, we consider the more recent approach of Robert Siegler.

Finally, we turn to the development of children's ability to understand what other people are thinking and feeling. This ability is of fundamental importance if children are to communicate effectively with other people.

Piaget's theory

Jean Piaget (1896–1980) is the most famous developmental psychologist of all time. He argued that children learn to adapt to the world around them by making use of two types of processes:

Developmental psychologist Jean Piaget, c. 1975.

- **Accommodation**: the individual adjusts to the outside world by changing his/her cognitive organisation.
- **Assimilation**: the individual adjusts his/her interpretation of the outside world to fit his/her existing cognitive organisation.

Imitation is a clear example of accommodation dominating assimilation. In imitation, the individual simply copies someone else's actions or ideas and contributes nothing from his/her previous knowledge. Play is a clear example of assimilation, with reality being interpreted according to the child's whim (e.g., a hairbrush is used as a microphone).

When a child cannot understand its experience in terms of its existing knowledge, he/she experiences conflict between what *actually* happens and what the child expected to happen. This creates an unpleasant state of disequilibrium. This leads to a process known as **equilibration**, in which the child uses accommodation and assimilation to restore a state of equilibrium.

KEY TERMS

Accommodation: changes in an individual's cognitive organisation designed to deal more effectively with the environment.

Assimilation: dealing with new environmental situations by using existing cognitive organisation.

Equilibration: responding to cognitive conflicts by using the processes of accommodation and assimilation to re-establish equilibrium.

An example of the dominance in play of assimilation over accommodation— pretending that a hairbrush is a microphone.

KEY TERMS

Clinical method: an informal question-based approach used to assess children's understanding of problems.

Object permanence: the belief that objects continue to exist even when they can't be seen.

What happens during the course of cognitive development? One possibility is that there are profound changes in the ways in which children think during childhood. Another possibility is that changes in how children think are modest, with cognitive development depending mostly on a dramatic increase in the knowledge they possess. Piaget strongly endorsed the former viewpoint.

Piaget's approach to research involved use of the **clinical method**: an informal interview involving the researcher (e.g., Piaget) and a child was used to assess the child's understanding of problems. This approach was very different to the experimental method discussed in Chapter 3. It is a relatively "natural" approach. However, it has the disadvantages of being unstructured and potentially open to bias in the researcher's choice of questions and his/her interpretations of the child's answers.

Piaget claimed that children pass through four stages of cognitive development each very different from the others:

1. Sensori-motor stage

This stage lasts from birth to about 2 years of age. It is the stage of intelligence in action in which the infant acquires much knowledge by moving around his/her environment. The key achievement of this stage is **object permanence**. This allows the child to be aware of the existence of objects even when they are not visible. Early in the sensori-motor stage, the infant has no awareness of the continued existence of objects – it is literally "out of sight, out of mind".

2. Preoperational stage

This crucial stage of development lasts between the ages of 2 and 7. Thinking during this stage is dominated by *perception*. This often leads to error because things are not always the way they look. Piaget argued that children in the

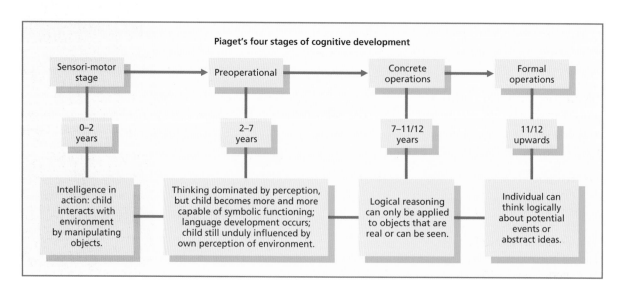

Piaget's four stages of cognitive development

Sensori-motor stage	Preoperational	Concrete operations	Formal operations
0–2 years	2–7 years	7–11/12 years	11/12 upwards
Intelligence in action: child interacts with environment by manipulating objects.	Thinking dominated by perception, but child becomes more and more capable of symbolic functioning; language development occurs; child still unduly influenced by own perception of environment.	Logical reasoning can only be applied to objects that are real or can be seen.	Individual can think logically about potential events or abstract ideas.

preoperational stage often pay attention to only part of a given situation: this is called **centration**.

How centration produces errors have been shown in studies of conservation. **Conservation** refers to an understanding that certain aspects of an object remain the same despite changes in one or more of its dimensions.

In classic research, Piaget gave children two glasses of the same size and shape containing the same quantity of liquid. When the child agreed there was the same quantity of liquid in both glasses, all the liquid from one glass was poured into a glass that was taller and thinner.

Preoperational children failed to show conservation. They argued there was more liquid in the new container ("because it's higher") or that there was more liquid in the original glass ("because it's wider"). In either case, the child centred (focused) on only one dimension (height or width).

According to Piaget, preoperational children also lack **reversibility** (the ability to realise that an object (or number) that has been changed can be restored to its original condition). In the study just described, reversibility involves knowing the effect of pouring the liquid from one container into another could be reversed by pouring it back.

Piaget argued that when children acquire the notion of reversibility, they should be able to succeed on most conservation tasks. In contrast, Piaget's critics argue that performance on conservation tasks also depends on experience and cultural factors. For example, Dasen (1994) carried out research on Australian Aborigines. On the problem with the two glasses, the Aborigines only showed conservation between the ages of 11 and 13 (about five or six years later than European children). However, they performed well on conservation tasks that involved spatial reasoning. These findings make sense – it is important (or least was so traditionally) for Aborigine children to develop good spatial skills for hunting or finding water holes, but the exact quantity of water found is of little importance.

McGarrigle and Donaldson (1975) argued that preoperational children presented with a conservation task assume the experimenter *intends* to change the amount of liquid or other substance. This biases them against showing conservation. McGarrigle and Donaldson tested this notion on various conservation tasks. Six-year-old children were presented with two rows of counters, and all agreed there were equal numbers of counters in each row. Then the experimenter deliberately messed up one of the rows or a "naughty" teddy bear did the same in an apparently accidental way.

What did McGarrigle and Donaldson (1975) find? Only 16% of the children showed conservation (arguing there were the same number of counters in each row) when the experimenter moved the counters. Four times as many children (62%) showed conservation when the counters were moved by naughty teddy. Thus, children's ability to show conservation can be greatly reduced when the experimenter deliberately changes the situation.

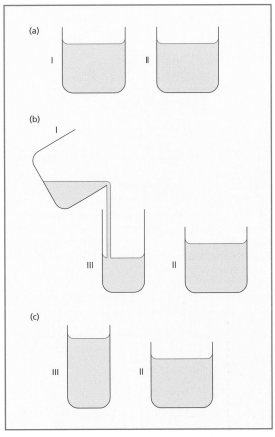

Piaget's study on conservation of quantity. (a) Children agreed that I and II both contained the same quantity of liquid, but when I's liquid was poured into a taller, thinner glass (b and c), the pre-operational children argued that the quantities differed.

KEY TERMS

Centration: the tendency of young children to attend to only part of the information available in a given situation.

Conservation: the child's understanding that various aspects of an object may remain constant even though other aspects are transformed or changed considerably.

Reversibility: the ability to undo mentally (reverse) some operation previously carried out (e.g., changing an object's shape).

McGarrigle and Donaldson found that when an experimenter rearranged one of a pair of rows of counters, relatively few 6-year-old children thought that the two rows still contained the same number of counters. However, when "naughty teddy" appeared to mess up the counters accidentally, most children said that the number in the rows was still the same.

An experimental situation used to show how Piaget overstated the amount of egocentrism shown by young children.

KEY TERMS

Egocentrism: an assumption made by young children that the ways other people see or think are the same as theirs; it is similar to being self-centred.

Decentration: the ability to focus on several aspects of a problem at once and make coherent sense of them.

Egocentrism

Preoperational children also show egocentrism. **Egocentrism** involves children assuming that how they see the world is the same as other people. Piaget obtained evidence of egocentrism using the three mountains task in which children were presented with a three-dimensional model of an imaginary scene consisting of three mountains. They looked at the scene from one angle and a doll was placed at a different location. Four-year-old children assumed that what the doll could see was exactly the same as what they could see: this is an example of egocentrism. Only when children reached the age of 7 or 8 did they work out accurately what the doll could see.

Hughes (1975) used a simpler and more realistic situation involving a boy doll and two policemen. When given the task of hiding the boy doll so neither of the policemen could see him, 90% of children between the ages of 3½ and 5 succeeded even though they could still see the doll. Thus, egocentrism can be avoided at a young age if the task relates to their experience.

Piaget did not distinguish clearly between egocentrism in two senses: (1) absolute failure to appreciate that other people have a different perspective and (2) some appreciation that others have a different perspective but an inability to use that information effectively (Kesselring & Müller, 2011). Consider an experiment by Aebli et al. (1968). Many children given the three mountains task showed egocentrism in the second sense but nevertheless admitted that a doll sitting at the other side of the model had a different perspective to them (lack of egocentrism in the first sense).

Children's shift from being egocentric to being non-egocentric is a very important aspect of cognitive development. For example, successful social interactions with others depend on having a reasonable awareness of their beliefs and values. More recent research on this topic is discussed near the end of the chapter (in the section on theory of mind).

3. Concrete operations stage

Piaget argued that the concrete operations stage lasts between the ages of 7 and 11 or 12. The main advance in this stage is that thinking becomes much less dependent on perception. This involves **decentration**, which involves children spreading their attention over several aspects of a problem and relating these aspects to each other. This is in marked contrast to the limited attentional focus or centration shown by younger children.

The development of various logical and mathematical operations underlies this advance. These operations include the actions denoted by symbols such as +, −, ÷, ×, > (more than), and < (less than). The most important aspect of such operations is reversibility (discussed earlier), in which the effects of a change can be cancelled out by imaging the reverse change. For example, we can turn 9 into 14 by adding and then return to 9 by subtracting 5 from 14.

Cognitive operations are usually organised into a system or structure (termed a **group** by Piaget). For example, an operation such as "greater than" should be considered jointly with "less than". Children have not fully grasped the meaning of "A is greater than B" unless they realise this statement means the same as "B is less than A".

The main limitation of children in this stage is that their thinking is limited to *concrete* situations based on their own experiences. The ability to escape from the limitations of immediate reality into the realm of abstract ideas is found only in the fourth (and final) stage of cognitive development.

4. Formal operations stage

Children from the age of 11 or 12 enter the stage of formal operations in which they develop the ability to think in terms of possible (rather than simply actual) states of the world. Thus, individuals in the stage of formal operations can manipulate ideas to a far greater extent than those in the concrete operations stage. In other words, they can think about thinking and have developed the ability to manage their own minds.

Piaget admitted that most adolescents do not attain the stage of formal operations across all complex cognitive tasks. This occurs in part because their performance on any given task depends on their interests and aptitudes.

Findings

Low and Hollis (2003) asked children to indicate where on the human body they would put a third eye and why. Children aged 6 to 12 typically suggested putting the third eye on the forehead. In contrast, adults produced useful suggestions (e.g., putting the third eye at the back of the head so the person could see behind them) showing evidence of formal operations (i.e., thinking of possible states of the world they had not experienced).

Shayer and Ginsburg (2009) compared the performance of 13- and 14-year-olds on tests of formal operations in 1976 and 2006/7. Many children showed little or no evidence of having attained the stage of formal operations. For reasons that are unclear, the mean level of performance was much lower in 2006/7.

There is a moderately strong relationship between performance on tests of formal operations and IQ (Bradmetz, 1999). This occurs because some of the cognitive abilities associated with formal thinking resemble those assessed by intelligence tests. It follows that adolescents and adults with relatively low IQs are unlikely to attain the stage of formal operations.

Describe children in the stage of formal operations.

KEY TERM

Group: the structure formed from the organisation of various related cognitive processes or operations.

EVALUATION

➕ Piaget's theory was a remarkably ambitious and comprehensive attempt to explain how children move from being irrational and illogical to rational and logical.

➕ Piaget discovered numerous fascinating aspects of cognitive development (e.g., object permanence; conservation; egocentrism).

➕ The notions that children learn certain basic operations (e.g., reversibility), and that these operations then allow them to solve numerous problems, are valuable ones.

➕ Piaget's ideas have had a great influence on educational practice (discussed later).

➖ Piaget exaggerated the differences between stages but minimised the differences within stages. Cognitive development is less neat and tidy than Piaget assumed.

➖ Piaget correctly emphasised the importance of internal motivation for cognitive development but de-emphasised external motivation provided by parents and teachers (see next section).

➖ The clinical method favoured by Piaget is not entirely scientific and is open to biased interpretations by the researcher.

➖ Piaget indicated *what* is involved in cognitive development but not *why* or *how* this development occurs. As a result, there is a "miraculous transition" (Siegler & Munakata, 1993) from one developmental stage to the next.

Vygotsky's theory

According to Vygotsky, when do children learn best?

There are many similarities between the theories proposed by Piaget and by Vygotsky. However, there is one crucial difference (Lourenço, 2012). Piaget emphasised the importance of children's *internal* motivation (self-discovery) as the driver of cognitive development: children are "little scientists". In contrast, Vygotsky saw children as "little apprentices", whose cognitive development was greatly facilitated by *external* social influences provided by parents, teachers, and other children. Note that there were mostly differences in emphasis between these two theorists rather than radical differences: they both acknowledged the importance of internal *and* external factors (Shayer, 2003).

According to Vygotsky, effective learning in children requires taking account of the zone of proximal development. The **zone of proximal development** is the gap between what children can achieve on their own and what they can achieve with the assistance of others. It has two basic aspects (Wass & Golding, 2014). First, children apparently lacking certain skills when tested on their own may perform at a higher level in the social context of someone having the necessary knowledge. Second, when children's level of understanding is moderately challenged, they are most likely to acquire new knowledge rapidly and without a sense of failure.

KEY TERM

Zone of proximal development: the gap between a child's current or actual problem-solving ability and his/her potential when provided with suitable guidance.

Vygotsky emphasised the importance of language in cognitive development. Language and thought in young children develop in parallel and have little impact on each other. Slightly older children use the speech of others and talking to themselves to assist their thinking and problem solving. By the age of 7, egocentric speech (i.e., speaking without paying attention to anyone else present) gives way to inner speech. This inner speech is of direct benefit to thinking.

Findings

Moss et al. (1992) reviewed research on mothers' use of the zone of proximal development. There were three main aspects to the mothers' strategies. First, the mother instructed her child in new skills the child could not perform on its own. Second, the mother encouraged her child to maintain useful problem-solving tactics it had shown spontaneously. Third, the mother persuaded the child to discard immature and inappropriate forms of behaviour. These strategies were generally successful in promoting children's effective learning.

Vygotsky's notion that inner speech assists children in their thinking has received support. Children using the most inner speech performed difficult tasks better than those making little use of inner speech (Jones, 2007). Benigno et al. (2011) studied children of 4 and 5 years as they practiced a planning task across several sessions. Some children showed sharp improvements in performance. These improvements were preceded by increased internal speech, which may have indicated the children were grappling actively with the task.

Vygotsky assumed children show a shift from egocentric or private audible speech to inner speech over the course of development, with egocentric speech almost disappearing after the age of 7. However, these assumptions have received only partial support. Martinez et al. (2011) gave children aged 4½, 6½, and 8½ the task of describing the organisation of a room in a picture so another child could recreate it. As predicted by Vygotsky, the youngest children produced very little inner speech but there was a marked increase in older ones. The findings for egocentric speech were less supportive of Vygotsky. There was a large increase in such speech between the ages of 4½ and 6½ and there were very little changes between 6½ and 8½ years.

EVALUATION

➕ Vygotsky correctly attached considerable importance to the social environment in promoting cognitive development.

➕ As Vygotsky predicted, inner speech helps the problem-solving activities of young children, perhaps because it is associated with an active involvement with the problem.

➖ Vygotsky de-emphasised the role played by internal motivation and curiosity in promoting cognitive development.

➖ Vygotsky failed to develop a systematic theory of cognitive development.

➖ Vygotsky did not specify clearly what kinds of social interaction are most beneficial for learning (e.g., general encouragement vs. specific instructions).

> **IN THE REAL WORLD: Cognitive Acceleration through Science Education (CASE)**
>
> The main ideas of Piaget and Vygotsky have often been used in the real world to enhance children's learning. Here we will consider the Cognitive Acceleration through Science Education (CASE) programme originally used in secondary schools in the UK (Shayer, 1999) and designed to foster effective thinking.
>
> The CASE programme has *five* main features and a typical lesson involves working through them in the order listed:
>
> 1. *Concrete preparations*: the teacher sets the scene and ensures students understand the scientific terms that will be used.
> 2. *Cognitive conflict*: students are exposed to unexpected ideas and/ or findings.
> 3. *Construction*: the cognitive conflicts created in stage 2 are resolved by group discussion.
> 4. *Metacognition*: students are asked open-ended questions requiring them to explain their thinking and focus on tricky issues.
> 5. *Bridging*: students' new understanding is related to their everyday experience.
>
> The CASE programme uses several of Piaget's and Vygotsky's ideas. First, the teacher's use of his/her greater knowledge is in line with Vygotsky's thinking. Second, the use of cognitive conflict resembles Piaget's emphasis on disequilibrium. Third, the metacognition stage requires students to engage in a process resembling Piaget's self-discovery. Fourth, the construction phase resembles Vygotsky's peer tutoring approach (involving guidance from other children).
>
> The CASE programme has proved very effective. As expected, CASE students showed improved performance on GCSE Science. In addition, however, they perform better at other GCSE subjects such as Mathematics and English (Adey, 1993). In Australia, students exposed to the CASE programme showed substantial improvements in scientific reasoning, and this was especially the case for those in academically selective schools (Venville & Oliver, 2015).
>
> In sum, the CASE programme has shown how theories of cognitive development can be used to enhance students' academic performance. It has proved so successful it has been extended to other subjects (e.g., Cognitive Acceleration through Mathematics Education; Cognitive Acceleration through the Arts).

Overlapping waves model

Piaget's central goal was to understand the cognitive changes occurring during children's development. To do this, he compared the cognitive abilities of children of different ages at a given point in time. However, this approach meant Piaget could not observe cognitive changes as they occurred and so was poorly suited to achieving his goal!

Siegler developed an experimental approach that allowed him to study more closely the nature of cognitive changes. This approach involved the **microgenetic method** – children perform the same cognitive task repeatedly over a short period of time.

Siegler (2007) put forward an overlapping waves model. Its key assumption is each child typically has various strategies or ways of thinking about problems of a given type at any point in time. As a result, they exhibit unexpectedly great *variability* in strategy use. According to Siegler (2007, p. 104), "Variability is omnipresent, occurring at all ages, in all domains [areas], and at all points in learning." This assumption is very different from Piaget's view that children at any given stage of development should show reasonable *consistency* in their cognitive processes.

How do children improve their strategy selection? According to the model, children acquire increasingly detailed knowledge by taking account of the speed and accuracy of problem solution with each strategy. This allows them to select the best strategy more often and to learn that a generally effective strategy may not be so for all types of problems.

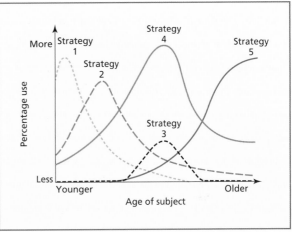

Siegler's overlapping waves model.

Findings

Variable strategy use occurs even when the same problem is presented on two occasions close in time (e.g., Siegler & McGilly, 1989). Many of these changes were *not* due to learning because they involved a shift from a more advanced to a less advanced strategy. In similar fashion, infants of 13½ and 18 months often vary how they go down stairs (walking; bumping down the stairs on their bottoms; going down backwards) from trial to trial (Berger et al., 2015).

According to Siegler, what does cognitive development involve?

Children who initially use several different strategies with a given type of problem generally learn faster than those using only one or two. Why is this? It is easier to replace a dominant (but ineffective) strategy when children have access to several other strategies (Siegler, 2007).

Siegler and McGilly (1989) studied how children learn new strategies. They gave 4- and 5-year-olds addition problems such as 3 + 8 = ? One of the most effective strategies used by young children is the count-on strategy – start with the larger number and count on from that point. In the example, start with 8 and count 9, 10, 11.

No children in the study by Siegler and McGilly (1989) used this strategy initially. With extensive practice, however, nearly all the children discovered the count-on strategy. Typically, the children took much longer than usual on the problem just before their first use of the new strategy. This suggests they were thinking carefully about the best strategy to use.

As predicted by the overlapping waves theory, the children continued to use other strategies much of the time after discovering the count-on strategy. However, they used the count-on strategy much more often following challenging problems (e.g., 2 + 26) that were very hard to solve with other strategies.

There was a final interesting finding from Siegler and McGilly's (1989) study. Several children who used the count-on strategy had little conscious understanding of it. Indeed, some even denied using the strategy in spite of

KEY TERM

Microgenetic method: an approach to studying children's changes in cognitive strategies by means of short-term longitudinal studies.

very clear videotape evidence! Thus, implicit knowledge (knowledge without conscious awareness) can guide children's choice of strategy.

Are the rapid strategy changes found with use of the microgenetic method similar to those shown by children in their everyday lives? This issue was addressed by Siegler and Svetina (2002), who studied problem solving in 6- and 7-year-olds. There were striking similarities between the patterns of change produced by the microgenetic method and by the natural environment.

EVALUATION

⊕ The microgenetic method has proved very useful for studying in detail the ways cognitive functioning changes over time.

⊕ The substantial variability in strategy use shown by individual children is predicted by the overlapping waves model but is inconsistent with previous theories (including Piaget's).

⊕ Much of cognitive development depends on *competition* among various cognitive strategies.

⊖ The model cannot easily be applied to learning on tasks that do not involve clearly defined strategies.

⊖ Much remains to be discovered about how children discover new strategies and how to speed up such discovery.

Theory of mind

At what age do children develop a theory of mind?

We saw earlier in the chapter that young children are egocentric. Thus, they are unaware that others' beliefs and the way they see the world are often different from their own. Piaget assumed that it was only when children reached the age of 7 or 8 that there was a substantial reduction in egocentrism. However, subsequent research (e.g., Hughes, 1975) found evidence of a lack of egocentrism in children a few years younger than that.

The ability to understand that other people's beliefs about the world may differ from their own is very important. Social communication is extremely limited if a child assumes everyone else has the same beliefs. Indeed, children who make that assumption typically find it hard to make friends and to enter successfully into group situations.

Recent research revolves around the notion of **theory of mind**, which is "the ability to make inferences about one's own and other people's mental states" (Schurz & Perner, 2015, p. 1). In other words, children and adults possessing theory of mind are "mind readers" who can understand what other people are thinking and feeling. Having a theory of mind helps to make humans more intelligent than any other species.

We can show the importance of having a theory of mind by considering children lacking the ability to infer the mental states of others. This ability is absent in **autism**, which involves very poor social interaction (e.g., failure to develop peer relationships; preference for solitary activities) and impaired communication (e.g., reluctance to maintain a conversation).

KEY TERMS

Theory of mind: the understanding by children and adults that other people may have different beliefs, emotions, and intentions than their own.

Autism: a severe disorder involving very poor communication skills, deficient social and language development, and repetitive behaviour.

How can we assess theory of mind? One of the main ways theory of mind has been studied is by using false-belief tasks. For example, Wimmer and Perner (1983) used models to present children with the following story. A boy called Maxi puts some chocolates in a blue cupboard. While he is out of the room, his mother moves the chocolate to a green cupboard. The children indicated where Maxi would look for the chocolate when he returned to the room.

Most 4-year-olds argued mistakenly that Maxi would look in the green cupboard. This indicates an absence of theory of mind – these children simply assumed Maxi's beliefs were the same as their own. In contrast, most 5-year-olds produced the right answer.

Findings

Wellman et al. (2001) reviewed numerous false-belief studies carried out in seven countries. Most 3-year-olds performed poorly whereas a substantial majority of 5-year-olds produced the correct answer. However, there is evidence that even infants possess some aspects of theory of mind. For example, Onishi and Baillargeon (2005) showed 15-month-old infants the following: an actor watched a watermelon slice being placed into a green box; the actor's view is blocked as the slice is placed in a yellow box; the actor reaches into one of the boxes. Infants looked longer at the display when the actor reached into the yellow box rather than the green box because there was a discrepancy between the actor's beliefs and actions.

How can we explain findings such as those of Onishi and Baillargeon (2005) apparently indicating children possess a theory of mind much younger than was previously thought to be the case (e.g., Wellman et al., 2001)? An influential answer was provided by Apperly and Butterfill (2009). They argued that successful performance on theory-of-mind tasks can involve two different systems. First, there is a relatively simple system that is cognitively efficient but limited and inflexible. Second, there is a more complex system that is flexible and that depends on knowledge of beliefs and the development of language. Infants possess the first system but not the second one, and so succeed on some theory-of-mind tasks but not complex ones requiring language and use of the second system.

Apperly and Butterfill's (2009) two-system approach makes sense of many of the experimental findings. However, it *underestimates* the abilities of children in the second year of life. Such children perform well on a wider range of theory-of-mind tasks than predicted by their approach (Christensen & Michael, 2016).

We turn now to autism. There is overwhelming evidence that autistic children have great difficulties with theory of mind. For example, Baron-Cohen et al. (1985) gave healthy 4-year-old children as well as autistic children with a mental age of at least 4 a false-belief problem. More than 80% of the healthy children but only 20% of the autistic child solved the problem.

The failure of autistic children to show theory of mind depends heavily on deficient general cognitive abilities. In a study by Pellicano (2010), 4-year-old autistic children were assessed for various executive functions (e.g., inhibitory control). They were also assessed for **central coherence**, which is the ability to use all the information when interpreting a situation. Their improvement in theory-of-mind performance between the ages of 4 and 7 was predicted by executive functioning and central coherence at the age of 4.

It has often been argued that autistic children's deficient theory of mind explains their very poor social skills when interacting with other children. However, there is some evidence suggesting matters may be more complex.

KEY TERM

Central coherence:
the ability to interpret information taking account of the context; the ability to "see the big picture".

Peterson et al. (2016) found that these children's poor social skills seemed to depend more on their deficient language ability than on their poor theory-of-mind understanding.

EVALUATION

➕ The development of a theory of mind is important in allowing children to acquire social skills.

➕ Some of the cognitive abilities (e.g., executive functions; central coherence; language) needed for the development of theory of mind have been identified.

➕ The importance of theory of mind in everyday life is indicated by the problems experienced by children lacking it (e.g., autistic children).

➖ The nature of the processing systems underlying theory-of-mind understanding remains unclear (Apperly & Butterfill, 2009; Christensen & Michael, 2016).

➖ Successful performance on false-belief tasks involves more than simply possessing a theory of mind. It also involves having the necessary motivation and processing resources (Samson & Apperly, 2010).

Chapter summary

- Piaget argued that adaptation to the environment requires accommodation and assimilation.
- Piaget identified four stages of development: (1) sensori-motor (intelligence in action), (2) preoperational (thinking dominated by perception), (3) concrete operations (cognitive systems can be applied to the real world), and (4) formal operations (cognitive systems can also be applied to possible worlds; thinking about thinking).
- Piaget exaggerated the importance of general cognitive operations and minimised the importance of specific learning experiences. He also underestimated children's cognitive skills and described rather than explained the stages of cognitive development.
- Vygotsky argued that external social influences are crucial in cognitive development whereas Piaget emphasised internal motivational influences and self-discovery.
- According to Vygotsky, children's learning is enhanced by strategies based on the zone of proximal development.
- There is support for Vygotsky's claim that children use inner speech to guide their thinking.
- The Cognitive Acceleration through Science Education (CASE) programme combines elements of Piaget's and Vygotsky's theorising and has proved very effective in enhancing students' examination performance.

- Siegler developed the microgenetic method in which children perform the same cognitive task repeatedly over a short period of time.
- Siegler found that children exhibit much more variability in strategy use on many tasks than was previously thought to be the case. Improved strategy use involves taking account of the speed and accuracy of problem solution with each strategy.
- Theory of mind (mindreading) typically develops at about the age of 4, but many aspects of theory of mind are present before the age of 2.
- Autistic children have very deficient theory-of-mind understanding. This is due to impaired executive functioning, a poor ability to use all available information, and deficient language skills.

Further reading

- Defeyter, M.A. (2011). Cognitive development. In A. Slater & G. Bremner (Eds.), *An introduction to developmental psychology* (2nd ed., pp. 287–318). Chichester, UK: Wiley-Blackwell. This chapter provides an overview of major approaches to cognitive development.

- Lourenço, O. (2012). Piaget and Vygotsky: Many resemblances, and a crucial difference. *New Ideas in Psychology, 30*, 281–295. Orlando Lourenço compares and contrasts the theoretical views of Piaget and Vygotsky.

- Newcombe, N.S. (2013). Cognitive development: Changing view of cognitive change. *Wiley Interdisciplinary Reviews: Cognitive Science, 4*, 479–491. Nora Newcombe provides a readable historical account of the major theories of cognitive development.

- Siegler, R.S. (2007). Cognitive variability. *Developmental Science, 10*, 104–109. The implications of his cognitive waves model for understanding cognitive development are discussed briefly and clearly by Robert Siegler in this article.

Essay questions

1. Describe Piaget's stage theory of cognitive development. What are its major strengths and limitations?

2. Assess Vygotsky's contributions to our understanding of cognitive development.

3. Describe Siegler's overlapping waves model. In what ways does it represent an improvement on previous approaches?

4. What is theory of mind? Why do most children develop a theory of mind but some do not?

Language is of enormous importance to the human species. Indeed, it is one of the most significant differences between us and all other species. Anyone lacking a reasonable ability to understand or use language is at a huge disadvantage because it is central to education and the work environment. In addition, making (and keeping) friends involves effective communication, which depends mostly on language.

Mastering language is a complex skill. However, nearly all children do so with apparent ease. Moreover, they do so at a very young age before their other cognitive abilities (e.g., thinking; reasoning) are well developed. How do you they manage to do this?

Several attempts have been made to teach language to chimpanzees. Do you think any of these attempts have been successful?

Language development

9

How can language be defined?

What is language? According to Harley (2013, p. 5), language is "a system of symbols and rules that enable us to communicate. Symbols stand for other things: words, either written or spoken, are symbols. The rules specify how words are ordered to form sentences". Hockett (1960) suggests various criteria, including the following, for distinguishing between language and non-language:

- *Semanticity*: the words or other units must have meaning.
- *Arbitrariness*: there is an arbitrary connection between the form or sound of the word and its meaning.
- *Displacement*: language can be produced even when the object being described is not present.
- *Prevarication*: language involves the ability to tell lies and jokes.
- *Productivity*: an essentially infinite number of ideas can be communicated using language.

It has often been argued that the apparently breathtaking speed with which young children acquire language is a remarkable achievement. From the age of 18 months onwards, children learn 10 or more new words every day. By the time they are 2 years old, most children use language to communicate hundreds of messages.

By the age of 5, children who may not even have started school have mastered most of the grammatical rules of their native language. This happens even though very few parents formally teach their children the rules of grammar. Indeed, most parents are not consciously aware of these rules! Thus, young children simply "pick up" the complex rules of grammar.

In what follows, I first describe the stages of language development. After that, we return to the fascinating issue of how children acquire something as complex as language so quickly and apparently effortlessly. Finally, we consider attempts to teach language to chimpanzees. There has been much controversy concerning the success (or otherwise) of such attempts.

KEY TERMS

Receptive language: the comprehension or understanding of language (e.g., the speech of others).

Productive language: this is language production that involves speaking or writing.

Phonology: the system of sounds within any given language.

Semantics: the meanings expressed by words and sentences.

Syntax: the grammatical rules that indicate the appropriate order of words within sentences.

Pragmatics: the rules involved in deciding how to make sure that what is said fits the current situation.

Telegraphic speech: children's early speech resembling a telegram in that much information is contained in two or (less often) three words.

Stages of language development

It is important to distinguish between **receptive language** (language comprehension) and **productive language** (language expression or speaking). Our central focus will be on productive language. However, there are close links between productive and receptive language.

Children (as well as adults) have better receptive than productive language. Thus, we would underestimate children's language skills if we assumed their speech reflects all their knowledge of language.

Children acquire *four* kinds of knowledge about language:

1. **Phonology:** the sound system of a language.
2. **Semantics:** the study of the meaning.
3. **Syntax:** the rules determining word order within any given language.
4. **Pragmatics:** the study of the influence of situational and contextual factors influencing the meanings of words and sentences.

It used to be assumed that children learn about language in the order listed above (i.e., starting with phonology and finishing with pragmatics). As we will see, that is an oversimplification. Of particular importance, children acquire knowledge of grammar at the same time as knowledge of words and their meanings.

Initial stages

Infants engage in vocalisation from a very early age. The early babbling of infants up to 6 months of age is similar in all parts of the world. By 8 months of age, however, infants' vocalisations show signs of the language they have heard. Adults can sometimes guess accurately from their babbling whether infants have been exposed to French, Chinese, Arabic, or English (De Boysson-Bardies et al., 1984).

Up until 18 months, infants are limited to single-word utterances (although they may be trying to convey a considerable amount of information). Almost two-thirds of the words used by infants are nouns referring to objects or people that interest them. Words sometimes cover more objects than they should (over-extension) as when my younger daughter Juliet referred to every man as "Daddy".

The second stage of language development starts at 18 months. It involves **telegraphic speech**, during which children's speech is abbreviated like a telegram. More specifically, content words such as nouns and verbs are included, but function words (e.g., *a*; *the*; *and*), pronouns, and prepositions are omitted. Even though children at this stage are mostly limited to two-word utterances, they can still communicate numerous meanings. For example, "Daddy chair" may mean "I want to sit in Daddy's chair", "Daddy is sitting in his chair", or "Daddy, sit in your chair!"

Infants engage in vocalisation from a very early age. Here, a baby boy (Sebastian) smiles at the face of his mother (Fleur), and responds to baby talk. At this age, vocalisations are the same in all parts of the world but by 8 months of age infants show signs of the language they have heard.

At about 24 months, most children start producing utterances of three words or longer. From 36 months on, children start using complete sentences and exhibit an increasingly accurate knowledge of grammar.

Vocabulary and grammar

Children's language develops considerably between 2 and 5 years of age. For example, the maximum sentence length increases from four morphemes (units of meaning) at 24 months to eight at 30 months (Fenson et al., 1994). Children gradually acquire various **grammatical morphemes** (modifiers that alter meaning). Examples includes prepositions, prefixes, and suffixes (e.g., *in*; *on*; plural – *s*; and *the*).

Children learn the various grammatical morphemes in the same order. They start with simple ones (e.g., including *in* and *on* in sentences). They then learn more complex ones (reducing *they are* to *they're*).

Children (especially young ones) often imitate adults' speech. Bannard et al. (2009) found much evidence of "blind imitation" in 3-year-olds – they copied everything an adult had just said even when some of it added nothing to the communication. Evidence that children do *not* merely imitate was reported by Berko (1958), who showed children two pictures of an imaginary animal or bird. They were told, "This is a wug. Now there are two . . ." Even young children produced the regular plural form "wugs" despite not having the word before.

More evidence that children often do not imitate comes from their grammatical errors (e.g., saying "The dog runned away" instead of "The dog ran away"). Such errors involve **over-regularisation** – using a grammatical rule in situations to which it does not apply. However, if such errors actually involve misapplying grammatical rules, we would expect to find much more over-generalisation than is actually the case. In fact, children's exposure to language is crucial – there is much less over-generalisation for irregular words children have heard many times than those they have heard infrequently (Gogate & Hollich, 2010).

It used to be thought that young children acquired vocabulary before grammar. However, Labrell et al. (2014) found among children between the ages of 17 and 42 months that vocabulary and grammar had very similar peaks of growth. Dionne et al. (2003) assessed vocabulary and grammar in children at the ages of 2 and 3. Vocabulary at age 2 predicted grammar at age 3, and grammar at age 2 predicted vocabulary at age 3. Such findings suggest that similar processes underlie vocabulary and grammar development.

In sum, the great majority of young children show massive advances in language between 18 and 36 months. Their vocabulary expands by hundreds or thousands of words, their sentences become much longer and more complete, and what they say is increasingly grammatical.

This is a wug

Now there is another one.
There are two of them.
There are two _____.

KEY TERMS

Grammatical morphemes:
prepositions, suffixes, and so on that help to indicate the grammatical structure of sentences.

Over-regularisation:
this is a language error in which a grammatical rule is applied to situations in which it isn't relevant.

Theories of language development

How do young children acquire language with such apparently amazing speed? Most theories can be categorised as inside-out or outside-in theories. Inside-out theorists (e.g., Chomsky; Pinker) argue that language development depends very much on innate factors and only modestly on the child's own experience. In contrast, outside-in theorists (e.g., Bruner; Tomasello) argue that language experience and other environmental influences are of central importance. We turn now to a discussion of the inside-out and outside-in theoretical approaches.

Inside-out theories

Explain the language acquisition device.

Chomsky (1957) argued that language has several unique features (e.g., grammar or syntax) and can only be acquired by humans. Of particular importance was Chomsky's claim that humans possess a language acquisition device consisting of an innate universal grammar (a set of grammatical principles found in all human languages). In Chomsky's own words, "Whatever universal grammar is, it's just the name for [our] genetic structure" (Baptista, 2012, pp. 362–363).

Chomsky (1986) later replaced the notion of a language acquisition device with the idea of a universal grammar common to all languages. This universal grammar consists of various **linguistic universals** (features common to nearly every language). Claimed examples of linguistic universals are word order and the distinction between nouns and verbs. In English, the typical word order is subject-verb-object (e.g., "The man kicked the ball"). Another contender as a linguistic universal is **recursion** (adding additional clauses within sentences to generate longer and longer sentences).

Why did Chomsky propose the notion of an innate universal grammar? First, he argued it explains why only humans develop language fully. Second, the broad similarities Chomksy claimed existed among the world's languages suggested there is a universal grammar. Third, Chomsky claimed the spoken language to which young children are exposed is too limited to allow them to develop language with the breathtaking speed they display.

According to Chomsky, language acquisition depends to a limited extent on children's exposure to (and experience with) the language environment provided by their parents and other people. Such experience determines *which* language a child will learn.

Pinker (1989) was broadly sympathetic to Chomsky's approach. However, he attached more importance to language exposure. For example, Pinker argued that children use "semantic bootstrapping" to allocate words to their appropriate word lass. Suppose a young child hears the sentence, "Williams is throwing a stone", while watching a boy perform that action. The child will realise from their observations that "William" is the actor, "stone" is the object acted on, and "is throwing" is the action. The child then uses its innate knowledge of word categories to work out that "William" is the subject of the sentence, "stone" is the object, and "is throwing" is the verb.

Bickerton (1984), influenced by Chomsky's views, proposed the language bio-programme hypothesis. According to this hypothesis, children will *create* their own grammar even if they are not exposed to a proper language during their early years.

Findings

Chomsky's views have attracted some support. For example, Greenberg (1963) considered word order in numerous languages. The subject preceded the object in

KEY TERMS

Linguistic universals: features (e.g., preferred word orders; the distinction between nouns and verbs) found in the great majority of the world's languages.

Recursion: turning simple sentences into longer and more complex ones by placing one or more additional clauses within them.

98% of the languages studied, and so it may be a linguistic universal determined by human genetics. However, there is an alternative explanation. The subject indicates what a sentence is about whereas the object is the person or thing acted upon by the subject. The central importance of the subject means it makes much sense for the subject to precede the object regardless of any genetic considerations.

Evidence supportive of the language bioprogramme hypothesis was provided by Senghas et al. (2004). They studied deaf Nicaraguan children at special schools in which attempts were made to teach them Spanish. Even though most of these attempts were unsuccessful, the children nevertheless acquired language. They developed a new system of gestures that expanded into a basic sign language passed on to successive groups of children who joined the school. Since their Nicaraguan Sign Language bore very little relation to Spanish or the gestures made by hearing children, it appears to be a genuinely new language that owes remarkably little to other languages.

The findings of Senghas et al. (2004) are consistent with the notion of a universal grammar. However, there is an alternative explanation. The findings may simply show that humans have a strong innate motivation to acquire language (including grammatical rules) and to communicate with others.

There are two main reasons for increasing scepticism concerning Chomsky's views. First, the world's languages differ much more from each other than assumed by Chomsky. Admittedly, the main European languages are all very similar. However, large differences appear when all the world's 6,000 to 8,000 languages are considered. Evans and Levinson (2009, p. 429) did precisely that and concluded, "There are vanishingly few universals of language in the direct sense that all languages exhibit them." For example, there is evidence that recursion (discussed earlier) is lacking in the Amazonian language Pirahã (Everett, 2005). It has proved very difficult to decide whether recursion exists in Pirahã. However, Futrell et al.'s (2016) thorough attempt failed to find any strong evidence for it.

Second, the language input to which young children are exposed is much richer than Chomsky believed. Most children are exposed to child-directed speech that is easy for them to understand. **Child-directed speech** involves very short, simple sentences; a slow rate of speaking; and use of a restricted vocabulary. Such speech should facilitate children's ability to learn language (see next section).

EVALUATION

➕ Inside-out theories such as Chomsky's potentially explain why nearly all children master their native language reasonably rapidly.

➕ Chomsky's theoretical approach is supported by evidence suggesting that language (or at least complex language) is uniquely human (discussed later).

➕ There is evidence that specific genes influence language acquisition.

➖ Languages change amazingly rapidly. For example, the entire range of Indo-European languages emerged from a common source in under 10,000 years (Baronchelli et al., 2012). Biological evolution (emphasised by Chomsky) could not possibly have kept pace with such changes.

KEY TERM

Child-directed speech: the short, simple, slowly-spoken sentences used by mothers, fathers, or other caregivers when talking to their young children; designed to be easy for children to understand.

> ⊖ The world's languages differ far more than Chomsky assumed and there are few (or no) linguistic universals.
>
> ⊖ Parents' use of child-directed speech means that the language input received by young children is much richer than implied by Chomsky.
>
> ⊖ Human ability to acquire language is probably due to our *general* abilities (e.g., perception; attention; learning; thinking) rather than any language-related genetic structures.

Outside-in theories

Outside-in theorists (e.g., Tomasello, 2005) emphasise the central roles of learning and experience in allowing young children to acquire language. In essence, outside-in theorists argue that the language input to which young children are exposed is sufficient for language acquisition. This is in sharp contrast to Chomsky's views. We saw earlier that parents talking to their young children use very short, simple sentences (child-directed speech), which should make it easier for young children to develop language.

According to Tomasello (2005), children's language development depends on their cognitive understanding of the scenes or events they experience. As a result, children's learning of specific language skills (e.g., grammar) tends to be *gradual*. In addition, young children's limited cognitive ability means their early use of language often consists of imitating or copying what they have heard.

Findings

There are several aspects to child-directed speech. Parents use sentences slightly longer and more complex than those produced by their child (Bohannon & Warren-Leubecker, 1989). **Expansions** consist of fuller and more grammatical versions of what the child has just said. For example, a child might say, "Cat out", with its mother responding, "The cat wants to go out."

How does child-directed speech help children acquire language skills?

Saxton (1997) argued that many expansions provide children with an immediate *contrast* between their own incorrect speech and the correct version. For example, a child may say, "He shooted bird!", to which the adult might reply, "He shot the bird!"

Unsurprisingly, the children of parents who use much child-directed speech typically show more rapid language development than other children (Rowe, 2008). The take-home message is that most parents are "in tune" with their child's current language abilities and so provide the environmental support required for language acquisition. Schieffelin (1990) reported an apparent exception to this conclusion among the Kaluli of New Guinea. Kaluli children develop language at the normal rate even though their parents talk to them as if they were adults. However, Kaluli children become involved in social and communal activities that promote shared understanding and language development (Ochs & Schieffelin, 1995).

KEY TERM

Expansions: utterances of adults that consist of fuller and more accurate versions of what a child has just said.

Outside-in theorists assume that young children master language much more slowly than implied by Chomsky. Children's speech for the first two years after they start to speak is remarkably limited (Bannard et al., 2009). For example, they use a small set of familiar verbs and often repeat back what they have just heard. Bannard et al. (2013) found 3-year-olds often engage in "blind copying" – they imitate everything an adult has just said even when part of it does not add any useful information.

Matthews et al. (2005) provided evidence that children learn grammar slowly. They presented 2- and 3-year-old children with short sentences in which the words were in an ungrammatical subject-object-verb order (e.g., "Bear elephant tugged"). The children in their own speech often copied the ungrammatical word order they had heard when they were not familiar with the verb in the sentence. However, they rarely spoke ungrammatically when they were very familiar with the verb.

These findings indicate that using the correct grammatical order is a *gradual* process. It starts with familiar verbs several months before being used with unfamiliar verbs. This is exactly what we would expect to find if children's language development is closely linked to their specific language experience.

EVALUATION

➕ Children's language acquisition benefits substantially from exposure to child-directed speech because it is carefully tailored to the need of young children.

➕ Children's limited cognitive abilities mean that language acquisition is gradual and error prone and often involves copying the language they hear.

➖ It is important to find out more about language acquisition in children with little exposure to child-directed speech.

➖ More needs to be discovered about the processes allowing young children to move from imitative speech to more creative speech.

Animal language

There are two main reasons why it is important to study language in other species. First, such research is directly relevant to Chomsky's theoretical assumption that language is unique to the human species. Second, studying language in other species forces us to consider precisely what we mean by language. As we will see, the great apes provide an interesting test case – they can acquire some (but not all) features of language. That makes it hard to decide whether or not they possess language.

According to Skinner, how does language develop?

There is one final point before we discuss research on great apes. Their vocal tracts are very different from those of humans and so they cannot produce human sounds. As a result, great apes have been trained to produce language in other ways (e.g., using sign language).

Findings

Two species of great apes (common and bonobo chimpanzees) are often regarded as being closest to the human species. Early research by Allen and Beatrice Gardner (1969) involved teaching American Sign Language to a female common chimpanzee called Washoe. After four years of training, she knew 132

With training, what aspects of language can chimpanzees learn to produce?

signs. She could also arrange signs meaningfully, suggesting she had grasped basic aspects of grammar. However, Terrace et al. (1979) disputed the Gardners' claim that Washoe had acquired language – most of the time she merely *imitated* the signs just made by her teacher. This suggests Washoe probably had little or no understanding of grammar.

IN THE REAL WORLD: case study of Kanzi and Panbanisha

Bonobos, a species of great ape, have developed better language skills than common chimpanzees. Two of the most famous bonobos are Kanzi, a male bonobo born on 28 October 1980, and his half-sister Panbanisha, born on 17 November 1985. In this case study, I discuss their language achievements.

Kanzi was taught language using a keyboard containing **lexigrams** (figures or symbols representing words). In 17 months, he learned to understand nearly 60 of them and could produce nearly 50 by pointing to relevant ones (Savage-Rumbaugh et al., 1986). His comprehension skills were especially good – he responded correctly to 109 words on a speech comprehension test. However, he differed from young children in that the length of his utterances increased only a little over time. Indeed, most of his utterances consisted of a single lexigram (the average length of his sentences was only 1.15 lexigrams).

Savage-Rumbaugh et al. (1993) compared Kanzi's language comprehension at the age of 8 with that of a 2-year-old girl Alia. Grammatical knowledge was tested by asking Kanzi and Alia to respond to commands. Kanzi responded correctly on 72% of trials and Alia on 66% of trials, suggesting Kanzi had a reasonable grasp of grammar. However, most commands did not require a knowledge of grammar. For example, "Take the snake outdoors" can only mean take the snake to the outdoors rather than take the outdoors to the snake! Kanzi performed only slightly better than chance when grammatical knowledge was needed to interpret the command (e.g., "Put the noodles on the hotdogs" vs. "Put the hotdogs on the noodles"). Overall, then, Kanzi showed little or no grasp of grammar.

Panbanisha was exposed to language from birth and arguably developed greater language skills than any other great ape. She used a specially designed keypad with about 400 lexigrams on it. When she pressed a sequence of keys, a computer translated the sequence into a synthetic voice. Panbanisha learned a vocabulary of 3,000 words by the age of 14 and combined symbols in the grammatically correct order (e.g., "Please can I have an iced coffee?"). When Bill Fields, one of the researchers, asked Panbanisha what was wrong, she replied, "Kanzi bad keyboard". She said this because Kanzi had recently broken a keyboard.

It has often been claimed that apes' language responses lack spontaneity and refer only to the present. However, that was not the case in a study by Lyn et al. (2011) on Panbanisha, Kanzi, and a common chimpanzee. They found 74% of the apes' utterances were spontaneous. In addition, the apes referred to the past as often as young children and produced more responses referring to future intentions. Subsequent research by Lyn et al. (2014) indicated that bonobos (including

---

KEY TERM

Lexigrams: symbols used to represent words in studies on communication.

Kanzi with researcher Sue Savage-Rumbaugh.

Panbanisha and Kanzi) can communicate about displaced objects (i.e., those no longer present), which is one of the criteria for language.

In sum, Kanzi and Panbanisha (especially Panbanisha) have greatly exceeded the achievements of Washoe and have shown an impressive ability to acquire many aspects of language. An evaluation of their language abilities (and those of other bonobos) is provided shortly.

Children's use of language is generally responsive to the reactions of the person to whom they are speaking. For example, they repeat a message if the recipient appears not to understand what they have said. Genty et al. (2015) found bonobos' communications were also responsive to the recipient. Bonobos often switched to new signals if their initial attempt at communication proved unsuccessful. Their signal production differed according to whether they knew the recipient (a human adult): they were more likely to repeat a message with a familiar recipient but to elaborate the original message with an unfamiliar recipient. Thus, bonobos resemble humans in varying their communications to accommodate the recipient's needs.

What are the main limitations in bonobos' language acquisition? First, bonobos' utterances are much less likely than those of young children (between 12 and 24 months) to reflect motivation to engage in social interaction. Young children make much use of statements referring to intentions, attention seeking, offering something to someone else, past activities, and so on, whereas only 5% of bonobos' utterances involve similar statements (Lyn et al., 2014). In contrast, 80% of bonobos' utterances are requests (e.g., for food). Thus, language is used in a much less communicative and cooperative fashion in bonobos than young children.

Second, children's language skills develop dramatically after the age of 2 and so become markedly superior to those of bonobos. For example, their language exhibits much more productivity (expressing numerous ideas) and is much more complex in terms of sentence length and use of grammatical structures.

In sum, we cannot provide a "Yes" or "No" answer to the question of whether chimpanzees can acquire language. They can acquire many aspects of language. However, their language learning falls substantially below that of even young children.

EVALUATION

➕ Great apes (especially bonobos) have learned hundreds of words in the form of lexigrams and show reasonable understanding of these lexigrams. Their achievements satisfy several criteria for language proposed by Hockett (1960), including semanticity, arbitrariness, and displacement.

➕ Bonobos communicate flexibly and are responsive to the recipient of their communications (e.g., communicating differently to familiar and unfamiliar recipients).

➕ Bonobos' language comprehension ability is similar to that of 2-year-old children in some ways.

➖ Bonobos' language is mostly confined to very short utterances and expresses much simpler ideas than those of children after the age of 2.

➖ Bonobos are much less likely than young children to use language to facilitate communication and cooperation.

➖ As Chomsky (quoted in Atkinson et al., 1993) pointed out, "If an animal had a capacity as biologically advantageous as language but somehow hadn't used it until now, it would be evolutionary miracle, like finding an island of humans who could be taught to fly."

Chapter summary

- Various criteria for language have been suggested. They include semanticity, arbitrariness, displacement, prevarication, and productivity.
- Children have better receptive than productive language. Productive language starts with one-word utterances followed by the telegraphic period in which the emphasis is on content words.
- Children sometimes imitate adults' speech, but they also seem to acquire grammatical rules.
- Chomsky argued that humans possess a language acquisition device and that there are language universals. Neither assumption is correct, and the world's languages are much more diverse than assumed by Chomsky.
- According to the language bioprogramme hypothesis, children will create a grammar even if exposed to very little language. There is some support for this hypothesis in research on deaf Nicaraguan children, which reveals the strong human motivation to communicate.

- Outside-in theorists argue that child-directed speech (tailored to children's needs) plays a vital role in language acquisition.
- According to outside-in theorists, children's language acquisition depends in part on their cognitive understanding of their everyday experiences. This leads to the prediction (which has research support) that children should acquire language gradually.
- Research on great apes is of relevance to the issue of whether there is something unique and specifically human about language.
- Bonobos can acquire large vocabularies and can communicate numerous messages.
- The communications of great apes are much more limited than those of young children. For example, there are few long utterances, and there is limited evidence they possess grammatical knowledge.

Further reading

- Christiansen, M.H., & Chater, N. (2015). The language faculty that wasn't: A usage-based account of natural language recursion. *Frontiers in Psychology*, 6 (Article 1182). Morten Christiansen and Nick Chater provide a readable account of the main problems with Chomsky's theories about language development.

- Harley, T.A. (2013). *The psychology of language: From data to theory* (4th ed.). Hove, UK: Psychology Press. Chapters 3 and 4 of this outstanding textbook by Trevor Harley deal with language development in children and animals.

- Mitchell, P., & Ziegler, F. (2012). *Fundamentals of developmental psychology*. Hove: Psychology Press. Chapter 12 in this textbook focuses on language development.

- Smith, P.K., Cowie, H., & Blades, M. (2015). *Understanding children's development* (6th ed.). Chichester: Wiley. Language development is discussed in Chapter 12 of this readable textbook.

Essay questions

1. Describe the early stages of language development. What are the main changes that occur?

2. What are the main assumptions of inside-out theories? How successful (or otherwise) have such theories been?

3. What are the main environmental influences that facilitate children's acquisition of language?

4. Has research on great apes shown they can acquire language?

Most children show considerable moral development as they grow up. Of particular importance, they achieve an increasingly clear understanding of appropriate and inappropriate ways of behaving and interacting with other people. In addition, their behaviour becomes increasingly influenced by moral values, and they experience guilt and shame when they fail to live up to reasonable moral standards.

What factors lead children to exhibit moral development during the course of their childhood? Does it depend mostly on their parents, on learning from other children, or on genetic factors? Do children behave in a moral way because they are imitating others' behaviour?

Moral development

10

This chapter deals with moral development occurring in children as they grow up into adults. What do we mean by 'morality'? According to Villegas de Posada and Vargas-Trujillo, (2015, p. 408), **morality** involves "acting in conformity with a code of conduct that prescribes what is right and wrong. It prohibits harming others . . . and promotes charitable activities."

Why is morality important? A crucial reason is that the smooth functioning of society requires reasonable agreement on what is right and what is wrong. Of course, there are some moral issues (e.g., animal experiments; nuclear weapons) on which individuals within any given society have very different views. However, society would become chaotic if there were controversy about all moral issues.

Human morality has three major components:

1. *Cognitive*: how we think about moral issues and decide what is right and wrong; this component involves moral reasoning.
2. *Emotional*: the feelings (e.g., guilt; pride) associated with moral thoughts and behaviour.
3. *Behavioural*: the extent to which we behave honourably or lie, steal, and cheat.

What are the main components of morality?

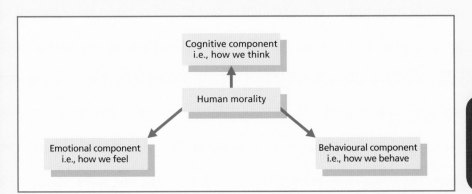

KEY TERM

Morality: A system of values that can be used to identify right and wrong ways of thinking and behaving.

Consistency of moral development

We might imagine that any given individual would show *consistency* among the three components of morality. For example, someone whose moral reasoning (cognitive component) was highly developed would exhibit high moral standards with respect to the emotional and behavioural components. In fact, however, there are sometimes large discrepancies among the three components.

Villegas de Posada and Vargas-Trujillo (2015) carried out a meta-analytic review based on numerous studies comparing moral reasoning (cognitive component) and the behavioural component. The behavioural component was assessed in various ways: (1) real life (e.g., small infringements of the law), (2) honesty (e.g., cheating in exams), and (3) altruism (e.g., helping and sharing). They discovered that there were significant positive associations between the cognitive component and all three measures of the behavioural component. However, these associations were fairly small, and so there is much inconsistency between the cognitive and behavioural components of morality.

Why are there discrepancies between moral reasoning and behaviour? An important reason is that individuals with a high level of moral reasoning sometimes behave in ways they know are wrong when faced with temptation. For example, someone who believes strongly that stealing is wrong may say nothing when given far too much change in a shop.

However, individuals sometimes behave *more* morally than they thought they would. Teper et al. (2011) gave students the opportunity to cheat on a maths test. In practice, they cheated less often than they had anticipated. Why was this? The students experienced more emotional arousal when given the chance to cheat than when they merely considered what they would do in that situation. Thus, emotional arousal acted as a "brake" on their temptation to cheat.

Structure of the chapter

I will start by discussing Kohlberg's theory of moral development, which focused mostly on the cognitive component of morality. After that, I discuss two theoretical approaches to understanding gender differences in morality.

After that, we will consider the influence of parents and peers (other children of the same age). Unsurprisingly, the extent to which children and adolescents exhibit moral behaviour depends to a large extent on both parents and peers.

Kohlberg's cognitive-developmental theory

Lawrence Kohlberg (1927–1987) was strongly influenced by Jean Piaget. Piaget claimed that cognitive development for all children involves an invariant sequence of stages, and Kohlberg argued the same is also true of moral development. According to Kohlberg, moral development relies heavily on changes in moral reasoning and on children's increasing cognitive abilities.

Kohlberg (e.g., 1963) tested his cognitive-developmental theory by presenting children and adolescents with moral dilemmas in which they chose between upholding some moral principle or law or rejecting the moral principle in favour of some basic human need. For example, what would you think of someone who stole a drug to save his dying wife because he could not afford the inflated price quoted by the pharmacist?

Kohlberg's theory revolves around three levels of moral development with two stages at each level:

At which level or stage in Kohlberg's theory do children have a punishment-and-obedience orientation?

- Level 1: **Pre-conventional morality**: what is regarded as right or wrong is determined by the rewards or punishments likely to follow rather than by moral issues.
- Level 2: **Conventional morality**: children at this level are very concerned to have others' approval and to avoid being blamed for behaving wrongly.
- Level 3: **Post-conventional morality**: there is an increasing recognition that the rights of others can override the need to obey laws and rules and more of a focus on abstract notions of justice.

KEY TERMS

Pre-conventional morality: the first level of moral development in Kohlberg's theory; at this level, moral reasoning focuses on rewards and punishments for good and bad actions.

Conventional morality: the second level of moral development in Kohlberg's theory; at this level, moral reasoning focuses on having the approval of others.

Post-conventional morality: the third level of moral development in Kohlberg's theory; at this level, moral reasoning focuses on justice and the need for others to be treated in a respectful way.

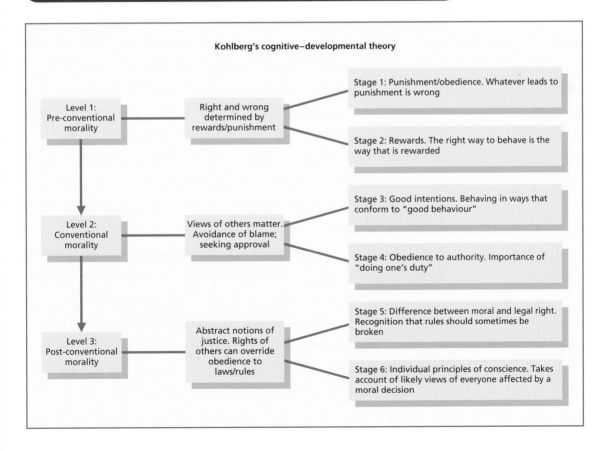

Kohlberg's cognitive–developmental theory

Level 1: Pre-conventional morality

Right and wrong determined by rewards/punishment

Stage 1: Punishment/obedience. Whatever leads to punishment is wrong

Stage 2: Rewards. The right way to behave is the way that is rewarded

Level 2: Conventional morality

Views of others matter. Avoidance of blame; seeking approval

Stage 3: Good intentions. Behaving in ways that conform to "good behaviour"

Stage 4: Obedience to authority. Importance of "doing one's duty"

Level 3: Post-conventional morality

Abstract notions of justice. Rights of others can override obedience to laws/rules

Stage 5: Difference between moral and legal right. Recognition that rules should sometimes be broken

Stage 6: Individual principles of conscience. Takes account of likely views of everyone affected by a moral decision

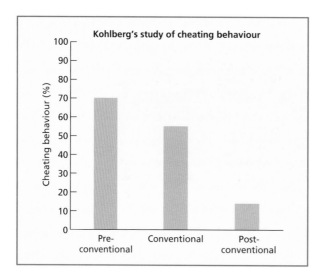

Kohlberg's study of cheating behaviour

Findings

The key assumption that all children follow the same sequence of stages has received some support. Colby et al. (1983) found in a 20-year longitudinal study that there was a large decrease in reasoning at Stages 1 and 2 (i.e., Level 1) and a corresponding increase in reasoning at Stages 3 and 4 (i.e., Level 2). Snarey (1985) reported that most individuals in 26 cultures went through the various stages of moral development in the same order.

However, people's moral reasoning is often inconsistent: a given individual will often exhibit a lower level of reasoning on some moral dilemmas than others. Krebs and Denton (2005, p. 633) explained this inconsistency as follows: "Moral development is defined more by an expansion in the range of structures of moral reasoning available to people than by the last structure they acquire." The fact that older children and adolescents have access to far more knowledge relevant to moral reasoning than younger children helps to explain why their responses to moral dilemmas often exhibit inconsistency.

It is reasonable to assume an individual's stage of moral development will predict their behaviour. There is some support for this prediction. Kohlberg (1975) found that cheating behaviour was approximately five times more common among students at the post-conventional level of morality than those at the pre-conventional level.

EVALUATION

➕ Kohlberg's stage theory of moral reasoning has been very influential.

➕ There is some support for the sequence of stages identified by Kohlberg from studies in the United States and cross-cultural studies.

➖ The notion of an invariant sequence of stages of moral reasoning is far too neat and tidy.

➖ Kohlberg's relative neglect of the emotional and behavioural components of morality means his approach is too narrow (Lapsley & Carlo, 2014).

- People's level of moral reasoning is often higher with the imaginary scenarios used by Kohlberg than the moral dilemmas of everyday life. This is because, "It's a lot easier to be moral when you have nothing to lose" (Walker et al., 1995, pp. 381–382).
- As we will see later, Kohlberg *underestimated* young children's moral development. His claims that young children are egocentric or self-focused and largely unaware of moral considerations have been disconfirmed.

Recent theoretical developments

There have been two major recent changes in research and theory on moral development since Kohlberg put forward his influential theory. First, it is increasingly recognised that a much broader approach to moral development is required. Such an approach needs to include an emphasis on moral emotions (e.g., empathy; sympathy; guilt; and shame) and on children's actual behaviour in many situations involving their interactions with other children and with adults.

Second, Kohlberg's assumption that young children have very limited moral development has been rejected. Instead, it is generally accepted they have "a non-egocentric awareness of the goals, feelings, and desires of people and of how those mental states are affected by others' actions" (Thompson, 2012, p. 426).

Findings: behaviour

Young children in the first year of life already exhibit some basic features of a moral perspective. For example, Hamlin (2015) studied 6-month-old infants. These infants preferentially attended to a character who had previously behaved in a helpful way towards another character rather than a character who had previously behaved unhelpfully towards another character. The infants' behaviour was also influenced – they were more likely to approach the helpful character than the unhelpful one.

Brownell et al. (2013) assessed whether 18- and 24-month-old children would share toys or food with an adult playmate who had none. They found that 73% of the older children and 28% of the younger ones shared spontaneously.

Why do children display helpful behaviour and a concern about others at a very young age? Many of our ancestors in our evolutionary past were engaged in a constant struggle to survive (e.g., finding enough food to eat). Accordingly, it was vitally important that even very young children made as much of a contribution as possible (Warneken, 2015).

Findings: theory of mind

An important aspect of moral development is the understanding that other people's beliefs about the world may differ from one's own. This involves **theory of mind**, "the ability to make inferences about one's own and other people's

> **KEY TERM**
>
> **Theory of mind:** the understanding that others may have different beliefs, emotions, and intentions from one's own.

mental states" (Schurz & Perner, 2015, p. 1). Children with a theory of mind are "mind readers".

Theory of mind has been assessed using false-belief tasks such as the following (Wimmer & Perner, 1983): A boy called Maxi puts chocolates in a blue cupboard. While he is out of the room, his mother moves the chocolates to a green cupboard. The children then indicated where Maxi would look for the chocolates when he returned to the room.

Most 4-year-olds argued mistakenly that Maxi would look in the green cupboard. This indicates an absence of theory of mind – these children simply assumed Maxi's beliefs were the same as theirs. In contrast, most 5-year-old children produced the right answer.

Children show evidence of theory of mind at four or five years of age when performance is assessed by verbal responses but at 12 months of age when performance is assessed by looking behaviour (Christensen & Michael, 2016). How can we explain this discrepancy? Apperly and Butterfill (2009) argued that infants have only a limited and inflexible system that permits success when performance is assessed by looking behaviour. Full theory of mind requires the development of language and only occurs at the age of four. This theory underestimates the abilities of infants – they show much more flexibility than assumed by Apperly and Butterfill and show convincing evidence of a theory of mind (Christensen & Michael, 2016).

In sum, infants possess many aspects of theory of mind. This indicates that they are less egocentric and have greater moral development than assumed by Kohlberg.

Gender differences: theoretical explanations

There has been much interest over the years in the issue of gender differences in morality. The first major theory to address this issue was put forward by Carol Gilligan (1977, 1982).

She disliked what she claimed was the sexist bias of Kohlberg's approach. Kohlberg initially based his theory only on interviews with male participants, and this may have introduced bias into his theory. More importantly, most women were classified at Stage 3 of moral development whereas most men were at Stage 4.

Gilligan argued that Kohlberg had failed to realise that moral development differs between boys and girls. More specifically, boys develop a **morality of justice** in which the focus is on the use of laws and moral principles. In contrast, girls develop a **morality of care** in which the focus is on human well-being and compassion for others. According to Gilligan, Kohlberg showed sexist bias by regarding the morality of justice as superior to the morality of care. More generally, Gilligan argued that theories of moral reasoning should give equal weight to the two types of morality.

Friesdorf et al. (2015) also focused on gender differences in moral reasoning. Their starting point was Greene's (2007) dual-process model of moral judgment. According to this model, the decisions we make when confronted by many major moral dilemmas can depend more on cognitive processes or

> **KEY TERMS**
>
> **Morality of justice:** the individual emphasises the importance of laws and moral principles when deciding what is morally acceptable.
>
> **Morality of care:** the individual emphasises the importance of compassion and human well-being when deciding what is morally acceptable.

on emotional ones. For example, consider the footbridge problem. There is a runaway trolley on a track that will kill five workmen. The only way to save their lives is to push a stranger over a footbridge. The stranger would be killed, but the workmen would survive.

What would you do in this situation? You could decide to sacrifice the stranger because it would save four lives compared to doing nothing – this decision is based on cognitive processes. Alternatively, you could decide not to push the stranger over the bridge because you were so concerned not to harm anyone directly – this decision is based on emotional processes.

Friesdorf et al.'s (2015) theory of moral reasoning was based on dilemmas such as the one just discussed. They argued that women experience stronger emotional responses than men to harming others. One reason for this is that women are better than men at identifying with the emotional states of other people (Hall & Schmid Mast, 2008). As a consequence, they predicted that women would be more likely than men to make decisions to moral dilemmas based on emotional processes.

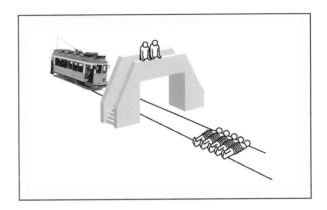

Findings

Attempts to test Gilligan's theory have produced mixed and inconsistent findings. The most thorough attempt was made by Jaffee and Hyde (2000), who reviewed numerous studies of moral reasoning comparing males and females. Overall, there was a very small tendency for males to show more justice reasoning than females. There was a slightly larger (but still small) tendency for females to show more caring reasoning than males.

Research has revealed some interesting cultural differences. For example, Skoe (1998) found as predicted by Gilligan that Canadian and American women between the ages of 17 and 26 showed more complex care-based understanding than men. However, there was no gender difference in care-based understanding in Norway, a culture emphasising gender equality in the workplace and in society generally.

According to Gilligan, which moralities do girls and boys develop?

We turn now to Friesdorf et al.'s (2015) theory. Fumagalli et al. (2010) used the footbridge problem. Men were more likely than women to sacrifice the stranger, indicating that they were less influenced by emotional considerations. This finding is consistent with the theory.

Friesdorf et al. (2015) carried out a meta-analysis (combining the findings from numerous studies) to test their theory of gender differences in moral reasoning. They reported two main findings. First, women were much more likely than men to resolve moral dilemmas by using emotional processes. Second, men were slightly more likely than women to use cognitive processes to resolve moral dilemmas. Their main conclusion was as follows: "Gender differences in moral dilemma judgments are due to differences in affective [emotional] responses to harm rather than cognitive evaluations of outcomes" (p. 696).

EVALUATION

➕ There is weak support for Gilligan's assumptions that women have a morality of care whereas men have a morality of justice.

➕ There is strong support for the notion that women's moral reasoning often relies more on emotional considerations than does men's moral reasoning. This probably reflects the greater empathy of women and their superior ability to identify with the emotional experiences of other people.

➕ The findings reported by Friesdorf et al. (2015) indicate there are important gender differences in moral reasoning that merit further research.

➖ Gilligan's theoretical approach is interesting but has not attracted much support from research.

Parents, peers, and genetic factors

It is of theoretical and practical importance to identify the factors that influence children's moral development. The strongest environmental influences typically come from the child's parents and his/her **peers** (children of the same age). We also need to consider possible genetic influences on moral development.

Parents

Which is the most effective of Hoffman's parenting styles for children's moral development?

Hoffman (1970) identified three major strategies used by parents in the moral development of their children:

1. *Induction*: explaining why a given action is wrong and could harm other people.
2. *Power assertion*: using spanking, removal of privileges, and harsh words to assert power over one's child.
3. *Love withdrawal*: withholding attention or love when one's child behaves badly.

Brody and Shaffer (1982) in a review found that induction improved moral development in 86% of the studies. In contrast, power assertion improved moral development in only 18% of studies and love withdrawal in 42%. Power assertion in the form of spanking typically reduces children's internalisation of moral values and leads to increased delinquent and antisocial behaviour (Gershoff, 2002).

Further support for the importance of induction was reported by Patrick and Gibbs (2012) in a study on adolescents. Parental induction (including parental disappointed expectations as well as focusing on the harm done to others) was the most used technique by mothers. Induction was perceived by adolescents as fairer and more appropriate than power assertion or love

KEY TERM

Peers: children of approximately the same age as any given child.

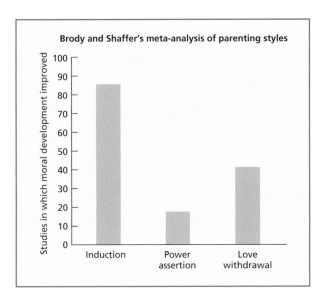

Brody and Shaffer's meta-analysis of parenting styles

withdrawal. Of most importance, parental induction was positively related to adolescents' development of a higher moral identity whereas power assertion and love withdrawal were not.

Why is induction so effective? Hoffman (2000) argued it is a direct way in which parental standards can be communicated to their children. Ideally, children should be in a state of mild emotional arousal while parental induction is occurring. This increases the probability that children will continue to follow parental demands even when they are not being observed.

IN REAL LIFE: moral development over time

We can obtain the clearest understanding of how moral development occurs in children's everyday lives by studying children over a period of several years. Such studies (known as longitudinal studies) shed light on causality – we can see how factors at one point in time are related to children's moral development at a later point in time. Impressive longitudinal studies were reported by Kochanska et al. (2008), Kochanska et al. (2010), and Kochanska and Kim (2014).

A key factor emerging from these studies was mutually responsive orientation between mother and child. **Mutually responsive orientation** "is a positively reciprocal, mutually binding, receptive, and cooperative parent-child relationship" (Kochanska & Kim, 2014, p. 9). Mutually responsive orientation during the first two years of life strongly predicted moral behaviour at 52 months (Kochanska et al., 2008). One reason is that strong emotional bonds between mother and child increase the chances the child will accept the mother's moral guidance.

KEY TERM

Mutually responsive orientation: a mutually cooperative relationship between parent and child.

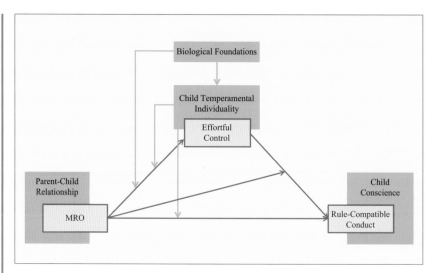

A model of the ways in which mutually responsive orientation (MRO) and effortful control influence moral behaviour (rule-compatible conduct). Additional relevant factors are shown in grey. From Kochanska and Kim (2014).

Kochanska et al. (2010) studied young children as they developed between 25 and 80 months and focused on various factors relevant to the children's moral development. First, there was internalisation of their parents' rules (assessed by their ability to resist the temptation to play with forbidden toys). Second, there was empathic concern towards their parents (assessed by their distress when led to believe, mistakenly, they had accidentally hit their parent on the finger and caused pain). Third, there was each child's **moral self** (assessed by asking many questions concerning their moral beliefs and behaviour). All three factors predicted subsequent levels of moral development.

Kochanska and Kim (2014) argued that differences in moral development among children also depend on genetic factors. They focused on **effortful control**, which is "the capacity to deliberately, actively suppress the dominant response. . . . It underpins children's capacity for self-regulated behaviour, including rule-compatible conduct" (p. 9). They also focused on mutually responsive orientation assessed through lengthy naturalistic interactions between parents and children. Moral development at 67 months was predicted by effortful control and mutually responsive orientation assessed several years earlier.

In sum, naturalistic longitudinal family studies have identified several major factors influencing children's moral development. These factors include mutually responsive orientation, internalisation of rules, empathic concern, the moral self, and effortful control. Of most importance is the way in which environmental factors (especially mutually responsive orientation) interact with biologically based individual differences in effortful control to influence children's later moral development.

KEY TERMS

Moral self: an individual's self-perception of their moral values, internalisation of rules, guilt, empathy, and so on.

Effortful control: a personality trait relating to the ability to suppress dominant responses (e.g., those involving rule-breaking behaviour).

Peers

Children and adolescents are often strongly influenced by their peers. Berndt (1979) asked individuals aged 9 to 18 how likely it was they would give in to peer pressure if their friends suggested carrying out various forms of antisocial behaviour. Children of all ages were influenced by peer pressure (especially 15-year-olds).

At what age are children especially influenced by peer pressure to behave antisocially?

Kandel (1973) studied marijuana use in adolescents whose parents and best friend did (or did not) use the drug. When the parents used marijuana but the best friend did not, only 17% of the adolescents smoked marijuana. In contrast, 56% of the adolescents smoked marijuana if their best friend did. Dishion and Owen (2002) found that having deviant friends increased the probability that adolescents would engage in substance abuse. In addition, however, engaging in substance abuse increased the probability of selecting deviant friends.

Evidence that peers can have *beneficial* effects on moral reasoning was reported by Schonert-Reichl (1999) in a study on early adolescents aged between 10 and 13. Adolescents who had the greatest number of close friends had more advanced moral reasoning than those with relatively few close friends.

In sum, friends have strong effects on moral development and behaviour in children and adolescents. Whether these effects are positive or negative depends on factors such as the prevailing culture and the friends' moral values.

Genetic factors

Individual differences in personality depend to a moderate extent on genetic factors (see Chapter 18). Accordingly, evidence that personality is associated with moral/immoral behaviour would suggest that genetic factors are relevant to moral behaviour. Such evidence was reported by Le et al. (2014). They measured personality in adolescents and then assessed counterproductive workplace behaviours (e.g., theft; absenteeism) 18 years later. Unsurprisingly, individuals high in agreeableness and conscientiousness displayed fewer counterproductive behaviours than those low in those personality dimensions.

Campbell et al. (2009) carried out a twin study. Identical twins resembled each other more in moral development than did fraternal twins. Since identical twins share 100% of their genes whereas fraternal twins share only 50% of theirs, this provides strong evidence that genetic factors influence moral development.

Chapter summary

- Morality can be divided into cognitive, emotional, and behavioural components.
- There are often discrepancies among the three components of morality. For example, individuals sometimes behave in ways they know are wrong.

- Kohlberg argued that moral developments always proceed in order from pre-conventional morality through conventional morality to post-conventional morality. There is some support for his viewpoint from cross-cultural studies.
- Kohlberg focused on the cognitive component of morality and de-emphasised the emotional and behavioural components. He also underestimated the rate at which children's moral development occurs: some basic aspects of a moral perspective are present during the first year of life.
- Gilligan argued that males develop a morality of justice whereas females develop a morality of care. There is only weak and inconsistent support for this position.
- The hypothesis that women's moral reasoning often relies more than men's on emotional considerations has received strong support.
- Children's moral development is helped by a parental style based on induction (explain why a given action could harm other people). In contrast, parental power assertion has negative effects on children.
- Children's moral development depends heavily on mutually responsive orientation between parents and children and on the extent to which they possess the personality trait of effortful control.
- Peers can have a negative influence on adolescents' moral behaviour (e.g., substance abuse). However, adolescents with many close friends have more advanced moral reasoning than those with few close friends.
- Twin studies indicate that moral development depends in part on genetic factors.

Further reading

- Hart, D., Watson, N., Dar, A., & Atkins, R. (2011). Prosocial tendencies, antisocial behavior, and moral development in childhood. In A. Slater & G. Bremner (Eds.), *An introduction to developmental psychology* (2nd. ed., pp. 334–356). Chichester, UK: Wiley-Blackwell. Factors that aid or hinder moral development are discussed in this chapter.

- Lapsley, D., & Carlo, G. (2014). Moral development at the crossroads: New trends and possible futures. *Developmental psychology*, *50*, 1–7. Daniel Lapsley and Gustavo Carlo indicate clearly how theory and research on moral development is now much broader in scope than previously.

- Leman, P., Bremner, A., Parke, R.D., & Gauvain, M. (2012). *Developmental psychology*. New York: McGraw-Hill. Chapter 14 in this textbook has detailed coverage of moral development.

- Thompson, R.A. (2012). Whither the preconventional child? Toward a life-span moral development theory. *Child Development Perspectives*, *6*, 423–429. Ross Thompson discusses theory and research showing that much moral development occurs at a surprisingly young age.

Essay questions

1. What are the major components of morality? Why are these components often not closely related to each other?

2. Describe Kohlberg's theory of moral development. Why is it now much less influential than the past?

3. Are there gender differences in morality? How can we account for these differences?

4. In what ways does the child's moral development depend on parental influences?

Most people are fascinated by the psychological differences between males and females. Are all the differences commonly assumed to exist between the sexes in their behaviour, abilities, and attitudes genuine, or do many of them simply reflect stereotypical views?

Why do most boys and girls prefer the company of other children of the same sex? Why do boys and girls differ so much in their preferred toys? Are these differences between boys and girls due more to heredity (nature) or environment (nurture)? Answers to these questions (and several others) are provided in this chapter.

Sex and gender

11

When a baby is born, a key question everyone asks is, "Is it a boy or a girl?" Afterwards, how it is treated by its parents and other people is strongly influenced by its sex. The growing child's thoughts about itself and its place in the world increasingly depend on whether it is a boy or a girl. By the age of 2, most children know whether they are male or female. By the age of 3, two-thirds of children prefer playing with other children of the same sex (La Freniere et al., 1984).

What is an individual's awareness of being male or female known as?

Before proceeding, I should say something about the terms "sex" and "gender". Sex refers to biological differences between boys and girls, whereas gender includes socially determined differences between them. Increasingly, however, gender is also used to refer to biological differences.

From the age of 3 or 4, children have fairly fixed beliefs about the activities (e.g., housekeeping) and occupations (e.g., doctor; nurse) appropriate for males and females. These are known as **gender-role stereotypes. Gender-typed behaviour** is behaviour consistent with the gender-role stereotypes within a given culture. In other words, it is the behaviour expected of a boy or girl within that culture.

Gender identity

One of the most important influences on **sex-typed behaviour** is **gender identity**, which is an individual's awareness of being male or female and is a major determinant of sex-typed behaviour. Halim et al. (2014) showed the importance of gender identity in a study on 3- to 6-year-old children. Approximately 50% of the children had insisted on wearing gender-typed clothing (e.g., dresses for girls) for a period of time. Children who scored highly on gender identity were more likely to wear gender-typed clothing than children with low scores. Of interest, the extent to which children wore gender-typed clothing was *not* associated with their parents' preferences.

Egan and Perry (2001) pointed out that gender identity involves feeling one is a typical member of one's sex, feeling content with one's own biologically determined sex, and experiencing pressures from parents and other children to conform to gender-role stereotypes. They assessed these aspects of gender identity in children aged between 10 and 14. Boys had much higher scores than girls on all three aspects. These findings suggest it is regarded as more important by children (at least in Western cultures) for boys to conform to stereotypical

KEY TERMS

Gender-role stereotypes: culturally-determined expectations concerning jobs and activities thought suitable for males and females.

Gender-typed behaviour: behaviour conforming to that expected on the basis of any given culture's gender-role stereotypes.

Sex-typed behaviour: this is behaviour that conforms to that expected on the basis of any given culture's sex-role stereotypes.

Gender identity: our awareness of being male or female; it depends to an important extent on social rather than biological factors.

views. More support was reported by Halim et al. (2014) in a study discussed earlier. Approximately 35% of boys had avoided other-gender clothes compared to under 10% of girls.

We have already seen most girls prefer to play with girls and most boys prefer to play with boys. This gender segregation is present throughout childhood from the age of 3 onward. What causes this gender segregation? Children are motivated to develop their sense of gender identity and can do so by playing with children of their own sex. In addition, children increasingly prefer to engage in gender-typed behaviour. This is easier to do in the company of other children of the same gender.

Observed gender differences

There are numerous gender-role stereotypes in most cultures. Thankfully, many of these stereotypes are in steep decline. For example, few people accept that men should go out to work and avoid looking after the home and children whereas women should stay at home all the time caring for the children.

Some gender-role stereotypes relate to aspects of intelligence and personality. For example, it is often assumed boys have superior spatial ability whereas girls have superior verbal ability. It is also assumed girls have more anxious personalities than boys and that boys are more aggressive.

There are two extreme positions concerning psychological gender differences. John Gray (1992) in his best-selling book, *Men are from Mars, Women are from Venus*, argued there are substantial sex differences. In contrast, Hyde (2005, p. 590) put forward the **gender similarities hypothesis**, according to which "males and females are alike on most – but not all – psychological variables".

Findings

The most thorough analysis of psychological gender differences was reported by Zell et al. (2015), who combined the findings from over 12 million participants. Their findings were mostly consistent with the gender similarities hypothesis. Of the 386 comparisons between males and females, 46% of the differences were small and a further 39% were very small.

However, Zell et al. (2015) found a few of the 386 gender comparisons showed large differences. Some of these gender differences (in descending order) are as follows:

1. Masculine vs. feminine traits (e.g., assertive and independent vs. gentle and understanding of others).
2. Mental rotation ability (**mental rotation** is the ability to imagine what would happen if an object were rotated and is an important aspect of spatial ability; it is greater in boys).
3. Peer attachment (greater in females).
4. Interest in people vs. things (greater in females).
5. Aggression (greater in males; see Chapter 7).
6. Film-induced fear (greater in females).

Since 85% of gender differences are small or very small, it is tempting to conclude that males and females are basically rather similar. However, that is not

KEY TERMS

Gender similarities hypothesis: the notion that there are only small differences between males and females with respect to the great majority of psychological variables (e.g., abilities; personality).

Mental rotation: a task used to assess spatial ability, which involves imagining what would happen if the orientation of an object in space were altered.

necessarily the case – perhaps the 15% of gender differences of medium size relate to factors more important or psychologically relevant than the 85% of smaller differences (Zuriff, 2015). Thus, the evidence supports (but does not conclusively prove) the gender similarities hypothesis.

What (if any) gender differences are there in intelligence? We have already seen that boys outperform girls in spatial ability as assessed by mental rotation tasks. There are also relatively large gender differences in writing skills: Reynolds et al. (2015) found females outperformed boys in written expression and spelling.

It is often assumed boys perform better than girls in mathematics. However, there is little support for this assumption. Lindberg et al. (2010) found in an analysis of findings from over one million individuals (mostly American) that there was no gender difference in mathematics performance. Else-Quest et al. (2010) found in a cross-cultural analysis of 69 countries that there was a very small overall tendency for boys to perform better than girls in mathematics. As expected, this gender difference was greatest in those countries where men make nearly all the decisions and girls have fewer opportunities than boys.

How can we explain the (small) gender differences in various aspects of intelligence? The media often claim there are large differences between "male brains" and "female brains". Recent neuroscience evidence suggests male brains are better designed than female ones for communication *within* each brain hemisphere. In contrast, female brains are better designed than male ones for communication *between* the brain hemispheres (Ingalhalikar et al., 2014). Male brains may be structured to facilitate connections between perception and action, whereas females' brains are designed to enhance communication between analytical and intuitive processing.

However, it is important not to exaggerate differences between male and female brains. Joel et al. (2015, p. 15,468) examined brain structure in more than 1,400 human brains and came to the following conclusion:

> Humans and human brains are comprised of unique "mosaics" of features, some more common in females compared with males, some more common in males compared to females, and some common in both females and males . . . human brains cannot be categorised into two distinct classes: male brain/female brain.

Personality

Else-Quest et al. (2006) reviewed numerous studies on gender differences in children's personality. Girls scored higher than boys on effortful control, especially its dimensions of perceptual sensitivity and inhibitory control. Boys scored higher than girls on surgency (similar to extraversion), especially its dimensions of activity and high-intensity pleasure. However, these sex differences were fairly modest. Cross-cultural research on adults in 55 countries revealed a small tendency for women to be higher than men in extraversion, agreeableness, conscientiousness, and neuroticism (tendency to experience negative emotions) (Schmitt et al., 2008).

These findings do *not* indicate there is a "male personality" and a "female personality". This is the case for two reasons. First, there is a substantial overlap and similarity between males and females on the great majority of personality traits. Second, most individuals exhibit a mixture of "male" and "female" personality traits. Thus, very few individuals could be regarded as having a male or female personality.

Theories of gender development

We saw earlier that most children exhibit considerable gender-typed behaviour. However, it is hard to identify the factors causing such behaviour. We will consider major relevant theories. Most focus on *environmental* factors (e.g., parental influence). Other theorists emphasise *biological* factors, and we will conclude this section with a discussion of the biological approach.

Social cognitive theory

According to social cognitive theory, what does the development of gender-role behaviour involve?

One of the most influential approaches to gender development is social cognitive theory. To understand this theory, it is useful to start with social learning theory (see Chapter 2), from which it developed. According to social learning theory (e.g., Bandura, 1977), gender development occurs as a result of children's experiences. Children learn to behave in ways that are rewarded and to avoid behaving in ways that are punished.

Since society has expectations about how boys and girls should behave, the use of rewards and punishments produces gender-typed behaviour. For example, many parents encourage girls (but not boys) to play with dolls, whereas the opposite is the case with guns (Leaper, 2013).

Bussey and Bandura (1999) in their social cognitive theory identified three forms of learning promoting gender development:

1. **Observational learning**: the child imitates aspects of others' behaviour he/she believes will increase feelings of mastery. Imitation is more likely with same-gender models.
2. **Direct tuition**: other people teach the child about gender identity (its awareness of being a boy or girl) and gender-typed behaviour.
3. **Enactive experience**: the child learns about gender-typed behaviour by discovering the outcomes resulting from its actions.

Findings

Nearly all infants and young children are much influenced by their parents' behaviour. For example, parents (especially fathers) tend to have more rigid expectations for their sons than their daughters (Leaper, 2013). As mentioned earlier, many parents provide their children with toys consistent with gender-role stereotypes. For example, girls are rewarded for playing with dolls and discouraged from climbing trees (Fagot & Leinbach, 1989). Those parents making the most use of direct tuition had children who behaved in the most gender-typed way.

However, the extent to which children acquire gender-role stereotypes varies across families. Children whose mothers were unmarried had less gender-typed knowledge than children whose mothers were married (Hupp et al., 2010). This occurred because unmarried mothers were more likely than married ones to behave in traditional "masculine" ways.

It is important not to exaggerate the impact of parents (e.g., through direct tuition) on their children's gender development. A review by Golombok and Hines (2002) indicated there is only a slight tendency for parents to encourage

KEY TERMS

Observational learning: learning based on watching others' behaviour, copying rewarded behaviour but not punished behaviour.

Direct tuition: a way of increasing a child's gender identity and sex-typed behaviour by receiving instruction from others.

Enactive experience: this involves the child learning which behaviours are expected of their gender within any given culture as a result of being rewarded or punished for behaving in different ways.

gender-typed behaviour or discourage behaviour that was not gender-typed. Golombok and Hines also found that boys and girls receive equal parental warmth, encouragement of achievement, discipline, and interaction.

Hallers-Haalboom et al. (2014) found *child* gender had practically no effect on the behaviour of fathers and mothers interacting with their children during free play. However, *parent* gender had an effect: mothers displayed more sensitivity and less intrusiveness than fathers with their children.

Peers (children of similar age) influence gender development. Kowalski (2007) studied the negative reactions of kindergarten children when a child played with a toy regarded as inappropriate. These reactions included ridicule, correction (e.g., "Give that girl puppet to a girl") and negating the child's gender identity (e.g., "Jeff is a girl"). These reactions are examples of enactive experience (discussed earlier).

More generally, much peer influence depends on **gender segregation** (young children prefer to play with same-sex peers rather than other-sex peers). The more time boys spend playing with other boys, the more "boy-like" their behaviour becomes (e.g., more active and aggressive). Girls who spend much time playing with other girls become more "girl-like" in their behaviour (Hanish & Fabes, 2014). Much of the gender development occurring as a result of gender segregation probably involves forms of learning such as observational learning, direct tuition, and enactive experience.

Young children are exposed to considerable gender-typed behaviour through the media (e.g., television; movies). They are also exposed to gender-typed behaviour through video games played by a substantial majority of children. Dill and Thill (2007) found many gender stereotypes are present in video games. For example, 33% of male characters in video games behave in a very "masculine" way and 62% of female characters are visions of beauty. In addition, more male than female characters are aggressive (83% vs. 62%, respectively).

EVALUATION

➕ Social cognitive theory correctly emphasises the social context in which gender development occurs.

➕ Factors such as observational learning, direct tuition, and enactive experience all contribute to gender development (Leaper, 2013). However, their effects are sometimes fairly modest.

➖ The theory focuses mainly on children's learning of *specific* forms of behaviour. However, as we will see shortly, children also engage in *general* learning (e.g., acquiring organised beliefs about their own gender).

➖ The theory assumes children are fairly passive individuals who are strongly influenced by others (e.g., parents; peers) and the rewards and punishments they provide. However, they can also actively influence their interactions with peers by selecting friends with similar interests and activities and can influence their parents' behaviour by what they say and do.

KEY TERM

Gender segregation: the tendency for young children from about 3 years to play mostly with same-sex peers.

Self-socialisation theory

According to self-socialisation theory, when do children acquire gender schemas of their own sex and of the opposite sex?

Self-socialisation theory (Martin & Ruble, 2004) developed out of gender schema theory (Martin & Halverson, 1987). A central assumption of self-socialisation theory is that children are "gender detectives" who are highly motivated to discover information about gender. The knowledge they acquire about gender influences how they organise and interpret gender-relevant information and influences their behaviour. Of central importance is the notion of gender identity ("I am a boy" or "I am a girl"). It is acquired at a very young age and provides children with a major social identity.

Over time, children acquire increasingly detailed gender-relevant knowledge. This knowledge includes **gender schemas** (organised beliefs about suitable activities and behaviour for each gender). Martin et al. (1990) argued there are three stages in the development of gender schemas:

1. Children learn specific information associated with each gender (e.g., boys play with guns girls play with dolls).
2. Children from 4 or 5 link together the information they possess about their own gender to form more complex gender schemas. This is done only with respect to their own gender.
3. Children from the age of 8 form complex gender schemas of the opposite gender as well as their own.

How does self-socialisation theory differ from social cognitive theory? According to self-socialisation theory, young children play a very *active* role in learning about gender and increasingly acquire fairly *general* knowledge and understanding of gender. In contrast, social cognitive theory regards young children as playing a more *passive* role and stresses their *specific* learning about gender-typed behaviour. According to social cognitive theory, young children learn gender-typed behaviour by observing (and then copying) the behaviour of same-gender models. For this to happen, however, they must know what gender they are – they need to have acquired some aspects of gender identity.

There is more emphasis on what *children* contribute to gender development in self-socialisation theory (e.g., their internal cognitive processes and structures). In contrast, there is more emphasis on what the *environment* contributes to gender development in social cognitive theory. In reality, of course, children themselves *and* the environment both contribute substantially to gender development.

KEY TERM

Gender schemas: organised knowledge stored in long-term memory in the form of numerous beliefs about forms of behaviour appropriate for each gender.

Boys and girls tend to prefer different toys—is this nature or nurture?

Findings

Martin et al. (1990) tested their three-stage theory. Children were provided with a description of someone of unspecified gender with a specific sex-typed characteristic (e.g., is a nurse) and predicted that person's other characteristics. Younger children performed poorly because they had not reached stage 2. Somewhat older children performed better when the gender-linked characteristic was appropriate to their own gender because they were more likely to have reached stage 2. Children of 8 or more had reached stage 3 and so performed well regardless of whether the gender-linked characteristic was appropriate to their own gender.

According to self-socialisation theory, much sex-typed behaviour is influenced by gender identity. Since children show gender-typed behaviour at an early age (often by 2 years), gender identity should also develop early. There is much support for this prediction (Halim & Lindner, 2013). For example, Zosuls et al. (2009) found 68% of children (especially girls) used gender labels (e.g., "boy"; "girl") by 21 months of age.

According to the theory, children who have acquired gender identity should exhibit more sex-typed behaviour than those who have not. Zosuls et al. (2009) obtained support for this prediction. Boys who used gender labels were more likely than other boys to play with trucks rather than dolls; the opposite was the case for girls.

Trautner et al. (2005) studied children for 5 years from kindergarten onwards. Boys' gender knowledge predicted their *preference* for gender-typed toys and activities (e.g., trucks; car washing) and their *avoidance* of toys and activities associated with girls (e.g., dolls; cooking). Girls' gender knowledge was much less predictive of their preferred (and avoided) toys and activities, probably because they perceived boys' toys and activities are more highly regarded.

Zosuls et al. (2009) and Trautner et al. (2005) found that gender knowledge is *associated* with gender-typed behaviour. However, that does not prove the former *causes* the latter. More direct evidence was reported by Bradbard et al. (1986). They presented children with gender-neutral objects (e.g., burglar alarms; pizza cutters) and told them some were "boy" objects whereas others were "girl" objects. Children spent much more time playing with objects they had been told were appropriate to their gender. Even a week later, the children remembered which objects were for boys and girls.

Weisgram et al. (2014) obtained similar findings with novel objects (e.g., nutcracker; shoe shaper) painted in a masculine colour (blue) or a feminine colour (pink) described as "for boys" or "for girls". Girls showed much more interest in objects that were "for girls" than those "for boys". They showed less interest in "boy" objects painted blue than those painted pink.

EVALUATION

⊕ The assumption that even young children are actively involved in making sense of the world and themselves using their schema-based knowledge is plausible. This cognitive approach has much support.

⊕ Children's knowledge in the form of gender identity and gender schemas often influences their actions (e.g., gender-typed behaviour).

⊖ "Few studies have examined gender self-socialisation beyond normative [normal], White, middle-class, or American children" (Halim & Lindner, 2013, p. 3).

⊖ The association between gender identity and behaviour is often not very strong. As Bussey and Bandura (1999, p. 679) pointed out, "Children do not categorise themselves as 'I am a girl' or 'I am a boy' and act in accordance with that schema across situations."

⊖ Little is known of the ways self-socialisation *interacts* with social factors such as parental and peer influences to determine gender-typed behaviour.

Biological approach

It is probable that biological differences between boys and girls play some role in gender development. For example, the "male sex hormone" testosterone is present in greater amounts in male than female fetuses from about six weeks, whereas the opposite is the case for the "female sex hormone" oestrogen.

It is very hard to disentangle the effects of biological and social factors in influencing gender development. Why is that? The main reason is that there are systematic biological *and* social differences between boys and girls. The best approach would be to study children who are biologically boys but treated as girls or biological girls treated as boys. Approximations to this approach are discussed in the following sections.

Another way of investigating the role of biological factors is by carrying out twin studies. This approach is considered briefly.

IN THE REAL WORLD: *Guevedoces* in the Dominican Republic

Dr. Julianne Imperato travelled to a remote area of the Dominican Republic in the 1970s because she had heard rumours about girls turning into boys. She discovered that the rumours were true. There were many children who were biologically male, but their external genitals appeared female and they were treated as girls. At puberty, they developed male genitals and looked like ordinary adolescents (apart from having only wispy beards). They were known as *Guevedoces* (penis at 12). The condition is caused by a deficient enzyme, but a large surge of testosterone (the male sex hormone) at around puberty largely corrects it.

Imperato-McGinley et al. (1974) studied the Batista family in the Dominican Republic. Four of the sons were *Guevedoces*. They were raised as girls in childhood and regarded themselves as females. In spite of that, they all adjusted to the male role in adolescence – they had "male" jobs, got married, and were generally accepted by society as men. Zhu and Imperato-McGinley (2008) reported on a larger sample (18 males) with the same condition. Seventeen of them (94%) managed successfully to change their gender identity from female to male at around the age of 16.

Some *Guevedoces* in the Dominican Republic adopt a relatively masculine approach to life even in the years prior to puberty. For example, Johnny (originally called Felicita) recalled his early childhood: "I never liked to dress as a girl and when they brought me toys for girls I never bothered playing with them – when I saw a group of boys I would stop to play ball with them."

In sum, the findings on *Guevedoces* indicate that gender identity does not *always* depend on social factors. In spite of being treated as females throughout childhood, the great majority of *Guevedoces* develop a male gender identity in adolescence.

Congenital adrenal hyperplasia

There is an interesting condition called **congenital adrenal hyperplasia**. This is a genetic disorder in which the foetus is exposed to high levels of **androgen** (male sex hormones). At birth, these hormonal levels are normalised. This disease affects boys and girls. Most research has focused on girls because they experience *conflict* between their social experiences (being reared as a girl) and their early high exposure to male sex hormones (a biological factor). This allows us to establish which factor has more impact on behaviour.

The evidence has been reviewed by Berenbaum and Beltz (2011) and Hines et al. (2015). Girls with congenital adrenal hyperplasia mostly exhibit male activity preferences (e.g., male-typical toys; male playmates). They nearly always have a weaker identification as a female than other girls and are more likely to enjoy rough sports. When they grow up, they are twice as likely as other women to choose male-dominant professions and are six times as likely (30% vs. 5%) not to have an exclusively heterosexual orientation.

KEY TERMS

Congenital adrenal hyperplasia: an inherited disorder of the adrenal gland causing the levels of male sex hormones in foetuses of both sexes to be unusually high.

Androgen: male sex hormones (e.g., testosterone) typically produced in much greater quantity by males than by females.

Why do females with congenital adrenal hyperplasia behave more like males than other females? It is probably due to biological factors directly associated with their prenatal exposure to male sex hormones. Alternatively, it may be that their parents encourage them to have male-type interests and behaviour. However, Pasterski et al. (2005) found that parents of daughters with congenital adrenal hyperplasia encouraged them to play with girls' toys. Indeed, they provided *more* positive feedback than parents of other girls when their daughter played with girls' toys.

Gender dysphoria

Finally, we consider a condition known as **gender identity disorder** (identification with the opposite gender and discomfort with one's biological gender). We can study the possible involvement of biological factors in this condition by carrying out a twin study and assessing the concordance rate (the probability that if one twin has the condition, the other also has it). If biological factors are important, identical twins (sharing 100% of their genes) should have a higher concordance rate than fraternal twins (sharing only 50% of their genes).

Heylens et al. (2012) reviewed the relevant literature. They found 39% of identical twins were concordant for gender identity disorder compared to 0% of fraternal twins. Thus, genetic factors clearly play a role in the development of gender identity disorder. However, the finding that the concordance rate was substantially below 100% for identical twins indicates that environmental factors are also of major importance.

> ### EVALUATION
>
> ➕ The notion that biological factors play an important role in gender development has been supported by research on *Guevedoces*, on congenital adrenal hyperplasia, and by twin studies.
>
> ➕ It is hard to provide a social or environmental interpretation of the male interests and behaviour of girls and women with congenital adrenal hyperplasia.
>
> ➖ The participants in much research have very rare conditions. This makes it difficult to know whether the findings generalise to the population at large.
>
> ➖ The biological approach is limited because it de-emphasises the role of social factors (e.g., parents; media; other children) on gender development.
>
> ➖ Some cross-cultural differences are hard to explain in purely biological terms. For example, Wood and Eagly (2002) found across 181 cultures that men were dominant in 67% of them whereas women were dominant in only 3%. This very large difference probably reflects environmental influences.

> **KEY TERM**
>
> **Gender identity disorder:** distress associated with a conflict between biological gender and the gender with which an individual identifies.

Masculinity and femininity

At one time it was common to distinguish between masculine qualities (based on an instrumental or achieving role) and feminine qualities (based on an expressive or communal role). It was also assumed that men were most likely to be psychologically well-adjusted if they possessed mainly masculine qualities whereas women should possess mainly feminine qualities. This is the congruence model.

Bem (e.g., 1985) disagreed with this viewpoint. She focused on **androgyny**, which describes someone having both masculine and feminine qualities. She argued that androgynous individuals have the greatest psychological well-being. This is the androgyny model.

Other theorists (e.g., Adams & Sherer, 1985) argued that society values masculine qualities (e.g., assertiveness). As a result, individuals (male or female) are likely to have greater psychological well-being if they possess many masculine qualities. This is the masculinity model.

What is Bem's term for those who are high on both masculinity and femininity?

Findings

There is some support for all three models. However, most of the support for the masculinity model was obtained several years ago. Bassoff and Glass (1982) reviewed 26 studies on mental health. Androgynous individuals on average had better mental health than those high in femininity. However, the mental health of androgynous individuals was no better than that of individuals high in masculinity. Thus, it seemed that high masculinity rather than androgyny itself was important for mental health.

Why was the possession of masculine characteristics so beneficial? Part of the answer was suggested by Williams and Best (1990). They asked students in 14 countries to describe their "current self" and their "ideal self". Men and women both included more masculine than feminine characteristics in their ideal self than in their current self.

More recent research has provided support for the androgyny model, suggesting the current world is less masculine-dominated. Cheng (2005) studied students coping with stressful situations during their first three months at university. Appropriate coping strategies were used most often by androgynous students.

What are the effects of androgyny on mental health? Lefkowitz and Zeldow (2006) found high masculinity and high femininity were both associated with good mental health. Those high in both masculinity and femininity (androgynous individuals) had the greatest mental health. In similar fashion, Flett et al. (2009) found depressed patients had low levels of both masculinity and femininity.

Finally, there is limited support for the congruence model. Udry and Chantala (2004) argued that adolescents would be attracted to members of the opposite sex whose personalities differed considerably from their own: "exotic is erotic". Couples were most likely to have sex (and to do so earlier in the relationship) when the boy was high in masculinity and the girl high in femininity.

> **KEY TERM**
>
> **Androgny:** used to describe an individual who possesses a mixture or combination of masculine and feminine characteristics.

Chapter summary

- According to the gender similarities hypothesis, males and females differ only slightly with respect to the great majority of psychological variables. Most of the evidence is consistent with this hypothesis.
- Women on average are higher than men in extraversion, agreeableness, conscientiousness, and neuroticism.
- According to social cognitive theory, gender development depends on observational learning, direct tuition, and enactive experience (positive or negative outcomes).
- Social cognitive theory exaggerates the extent to which children are passive and engage in very specific forms of learning about gender.
- According to self-socialisation theory, children are "gender detectives" who play an active role in learning about gender and acquire fairly general knowledge and understanding.
- Most biological males reared as females until adolescence adjust successfully to the male role.
- Girls exposed to high levels of male sex hormones in the womb are more likely than other girls to have a non-heterosexual orientation and to pursue male-dominant professions.
- Biological theories fail to account for the impact of social and cultural factors on gender development.
- It is often assumed masculine qualities involve an instrumental or achieving role whereas feminine qualities involve an expressive or communal role. However, androgynous individuals combine masculine and feminine qualities.
- Early research indicated that masculinity was associated with the greatest psychological and physical well-being. However, recent research suggests androgyny is associated with the greatest well-being.

Further reading

- Halim, M.L., & Lindner, N.C. (2013). Gender self-socialisation in early childhood. In R.E. Tremblay, M. Boivin, & R.De.V. Peters (Eds.), *Encylopaedia on early childhood development* (pp. 1–6). Montreal, Quebec: Centre of Excellence for Early Childhood Development and Strategic Knowledge Cluster on Early Child Development. The authors provide a brief review of self-socialisation theory and research designed to test it.
- Hanish, L.D., & Fabes, R.A. (2013). Peer socialisation of gender in young boys and girls. In R.E. Tremblay, M. Boivin, & R.De.V. Peters (Eds.), *Encylopaedia on early childhood development* (pp. 1–4). Montreal, Quebec: Centre of Excellence for Early Childhood Development and Strategic Knowledge Cluster on Early Child Development. The various ways in which peers influence children's gender development are reviewed in this article.

- Hines, M., Constantinescu, M., & Spencer, D. (2015). Early androgen exposure and human gender development. *Biology of Sex Differences*, 6, 1–10. This article reviews research on biological influences on gender development.
- Zell, E., Krizan, Z., & Teeter, S.R. (2015). Evaluating gender similarities and differences using meta-synthesis. *American Psychologist*, 70, 10–20. Ethan Zell and his colleagues provide a thorough review of numerous studies on gender differences.

Essay questions

1. It is often assumed there are many important gender differences in behaviour and personality. Discuss this assumption with reference to research on the gender similarities hypothesis.

2. Describe the biological approach to understanding gender development and gender differences. How successful has this approach been?

3. Compare and contrast the social cognitive and self-socialisation theories of gender development.

Part 3

Social approach

This section is devoted to social psychology, which is, "The scientific investigation of how the thoughts, feelings and behaviour of individuals are influenced by the actual, imagined or implied presence of others" (Hogg & Vaughan, 2005, p. 655).

You may have noticed that you can run faster when competing with a friend than when alone—this means your performance has been affected by the presence of another person. You may have laughed at a joke because your friends did even though you didn't really understand it. Thus, others can influence our behaviour even though no-one asked you to behave differently.

Chapter 12 • Attachment and deprivation

The vital importance of loving attachments to young children (and the potentially devastating effects of being deprived of such attachments) are discussed.

Chapter 13 • Prejudice and discrimination

The reasons why some people are prejudiced against other groups are discussed, together with practical suggestions for reducing prejudice.

Chapter 14 • Prosocial behaviour

Some of the reasons why we often help other people (but sometimes fail to!) are discussed in this chapter.

Chapter 15 • Social influence

The surprising extent to which most of us conform to the behaviour of others and obey authority is shown and reasons why social influence is so strong are identified.

Chapter 16 • Social perception and attraction

Reasons why we find some people more attractive than others are discussed as are how we decide what motivates other people to behave in the ways they do.

Most infants develop a close attachment to their mother, and this plays a major role in their emotional development. Why does this happen? Do you think this attachment happens naturally or does it depend on the nature of the interactions between mother and infant? The attachments a child forms with its parents can be disrupted by events such as child care and divorce. What factors do you think might determine whether children cope successfully with such events?

Attachment and deprivation

12

Infants rapidly start to learn about other people and their environment. Crucial aspects of this early learning are in the area of emotion. In this chapter, we will focus on factors influencing (and facilitating) children's emotional development. We also consider factors (e.g., separation; parental divorce) making it harder for children to develop close bonds with other people, finishing with a discussion of the effects of child care on young children.

Attachment

A key feature of emotional development is attachment. **Attachment** is "the strong, affectionate tie we have with special people in our lives that leads us to experience pleasure and joy when we interact with them and to be comforted by their nearness in times of stress" (Berk, 2013, p. 426). An infant's most important attachment is typically to its mother. However, strong attachments are often formed to other people with whom the infant has regular contact. Main and Weston (1981) found one-quarter of infants were securely attached to both parents, another one-quarter only to their mother, and a further one-quarter only to their fathers.

Schaffer and Emerson (1964) found that by the age of 18 months, very few (13%) infants are attached to only one person, and 32% have five or more attachments. These attachments often included the father, grandparent, or older siblings as well as the mother.

Bowlby (1969, 1988) argued the development of attachment involves five phases:

1. The infant responds similarly to everyone.
2. At 5 months, the infant starts to *discriminate* among other people (e.g., smiling mainly at his/her mother).
3. At 7 months, the infant remains close to his/her mother or caregiver. He/she shows "separation protest" by becoming upset when the mother leaves.
4. From 3 years, the child takes account of the caregiver's needs.
5. From 5 years, the child has an internal representation of the child-caregiver relationships. As a result, the attachment remains strong even when the child does not see the caregiver for some time.

> **KEY TERM**
>
> **Attachment:** a powerful emotional relationship between two people (e.g., mother and child).

According to Ainsworth, most American infants exhibit which type of attachment to their mothers?

Attachment types

How can we assess attachment between mother and child? The most-used method is the Strange Situation test (Ainsworth & Bell, 1970). The infant (typically about 12 months old) is observed during eight short episodes. Some of the time the infant is with its mother, whereas at other times it is with its mother and a stranger, just with a stranger, or entirely on its own.

The child's reactions to the stranger, to separation from the mother, and especially to being reunited with its mother, are all recorded in the Strange Situation test. These reactions allow the infant's attachment to its mother to be assigned to one of three categories:

1. **Secure attachment:** The infant is distressed by the mother's absence, but rapidly returns to contentment after the mother's return, immediately seeking contact with her. There is a clear difference in reaction to the mother and to the stranger. About 70% of American infants show secure attachment.
2. **Resistant attachment:** The infant is insecure in the presence of the mother, becomes very distressed, resists contact when she returns, and is wary of the stranger. About 10% of American infants are resistant.
3. **Avoidant attachment:** The infant does not seek contact with the mother, shows little distress when separated from her, and avoids contact with her when she returns. The infant treats the stranger similarly to the mother. About 20% of American infants are avoidant.

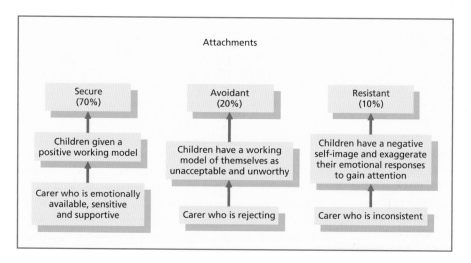

Ainsworth and Bell's (1970) attachment types.

KEY TERMS

Secure attachment: a strong and contented attachment of an infant to its mother, including when she returns after an absence.

Resistant attachment: an insecure attachment of an infant to its mother combined with resistance of contact when she returns after an absence.

Avoidant attachment: an insecure attachment of an infant to its mother combined with avoidance of contact with her when she returns after an absence.

Main et al. (1985) identified a fourth type of attachment behaviour: disorganised and disoriented attachment. Infants with this type of attachment lacked any coherent strategy for coping with the Strange Situation – their behaviour was a confusing mixture of approach and avoidance.

Dimensional approach

Assigning all children to three (or four) attachment categories is neat and tidy. However, reality is not neat and tidy. Fraley and Spieker (2003) used *dimensions* (going from very low to very high) rather than *categories*. They identified two attachment dimensions:

1. *Avoidant/withdrawal vs. proximity-seeking strategies*: the extent to which the child tries to maintain physical closeness with his/her mother.
2. *Angry and resistant strategies vs. emotional confidence*: the child's emotional reactions to the attachment figure's behaviour.

Why is this dimensional approach preferable to Ainsworth and Bell's (1970) categorical approach? It provides a more accurate assessment of each child's attachment behaviour because it takes more account of small individual differences.

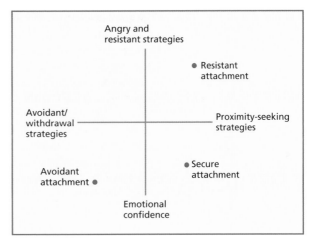

Theories of attachment

Why do some infants have a secure attachment with their mothers whereas others do not? An influential answer was provided by Ainsworth et al. (1978) in their maternal sensitivity hypothesis. According to this hypothesis, the sensitivity of the mother (or other caregiver) is of crucial importance – mothers of securely attached children are sensitive to their needs and respond rapidly and appropriately.

De Wolff and van IJzendoorn (1997) found there was a positive (but fairly weak) association between maternal sensitivity and security of infant attachment. Other aspects of mothers' behaviour were also important: they included stimulation (any action of the mother directed at her infant) and attitude (mother's expressions of positive emotion towards her infant).

The maternal sensitivity hypothesis exaggerates the mother's role. Infants' attachment security also depends on *paternal* sensitivity, although to a lesser extent than maternal sensitivity (Lucassen et al., 2011). Surprisingly, the importance of paternal sensitivity has *not* increased in recent times in spite of the gradually increasing involvement of fathers in child care.

The maternal sensitivity hypothesis ignores the possible role played by the infant him/herself in influencing attachment type. For example, Kagan (1984) put forward a temperament hypothesis according to which the infant's temperament or personality (moderately determined by genetic factors) influences its attachment to its mother. There is limited evidence that the child's genetic make-up is important. O'Connor and Croft (2001) found that identical twins (who share 100% of their genes) showed more agreement in attachment style than did fraternal twins (who share only 50% of their genes).

The locations of secure, resistant, and avoidant attachments within a two-dimensional framework (proximity seeking vs. avoidance/withdrawal, angry and resistant vs. emotional confidence).

If the child's temperament is important, we might imagine that anxious infants would be less likely than non-anxious ones to form a secure attachment with their mother. In fact, however, most evidence indicates the infant's temperament has only a small effect on its attachment type. More specifically, an infant's attachment type depends on a combination of its genetic make-up and maternal sensitivity. Spangler et al. (2009) found disorganised attachment was present mostly in infants having specific genes. However, this genetic influence was found only in infants whose mothers were insensitive. These findings (and other similar ones discussed by Spangler, 2013) suggest maternal sensitivity can be especially valuable with genetically at-risk infants.

Advantages and disadvantages of attachment types

Unsurprisingly, secure attachment is the one most closely associated with healthy emotional and social development. For example, Stams et al. (2002) found children securely attached to their mother at 12 months had superior social and cognitive development at the age of seven. However, several studies have reported that secure attachment in infancy is only moderately predictive of secure attachment a few years later (Pinquart et al., 2013).

Groh et al. (2015) considered relationships between attachment type and externalising (e.g., aggression; antisocial behaviour) and internalising (e.g., anxiety; depression) symptoms in children. Disorganised attachment, avoidant attachment, and resistant attachment were all associated with externalising symptoms whereas only avoidant attachment was associated with internalising symptoms.

Are there any advantages associated with avoidant or resistant attachment? Evidence that the answer is "Yes" was discussed by Ein-Dor (2015). Individuals with resistant attachment are very vigilant to threats. Compared to other people, they respond faster to threats (e.g., a fire alarm going off) and are better at detecting deceit. Individuals with avoidant attachment focus more than others on self-preservation and so are likely to be good at finding escape routes when danger looms.

Cross-cultural differences

Mother-infant attachment behaviour may depend heavily on cultural expectations concerning what is appropriate. If so, we would expect large differences in attachment behaviour from culture to culture. Sagi et al. (1991) studied this issue using the Strange Situation test in four countries. German infants were least likely to be securely attached and most likely to be avoidant. Why was this? German parents prefer their infants to be independent, non-clinging, and obedient (Grossman et al., 1985).

None of the Japanese infants were avoidant. Japanese mothers in the 1980s practically never left their infants with a stranger and so the infants in the Strange Situation were faced with the totally new experience of being on their own with a stranger. The Japanese think of infants' secure attachment as involving *amae* (a-mah-yeh), which means emotional dependence. Infants showing much clinging behaviour and need for attention are regarded as showing good adjustment in Japan but insecure attachment in Western countries (Rothbaum et al., 2000).

Sagi et al. (1991) found few Israeli infants were avoidant. These infants lived on a kibbutz (collective farm) and were mostly looked after by strangers. However, they had a close relationship with their mothers, and so tended not to be avoidant.

Which type of attachment to their mothers is exhibited by very few Japanese infants?

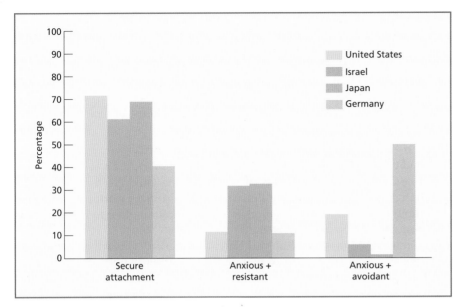

Children from different countries vary in their attachment types. The graph summarises research from Sagi et al. (1991).

We must not exaggerate cultural differences. Van IJzendoorn and Kroonenberg (1988) analysed numerous studies using the Strange Situation. Variations in findings *within* countries were much greater than those *between* countries. Thus, there is not a *single* culture in the UK, the United States, or most other countries.

EVALUATION

➕ There is much support for Ainsworth's three attachment types.

➕ Secure attachment is associated with superior subsequent emotional and social development. However, there are also some (more minor) advantages associated with resistant and avoidant attachment.

➕ Maternal sensitivity predicts security of infant attachment (especially among infants genetically at-risk).

➖ A dimensional approach to individual differences in infant attachment provides a more accurate assessment than does the traditional categorical approach.

➖ Paternal sensitivity is often ignored even though it predicts infant attachment to some extent.

➖ Most theories are oversimplified because they do not consider complex interactions (e.g., gene-environment interactions) between the factors influencing attachment type.

➖ There are important cross-cultural differences in attachment behaviour. However, we do not yet have a clear understanding of the factors producing these differences.

According to Bowlby's maternal deprivation hypothesis, what are the effects of a breaking of the maternal bond, and how serious are they?

Effects of deprivation and privation

So far we have considered factors influencing the type of attachment an infant forms with its mother or caregiver. In the real world, unfortunately, several events (e.g., divorce; death of a parent) can disrupt an infant's attachments or even prevent them being formed in the first place. In this section, we discuss the effects on infants of being separated from the most important adult(s) in their lives.

Maternal deprivation hypothesis and beyond

The child psychoanalyst John Bowlby (1907–1990) proposed a very influential theory concerned with the effects of separation on children. Bowlby (1951) argued that "an infant and young child should experience a warm, intimate and continuous relationship with his mother (or permanent mother figure) in which both find satisfaction and enjoyment."

No-one would disagree with this statement. However, Bowlby (1951) also proposed the more controversial **maternal deprivation hypothesis**. According to this hypothesis, a breaking of the maternal bond with the child early in life often has serious effects on its intellectual, social, and emotional development. He also claimed these negative effects of maternal deprivation were permanent or irreversible in 25% of children.

Bowlby made two other important assumptions. First, he argued in his **monotropy hypothesis** that infants form only *one* strong attachment (typically with the mother). Second, he argued there is a **critical period** during which the infant's attachment to the mother or caregiver must occur. This critical period ends at some point between 1 and 3 years of age. After that, it is not possible to establish a powerful attachment to the mother or caregiver.

Rutter (1981) claimed Bowlby's ideas were oversimplified in three ways. First, Bowlby failed to distinguish between deprivation and privation. **Deprivation** occurs when a child has formed a close attachment and is then separated from its major attachment figure. **Privation** occurs when a child has never formed a close attachment. Rutter argued privation is more serious than deprivation. He found that many of the adverse effects Bowlby had attributed to deprivation were actually due to privation.

Second, Rutter (1981) disagreed with Bowlby's notion that deprivation typically causes long-term difficulties. Rutter argued instead that the effects of deprivation depend on the *reasons* for the separation.

Third, Rutter (1981) was sceptical of Bowlby's assumption that it is very hard to reverse the negative effects of long-term maternal deprivation. He argued these effects can generally be reversed if deprived children are placed with a loving family.

Findings

Studies Bowlby relied on to support his hypothesis that maternal deprivation can be very damaging involved children placed in institutions (e.g., orphanages). For example, Spitz (1945) found that children living in very poor orphanages and other institutions in South America became apathetic and suffered from helplessness and loss of appetite. Goldfarb (1947) studied children who had spent their early life in a poor and inadequately staffed orphanage before being fostered. Those who had spent longer in the orphanage (3 years) were

KEY TERMS

Maternal deprivation hypothesis: the notion that a breaking of the bond between child and mother during the first few years often has serious long-term effects.

Monotropy hypothesis: Bowlby's notion that infants have an innate tendency to form special bonds with one person (generally the mother).

Critical period: according to the maternal deprivation hypothesis, a period early in life during which infants must form a strong attachment if their later development is to be satisfactory.

Deprivation: the state of a child who has formed a close attachment to someone (e.g., its mother) but is later separated from that person.

Privation: the state of a child who has never formed a close attachment with another person (e.g., its mother)

more likely to become loners and aggressive individuals than those who spent only a few months there.

The evidence from studies such as those discussed earlier is hard to interpret. Maternal deprivation (or privation) might have been responsible for the negative effects on the children. However, some of these effects were probably due to deficiencies in the institutions. For example, the children studied by Goldfarb (1947) received little attention or warmth from the staff.

Bowlby argued that lengthy separation from the mother is damaging to children regardless of the underlying reasons. Rutter (1970) reported contrary evidence in a study of boys aged between 9 and 12 years deprived of their mother for a period of time when they were younger. Some of these boys were well-adjusted whereas others were not. The well-adjusted boys had been separated from their mother because of factors such as housing problems or physical illness. In contrast, the maladjusted boys had mostly been separated because of family problems (e.g., psychiatric illness). Thus, family discord rather than simply separation causes problems for children.

Bowlby assumed the negative effects of maternal deprivation are often irreversible. Counterevidence was reported by Hodges and Tizard (1989) in a study of privation. They studied boys who had spent their early years in an institution where they had on average been looked after by 24 different caregivers by the age of two. Some of the children subsequently returned to their own families whereas others were adopted. Most of the adopted children had formed close relationships with their adoptive parents, but this was less the case with children returned to their own parents. The reason was that their own parents were often unsure whether they wanted their children back. Both groups of children exhibited attention-seeking behaviour at school and were over-friendly. As a result, they were not popular.

Hodges and Tizard (1989) found the family relationships of the adopted children at the age of 16 were as good as those of ordinary families. However, there was little affection between the 16-year-olds who had returned to their families and their parents. Both groups were less likely than other children to have a special friend or to regard other adolescents as sources of emotional support.

Hodges and Tizard's (1989) important research showed the long-term effects of separation depend very much on what happens *following* deprivation or privation. The love and involvement provided by adoptive parents can allow deprived children to develop close relationships and to become well-adjusted. However, if deprived children are returned to their own families when they are not wanted, the outlook is much less favorable.

In sum, we have considered some research that appears to support Bowlby's maternal deprivation hypothesis and other research that does not. There is a summary of both types of research in the figure.

Extreme privation

As we have seen, the adverse effects of maternal deprivation are generally reversible. We turn now to privation, in which children have never experienced a close and loving relationship with anyone. Extreme privation occurs when such children spend several years in terrible conditions before being adopted. In line with Bowlby's theoretical approach, it would be predicted that such children would suffer irreversible damage. Surprisingly, that is often *not* the case.

Does research support Bowlby's maternal deprivation hypothesis?

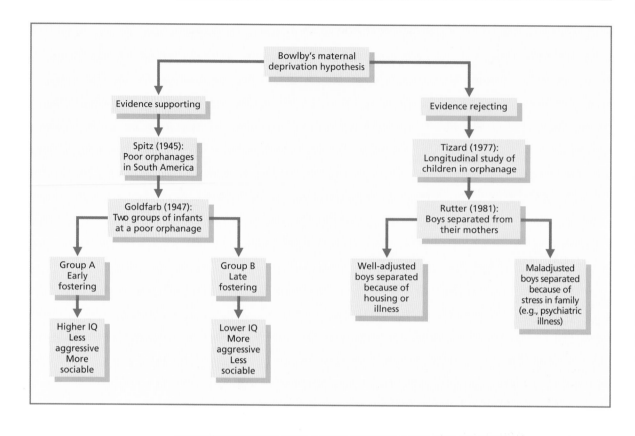

News reports in the 1980s highlighted deprivation in Romanian orphanages, with many children becoming depressed, having received basic sustenance but little human warmth or contact.

Koluchová (1976) studied twin boys (Andrei and Vanya) who spent most of their first 7 years locked in a cellar being treated very badly. They could barely talk and relied mainly on gestures. Fortunately, they were adopted by very dedicated women when they were about 9. By the time they were 14, their behaviour was essentially normal. By the age of 20, they had above-average intelligence and excellent relationships with their foster family. They took further education and both married and had children.

IN THE REAL WORLD: Cezarina

Jean Riley (54) and her husband Peter (58) adopted a child from Romania. Cezarina was 8 years old when they met her at an orphanage in Bucharest. She had not had a visit from her family during her entire time there. Cezarina was filthy and was not house-trained at all. Her muscles were wasted through lack of exercise, and she had frequently been beaten. She had the social skills of a two-year-old.

In England, Cezarina initially ran around like "a wild animal" and always wanted to be the centre of attention. Even though she had had very little schooling in Romania, she was very intelligent and managed to get into a grammar school. Cezarina became much happier and developed social skills during her first few years with the Riley family. However, she was still rather naïve and emotionally immature. When she became a teenager, Cezarina liked the same things as other teenagers (e.g., fashion; pop music) but regarded herself as different from other girls. She found it hard to show affection and did not like to be hugged or kissed. According to Jean Riley, "Children with years of abuse find it difficult to understand or cope with relationships."

One of the positive developments in Cezarina's progress occurred when the Rileys adopted Augustina, who was another orphan from Romania. Cezarina was very happy to share her bedroom with Augustina, who was 8 years younger than her. She was delighted when Augustina arrived and took an active role in helping to bathe and feed her when she was little.

Another positive feature is that Cezarina refused to blame her biological mother: "I know she was young, she had me at school at about 15 or 16, her name was Violeta. I remember when I was 16. If I had had a child I wouldn't have had a clue what to do, so I place no blame on her at all. I don't feel bitter."

(Account based on an article in the *Independent*, 15 December 1995.)

Important evidence on the long-term effects of privation has emerged from the English & Romanian Adoptees Study. This study focuses on Romanian children who had often spent several years in very poor-quality institutions before being adopted by caring British families. These children were tested several times up to the age of 15.

There were four main findings from the study:

1. Most of these Romanian children showed substantial catch-up in their social and intellectual development following adoption (O'Connor et al., 2000).
2. The outcomes varied from child to child (Rutter et al., 2010). Most children recovered almost totally from their institutional experiences, but a minority did not.

3. There were surprisingly few long-term negative effects of early institutionalisation on emotional development, behavioural problems, or interactions with children of their own age. These findings are inconsistent with Bowlby's maternal deprivation hypothesis.

4. A minority of these children had problems including cognitive impairment, excessive friendliness with complete strangers, inattention, and overactivity. Of central importance are deficits in social cognition and behaviour (as found with Cezarina discussed earlier). These negative consequences of deprivation have been labelled **deprivation-specific problems** (Kumsta et al., 2015) because they differ from the problems of children with other forms of early adversity (e.g., physical and/or sexual abuse).

OVERALL EVALUATION

➕ Children's early experiences often have long-term effects on their social and emotional development; many of these negative effects are deprivation-specific problems.

➕ Rutter's assumption that the adverse effects of privation are greater than those of deprivation has received support.

➕ Rutter's assumption that most negative effects of maternal deprivation can be reversed is strongly support by research.

➕ Rutter's argument that the effects of deprivation depend on the reasons for the separation is correct.

➖ Bowlby failed to distinguish clearly between deprivation and privation.

➖ Bowlby de-emphasised the extent to which a loving environment can reverse the adverse effects of previous deprivation or privation.

According to Hetherington et al. (1982), what typically happens in the period following divorce?

Effects of divorce and child care

Some major sources of disruption in children's attachments in Western societies (and many other cultures) have become much more common in recent decades. For example, fewer than 5% of marriages in the United Kingdom ended in divorce 60 years ago. Nowadays the figure is 40% and is even higher in the United States.

There has also been a large increase in the number of young children put into child care for several days a week while their mothers are at work. In the United States, 80% of children under the age of 6 spend an average of 40 hours in non-parent care every week. The effects of divorce and day care on children's well-being are the focus of this section.

Divorce

Divorce involves various stages, each requiring children to adjust. First, there are marital conflicts that are distressing to children. Second, there is the actual separation followed by divorce. Third, children often have to cope with moving

KEY TERM

Deprivation-specific problems: problems (e.g., social deficits; interests that are intense but very limited) sometimes found following deprivation but uncommon following other kinds of childhood adversity.

house and reacting to new relationships as their parents find new partners and perhaps remarry.

Hetherington et al. (1982) reported the effects of divorce on 4-year-old children over a two year period. The first year after the divorce was the **crisis phase**. During that time, mothers became stricter and less affectionate than before. In return, the children (especially boys) behaved in more aggressive and unchanging ways. During this first year, the fathers became less strict and often gave treats to their children.

The **adjustment phase** was usually reached about two years after divorce. There was more routine and order about the children's everyday lives. In addition, the mothers had returned to treating their children with more patience and understanding. Overall, there was less emotional distress than during the crisis phase. However, the boys of divorced parents had worse relations and showed more disobedient behaviour than boys whose parents had not divorced.

The negative effects of divorce depend in part on the child's age at the time of the divorce (Lansford, 2009). Children experience more behavioural problems if they are relatively young at the time of divorce. However, they experience more problems with academic achievement and with romantic relationships if they are older when their parents divorce. Hetherington and Kelly (2002) found 25% of children with divorced parents had serious long-term social, emotional, or psychological problems compared to 10% of children whose parents had not divorced. Even 10 years after a divorce, the children involved regarded it as the most stressful event in their lives (Wallerstein, 1984).

Parents who divorce do not only provide their children with a hard and stressful home environment. They also provide their children's genes. It is thus possible that some negative effects of divorce on children are to the genes they have inherited rather than divorce itself. O'Connor et al. (2003) studied

What are the short- and long-term effects of divorce on girls and on boys?

KEY TERMS

Crisis phase: the first period following divorce; during this period, the mother is less affectionate than usual.

Adjustment phase: the second period following divorce; it follows the crisis phase and is marked by less emotional distress than that phase.

Erel et al.'s (2000) review of studies on day care found that there were no significant effects on measures of child development such as social interaction with peers and attachment to mother.

children at genetic risk because their parents had anxious personalities. This genetic risk strongly predicted poor adjustment in children whose parents had separated but not in those that had remained together. Thus, the negative effects of parental separation were much greater on children at genetic risk.

In sum, the great majority of children experience the divorce of their parents as extremely stressful. Adults whose parents divorced when they were children are more vulnerable than other adults to emotional and psychological problems. Some of this vulnerability is due to the genes these adults inherited from their parents rather than the divorce itself.

Child care

The studies discussed earlier in the chapter concerned long and distressing periods of separation of children from their mothers. However, 50% of infants in Western societies experience short periods of separation several days a week because their mothers are working. Do these infants suffer as a result? Perhaps surprisingly, the answer is mostly, "No". However, it is important to consider the mother's attitude towards working. Harrison and Ungerer (2002) studied mothers who had returned to paid employment during the first year of their infant's life. Infants were less likely to be securely attached to their mother if she was not committed to work and had anxieties about using child care.

Erel et al. (2000) carried out a thorough review of studies on the effects of child care (also known as day care) using seven measures of child development:

1. *Secure vs. insecure attachment to the mother.*
2. *Attachment behaviours*: Avoidance and resistance (reflecting insecure attachment), and exploration (reflecting secure attachment).
3. *Mother-child interaction*: Responsiveness to mother, smiling at mother, obeying mother, and so on.
4. *Adjustment*: Self-esteem, lack of behaviour problems, and so on.
5. *Social interaction with peers* (children of the same age).
6. *Social interaction with non-parental adults* (e.g., relatives; teachers).
7. *Cognitive development*: School performance, IQ, and so on.

Erel et al. (2000) found child care had non-significant effects on all seven measures described. This was the case regardless of the amount of child care per week, the number of months the child had been in child care, and the child's gender.

The National Institute of Child Health and Development (NICHD) carried out very large studies into the effects of child care. In one study (NICHD, 2003), levels of aggression (e.g., fighting) and assertiveness (e.g., demanding attention) were higher in infants who had received the most child care. However, there are many kinds of child care (e.g., being looked after by grandparents; babysitting at home; child-care centres). Love et al. (2003) re-analysed the data from the NICHD (2003) study, finding that child care provided by relatives did *not* lead to an increase in aggression or assertiveness.

Huston et al. (2015) confirmed previous findings. There were no effects of extensive child care on young children's positive behaviour (e.g., cooperation) or peer interactions, but there were slight increases in aggression and reduced self-control. The negative effects of child care on aggression and self-control were due to poor relationships between the children and those providing child care and negative interactions with other children (peers) rather than reduced attachment to mothers.

When focusing on the effects of child care on young children, we need to consider the impact on mother-child attachment caused by mothers going out to work. Overall, there is typically no effect. However, that non-significant effect camouflages various effects on mothers. On the positive side, mothers who go out to work generally have higher self-esteem and fewer depressive symptoms than those who stay at home. On the negative side, mothers who go out to work are less sensitive to the needs of their children and provide less stimulation.

At what age do infants generally do better in day care, and do the mother's circumstances matter?

Chapter summary

- It has been found with the Strange Situation test that American infants' attachment to their mother is secure in 70% of cases, avoidant in a further 20%, and resistant in the remaining 10%.
- Individual differences with the Strange Situation test can be seen in terms of the two dimensions of avoidant/withdrawal vs. proximity seeking, and angry and resistant vs. emotional confidence.
- Ainsworth argued in her maternal sensitivity hypothesis that an infant's attachment to his/her mother depends mainly on the mother's sensitivity. This de-emphasises the roles played by the infant's father and the infant's personality.
- Any given child's attachment type depends on complex interactions between various factors (e.g., genes; maternal responsiveness).
- There are significant cross-cultural differences in attachment types. However, the differences are greater within than between cultures.
- Bowlby argued it is very important for children to have a warm and continuous attachment to their mother. According to him, infants experiencing maternal deprivation may suffer severe and irreversible emotional and other problems.
- In Bowlby's monotropy hypothesis, he argued that babies are born with a tendency to become strongly attached to only one individual. There is little support for this theory.
- Bowlby exaggerated the adverse effects of maternal deprivation, which are typically reversible. In most cases, family discord rather than separation is the major problem.
- Children generally experience more problems when exposed to privation (never having had a close relationship) than when exposed to deprivation. However, even the adverse effects of extreme privation are mostly reversible.

- There are two stages of reaction to divorce within families. There is an initial crisis phase followed by an adjustment phase.
- Some negative effects on children within families experiencing divorce are due to the genes they have inherited.
- Child care typically has few (if any) negative effects on children's social, emotional, or cognitive development. However, increased aggression and assertiveness in children are associated with some forms of child care.

Further reading

- Berk, L.E. (2012). *Child development* (9th ed.). New York: Pearson. There is accessible coverage of child attachment in Chapter 10 of this textbook.

- Kumsta, R., Kreppner, J., Kennedy, M., Knights, N., Rutter, M., & Sonuga-Barke, E. (2015). Psychological consequences of early global deprivation: An overview of findings from the English & Romanian Adoptees Study. *European Psychologist*, *20*, 138–151. This article provides an excellent overview of the authors' important research on the effects of severe privation on children's subsequent development.

- Leman, P., Bremner, A., Parke, R.D., & Gauvain, M. (2012). *Developmental psychology*. New York: McGraw-Hill. Chapter 7 in this textbook has detailed coverage of children's attachment.

- Meins, E. (2011). Emotional development and early attachment relationships. In A. Slater & G. Bremner (Eds.), *An introduction to developmental psychology* (2nd ed., pp. 141–164). Chichester: Wiley-Blackwell. Elizabeth Meins reviews research concerned with attachments in early life.

Essay questions

1. Discuss the categorical and dimensional approaches to infants' attachment to their mothers. Which approach is preferable, and why?

2. What are some of the main factors influencing the nature of infants' attachment to their mothers?

3. Compare and contrast the effects on children of deprivation and privation. What can be done to maximise the chances of children recovering from deprivation or privation?

4. Compare and contrast the effects of divorce and child care on young children.

Some of the people you know are probably prejudiced against one or more minority groups. If you are a member of a minority group yourself, you have probably been on the receiving end of prejudice from others. Why do you think people are prejudiced? Is it because of their personality, their experiences, the influence of other people, or some other factor?

In view of the harm and misery caused by prejudice, it is clearly very desirable that society takes steps to reduce and eliminate it. This is likely to prove difficult to achieve. How do you think the authorities might attempt to make our society less prejudiced?

Prejudice and discrimination

13

Many people regard prejudice and discrimination as meaning the same thing. In fact, there is an important distinction between them. **Prejudice** is "an attitude towards a person on the basis of his or her group membership. Prejudice may reflect preference towards ingroup members or dislike of outgroup members and it is typically imbued with affect [emotion]" (Amodio, 2014, p. 671). In other words, prejudice has a cognitive component (i.e., attitude or belief) and an emotional component (e.g., fear; anger). In contrast, **discrimination** refers to behaviour or action (e.g., aggression; exclusion from society) against another group.

What is the difference between prejudice and discrimination?

Most research has found only a modest association between prejudice and discrimination (Dovidio et al., 1996). One reason is that there are generally greater social pressures to avoid discrimination (which is easily observable by others) than to avoid prejudice (which is less obvious to other people). Schütz and Six (1996) found across 60 studies that there was a moderate relationship between prejudice and discrimination (the correlation was +.36). However, the relationship between prejudice and the *intention* to discriminate was somewhat stronger (the correlation was +.45). Thus, prejudice is more closely related to what people say they will do than it is to what they actually do.

An important contribution to understanding the relationship between prejudice and discrimination was made by Talaska et al. (2008). They argued there is an important distinction between emotional prejudice and attitudinal prejudice (i.e., beliefs and stereotypes). Their key finding was that emotional prejudice was much more closely associated with discrimination than was attitudinal prejudice. Strong emotional reactions to another group provide the motivational impetus to turn prejudice into action (i.e., discrimination).

Discrimination can take many forms. In some situations (e.g., Nazi Germany) there is a rapid increase in discrimination. Allport (1954) identified five stages of increasingly harsh discrimination:

1. *Anti-locution*: verbal attacks are directed against some group.
2. *Avoidance*: the other group is systematically avoided; this can involve ways of making it easier to identify members of that group (e.g., the Star of David worn by Jews in Nazi Germany).
3. *Discrimination*: the other group is treated worse than other group in civil rights, job opportunities, and so on.

> **KEY TERMS**
>
> **Prejudice:** attitudes and feelings (typically negative) about the members of some group solely on the basis of their membership of that group.
>
> **Discrimination:** negative actions of behaviour directed towards the members of some other group.

Discrimination against specific groups is sometimes aided by distinguishing visual characteristics such as skin colour, or style of dress. Sometimes, however, minority group members are not clearly distinguishable from the majority, and are forced to identify themselves. This was the case in Nazi Germany where Jews had to wear a Star of David on their clothing, making them a focus for racial hatred.

4. *Physical attack*: group members are attacked and their property destroyed.
5. *Extermination*: there are deliberate attempts to kill members of the other group (e.g., the gas chambers built by the Nazis).

Is prejudice in decline?

Much evidence suggests that prejudice is in decline in many countries. For example, only 10% of those living in Western countries have obvious racial biases (much less than 50 or 60 years ago). In the United States, for example, self-reported racial attitudes became much more positive between 1972 and 2010 (Smith et al., 2011). However, up to 80% of white Americans possess more subtle racial prejudice leading to "awkward social interactions, embarrassing slips of the tongue, unchecked assumptions, stereo-typic judgments, and spontaneous neglect" (S.T. Fiske, 2002, p. 124).

The term "modern racism" is used to describe various subtle prejudicial attitudes towards other racial groups. It manifests itself in various ways including the following (Swim et al., 1995):

1. denial there is prejudice and discrimination against minority groups;
2. annoyance because minority groups demand equal treatment with the majority group;
3. resentment at minority groups receiving positive action to assist them.

Subtle racism can influence basic perceptual processes. Payne (2001) presented briefly a photograph of a male white or black face followed by the photograph of an object. Participants decided whether the object was a handgun or hand-tool. They were more likely to misidentify a tool as a handgun when it was preceded by a black face than by a white one.

Many individuals express greater racial prejudice when they are reminded of their concerns about other racial groups. In the United States, it is predicted that non-Hispanic whites will form a minority of the American population by 2042. When white Americans were reminded of this prediction through a newspaper article, they expressed more direct and subtle racial bias (Craig & Richeson, 2014).

Stereotypes

KEY TERM

Stereotype: an oversimplified generalisation (typically negative) concerning some group in society.

Prejudiced people generally regard all (or nearly all) members of a disliked minority as being similar to each other; this involves stereotyping. Stereotypes can be regarded as the *cognitive* component of prejudice. A **stereotype** is an oversimplified (and usually negative) cognitive representation of a group (e.g., black people; the French) that ignores individual differences within that group. For example, many people have a stereotype of the English as intelligent, tolerant, and reserved even though they know many English people who are totally different! A stereotypical Italian mother is shown in the photograph.

How accurate are stereotypes? They are nearly always oversimplified and represent distorted views of other groups. However, stereotypes often contain a kernel of truth. For example, Lóchenhoff et al. (2014) considered gender stereotypes of personality across 26 countries with respect to five major personality factors (see Chapter 18). Such gender stereotypes were similar across countries: women were perceived as slightly higher than men in agreeableness, conscientiousness, openness, some aspects of neuroticism (e.g., anxiety; vulnerability) and some aspects of extraversion (e.g., warmth; positive emotions). Lóchenhoff et al.'s key finding was that there was reasonable agreement between perceived gender stereotypes and actual gender differences in personality.

The stereotypical image of Italian matriarchs being wonderful cooks has given rise to several advertising campaigns for Italian food products.

Other stereotypes are typically much less accurate than is the case with gender stereotypes. Terracciano et al. (2005) compared stereotypical views of national character in 49 cultures with actual average personality. There was no validity to these stereotypes. For example, the average level of conscientious among Germans was almost identical to that among Chileans in spite of the stereotypical view that the Germans are more conscientious.

Why do stereotypes differ in accuracy? First, stereotypes based on numerous observations (e.g., gender stereotypes) are likely to be more accurate than those not so based (e.g., national character stereotypes). Second, stereotypes are more inaccurate when they involve groups evoking strong emotions. For example, people may be positively biased when assessing the national character of their own country but negatively biased when assessing the national character of another country with which they have been at war.

Assessing stereotypes

Historically, stereotypes were assessed mainly by questionnaires. A major limitation with this approach is that individuals may pretend their stereotypes of disliked other groups are less negative than is actually the case. Cunningham et al. (2001) addressed this issue in a study in which white participants completed the Implicit Association Test. In condition 1, participants pressed one key if a white face or a good word (e.g., *love*) was presented and a different key if a black face or bad word (e.g., *terrible*) was presented. In condition 2, white faces and bad words involved one key and black faces and good words the second key.

Reaction times were much faster in condition 1 than in condition 2, which suggests the existence of implicit or unconscious pro-white and anti-black stereotypes. There was a modest tendency for participants showing much conscious or explicit prejudice on a questionnaire to also show unconscious prejudice.

There has been some controversy concerning the meaning and importance of findings obtained from the Implicit Association Test. When all the evidence is considered, it indicates there are theoretically predictable effects of prejudice assessed by the Test on intergroup discrimination (Greenwald et al., 2015). These effects are relatively small but nevertheless have some value when trying to identify prejudiced individuals

Why do we have stereotypes?

Nearly everyone has numerous stereotypes, which suggests (but does not prove!) they fulfil important functions. Two major functions have been identified. First, stereotypes reduce processing effort by providing a simple way of perceiving the world around us. For example, we can easily categorise a stranger based on their sex, age, clothing, and so on.

Second, stereotypes also fulfil major social and motivational functions. How we think about ourselves is influenced by the various social groups (e.g., school; clubs) to which we belong. Stereotypes allow us to distinguish ourselves (and our groups) clearly from other groups (Oakes et al., 1994). For example, the stereotype of the British as reserved and industrious became stronger when British students compared the British against Italians. This happened because the British students wanted to *emphasise* the differences between the two nationalities (Cinnirella, 1998).

Why are stereotypes hard to change?

We can attribute other people's behaviour to *internal* causes (e.g., personality) or *external* or *situational* causes (see Chapter 16). If we attribute someone's behaviour to internal causes, we generally expect that behaviour to be repeated in future. However, we expect behaviour attributed to external causes to change when the situation changes.

Sherman et al. (2005) argued that the attributions we make about others' behaviour help to explain why it is generally hard to produce lasting changes in someone's negative stereotypes about some minority group. They assessed people's attribution for the behaviour of a gay man called Robert. Individuals prejudiced against homosexuals gave *internal* attributions to Robert's stereotype-consistent behaviour but *external* attributions to his stereotype-inconsistent behaviour. Thus, even prejudiced individuals found some of Robert's behaviour inconsistent with their stereotypical views of gays. However, they still expect he would mostly behave in a stereotype-consistent way in future.

Explanations of prejudice

KEY TERM

Outgroup: a group to which the individual does not belong; such groups are often regarded negatively and with prejudice.

There are *three* main causes of prejudice. First, the individual's personality (which depends in part on genetic factors) can influence prejudice. Second, environmental factors (e.g., a dramatic increase in unemployment) may lead to greater prejudice against minority groups. Third, simply belonging to a group may cause prejudice. The groups to which an individual belongs (ingroups) may be regarded favourably whereas other groups (**outgroups**) are regarded unfavourably or with prejudice.

Personality

Adorno et al. (1950) argued that prejudiced individuals tend to have an **authoritarian personality**. It includes rigid beliefs in conventional values, general hostility towards other groups, intolerance of ambiguity, and submissive attitudes towards those in authority. Adorno et al. devised the F (Fascism) Scale to measure attitudes associated with the authoritarian personality. Here is a sample item: "Most of our social problems would be solved if we could somehow get rid of the immoral, crooked, and feeble-minded people."

According to Adorno et al., children having a harsh upbringing with little affection and much punishment from their parents are most likely to develop an authoritarian personality. The treatment they receive from their parents creates hostility, but they cannot express it towards their parents. As a result, they re-direct it towards minority groups.

What attitude do individuals with an authoritarian personality have towards authority figures and values?

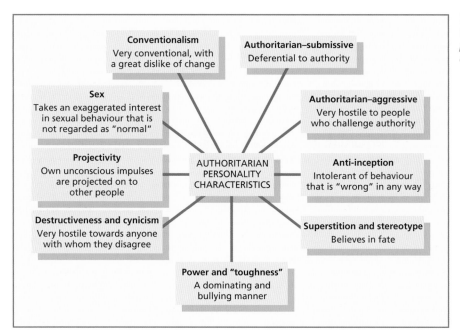

The nine personality traits of the authoritarian personality from Adorno et al.'s F-Scale.

Findings

Adorno et al. (1950) found adults with an authoritarian personality had often been treated harshly by their parents. They interpreted this as meaning that the harsh family environment caused the development of an authoritarian personality. However, there is an alternative biological explanation: genetic factors may mean authoritarian parents tend to have authoritarian children.

We can investigate theoretical explanations of the origins of the authoritarian personality by carrying out twin studies. Identical twins share 100% of their genes whereas fraternal twins share only 50% of theirs. If individual differences in the authoritarian personality depend in part on genetic factors, we would expect identical twins to be more similar to each other than fraternal twins. Hatemi et al. (2014) considered the findings from over 12,000 twin pairs. They found that about 40% of individual differences in the authoritarian personality

> **KEY TERM**
>
> **Authoritarian personality:** a type of personality consisting of intolerance of ambiguity, hostility towards other groups, rigid beliefs, and submissiveness towards authority figures.

and other political attitudes were due to genetic factors. Note, however, that these findings leave open the possibility that a harsh family environment may also play a role in causing children to develop the authoritarian personality.

We must not exaggerate the role of personality in creating prejudice. Prejudice can depend more on cultural norms than on personality. For example, Pettigrew (1958) found there was much more prejudice towards black people in South Africa than in the United States even though the levels of authoritarianism were similar in the two countries.

Major historical events can increase prejudice. Consider the impact of the attack on the US fleet in Pearl Harbor on Americans' attitudes to the Japanese. There was an immediate large increase in prejudice against Japanese people among those with (and without) authoritarian personalities. Such widespread prejudice cannot be explained by Adorno et al.'s theory.

EVALUATION

⊕ Individual differences in prejudice can be assessed by the F-Scale.

⊕ Genetic factors (and various environmental ones) help to determine whether someone will develop an authoritarian personality.

⊖ Prejudice generally depends more on cultural and social factors than on personality. This can be seen when there are rapid increases in prejudice within a society (e.g., Nazi Germany).

⊖ Adorno et al. (1950) exaggerated the role of the family environment in producing the authoritarian personality.

According to realistic conflict theory, what does prejudice result from?

Realistic group conflict

Sherif (1966) proposed in his realistic conflict theory that prejudice often results from conflict between groups. When two groups compete for the same goal, the members of each group become prejudiced against those of the other group. In contrast, if two groups work together to achieve the same goal, they will cooperate and there will be no prejudice.

Findings

The origins of realistic conflict theory lie in the Robbers Cave study (Sherif et al., 1961). Twenty-two boys spent two weeks at an American summer camp. They were put into two groups (Eagles and Rattlers) and were told that the group that performed better in various sporting events and competitions would receive a trophy, knives, and medals. As a result of this competition, a fight broke out between the members of the two groups and the Rattlers' flag was burned.

Prejudice was shown in the Robbers Cave study – each group regarded its own members as friendly and courageous whereas those of the other group were perceived as smart-alecks and liars. On average, the boys indicated 93% of their friends in the study were members of their own group. However, prejudice was greatly reduced (and there were more other-group friends) when the researchers replaced the competitive situations with a cooperative one in which success required the cooperation of both groups.

Filindra and Pearson-Merkowitz (2013) assessed the impact of a perceived increase in the number of foreign immigrants in New England states on views towards a strict anti-immigration law. A perceived increase in immigration was associated with support for anti-immigration measures among those pessimistic about the economic future but not those who were optimistic. As predicted by realistic conflict theory, negative views about immigration were associated with fears of competition for resources from immigrants.

Ember (1981) studied 26 small societies. As predicted by realistic conflict theory, intergroup violence was much more frequent when societies competed for resources because of population pressures or severe food shortages.

EVALUATION

➕ Sherif was one of the first psychologists to provide strong evidence that individuals "see the world through the lens of their group membership" (Platow & Hunter, 2014, p. 840).

➕ Competition between groups can lead to prejudice.

➕ Realistic conflict theory helps to explain the large increases in prejudice found when countries are at war with each other.

➕ Replacing competition with cooperation can reduce prejudice.

➖ Sherif (1966) argued that conflicts arise when group interests are threatened, but defined group interests vaguely: "A real or imagined threat to the safety of the group, an economic interest, a political advantage, a military consideration, prestige, or a number of others" (Sherif, 1966, p. 15).

➖ Tyerman and Spencer (1983) failed to replicate Sherif et al.'s (1961) study among scouts who knew each other well before attending scout camp. They argued that competition and realistic conflict only cause prejudice when those involved do not already have established friendships.

➖ The Robbers Cave study was biased (Perry, 2014). For example, the researchers deliberately chose highly athletic boys because they would be more likely to be competitive than other boys. Those involved in running the study facilitated the development of conflict among the children (e.g., a staff member pulled down a tent hoping one group would blame the other).

Social identity

Suppose someone asked you to describe your best friend. Your description would certainly refer to their personal qualities (e.g., personality). It would also probably include some indication of the groups to which they belong

What does social identity theory assume about people?

(e.g., student at college; hockey team member). Tajfel and Turner (1979) argued in their social identity theory (see Chapter 19) that we all have various **social identities** based on the different groups to which we belong. Our sense of self is strongly influenced by our social identities. Note that Sherif et al.'s (1961) group-based study can be regarded as a forerunner of social identity theory.

Why is it important for us to possess social identities? Having a positive social identity makes us feel good about ourselves and enhances our self-esteem. We can achieve a positive social identity by comparing a group to which we belong (an ingroup) favourably to some other group (an outgroup). This produces **ingroup bias** (favouring one's ingroup over outgroups) and can lead to prejudice.

There is another way prejudice can occur. When someone belongs to a group, they generally accept that group's values or norms. If those norms include negative views about a given outgroup, prejudice will result.

Findings

Barlow et al. (2010) studied prejudice in Asian Australians who felt rejected by Aboriginal Australians. Those Asian Australians who identified themselves most strongly with their ingroup had greater prejudice towards Aboriginal Australians than those who identified less strongly.

Mullen et al. (1992) reviewed numerous studies. Members of poorly regarded minority groups showed *favouritism* towards more highly regarded outgroups. This is the opposite of what is predicted by social identity theory and probably occurred in part because of the greater power possessed by the outgroups.

Prejudice towards other groups does not occur in an automatic and unthinking way. For example, children are more likely to show prejudice and socially exclude members of an outgroup if they think such behaviour is approved of by other members of their ingroup (Nesdale, 2013).

KEY TERMS

Social identities: each of the groups with which we identify produces a social identity; our feelings about ourselves depend on how we feel about the groups with which we identify.

Ingroup bias: the tendency to view one's own group(s) more favourably than other groups.

EVALUATION

➕ Group membership and social identities can have strong effects on attitudes towards ingroups and outgroups.

➕ An individual's social identities can lead to prejudice and discrimination.

➖ Social identity theory does not provide a clear account of how prejudice develops.

➖ A strong ingroup identity often fails to lead to prejudice against outgroups if they are more powerful than the ingroup.

➖ Individuals with a strong ingroup identity are less likely to show prejudice and discrimination against outgroups if they perceive other ingroup members do not approve of such behaviour.

Reducing prejudice and discrimination

It is very important to find ways of reducing (and ideally eliminating) prejudice and discrimination. Here we will discuss briefly various approaches taken by psychologists.

Changing stereotypes

Er-rafiy and Brauer (2013) argued that many people are prejudiced because they possess stereotypical views about some minority group. If so, we could reduce prejudice by increasing the perceived *variability* of members of that group (thus reducing stereotypical views). Er-rafiy and Brauer presented French participants with a poster designed to increase perceived variability of Arabs. This simple procedure successfully reduced stereotyping, prejudice, and discrimination.

Intergroup contact theory

Allport (1954) argued in his contact hypothesis that we can reduce prejudice by increasing direct social contacts between members of different groups. Such social contact may make it clear to prejudiced individuals that the members of the other group are more similar to themselves than previously thought. In addition, social contact may reduce mistaken stereotypical views about the other group.

Allport (1954) argued successful social contact requires that *four* conditions are met:

1. The two groups have equal status within the situation in which the contact takes place.
2. The two groups are working towards common goals.
3. Efforts to achieve these common goals are based on intergroup cooperation.
4. There is formal institutional support for intergroup acceptance.

Allport's original hypothesis focused on the benefits of direct (face-to-face) contact. This hypothesis has been extended (e.g., by assuming that indirect contact without physical interactions is also effective). It is now referred to as the intergroup contact theory (Pettigrew & Tropp, 2011). A key assumption of the original hypothesis and the later theory is that prejudice is partly based on ignorance and that social contact can remove ignorance and thus reduce prejudice.

Findings

Lemmer and Wagner (2015) provided a thorough review of research on the effects of social contact in real-life situations. They reported three main findings. First, direct and indirect social contacts were equally effective at reducing prejudice. Second, the beneficial effects of social contact were as great several months afterwards as immediately. Third, intergroup contact reduced prejudice within majority and minority groups, but the effects were greater for majority groups. The effects may be smaller within minority groups because of their members' concerns about experiencing prejudice and discrimination from majority group members.

How does intergroup contact reduce prejudice?

Pettigrew and Tropp (2008) found reduced prejudice among majority group members following intergroup contact was due to three reasons:

1. Intergroup contact reduced anxiety about interacting with minority group members.
2. It increased empathy (understanding of the feelings of minority group members).
3. It increased knowledge about the other group.

Allport (1954) de-emphasised individual differences in the effects of intergroup contact. Dhont et al. (2011) considered the effects of intergroup contact on individuals varying in need for closure (preference for firm answers and an aversion to ambiguity). Intergroup contact reduced prejudice more in those high in need for closure because it reduced their anxiety about the other group.

EVALUATION

➕ Social contact (especially between groups of equal social status) can reduce prejudice; this is the case with both direct and indirect contact.

➕ Key factors (reduced anxiety; empathy; increased knowledge) responsible for the beneficial effects of social contact have been identified.

➖ Intergroup contact typically has relatively little effect on prejudice within minority groups.

➖ The intergroup contact theory does not indicate clearly how positive contact with individual members of an outgroup might generalise to include other members of that outgroup.

➖ Individual differences (e.g., in need for closure) are more important in determining the effects of intergroup contact than assumed by the theory.

Salient categorisation

Suppose someone meets (and likes) a member of an outgroup. This may not lead to a reduction in prejudice with respect to that group if that person is regarded as "an exception to the rule". The outgroup member needs to be perceived as *typical* of his/her group to reduce prejudice. This can be done by making his/her group membership as salient or obvious as possible. Thus, **salient categorisation** is the key.

Van Oudenhouven et al. (1996) tested this hypothesis. Dutch participants spent 2 hours interacting with a Turkish person in the following two conditions:

1. The experimenter never mentioned the person was Turkish (low salience).

KEY TERM

Salient categorisation: the notion that someone needs to be regarded as typical or representative of a group in order for positive encounters with that individual to lead to reduced prejudice towards the entire group.

2. The fact that the person was Turkish was emphasised throughout (high salience).

Attitudes towards Turks in general were more favorable in the second condition than in the first, indicating the importance of salient categorisation.

Much research has focused on multiculturalism, which involves the acceptance and promotion of group differences. It resembles salient categorisation and is effective in improving intergroup relations (Hahn et al., 2015). However, there are two potential problems with salient categorisation. First, it can be hard to persuade someone that a given member of an outgroup is actually a typical member of that group. Second, if the interaction with the outgroup member who is allegedly typical of that group goes badly, there is a danger the entire outgroup will be perceived negatively.

Common ingroup identity model

We saw earlier that most individuals have much more positive attitudes towards their own ingroup or ingroups than to outgroups. It follows that one potentially effective way of reducing prejudice would involve **recategorisation** – the ingroup and outgroup are combined to form a single common ingroup. Recategorisation leads individuals to perceive members of this common ingroup as being similar to each other. The notion of forming a common overarching identity is of central importance within the common ingroup identity model (e.g., Gaertner & Dovidio, 2012). Note that the creation of a common ingroup identity does *not* require each group to forsake its original group identity: individuals can have a dual identity.

Findings

Recategorisation can help to reduce prejudice and discrimination (Gaertner & Dovidio, 2012). For example, Dovidio et al. (2004) showed white participants a video showing examples of racial discrimination. Those previously exposed to a recategorisation manipulation (told a terrorist threat was directed at both black and white Americans) showed reduced prejudice following the video. More evidence indicating the beneficial effects of recategorisation is discussed in the box on E-contact.

Recategorisation does not *always* have beneficial effects. Turner and Crisp (2010) asked British students to think of themselves as Europeans. This recategorisation reduced prejudice against the French among British students who did not identify very strongly with being British. However, it *increased* prejudice against the French among students strongly identified with being British. These students wanted to preserve a strong sense of British identity, and this was threatened when told to think of themselves as European.

Dovidio et al. (2015) also found recategorisation can have negative effects on prejudice and discrimination. If everyone is perceived as belonging to the same common ingroup, this can make it less likely that high-status group members will recognise and respond to injustices suffered by low-status members. Banfield and Dovidio (2013) asked white participants to read a scenario in which a black candidate was not offered a job through discrimination. When the discrimination was subtle, emphasising common identity reduced the perception of bias and the willingness to protest about the injustice.

KEY TERM

Recategorisation: merging the ingroup and outgroup to form a single large ingroup.

What does reducing prejudice by recategorisation involve?

EVALUATION

➕ Recategorisation often reduces prejudice even among those whose initial level of prejudice is high.

➕ Recategorisation has been shown to reduce prejudice with indirect electronic contact between groups (see the box on E-contact).

➖ Recategorisation can increase prejudice among those who identify strongly with their ingroup and so do not want to recategorise.

➖ Recategorisation can make high-status members of the common ingroup less sensitive to the problems and injustices experienced by low-status members.

IN THE REAL WORLD: electronic (E)-contact

Most research on prejudice reduction takes place in the artificial environment of the experimental laboratory. That is no longer necessary given that nearly 80% of households in the Western world have Internet access. Accordingly, White et al. (2014) carried out a study involving electronic (E)-contact between Christian and Muslim students; E-contact is a form of indirect contact. Four-person teams (two of each religion) discussed ways their religions could work together (e.g., to develop recycling solutions) to enhance the sustainability of the Australian environment. This approach involved dual-identity recategorisation: there was recategorisation (i.e., shared Australian identity), but all participants retained their subgroup identity (i.e., their religious affiliation). The programme lasted for nine weeks. There was also a control condition not involving recategorisation.

What did White et al. (2014) find? The dual-identity recategorisation group showed greater reduction in prejudice towards members of the other religion than did the control group. Impressively, this reduced prejudice was maintained for 12 months after the end of the programme. However, there was much stronger evidence of reduced prejudice among the Muslim students than the Christian ones. This reduced prejudice over time occurred in part because of reduced anxiety about the other group and the development of friendships with Christian participants.

White et al. (2015a) analysed the language used during the programme by the two groups. The dual-identity recategorisation group used more positive emotion words and fewer anger and sadness words than the control group. Further analysis revealed that the greater reduction in intergroup prejudice in the recategorisation group occurred in part because they expressed negative emotions less often.

The advantage of using E-contact to reduce prejudice is that it involves a relatively natural and easy-to-use approach that is engaging for most young people. It could be used to reduce prejudice in vastly

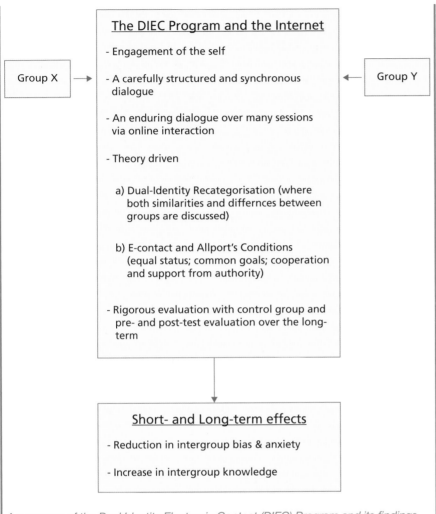

The DIEC Program and the Internet

- Engagement of the self

- A carefully structured and synchronous dialogue

- An enduring dialogue over many sessions via online interaction

- Theory driven

    a) Dual-Identity Recategorisation (where both similarities and differnces between groups are discussed)

    b) E-contact and Allport's Conditions (equal status; common goals; cooperation and support from authority)

- Rigorous evaluation with control group and pre- and post-test evaluation over the long-term

Group X →

Group Y ←

Short- and Long-term effects

- Reduction in intergroup bias & anxiety

- Increase in intergroup knowledge

A summary of the Dual Identity Electronic Contact (DIEC) Program and its findings.

greater numbers of people than can receive interventions under laboratory conditions. The main potential disadvantage is that the relatively anonymous nature of the Internet means that E-contact can have negative consequences (e.g., cyberbullying). To prevent that, "E-contact must involve structured tasks that seeks to engender co-operation and collaboration between group members, and where common . . . goals that are important to all group members are pursued" (White et al., 2015b, p. 135).

Conclusions and synthesis

We can distinguish two very different approaches to reducing prejudice. An emphasis on salient categorisation implies that we should *emphasise* differences between groups. This approach is often known as multiculturalism and involves agreeing to statements such as, "We must appreciate the unique characteristics of different ethnic groups to have a co-operative society" (Hahn et al., 2015, p. 1662).

In contrast, recategorisation implies we should *minimise* differences between groups. It is associated with a colour-blind approach summed up by the following statement: "All humans are fundamentally the same, regardless of where they come from or what their background is" (Hahn et al., 2015, p. 1662).

Most research indicates that both approaches are effective. For example, Wolsko et al. (2000) found a colour-blind message (recognise group differences as enriching) and a multicultural message (recognise our sameness) both increased the warmth expressed towards ethnic outgroups.

Hahn et al. (2015) identified a "dark" side to colour-blindness and to multiculturalism. The dark side with colour-blindness is that sameness across groups is defined with respect to the dominant group's norms and beliefs. Thus, for example, those favouring the colour-blind approach often endorse statements such as, "People from all ethnic backgrounds living in America should embrace the American dream of hard work and success" (Hahn et al., 2015, p. 1662)

The dark side with multiculturalism is that the emphasis on group differences can lead to the conclusion it would be best if different groups live separately. For example, those favouring multiculturalism often agree with statements such as, "It is important for different ethnic groups to stick to themselves to some degree to preserve the uniqueness of their cultures" (Hahn et al., 2015, p. 1662).

In sum, approaches based on multiculturalism and colour-blindness have both proved of value in reducing prejudice and discrimination. However, these approaches must be used sensitively to prevent the "dark" side of each approach from emerging. The best approach involves combining the two approaches as was done in the E-contact study by White et al. (2014). In other words, individuals adopt a dual identity (Dovidio et al., 2010): they have a common identity deriving from recategorisation while at the same time retaining their original group identity.

Chapter summary

- Prejudice involves negative attitudes (cognitive component) and emotions towards the members of some group. In contrast, discrimination involves negative actions directed at the members of another group.
- There has been a decline in overt racism, but this has largely been replaced by more subtle forms of racism.
- Stereotypes are useful because they provide a simple way of perceiving the world. They also serve social and motivational purposes.
- Adorno et al. argued that prejudiced people have an authoritarian personality stemming from a harsh and affectionless childhood.
- Adorno et al. minimised the role of genetic factors in producing individual differences in prejudice. They also minimised the importance of cultural and intergroup factors.
- According to realistic conflict theory, competition between two groups for the same goal can cause intergroup conflict and prejudice.
- Realistic conflict is often neither necessary nor sufficient to produce prejudice; for example, prejudice does not occur if there are pre-existing friendships between groups experiencing conflict.

- Individuals' social identities can produce ingroup bias, leading to prejudice against outgroups. However, there is less prejudice when outgroups are more powerful than the ingroup and when individuals perceive that other ingroup members do not approve of prejudice and discrimination.
- Intergroup contact can reduce prejudice by reducing anxiety about the other group and by increasing empathy for (and knowledge of) that group. However, the beneficial effects of intergroup contact often fail to generalise to all members of the other group.
- Prejudice can be reduced when salient categorisation is used so that a member of another group is perceived as typical of that group.
- Prejudice can also be reduced by recategorisation in which the ingroup and outgroup are combined to form a single common ingroup.
- Multiculturalism (resembling salient categorisation) has the downside that it can lead to separation of different groups in society. Colour-blindness (resembling recategorisation) has the downside that it implies that everyone should adopt the norms of the dominant group.

Further reading

- Lemmer, G., & Wagner, U. (2015). Can we really reduce ethnic prejudice outside the lab? A meta-analysis of direct and indirect contact interventions. *European Journal of Social Psychology*, 45, 152–168. Gunnar Lemmer and Ulrih Wagner provide a thorough review of the effects of intergroup contact on prejudice in real-world settings.
- Richeson, J.A., & Sommers, S.R. (2016). Toward a social psychology of race and race relations for the twenty-first century. *Annual Review of Psychology*, 67, 439–463. This chapter is concerned with ways in which theory and research on race issues in the United States can be used for the benefit of society.
- Vaughan, G.M., & Hogg, M.A. (2014). *Social psychology* (7th ed.). London: Prentice Hall. Chapter 10 of this leading textbook in social psychology is concerned with prejudice and discrimination.

Essay questions

1. Define prejudice and discrimination. Why is the relationship between prejudice and discrimination relatively modest?
2. What are stereotypes and how can they be assessed? What functions do they serve?
3. What are the main factors leading to prejudice and discrimination?
4. What advice would you give to a government seeking to reduce prejudice and discrimination in society?

You must have met many people who were very helpful and cooperative and others who were the exact opposite. What reasons lead some individuals to behave in a prosocial or cooperative way? It is often claimed that people living in Western societies are more self-centred and less helpful than those in non-industrialised societies. Is that true or simply a myth?

Bystanders seeing someone needing help (e.g., someone injured while crossing the road) often fail to go to that person's assistance. Why do you think bystanders are often so reluctant to help? Is it a reflection of increased selfishness in contemporary society?

Prosocial behaviour

14

The central focus of this chapter is on cooperative and helpful behaviour and on the factors determining whether someone will behave in that way. **Prosocial behaviour** is any behaviour of benefit to someone else; it includes actions that are cooperative, affectionate, and helpful to others. Such behaviour may or may not be costly to the person engaging in such behaviour. In fact, it is often as beneficial to that person as to the person being assisted.

Altruism is an especially important type of prosocial behaviour. It is helping behaviour that is potentially costly to the individual being altruistic. In other words, altruism is based on a desire to help someone else rather than on possible rewards for the person doing the rewarding. It is often assumed altruism depends on **empathy** – the ability to share another's emotions and understand their point of view.

We will initially discuss factors involved in the development of prosocial behaviour in children. For example, when do young children start to show signs of wanting to help others?

After that, we will consider prosocial and altruistic behaviour from the evolutionary perspective. According to that perspective, prosocial behaviour helps to ensure the survival of the human species.

Most research on prosocial behaviour has been carried out in a small number of relatively affluent Western societies, differing markedly from most other human cultures. As a result, it is important to assess the similarities and differences in prosocial behaviour across numerous cultures.

It is often argued that most individuals in Western cultures are selfish and that this state of affairs is undesirable. As a result, it is important to devise ways of encouraging children and adults to engage in more prosocial behaviour. That is the fourth topic discussed in this chapter.

A form of prosocial behaviour that has been studied in detail is **bystander intervention**. Those who study bystander intervention want to understand the factors determining whether or not bystanders give help to a victim. This research is discussed later in the chapter.

KEY TERMS

Prosocial behaviour: behaviour that is positive (e.g., cooperative; affectionate) and that is designed to be of benefit to someone else.

Altruism: a form of prosocial behaviour that is generally costly to the altruistic person, and which is motivated by the desire to help someone else.

Empathy: the capacity to enter into another person's feelings and more generally to understand that person's perspective.

Bystander intervention: an area of research focusing on the reasons why bystanders to a crime or incident decide whether to help the victim.

Development of prosocial behaviour

Do young children exhibit prosocial behaviour? Several famous psychologists (including Freud and Piaget) emphasised children's tendency to engage in anti-social rather than prosocial behaviour. In the words of Schaffer (1996, p. 269), "The child emerged from these accounts as a selfish, self-centred, aggressive, and uncooperative being, with little . . . understanding of anyone else's needs."

Findings

This account provides an exaggerated account of children's selfishness. Zahn-Waxler et al. (1992) found children between 13 and 20 months showed empathic concern (e.g., sad or upset expression) on 10% of occasions on which someone else's distress was not caused by the child. This more than doubled among children 23–25 months old.

Zahn-Waxler et al. (1992) also found young children engaged in prosocial behaviour (e.g., sharing food; hugging) in response to another person's distress. There was a marked increase with age in prosocial behaviour in response to distress not caused by the child.

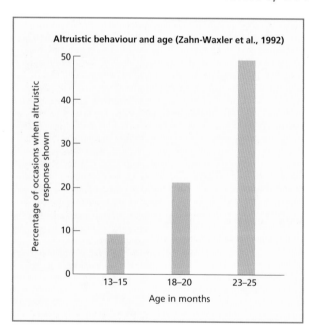

Altruistic behaviour and age (Zahn-Waxler et al., 1992)

Percentage of occasions when altruistic response shown

Age in months

Note that the prosocial behaviour of young children is typically limited in scope. Svetlova et al. (2010) studied three kinds of prosocial behaviour in 18- and 30-month-olds:

1. *Instrumental helping*: assisting another person to achieve an action-based goal (e.g., finding a toy).
2. *Empathic helping*: showing concern about another person.
3. *Altruistic helping*: giving up an object owned by the child.

The children showed much instrumental helping, rather less empathic helping, and little altruistic helping. The altruistic helping they exhibited was rarely costly and was mostly produced in response to an adult's direct request rather than spontaneous.

Much "helping" behaviour in young children is not based on cooperation and altruism. Instead it indicates an interest in participating in the activity of others (Carpendale et al., 2015). For example, my grandson Sebastian at the age of two insisted on helping his grandparents to tidy up the garden using his little spade and brush. His behaviour was helpful but seemed mostly motivated by the desire to behave in an adult-like way.

Individual differences

Which environmental factors produce individual differences in children's pro-social behaviour? Daniel et al. (2016) studied children between the ages of 18 and 54 months. Their key finding was that the mother's warmth and the father's warmth were both associated with increased prosocial behaviour by their offspring.

Genetic factors also play a role. Knafo et al. (2011) found 45% of individual differences in prosocial behaviour in young twins were due to genetic factors. In an earlier study, Knafo et al. (2008) focused on empathy (often associated with prosocial behaviour). In young children of 24 and 36 months, 25% of individual differences in empathy depended on genetic factors. In addition, the amount of prosocial behaviour shown by children depended in part on their empathy level.

Summary

Many infants display some prosocial behaviour below the age of 2, and the percentage increases rapidly thereafter. However, much of this behaviour does not indicate genuine altruism. Some of it is motivated by the wish to participate in the activity of others or to receive reward (e.g., parental attention and praise).

What explains altruism?

It is often argued that it is natural for individuals to behave selfishly to further their own ends. Why, then, do people sometimes behave unselfishly or altruistically? An influential account of altruistic behaviour has come from **evolutionary psychology**, an approach assuming human behaviour can be explained in evolutionary terms.

According to evolutionary psychologists, individuals are highly motivated to ensure their genes survive even if they are not consciously aware of it. Two concepts are important here: inclusive fitness and kin selection. **Inclusive fitness** is the notion that natural selection favours organisms that maximise replication of their genes. **Kin selection** is the notion that organisms are selected to favour their own offspring and other genetically related individuals. These notions are important for the following reason: "If a mother dies in the course of saving her three offspring from a predator, she will have saved 1½ times her own genes (since each offspring inherits one half of its mother's genes). So, in terms of genes, an act of apparent altruism can turn out to be extremely selfish" (Gross, 1996, p. 413).

Parents invest a lot of time and resources in their children, which may be explained by biological theories of relationships—the parents' chances of passing on their genes are improved if they can help their children to survive and succeed.

So far, we have seen why individuals might behave altruistically towards their own family. However, most people also behave altruistically towards non-relatives. Evolutionary psychologists explain this by **reciprocal altruism**: "I'll scratch your back if you scratch mine." Trivers (1971) argued reciprocal altruism is most likely to be found in two conditions:

1. The costs of helping are fairly low and the benefits are high.
2. We can identify those who cheat by receiving help but not helping in return.

> **KEY TERMS**
>
> **Evolutionary psychology:** an approach to psychology based on the assumption that much human behaviour can be explained by Darwin's theory of evolution.
>
> **Inclusive fitness:** the successful transmission of one's genes *directly* via reproduction and *indirectly* by helping genetically related individuals.
>
> **Kin selection:** helping genetically related relatives to enhance inclusive fitness.
>
> **Reciprocal altruism:** the notion that someone will show altruism in their behaviour towards someone else if they anticipate that person will respond altruistically.

Matters become more complicated when we consider that many individuals behave altruistically even when those they help are unlikely to reciprocate (return the favour). Why does this happen? Fehr and Fischbacher (2003) argued that it allows those individuals to gain a reputation for behaving altruistically. This increases the chances they will be assisted by others in the future.

Most societies have norms (socially accepted standards of behaviour) that involve treating others fairly. One example is the distribution norm (goods should be distributed equally). Suppose one person (X) is given some money and decides to give very little of it to another person (Y). You are person Z. If you believe strongly in the distribution norm, you might punish person X by removing some of their money even if it involved a sacrifice (e.g., of money) on your part. This is known as **third-party punishment** (Fehr & Fischbacher, 2004). Such punishment can reduce selfishness and increase cooperation.

Other evolutionary explanations of the origins of altruism have been put forward. Tomasello et al. (2012) proposed the interdependence hypothesis. According to this hypothesis, altruistic behaviour developed when our ancestors discovered the benefits of **mutualistic collaboration** (cooperation between people that is mutually beneficial). An example of such collaboration is the stag hunt. Imagine that in our ancestral past you and I were both hunting alone for small animals (e.g., hares). If either of us spots a stag, it is in both our interests to abandon our pursuit of hares and collaborate on killing the stag.

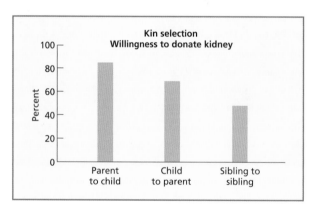

Findings

Much research shows the importance of genetic relatedness or kinship, especially in life-and-death situations. Fellner and Marshall (1981) found 86% of people were willing to be a kidney donor for their children, 67% would do the same for their parents, and 50% would be a kidney donor for their siblings.

Hackman et al. (2015) distinguished between emotional closeness and genetic relatedness. They asked participants how much money they would sacrifice to ensure a given other person (e.g., biological kin; friend) received $75 (£55). The amount sacrificed was greater for biological kin and friends to whom participants felt emotionally close. As predicted by the evolutionary approach, the amount sacrificed was greater for biological kin than friends when the effects of emotional closeness were removed.

Fehr and Fischbacher (2003) considered the role played by individuals' desire to have a reputation for altruism. Participants decided whether to help another person who could not reciprocate that help. Help was provided by 74% of those who could gain a reputation for altruism but by only 37% of those who could not. Bateson et al. (2006) also showed the impact of reputational concerns. Individuals making tea or coffee were supposed to put money in a box. As they did so, they saw a photo of a pair of eyes or flowers. They paid almost three times as much for their drinks when they saw a pair of eyes because this increased their concerns about their reputation for making a fair contribution.

Henrich et al. (2006) obtained evidence of third-party punishment in 15 cultures in Africa, North America, Asia, and Oceania. However, the percentage

KEY TERMS

Third-party punishment: punishing someone else who has treated a third party unfairly even though it involves a personal sacrifice.

Mutualistic collaboration: cooperation between two or more humans on a joint goal (e.g., survival) that is beneficial to all of them.

of individuals willing to lose their own money to punish others who violated the distribution norm varied. The incidence of third-party punishment was greatest in the most altruistic cultures, suggesting third-party punishment is an altruistic way of behaving.

Roos et al. (2014) argued that third-party punishment is most effective in groups characterised by strong social ties (individuals interact frequently) and low mobility (individuals cannot easily switch groups). In such conditions, recipients of third-party punishment have the strongest incentive to cooperate with other members of their group and to behave altruistically. Roos et al. discussed support for their argument based on research with various groups.

Would we expect to find basic forms of altruistic behaviour in other species? If such behaviour depends on complex socialisation processes, then the answer is, "No". However, if altruistic behaviour depends in part on biological processes rooted in our evolutionary past, then the answer might well be, "Yes". Warneken (2015) discussed evidence indicating chimpanzees show basic forms of altruism (e.g., helping humans pick up dropped objects; helping another chimpanzee by selecting the tool they need). This evidence supports the evolutionary approach. However, chimpanzees rarely exhibit altruistic behaviour spontaneously – it nearly always occurs when the other person or chimpanzee signals a need for help.

The emphasis of the evolutionary approach is on *general* principles underlying altruistic behaviour and so it de-emphasises individual differences. For example, John et al. (2008) found that individuals high in agreeableness (e.g., warmth; generosity) were much more altruistic than low scorers.

EVALUATION

➕ Evolutionary psychologists focus on the key issue of *why* altruism is so important to the human species.

➕ The evolutionary approach explains why costly altruistic behaviour is shown more often to close relatives than non-relatives.

➕ Evolutionary psychologists have provided plausible reasons for altruistic or unselfish behaviour towards non-relatives and even strangers. These reasons include reciprocal altruism, the desire to have a reputation for altruism, and the risk of third-party punishment.

➕ The presence of basic forms of altruism in chimpanzees supports the evolutionary approach.

➖ The evolutionary approach de-emphasises the role of environmental factors (e.g., parental support; socialisation) in producing altruistic behaviour in children (discussed later).

➖ The evolutionary approach largely ignores factors (e.g., emotional closeness; the individual's personality) that influence the extent to which an individual will behave altruistically in a given situation.

➖ The evolutionary approach minimises the role played by mutualistic collaboration in producing altruistic behaviour.

Is it the case that children in non-industrialised societies are given family responsibilities, and that this increases their altruism?

Cross-cultural differences

Most research on altruism and other forms of prosocial behaviour has been carried out in the United States. However, what is true in the American culture may well not be the case in other cultures. Evidence that the selfish approach dominant in the American culture differs from that of other cultures was reported by Whiting and Whiting (1975). They studied young children in six cultures: United States, India, Okinawa (a Japanese island), the Philippines, Mexico, and Kenya. A smaller percentage of American children were altruistic than in any other culture (especially Kenya).

How can we explain these findings? First, the emphasis on competition and personal success found in individualistic cultures (see Chapter 1) such as the United States and Okinawa reduces cooperation and altruism. Second, the emphasis in collectivistic cultures (e.g., Kenya; Mexico) on the group's needs rather than the individual's means children are often given major family responsibilities (e.g., caring for younger siblings) that develop altruistic behaviour.

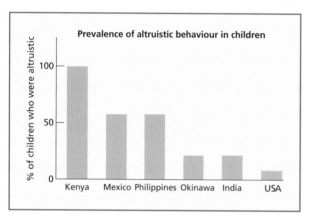

In spite of the differences between individualistic and collectivistic cultures, they are more similar than sometimes recognised. Fijneman et al. (1996) found those living in collectivistic cultures expect more help from others than those living in individualistic cultures. Both kinds of cultures are similar in that individuals anticipate giving only a little more help than they expect to receive. Thus, a norm of reciprocity or mutual exchange applies in both types of cultures and so they may differ relatively little in altruism.

Klein et al. (2015) discovered other similarities across seven countries (China, Russia, UK, USA, Turkey, Austria, and Denmark). Individuals who behaved generously were evaluated positively in all seven countries whereas those who behaved selfishly were evaluated negatively. Across all seven countries, negative evaluations were strongly influenced by the extent of another person's selfishness whereas positive evaluations were relatively insensitive to the extent of their generosity. The take-home message is that, "It pays to be nice, but pays no more to be really nice" (Klein et al., 2015, p. 361).

How can we explain these findings? If an individual behaves selfishly, we tend to interpret this as reflecting what they really think and feel. In contrast, an individual may behave generously because they wish to convey the impression of being kind-hearted rather than because they actually feel generous. If selfish behaviour tells us more about the other person than does generous behaviour, it is unsurprising that we are especially sensitive to very selfish behaviour.

EVALUATION

➕ There are substantial cross-cultural differences in prosocial behaviour and altruism.

➕ There is more apparently altruistic behaviour in collectivistic than individualistic cultures.

- Collectivistic cultures resemble individualistic ones in that most individuals expect to give only slightly more help than they receive.

- Most cultures are similar in that people are more sensitive to increasing levels of selfishness than to increasing levels of generosity.

- Collectivistic cultures differ in their levels of prosocial and altruistic behaviour, and the same is true of individualistic ones.

- What is true at the cultural level is generally not true at the level of all individuals within any given culture (see Chapter 1).

Factors influencing prosocial behaviour and altruism

How can children be encouraged to behave more prosocially? There are many answers, and we will consider a few of the more important ones.

Television

How do the effects of prosocial television programmes on prosocial behaviour compare to those of violent television programmes on aggressive behaviour?

Mares and Woodard (2005) reviewed 34 studies concerned with the effects on children's behaviour of watching prosocial television programmes. The effects were consistently moderately positive. This was especially the case when children viewed altruistic behaviour that was easy to imitate.

In spite of the existence of many studies showing that watching prosocial television is associated with increased prosocial behaviour (Valkenburg et al., 2016), there are two major limitations with much of the evidence. First, we cannot assume the only reason for this association is because watching prosocial television enhances prosocial behaviour. In addition, children who already display much prosocial behaviour are probably more likely than other children to watch prosocial television. Padilla-Walker et al. (2015) addressed this issue in a long-term or longitudinal study. Watching prosocial television increased subsequent prosocial behaviour *and* acting prosocially increased the amount of prosocial television watched.

Second, most studies have considered only short-term effects of prosocial television on prosocial behaviour. This is important because long-term effects are often rather weak or even non-existent (Sagotsky et al., 1981).

Video games

It is important to assess the impact of video games on behaviour given that there are several countries in which more than 80% of teenagers play such games. Greitemeyer and Mügge (2014) reviewed studies concerned with the effects of playing prosocial video games. Playing prosocial video games increased prosocial emotions, cognitions, and behaviour and also reduced aggressive behaviour. Most of the effects were reasonably consistent although relatively small in size.

Most studies simply show an association or correlation between playing prosocial games and prosocial behaviour. Such findings do not indicate causality – it could be that playing prosocial games enhances prosocial behaviour or that exhibiting prosocial behaviour leads to increased game playing

(Valkenburg et al., 2016). Gentile et al. (2009) reviewed studies indicating that the causality operates in both directions.

What processes cause the playing of prosocial video games to increase prosocial behaviour? Prot et al. (2014) carried out a two-year study across seven countries. Increases in prosocial-video-game use were followed by increased prosocial behaviour in all seven countries, suggesting that the former caused the latter. This effect occurred in part because increased prosocial-video-game use led to an increase in empathy (understanding of another person's feelings).

IN THE REAL WORLD: parental influence

For the great majority of children, their parents are easily the most important adults in their lives. How can parents promote prosocial behaviour in their offspring? Schaffer (1996) argued that several types of parental behaviour are of special value in teaching children to be prosocial and altruistic, including the following factors:

1. *Provisions of clear and explicit guidelines* (e.g., "You mustn't hit other people because you will hurt and upset them").
2. *Emotional convictions:* guidelines to children should be given in a fairly emotional way.
3. *Parental modeling*: parents should behave altruistically towards their children.
4. *Empathic and warm parenting*: parents should have a good understanding of their children's needs and emotions.

There is support for all these parental factors. With respect to the first factor, Krevans and Gibbs (1996) found children exhibited more prosocial behaviour when their mothers repeatedly told them to consider the effects of their behaviour on others. With respect to the second factor, children showed altruistic behaviour twice as often (42% vs. 21% of occasions) when their mother frequently used emotional explanations. With respect to the third factor, Burleseon and Kunkel (2002) found that mothers' comforting skills predicted their children's emotional support skills. With respect to the fourth factor, Robinson et al. (1994) found children having a warm and loving relationship with their parents were most likely to show prosocial behaviour. In a study by Davidov and Grusec (2004), mothers' responsiveness to distress (e.g., encouraging their children to discuss their troubles) predicted the children's empathic capacity and prosocial behaviour towards distressed others.

As we have seen, parents have a major influence on children's prosocial behaviour. However, we must not exaggerate the extent of that influence because genetic factors are also very important. Knafo-Noam et al. (2015) carried out a twin study and discovered 69% of individual differences in children's prosociality were due to genetic factors. Knafo and Plomin (2008) found that children's prosocial behaviour was negatively associated with parental negativity (e.g., punitive discipline). Of importance, this association was due in part to genetic factors. For example, children genetically predisposed to be low in prosociality may increase the likelihood of their parents responding negatively to them. Children's prosocial behaviour was positively associated with parental positivity (e.g., expressing positive feelings) but this association did not depend on genetic factors.

OVERALL EVALUATION

➕ Evidence from longitudinal (long-term) studies indicates that watching prosocial television programmes and/or playing prosocial video games slightly increases prosocial behaviour.

➕ Several types of parental behaviour that increase their children's prosocial behaviour have been identified.

➖ Some of the effects of prosocial television and playing prosocial video games are relatively small and may not be long-lasting.

➖ Some of the association between prosocial television programmes and children's prosocial behaviour (and between prosocial video games and prosocial behaviour) occurs because prosocial children are more likely to watch such programmes and play such games.

➖ There has been a tendency to exaggerate the impact of environmental factors on children's prosocial behaviour. There is much evidence that genetic factors are also important.

Bystander effect

A haunting image of our time is of someone being attacked violently in the middle of a city with no-one coming to their assistance. Consider the case of Kitty Genovese, who was stabbed to death as she returned home at 3 a.m. on 13 March 1964. According to the *New York Times*, 38 witnesses saw Kitty Genovese being attacked three times over a 30-minute period. However, no-one intervened, and only one person called the police.

There is just one problem with this account – it is grossly exaggerated. In fact, only *three* people saw either of the stabbings (there were two not three). Even those three eyewitnesses saw Kitty being attacked for only a few seconds (Manning et al., 2007).

Darley and Latané (1968) were very interested in the Kitty Genovese case (but did not realise how distorted the newspaper account was). This led them to initiate research on the **bystander effect** (the reluctance for bystanders to provide assistance to the victim of a crime or incident). Darley and Latané hypothesised that a victim is less likely to receive help when there are several bystanders rather than one. Why is this? Their answer was **diffusion of responsibility** – when several bystanders are present, each one bears only a small portion of the blame for not helping.

Kitty Genovese.

Is a bystander more or less likely to help a victim if there are several other bystanders?

KEY TERMS

Bystander effect: the finding that a victim is less likely to be helped as the number of bystanders increases.

Diffusion of responsibility: the larger the number of bystanders who observe what happens to a victim, the less the sense of personal responsibility to help experienced by each one.

Findings

Darley and Latané (1968) obtained support for their hypothesis in a study in which participants were placed in separate rooms. They believed they were taking part in a discussion when they heard one of the other people in the discussion apparently having an epileptic fit. Of those participants thinking they were the only person to hear the epileptic fit, 100% left the room and reported the emergency. In contrast, only 62% of participants responded if they thought five other bystanders had heard the fit, and those who responded took longer than participants thinking they were the only bystander.

Darley and Latané (1968) reported two other findings. First, participants who believed there were five other bystanders denied this had influenced their behaviour. Thus, they were not fully aware of the factors determining their behaviour. Second, those participants who failed to report the emergency were not uncaring. Most had trembling hands and sweating palms and seemed more emotionally aroused than participants who reported the emergency.

Is it always bad news for victims when there are several bystanders rather than only one? The answer is, "No". In Darley and Latané's (1968) research, the bystanders did not know each other. Fischer et al. (2011) reviewed research in which the bystanders knew each other beforehand. The likelihood of a victim being helped increased when there were more bystanders who knew each other. Thus, there can be strength in numbers (rather than diffusion of responsibility) when bystanders share social relationships.

Several other factors influence bystanders' behaviour, and we will briefly mention five. First, bystanders are more likely to help a victim perceived as *similar* to themselves. Levine (2002) found victims were more likely to receive help when they were described as belonging to the bystanders' ingroup (with which they identified) rather than to an outgroup. Second, bystanders are more likely to help "deserving" victims. A man who staggered and collapsed on a New York subway was more likely to be helped if he appeared to be sober rather than drunk (Piliavin et al., 1969).

Third, bystanders are reluctant to become involved in strangers' personal lives. Bystanders witnessing a fight between a man and a woman were *three* times more likely to intervene when they thought the fight involved strangers rather than a married couple (Shotland & Straw, 1976). Fourth, bystanders' willingness to help depends on what they were doing before the incident. Batson et al. (1978) used a situation in which participants passed a male student slumped on the stairs coughing and groaning as they were on

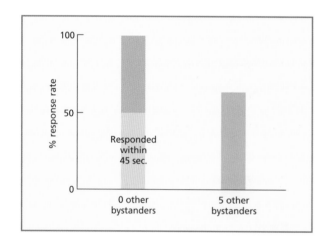

Bystanders who have some relevant skill to offer are more likely to get involved than those who don't know what to do.

their way to perform a task. Only 10% of those told their task was important stopped to assist the student compared to 80% told the task was trivial. Fifth, bystanders with relevant skills or expertise (e.g., first-aid) are especially likely to provide assistance (Huston et al., 1981).

What can be done to increase bystander intervention? One simple approach is to provide people with detailed information about the factors that inhibit helping behaviour in emergency situations. Beaman et al. (1978) found that a man sprawled across a wall received help from 42% of bystanders following the provision of such information compared to only 25% who had received the information.

Arousal: cost-reward model

According to the arousal: cost-reward model, when does a bystander give help?

Fischer et al. (2011) reviewed research on the bystander effect. They found the bystander effect was smaller when the situation was perceived as dangerous rather than non-dangerous, when the perpetrator (person responsible for harming the victim) was present, and when the costs of intervention were physical rather than non-physical.

How can we explain these (and other) findings relating to the bystander effect? Piliavin et al.'s (1981) arousal: cost-reward model can be used to provide an answer. According to this model, bystanders go through five stages before deciding whether to assist a victim:

1. Becoming aware of someone's need for help; this depends on attention.
2. Experience of arousal.
3. Interpreting cues and labeling their state of arousal.
4. Working out the rewards and costs associated with different actions.
5. Making a decision and acting on it.

Findings

How can this model explain the lack of a bystander effect with dangerous situations? According to the model, dangerous situations should be recognised faster as real emergencies (Stage 1). This produces heightened arousal (Stage 2), which is then interpreted as indicating a serious emergency (Stage 3). As a result, bystanders observing a dangerous situation provide assistance, which serves to reduce their arousal level.

Research discussed earlier indicates the importance of various rewards and costs associated with helping or not helping:

- *Costs of helping*: Physical harm, delay in carrying out other activities (Piliavin et al., 1969; Batson et al., 1978).
- *Costs of not helping*: Ignoring personal responsibility, guilt, criticism from friends, ignoring perceived similarity (Darley & Latané, 1968; Fischer et al., 2011; Levine, 2002).
- *Rewards of helping*: Praise from victim, satisfaction from having been useful when relevant skills are possessed (Huston et al., 1981).
- *Rewards of not helping*: Able to continue with other activities as normal (Batson et al., 1978).

EVALUATION

➕ The model provides a comprehensive account of factors influencing bystanders' behaviour when an incident occurs.

➕ As predicted by the model, there is much more evidence for a bystander effect with non-dangerous situations than dangerous ones.

➕ The model argues correctly that various potential rewards and costs associated with helping or not helping strongly influence bystanders' behaviour.

➖ The model emphasises the notion that bystanders engage in *deliberate* processing when observing an emergency situation. This is oversimplified. For example, there is less *automatic* activation of brain regions concerned with action preparation when several other bystanders are present (Hortensius & de Gelder, 2014). This helps to explain the bystander effect. In addition, bystanders often respond impulsively and without deliberation.

➖ It is not essential for bystanders to become aroused for them to provide help to a victim. Bystanders with much relevant experience (e.g., a doctor observing someone have a heart attack) may provide efficient help without becoming very aroused.

Chapter summary

- Young children under the age of 2 exhibit much prosocial behaviour (especially instrumental helping). However, altruistic helping is rare, and much apparently helping behaviour is motivated by an interest in participating in the activity of others.
- Differences among children in empathy and prosocial behaviour depend on environmental factors (e.g., parental warmth) and genetic factors.
- According to evolutionary psychologists, altruistic behaviour is motivated by a desire to maximise replication of one's genes. Other reasons for altruistic behaviour include the desire to gain a reputation for behaving altruistically and third-party punishment.
- The evolutionary approach de-emphasises environmental factors influencing children's prosocial and altruistic behaviour.
- Altruistic behaviour is more common in collectivistic than in individualistic cultures. This occurs in part because individuals in collectivistic cultures expect to receive more help.
- Watching prosocial behaviour on television and playing prosocial video games can increase children's and adolescents' prosocial behaviour by increasing empathy and the accessibility of prosocial thoughts. However, the beneficial effects on behaviour are often short-lived.
- Parents can encourage prosocial behaviour in their children by providing clear guidelines in an emotional way, by behaving altruistically themselves, and by providing warm and empathic parenting.
- Some of the associations between parental behaviour and children's prosocial behaviour are due in part to genetic factors rather than purely environmental ones.
- Bystanders often fail to assist a victim because of diffusion of responsibility. Bystander intervention is more likely when the bystanders are friends, when the victim is similar to them, or when he/she seems deserving of assistance.
- According to the arousal: cost-reward model, bystanders decide what to do after working out the rewards and costs associated with different actions.
- The finding that bystanders often respond rapidly without engaging in a complex assessment of rewards and costs seems somewhat inconsistent with the arousal: cost-reward model.

Further reading

- Feygina, I., & Henry, P.J. (2015). Culture and prosocial behaviour. In D.A. Schroeder & W.G. Graziano (Eds.), *The Oxford handbook of prosocial behaviour* (pp. 188–208). Oxford: Oxford University Press. Cultural similarities and differences in prosocial behaviour are discussed fully by Irina Feygina and Patrick Henry.

- Fischer, P., Krueger, J.I., Greitemeyer, T., Vogrincic, C., Kastenmuller, A., Frey, D., et al. (2011). The bystander effect: A meta-analytic review on bystander intervention in dangerous and non-dangerous emergences. *Psychological Bulletin, 137*, 517–537. Peter Fischer and his colleagues provide a thorough review of research on bystander intervention.

- Vaughan, G.M., & Hogg, M.A. (2014). *Social psychology* (7th ed.). London: Prentice Hall. There is comprehensive coverage of research and theory on prosocial behaviour in Chapter 13 of this leading textbook.

- Warneken, F. (2016). Insights into the biological foundation of human altruistic sentiments. *Current Opinion in Psychology, 7*, 51–56. Felix Warneken discusses how biology and socialisation combine to produce prosocial behaviour in young children.

Essay questions

1. How do evolutionary psychologists account for altruistic behaviour? What are the strengths and limitations of this account?

2. Describe cross-cultural differences and similarities in altruistic or prosocial behaviour. How can we explain these cross-cultural findings?

3. What recommendations would you make for increasing children's prosocial behaviour?

4. When are bystanders likely to help a victim? When are they unlikely to help a victim?

Humans are social animals who spend much of their time interacting with other people. How far are we willing to go to fit in with the expectations of others? For example, would you go along with the views of the members of a group even though you were confident they were wrong? Would you obey the orders of an authority figure if you thought the orders were mistaken? In what circumstances are you most likely to obey authority figures? Why do people in crowds often behave differently from how they behave on their own?

Social influence 15

What we say and *how* we behave are influenced by other people. We want to be liked and to fit into society. As a result, we often hide what we really think and try to behave in ways that will meet the approval of others. Research by social psychologists has shown that we are influenced much more by other people than we think we are. This is **social influence**, "the process whereby attitudes and behaviour are influenced by the real or implied presence of other people" (Vaughan & Hogg, 2014, p. 214).

In this chapter, we consider the main ways social influence manifests itself. These include conformity behaviour, obedience to authority, groupthink, group polarisation, social power, and crowd behaviour.

Conformity

Conformity involves yielding to group pressure, something nearly all of us do sometimes. Suppose, for example, you go with friends to see a movie. You did not enjoy it much, but all your friends thought it was brilliant. You might be tempted to conform by pretending to agree with their verdict on the movie rather than being the odd one out.

Most textbook writers argue that conformity is undesirable. However, conformity sometimes makes sense. Suppose your friends who are also studying psychology have the same view on a given topic in psychology, but it differs from yours. If they know more about the topic, it is probably a good idea to conform to their views!

Solomon Asch: majority influence

Solomon Asch (1951, 1956) carried out the best-known research on conformity. He used a situation in which several people (typically seven) sat looking at a display. Their task was to say aloud which one of three lines (A, B, and C) was the same length as a given stimulus line, with the experimenter working his way around the group members in turn. This was a very easy task (99% of judgments were correct under control conditions).

All group members (except for one genuine participant) were confederates working with the experimenter and had been told to give the same wrong

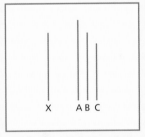

Asch showed lines like the above to his participants. Which line do you think is the closest in height to line X? A, B, or C? Why do you think over 30% of participants answered A?

KEY TERMS

Social influence: efforts by individuals or groups to change the attitudes and/or behaviour of others.

Conformity: changes in behaviour and/or attitudes that occur in response to group pressure.

answers on some trials. The only genuine participant was the last (or last but one) to provide his/her opinion.

Findings

In what type of culture is Asch's conformity effect stronger?

What do you think the genuine participants did when faced with the conflict between what the other group members said and what they knew was the right answer on this very easy task? They gave the wrong answer on 37% of these critical trials. Only 25% of participants made no errors throughout the experiment. Conformity increased as the number of confederates increased from one to three but did not increase after that (Asch, 1956).

Although Asch's research is famous within social psychology, there was not anything very social about it – he used groups of strangers! Abrams et al. (1990) studied the role of social factors using psychology students as participants. The confederates were said to be psychology students from a nearby university or students of ancient history.

Abrams et al. (1990) predicted that participants would exhibit more conformity when the confederates appeared similar to them. In these circumstances, participants would have more identity with the group and would be motivated to maintain group cohesion by conforming. As predicted, there was conformity on 58% of trials when the confederates were described as psychology students but only 8% when they were described as students of ancient history.

Asch's research was carried out in the United States in the late 1940s and early 1950s. Since then, there has been a significant increase in people's need for social approval, and so we might expect conformity levels to have reduced over time. That is, indeed, the case. However, even recent studies have produced clear conformity effects (Smith & Bond, 1993).

We would expect greater conformity in collectivistic cultures (which emphasise group belongingness) than individualistic ones (which emphasise personal responsibility). As predicted, conformity is greater in collectivistic cultures in Asia, Africa, and elsewhere (37% of trials) than individualistic cultures in North America and Europe (25%) (Bond & Smith, 1996b).

When does conformity break down? The findings were very different when *one* confederate gave the correct answer (Asch, 1956). In those conditions, conformity occurred on only 5% of trials. The comforting feeling of not being entirely isolated made it much easier for the participants to avoid conforming.

Why does conformity occur?

Deutsch and Gerard (1955) identified two reasons why individuals conform in Asch-type studies. First, there is **normative influence**: they conform to be liked or respected by group members. There was strong normative influence in the study by Abrams et al. (1990; discussed earlier) when the other group members were perceived as similar to the participants.

Second, there is **informational influence**: they conform because of others' superior knowledge. For example, Lucas et al. (2006) found participants who doubted their mathematical ability showed greater conformity through informational influence than those with more confidence in their mathematical ability when the task involved hard mathematical problems.

KEY TERMS

Normative influence: conformity based on people's desire to be liked and/or respected by others.

Informational influence: conformity based on the perceived superior knowledge or judgment of others.

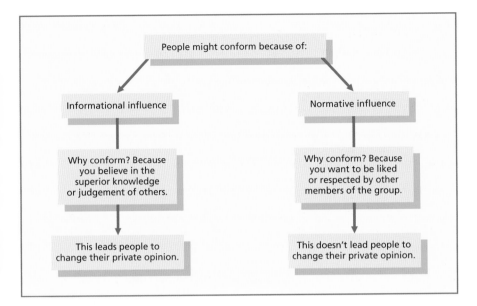

People might conform because of:

Informational influence

Why conform? Because you believe in the superior knowledge or judgement of others.

This leads people to change their private opinion.

Normative influence

Why conform? Because you want to be liked or respected by other members of the group.

This doesn't lead people to change their private opinion.

Bond (2005) reviewed 125 Asch-type studies. Normative influence was stronger when participants made public responses and were face-to-face with the majority (as in Asch's research). In contrast, informational influence was stronger when participants made private responses and communicated only indirectly with the majority.

Erb et al. (2002) found normative influence was dominant when an individual's previously formed opinions were strongly opposed to the majority. However, the influence was mostly informational when an individual's previous opinions differed only moderately from those of the other group members. Thus, the extent of conflict between an individual's opinions and those of the group determines the type of influence that is dominant.

Theoretical considerations

It is often argued that participants in Asch's studies had a moral obligation to tell the truth. From that perspective, it is regrettable that 75% produced the wrong answer in response to group pressure at least once and so exhibited mindless conformity. In fact, this argument is flawed in various ways.

First, we must not overstate the amount of conformity. Nearly 70% defied the group on over 50% of trials, and 25% did not conform at all. Thus, we have to explain lack of conformity as well as conformity.

Second, Asch found many participants became aroused and somewhat distressed. Thus, they were aware of a conflict between producing the correct answer and their desire not to ignore the group.

Third, the behaviour of most participants can be regarded as entirely reasonable. It makes sense for an individual to regard the unanimous judgments of all other group members as providing useful information (Toelch & Dolan, 2015). Of great importance, most participants provided a mixture of incorrect and correct answers. Their incorrect answers allowed them to avoid being disrespectful to other group members and to exhibit group solidarity (Hodges, 2014). Their correct answers allowed them to show their perceptual accuracy and perhaps persuade other group members to reconsider their judgments (Hodges, 2014). Perhaps Asch's participants should be praised rather than criticised!

EVALUATION

➕ There is much more conformity than most people would predict on such an easy task in which the correct answer is obvious.

➕ Several factors influencing conformity (e.g., number of confederates; presence vs. absence of a supporter; type of culture) have been identified.

➕ Many findings can be explained by normative and informational influence.

➖ Asch used a trivial task in which participants' deeply held beliefs were not called into question.

➖ The behaviour of most participants on Asch-type tasks has been criticised. However, their behaviour can be seen as an effective way of showing respect to the other group members and also exhibiting accurate visual perception.

Is conversion or compliance involved when a majority influences a minority?

Serge Moscovici: minority influence

Asch studied the influence of the majority on a minority (typically of one) within a group. However, minorities can also influence majorities. Serge Moscovici is a central figure in research on minority influence and so we will focus on his contribution.

Moscovici (1980) addressed the issue of how a majority influences a majority in his dual-process theory. In this theory, he distinguished between compliance and conversion. **Compliance** is often involved when a majority influences a minority. It is based on the majority's power and usually involves public (but not necessarily private) agreement with the majority. Compliance often occurs rapidly and without much thought.

Conversion is how a minority can influence a majority. It involves convincing the majority that the minority's views are correct. This is most likely to occur under the following conditions:

1. *Consistency*: the minority must be consistent in their viewpoint.
2. *Flexibility*: the minority must not appear to be rigid and dogmatic in how they present their viewpoint.
3. *Commitment*: a committed minority will lead the majority to re-think their position.

Conversion often produces private as well as public agreement among majority members. It is generally more time-consuming than compliance and occurs after cognitive conflict and much thought.

KEY TERMS

Compliance: the influence of a majority on a minority based on its power; this influence is generally on public behaviour rather than private beliefs.

Conversion: the influence of a minority on a majority based on convincing the majority that its views are correct; this influence is on private beliefs more than public behaviour.

Findings

Wood et al. (1994) identified three conformity effects predicted by Moscovici's dual-process theory:

1. *Public influence*: in which the individual's behaviour in front of the group is influenced by others' views. This should occur mostly when majorities influence minorities.
2. *Direct private influence*: in which there is a change in the individual's private opinions about the issue discussed by the group. This should be found mainly when minorities influence majorities.
3. *Indirect private influence*: in which the individual's private opinions about related issues change. This should also be found mostly when majorities are influenced by minorities.

Wood et al. (1994) reviewed studies relevant to these three effects. As predicted, majorities in most studies had more public influence than minorities. Also as predicted, minorities had more indirect private influence than majorities, especially when their opinions were consistent. However, majorities had more direct private influence than minorities, which is contrary to Moscovici's theory.

Nemeth et al. (1990) found minorities can make group members engage in more thorough processing than majorities as predicted by Moscovici. Participants listened to word lists. The majority or the minority consistently drew attention to words belonging to certain categories. There was then a recall test for the words. There was much better recall when a minority had drawn attention to them, presumably because they had been processed more thoroughly.

David and Turner (1999) argued minority influence will be found *only* when the minority is perceived as part of the ingroup. The participants were moderate feminists exposed to the minority views of extreme feminists. These views influenced the participants when the situation was set up as feminists vs. non-feminists – the extreme feminists were part of the ingroup. The views of the extreme feminists had little impact when there was a contrast between a moderate feminist majority and an outgroup of extreme feminists.

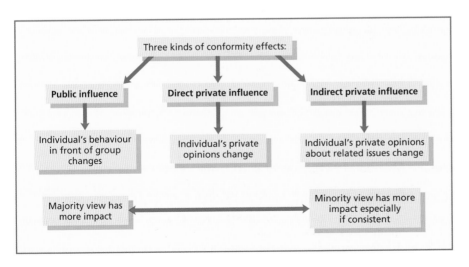

EVALUATION

➕ Minorities often influence majorities.

➕ The influence of minorities on majorities is mainly in the form of private rather than public agreement. The opposite pattern is found when majorities influence minorities.

➖ Minorities generally differ from minorities in several ways (e.g., power; status). Differences in the social influence exerted by majorities and minorities may depend on their power or status rather than on their majority or minority position within the group.

➖ Moscovici exaggerated the differences between majority and minority influence. As Smith and Mackie (2000, p. 371) pointed out, "Minorities are influential when their dissent offers a consensus, avoids contamination [i.e., obvious bias], and triggers private acceptance – the same processes by which all groups achieve influence."

Obedience to authority

In nearly all societies, certain people are given power and authority over others. In our society, parents, teachers, and managers are invested with varying degrees of authority. This generally makes sense – if a doctor tells us to take some tablets three times a day, he/she is the expert, and we do as are told without thinking any more about it.

Obedience to authority resembles conformity in that both involve social influence. However, research on obedience to authority differs in three ways from research on conformity. First, the participants are ordered to behave in certain ways rather than being fairly free to decide what to do. Second, the participant is typically of lower status than the person issuing the orders, whereas in conformity research the participant is usually of equal status to the other group members. Third, participants' behaviour in obedience studies is determined by **social power**, whereas in conformity studies it is influenced mostly by the need for acceptance.

It is important to see how far individuals are willing to go in obeying an authority figure. What would happen if you were asked to do something wrong? The best-known attempt to answer that question was by Stanley Milgram (see the next section).

Did Milgram's research on obedience to authority produce more or less obedience than most people predicted?

Stanley Milgram

In Milgram's studies at Yale University in the early 1960s (reported in book form by Milgram, 1974), pairs of participants were used in a simple learning task. The "teacher" gave electric shocks to the "learner" for wrong answers, increasing the shock intensity each time. At 180 volts, the learner yelled, "I can't stand the pain!" and by 270 volts his only response was an agonised scream. The maximum shock was 450 volts.

Would you give the maximum (and potentially deadly) 450-volt shock in this situation? Psychiatrists at a leading medical school predicted only one

KEY TERM

Social power: the force that can be used by an individual to change the attitudes and/or behaviour of other people.

The photographs show the electric shock machine used in Milgram's classic experiment where 65% of the participants gave a potentially lethal shock to the "learner", shown in the bottom left photograph. The learner was actually a confederate of the experimenter, a 47-yearold accountant called "Mr Wallace". The photographs show the experimenter (in the overall) and the true participant, the "teacher".

person in a thousand would go to the 450-volt stage. In fact, 65% of Milgram's participants gave the maximum shock – 650 times as many as the expert psychiatrists had predicted!

Milgram found two main ways that obedience to authority could be reduced:

1. Increasing the obviousness of the learner's plight.
2. Reducing the authority or influence of the experimenter.

The first way was studied by comparing obedience in four situations (the percentage of totally obedient participants is in brackets):

- *Remote feedback*: the victim could not be seen or heard, but his thumping on the wall could be heard (66%).
- *Voice feedback*: the victim could be heard but not seen (62%),
- *Proximity*: the victim was only 1 metre away from the participant (40%).
- *Touch-proximity*: this was like the proximity condition, except the participant had to force the learner's hand onto the shock-plate (30%).

In one experiment, Milgram reduced the authority of the experimenter by carrying out the experiment in a run-down office building rather than at Yale University. The percentage of obedient participants went down from 65% at Yale University to 48% in the run-down building. When the experimenter's influence was reduced by having him give orders by phone, obedience fell to only 20%.

All the factors discussed earlier were effective in reducing obedience because they increased the extent to which participants identified with the learner/victim (Reicher et al., 2012). In contrast, reducing the obviousness of the learner's plight and increasing the experimenter's authority led to greater obedience because participants identified with the experimenter (Reicher et al., 2012).

Reducing obedience to authority was achieved by:			
Increasing the obviousness of the learner's plight...		**Reducing the authority or influence of the experimenter...**	
		at Yale University	65%
victim not seen or heard	66%	at a run-down office	48%
victim not seen but heard	62%	with experimenter sitting next to participant	65%
victim one metre away	40%	with experimenter giving orders via telephone	20.5%
victim's hand placed on shock plate	30%	when confederates of experimenter refused to give shocks	10%

Very high levels of obedience were reported in most research using Milgram's set-up. The percentage of totally obedient participants was 80% or more in Italy, Spain, Germany, Austria, and Holland (Bond & Smith, 1996a).

Reasons for obedience

Burger (2011) argued that Milgram only obtained high levels of obedience because of several features of his situation. First, the experimenter told concerned participants he took full responsibility for what happened. This is very important because there is much less obedience when participants are told they are responsible for any harm (Tilker, 1970).

Second, it was only when participants delivered the *tenth* shock that the learner first protested. More participants would have refused to obey the experimenter if the learner's anguish had been obvious earlier.

Third, the shocks increased slowly in 15-volt increments. This made it hard for participants to notice when they were being asked to behave unreasonably.

Real-life situations

Milgram's studies were laboratory-based. However, similar findings have been obtained in the real world. In a study by Hofling et al. (1966), nurses were phoned up by someone claiming to be Dr. Smith. He instructed them to give 20 mg of a drug called Astroten to a patient. The nurses should have refused because they did not know Dr. Smith and the dose was much higher than the maximum safe dose. However, 95% of the nurses obeyed the instruction.

Similar findings were obtained in a study on medication errors in American hospitals (Lesar et al., 1997). However, Rank and Jacobsen (1977) found only 11% of nurses obeyed a doctor's instructions to give an overdose of Valium to patients. This low level of obedience occurred because the nurses discussed the issue with other nurses before deciding what to do.

KEY TERM

Agentic state: feeling controlled by an authority figure and therefore lacking a sense of personal responsibility.

Theoretical considerations

Milgram (1974) argued that a key reason why so many people were fully obedient in his situation is because they were in an **agentic state**. In this state, they became the instrument of an authority figure (i.e., the experimenter) and so ceased to act according to their conscience. Someone in an agentic state thinks, "I am not responsible because I was ordered to do it!" As we saw earlier, Milgram explicitly told many participants that he would accept full responsibility if anything went wrong – thus, he loaded the dice in favour of his agentic state theory.

According to Milgram, this tendency to adopt the agentic state "is the fatal flaw nature has designed into us". This led him to claim there were links between his findings and the horrors of Nazi Germany. Milgram's claims are exaggerated. Many participants were very tense and distressed, which suggests they had not surrendered all personal responsibility. These participants experienced a strong conflict between the experimenter's demands and their own conscience, whereas most Nazis seemed unconcerned about moral issues.

There are other important differences. First, the values underlying Milgram's studies were the positive ones of understanding more about human learning and memory in contrast to the vile ideas of racial superiority in Nazi Germany. Second, most participants in Milgram's studies had to be watched closely to ensure their obedience, which was not necessary in Nazi Germany.

Haslam et al. (2015) favoured a different explanation for obedience in the Milgram situation. They argued that many participants identified with the experimenter and with the scientific goals underpinning the experiment. In essence, they displayed "engaged followership" rather than the passive obedience emphasised by Milgram. This interpretation was supported by participants' reports after taking part in Milgram's research. Almost half were highly engaged in the experiment and were positive about their involvement.

Haslam et al. (2015, p. 79) concluded as follows: "People are able to inflict harm on others not because they are unaware that they are doing wrong, but rather because – as engaged followers – they know full well what they are doing and *believe it to be right*."

EVALUATION

➕ Milgram's important findings are among the most surprising in the history of psychology (although less surprising when you consider in detail the set-up of his research).

➕ Milgram's findings are of direct relevance to many everyday situations (e.g., doctor and nurse interactions).

➖ There are limitations with Milgram's notion of an agentic state – most participants found it emotionally distressing to obey the experimenter.

➖ Milgram de-emphasised the extent to which his participants were motivated by "engaged followership".

➖ Milgram exaggerated the extent to which his findings apply to the horrors of Nazi Germany.

➖ There are serious ethical problems with Milgram's research. Participants did not give their informed consent and weren't free to leave the experiment if they wanted to.

Group decision making

It is often believed that groups tend to be more cautious than individuals in their decision making. For example, it may be that group decisions reflect the average views of all (or most) of its members. In fact, what typically happens is **group polarisation**, "the tendency for group discussion to produce more extreme group decisions than the mean of members' pre-discussion opinions" (Vaughan & Hogg, 2014, p. 314).

What factors influence group polarisation? First, there is social comparison. Individuals want to be positively evaluated by other group members. If they see other group members endorsing positions closer to some socially desired goal than their own, they will change their position towards that goal. Isenberg (1986) reviewed numerous studies. Social comparison had a reasonably strong effect on group polarisation, especially when value- or emotion-laden issues were discussed rather than factual ones.

Second, group polarisation is influenced by persuasive arguments. Suppose most group members initially favour a given type of decision. During the discussion, individuals are likely to hear new arguments supporting their position (Larson et al., 1994). As a result, their views will often become more extreme. Isenberg's (1986) review indicated persuasive arguments produced more group polarisation with factual than emotional issues.

Third, members of an ingroup often want to distinguish their group from other groups. Suppose an ingroup has a confrontation with a cautious outgroup (not part of the ingroup). They can distinguish themselves from that group by becoming riskier in their decision making (Hogg et al., 1990). In similar fashion, an ingroup encountering a risky outgroup can distinguish itself by becoming more cautious (Hogg et al., 1990).

Groupthink

Is groupthink found more in groups with a strong or a weak leader? Is it useful or dangerous?

The processes leading to group polarisation can have serious consequences. This is especially the case when groups engage in **groupthink**, "a mode of thinking in highly cohesive groups in which the desire to reach unanimous agreement overrides the motivation to adopt proper rational decision-making procedures" (Vaughan & Hogg, 2014, p. 312). Features of groupthink include suppression of dissent, exaggerating the group consensus, and a sense of group invulnerability.

Groupthink has led to catastrophic decisions in the real world. For example, Sorkin (2009) analysed factors behind the near-collapse of several very large American banks in 2008. There was a culture of risk taking that produced huge profits for a few years. Individuals in those banks working on risk assessment who expressed concerns about the excessive risks the banks were taking were ignored or sacked.

Janis (1982) argued that *five* factors increase the chances of groupthink occurring:

1. The group is very cohesive.
2. The group considers only a few options.
3. The group is isolated from information coming from outside the group.
4. There is much stress (e.g., time pressure; threatening circumstances).
5. The group is dominated by a very directive leader.

KEY TERMS

Group polarisation: the tendency of groups to produce fairly extreme decisions.

Groupthink: group pressure to achieve general agreement in groups in which dissent is suppressed; it can lead to disastrous decisions.

Findings

Tetlock et al. (1992) considered eight of the real-world cases Janis (1982) used to support his groupthink theory. Groups showing groupthink typically had a strong leader and much conformity. Contrary to Janis's theory, groups showing groupthink were generally *less* cohesive than other groups, and exposure to stressful circumstances was not an important factor. In the workplace, high group cohesion is associated with positive outcomes such as greater loyalty and increased productivity (Haslam et al., 2006).

Baron (2005) argued (with strong supporting evidence) that groupthink symptoms (e.g., suppression of dissent) are present in most groups (not only those making catastrophic decisions). Peterson et al. (1998) studied top management teams when making good and bad decisions. Contrary to Janis' theory, the symptoms of groupthink were present almost as much during good as poor decision making.

Baron (2005) reviewed research on the five factors Janis (1982) identified as leading to groupthink. He argued these factors sometimes increase the chances of groupthink occurring. However, they are not *necessary* for groupthink to occur because most groups naturally strive for consensus even in their absence.

Baron (2005) concluded that groups making good and bad decisions often use the same processes. What, then, determines whether a group's decision making is good or bad? Much depends on the quality of shared knowledge within a group. Bad decisions are mostly made by groups possessing biased or task-inappropriate shared knowledge whereas good decisions are made by groups with unbiased and appropriate knowledge (Tindale et al., 2012).

EVALUATION

➕ Groupthink has played a role in many real-world catastrophic decisions.

➕ As Janis predicted, factors such as a strong leader and pressures towards conformity increases the chances of groupthink.

➖ Janis exaggerated the roles of group cohesion and exposure to threatening circumstances in producing groupthink.

➖ The symptoms of groupthink are present in most groups (successful as well as unsuccessful) and are found far more often than assumed by Janis.

Power: social roles

Social roles are the parts we play every day as members of various social groups. Most days your social roles probably include those of friend and student. The best-known study to assess how social roles influence behaviour was the Stanford prison experiment (discussed in the next section). It was based on assumption that guards and prisoners in prisons have very clear social roles with the former exerting their power over the latter.

KEY TERM

Social roles: the parts we play as members of social groups based on certain expectations about the behaviour that is appropriate.

Stanford prison experiment

In the 1960s, there were numerous brutal attacks by prison guards on prisoners in American prisons. Why did this brutality occur? Perhaps prison guards have aggressive or sadistic personalities. Alternatively, the social environment of prisons (including a rigid power structure) might be responsible.

Zimbardo carried out the Stanford prison experiment (Haney et al., 1973) to decide between these two possibilities. Emotionally stable students agreed to act as "guards" and "prisoners" in a mock prison. If hostility were found in spite of not using sadistic guards, this would suggest the social environment of prisons (and the social role of guards) create hostility.

What happened? The experiment was stopped after 6 days instead of the intended 14 days! Violence and rebellion broke out within two days of the start. The prisoners ripped off their clothing and shouted and cursed at the guards. In return, the guards violently put down this rebellion using fire extinguishers. One prisoner exhibited so much emotional disturbance (e.g., disorganised thinking; uncontrollable crying) he had to be released after only one day.

Over time, the prisoners became more subdued and submissive, often slouching and keeping their eyes fixed on the ground. At the same time, force, harassment, and aggression by the guards increased. For example, the prisoners were sleep deprived, put in solitary confinement, and forced to clean the toilets with their bare hands.

Zimbardo argued that the mock guards became aggressive because of the role they occupied. However, it emerged many years later that Zimbardo was much more centrally involved in what happened than he indicated at the time. He briefed the guards as follows: "You can create in the prisoners . . . a sense of fear to some degree. . . . We have total power in the situation. They have none" (Zimbardo, 2007, p. 55).

British study

In December 2001, British researchers carried out a study similar to the Stanford prison experiment. However, the findings were very different (Reicher & Haslam, 2006). The guards failed to identify with their role whereas the prisoners increasingly identified with theirs. As a result, the guards were reluctant to impose their authority on the prisoners and so were overcome by them.

Why were the findings so different from those of the Stanford prison experiment? First, the pressure applied to the guards by Zimbardo to act aggressively was missing from the BBC study. Second, the guards in the BBC prison study knew their actions would be seen by millions on television.

EVALUATION

➕ Zimbardo apparently showed that situational factors can have dramatic effects on behaviour.

➕ Zimbardo found that even stable individuals often abuse their power.

➖ Several guards did *not* act brutally which shows that the situation was *not* all-important (Haslam & Reicher, 2012).

- Much of the brutality exhibited by the guards occurred because they were simply doing what Zimbardo had told them to do. According to one of the guards (John Mark), "Zimbardo went out of his way to create tension. Things like forced sleep deprivation – he was really pushing the envelope . . . he knew what he wanted and then tried to shape the experiment" (Mark, 2011).

- The failure of the BBC study to repeat Zimbardo's findings casts doubt on the importance of situational factors on behaviour.

- Haney and Zimbardo (2009) claimed that the findings of the Stanford prison experiment showed that individual differences in personality were unimportant. However, they did not compare the effects on behaviour of different types of personality, and so they cannot know whether personality makes a difference.

- There are serious ethical problems in exposing people to degradation and hostility.

Crowd behaviour

Individuals often behave differently when in a crowd than when on their own or with a few friends. For example, lynch mobs in the southern United States murdered 2,000 people (mostly blacks) in the twentieth century. It is unlikely that those involved would have behaved like that if they had not been part of a highly emotional crowd. Much more recently, groups of people were involved in most of the rioting in London and other cities in August 2011.

Le Bon (1895) argued that the anonymity of individuals in a crowd or mob can remove normal social constraints and so lead to violence and panic. In similar fashion, Zimbardo (1970) argued for the importance of **deindividuation**, the loss of a sense of personal identity occurring in conditions of high arousal and anonymity.

Negative views of crowd behaviour remain popular. Schweingruber and Wohlstein (2005) identified the following characteristics often ascribed to crowds: (1) spontaneous, (2) destructive, (3) irrational, (4) highly emotional, and (5) suggestible (the last two characteristics occur due to anonymity and unanimity within the crowd).

When members of a crowd become deindividuated, do they tend to follow or ignore society's norms and group norms?

These ideas imply that crowds will typically behave in antisocial and aggressive ways. Reicher et al. (1995) proposed a more positive approach to crowd behaviour in their social identity model. They disagreed with the notion that deindividuated individuals become uninhibited and freed from social constraints. Reicher et al. argued almost the opposite is the case – the behaviour of deindividuated individuals is strongly influenced by the crowd's **norms** (standards of behaviour) and so may not lead to antisocial behaviour.

Drury and Reicher (2010, p. 61) developed the notion: "People in a crowd develop a shared social identity based on their common experience during an emergency. This shared identity promotes solidarity, which results in coordinated and beneficial actions – or what we call 'collective resilience'."

> **KEY TERMS**
>
> **Deindividuation:** loss of a sense of personal identity; it can occur in a large group or crowd.
>
> **Norms:** standards or rules of behaviour that operate within a group or within society generally.

IN THE REAL WORLD: mass panic?

As Drury and Reicher (2010, p. 60) pointed out, "Hardly any self-respecting Hollywood disaster movie would be complete without one scene of people running wildly in all directions and screaming hysterically." That is consistent with what is generally assumed – 80% of individuals believe crowds panic in threatening situations (see Dezecache, 2015).

There is apparent support for this assumption in reports of theatre fires (e.g., 492 people died in a fire at the Coconut Grove Theatre in Boston in 1942). However, careful analysis of such fires indicates that the inadequate structure of the buildings and insufficient emergency exits played a larger role than panic (Chertkoff & Kushigian, 1999).

In what follows, we discuss the alleged tendency of crowds to panic when confronted by an emergency. As we will see, there is very little support for this viewpoint.

Drury and Reicher (2010) interviewed many of those present during the bombings in London on 7th July 2005. Most experienced a sense of togetherness on that day and used a wide range of positive terms to describe their feelings (e.g., "unity"; "affinity"; "part of a group"; "warmness"). I was working in central London when the bombings occurred and can vouch for the solidarity and calm exhibited by most Londoners.

Dezecache (2015) discussed many other examples of mass emergency situations. Most of the evidence was entirely consistent with that of Drury and Reicher (2010). For example, Proulx and Fahy (2004) analysed first-hand reports from 435 survivors of the attacks on the World Trade Centre in New York on 9th September 2001. Mutual help was highlighted in 46% of the reports, and 57% of the survivors perceived other people as reacting calmly to the situation.

Drury et al. (2009) analysed interviews with survivors of 11 mass emergency events. They found that 57% of those interviewed identified strongly with other crowd members. Those who identified strongly were more likely to experience feelings of a shared fate with other crowd members, and they were also more likely to help other survivors.

In sum, crowd members typically respond by developing a shared social identity when confronting a mass emergency situation. This shared identity often makes crowd members feel safer and increases their expectations that others will be supportive (Alnabulsi & Drury, 2014). As a result, they generally assist others rather than panicking and behaving selfishly. As Dezecache (2015, p. 209) concluded, "Far from leading to the breakdown of the social fabric, the presence of a common threat can strengthen social bonds."

Findings

There is some support for Zimbardo's (1970) deindividuation theory. Mann (1981) analysed newspaper reports of individuals threatening to commit suicide by jumping from a bridge or building. Crowd members who were watching were most likely to encourage the potential suicide to jump when they were fairly anonymous and deindividuated (the crowd was large or the incident took place after dark).

Silke (2003) analysed 500 violent attacks carried out in Northern Ireland. Disguised offenders (who can be regarded as deindividuated) inflicted more serious physical injuries on their victims.

Postmes and Spears (1998) reviewed studies on group and crowd behaviour. On average, deindividuation (produced by anonymity, large groups, and so on) was associated with a very small increase in anti-social behaviour. More importantly, deindividuation increased individuals' adherence to group norms. This often produced positive effects (see earlier Box).

EVALUATION

➕ Individuals in crowds often experience deindividuation.

➕ There is strong evidence that deindividuation increases adherence to group norms.

➕ The social identity model accounts for most of the findings, including the varying effects of deindividuation on crowd behaviour.

➖ Members of a crowd may experience exhilaration or great excitement, but the social identity model has little to say about such emotional states.

➖ It is sometimes hard to measure "social identity" and "group norms".

Chapter summary

- There is a moderately strong conformity effect in the Asch situation, especially when participants regard other group members as similar to themselves.
- Conformity in the Asch situation depends on normative and informational influence.
- Majorities often influence minorities through compliance whereas minorities influence majorities through conversion.
- In Milgram's research, the percentage of fully obedient participants went down when the obviousness of the learner's plight increased and/or the experimenter's authority was reduced.
- Milgram exaggerated the extent to which his participants entered into an agentic state. In fact, many were positively engaged and believed their behaviour was appropriate.
- Group polarisation is influenced by social comparison, persuasive arguments, and group members' desire to distinguish their group from other groups.
- Groupthink, which is more likely when a group has a strong leader and there are pressures towards conformity, is present in successful as well as unsuccessful groups.
- The Stanford prison experiment suggested brutality in American prisons is due to the power structure within prisons. However, the experiment was poorly designed, and the findings have not been replicated.
- It has been claimed that deindividuation within crowds produces uninhibited and aggressive behaviour; in fact, it increases individuals' adherence to group norms.
- It is often assumed that crowds confronted by a serious emergency will tend to panic. In fact, what is much more common is that crowds react calmly, develop a shared social identity, and engage in mutual help.

Further reading

- Burger, J.M. (2011). Alive and well after all these years. *Psychologist*, 24, 654–657. Jerry Burger shows very clearly how Milgram set up his research so most participants felt they had no alternative but to show extreme obedience to authority.

- Dezecache, G. (2015). Human collective reactions to threat. *Wiley Interdisciplinary Reviews: Cognitive Science*, 6, 209–219. This article discusses much evidence that indicates crowds typically respond to threatening situations with solidarity rather than collective panic.

- Hodges, B.H. (2014). Rethinking conformity and imitation: Divergence, convergence, and social understanding. *Frontiers in Psychology*, 5 (Article 726). Bert Hodges show how Asch's conformity research has been misunderstood and misinterpreted.

- Vaughan, G.M., & Hogg, M.A. (2014). *Social psychology* (7th ed.). London: Prentice Hall. Chapter 7 in this textbook contains comprehensive coverage of the topics discussed in this chapter.

Essay questions

1. What are some of the main reason why people conform? To what extent should we criticise people for conforming?

2. Discuss the strengths and limitations of research on obedience to authority. How relevant is this research to real-life situations?

3. "The Stanford prison experiment proved that prison guards behave aggressively because of the power structure in prisons rather than because of their personality." Discuss.

4. How do crowds typically behave when confronted by a serious emergency? What factors are important in determining their behaviour in such circumstances?

You probably like most of the people you meet but dislike others. What kinds of information do you think influence your reactions to other people? Are you most affected by their personality, their intelligence, or their personal appearance? Why do you find some individuals more attractive than others? Do the factors determining romantic attraction to members of the opposite sex differ between men and women?

Social perception and attraction

This chapter deals with **social perception** – how we perceive and understand other people and form impressions of them. Humans are social beings who spend much of their time interacting with other people within the family, at work, and at various leisure and social activities.

When we meet someone for the first time, we nearly always form an impression of that person. We find him/her friendly or unfriendly, aggressive or timid, clever or unintelligent. Such impressions are typically formed very rapidly, and it is often hard to know exactly why our immediate impressions are positive or negative.

This chapter is divided into two main sections. First, we discuss the major mechanisms involved in social perception. For example, how do we interpret or make sense of other people's behaviour? Are some of their personality traits more important than others in forming a global impression of them?

Second, we consider why we find someone attractive or unattractive. Relevant factors include physical attractiveness; our familiarity with the other person; and their similarity to us in beliefs, attitudes, personality, and so on. The factors involved in romantic attraction are also discussed.

When deciding why someone has behaved in a certain way, what types of information do we typically use?

Attributions about others' behaviour

Most of the behaviour other people display towards us is *ambiguous* – it can be interpreted in various ways. For example, someone you meet is very friendly towards you. This may mean they are naturally warm and friendly, or they especially like you, or they want something from you. It is thus important to try to understand the reasons for their apparent friendliness.

Heider (1958) argued that people are naïve scientists who relate observable behaviour to unobservable causes. We produce **attributions**, which are beliefs about the reasons why other people behave as they do. He distinguished between dispositional or internal attributions and situational or external attributions. A **dispositional attribution** is made when we decide someone's behaviour is due to their personality or other characteristic. In contrast, a **situational attribution** is made when someone's behaviour is attributed to the current situation.

These two types of attributions can be applied to the behaviour of a man at a social gathering who virtually ignores everyone. He may have an unsociable personality (dispositional attribution). Alternatively, he may be very worried

KEY TERMS

Social perception: the processes involved when one person perceives, evaluates, and forms an impression of someone else.

Attributions: our inferences concerning the causes of behaviour patterns in other people and in ourselves.

Dispositional attribution: deciding that someone's behaviour is due to their personality rather than to the situation.

Situational attribution: deciding that someone's behaviour is due to the situation in which they find themselves rather than to their personality.

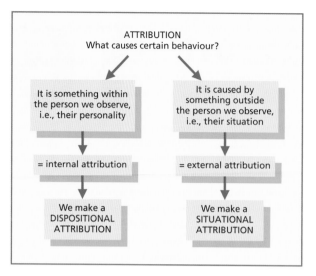

ATTRIBUTION
What causes certain behaviour?

It is something within the person we observe, i.e., their personality

It is caused by something outside the person we observe, i.e., their situation

= internal attribution

= external attribution

We make a DISPOSITIONAL ATTRIBUTION

We make a SITUATIONAL ATTRIBUTION

about personal matters (e.g., his partner's health) (situational attribution).

Why does it matter whether we make dispositional or situational attributions? When we make a dispositional attribution, we generally expect the behaviour in question to be repeated frequently in the future. However, that is not the case when we make a situational attribution for the same behaviour.

Heider's theoretical ideas led subsequent researchers to identify biases in our attributions for the behaviour of others and of ourselves. First, there is the **fundamental attribution error** – we tend to exaggerate the extent to which other people's actions are due to their personality or other dispositions and minimise the role of the situation. Second, there is **actor-observer bias**. This is the tendency for individuals to attribute their own actions to situational factors but to attribute the same actions to dispositional factors if performed by someone else.

Are we more likely to assume this man is sleeping rough because of situational factors (he's been taken ill, forgotten his house keys) or dispositional factors (he can't keep a job, he's drunk and rowdy in accommodation, for example)?

KEY TERMS

Fundamental attribution error: the tendency to think that the behaviour of other people is due more to their personality and less to the situation than is actually the case.

Actor-observer bias: others' actions tend to be attributed to internal dispositions whereas our own actions are attributed to the current situation.

Findings

Most textbooks on social psychology claim there is substantial evidence for the actor-observer bias. In fact, that is not the case. Malle (2006) carried out a meta-analysis (combining findings from numerous studies) and found practically no evidence of the actor-observer bias. Why was this? Malle et al. (2007) discovered the theoretical emphasis on dispositional attributions is misplaced – in their research, only 5% of all explanations of behaviour (one's own or another person's) referred to stable internal traits. In contrast, 44% of explanations of behaviour referred to mental states or reasons (i.e., beliefs and desires).

Malle et al. (2007) found an important difference between the attributions participants made about their own behaviour and that of another person. For example, they had to explain why they themselves or someone called Ian had chosen to work 14 hours a day last month. They tended to use *beliefs* (e.g., "A project was due") to explain their own behaviour but *desires* (e.g., "To make more money") to explain Ian's behaviour. Participants avoided belief explanations of another's behaviour because it is hard to decide which out of numerous beliefs motivated him/her.

There is some support for the fundamental attribution error. It is useful – it makes our lives seem more predictable if other people's behaviour is determined by their personality and so changes little across situations. However, there are many circumstances in which observers do not minimise the role of situational factors in determining someone else's behaviour (Gawronski, 2004). For example, suppose a teenage girl is asked by her mother to help an elderly neighbour by mowing her lawn. If she agrees while grumbling, we attribute her behaviour to the situation (i.e., her mother's influence) (Krull et al., 2008). Thus, if there are powerful situational reasons why someone behaves in a given way, we often interpret their behaviour using a situational attribution.

Cultural differences

The findings on the fundamental attribution error discussed earlier were obtained in individualistic cultures (e.g., UK; United States) in which the emphasis is on individual responsibility and independence (see Chapter 1). However, many cultures are collectivistic (especially in the Far East) and emphasise group cohesiveness. We might expect people in such cultures to focus on situational explanations of others' behaviour because their behaviour is responsive to others' wishes. As a result, the fundamental attribution error would be less.

There is reasonable support for this prediction (see Heine & Buchtel, 2009, for a review). For example, Norenzayan et al. (2002) found that East Asians show a greater tendency than Americans to infer that others' behaviour is strongly controlled by the situation.

In what type of culture is the fundamental attribution error more common?

EVALUATION

➕ We spend much time trying to understand others' behaviour by making attributions about it.

➕ It is important to distinguish between internal and external attributions for behaviour.

➕ We often attribute our own behaviour to our beliefs whereas we are more likely to attribute others' behaviour to their desires.

➖ There is little support for actor-observer bias and limited support for the fundamental attribution error.

➖ The traditional focus on dispositional and situational dispositions de-emphasises the role of mental states (reasons) in explaining behaviour.

➖ There is less evidence of the fundamental attribution error in collectivistic cultures than individualistic ones.

According to implicit personality theory, what do we assume about others? What does the primacy effect mean?

Implicit personality theory

What is of most importance in person perception? Fiske et al. (2007) argued there are two major dimensions: warmth (social desirability) and competence (intellectual desirability). Another person's warmth or coldness indicates whether they have good or bad intentions. Their competence or incompetence indicates whether they have the ability to act effectively on those intentions. Thus, warmth is judged before competence, and Fiske et al. argued that it carries more weight than competence in person perception.

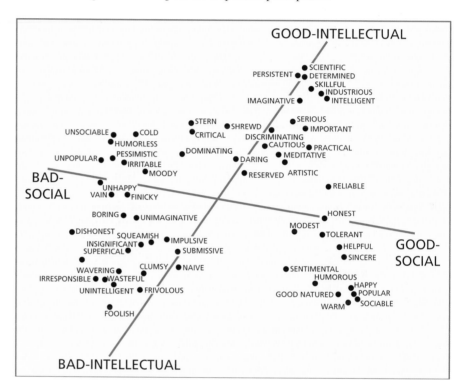

Fiske et al.'s (2007) views represent a development of the earlier theoretical approach to Asch (1946). He distinguished between key aspects of personality (*central* traits) and less important ones (*peripheral* traits). Central traits (e.g., warmth) have much more influence on our impressions of another person than peripheral ones. These ideas led to the development of **implicit personality theory** – when we form impressions of other people, we assume that someone who has one particular personality trait will typically have other, related traits. That is a major reason why warmth and competence are so important – we attribute a wide range of positive traits to anyone we perceive as being warm and competent.

Asch (1946) also claimed that the initial information we obtain about another person affects our perception of him/her more than information presented later. The term **primacy effect** refers to the special importance of first impressions.

KEY TERMS

Implicit personality theory: the tendency to believe (sometimes mistakenly) that someone who has a given personality trait will also have other, related traits.

Primacy effect: the finding that first impressions are more important than later ones in determining our opinions of others.

Findings

What causes the primacy effect?

In early research, Asch (1946) found evidence that whether someone is warm or cold can be of special importance. He gave his participants seven adjectives describing an imaginary person called X. They all received the following seven adjectives: intelligent, skillful, industrious, determined, practical, and cautious. The final adjective was warm, cold, polite, or blunt.

The adjectives "warm" and "cold" had a major impact on how all the information about X was interpreted. When he was warm, 91% of the participants thought he was generous and 94% thought he was good-natured. When he was cold, however, only 8% thought he was generous and 17% thought he was good-natured. In contrast, the adjectives "polite" and "blunt" had little impact on overall impression formation.

Subsequent research has indicated our overall impressions are often much influenced by their perceived warmth or coldness and by their competence or incompetence (Fiske et al., 2007). For example, Wojciszke et al. (1998) found that warmth judgments were more than twice as important as competence judgments in determining individuals' global impressions of familiar other people.

It is important not to exaggerate the importance of "warmth" in determining person perception. Nauts et al. (2014) carried out a modified version of Asch's (1946) study in which some participants received the six adjectives he used plus the trait "warm" and indicated their overall impression of the person described. After that, they chose the adjective most influential in shaping that impression. Only 19% chose "warm" compared to 55% choosing "intelligent".

Goodwin et al. (2014) argued that our perception of other people is greatly influenced by their moral character. This makes sense because individuals with bad moral character are more likely than those with good moral character to do us harm. Goodwin et al. asked participants to rate various real people (e.g., a close friend; mother or father; Barack Obama) on various traits including some focusing on high morality rather than warmth (e.g., courageous; principled; honest) and others focusing on high warmth rather than morality (e.g., sociable; enthusiastic; playful). Overall impressions were influenced by moral character and by warmth but more so by moral character.

There are cultural differences in people's implicit personality theories. Hoffman et al. (1986) asked bilingual English-Chinese speakers to read descriptions of individuals and then interpret their personality using the Chinese or English language. Some of their interpretations involved English or Chinese stereotypes. For example, there is a stereotype of the artistic type in English (moody and intense temperament; a bohemian lifestyle) but not in Chinese. Participants only used stereotypes relevant to the language in which they spoke.

Asch (1946) found clear evidence for a primacy effect. Some participants were told another person was "intelligent, industrious, impulsive, critical, stubborn, and envious". In other words, positive traits were presented first, followed by negatives ones. Other participants were given the same adjectives in reverse order. As predicted, those hearing the positive traits first formed a much more favourable impression than those hearing the negative ones first.

The primacy effect is not always obtained, especially when the information provided about another person focuses on their behaviour rather than their personality traits. Ybarra (2001) found there was no primacy effect when positive information was followed by negative information. However, there was a primacy effect when negative information was followed by positive information. Why was this? Positive behaviour (e.g., "completed his time sheet accurately at work") is often attributed to situational demands rather than the individual's personality. In contrast, negative behaviour is generally attributed to the individual's personality.

EVALUATION

➕ There is much support for implicit personality theory and for the notion that some traits are of more central importance than others.

➕ The dimensions of warm-cold and competent-incompetent are of central importance in impression formation.

➕ There is a primacy effect in impression formation based on information about personality traits.

➖ Most research has de-emphasised the importance of moral character in impression formation.

➖ Much research has involved asking participants to form impressions of imaginary others on the basis of lists of adjectives. This is very artificial and may involve different processes to those used in everyday life.

Physical attractiveness

The first thing we generally notice when meeting a stranger is their physical appearance. This includes how they are dressed and whether they are clean or dirty. It also often includes an assessment of their physical attractiveness.

There is reasonable consensus as to whether someone is physically attractive or not. Women whose faces resemble those of young children are often perceived as attractive. Thus, photographs of females with fairly large and widely separated eyes, a small nose, and a small chin are regarded as more attractive. However, wide cheekbones and narrow cheeks are also seen as attractive (Cunningham, 1986), and these features are not usually found in young children.

Cunningham (1986) also studied physical attractiveness in males. Men having features such as a square jaw, small eyes, and thin lips were found attractive by women. These features can be regarded as indicating maturity, since they are rarely found in children.

Perhaps the most important factor associated with facial attractiveness is averageness faces resembling the average face in the population are generally regarded as highly attractive (Trujillo et al., 2014). That may sound unlikely – who wants to look average? However, this notion makes sense when you consider non-average faces can be asymmetrical, have one or more blemishes, and can have features (e.g., nose; eyes) out of proportion with the rest of the face.

Cheryl Cole (top left) fits Cunningham's "attractive female" characteristics — note how her features are similar to the little girl's (top right). Colin Firth (bottom left), however, looks very different from the little boy (bottom right).

How important is physical attractiveness in everyday life? Physically attractive individuals are thought to have more positive traits and characteristics than less attractive ones (Dion et al., 1972). These findings may be due either to the "beauty-is-good" stereotype or to the "unattractiveness-is-bad" stereotype. Griffin and Langlois (2006) found being unattractive is a disadvantage rather than being attractive is an advantage.

So far we have considered only people's *beliefs* about physically attractive and unattractive people. A saying such as "You can't judge a book by the cover" suggests physical attractiveness is relatively unimportant in real life. However, the evidence indicates otherwise. Langlois et al. (2000) found there were many significant differences between physically attractive and unattractive adults. Below are the percentages of each group having each characteristic (attractive people first). Attractive individuals had more self-confidence (56% vs. 44%), better social skills (55% vs. 45%), better physical health (59% vs. 41%), more extraversion (56% vs. 44%), and more sexual experience (58% vs. 42%). Thus, beauty is more than skin deep!

Nedelec and Beaver (2014) examined the relationship between physical attractiveness and physical health in more detail. There was a small (but consistent) tendency for high physical attractiveness to be associated with fewer sick days, fewer minor diseases, and fewer chronic diseases.

Cultural variations

The ideal female figure in Western cultures is often regarded as one that is slim (Swami, 2013). For example, Rubinstein and Caballero (2000) found there was a steady decrease in the body mass of winners of Miss America during the 1990s. Towards the end of that decade, several winners had a low body mass suggestive of undernourishment.

Anderson et al. (1992) studied body size preferences for females in 54 cultures. Heavy women were preferred to slender ones in most cultures, especially those in which the food supply was moderately or very unreliable. Heavy women in cultures with unreliable food supplies are better equipped than slender women to survive food shortages and provide nourishment for their children.

More recent research by Swami et al. (2010) obtained very different results in a study of 26 cultures. There were very small differences between Western and non-Western cultures in preferred female body size. Of interest, the greatest differences in preferred body size are found *within* cultures – the ideal body size is larger among groups of low socio-economic status than those of high status. Perhaps the former regard heavier women as having more resources than lighter ones.

Are heavy women regarded as more attractive than slender women in most, some, or no cultures? How does the reliability of the food supply affect this perception?

FOOD SUPPLY				
Preference	**Very unreliable**	**Moderately unreliable**	**Moderately reliable**	**Very reliable**
Heavy body	71%	50%	39%	40%
Moderate body	29%	33%	39%	20%
Slender body	0%	17%	22%	40%

Similarity

Two individuals can be similar in many ways, including in personality, attitudes, and demographic characteristics (e.g., age, race, gender). We start by considering similarity in personality. The saying, "Opposites attract", implies we are most likely to be attracted to those very different from us. However, another saying, "Birds of a feather flock together", implies we are attracted to similar people.

Actual vs. perceived similarity

We need to distinguish between *actual* and *perceived* similarity. This is important because there is much evidence for the **false consensus effect** – we tend to overestimate how similar other people are to us in their opinions, behaviour,

KEY TERM

False consensus effect: the mistaken belief that most other people are similar to us in their opinion, behaviour, and personality.

and personality. For example, Krueger and Clement (1994) found individuals consistently overestimated the percentage of the population who would provide the same answers as them on a personality test.

Montoya et al. (2008) carried out a meta-analysis (review of numerous studies) on similarity in attitudes and personality. Actual similarity and perceived similarity were both important when individuals interacted only briefly. Within existing relationships, attraction continued to be well predicted by perceived similarity. However, attraction within such relationships was *not* predicted by actual similarity. What is going on here? Attraction within relationships leads to perceived similarity (and high relationship satisfaction) even in the absence of actual similarity.

Findings

Most findings indicate we are attracted to individuals similar to us in personality. Burgess and Wallin (1953) found that engaged couples showed significant similarity for 14 personality characteristics (e.g., feelings easily hurt; leader at social events), and there was no evidence that opposites attract. Sprecher (1998) studied similarity in romantic relationships, opposite-sex friendships, and same-sex friendships. Similarity of interests and leisure activities was more important than similarity of attitudes and value in same- and opposite-sex friendships. However, the opposite was the case for romantic relationships.

Byrne (1971) found that people rated strangers with similar attitudes to themselves as more attractive than those with dissimilar attitudes. Is this difference due to our liking of those with similar attitudes or our dislike of those having dissimilar attitudes? Rosenbaum (1986) found dissimilarity of attitudes increased disliking more than attitude similarity increased liking. This may happen because we feel threatened and fear disagreements when we discover the other person has very different attitudes.

Are there exceptions to the general rule that we are attracted to those who are (or appear to be) similar to us? The answer is, "Yes". Heine et al. (2009) considered several kinds of similarity (e.g., personality; activities; attitudes). There was a stronger impact of similarity on attraction in Americans than in the Japanese. Why is this? Americans attach more importance than the Japanese to having a high level of self-esteem. As a result, Americans are more attracted to those who are like them because such individuals confirm their own level of self-esteem.

Conclusions

There is convincing evidence that we are generally more attracted to those similar to us in attitudes and personality. Of importance, what really matters in established relationships is perceived rather than actual similarity – attraction makes us perceive the other person as more similar to us than is actually the case.

However, there are cultural differences. Similarity plays a more important role in attraction within American than Japanese society. Americans' self-esteem is confirmed by forming relationships with those who are very similar to them, whereas the Japanese attach little value to high self-esteem.

Familiarity

How attractive we find another person often changes over time. Friends can become enemies ("Familiarity breeds contempt") and enemies can become friends. Here we briefly consider some of the factors involved.

Reis et al. (2011) identified three factors leading two same-sex strangers to become increasingly attracted to each other the more they interacted:

1. increased knowledge about the other person;
2. increased comfort and satisfaction over time;
3. increased responsiveness of the other person.

An especially important aspect of increased knowledge involves **self-disclosure,** in which revealing information of a personal nature is communicated. Research indicates that individuals engage in more self-disclosure with others whom they already like than those about whom they are more neutral (Collins & Miller, 1994). Individuals disclosing personal information to someone else tend to like that person more as a result and are also more liked by him/her.

Finkel et al. (2015) put forward a model to account for the various effects of familiarity on attraction. Their key assumption was as follows: "The link between familiarity and attraction is likely to be especially positive to the degree that the target [other person] facilitates the individual's goals and especially negative to the degree that the target undermines the individual's goals."

According to Finkel et al. (2015), greater familiarity is more likely to increase attraction between two individuals if most of their interactions occur in cooperative rather than competitive situations. In competitive situations, the two individuals are likely to thwart each other's goals. The effects of increasing familiarity on attraction also depend on discovering more about the other person's qualities: if those qualities are mostly appealing ones, this leads to increased attraction. If those qualities are unappealing, however, greater familiarity typically leads to reduced attraction.

A third factor identified by Finkel et al. (2015) is the strength and diversity of the other person's influence. If this influence is considerable, then familiarity can lead to conflict and decreased attraction. This negative impact of familiarity is found in many marriages (Norton et al., 2013). It helps to explain why college roommates on average like each other less over time (West et al., 2009).

Conclusions

KEY TERM

Self-disclosure: revealing personal or private information about oneself to another person.

We are a social species, and so increasing familiarity with another person mostly leads to increased attraction and friendship. Familiarity allows for increasing self-disclosure and an increased understanding of the other person. However, increasing familiarity can lead to reduced liking and attraction in competitive social contexts, when the other person's unappealing qualities become more apparent, or when the strength and diversity of their influence is excessive.

Romantic attraction

So far we have discussed factors determining how attractive (or unattractive) another person is to us. Unsurprisingly, most of these factors are also relevant when explaining romantic attraction.

Sex differences

It is generally assumed that the factors associated with romantic attraction show major differences between men and women. Of importance here is the approach adopted by evolutionary psychologists, who argue we can understand sexual attraction and behaviour in terms of natural selection (Buss, 2013).

According to evolutionary psychologists, what men and women find attractive in the opposite sex are features maximising the chances of producing offspring who will survive and prosper. The reason is that we want our genes to carry over into the next generation. It follows that men should prefer younger women to older ones because such women are more likely to be able to have children. Men should also prefer physically attractive women because they are more likely to be fertile. In contrast, women should prefer older men (especially those with high levels of resources) because they are more likely to provide for their offspring's needs.

Evolutionary psychologists argue that humans are highly motivated to ensure the survival of their genes. Men can best achieve that goal by having numerous sex partners. In contrast, women can only have a limited number of children in their lives and typically have a very large investment in their children. As a result, it is optimal for women to be selective in their choice of mates and to have a partner who will provide for their offspring. To oversimplify somewhat, men prefer *quantity* of mates whereas women prefer *quality* according to the evolutionary approach.

Stewart-Williams and Thomas (2013) argued that this evolutionary theory is much more applicable to some other species than to humans. Sex differences in parental investment are fairly small, and most men and women are very concerned to find a high-quality long-term partner with whom to have children. In sum, the traditional evolutionary theory "has led to the exaggeration of the magnitude of human sex differences" (Stewart-Williams & Thomas, 2013, p. 137).

Findings

Some support for the evolutionary approach was reported by Buss (1989). Across 37 cultures, men expressed a preference for younger women as mates whereas women preferred older men in nearly all cultures except Spain. If men prefer younger women because they are more likely to be fertile, this preference should increase as men become older. This is, indeed, the case (Kenrick & Keefe, 1992).

It has been argued from an evolutionary perspective that men attach more importance than women to physical attractiveness (they seek "sex objects"). In contrast, women attach more importance than men to social status and resources (they seek "success objects"). Shackelford et al. (2005) re-analysed Buss's (1989) data and found the predicted gender differences.

Fales et al. (2016) found that men attached more importance than women to the following characteristics: good-looking (92% vs. 84%), and slim (80% vs. 58%). In contrast, women attached more importance than men to the following aspects: steady income (97% vs. 74%), has made/will make a lot of money (69% vs. 47%), and a successful career (61% to 33%).

We must not exaggerate gender differences in the factors associated with romantic attraction. If we return to Buss's (1989) cross-cultural study, we find that the personal qualities of kindness and intelligence were regarded as important by both sexes in virtually every culture. In similar vein, Bryan et al. (2011) found men and women both attach much importance to agreeableness when looking for a serious relationship. They also discovered that agreeableness was the strongest predictor of current and future relationship satisfaction.

IN THE REAL WORLD: personal ads, online dating, and speed dating

In the twenty-first century, men and women seek romantic partners in far more ways than in the past (e.g., personal ads; online dating; speed dating). We will consider relevant sex differences in partner preferences and then provide an overall account.

Research on personal ads and online dating has provided evidence generally supportive of the evolutionary approach. Goode (1996) studied response rates to personal ads. More men responded to an ad describing a physically attractive but low-income woman than an unattractive, high-income one, whereas the opposite was the case with women responding to male ads. Hitsch et al. (2010) obtained similar findings in a study of online dating. A potential partner's physical attractiveness had a somewhat greater impact on men than women, whereas his/her income had a much stronger impact on women than men.

We turn now to speed dating. Luo and Zhang (2009) found physical attractiveness was the strongest predictor of romantic interest for both sexes following 5-minute interactions. Women's interest was almost unrelated to men's personality. In contrast, men tended to be more attracted to women high in extraversion, agreeableness, and conscientiousness, but low in neuroticism (anxiety and depression).

Eastwick et al. (2014) carried out a meta-analysis of numerous studies on romantic attraction where the two individuals had had face-to-face contact (e.g., speed dating; relationships). Romantic attraction was moderately associated with physical attractiveness (the correlation was +.43 for men and +.40 for women). It was also associated (but less so) with earning prospects (correlation of +.09 for men and +.12 for women).

Eastwick et al. (2014) made coherent sense of these findings by making use of the three-stage approach to relationships put forward by Levinger and Snoek (1972):

1. *awareness*: two individuals form impressions of each other in the absence of face-to-face contact (e.g., online dating).
2. *surface contact*: two individuals have interacted and shared some information (e.g., speed dating).
3. *mutuality*: two individuals have formed a relationship.

Research has consistently indicated that the gender differences in partner preference predicted by the evolutionary approach are obtained during the initial awareness stage. However, gender differences in preference largely or completely disappear during the subsequent surface contact and mutuality stages. How can we explain the changes across relationship stages? Before you have met a potential partner, your preferences are dominated by rather abstract and stereotyped views. When you have met a potential partner, however, your preferences soon become strongly influenced by detailed information about the other person. As a result, you no longer make much use of stereotyped information and so the evolutionary approach ceases to predict your preferences.

Similarity

We saw earlier that people are more attracted to those similar to us. Similarity with respect to several factors is also important in determining the person we choose to marry. Lykken and Tellegen (1993) found married couples were moderately similar with respect to physical attractiveness and educational attainment and slightly less so with respect to intelligence and personal values. Finally, there was a modest tendency for married couples to have similar personalities.

Hunt et al. (2015) wondered whether similarity in physical attractiveness is always important. They studied long-term couples (mostly married). There was much less similarity in physical attractiveness in couples who had been friends before starting their relationship than those that had not. How can we explain these findings? Couples who had previously been friends possessed much more information about each other prior to starting their relationship. As a result, factors totally unrelated to physical attractiveness were of major importance in leading them to start their relationship.

Chapter summary

- According to attribution theory, we try to understand our own and others' behaviour by making dispositional or situational attributions.
- Attribution theorists claim we are biased to produce dispositional attributions of other people's behaviour whereas we make situational attributions of our own behaviour (fundamental attribution error; actor-observer bias). There is little evidence for actor-observer bias, and the fundamental attribution error is less common in collectivistic cultures than individualistic ones.
- According to implicit personality theory, we assume an individual having one particular personality trait will have other related traits. It is of central importance whether someone is warm or cold and competent or incompetent. Our evaluation of another person also depends very much on our assessment of their moral character.
- There is a primacy effect in impression formation, but more so when the information about another person is based on their personality rather than their behaviour.
- Faces that resemble average faces in the population are generally perceived as more attractive than non-average ones.
- Physically attractive individuals are perceived as possessing more positive qualities than unattractive ones. There is some validity to these perceptions, and more attractive individuals have better physical health than unattractive ones.
- Heavy women used to be preferred to slender ones in many non-Western cultures, especially those in which the food supply was unreliable. Increasingly, however, most cultures (Western and non-Western) have a preference for slim women.
- We overestimate the similarity of other people's opinions, behaviour, and personality: the false consensus effect.
- Attraction within existing relationships is associated more with perceived than actual similarity: attraction makes us perceive the other person as more similar to us than is actually the case.
- Similarity has a greater effect on attraction among Americans than among the Japanese. This is because Americans' self-esteem is confirmed by forming relationships with those resembling themselves.
- According to evolutionary psychologists, men prefer quantity of mates whereas women prefer quality. This is an exaggerated view of gender differences: men and women both attach considerable importance to kindness, agreeableness, and intelligence in a romantic partner.
- It is often argued that men attach more importance than women to physical attractiveness in a potential partner whereas women attach more importance than men to income.

Further reading

- Eastwick, P.W., Luchies, L.B., Finkel, E.J., & Hunt, L.L. (2014). The predictive validity of ideal partner preference: A review and meta-analysis. *Psychological Bulletin, 140,* 623–665. Paul Eastwick and his colleagues provide a thorough review of sex differences and similarities in partner preferences.

- Little, A.C. (2014). Facial attractiveness. *Wiley Interdisciplinary Reviews: Cognitive Science, 5,* 621–634. Anthony Little provides a comprehensive review of research on facial attractiveness.

- Vaughan, G.M., & Hogg, M.A. (2013). *Social psychology* (7th ed.). London: Prentice Hall. Chapters 3 and 14 of this excellent textbook cover many topics related to social perception and attraction.

Essay questions

1. What is attribution theory? Identify its strengths and limitations.

2. Describe implicit personality theory. To what extent does the evidence support this theory?

3. Describe the evolutionary approach to romantic attraction. What are the problems and limitations of this approach?

Part 4

Individual differences

The extraordinary diversity of human behaviour is obvious to us nearly all the time in the course of our everyday lives. As a result, psychologists have devoted considerable research to trying to identify (and understand) some of the most important aspects of individual differences.

Individual differences have a great influence on our behaviour. For example, if you have a problem, you would probably discuss it with a friend who is warm and approachable rather than one lacking those qualities.

Chapter 17 • Intelligence

Issues such as what we mean by "intelligence" and why some individuals are more intelligent than others will be discussed.

Chapter 18 • Personality

We will address issues such as the number and nature of personality dimensions and why individuals differ in terms of those dimensions.

Chapter 19 • The self-concept

We will consider major aspects of our self-concept and the ways in which the self-concept differs as a function of gender and culture.

Some of the people you meet from day to day seem very intelligent whereas others are much less. How do you think we could best measure intelligence: Are intelligence or IQ tests adequate? Do you think that people can be intelligent in several different ways? If so, what are the major dimensions of intelligence?

Finally, there is an especially difficult and controversial issue: Where do you think intelligence comes from? Is it something we are born with, or is it largely determined by education and other environmental factors? Alternatively, does an individual's level of intelligence depend on a combination of genes and environment?

Intelligence

17

There has been much controversy about the meaning of the term "intelligence". Historically, it was assumed that individuals good at abstract reasoning, problem solving, decision making, mathematics, vocabulary, and language are more intelligent than those poor at these mental activities. Most intelligence tests have been based on this assumption, and it does capture much of what is important about intelligence (at least in most Western cultures). However, as we see later, there are two major problems with this approach.

First, it is too limited because it de-emphasises the practical skills needed for success in life. A more comprehensive view was provided by Sternberg (2015a, p. 230): "Intelligence is (1) the ability to achieve one's goals in life, given one's sociocultural context; (2) by capitalising on strengths and correcting or compensating for weaknesses; (3) in order to adapt to, shape, and select environments; (4) through a combination of analytical, creative, and practical abilities."

Second, and related to the first point, cultures differ in the meaning of "intelligence". For example, social considerations loom larger in definitions of "intelligence" in collectivistic cultures (with an emphasis on group solidarity) than individualistic ones (Western cultures with an emphasis on personal responsibility) (Sternberg & Kaufman, 1998). For example, the word for intelligence in Zimbabwe is *ngware*, meaning "to be careful and prudent in social relationships." In similar fashion, the Taiwanese Chinese people emphasise interpersonal intelligence (the ability to understand and to get on well with other people).

Sternberg (2015b) illustrated the importance of taking account of cultural context in a discussion of people living in a Yup'ik fishing village in a remote area of Alaska. Most Yup'ik children do not score well on traditional intelligence tests. However, they show intelligence by coping well with the demands of everyday life: coping with their bleak surrounds by developing skills of ice fishing, hunting, gathering, and navigating.

In sum, the term "intelligence" includes cognitive skills such as mathematics, reasoning, problem solving, and so on. It should also include various practical skills of value in everyday life and in so doing take account of differences in the everyday challenges faced by individuals from different cultures. Note, however, that "intelligence" cannot be defined with precision. For example, should "emotional intelligence" (sensitive handling of interpersonal relationships) be regarded as a form of intelligence? The skills associated with emotional intelligence are of practical value in our lives, which suggests the answer is "Yes". However, as discussed later, individual differences in emotional intelligence depend heavily on personality, which suggests the answer is "No".

Intelligence testing

How is the intelligence quotient usually assessed? What is the average IQ and standard deviation?

The first proper intelligence test was produced by the French psychologist Alfred Binet and his associate Théophile Simon in 1905. It assessed comprehension, memory, and other psychological processes. Subsequent well-known intelligence tests include the American Stanford-Binet test, the Wechsler Intelligence Scale for Children, and the British Ability Scales.

These tests typically contain mathematical items and vocabulary tests in which individuals define the meanings of words. They often include problems based on analogies (e.g., "Hat is to head as shoe is to ____") and tests of spatial ability. A sample item might be as follows: "If I start walking northwards, then turn left, and turn left again, what direction will I be facing?"

Reliability and validity

Should intelligence tests possess high/low reliability and/or validity?

Useful intelligence tests have high reliability and validity. **Reliability** refers to the extent to which a test provides consistent findings. **Validity** refers to the extent to which a test measures what it is claimed to be measuring.

Reliability

Suppose someone obtains an IQ of 135 when taking an intelligence test on one occasion but an IQ of 80 when retaking the test shortly afterwards. The test would obviously be unreliable and so could not possibly be an adequate measure of something as relatively unchanging as intelligence.

Reliability is usually worked out using the test-retest method. A group of people take the same test on two occasions, and their scores on the two occasions are compared. The higher the correlation (a measure of the relationship between the two scores), the greater is the test's reliability. The highest possible correlation is +1.0, which indicate perfect agreement or reliability. In contrast, a correlation of 0.0 would indicate no reliability. Reliability correlations for most major intelligence tests are about +.80 to +.85, which is not far from perfect reliability. This is especially impressive given that some individuals show a practice effect – they perform better on the second testing occasion.

Validity

Validity is harder to assess than reliability. The most direct approach to validity involves relating IQ to some external criterion or standard. For example, we would expect highly intelligent individuals to do well at school, to succeed in their careers, and so on. This approach has its limitations because academic and career success depend on several factors (e.g., motivation; quality of teaching) as well as the individual's level of intelligence.

Validity studies indicate that IQ generally correlates about +.5 with school or college academic performance (Mackintosh, 1998). There is thus a moderate

KEY TERMS

Reliability: the extent to which an intelligence (or other) test gives consistent or similar findings on different occasions.

Validity: the extent to which an intelligence (or other) test measures what it is supposed to be measuring.

tendency for more intelligent students to perform better academically than less intelligent ones. Krapohl et al. (2014) found school educational achievement was best predicted by intelligence. However, educational achievement was also predicted moderately well by other factors such as self-efficacy (belief in one's ability to succeed) and personality.

The validity of intelligence tests can also be assessed by considering the relationship between IQ and occupational performance. Most lawyers, doctors, and accountants have IQs within the top 10% of the population (Mackintosh, 1998). Hunter (1986) found IQ correlated moderately highly (+.58) with work performance among individuals having high-complexity jobs. However, most researchers have relied on supervisor ratings to assess work performance. Such ratings are likely to provide a rather subjective and imprecise assessment (Richardson & Norgate, 2015).

Calculating IQ

All the major intelligence tests are **standardised tests.** This means the test has been given to large, representative samples of the age groups covered by the test. As a result, the meaning or significance of an individual's score on the test can be assessed. For example, we can only interpret an individual's score of, say, 47 out of 70 on an intelligence test by comparing it against the scores obtained by numerous other people.

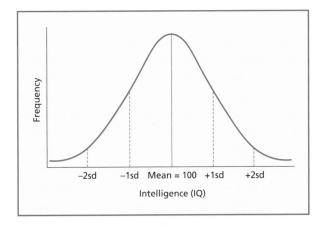

The best-known measure obtained from intelligence tests is IQ or **intelligence quotient.** This is based on performance across all the sub-tests contained in the overall test. It thus provides an overall measure of intellectual ability.

All major intelligence tests have manuals indicating how the test should be administered. This is important because the precise instructions given to those taking the test can influence their score.

An individual's IQ is generally assessed by comparing his/her test performance against that of others of the same age. Most intelligence tests are devised so IQs from the general population are normally distributed. The normal distribution is a bell-shaped curve in which there are as many scores above the mean as below it. Most scores are close to the mean, and there are fewer and fewer scores as we move away from the mean in either direction.

The spread of scores in a normal distribution is usually indicated by a statistical measure known as the standard deviation (sd). In a normal distribution, 68% of the scores fall within one standard deviation of the mean or average, 95% fall within two standard deviations, and 99.73% are within three standard deviations.

Intelligence tests are designed to produce a mean IQ of 100 and a standard deviation of about 16. Thus, an individual with an IQ of 116 is more intelligent than 84% of the population. That is so because 50% of people are below the mean and a further 34% are between the mean and one standard deviation above it.

KEY TERMS

Standardised tests: tests that have been given to large representative samples, and on which an individual's ability (or personality) can be compared to that of other people.

Intelligence quotient (IQ): a measure of general intelligence; the average IQ is 100 and most people have IQs between 85 and 115.

EVALUATION

⊕ Most intelligence tests have good reliability.

⊕ Intelligence have proved useful for predicting academic performance and career success. Thus, they possess reasonable validity.

⊖ Most intelligence tests are somewhat narrow in scope. They focus on individuals' thinking ability and de-emphasise their ability to interact successfully with other people (emotional intelligence).

⊖ IQ is a very *general* measure of intelligence. It can obscure the fact that intelligence also involves more specific abilities (e.g., spatial; numerical; verbal).

⊖ Most intelligence tests have been devised by white, middle-class psychologists from Western societies. Such tests may be biased against those from other cultures.

Heredity and environment

Where do individual differences in intelligence come from? One possibility is that they depend on heredity. In other words, our level of intelligence might be based mainly on the genes we inherit from our parents. Another possibility is that individual differences in intelligence depend on the environment. According to this view, some individuals are more intelligent than others because of more favourable environmental conditions (e.g., good teaching; supportive family and friends). Finally, and most plausibly, individual differences in intelligence may depend on genetic factors *and* on environmental ones.

It is perhaps natural to think of heredity and environment as having entirely separate or *independent* effects. However, the reality is very different because our genetic make-up influences our environmental experiences. Individuals with high genetic ability are much more likely than those with less ability to read many books and go to university. As Dickens and Flynn (2001, p. 347), pointed out, "Higher IQ leads one into better environments causing still higher IQ, and so on." In other words, to him (or her) that hath shall be given. I will return to this point later.

Twin studies

What is generally found in studies of intelligence on identical and fraternal twins?

Some of the most important work on individual differences in intelligence has made use of twins. Identical twins (technically known as monozygotic twins) have the same heredity, meaning they inherit the same genes. Fraternal twins (known as dizygotic twins) share 50% of their genes. They are thus no more similar genetically than ordinary brothers and sisters.

What predictions can we make? If heredity is important in producing individual differences in intelligence, we would expect identical twins to be more similar in intelligence than fraternal twins. However, if the environment is the *only* important factor determining individual differences in intelligence, we would expect that identical twins would be no more similar in intelligence than fraternal twins.

The degree of similarity in intelligence shown by pairs of twins is usually reported in the form of a correlation. A correlation of +1.0 would mean both twins in a pair have exactly the same IQ, whereas a correlation of 0.0 would mean there was no relationship.

McCartney et al. (1990) found across numerous twin studies that the mean correlation for identical twins was +.81 compared to +.59 for fraternal twins. Thus, identical twins are more alike in intelligence than fraternal

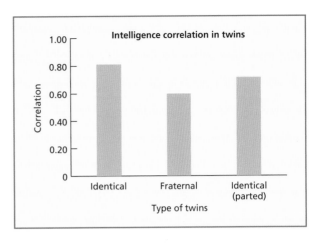

twins, suggesting that genetic factors influence individual differences in intelligence. However, identical twins tend to have more similar environments than fraternal twins. For example, identical twins spend more time together than fraternal twins, and their parents are more likely to try to treat them exactly the same (Loehlin & Nichols, 1976). As a result, the higher correlation for identical twins might be due to environmental factors. In fact, however, the more similar environments of identical than fraternal twins play a very minor role in accounting for their greater similarity in intelligence (Loehlin & Nichols, 1976).

We can clarify the roles of heredity and environment by considering identical twins separated early in life and then reared apart. Such twins have the same heredity but grow up in a different environment. If heredity is of major importance, such twins should have very similar intelligence. If environment is of more importance, there should be little similarity in intelligence. Bouchard et al. (1990) studied adult identical twin pairs separated on average at 5 months. Their IQs correlated +.75, and this high degree of similarity in intelligence depended very little on their age at separation or on the total amount of contact with each other. However, over 50% of the twin pairs were brought up in different branches of the same family and so their environments may well have been rather similar.

Adoption studies

Adoption studies provide another way of assessing the extent to which genetic and environmental factors influence individual differences in intelligence. In principle, adopted children's IQs should be more similar to those of their biological parents than their adoptive parents if heredity is more important than environment. However, the opposite pattern should be found if environment is more important.

The IQs of adopted children are generally more similar to those of their biological parents than their adoptive parents. This finding suggests heredity may be more important than environment in determining individual differences in intelligence. However, there is a potential problem. Adoption agencies often try to place infants in homes with similar educational and social backgrounds to those of their biological parents: this is **selective placement**.

Do adoption studies indicate that the IQ of adopted children is more similar to that of their biological mother or their adoptive mother?

KEY TERM

Selective placement: placing adopted children in homes resembling those of their biological parents in social and educational terms.

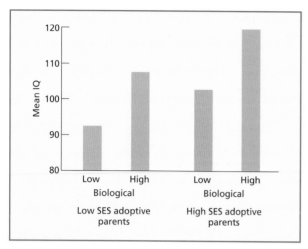

Mean IQs of adopted children as a function of socioeconomic status (SES) of their biological parents (low vs. high) and their adoptive parents (low vs. high). Data from Capron and Duyme (1989).

Capron and Duyme (1989) carried out an important study in which there was little evidence of selective placement. Adopted children's IQs were comparably influenced by the socioeconomic status of the biological parents than that of the adoptive parents. Thus, favourable heredity and favourable environment were both associated with similar increases in the adopted children's level of intelligence.

Environmental factors

Extreme environmental conditions can have large effects on intelligence. For example, Wheeler (1942) found children's IQs were very low on average in an isolated community in East Tennessee. When this community became more integrated into society, children's IQs increased by 10 points on average.

Hall et al. (2010) identified several environmental factors associated with children's intelligence. Some were at the *child* level (e.g., whether he/she was part of a large family; whether the first language was English). Other factors were at the *family* level (e.g., whether the father was employed; father's social class; the mother's qualifications).

Evidence that environmental factors influence intelligence was reported by Flynn (1987). He identified the **Flynn effect**, which is a surprisingly rapid rise in mean IQ in numerous Western countries over the past 50 years. Trahan et al. (2014) tested for the Flynn effect in a very large meta-analysis (statistical review of many studies). On average, there was an increase of 2.31 IQ points per decade, and the rate of increase has increased slightly in recent decades.

Why does the Flynn effect occur? General factors are involved – Ang et al. (2010) found it occurred in *all* American groups regardless of gender, race, or rural vs. urban living. Education is an important factor. In 1950, 12% of Americans had received tertiary education (education following the end of schooling); the current figure is 52%. Bordone et al. (2015) found the Flynn effect depends in part on increasing years of education. It also depends on increasing use of modern technology (computers and mobile phones).

Conclusions

Heredity and environment are both very important in determining individual differences in intelligence. However, it would be wrong to assume that the role of genetic factors in determining individual differences in intelligence can be expressed as an overall percentage figure. The reason is that any estimate of the impact of genetic factors is relevant only *within a given population* (see Chapter 4).

Evidence supporting this point comes in research by Tucker-Drob et al. (2013) in which they combined the findings from several twin and adoption studies. They assessed the importance of genetic factors, family environment (shared environmental influences), and unique environment (non-shared environmental influences) on intelligence across various ages. The findings were dramatic. Genes accounted for less than 25% of individual differences in

KEY TERM

Flynn effect: the progressive increase in IQ in numerous countries over the past 50 or 60 years.

intelligence in infancy but 70% in adolescence. In contrast, family environment became considerably less important with increased age (from 65% in infancy to close to 0% in adolescence), and unique or non-shared environment had a comparable impact (approximately 20%) at all ages.

Why do genetic factors become increasingly important during childhood and adolescence? As children grow up, they increasingly select environmental conditions in line with their genetic endowment. For example, children with the genes for high intelligence will typically seek out intellectually stimulating activities (e.g., reading books; accessing information on the Internet) more than other children. Thus, genetic factors have an *indirect* impact on intelligence via their influence on environment selection as well as a *direct* impact on learning ability.

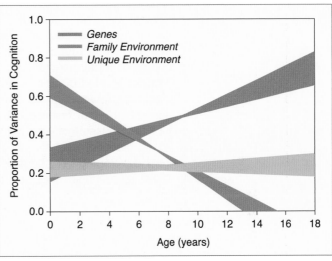

Dramatic evidence that genetic influences on individual differences in intelligence vary greatly across population was reported by Turkheimer et al. (2003) in a study on American children (see Chapter 4). Within affluent families high in socio-economic status, genetic factors accounted for 72% of individual differences in intelligence. In contrast, the figure was only 10% within impoverished families low in socio-economic status.

Why was there this very large difference? If the great majority of children within a population have a *similarly* supportive environment, individual differences in intelligence will depend heavily on genetic factors. That was the case for the high socio-economic status children. In contrast, the environmental conditions of the low socio-economic status children varied much more, which increased considerably the impact of environmental factors.

Proportion of variance in intelligence attributable to genetic influences, family environment, and unique environment during childhood and adolescence up to 18 years. From Tucker-Drob et al. (2013).

IN THE REAL WORLD: "We only use 10% of our brains"

You have probably heard people claim, "We only use 10% of our brains". If so, it is possible humans might become much more intelligent than they are today. After all, the human brain has 100 billion neurons each having between 1,000 and 10,000 synapses (connections) to other neurons (Rolls, 2010). Next, we discuss evidence apparently supporting this claim.

Lorber (1981) studied a patient suffering from **hydrocephalus**, a condition in which large quantities of cerebrospinal fluid accumulate within the brain ventricles (cavities). This creates pressure causing the cerebral cortex to be forced outwards towards the skull. Lorber estimated that the patient's brain weighed only about 10% of that of healthy individuals. Nevertheless, he had an IQ of 126 (in the top 5% of the population) and obtained a university degree. Note, however, that Lorber had previously studied many other patients with hydrocephalus who were very delayed intellectually.

KEY TERM

Hydrocephalus: a condition known non-technically as "water on the brain" in which excessive cerebrospinal fluid crushes the cerebral cortex against the skull.

Subsequently, there have been a few other reported cases of individuals whose brains had been crushed by hydrocephalus but who had reasonable intelligence. This was especially the case when the hydrocephalus has been treated by implanting catheters to drain cerebrospinal fluid away from the brain. Several such cases were discussed by de Oliviera et al. (2012). What is notable is that the extent of brain damage is often rather similar in patients with and without cognitive impairment.

What can we conclude? It is clear the brain sometimes shows surprisingly great resilience after very severe crushing. Brain resilience has also been found in children whose cognitive functioning showed only small impairment following the removal of one entire brain hemisphere (Pulsifer et al., 2004). It is also probable we have some unused brain capacity. However, there are various reasons for disbelieving that we use only 10% of our brain (Beyerstein, 1999). First, it is hydrocephalus typically causes the brain to be compacted rather than destroyed (Rolls, 2010). Second, evolutionary pressures would have prevented humans from developing very inefficient brains, 90% of which were not used. Third, neuroimaging indicates large areas of the brain are active whenever we are engaged in a complex task (Eysenck & Keane, 2015).

Types of intelligence

So far we have focused mainly on IQ, which is a very general measure of intelligence. However, we also need to take account of more specific abilities. For example, some individuals with average IQs have highly developed abilities in language, mathematics, or some other aspect of intelligence. In this section, we discuss the main types or varieties of intelligence.

Factor theories

What is the range of factor types in the hierarchical model of intelligence?

During the first half of the twentieth century, theorists such as Spearman, Thurstone, and Burt tried to identify the main general and specific forms of intelligence. They used a statistical technique known as **factor analysis**, in which the first step involves obtaining scores from numerous individuals on a series of tests.

What happens next? The extent to which individuals performing well on one test perform well on other tests is assessed. If individuals performing well on test A also tend to perform well on test B (i.e., performance on the two tests is highly correlated), it is assumed both tests assess the same aspect (or factor) of intelligence. In contrast, if you cannot predict an individual's performance on test B from their performance on test A, it is assumed the two tests assess different aspects of intelligence.

Hierarchical theory

Carroll (1993) reviewed the evidence based on factor analysis of over 460 data sets obtained from more than 130,000 individuals. The findings suggested a hierarchical theory having three levels:

- At the top level, there is a general factor of intelligence; its existence is supported by the finding that nearly all aspects of intelligence are positively correlated.

KEY TERM

Factor analysis: a statistical technique used to find out the number and nature of the aspects of intelligence (or personality) measured by a test.

- At the middle level, there were eight fairly general group factors including crystallised intelligence (acquired knowledge and ways of thinking) and fluid ability (used when dealing with novel problems).
- At the bottom level, there were very specific factors associated with only one or a small number of tests.

Carroll's theory has been integrated with similar theories proposed by Cattell and by Horn to produce the Cattell-Horn-Carroll theory of intelligence (McGrew, 2009). This theory has general intelligence at the top and 10 fairly general abilities at the second level of the hierarchy. There is reasonable consensus (but not total agreement) concerning the number and nature of abilities at this second level.

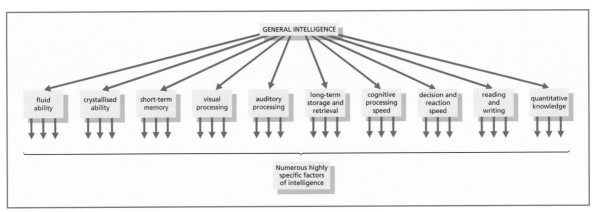

A three-level hierarchical model of intelligence.

EVALUATION

➕ There is much support for the notion that intelligence has a hierarchical structure.

➕ Evidence for the existence of a general factor of intelligence justifies the widespread use of IQ as a general measure of intelligence.

➖ Factor theories *describe* the structure of intelligence. However, they do not *explain* the processes and mechanisms underlying intelligent behaviour.

➖ Factor analysis resembles a sausage machine: what you get out depends on what you put into it in the first place. For example, if no mathematical tests are given to participants, then no factor of mathematical ability will emerge from the subsequent factor analysis.

Gardner's multiple intelligences

Howard Gardner (1983, 1993) argued most intelligence tests (and theories of intelligence) are based on a very narrow view of intelligence. Traditionally, intelligence tests have assessed language ability, spatial ability, and mathematical ability but have failed to consider other abilities required to cope successfully with the environment.

According to Gardner (1983, 1993), there are at least seven intelligences which are allegedly reasonably separate or independent of each other:

1. *Logical-mathematical intelligence*: This is used to handle abstract problems of a logical or mathematical nature.
2. *Spatial intelligence*: This is used when deciding how to go from one place to another, how to arrange suitcases in a car boot or trunk, and so on.
3. *Musical intelligence*: This is used for active musical processes (e.g., playing an instrument) and more passive processes (e.g., appreciating music).
4. *Bodily/kinaesthetic intelligence*: This is involved in the fine control of bodily movements (e.g., in sport and dancing).
5. *Linguistic intelligence*: This is involved in language activities (e.g., reading; writing; speaking).
6. *Intrapersonal intelligence*: This intelligence "depends on core processes that enable people to distinguish among their own feelings" (Gardner et al., 1996, p. 211); it closely resembles self-awareness.
7. *Interpersonal intelligence*: This intelligence involves understanding other people; high scorers are regarded as warm and sympathetic.

The order in which the intelligences are presented here does *not* reflect their importance. Indeed, Gardner (1993, p. 6) argued that "All seven of the intelligences have equal claim to priority." As a result, children should be encouraged to develop those intelligences for which they have the greatest potential.

Findings

Gardner (1993) supported his theory by selecting individuals having outstanding creativity with respect to one of the intelligences. The seven individuals were Albert Einstein (logical-mathematical intelligence), Pablo Picasso (spatial intelligence), Igor Stravinsky (musical intelligence), the poet T.S. Eliot (linguistic intelligence), the dancer and choreographer Martha Graham (bodily/kinaesthetic intelligence), Sigmund Freud (intrapersonal intelligence), and Mahatma Gandhi (interpersonal intelligence).

There is also support for the notion that students differ considerably in their personal preferences for the various intelligences. Lisle (2007) studied adults with intellectual difficulties. Among these adults, 34% expressed a preference for learning through visual presentation of material, 34% through auditory presentation, 23% through kinesthetic presentation, and 9% through multi-modal presentation.

EVALUATION

➕ Gardner was correct in arguing that traditional intelligence tests ignore some aspects of intelligence.

➕ Emotional intelligence (basically a combination of Gardner's intrapersonal and interpersonal intelligences) has attracted enormous interest in recent years (see next section on emotional intelligence).

⊕ Gardner's notion that students differ in their preferred ways of learning has strongly influenced educators.

⊖ The genius-based approach to identifying intelligences is open to criticism. As Jensen (in Miele, 2002, p. 58) pointed out sarcastically, the logic of this approach is that we could claim that, "Al Capone displayed the highest level of 'Criminal Intelligence', or that Casanova was 'blessed' with exceptional 'Sexual Intelligence'."

⊖ What Gardner tried to identify was "forms of knowledge of tremendous importance in many . . . societies" (Gardner, 1983, p. 241). That is not the same as identifying different intelligences (White, 2005).

⊖ Nearly all aspects of intelligence correlate positively with each other, leading to a strong general factor of intelligence. Thus, Gardner's seven intelligences are much less independent or separate than he claimed.

⊖ The seven intelligences are *not* all equally important. The musical and bodily kinaesthetic are less important than the other intelligences in everyday life. You can be tone-deaf and poorly coordinated and still lead a very successful life.

⊖ The theory is descriptive rather than explanatory – it fails to explain *how* each intelligence works or *why* some individuals are more intelligent than others.

Emotional intelligence

Over the past 35 years, there has been a dramatic increase in research on the more social and interpersonal aspects of intelligence (especially emotional intelligence). **Emotional intelligence** can be defined as "the ability to monitor one's own and other people's emotions, to discriminate between different emotion and label them appropriately, and to use emotional information to guide thinking and behaviour" (Colman, 2009, p. 248).

We can distinguish between two types of tests used to assess emotional intelligence. First, there are self-report tests based on the assumption that emotional intelligence "encompasses a constellation of personality traits, affect [emotion], and self-perceived aptitude" (Joseph et al., 2015, p. 298). Second, there are ability tests based on the assumption that emotional intelligence involves the ability to think accurately about one's own and other people's emotions. Thus, self-report tests relate emotional intelligence mostly to personality whereas ability tests relate it more to intelligence.

The difference between these two types of tests is important. Joseph and Newman (2010) found in a meta-analysis (combining the findings from many studies) that there was only a modest correlation of +.26 between self-report and ability tests. This indicates that they assess rather different aspects of emotional intelligence.

KEY TERM

Emotional intelligence: an individual's level of sensitivity to his/her own emotional needs and those of others.

There are several self-report measures of emotional intelligence. One example is the Emotional Quotient Inventory (EQ-i) (Bar-On, 1997, 2006). It contains 133 items relating to intrapersonal skills (e.g., emotional self-awareness), interpersonal skills (e.g., empathy), stress management, adaptability, and general mood.

Probably the best-known ability test of emotional intelligence is the Mayer-Salovey-Caruso Emotional Intelligence Test (MSCEIT) (Mayer et al., 2003). Individuals' ability to perceive emotions in faces, to use emotions to facilitate thought and action, to understand emotions, and to manage emotions is assessed.

Findings

Many studies apparently indicate that emotional intelligence is important. For example, O'Boyle et al. (2011) found in a meta-analysis combining the findings from many studies that ability and self-report measures of emotional intelligence both predicted job performance to some extent. The MSCEIT predicted deviant behaviour in male adolescents (Brackett et al., 2004) over and above the effects of major personality dimensions. Brackett et al. also found that heterosexual couples in which both individuals had high MSCEIT scores were much happier than those in which both had low scores.

Lopes et al. (2004) compared workers having low and high scores on the MSCEIT. Those with high scores were rated by colleagues as easier to deal with, more interpersonally sensitive, more tolerant of stress, and more sociable.

Some findings showing the MSCEIT can predict job performance are less impressive than they appear. This is because the MSCEIT in part assesses aspects of ability and personality duplicating those assessed by previous tests. For example, Rossen and Kranzler (2009) found the MSCEIT predicted academic achievement, psychological well-being, peer attachment, positive relations with others, and alcohol use. However, most of these effects occurred because high scorers on the MSCEIT differed from low scorers in traditional measures of personality (e.g., extraversion; neuroticism) and intelligence. Thus, the individual differences identified by the MSCEIT resemble those identified by well-established measures of personality and intelligence.

The EQ-i (a self-report measure of emotional intelligence discussed earlier) correlates positively with extraversion and negatively with neuroticism (Geher, 2004; see Chapter 18). However, it often fails to correlate with IQ (Geher, 2004). The correlations are sufficiently high to suggest the EQ-i mainly involves re-packaging well-established personality dimensions and has little to do with intelligence as conventionally defined. The same limitations apply to most other self-report measures of emotional intelligence (Zeidner et al., 2009).

In the study by O'Boyle et al. (2011) discussed earlier, they found self-report measures of emotional intelligence correlated with major personality dimensions (extraversion and neuroticism). They also found that ability measures correlated with traditional measures of intelligence. However, their key finding was that self-report and ability measures of emotional intelligence both predicted job performance to some extent over and above the contribution from traditional measures of personality and intelligence.

EVALUATION

➕ As suggested by the term "emotional intelligence", success at school and in life generally depends on social and emotional factors as well as intelligence. Support for this statement with respect to educational achievement was reported by Krapohl et al. (2014; discussed earlier).

➕ Self-report and ability measures of emotional intelligence have had some success in predicting various aspects of job performance and relationship satisfaction over and above the effects of traditional measures of personality and intelligence.

➖ Self-report measures of emotional intelligence mostly assess well-established personality dimensions (especially extraversion and neuroticism).

➖ Ability measures of emotional intelligence mostly assess the general factor of intelligence as measured by conventional intelligence tests.

Chapter summary

- Intelligence involves abilities such as problem solving and reasoning. Of importance, it also involves successful adaptation to one's cultural environment.
- Intelligence tests assess IQ. It is a general measure of intelligence having a population average of 100 and with two-thirds of individuals having IQs between 85 and 115.
- All good intelligence tests have high reliability (consistency of measurement) and validity (e.g., ability to predict career success).
- Identical twins (even those reared apart) are more similar in IQ than fraternal twins. Thus, genetic factors influence individual differences in IQ.
- The rapid rise in IQ in recent decades (the Flynn effect) is due to several environmental factors (e.g., increased years of education).
- The impact of genetic factors on individual differences in intelligence is much greater in adolescents and adults than in young children because the former can select and control their environment to a greater extent.
- Factor theories suggest that intelligence has a hierarchical structure with a general factor at the top and approximately 10 factors at the second level. Such theories are descriptive rather than explanatory.
- Gardner proposed an approach based on multiple intelligences. This approach has been influential within education. However, he exaggerated the independence of the intelligences from each other.

- Self-report and ability tests of emotional intelligence correlate with traditional measures of personality and intelligence. However, they have shown some ability to predict job performance and other outcomes over and above the contributions of these traditional measures.

Further reading

- Deary, I.J. (2012). Intelligence. *Annual Review of Psychology, 63,* 453–482. This chapter by Ian Deary provides a comprehensive discussion of theory and research on intelligence.

- Mackintosh, N.J. (1998). *IQ and human intelligence.* Oxford: Oxford University Press. This is an excellent book by a leading British psychologist. It stands out for providing a balanced and insightful account of the controversial topic of human intelligence.

- O'Boyle, E.H., Humphrey, R.H., Pollack, J.M., Hawver, T.H., & Story, P.A. (2011). The relation between emotional intelligence, and job performance: A meta-analysis. *Journal of Organizational Behavior, 32,* 788–818. The relationships between different measures of emotional intelligence, cognitive ability, personality and job performance are explored in a review of the research literature.

- Plomin, R., & Deary, I.J. (2014). Genetics and intelligence differences: Five special findings. *Molecular Psychiatry, 20,* 98–108. Robert Plomin and Ian Deary provide an up-to-date account of what is known about the influence of genetic factors on individual differences in intelligence.

Essay questions

1. Discuss possible definitions of intelligence. What are the main features of a good intelligence test?

2. Discuss ways of assessing the relative roles of heredity and environment in influencing individual differences in intelligence. Why do the findings vary considerably depending on the population being studied?

3. Discuss ways in which emotional intelligence can be measured? To what extent has the notion of emotional intelligence proved useful?

4. Describe Gardner's theory of multiple intelligences. To what extent has this theory received research support?

One of the most interesting and fascinating things in our lives is the rich diversity of people we meet. Of course, they differ in numerous ways. However, one of the most important ways in which they differ is in terms of their personality. In view of the richness and variety of humans' personality, is it really possible to assess it? How can we sure we have assessed it accurately?

What do you think are the most important ways in which people's personalities differ? Is personality determined largely by heredity, or does it depend more on the experiences we have had during our lives?

Personality

■ ■ ■ ■ ■ ■ ■ ■ ■ □

18

Introduction

Some of the people we know are nearly always cheerful and friendly. In contrast, others tend to be unfriendly and depressed, and still others are aggressive and hostile. This chapter is concerned with attempts to understand these individual differences in personality.

What is meant by the word "personality"? According to Child (1968, p. 83), personality consists of "the more or less stable, internal factors that make one person's behaviour consistent from one time to another, and different from the behaviour other people would manifest in comparable situations".

There are *four* key words in this definition:

- *Stable*: personality remains relatively constant or unchanging over time.
- *Internal*: personality lies within us, but how we behave is determined in part by our personality.
- *Consistent*: if personality remains constant over time, and if personality determines behaviour, then we would expect people to behave fairly consistently.
- *Different*: when we talk of personality, we assume there are large individual differences leading different people to behave differently in similar situations.

Cross-cultural differences

I have suggested so far that an individual's personality remains fairly stable over time. However, that is less true of collectivistic cultures (e.g., China; Japan) that emphasise interdependence and group membership than individualistic ones (e.g., UK; United States) that emphasise independence and personal responsibility. Why is that? Individuals living in collectivistic cultures are supposed to fit in *flexibly* with group expectations.

These views have been supported by research using the Twenty Statements Test in which people describe themselves. Those from collectivistic cultures use fewer personality characteristics than those from individualistic ones to describe themselves. Instead, the focus is more on their various social roles (e.g., parent; teacher; club member) (Heine & Buchtel, 2009).

Further evidence was reported by English and Chen (2007). They asked European Americans and Asian Americans to describe their personality in different relationship contexts (e.g., friends; parents). The European Americans showed more consistency than the Asian Americans across contexts. English and Chen (2011) considered European Americans and Asian Americans whose personalities were inconsistent across different relationship contexts. The former interpreted this inconsistency negatively as indicating they were not being "true to themselves" whereas the Asian Americans did not interpret it negatively. Thus, those living in individualistic cultures regard it as more important than those living in collectivistic cultures to behave consistently across different relationships and contexts.

Personality assessment

What is the greatest problem with personality questionnaires?

There are several ways of assessing personality. As with intelligence tests, however, any good personality tests must possess three important characteristics:

1. *Reliability*: the test produces similar results on different occasions. A test indicating that a given individual is very extraverted on the first testing occasion but very introverted on the second occasion would be useless.
2. *Validity*: the test measures what it is claimed to measure. For example, we would expect patients with anxiety disorders to score highly on a test designed to assess the extent to which people have an anxious personality.
3. *Standardisation*: this involves giving the test to large representative samples of people to establish the meaning of any given individual's scores. For example, a score of 19 on a test of extraversion has no meaning on its own but becomes meaningful if we know that only 10% of the population have such a high score.

Questionnaires

You have probably filled in several personality questionnaires. The items on these questionnaires relate to your thoughts, feelings, and behaviour (e.g., "Do you tend to be moody?"; "Do you have many friends?"). The obvious advantage of the questionnaire-based approach is that you know more about yourself than do other people.

The greatest disadvantage is that individuals may fake their responses. Most such faking involves **social desirability bias** (the tendency to respond to questionnaire items in the socially desirable, but incorrect, way). Paulhus (2002) identified two forms of social desirability bias: (1) self-deception (when you are unaware of the bias); and (2) impression management (when you are aware of the bias). Evidence for this bias has been obtained using the **bogus pipeline** – participants are told (incorrectly) they are connected to a lie detector that can detect the increased arousal produced by dishonest answers. In one study (Derakshan & Eysenck, 1999), participants reported significantly less defensiveness on a personality questionnaire under bogus pipeline conditions than under standard conditions.

The most common method used to detect social desirability bias is to use a Lie scale consisting of items where the socially desirable answer is very unlikely to be the honest one (e.g., "Do you ever gossip?"; "Do you know anyone you really dislike?"). It is assumed that someone who answers most such questions in the socially desirable direction is faking their responses.

KEY TERMS

Social desirability bias: the tendency to provide socially desirable responses on personality questionnaires even when those responses are incorrect.

Bogus pipeline: a sham lie detector used to elicit honest answers when individuals complete personality questionnaires.

Reliability

How can we assess reliability? The most common approach involves giving a personality questionnaire to a group of people on two occasions (the test-retest method). The test has high reliability if most individuals have similar scores on both occasions, as is the case with the great majority of personality questionnaires.

Validity

How can we assess validity? One approach is to consider behavioural differences between low and high scorers on some personality dimensions. For example, we might expect that individuals high in extraversion would be more popular and attend more parties than those low in extraversion. We would expect those high in conscientiousness to have higher levels of academic performance and to be more honest than those low conscientiousness. These and other predictions have been confirmed (Paunonen & Ashton, 2001).

Another method for assessing validity involves comparing other-ratings (someone who knows a given individual well provides an assessment of his/her personality) with self-reports (the individual assesses his/her own personality). A questionnaire has good validity if there is much similarity between self-report and rating scores. McCrae and Costa (1990) compared other-ratings from spouses with self-reports. There was good agreement between other-ratings and self-reports for all five personality factors assessed. Costa and McCrae (1992) reported a moderate average correlation of +.43 between self-reports and friend-reports across five personality factors.

Are self-reports or other-ratings likely to be more valid when there are disagreements between them? There is no simple answer to that question because both measures have significant limitations (Paunonen & O'Neill, 2010). Other-ratings have the disadvantage that raters typically only have knowledge of the target person's behaviour in limited contexts (e.g., in college). Another issue is that other-ratings typically become more positive over time as the rater becomes increasingly friendly with the target person.

Theories of personality

What factors determine individual differences in adult personality? As we will see, there are several answers to that question. Freud argued that adult personality is influenced mainly by childhood experiences although he accepted that biological factors are also important. In contrast, trait theorists such as Raymond Cattell and H.J. Eysenck emphasised the importance of genetic factors in determining personality. The trait approach remains very influential. Several theorists (e.g., McCrae & Costa, 1985) have argued there are five major personality factors (the so-called Big Five model). In contrast, Bandura argued that individual differences in personality depend to a large extent on the particular learning experiences we have had.

Which of these views is correct? There is some truth in all the views – thus, a complete account of the determinants of personality would combine the factors emphasised by each theorist.

Freud's psychoanalytical approach

Freud argued that children's experiences during the first 5 years of life have a strong influence on their subsequent adult personality. He identified five stages of psychosexual development: oral stage (focus on mouth and lips; 0–18 months), anal stage (focus on anal area; 18–36 months), phallic stage (focus on the penis or clitoris; 3–6 years), latency stage (few sexual feelings; 6 years – puberty), and genital stage (focus on sexual pleasure with another person; puberty onwards).

If children experience great satisfaction or problems at any given psychosexual stage, this influences their adult personality. For example, individuals who focus excessively on the phallic stage become self-assured, vain, and impulsive adults.

There is some support for Freud's general approach in that childhood experiences and personality clearly influence the development of adult personality. For example, Franz et al. (1996) reported evidence suggesting that childhood experiences have a long-term impact. Adult levels of depression at the age of 41 were predicted well by parental coldness when they were only 5 years old. In addition, an overall measure of difficult childhood experiences (e.g., parental divorce; frequent moves; loss) predicted depression in middle age.

Mickelson et al. (1997) found parental loss or separation in childhood was associated with insecure attachment in adults. In addition, adults who experienced serious traumas in childhood (e.g., sexual abuse; severe neglect) were more likely than other adults to have anxious attachments to other people.

The strengths of Freud's approach are that he put forward the first systematic theory of personality, and his assumption that adult personality depends in part on the experiences of early childhood is correct. However, there are several limitations. First, individual differences in personality depend much more on genetic factors that assumed by Freud (discussed later). Second, Freud's stage-based theory assumes that personality development occurs in a neater and tidier way than is actually the case. Third, the evidence does not support Freud's assumptions concerning the relationships between the 5 stages of psychosexual development and adult personality.

Trait theories

We may think of Susan as "sociable", Fred as "neurotic", and Catherine as "aggressive". This involves focusing on their **traits** (stable aspects of a person that influence their behaviour). For example, Susan is sociable because she is talkative, smiles a lot, is much involved in social events, and has many friends. Personality traits are typically assessed by questionnaires. As we have just seen, such questionnaires provide a reliable and valid assessment of human personality.

One of the main goals of trait theorists is to provide a comprehensive description that includes *all* the major personality traits. Unfortunately, no method is guaranteed to achieve that goal. However, a useful approach is based on the **fundamental lexical hypothesis**. According to this hypothesis, every language has words in it referring to those personality characteristics of most importance to those speaking that language (Allport & Odbert, 1936, identified 4,500 such words). Several theorists (e.g., Cattell, 1943; Goldberg, 1990) have used the fundamental lexical hypothesis in their research.

KEY TERMS

Traits: aspects or dimensions of personality that exhibit individual differences and are moderately stable over time; they have direct and indirect influences on behaviour.

Fundamental lexical hypothesis: the assumption that dictionaries contain words referring to all of the most important personality traits.

Cattell's trait theory

Cattell (1943) used the fundamental lexical hypothesis to reduce Allport and Odbert's (1936) 4,500 personality-related terms to 160 trait words by eliminating unfamiliar words and synonyms. Cattell (1943) then added 11 traits from the personality literature producing a total of 171 trait names claimed to cover the whole of personality. These trait names were used to construct the Sixteen Personality Factor (16PF) test to measure 16 personality traits.

The factors of Cattell's 16PF

Reserved	Outgoing
Less intelligent	More intelligent
Affected by feelings	More emotionally stable
Humble	Assertive
Sober	Happy-go-lucky
Expedient	Conscientious
Shy	Venturesome
Tough-minded	Tender-minded
Trusting	Suspicious
Practical	Imaginative
Forthright	Shrewd
Placid	Apprehensive
Conservative	Experimenting
Group-dependent	Self-sufficient
Casual	Controlled
Relaxed	Tense

The 16PF is one of the world's most popular personality tests. However, systematic analysis has indicated that it does not measure anything like 16 different personality traits. For example, Barrett and Kline (1982) found evidence for only seven to nine factors, most of which did not relate closely to those proposed by Cattell.

Why have findings with the 16PF been so disappointing? The key problem is that many of the 16 traits resemble each other very closely. For example, the tense and apprehensive traits are very similar, and both are almost the opposite of emotionally stable.

EVALUATION

➕ Cattell was a pioneer in his use of the fundamental lexical hypothesis to identify the main personality traits.

➕ Cattell was one of the first psychologists to demonstrate that similar personality traits can be found in self-report and other-rating data.

➖ There are only about 8 different personality traits in the 16PF. Thus, Cattell's main questionnaire is seriously flawed.

➖ Cattell's approach was not very theoretical or explanatory. As Cattell (1957, p. 50) admitted, "I have always felt justifiably suspicious of theory built much ahead of data."

H.J. Eysenck's trait theory

What did Cattell find in relation to personality traits using life, questionnaire, and objective test data?

Cattell identified numerous *correlated* personality traits, many of which were very similar. In contrast, H.J. Eysenck argued it is preferable to focus on a small number of uncorrelated or *independent* factors entirely separate from each other.

H.J. Eysenck identified three major personality traits or "superfactors". All these superfactors are measured by the Eysenck Personality Questionnaire (EPQ; Eysenck & Eysenck, 1975):

- **Extraversion**: those scoring high on extraversion (extraverts) are more sociable and impulsive than those scoring low (introverts).
- **Neuroticism**: those scoring high on neuroticism are more anxious and depressed than those scoring low.
- **Psychoticism**: those scoring high are aggressive, hostile, and uncaring.

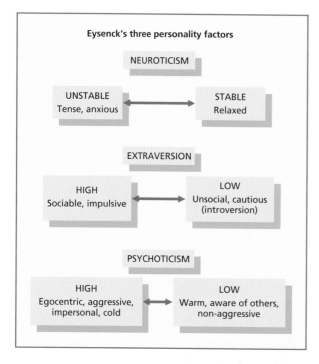

You probably feel there must be more to personality than just these three factors (and you are right!). However, many aspects of personality can be understood as *combinations* of two (or even all three) of these factors. For example, optimistic individuals are high in extraversion and low in neuroticism.

What causes individual differences in extraversion, neuroticism, and psychoticism? According to Eysenck (1979), 60% to 80% of individual differences in each trait are due to genetic factors. These genetic factors influence the physiological system. Introverts were assumed to have a high level of cortical arousal (brain activity). As a result, they can become over-aroused and so prefer reading books to going to exciting parties.

Those high in neuroticism were assumed to have high activation of the visceral brain. This consists of several parts of the brain including some (e.g., **amygdala**) involved in fear processing, and helps to explain why individuals high in neuroticism have strong negative emotions. Differences in brain functioning associated with psychoticism are unclear.

Gray (1981) developed H.J. Eysenck's theory by providing an alternative biological explanation. According to his theory, trait anxiety (consisting mainly of neuroticism but also including some introversion) is associated with brain systems concerned with susceptibility to punishment. In contrast, extraversion (especially impulsivity) is associated with brain systems concerned with susceptibility to reward.

KEY TERMS

Extraversion: a personality trait reflecting individual differences in sociability and impulsiveness.

Neuroticism: a personality trait reflecting individual differences in negative emotional experiences (e.g., anxiety; sadness).

Psychoticism: a personality trait that reflects individual differences in hostility, coldness, and aggression.

Amygdala: a small, almond-shaped part of the brain buried deep within the temporal lobe; it is associated with several emotional states (e.g., fear).

Individuals high in neuroticism should experience more negative mood states than low scorers, and individuals high in extraversion should experience more positive mood states than low scorers.

What do studies based on H.J. Eysenck's theory indicate about major personality traits?

Findings

Vukasović and Bratko (2015) assessed the percentage of individual differences in each Eysenckian dimension due to genetic factors in a meta-analysis combining the findings from many studies. For extraversion, it was 39%; for neuroticism, it was 42%; and for psychoticism it was 30%.

Is it preferable to describe personality in terms of 3 factors (H.J. Eysenck) or 16 (Cattell)? Saville and Blinkhorn (1976) provided part of the answer. They analysed Cattell's 16PF questionnaire to discover which independent or separate factors it contained. They found it largely measured extraversion and neuroticism (but not psychoticism).

Shortly we discuss the most influential trait approach (the Big Five model). Extraversion and neuroticism are both included among its five personality factors, but psychoticism is not. Why are extraversion and neuroticism so important? Extraverts (who have high susceptibility to reward) experience more positive moods than introverts. Those high in neuroticism (having high susceptibility to punishment) experience more negative moods than those low in neuroticism (Meyer & Shack, 1989). Thus, individual differences in mood state (positive and negative) are well predicted by an individual's level of extraversion and neuroticism.

EVALUATION

- It has proven more useful to identify a few unrelated or independent personality traits (as in H.J. Eysenck's approach) than a much larger number of related ones (as in Cattell's approach).

- There is convincing evidence that extraversion and neuroticism are major personality traits or factors.

- H.J. Eysenck tried to provide an explanatory account of his three personality factors by focusing on genetic factors and physiological mechanisms.

- The role of genetic factors in influencing individual differences in personality is much smaller than claimed by H.J. Eysenck.

- H.J. Eysenck was only partially successful in identifying the underlying physiological mechanisms. Gray's (1981) theory based on susceptibility to reward and punishment has proved more valid.

- Psychoticism is not a major personality trait. It is also poorly named in that it is more closely related to antisocial personality disorder than psychotic disorders such as schizophrenia (Corr, 2010).

> **IN REAL LIFE: identical twins brought up apart**
>
> There is substantial evidence that identical twins brought up together are much more similar in personality than fraternal twins brought up together. It seems obvious to explain these findings in terms of genetic factors. However, parents try to treat identical twins more similarly than fraternal twins (Loehlin & Nichols, 1976), and this may make the environments of identical twins more similar than those of fraternal twins. The best solution is to study identical twins reared apart. Bouchard et al. (1990) studied identical twins who were reared apart throughout the great majority of their childhoods and compared them against identical twins reared together. They found there was moderately high similarity in personality between identical twins reared together, and the degree of similarity was very similar between identical twins reared apart. These findings suggest environmental factors have a very modest impact on the development of personality.

Big five model

McCrae and Costa (e.g., 1985) argued that there are five major personality traits (the Big Five):

1. *Openness* (curious, imaginative, creative)
2. *Conscientiousness* (hard-working, ambitious, persistent)
3. *Extraversion* (sociable, optimistic, talkative)
4. *Agreeableness* (good-natured, cooperative, helpful)
5. *Neuroticism* (anxious, insecure, emotional)

The first letters of the five traits or factors form the word OCEAN – this may help you to remember the trait names!

Costa and McCrae (1992) produced the revised NEO-PI Five-Factor Inventory to measure these five factors. They assumed these five traits or factors were all independent or *unrelated* to each other (like the H.J. Eysenck's factors). They also assumed that individual differences in each trait depend importantly on genetic factors.

Findings

Five traits or factors closely resembling those put forward by McCrae and Costa (1985) have been reported many times. McCrae and Costa (1997) identified the Big Five factors in a cross-cultural study involving German, Portuguese, Hebrew, Chinese, Korean, and Japanese translations of their English-version questionnaire. Goldberg (1990) confirmed the importance of these five factors in a study in which he made use of the fundamental lexical hypothesis (discussed earlier) to identify all the major personality factors.

Vukasović and Bratko (2015) found in a meta-analysis that the percentages of individual differences attributable to genetic factors for each of the

Big Five factors were as follows: openness: 41%, conscientiousness: 31%, extraversion: 36%, agreeableness: 35%, and neuroticism: 37%. Thus, there are moderately strong genetic influences on individual differences in all five factors.

Are the Big Five factors important in everyday life? There is much evidence that they are. Paunonen (2003) compared introverts and extraverts. Extraverts consumed more alcohol, were more popular, attended more parties, and had more dating variety. Those high in conscientiousness had higher academic achievement, were more intelligent, and more honest than those low in conscientiousness. The other factors (neuroticism, agreeableness, and openness) also predicted aspects of behaviour.

Fleeson and Gallagher (2009) asked participants to report on their behaviour several times a day for two weeks. Most individuals' behaviour was reasonably consistent and predictable over time. Extraverted individuals behaved in an extraverted way much more often than introverted ones, those high in conscientiousness behaved more often in a conscientious way than low scorers, and so on.

The Big Five factors are also relevant to mental disorder. Kotov et al. (2010) found that patients suffering from a wide range of mental disorders were high in neuroticism and low in conscientiousness, and also tended to be low in extraversion. These findings suggest that individuals with certain types of personality may be vulnerable to the development of mental disorders. However, it is also possible that having a mental disorder leads to high neuroticism and low extraversion.

Wood (2015) used the fundamental lexical hypothesis to identify 498 adjectives describing personality. Participants rated the importance of each personality characteristic when considering someone as a potential friend, romantic partner, or work colleague. Those personality characteristics most strongly related to the Big Five factors were rated as of most social importance.

Why are the Big Five factors so important? Buss (1995) argued that these personality factors are all crucial to group living. For example, agreeable individuals increase group cooperation, extraverted ones enhance group cohesion by being people-oriented, and conscientious individuals can be trusted to work effectively towards group goals. In addition, those low in neuroticism remain calm when the group faces threats, and those high in openness help the group to plan for the future.

If the Big Five factors are of fundamental importance, we might expect to find evidence of them in nonhuman species. That is, indeed, the case. The personality dimensions of extraversion, neuroticism, and agreeableness have been identified in several species (Gosling & John, 1999), and there is some evidence that the same is true of openness. The conscientiousness dimension is found only in chimpanzees.

It is assumed within the Big Five model that the factors are all independent of each other. This assumption is not entirely correct. High neuroticism is associated with low conscientiousness, low extraversion, and low agreeableness, and high extraversion is associated with high openness and high conscientiousness (van der Linden et al., 2010).

EVALUATION

➕ The Big Five personality traits or factors have been obtained repeatedly in self-report and rating studies.

➕ Use of the fundamental lexical hypothesis suggests that the Big Five approach provides a comprehensive description of personality.

➕ The Big Five factors all have high social relevance and importance, and four of them have been identified in other species.

➕ Genetic factors account for between 31% and 41% of individual differences in each of the Big Five factors.

➖ The Big Five factors are more related to each other than assumed theoretically.

➖ The Big Five approach works well as a description of personality but is less developed theoretically. In spite of the efforts of Buss (1995), it is not entirely clear *why* these five factors are of central importance to human personality.

Social cognitive theory

What are the main differences between Bandura's social cognitive theory of personality and the trait theories?

Albert Bandura, an American psychologist born in 1925, has developed a social cognitive approach to personality. He has consistently argued that the trait approach to personality is *oversimplified*. According to him, we need to consider personal factors (personality), environmental factors, and the individual's own behaviour to achieve a comprehensive understanding.

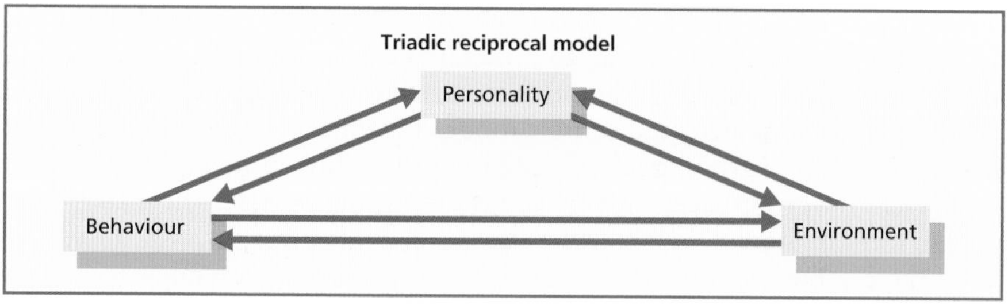

Triadic reciprocal model

As the figure shows, Bandura assumed that personality, behaviour and the environment influence each other in complex ways. The environment influences our behaviour, but our personality and behaviour also help to determine the environment. For example, extraverts choose to spend more of their time in social situations than do introverts.

Bandura's approach is more comprehensive than that of traditional trait theorists. Trait theorists emphasise the notion that personality influences behaviour, which corresponds to *only* one of the six arrows in Bandura's approach. Trait theorists also argue that the environment influences behaviour (a second arrow in Bandura's model). However, few trait theorists focus on the other four arrows. This is a real limitation. People's personalities influence the situations in which they find themselves as well as how they behave in those situations. For example, extraverts actively seek out social situations more often than introverts (Furnham, 1981).

There are two other important differences between Bandura's social cognitive approach and trait theories. Bandura argued we must take full account of the *specific* situation in which individuals find themselves to predict their behaviour. In contrast, most trait theorists claim an individual's personality will influence their behaviour similarly in most situations.

Second, Bandura argued that individual differences in behaviour depend on *cognitive* processes and strategies. In contrast, the neglect of the cognitive system is one of the greatest limitations of most trait theories.

Self-efficacy

Bandura emphasises the importance of **self-efficacy**, which refers to the beliefs individuals have about their ability to cope with a given task or situation and to achieve the desired outcomes. In the words of Bandura (1977, p. 391), self-efficacy judgments are concerned "not with the skills one has but with judgments of what one can do with the skills one possesses". It is assumed that high self-efficacy increases task motivation and thus enhances performance.

What determines an individual's level of self-efficacy in any given situation? First, there are the individual's experiences of success and/or failure in that situation. Second, there are relevant second-hand experiences – if you see someone else cope successfully with that situation, it will increase your self-efficacy beliefs. Third, there is social persuasion – your level of self-efficacy will increase if someone argues persuasively you have the necessary skills to succeed in that situation. Fourth, self-efficacy will be reduced if you experience the high level of arousal associated with anxiety and failure.

Findings

There is much evidence for a positive association between self-efficacy and performance. For example, Stajkovic and Luthans (1998) found across 114 studies that high self-efficacy was associated with a 28% increase in work performance. Self-efficacy was more strongly associated with high task performance on easy than complex tasks, and the strength of the association was higher in laboratory settings than in more naturalistic ones.

Why did these differences occur? We would expect the relationship between self-efficacy and performance to be greater when participants possess detailed information about task demands, the best strategy to adopt, and so on. People performing difficult tasks in real-world settings often lack sufficient information to make accurate self-efficacy judgments.

Findings such as those of Stajkovic and Luthans (1998) are hard to interpret because we do not know whether high self-efficacy enhances performance or whether high performance increases self-efficacy. Hwang et al. (2016) addressed this issue in a study on academic achievement in students over a 5-year period. They found past academic achievement predicted subsequent self-efficacy beliefs and that self-efficacy beliefs predicted subsequent academic performance. The former effect was stronger than the latter.

How does self-efficacy relate to standard personality factors in its ability to predict behaviour? Judge et al. (2007) reviewed studies on work-related performance. Self-efficacy predicted performance to a modest extent, but this did not

> **KEY TERM**
>
> **Self-efficacy:** the beliefs about being able to perform a task so as to achieve certain goals.

seem to be due to self-efficacy itself. Instead, it occurred mainly because individuals high in self-efficacy tended to be high in intelligence, conscientiousness, and extraversion, and low in neuroticism. Performance was better predicted by intelligence and conscientiousness than by self-efficacy.

Self-regulation

Bandura (1986) argued that our behaviour is influenced by **self-regulation** as well as by self-efficacy. Self-regulation involves using cognitive processes to regulate and control your own behaviour.

EVALUATION

➕ Bandura's theory has clarified how individual differences in behaviour depend on interactions among cognitive, social, and motivational factors.

➕ The extent to which people adopt healthy forms of behaviour (e.g., giving up smoking; losing weight; taking exercise) depends to an important extent on self-efficacy and self-regulation.

➖ Bandura's social cognitive approach de-emphasises emotional factors. In fact, motivation and behaviour are often influenced by our emotions rather than by cognitions.

➖ Bandura emphasises the importance of learning in determining an individual's self-efficacy beliefs. However, individual differences in self-efficacy depend mostly on genetic factors (e.g., Waaktaar & Torgersen, 2013).

➖ Bandura has focused on predicting and understanding people's behaviour in *specific* situations. It is unclear whether his approach can account for individual differences in *broad* areas of life.

➖ Vancouver (2012, p. 466) referred to "the informal nature of Bandura's theorising." For example, many terms (e.g., "belief"; "motivation") are not clearly defined.

➖ Bandura has focused on predicting and understanding people's behaviour in *specific* situations. His theoretical approach is unable to account properly for individual differences in *broad* areas of life.

KEY TERM

Self-regulation: the notion that individuals learn to reward and punish themselves internally to regulate their own behaviour and achieve desired outcomes.

Chapter summary

- The notion that our behaviour is strongly influenced by our personality characteristics is more relevant in individualistic than collectivistic cultures.
- Personality tests need to be standardised and to have high levels of reliability and validity.

- Freud argued correctly that childhood experiences influence adult personality. However, there is little empirical support for the detailed predictions from his theory of psychosexual development.
- Cattell argued there are 16 personality traits, many of which are closely related. However, there are no more than 8 personality traits in his questionnaire designed to assess 16.
- H.J. Eysenck identified three unrelated superfactors (extraversion, neuroticism, psychoticism). Genetic factors account for about 40% of individual differences in all three superfactors.
- Costa and McCrae argued there are five major personality factors (the Big Five: openness, conscientiousness, extraversion, agreeableness, and neuroticism). Individual differences in all five factors depend in part on genetic factors.

Further reading

- Bandura, A. (2012). On the functional properties of perceived self-efficacy revisited. *Journal of Management, 38*, 9–44. Albert Bandura evaluates research supporting and criticising his notion of self-efficacy.

- Cervone, D., & Pervin, L.A. (2016). *Personality: Theory and research* (13th ed.). Hoboken, NJ: Wiley. This well-established textbook has full discussions of all the theoretical approaches included in this chapter.

- Eysenck, M.W. (2016). Hans Eysenck: A research evaluation. *Personality and Individual Differences, 103*, 209–219. In this article, I provide an assessment of the strengths and limitations of my father's contribution to our understanding of personality.

- Turkheimer, E., Pettersson, E., & Horn, E.E. (2014). A phenotypic null hypothesis for the genetics of personality. *Annual Review of Psychology, 65*, 515–540. The role of genetic factors in determining individual differences in personality is discussed fully in this chapter.

Essay questions

1. How would you set about designing a questionnaire to assess personality?

2. Describe Cattell's and H.J. Eysenck's theories of personality. What do they have in common? How do they differ?

3. What is the Big Five approach to personality? What are the strengths and limitations of this approach?

4. Describe and evaluate Bandura's social cognitive theory.

How we see ourselves is our self-concept. Like everyone else, you have numerous thoughts and feelings about yourself, about the kind of person you are, and about your relationships with other people. What are the most important influences that have shaped your self-concept? Has your self-concept been influenced by other people (especially those who play or have played major roles in your life)?

In Western cultures, most people have a sense of themselves as individuals whose behaviour is determined by their personality, personal goals, and so on. Do you think this Western view of the self is universal? More specifically, do you think people living in very different cultures (e.g., the Far East) have a sense of self revolving around their social roles and obligations?

The self-concept

19

What is the **self-concept**? According to Grilli and Verfaellie (2015, p. 1684), it is "the conception of oneself that enables each individual to construct a personal identity". Baumeister (2011) argued the self has three major aspects:

1. A *knowledge structure*: we all possess a huge amount of information about ourselves, and this gives us our awareness of having a self.
2. An *interpersonal being*: the self exists almost entirely within social contexts and is used when relating to others.
3. An *agent*: the self is a doer in that it makes decisions and causes us to behave in certain ways.

Our self-concept is influenced by many factors. However, our relationships with other people are of crucial importance. Charles Cooley (1902) used the term "looking-glass self" to convey the notion that our self-concept reflects other people's evaluations – we tend to see ourselves as others see us. Those of greatest importance in our lives (e.g., partners, parents, close friends) influence our self-concept the most. However, changes in our self-concept do not depend only on *passively* accepting the views of others. Yeung and Martin (2003) found that over time we can *actively* change our self-concept and how we are perceived by others.

William James (1890) distinguished between two aspects of the self-concept: the "I" or self as the *subject* of experience and the "me" or self as the *object* of experience. Young children start to develop a sense of being separate from other people: this is the "I". The "I" is the doer that experiences the immediate present. After that, the "me" develops; this involves awareness of the self as an object that can be perceived by others. It takes account of the past and future and provides a sense of permanence in our self-concept.

It seems natural for people living in Europe or the United States to think in terms of a self-concept. These cultures are individualistic ones in which the emphasis is on personal responsibility and achievement (see Chapter 1). This way of thinking is less common in collectivistic cultures in which the emphasis is on the group rather than the individual. For example, the Chinese word *ren* (meaning person) refers to the ways in which an individual's behaviour fits (or fails to fit) group standards.

> **KEY TERM**
>
> **Self-concept:** the organised information about ourselves that we have stored away in long-term memory.

Development of the self-concept

The self-concept develops during the early years of life. It is hard to study its development because young children have a very limited command of language. In spite of this, progress has been made in understanding when and how infants start to have a self-concept.

Self-recognition

One of the earliest signs that infants are starting to develop a sense of self is when they can recognise themselves in a mirror (the mirror self-recognition test). A red spot is applied secretly to the infant's nose and then he/she is held up to a mirror. It has been argued that infants who reach for their own nose (and so recognise their own reflection) show some evidence of self-awareness. Very few infants in the first year of life showed self-awareness compared to 70% of those aged between 21 and 24 months.

Success on the mirror self-recognition test only requires that infants have a very basic sense of self. A more developed sense of self is required for successful performance of the delayed self-recognition test. On this test, a large sticker is secretly placed in the child's hair, and this event is videotaped or photographed. After three minutes, the child is shown the videotape or photograph, and success is defined as reaching up to remove the sticker.

The delayed self-recognition test is harder than the mirror self-recognition test – children given some prior training are nevertheless typically 3 years old before they succeed on it. Success on the delayed test is generally associated with the development of a temporally extended self (Lazaridis, 2013). In other words, they understand the self remains the same through time (past, present, and future).

What are the changes in the self-concept during childhood?

According to Howe and Courage (1997), the initial development of a sense of self is crucial to the emergence of **autobiographical memory** (concerned with our memories of events we have experienced). Support for this hypothesis was reported by Howe et al. (2003). Among infants aged between 15 and 23 months, self-recognisers had better memory for personal events than infants who were not self-recognisers. More strikingly, not a single child showed good performance on a memory test for personal events *before* achieving self-recognition.

Autobiographical memory

We can study the development of the self-concept in childhood and adolescence by focusing on autobiographical memory. Habermas and de Silveira (2008) compared the narrative accounts of individuals in late childhood and adolescence. The adolescents' accounts showed greater causal coherence (e.g., explaining how early events caused later ones) and coherence (identifying organising themes in their lives). These findings suggest that a complete self-concept only emerges during adolescence.

Further support for the notion that the self-concept is still developing in late adolescence and early adulthood was reported by Bluck and Alea (2009). They asked young and older adults why they thought and talked about the past. The younger group used autobiographical memory more often to direct future plans and to produce a sense of self-continuity.

There are other interesting changes in autobiographical memory during childhood and adolescence. Pasupathi and Wainryb (2010) asked children

KEY TERM

Autobiographical memory: memory across the lifespan for events involving the individual (especially those of personal significance).

and adolescents to construct autobiographical memory narratives. Adolescents were much more likely than children to focus on their desires, emotions, and beliefs in their narratives. Thus, the notion of a self that can succeed or fail only fully develops during adolescence.

Self-descriptions

We can also study the development of the self-concept in older children and adolescents by asking them to describe themselves. However, this approach has some limitations. Children may *distort* their self-descriptions to impress the researcher. Alternatively, they may ignore important aspects of their self-concept when providing self-descriptions. Nevertheless, the use of self-descriptions is a valuable approach.

Tanti et al. (2008) asked Australian pre-adolescent (9 years), early-adolescent (12 years), mid-adolescent (15 years), and late-adolescent (18) groups to provide self-descriptions. They analysed the data based on the assumption that the self-concept has three levels of self-representation:

1. *Individual self*: this differentiates the person from others as a unique individual.
2. *Relational self*: this reflects the individual's important interpersonal relationships.
3. *Collective self*: this is based on the person's group memberships or group identities.

What did Tanti et al. (2008) find? The individual and collective selves were more prominent in the older groups, whereas the relational self became less so. The main reason why the relational self became less prominent was because there was a marked decrease in relational family descriptions only partially compensated for by an increase in relational friend descriptions. Another key finding was that the individual self was much more socially oriented later in adolescence than earlier.

In sum, the years between late childhood and late adolescence see a large increase in the importance of friends and group memberships to the self-concept. The same time period sees a large decrease in the importance of family and non-socially oriented individual descriptions to the self-concept.

IN THE REAL WORLD: depression and the self-concept

Depressed individuals have a very negative self-concept, seeing themselves as helpless, worthless, and inadequate. Dalgleish et al. (2011) studied the self-concept of depressed patients by asking them to list their main lifetime periods (e.g., years at primary school; time spent living abroad). They then decided which positive and negative items applied to each lifetime period. The patients' perceived self was predominantly negative and showed increased coherence and repetition of negative information across lifetime periods. In contrast, there was reduced coherence and repetition of positive information across lifetime periods. These findings occur in part because depressed patients have biases towards accessing emotionally negative personal information and reduced access to positive personal information.

Depressed patients typically produce overgeneral memories (mostly negative) when producing autobiographical memories to a cue (e.g., "party"). Healthy controls mostly produce specific memories (e.g., "My 12th birthday party was very exciting!") whereas depressed patients produce very general ones (e.g., "Every birthday party I have attended turned out badly"). Recalling such negative overgeneral memories strengthens depressed patients' very negative self-concept.

Finally, depressed individuals have an altered relationship to their emotional memories. More specifically, they often try to suppress their painful memories. However, the attempt to suppress a given painful memory can be counterproductive, leading to increased focus on other painful memories.

We have seen that biased autobiographical memory processing in depressed patients plays a role in the development and maintenance of their negative self-concept and thus increases their level of depression. In addition, a negative self-concept and depression increase the extent of the various biases.

What can be done to reduce the various biases producing a negative self-concept? Dalgleish and Werner-Seidler (2014) addressed that issue.

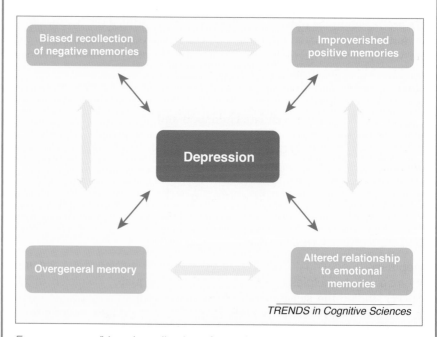

TRENDS in Cognitive Sciences

Four processes (biased recollection of negative memories, impoverished positive memories, overgeneral memory, and altered relationship to emotional memories that interact so maintain and increase depression. From Dalgleish and Werner-Seidler (2014).

One approach that shows promise is Memory Specificity Training (MEST), which is designed to reduce depressed individuals' tendency to produce overgeneral negative memories. MEST has proved successful in reducing depressive symptoms (Dalgleish & Werner-Seidler, 2014).

Another approach is to enhance depressed individuals' self-concept by using the method of loci. In essence, depressed individuals recalled and elaborated several positive personal memories. After that, they associated these memories with locations along a familiar route. This approach shows promise because it increases the subsequent accessibility of the positive personal memories.

Self-knowledge

Do we know ourselves better than anyone else? Most people believe the answer is "Yes". That makes sense because we possess detailed knowledge about our own lives, thoughts, and feeling not available to other people. However, many people have "blind spots" concerning their faults and limitations (especially in individualistic cultures in which the emphasis is on being independent). Research in individualistic cultures is discussed briefly here – individualistic and collectivistic cultures are compared in the later section on self-esteem.

Vazire and Carlson (2011) discussed research in which personality ratings were obtained from the participants themselves and from their friends. These self-ratings and friend-ratings were then compared with the participants' actual behaviour. In general, friend-ratings predicted behaviour better than self-ratings for very desirable or undesirable traits, whereas self-ratings predicted behaviour better than friend-ratings for more neutral traits.

However, Bollich et al. (2015) discovered most people have reasonable insight into their biased views of their own personality traits. Individuals whose self-concepts were more positive than indicated by friends' ratings of them described themselves as positively biased. In contrast, individuals whose self-concepts were more negative than friends' ratings described themselves as negatively biased. Thus, people have more accurate and sophisticated knowledge of themselves than is generally assumed.

Balcetis and Dunning (2013) found we are better at judging other people's helpfulness than our own. Some participants predicted whether they would help to clear up a mess (3,000 spilled jigsaw pieces) when on their own or when other participants were present. Additional participants predicted whether other people would help.

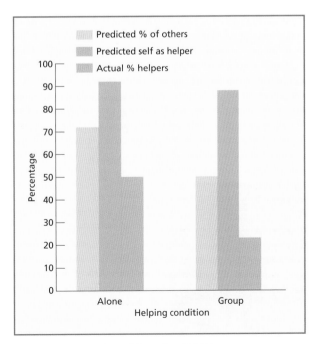

Data from Balcetis and Dunning (2013).

Help was much more likely to be given when participants were on their own than when with other participants. The participants predicted this pattern when judging whether others would help. However, they predicted wrongly that they personally would be equally likely to help in both conditions. The participants exaggerated their own helpfulness more than that of other people. Help was offered 36% of the time. However, 90% of the participants predicted they would help and that 61% of the other participants would do so.

There are two key take-home messages from this study. First, most people have a more flattering view of themselves than of others. This is consistent with other evidence. For example, 31% of adult Americans are obese. However, only 5% of adult Americans consider themselves obese although they estimate that 37% of other Americans are.

Second, participants' predictions of whether they would help virtually ignored the impact of the situation (i.e., being on their own vs. with others) on their behaviour. In similar fashion, Balcetis and Dunning (2013) found people claimed they would be equally likely to donate money to charity whether in a good or bad mood. In fact, they were much more likely to do so when in a good mood (58%) than a bad one (35%).

In sum, we find a complex picture. People in individualistic cultures sometimes seem to have reasonably good self-knowledge. However, that is often not the case, and they have a tendency to regard themselves and their behaviour too positively (see later section on self-esteem).

Cross-cultural and gender differences

Markus and Kitayama (1991) argued there are important cultural differences in the self-concept. Those living in individualistic cultures (e.g., the United Kingdom; the United States) have an **independent self** – the individual is seen as "an independent, self-contained autonomous entity who (1) encompasses unique configuration of internal attributes (e.g., traits, abilities, morals, and values), and (2) behaves primarily as a consequence of these internal attributes" (p. 224).

In contrast, those living in collectivistic cultures (especially those in East Asia) have an **interdependent self**. They define themselves mainly with respect to their relationships and group memberships.

Cross and Madsen (1997) argued the distinction between an independent self and an interdependent self also applies to gender differences: "Men in the United States are thought to construct and maintain an independent self-construal, whereas women are thought to construct and maintain an interdependent self-construal" (p. 5). What Cross and Madson had in mind was that men and women differ *on average* in the nature of the self-concept – they accepted that some men have an interdependent self and some women have an independent self.

Findings

Cultural differences in the self-concept have been studied using the Twenty Statements Test, which requires individuals to provide 20 answers to the question, "Who am I?" Triandis et al. (1990) found there was much more emphasis on the individual as a member of a social group or category among students from a collectivistic culture (China) than individualistic cultures (e.g., United States; Greece).

Gudykunst et al. (1996) showed that cultural differences in the self-concept influence social processes. American and British participants reported greater

Is the interdependent self found mainly in men and/or women, and in members of collectivistic and/or individualistic societies?

KEY TERMS

Independent self: a type of self-concept in which the self is defined with respect to personal responsibility and achievement.

Interdependent self: a type of self-concept in which the self is defined with respect to one's relationships with others.

monitoring of *their own behaviour* in social situations than Japanese and Chinese. This suggests their self-concept is mostly concerned with themselves as individuals.

In contrast, the Japanese and Chinese participants monitored *others' behaviour* more in social situations. That is expected given that their self-concept is concerned with their relationships with others.

Cross and Madson (1997) reviewed many studies supporting predicted gender differences in self-concept. Men typically evaluated themselves more strongly on independence (e.g., power; self-sufficiency) than interdependence (e.g., sociability; likeability). In contrast, the opposite pattern was found in women.

Stein et al. (1992) found a measure of interdependence predicted self-esteem two years later for women but not men, suggesting interdependence is more important for women. In addition, a measure of independence predicted self-esteem two years for men but not women. Thus, men's self-concept depends more than women's on independence.

Berger and Krahé (2013) pointed out that most previous research on gender differences had ignored *negative* aspects of the self-concept. They found men's self-concepts were more likely than women's to include negative attributes such as "boastful", "harsh", and "power-hungry", most of which related to independence. In contrast, women's self-concepts were more likely than those of men to include negative attributes relating to interdependence (e.g., "anxious", "oversensitive", and "self-doubting").

Berger and Krahé (2013) also found that "masculine" and "feminine" attributes were rated by both men and women as being comparably desirable. That is a great advance on previous studies from the 1970s and 1980s in which men and woman both rated "masculine" attributes as more desirable than "feminine" attributes.

EVALUATION

⊕ The distinction between independent and interdependent selves captures important cultural differences in the self-concept.

⊕ The distinction between independent and interdependent selves sheds light on gender differences in the self-concept for both positive and negative attributes.

⊖ It is an oversimplification to use only two categories (independent and interdependent) to describe the self-concept. In addition, some people living in individualistic cultures have an interdependent self – as we saw earlier, Tanti et al. (2008) found in an individualistic culture (Australia) that the self-concept of most adolescents becomes more socially oriented and interdependent over time.

⊖ The notion that women's self-concepts are more interdependent than men's is oversimplified. It is rather the case that there is a gender difference in the type of interdependence represented in the self-concept. Interdependence in women's self-concepts tends to involve a bond with another individual (e.g., sister; teammate). In contrast, in men's self-concepts, interdependence tends to involve a group of individuals (e.g., family; netball) (Foels & Tomcho, 2009).

Multiple selves

Our discussion so far has implied we all have a *single* self-concept. However, that is an oversimplification. McDonnell (2011, p. 1) proposed an alternative approach: "The multiple self-aspects framework (MSF) conceives of the self-concept as a collection of multiple, context-dependent selves". For example, your selves may include those of a student, a daughter or son, and a woman or man.

What determines which self is dominant at any given time? The most important factor is the current situation. For example, your student self is probably most important when you are at college or university chatting with other students. In contrast, your daughter/son self is dominant when you go home to see your parents.

McDonnell (2011) asked American university students to identify their various selves. Very few of them reported having a unitary self-concept. On average, the students listed 4.23 self-aspects or selves. The most frequent selves related to social situations, followed by relationship selves and social role selves.

There are reasons for arguing that the self-concept should be more unitary in individualistic cultures emphasising independence than in collectivistic ones emphasising interdependence (see Chapter 1). In collectivistic cultures, individuals are supposed to fit in flexibly with group expectations, and so their self-concept should be more influenced by the immediate social context. Support for this viewpoint has come from studies using the Twenty Statements Test in which individuals provide descriptions of their self-concept. Those living in collectivistic cultures emphasise their various social roles (e.g., parent; teacher; club member) more than living in individualistic cultures (Heine & Buchtel, 2009).

Further evidence was reported by English and Chen (2011). East Asian Americans (from a collectivistic culture) and European Americans (from an individualistic culture) described their self-concept when with a friend, with their mother, and with their romantic partner. As predicted, the self-concept varied more across these three different contexts for East Asian Americans than European Americans.

Dissociative identity disorder

It is important for our psychological well-being that there is reasonable coherence and integration among our various selves or self-aspects. What happens if someone has several very different selves? This is the case in patients with dissociative identity disorder (formerly called multiple personality disorder). The key symptom of **dissociative identity disorder** is the presence of at least two separate identities controlling the individual's behaviour at different times.

The case of Chris Sizemore, who suffered from dissociative identity disorder, was turned into a movie called *The Three Faces of Eve* in 1957. She had three very different selves or identities: Eve White was timid and self-effacing, Eve Black was wild and fun-loving, and Jane was stable and sensible. Eve Black has full knowledge of Eve White, but Eve White is totally unaware of Eve Black. Jane, the last self or identity to appear, gradually develops an understanding of all three identities.

Why do individuals develop dissociative identity disorder? They nearly always have a history of chronic childhood trauma (e.g., physical and/or

KEY TERM

Dissociative identity disorder: a mental disorder in which the patient has two or more separate personalities or identities, which alternate in controlling behaviour; there is also amnesia or forgetting of autobiographical information.

Chris Sizemore.

physical abuse). Developing several identities or selves provides defence against the intense and conflicting emotions created by these traumatic events (Dorahy et al., 2014). However, the co-existence of several identities within a single individual is very disruptive and causes great problems in relating to other people.

Self-esteem

Self-esteem is of major importance within the self-concept. It is the evaluative part – "the overall sense of worthiness and value that people places on themselves" (Gebauer et al., 2015, p. 527). Several theorists (e.g., Baumeister, 1998) argued that most people are highly motivated to maintain or enhance their self-esteem. As a result, we have the goal of maximising self-esteem (e.g., by being positively evaluated by others). The motivation to maximise self-esteem helps to explain why many people have excessively positive self-concepts.

Why are most people so determined to have high self-esteem? Leary and Baumeister (2000, p. 10) provided an answer in their sociometer theory: "The self-esteem system is designed to *monitor and respond* to others' responses, specifically in regard to social inclusion and exclusion." Thus, self-esteem reflects an individual's acceptability for inclusion in social groups and relationships. It is very important because social exclusion in our evolutionary history greatly reduced the chances of survival.

Findings

Evidence that social exclusion has very negative effects as predicted by sociometer theory was discussed by MacDonald and Leary (2005). Their key conclusion was that social exclusion and physical pain are associated with activity in common brain systems. In addition, they have similar effects on thoughts, emotion, and behaviour. Thus, social exclusion produces social pain.

KEY TERM

Self-esteem: the part of the self-concept concerned with the feelings (positive and negative) that an individual has about himself/herself.

Leary et al. (1998) also provided support for sociometer theory. Individuals who were evaluated positively showed enhanced self-esteem. In contrast, those evaluated negatively suffered decreased self-esteem.

Pass et al. (2010) discovered gender differences in reactions to different kinds of negative evaluation. Women's self-esteem was reduced when they were rejected as a potential mate because of their low physical attractiveness but not when they were rejected due to poor competence and status. In contrast, men's self-esteem was only lowered by rejection on the grounds of inadequate competence and status.

Is high self-esteem desirable?

I imagine your answer to this question is "Yes". In Western cultures, it is generally accepted that high self-esteem confers benefits. These alleged benefits include being less likely to be depressed or anxious than those having low self-esteem.

Does low self-esteem lead to anxiety and depression, or do anxiety and depression lead to low self-esteem? Trzesniewski et al. (2006) assessed self-esteem in adolescents and then followed them up for 11 years. Of those having several problems (e.g., major depressive disorder; anxiety disorder; criminal convictions) in adulthood, 65% had had low self-esteem in adolescence compared to only 15% of those with high self-esteem. Of adults with no problems, 16% had had low adolescent self-esteem but 50% had had high self-esteem. Stieger et al. (2014) found individuals with low self-esteem in adolescence were more likely to exhibit symptoms of depression two decades later. Thus, low self-esteem increases the probability of subsequent depression and anxiety.

Other research indicates that high self-esteem can have negative consequences. Colvin et al. (1995) studied individuals with inflated self-esteem (their self-descriptions were more positive than acquaintances' descriptions of them). They had poor social skills and signs of psychological maladjustment (e.g., hostility towards others; distrustful of people; self-defensive).

Bushman et al. (2009) studied the effects of threat (receiving negative feedback on an essay) on aggression among students with varying levels of self-esteem. There was no overall effect of self-esteem on aggression. However, high self-esteem students also high in narcissism (self-love, entitlement, and admiration seeking) were more aggressive than any other students. This was because the negative feedback they received greatly threatened their very high opinion of themselves.

We can make sense of the apparently conflicting findings by identifying two forms of high self-esteem. For example, Kernis (2003) distinguished between secure and fragile high self-esteem. Secure high self-esteem is genuine and stable over time, whereas fragile high self-esteem is defensive and changeable over time. Those with fragile high self-esteem have an excessively positive view of themselves and are often partly aware of this. Unsurprisingly, secure high self-esteem is much more desirable than fragile high self-esteem (Kernis, 2003).

Cross-cultural differences

Are members of collectivistic societies highly motivated to have high self-esteem, and do they show self-serving bias?

So far I have focused on the role of high self-esteem within individualistic cultures (especially the United States) in which the emphasis is on individual achievement. In contrast, high self-esteem or self-confidence is sometimes regarded as relatively undesirable in collectivistic cultures in which the emphasis is on the group and social cohesion rather than the individual. Why is this the case? According to Heine et al. (1999, p. 785), "In Japanese culture, . . . to say that an individual is self-confident has negative connotations because it reflects how self-confidence gets in the way of interdependence, or it reveals one's failure to recognise higher standards of excellence, and thus to continue to self-improve, or both."

Findings

The obvious prediction is that people living in collectivistic cultures should be less inclined than those in individualistic cultures to show biases designed to enhance self-esteem. Most findings support this prediction. Mezulis et al. (2004) found that **self-serving bias** was much weaker in collectivistic cultures than individualistic ones. The self-serving bias is weak (or non-existent) in collectivistic cultures because they attach much importance to being self-critical.

Heine and Hamamura (2007) reviewed numerous biases relating to self-esteem. One example is the **false uniqueness bias** (the tendency to regard oneself as better than most other people). Those living in individualistic societies possessed all the biases, whereas those living in East Asia (collectivistic cultures) had practically none. East Asians do not show these biases because they are concerned that their claims about themselves match other people's judgments about them.

Lee et al. (2010) argued that the individual's **cultural mindset** (culturally-determined way of thinking about things) is important. Bilingual Chinese students in Hong Kong decided whether desirable and undesirable personality traits applied more (or less) to them than the average student. There was more evidence of false uniqueness bias when they responded in English than when they responded in Chinese. Thus, the language they used influenced the cultural mindset that was activated.

Lo et al. (2011) argued we should not exaggerate the self-enhancing tendencies of people in individualistic cultures or the self-critical tendencies of people in collectivistic cultures. In their study, Lo et al. asked participants to write down five important positive qualities and five important negative qualities they possessed. Participants from individualistic and collectivistic cultures had both self-enhancing and self-critical tendencies. However, those from collectivistic cultures were less self-enhancing and more self-critical than those from individualistic cultures.

It seems likely that people's self-esteem depends on the extent to which they possess the values regarded as important within their own culture. Becker et al. (2014) tested this idea among people living in 20 cultural groups in several different areas of the world. They identified two dimensions of importance when considering individual or cultural differences in values. One dimension runs from controlling one's life to doing one's duty; individualistic cultures generally emphasise the former whereas collectivistic cultures emphasise the latter. The other dimension runs from self-regard based on achieving social status to self-regard based on benefiting others; individualistic cultures emphasise the former and collectivistic cultures the latter.

To what does the self-serving bias attribute success and failure?

KEY TERMS

Self-serving bias: the tendency to attribute your successes to your own efforts and ability, but to attribute your failures to task difficulty and bad luck; it is used to maintain self-esteem.

False uniqueness bias: the mistaken belief that one's abilities and behaviour are superior to those of most other people.

Cultural mindset: the beliefs and values that are active at any given time; individuals who have extensive experience of two cultures have two cultural mindsets, with the one that influences thinking and behaviour being determined by the immediate social context.

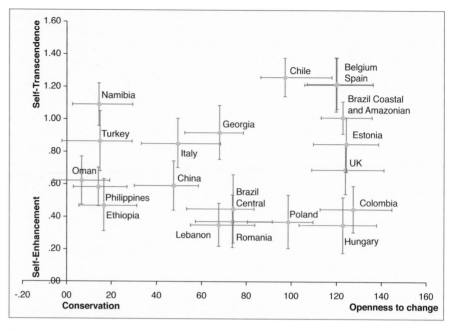

The locations of 20 cultural groups on two dimensions: (1) self-enhancement (self-regard based on achieving social status) to self-transcendence (self-regard based on benefiting others); (2) conservation (doing one's duty) to openness to change (controlling one's own life). From Becker et al. (2014).

Becker et al.'s (2014) key finding was that individuals' self-esteem across the 20 cultures depended mostly on whether their values matched those emphasised within their culture. This finding was replicated by Gebauer et al. (2015) in a study including 2.7 million participants from 106 countries. Gebauer et al. also tested the alternative hypothesis that self-esteem depends on getting ahead by achieving social dominance. There was much stronger support for this hypothesis than the notion that an individual's self-esteem depends on him/her having the values emphasised within their culture.

Conclusions

Most of the biases used by people in individualistic cultures to enhance their self-esteem are not present among those living in collectivistic cultures. There are various reasons for this, including the greater emphasis on social cohesion and the need for self-improvement rather than self-congratulation in collectivistic cultures. There is some truth in the notion that members of collectivistic cultures are self-critical whereas those in individualistic cultures are self-enhancing. However, most people in both cultures show evidence of self-critical and self-enhancing tendencies.

These differences are present when we compare individualistic and collectivistic *cultures*. However, there is evidence that there are important similarities when we consider *individuals* within different cultures. Gebauer et al. (2015) found across 106 countries that high self-esteem was typically associated with getting ahead by demonstrating social dominance.

Chapter summary

- The self-concept corresponds to the set of ideas individuals have about themselves. It depends crucially on social interaction and social relationships.
- Infants develop basic self-awareness (indexed by self-recognition) during the second year of life. The development of a self that remains fairly constant over time (indexed by delayed self-recognition) occurs at about three years of age.
- Autobiographical memory is of much relevance to the self-concept because it provides us with a sense of personal continuity over time.
- During adolescence, the individual and collective selves become more prominent.
- Depressed individuals have several autobiographical memory biases that maintain and increase their level of depression.
- Those living in individualistic cultures have an independent self whereas those living in collectivistic cultures have an interdependent self.
- American men have a more independent self than American women, whereas women have a more interdependent self than men.
- Most individuals possess multiple selves; these selves are more integrated in individualistic than collectivistic cultures. Possessing several very different selves can be associated with severe problems (as in dissociative identity disorder).
- In Western cultures, individuals with high self-esteem suffer less than those with low self-esteem from anxiety and depression. However, individuals whose self-descriptions are exaggerated are more susceptible to psychological maladjustment.
- High self-esteem in Western cultures (but not Eastern ones) is maintained by various biases (e.g., self-serving bias).
- It is true of most cultures that individuals with high self-esteem possess the values regarded as important within their culture and have high social dominance.

Further reading

- Baumeister, R.F. (2011). Self and identity: A brief overview of what they are, what they do, and how they work. *Annals of the New York Academy of Sciences, 1234*, 48–55. Roy Baumeister discusses key issues relating to the self-concept.

- Dalgleish, T., & Werner-Seidler, A. (2014). Disruptions in autobiographical memory processing in depression and the emergence of memory therapeutics. *Trends in Cognitive Sciences, 18*, 596–604. Tim Dalgleish and Aliza Werner-Seidler discuss how depression is associated with several biases in the self-concept and how these biases can be reduced.

- Gilovich, T., Keltner, D., Chen, S., & Nisbett, R.E. (2015). *Social psychology* (4th ed.). New York: W.W. Norton. Chapter 3 of this textbook focuses on the social self.

- Vaughan, G.M., & Hogg, M.A. (2014) *Social psychology* (7th ed.). Frenchs Forest, NSW: Pearson Australia. Chapter 4 of this excellent textbook is devoted to self and identity.

Essay questions

1. What are the main aspects of the self-concept? How does it develop during childhood and adolescence?

2. How is the conception of the self influenced by cross-cultural and gender differences?

3. Are most people motivated to enhance their self-esteem? What are the advantages and disadvantages of having high self-esteem?

Part 5

Cognitive approach

Cognitive psychology is concerned with our internal mental processes (e.g., perception; attention; memory) and with the ways these mental processes influence our behaviour. We differ from other species in many ways, but perhaps the most important are in terms of cognitive abilities such as thinking, reasoning, and problem solving.

Cognitive psychology is of major relevance to most of the other approaches discussed in this book. For example, our behaviour in social situations depends in part on our perceptions of others and on our beliefs and attitudes.

Chapter 20 • Abnormal psychology

We will explore the question 'what is abnormal behaviour?' and consider how our perception of this influences our approach to categorising and diagnosing mental disorders.

Chapter 21 • Visual perception

We will examine how it is that we generally manage to make sense of visual information in order to perceive the world accurately.

Chapter 22 • Memory

We will look at the ways in which we remember information and also why it is that we often forget things we wanted to remember.

Chapter 23 • Problem solving, expertise, and creativity

We will consider some of the factors that allow us to succeed at solving complex problems and showing creativity when it is required.

Suppose you observe someone who appears to be behaving abnormally. How can you tell whether they are suffering from a mental disorder rather than merely behaving eccentrically or struggling with serious issues in their personal lives? What is the best way of categorising the precise mental disorder from which someone is suffering? Probably the best-known form of therapy for mental disorders is psychoanalysis, which was introduced by Sigmund Freud over 100 years ago. What progress has been made in treating mental disorders over the past century?

Abnormal psychology

20

This chapter is devoted to key issues with respect to abnormal psychology. First, I discuss the surprisingly tricky question, "What is abnormality?" As we will see, there is no simple answer! Second, I consider various approaches to diagnosing mental disorders. Third, I focus on the causes of mental disorders. For example, do genetic factors play a role or are mental disorders simply caused by the experiences individuals have had? Fourth, there is the issue of how to treat mental disorders. Has any approach shown itself to be more effective than any other?

What is abnormality?

It might seem easy to define "abnormality". We might argue that individuals whose behaviour differs considerably from that of most other people are behaving abnormally and thus suffer from a mental disorder. However, that argument is only partially correct. Some individuals are socially deviant because they have chosen a non-conformist lifestyle or because their behaviour is motivated by high principles. Eccentrics behave differently to most people but most are happy and less prone to mental illness than other people (Weeks & James, 1995).

Szasz (1960) argued that it can be dangerous to define abnormality in terms of social deviancy. This definition can be used by the state to control the behaviour of its citizens. For example, throughout much of the twentieth century, those who disagreed with the communist government in Russia were called "dissidents" and confined in mental hospitals. In the nineteenth century in England, single women who became pregnant were regarded as social deviants, and some were even locked up in psychiatric institutions.

So far we have focused on an individual's *behaviour* as an indication of whether or not they are abnormal. However, we must also consider what is going on *inside* individuals. For example, someone with severe depression may try very hard to ensure their public behaviour appears normal. Thus, abnormality is typically associated with suffering and distress. However, there is nothing abnormal about the prolonged distress caused by loss of a loved one. In addition, some abnormal individuals (e.g., psychopaths or those with anti-social personality disorder) treat other people very badly without suffering themselves.

Most individuals seeking therapy from a clinical psychologist or psychiatrist report an inability to cope in their work and/or personal lives. Thus, an inability to function adequately in society can indicate abnormality. However, a given individual's work performance may be inadequate because they lack the necessary skills or intelligence to perform effectively. In addition, some individuals who are clearly abnormal appear to function adequately in their everyday lives. For example, consider the English doctor Harold Shipman who was responsible for the deaths of more than 200 of his patients. In spite of his appalling crimes, Shipman functioned adequately enough to escape detection for many years.

In sum, "abnormality" is an imprecise notion. Abnormal behaviour can take different forms and involve different features. Of special importance, no *single* feature reliably distinguishes between normal and abnormal behaviour. As Lilienfeld and Marino (1995, p. 416) pointed out, abnormality has "unclear boundaries and an absence of defining features".

In spite of the complexity and imprecision of the notion of "abnormality", it is still possible to provide a reasonable definition. Clinical psychologists and psychiatrists use the *Diagnostic and Statistical Manual of Mental Disorders (DSM)* to assess abnormality. According to the current version of DSM (DSM-5; American Psychiatric Association, 2013), a mental disorder (abnormal condition) is

> a syndrome [set of symptoms] characterised by clinically significant disturbance in an individual's cognition, emotion regulation, or behaviour that reflects a dysfunction in the psychological, biological, or developmental processes underlying mental functioning. Mental disorders are usually associated with significant distress in social, occupational, or other important activities.

This definition refers to several important aspects of abnormality. First, there are disturbances in an individual's behaviour. Second, there are disturbances in his/her cognition and emotion regulation. Third, there is impaired functioning in everyday life (e.g., social and occupational settings).

Diagnosing mental disorders

The starting point for diagnosing mental disorders is to identify the individual's symptoms. Clinical psychologists and psychiatrists use that information to diagnose the mental disorder or disorders from which he/she is suffering. This is typically done with reference to a classificatory system. The two most-used such systems are ICD-10 (full name International Statistical Classification of Diseases and Related Health Problems), published by the World Health Organisation in 2016, and DSM-5. Here we focus on DSM. The number of mental disorders identified by DSM has increased considerably – DSM-I (1952) contained 128 mental disorders whereas DSM-5 (2013) contains 541!

All editions of DSM make use of **categorical classification** – patients are assumed to have (or not have) a given mental disorder. This is problematical given there is no sharp dividing line between normality and abnormality. For example, consider DSM-5's approach to **major depressive disorder** (involving

KEY TERMS

Categorical classification: an all-or-none approach to diagnosis in which each mental disorder is regarded as a category applicable or not applicable to any given patient.

Major depressive disorder: a common mental disorder characterised by depressed mood, tiredness, lack of interest and pleasure in activities, and feelings of worthlessness or excessive guilt.

a relatively long-lasting sad, depressed mood). An important criterion for diagnosing major depressive disorder is that an individual has experienced at least 5 out of 9 symptoms for at least two weeks. That means an individual who has experienced 7 symptoms for only 10 days does not have the disorder – it is clearly arbitrary to identify the former individual as abnormal but not the latter one!

We might imagine any given patient would be diagnosed with only one mental disorder. In fact, many patients are diagnosed with two or more disorders: this is known as **comorbidity**. For example, up to 65% of patients with one anxiety disorder are diagnosed with one or more additional anxiety disorders.

Another problem is gender bias – exaggerating the importance of stereotypes about male and female behaviour in diagnosis. Ford and Widiger (1989) presented therapists with case studies of a patient with histrionic personality disorder (involving excessive emotionality) and another with antisocial personality disorder (involving aggressive and irresponsible behaviour). The therapists had to decide on the appropriate diagnosis. Histrionic personality disorder was much less likely to be diagnosed correctly when the patient was described as male rather than female. In contrast, antisocial personality disorder was much less likely to be diagnosed when the patient was described as female rather than male.

In what ways is the DSM approach limited?

Culture-bound syndromes

It is very easy to assume that what is regarded as abnormal is very similar across all cultures. That assumption is wrong because definitions of abnormality are culturally specific: the notion of **cultural relativism** means value judgments are relative to individual cultural contexts. For example, believing in witchcraft is common in many cultures but is regarded as abnormal in others.

We can see the importance of cultural differences with **culture-bound syndromes** (patterns of abnormal behaviour typically found in only one culture). *Dhat syndrome* (found among men of the Indian subcontinent) is an example of a culture-bound syndrome. Sufferers from this syndrome blame their physical and mental exhaustion on the presence of semen in their urine. There is some overlap between *dhat syndrome* and depression, but some sufferers from *dhat syndrome* are not depressed (Prakash & Mandal, 2014).

> **KEY TERMS**
>
> **Comorbidity:** the simultaneous presence of two or more mental disorders in a given individual.
>
> **Cultural relativism:** the notion we should view each culture from within that culture rather than the observer's own culture.
>
> **Culture-bound syndromes:** patterns of abnormal behaviour found in one or a small number of cultures.

EVALUATION

➕ DSM-5 provides a reasonably reliable and valid classificatory system for mental disorders.

➕ DSM-5 goes further than previous editions of DSM in acknowledging the importance of culture-bound syndromes.

➖ DSM-5 involves pigeonholing with individuals being assigned to diagnostic categories. A dimensional system (accepting that individuals have varying degrees of symptoms such as anxiety and depression) seems more realistic.

🔘 DSM-5 identifies over 500 mental disorders and has lenient criteria for diagnosing many disorders. As a result, "Many millions of people with normal grief, gluttony, distractibility, worries, reactions to stress, the temper tantrums of childhood, the forgetting of old age, and 'behavioural addictions' will soon be mislabelled as psychiatrically sick" (Frances, 2012).

🔘 Pilgrim (e.g., 2007) is sceptical about *all* diagnostic systems. His central argument is that diagnoses are based on symptoms and de-emphasise the personal and social context in which these symptoms occur.

Causes of mental disorders

It is important to establish the causes of mental disorders, in part because the knowledge gained can be used to reduce the incidence of such disorders in the future. It is a complex matter to find out why some individuals suffer from any given mental disorder. We start by distinguishing between one-dimensional and multi-dimensional models. According to one-dimensional models, the origins of a mental disorder can be traced to a *single* underlying cause. For example, depression might be caused by a major loss (e.g., death of a loved one). One-dimensional models are very oversimplified. As a result, they have been replaced by multi-dimensional models based on the assumption that mental disorders are caused by *several* factors in interaction.

The **diathesis-stress model** exemplifies the multi-dimensional approach. In this model, the occurrence of mental disorders depends on two types of factors:

1. *Diathesis*: a vulnerability or predisposition to disorder within the individual; it is often a genetic vulnerability.
2. *Stress*: some severe or distressing environmental event.

According to the diathesis-stress model, what determines whether any given individual develops a mental disorder is the *combination* of diathesis and stress. Thus, individuals exposed to high stress who also possess high vulnerability (diathesis) are most likely to develop a mental disorder. Individuals with high stress but lacking internal vulnerability and those with high internal vulnerability but not exposed to stress are unlikely to develop a mental disorder.

In the following sections, we show the superiority of the multi-dimensional model to the one-dimensional model. This is done with respect to two of the commonest mental disorders: major depressive disorder and social anxiety disorder.

KEY TERM

Diathesis-stress model: the notion that mental disorders are caused jointly by a diathesis (personal vulnerability) *and* a distressing event.

IN THE REAL WORLD: posttraumatic stress

On 22 November 2013, a leaking pipeline in Qingdao in eastern China caught fire and exploded. It ripped roads and pavements apart, turned cars over, killing 62 people and injuring 136. Guo et al. (2015) found the catastrophe caused 87 adolescents attending a school very close to the explosion to suffer symptoms of **posttraumatic stress disorder (PTSD)** such as increased arousal and re-experiencing of the event. However, 575 other adolescents at the school did not develop these symptoms.

The devastation caused by the pipeline in Qingdao in eastern China catching fire in 2013.

What determined which adolescents developed PTSD symptoms? According to the diathesis-stress model, those exposed to the most stress should have been more likely than those exposed to lower levels of stress to develop PTSD symptoms. In addition, individuals with high personal vulnerability should have been at high risk of PTSD symptoms. Guo et al. (2015) assessed the personality dimension of neuroticism (tendency to experience negative emotions such as anxiety;

KEY TERM

Posttraumatic stress disorder (PTSD): a mental disorder triggered by a very distressing event and involving re-experiencing of the event, avoidance of stimuli associated with the event, and increased fear and arousal.

see Chapter 18). Individuals high in neuroticism are more vulnerable than those low in neuroticism and so the former should have been more likely to experience PTSD symptoms.

Guo et al. (2015) assessed each individual's trauma severity based on the following measures: (1) injury or death to relatives, (2) impact of the explosion on their house, and (3) impact of the explosion on the individual. The number of PTSD symptoms was predicted by stress level (trauma severity) and by their vulnerability or diathesis (neuroticism). As predicted by the diathesis-stress model, the individuals most seriously affected by the pipeline explosion were those who had the combination of high vulnerability and high stress.

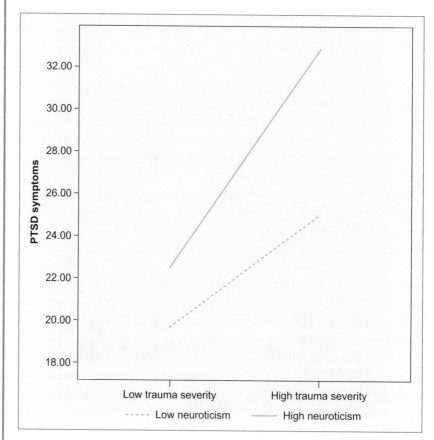

The mean number of posttraumatic stress disorder (PTSD) symptoms as a function of trauma severity (low vs. high) and neuroticism (low vs. high). From Guo et al. (2015).

In sum, this study shows how the effects of traumatic events in the real world can be understood within the framework of the diathesis-stress model. More specifically, we would only have a partial understanding if we considered stress or vulnerability in isolation rather than considering the interaction between them.

Major depressive disorder

Research has identified many factors of relevance to the development of major depressive disorder. Here we will focus on the most important ones.

Cognitive factors

Many experts (e.g., Aaron Beck) argue that cognitive factors are of great importance in the development of depression. Of particular importance is the notion of a **cognitive schema**, which is "a well-organised cognitive structure of stored information and memories that forms the basis of core beliefs about self and others" (Beck & Dozois, 2011). Depressed individuals' cognitive schemas are extremely important. These schemas influence *what* they attend to in the environment, *how* they interpret it, and *which* information they retrieve from long-term memory. Cognitive schemas in depressed individuals relate to the **cognitive triad** – the unrealistic negative thoughts in the three areas of themselves, the world, and the future.

What cognitive factors are involved in the development of depression?

Beck and Dozois (2011) argued that maladaptive cognitive schemas develop early in life. However, these schemas typically remain dormant and only cause symptoms when activated by external events (e.g., severe life events or problems). When activated, they cause the depressed individual to have negative views about themselves, the world, and the future.

The crucial issue for the cognitive approach is whether the distorted and unrealistic thoughts of depressed patients play a direct role in the development of the disorder. Perhaps patients only start having these unrealistic thoughts *after* developing depression. If so, it would mean distorted thoughts have nothing to do with causing depression!

Evidence that negative thoughts play a causal role in major depressive disorder was reported by Lewinsohn et al. (2001). They assessed negative thinking in adolescents not having major depressive disorder. One year later, they assessed the negative life events experienced by these adolescents over the 12-month period. Those experiencing many negative life events had an increased likelihood of developing major depressive disorder only if they were initially high in negative attitudes. Since these negative attitudes were assessed *before* the onset of depression, they form a risk factor for developing that disorder when exposed to stressful life events.

Genetic factors

According to the biological approach, genetic factors influence the development of depression. In other words, some individuals' genetic make-up makes them more vulnerable than other people to depression. We can test this approach with twin studies using monozygotic (identical) and dizygotic (fraternal) twins. The key measure is the **concordance rate** – the probability that if one twin has a given disorder the other twin also has it. If genetic factors are important, the concordance rate should be higher for identical twins than fraternal ones. In a review, McGuffin and Rivera (2015) concluded that the development of depression depends moderately on genetic factors. However, environmental factors were also important.

Life events

It is reasonable to assume that individuals experiencing stressful life events (e.g., death of a loved one; divorce) would be more vulnerable to depression than those not experiencing such events. Brown and Harris (1978) found 61% of

KEY TERMS

Cognitive schema: organised information stored in long-term memory and used by individuals to form interpretations of themselves and the world in which they live.

Cognitive triad: a depressed person's negative views of the self, the world, and the future.

Concordance rate: in twin studies, the probability that if one twin has a disorder, the other twin has the same disorder.

depressed women had experienced at least one very stressful life event recently compared to 19% of non-depressed women. However, the impact of life events depended on *personal context* – of those women who had experienced a serious life event, 37% of those without any intimate friends became depressed compared to only 10% having a very close friend.

There is another important issue concerning life events. Many life events (e.g., miscarriage; death of a romantic partner) are outside an individual's control. However, individuals have some control over other life events (e.g., unwanted pregnancy; conviction for a crime; end of romantic relationship).

Individuals experiencing stressful life events over which they have control are more likely than those not experiencing such events to develop depression. However, this does *not* occur because such life events increase vulnerability to depression. In fact, genetic influences make some individuals more susceptible to experiencing controllable life events *and* to depression (Boardman et al., 2011). Uncontrollable life events are also associated with major depressive disorder, but such events do not depend on genetic factors at all (Boardman et al., 2011).

In sum, uncontrollable stressful life events play a role in triggering major depressive disorder. However, their impact depends on any given individual's personal context and circumstances. For example, losing one's job is much more serious for a parent bringing up several children single-handedly than for someone who is wealthy and nearing retirement. Controllable stressful life events are related to depression. However, the association is due to genetic influences and does not indicate that such events help to cause depression.

Summary

The development of major depressive disorder depends on cognitive and genetic factors and the occurrence of serious life events. The findings are much more consistent with multi-dimensional models than one-dimensional models. More specifically, they are consistent with the diathesis-stress model – the diathesis involves genetic factors, and stress stems from the occurrence of life events.

Social anxiety disorder

Social anxiety disorder (also known as social phobia) is a very common anxiety disorder. In DSM-5 (2013), it is defined as "a marked and persistent fear of one or more social situations in which the person is exposed to unfamiliar people or to possible scrutiny by others". Of importance, this fear is so strong that it often leads those with the disorder to avoid most social situations.

Life events

Marteinsdottir et al. (2007) studied the role of severe life events in social anxiety disorder. Individuals with the disorder had experienced more life events than controls during childhood. Of most importance, they had experienced more negative life events in the year during which the social anxiety disorder first manifested itself.

It seems likely that very negative experiences in social situations would be especially likely to play a role in the development of social anxiety disorder. One approach based on this assumption claims that the disorder can be caused by classical conditioning (see Chapter 2). In essence, a conditioned stimulus (e.g., social situation) is associated with a very unpleasant unconditioned stimulus

KEY TERM

Social anxiety disorder: a disorder in which the individual has excessive fear of social situations and often avoids them; also known as social phobia.

creating fear (e.g., being exposed to public humiliation). As a consequence, subsequent exposure to a social situation produces great fear.

There is support for this approach. Hackmann et al. (2000) found 96% of patients with social anxiety disorder remembered socially traumatic experiences that had happened to them (often in adolescence). Most of these patients had recurrent negative images that often reminded them of those earlier traumatic experiences.

Social factors

Unsurprisingly, how parents treat their children influences the children's likelihood of developing social anxiety disorder. Two forms of parental behaviour have been studied in detail: (1) parental rejection (making children feel unloved) and (2) parental overprotectiveness (giving children little control over their social lives). Parental rejection and parental overprotectiveness are both associated with an increased risk of developing social anxiety disorder (Lieb et al., 2000). Parental rejection reduces children's confidence in themselves, and parental overprotectiveness reduces their ability to develop social skills.

Genetic factors

We can establish whether the development of a mental disorder depends partly on genetic factors with twin studies. Scaini et al. (2014) carried out a meta-analysis (combining findings from many studies). Genetic factors were important regardless of the age the social anxiety disorder started. However, such factors were especially important for patients whose disorder started in childhood: for them, genetic factors were more important than environmental ones.

OVERALL EVALUATION

➕ All mental disorders are multiply determined, meaning that biological, social, and cognitive factors all contribute to their development.

➕ The diathesis-stress model provides a valuable framework within which to consider interactions among factors causing mental disorders.

➖ There are large differences among mental disorders in the involvement of genetic factors, but we do not understand why that is the case. For example, only 1% of the population suffers from schizophrenia, but the figure is 48% for individuals having an identical twin with the disorder (Gottesman, 1991). In contrast, genetic factors are of minor importance with situational phobia (e.g., fear of confined spaces; van Houtem et al., 2013).

➖ There is an association between life events and most mental disorders (including major depressive disorder and social anxiety disorder). However, it is often hard to establish causality: some life events influence the development of mental disorders whereas others (controllable ones) occur in part because of the personal characteristics of individuals with mental disorders.

Treating mental disorders: depression and anxiety

Individuals with mental disorders exhibit diverse symptoms. There may be problems with thinking and cognition (e.g., schizophrenics' hallucinations), behaviour (e.g., the avoidance of social situations by individuals with social anxiety disorder), or physiological and bodily processes (e.g., the highly activated physiological system of someone with posttraumatic stress disorder). Note, however, that thinking, behaviour, and physiological processes are all highly interdependent.

Therapeutic approaches to mental disorders could focus on producing changes in thinking, behaviour, or physiological functioning. At the risk of oversimplification, this is precisely what has happened. The psychodynamic approach and cognitive therapy are designed to change thinking, behaviour therapy emphasises changing behaviour, and drug therapy focuses on physiological and biochemical changes. Of increasing importance is cognitive behavioural therapy which (as the name implies) combines cognitive therapy and behaviour therapy.

In this section, we focus on therapy for the two very common disorders discussed earlier: major depressive disorder and social anxiety disorder. In the following section, we will broaden out the discussion to consider the general effectiveness of various forms of therapy.

Depression: cognitive behavioural therapy

Beck's cognitive behavioural therapy for depression is based on three main hypotheses (Beck & Dozois, 2011):

1. *Access hypothesis*: if depressed individuals receive appropriate training, they become aware of the content of their own thinking.
2. *Mediation hypothesis*: how depressed individuals think about and interpret life's events influences their emotions and behaviour.
3. *Change hypothesis*: individuals can recover from depression by intentionally modifying their cognitive and behavioural reactions to life's events.

Beck's cognitive behaviour therapy involves collaborative empiricism, guided discovery, and Socratic dialogue to challenge the patient's irrational thoughts. Collaborative empiricism involves the therapist and patient agreeing on the problem and therapeutic goals. Thoughts are treated as hypotheses rather than facts. This means the patient's thoughts can be tested to see whether they are valid.

Guided discovery is then used to allow patients to test their thinking through their own observations and experiments (as we do with hypotheses). Here is an example. A depressed patient who argues people are always avoiding him/her keeps a diary of specific occasions on which this happens. This probably happens much less often than the patient imagines.

Socratic dialogue (a form of guided discovery) involves the therapist asking patients questions so they can challenge their maladaptive thoughts. Suppose a depressed patient argues she is dislikeable. Possible Socratic questions are as follows: "Have you met anyone who did seem to like you?"; "Do you have any qualities you regard as likeable?"

One goal of these techniques is to modify the patient's core beliefs and schemas. Another goal is to teach patients "how to become scientific investigators of their own thinking – to treat thoughts as hypotheses . . . and to put these thoughts to the test" (Beck & Dozois, 2011, p. 400). Achieving this goal involves patients changing their behaviour in desirable ways to facilitate them changing their maladaptive thoughts.

Depression: drug therapy

Serotonin is a chemical substance of much relevance to mood regulation and plays a significant role in depression. There is considerable evidence that serotonin levels in depressed individuals are lower than in healthy ones (e.g., Paul-Savoie et al., 2011). As a consequence, most drugs for depression increase serotonin levels. The most used of such drugs are the serotonin reuptake inhibitors (SSRIs) such as Prozac, which are prescribed for depressed individuals literally millions of times every year.

What are the disadvantages of using drug therapy to treat depression?

How effective is drug therapy for major depressive disorder? DeRubeis et al. (2005) compared drug therapy involving SSRIs with cognitive therapy. Approximately 58% of the patients with each form of treatment showed considerable improvement. Hollon et al. (2005) studied those depressed patients responding to treatment in the DeRubeis et al. (2005) study for 12 months following treatment. Of those patients who had received drug therapy, 76% suffered a relapse compared to only 31% of those who had received cognitive therapy.

These findings suggest drug therapy is mostly a palliative treatment – it suppresses depressive symptoms but does not change the underlying processes. As a result, the symptoms of depression often recur when therapy stops.

Social anxiety disorder: cognitive behavioural therapy

Cognitive behavioural therapy is the most effective form of treatment for social anxiety disorder and so is the focus of discussion. I will start with the main assumptions cognitive behavioural therapists make about the problems of patients with social anxiety disorder.

First, and most importantly, it is assumed patients avoid social situations because such avoidance reduces the anxiety they associate with such situations. Avoiding social situations obviously has a disruptive effect on patients' lives.

Second, an **interpretive bias** is the tendency to interpret ambiguous situations in excessively negative ways. Individuals with social anxiety disorder have an interpretive bias for social situations. They also have an interpretive bias for their own social behaviour, imagining that they appear less socially skilled than is actually the case.

Third, Clark and Wells (1995) argued that individuals with social anxiety disorder have an *internal* focus of attention in social situations rather than an *external* one on those with whom they are interacting. This makes them very aware of their internal anxious feelings and leads them to imagine other people are fully aware of how anxious they feel.

KEY TERM

Interpretive bias: negative biased or distorted interpretations of ambiguous stimuli and/or situations.

Fourth, patients tend to catastrophise in social situations (e.g., imagining they may suffer total social humiliation). This is odd because they typically admit that such catastrophes have rarely if ever happened to them. How can we explain this? The answer is that patients often believe that catastrophes are avoided because they use various **safety behaviours** (e.g., avoiding eye contact; speaking very little) to reduce anxiety.

How does cognitive behavioural therapy attempt to eliminate these four problems? First, avoidance behaviour by patients with social anxiety disorder is reduced via exposure therapy (see Chapter 2). **Exposure therapy** involves placing patients repeatedly in feared situations (e.g., a discussion group with several strangers) from which escape is hard or impossible. There is convincing evidence that exposure therapy is effective in treating social anxiety disorder (e.g., Clark et al., 2006).

Second, the tendency of patients to exaggerate the inadequacy of their social behaviour can be addressed by presenting with videotaped feedback concerning their social behaviour. Such feedback has proven effective. For example, Laposa et al. (2014) found that videotaped feedback decreased anxiety and enhanced social behaviour in patients with social anxiety disorder.

Third, Wells and Papageorgiou (1998) considered the effects of exposure therapy in the treatment of patients with social anxiety disorder. Exposure therapy that also involved techniques to increase patients' external attentional focus reduced anxiety more than exposure therapy on its own.

Fourth, Morgan and Raffle (1999) compared exposure with and without instructions to patients to avoid safety behaviours. The beneficial effects of therapy were greater for patients avoiding safety behaviours.

Clark et al. (2006) compared two forms of treatment for social anxiety disorder: cognitive therapy (designed to combat all four problems discussed earlier) and exposure therapy plus applied relaxation. The findings were clear-cut: of the patients receiving cognitive therapy, 84% recovered compared to only 42% of those receiving exposure therapy plus applied relaxation.

Which forms of therapy are most effective?

It has often been argued that several different forms of therapy are all comparable in terms of their effectiveness. This conclusion is sometimes known as the "Dodo Bird verdict": In Lewis Carroll's *Alice in Wonderland*, the Dodo Bird declared after a race that, "Everyone has won, and all must have prizes". Support for that verdict was reported by Matt and Navarro (1997). They considered 63 meta-analyses (combining data from numerous studies). On average, 75% of patients receiving treatment improved more than the average untreated patient. Of importance, moderately beneficial effects were found with all forms of therapy.

Matt and Navarro (1997) actually found behaviour therapy and cognitive therapy tended to be more effective than psychodynamic therapy. However, they argued these differences were more apparent than real because patients treated by behaviour or cognitive therapy often had less serious symptoms than those treated by psychodynamic therapy.

KEY TERMS

Safety behaviours: actions designed to reduce patients' level of anxiety and avoid catastrophes in social situations.

Exposure therapy: a form of treatment in which patients are repeatedly exposed to stimuli or situations they fear greatly.

Unsurprisingly, the Dodo Bird verdict is oversimplified (see Roth et al., 2005, for a review). Cognitive behavioural therapy is probably the most effective treatment for major depressive disorder and social anxiety disorder. It is also more effective than other forms of therapy in the treatment of panic disorder and generalised anxiety disorder (a disorder characterised by excessive worry). In contrast, psychodynamic therapy (psychoanalysis and developments of psychoanalysis) is often somewhat less effective than other forms of treatment.

Issues with assessing therapeutic effectiveness

Finally, I will briefly discuss some issues involved in interpreting the findings from studies of therapeutic effectiveness. First, there are two different kinds of reasons why a given form of therapy may prove effective in treating a given mental disorder. The obvious reason is that the therapy contains specific features that help patients to recover. However, another possible reason is that therapeutic effectiveness depends on non-specific factors common to most forms of therapy. Examples include therapist warmth and therapist empathy.

What problems arise when assessing therapeutic effectiveness?

Stevens et al. (2000) reviewed 80 studies to assess the relative importance of specific and non-specific factors. With the less severe disorders, the impact of specific and non-specific factors was similar. With the more severe disorders, in contrast, *only* specific factors influenced the outcome. As Bjornsson (2011) pointed out, we need a better theoretical understanding of how specific and non-specific factors combine to make therapy effective.

Second, there is a conflict at the heart of many studies of therapeutic effectiveness. This conflict involves deciding whether to adopt a scientific approach with a high level of control over what happens or to adopt a more realistic approach rooted in clinical practice. Seligman (1995) distinguished between the two approaches: he used the term "efficacy studies" to refer to those using a scientific approach and "effectiveness studies" to refer to those based on actual clinical practice.

Efficacy and effectiveness studies are both useful (Rush, 2009). Efficacy studies can provide convincing evidence that a given form of treatment successfully treats a given mental disorder. After that, effectiveness studies can assist in identifying the types of individuals benefiting most (and least) from that form of treatment.

Third, relatively few clinical psychologists use a single approach when treating patients. Instead, most adopt an **eclectic approach** using techniques drawn from several types of therapy. If therapists combine elements of two or three forms of therapy, it is hard to assess the contributions each has made to therapeutic improvement.

Fourth, as Strupp (1996) pointed out, we can consider therapeutic effectiveness from three different perspectives:

1. society's perspective (e.g., the client's ability to function in society);
2. the client's own perspective, including his/her overall subjective well-being;
3. the therapist's perspective (e.g., has the client developed a healthy personality structure?).

There is some overlap among these perspectives. However, the apparent effectiveness of treatment often varies from one perspective to another (Strupp, 1996).

KEY TERM

Eclectic approach: the use of a range of different forms of treatment by therapists.

Chapter summary

- Defining abnormality in terms of unusual behaviour is flawed because many healthy individuals (e.g., eccentrics) behave in unusual ways.
- Abnormality is often associated with suffering and distress and/or an inability to function adequately. However, these criteria are of limited applicability (e.g., suffering and distress are natural reactions to the loss of a loved one).
- "Abnormality" is an imprecise notion and cannot be defined by any single feature.
- ICD-10 and DSM-5 are the two most important classificatory systems for mental disorders. There is a real danger that healthy individuals are sometimes wrongly diagnosed as having mental disorders by DSM-5.
- There is increasing recognition that many mental disorders occur only in certain cultures.
- Mental disorders are caused by several different factors in combination. According to the diathesis-stress model, there is a diathesis (vulnerability or predisposition) combined with stress (distressing environmental events).
- The onset of major depressive disorder depends on negative cognitive schemas, genetic factors, and severe life events.
- The onset of social anxiety disorder depends on life events, parental rejection and overprotectiveness, and genetic factors.
- Major depressive disorder is treated successfully by cognitive behavioural therapy involving challenging patients' irrational thoughts and persuading them to behave in ways that will reduce such thoughts.
- Drug therapy for major depressive disorder typically reduces the symptoms for the duration of treatment but often leads to subsequent relapse.
- Cognitive behavioural therapy has proven very effective in treating social anxiety disorder. It focuses on eliminating avoidance behaviour, reducing patients' interpretive biases, producing an external focus of attention, and reducing patients' use of safety behaviours.
- Most forms of therapy are moderately effective. However, cognitive behavioural therapy is typically more effective than other forms of therapy in treating most anxiety disorders and depression.
- Comparing different therapies is complicated because many therapists adopt an eclectic approach, and therapeutic success varies depending on whether we adopt the perspective of society, the patient, or the therapist.

Further reading

- Comer, R.J. (2015). *Abnormal psychology* (9th ed.). New York: Palgrave Macmillan. Key issues in abnormal psychology are discussed in a thorough and accessible way in this up-to-date textbook.

- Durand, V.M., & Barlow, D.H. (2016). *Essentials of abnormal psychology* (7th ed.). Belmont, CA: Thomson/Cengage. This textbook covers in detail all the major topics within abnormal psychology.

- Lilienfeld, S.O., & Arkowitz, H. (2012). Are all psychotherapies created equal? *Scientific American*, 1 September, 47–50. Various reasons why the Dodo Bird verdict is oversimplified are discussed in this article.

- Pomerantz, A.M. (2014). *Clinical psychology: Science, practice, and culture* (3rd ed.). Thousand Oaks, CA: Sage. This textbook provides a readable and up-to-date account of abnormal psychology.

- Wakefield, J.C. (2016). Diagnostic issues and controversies in DSM-5: Return of the false positives problem. *Annual Review of Clinical Psychology*, 12, 105–132. Jerome Wakefield discusses key issues relating to the diagnosis of mental disorders within the context of DSM-5.

Essay questions

1. What is "abnormality"? How can we decide whether a given individual's behaviour should be categorised as "abnormal"?

2. Discuss approaches to identifying the causes of mental disorders and possible problems in establishing the precise causes.

3. Compare and contrast therapeutic approaches in the treatment of major depressive disorder.

4. "Most forms of therapy are of comparable effectiveness." Discuss ways in which this statement is oversimplified and misleading.

Our visual perception is typically very rapid and accurate in spite of the problems we face in making sense of visual information. When looking at the world, we have to turn a two-dimensional retinal image into a rich three-dimensional perception of the environment. What kinds of cues do you think we use to see the world as it is rather than as it appears on the retina?

In spite of our perceptual abilities, we are nevertheless fooled by many visual illusions. We think we have a clear picture of the visual scene in front of us. However, we often fail to notice even fairly large changes in that scene. Why is visual perception so prone to such errors?

Visual perception

21

This chapter is concerned with the area of psychology known as **visual perception,** which involves seeing and making sense of the visual information presented to our eyes. Vision is our most important sense and, unsurprisingly, more of the brain is devoted to visual processing than to processing in any other sense modality.

Visual perception typically seems effortless – we simply look around us and almost immediately make coherent sense of the objects in front of us. In fact, however, the information arriving at the retina is generally confused and disorganised. There is a mosaic of colours, and the retinal shapes and sizes of objects are often very different from their actual shapes and sizes. Another complication is that the retinal image is two-dimensional. In spite of that, we perceive the world as well-organised and three-dimensional.

We can see the complexities of visual perception by considering **CAPTCHAs** (Completely Automated Public Turing tests to tell Computers and Humans Apart). CAPTCHAs require the observer to identify visual stimuli (typically letters and digits) presented in a distorted form.

CAPTCHAs are designed to be easy for humans to solve but difficult for machines and are used to prevent problems such as automatic spamming of everyone on Facebook. The fact that we greatly outperform machines with these distorted stimuli shows the sophistication of our visual perception abilities. As you have discovered, however, human sometimes struggle to solve CAPTCHAs (Bursztein et al., 2010)!

In what follows, we consider how we manage to do this. We will also consider some of the deficiencies in visual perception. For example, we sometimes misperceive visual stimuli. We also find it surprisingly hard to detect changes in the visual world around us.

Perceptual organisation

It would be fairly easy to work out which parts of the visual information available to us at any given time belong together and so form objects if those objects were spread out in space. However, the visual environment is typically complex and confusing – some objects overlap others and so hide parts of them from view. As a consequence, it can be hard to achieve perceptual segregation of visual objects.

KEY TERMS

Visual perception: the processing of visual information to see objects in the world.

CAPTCHAs: Completely Automated Public Turing tests to tell Computers and Humans Apart involve identifying distorted visual stimuli; they are typically very hard for machines to solve but relatively easy for humans.

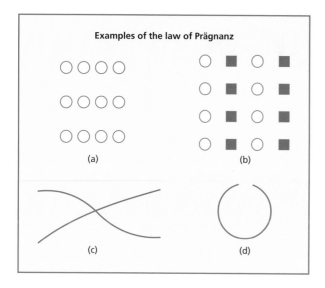

Examples of the law of Prägnanz

(a)

(b)

(c)

(d)

The Gestaltists (German psychologists including Koffka, Köhler, and Wertheimer) studied perceptual organisation in the early part of the twentieth century. Their fundamental principle was the **law of Prägnanz**, according to which we typically perceive the simplest possible organisation of the visual world.

We can see what the Gestaltists had in mind by considering some examples. Pattern (a) is more easily seen as three horizontal lines of dots than four vertical lines. It shows the Gestalt law of proximity, according to which visual elements close to each other tend to be grouped together.

In pattern (b), vertical columns rather than horizontal rows are seen. This fits the law of similarity, according to which similar visual elements are grouped together. In pattern (c), we see two crossing lines rather than a V-shaped line and an inverted-V-shaped line. This fits the law of good continuation: those visual elements producing the fewest interruptions to smoothly curving lines are grouped together.

Finally, pattern (d) shows the law of closure. The missing parts of a figure are filled in to complete it (in this case, a circle). All four laws discussed here are more specific statements of the basic law of Prägnanz.

Where do these organisational processes come from? The Gestaltists claimed most perceptual organisation depends on innate factors. In other words, we naturally organise our perceptual experience in line with the law of Prägnanz. Alternatively, we may *learn* that visual elements close (or similar) to each other generally belong to the same object. Bhatt and Quinn (2011) reviewed research indicating that infants as young as 3 or 4 months show grouping by good continuation, proximity, and connectedness. This seems consistent with the Gestalt position. However, other grouping principles (e.g., closure) were only used later in infancy. In addition, infants made *increased* use of grouping principles over a period of months. Thus, learning plays an important role in perceptual grouping.

The Gestaltists argued that the grouping of visual elements occurs ahead of most other visual processes. An important aspect of perceptual organisation is **figure-ground segregation**. One part of the visual field is identified as the figure (central object). The rest of the visual field is less important and forms the ground. When does figure-ground segregation occur? According to the Gestaltists, this happens very *early* in visual processing and always precedes object recognition.

You can check the validity of these claims by looking at the faces-goblet illusion. When the goblet is the figure, it seems to be in front of a dark background. In contrast, the faces are seen in front of a light background when they form the figure.

The faces–goblet ambiguous figure is an example of figure and ground—which is figure and which is ground?

KEY TERMS

Law of Prägnanz: the notion that visual perception will tend to be organised as simply as possible.

Figure-ground segregation: perception of the visual scene as consisting of an object or figure standing out from a less distinct background.

Findings

The Gestaltists used artificial figures, and it is important to check their findings apply to more realistic stimuli. Elder and Goldberg (2002) found using pictures of natural objects that proximity (closeness) and good continuation were both used when deciding which contours belonged to which objects.

Does the grouping of visual elements always occur early in processing as predicted by the Gestaltists? Rock and Palmer (1990) obtained evidence that the answer is "No" when they presented observers with luminous beads on parallel strings in the dark. These beads were closer together in the vertical direction than the horizontal one. However, the situation was more complex when the display was tilted backwards. Now the beads were closer to each other horizontally than vertically in the two-dimensional retinal image but remained closer to each other vertically in three-dimensional space.

What did the observers report? If the grouping of the beads occurred *before* depth perception (as predicted by the Gestaltists), they should have seen the beads organised in horizontal rows. If grouping occurred *after* depth perception, however, the observer should have seen the beads organised in vertical columns. That latter is what actually happened.

The Gestaltists assumed figure-ground segregation does not depend on past experience or learning. Contrary evidence was reported by Barense et al. (2012). Observers were shown drawings of familiar objects (e.g., a guitar) or drawings with the objects parts re-arranged and asked to indicate the figure region in each case. Healthy individuals identified regions containing familiar objects as the figure more often than those containing re-arranged parts. In contrast, amnesic patients (whose memory problems caused them to have difficulty in identifying the objects presented) showed no difference in performance between the two types of drawings. Thus, figure-ground segregation in healthy individuals depends on past experience based on object familiarity and so is not entirely innate.

EVALUATION

➕ The Gestaltists correctly emphasised the importance of perceptual organisation and figure-ground segregation.

➕ Nearly all the laws of grouping proposed by the Gestaltists have stood the test of time.

➕ The notion that observers perceive the simplest possible organisation of the visual environment (i.e., the law of Prägnanz) remains very influential (Wagemans et al., 2012).

➖ Experience and learning influence perceptual organisation to a greater extent than assumed by the Gestaltists.

➖ The Gestalt laws are *descriptive* rather than *explanatory*. They do not tell us *why* similar elements (or those close together) are grouped.

➖ The Gestaltists' approach was too inflexible – they did not realise that perceptual grouping and figure-ground segregation can occur early or late in processing depending on the nature of the stimuli and the task.

Texture gradients communicate texture and depth. The flowers appear to become closer together as they recede into the distance.

Depth perception

A central achievement of visual perception is our ability to use the information contained in the *two-dimensional* image on the retina to produce *three-dimensional perception*. This is one of the key issues of depth perception. Good depth or distance perception is very important. For example, we need to know how far away cars are so that we can cross the road safely. As we are about to discover, we use many different cues to achieve accurate depth perception.

Monocular cues

We start with **monocular cues**. Such cues only require the use of one eye but can also be used when someone has both eyes open. You can see the importance of monocular cues by closing one eye and discovering that the world still retains a sense of depth. Monocular cues are sometimes called pictorial cues because artists use them to create the impression of three-dimensional scenes when painting. One such cue is **linear perspective**. Parallel lines pointing away from us (e.g., railway lines) seem to get closer into the distance.

Texture provides another cue to perspective. Most objects (e.g., cobbled roads; carpets) possess texture, and textured objects slanting away from us have a **texture gradient** – the texture becomes more dense as you look from the front to the back of a slanting object.

Interposition is another cue in which a nearer object hides part of a more distant one from view. The power of this cue can be seen in Kanizsa's (1976) illusory square. It looks as if there is a square in front of four circles even though most of the square's contours are missing.

Finally, there is **motion parallax**. This refers to the movement of an object's image over the retina due to movement of the observer's head. If you look into the far distance through the window of a moving train, the apparent speed of objects passing by seems faster the closer they are to you. In addition, distant objects seem to move in the same direction as the train whereas nearby ones apparently move in the opposite direction.

Cues such as linear perspective, texture, and interposition allow observers to perceive depth even in two-dimensional displays. However, depth is often underestimated in such displays (Domini et al., 2011). A plausible explanation is that two-dimensional displays provide cues to flatness (the binocular and oculomotor cues discussed next), and these flatness cues reduce the impact of cues suggesting depth.

Binocular and oculomotor cues

Binocular cues are ones that can be used only when someone has both eyes open. The most important of such cues is **stereopsis**, which depends for its effectiveness on the fact that there are slight differences between

KEY TERMS

Monocular cues: cues to depth that only require the use of one eye.

Linear perspective: a strong impression of depth in a two-dimensional drawing created by lines converging on the horizon.

Texture gradient: a depth cue provided by the increased rate of change in texture density of a slanting object from the nearest part to the furthest part.

Interposition: a depth cue in which a closer object partly hides another object further away.

Motion parallax: a depth cue provided by the movement of an object's image across the retina.

Binocular cues: depth cues requiring the use of both eyes.

Stereopsis: a depth cue based on slight differences in the images on the retinas of the two eyes.

the two retinal images of objects. Stereopsis plays an important role in three-dimensional movies. What happens is that each scene is recorded with two cameras to simulate what can be seen with the left and right eyes. When people watch the movie, they wear special glasses so that the visual input to the spectator's two eyes corresponds to what each eye would have seen in the original scene.

The effectiveness of stereopsis depends on the disparity or discrepancy in the retinal images of the visual scene. This disparity in an object's retinal images decreases dramatically as distance increases. As a result, stereopsis is only effective at relatively short distances.

Oculomotor cues depend on the sensations from muscles around the eye. One such cue is convergence – the eyes turn inwards more to focus on an object when it is very close than when it is further away. **Accommodation** refers to the variation in optical power produced by a thickening of the eye's lens when focusing on a close object. **Convergence** and accommodation are only of use with objects very close to the observer.

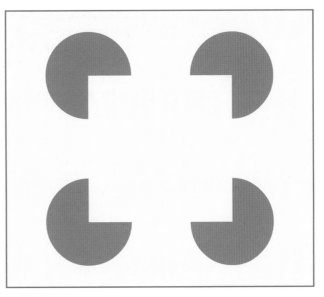

Kanizsa's illusory square—although no square is present, people see the diagram as if it were four circles with a square lying on them.

Integrating cue information

So far we have considered depth cues one at a time. In the real world, however, we typically have access to many such cues at the same time. How do we combine or integrate information from different cues? Perhaps observers attach equal importance to all available cues. In contrast, Jacobs (2002) argued that observers assign more weight or importance to *reliable* cues than unreliable ones. Cues can be reliable in two ways: (1) they provide unambiguous information; (2) they provide information consistent with that provided by other cues.

Support for the prediction that observers attach most importance to cues providing unambiguous information was reported by Triesch et al. (2002). They used a virtual reality situation in which observers tracked an object defined by three attributes (colour, shape, and size). On each trial, two attributes were ambiguous and one was unambiguous. Observers attached increased weight to the reliable cue and less to the ambiguous ones.

Support for the prediction that observers favour cues providing information consistent with that from other cues was reported by Atkins et al. (2001). They used a virtual reality environment in which observers viewed and grasped cylinders using three cues: texture, motion, and touch. When only one of the visual cues (e.g., texture or motion) indicated the same distance as the touch cue, that cue was preferred.

In sum, observers do *not* attach equal importance to all available visual cues. Instead, they attach most importance to the information provided by reliable ones. This typically works well. For example, Lovell et al. (2012) tested

KEY TERMS

Oculomotor cues: depth cues based on contractions of muscles around the eye.

Accommodation: a depth cue involving a thickening of the eyes' lenses when focusing on close objects.

Convergence: a depth cue provided by greater inward turning of the eyes when looking at a close object than one further away.

the effect of making a very reliable cue (stereopsis) less reliable over trials. Observers responded by attaching less weight to stereopsis, and their depth perception was optimal.

Object recognition

What processes are involved in object recognition?

All day long we identify or recognise objects in the world around us. At this very moment, you are looking at this book (possibly with your eyes glazed over). If you lift your gaze, perhaps you can see a wall, windows, and so in front of you.

Object recognition is much more complex than you might imagine. For example, many objects (e.g., chairs; houses) vary enormously in their visual properties (e.g., colour; size; shape), and yet we can still recognise them. We can also recognise objects over numerous viewing distances and orientations. For example, most plates are round, but we can easily identify them seen from an angle so they appear elliptical. Thus, there is much more to object recognition than might initially be supposed (than meets the eye?).

Recognition-by-components theory

What processes are involved in object recognition? According to Biederman's (1987) recognition-by-components theory, objects consist of basic shapes or components known as **geons** (geometric ions). Examples of geons are blocks, cylinders, spheres, arcs, and wedges. Biederman argued there are about 36 different geons. This sounds suspiciously few to describe thousands of different objects. However, these geons can be combined in a huge number of different ways. For example, a cup is an arc connected to the side of a cylinder whereas a pail is an arc connected to the top of a cylinder. Similarly, we can identify enormous numbers of English words even though there are only about 44 phonemes in our language.

Geon-based information about common objects is stored in long-term memory. As a result, object recognition depends crucially on the identification of geons. Since an object's geons can be identified from numerous viewpoints, object recognition should generally be easy unless one or more geons are hidden from view. This is known as **viewpoint-invariant perception**.

How do we recognise objects when only some of the relevant visual information is available? According to Biederman (1987), the concavities (hollows) in an object's contour provide especially useful information for identifying an object's geons.

Findings

Biederman (1987) presented observers with degraded line drawings of objects. As he predicted, object recognition was much harder to achieve when parts of the contour providing information about concavities were omitted than when other parts were deleted. Leek et al. (2012) studied observers looking at objects, and found most of their eye movements were directed to concavities within the objects.

KEY TERMS

Geons: basic shapes or components combined in object recognition; an abbreviation for "geometric ions" proposed by Biederman.

Viewpoint-invariant perception: the notion that it is equally easy to recognise objects from many different viewpoints.

Form a visual image of a bicycle. Your image probably involved a side view with the bicycle's two wheels clearly visible. Suppose some observers saw a picture of a bicycle from a typical viewpoint similar to your mental image whereas others saw the same bicycle viewed end on or from above. Would the observers given the typical view identify the bicycle faster than the others?

Biederman (1987) claimed object recognition should be equally rapid and easy regardless of the viewing angle (i.e., viewpoint-invariant perception). However, it is possible object recognition is generally faster and easier when objects are seen from typical angles (**viewpoint-dependent perception**).

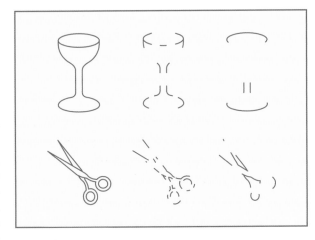

Intact figures (left-hand side), with degraded line drawings either preserving (middle column) or not preserving (far-right column) parts of the contour providing information about concavities.

As you may have guessed, object recognition is sometimes viewpoint-invariant and sometimes viewpoint-dependent. Two factors play a major role. First, it matters whether object recognition involves *categorisation* (e.g., is the object a dog?) or *identification* (e.g., is the object a poodle?) which requires within-category discriminations. Categorisation is often viewpoint-invariant whereas identification is viewpoint-dependent (Milivojevic, 2012). Identification requires more detailed processing of visual stimuli than categorisation and is harder to do when an object is viewed from an unusual angle.

Second, learning is important. Zimmermann and Eimer (2013) gave observers the task of deciding whether two faces presented together were the same or different on 640 trials. Face recognition was initially viewpoint-dependent but became more viewpoint-invariant over trials. More information about each face was stored in long-term memory with learning, and this facilitated rapid access to visual face memory regardless of face orientations.

Biederman (1987) emphasised the processing of object features or geons (bottom-up processing) in object recognition. However, top-down processing (e.g., expectation; knowledge) is often important especially when object recognition is hard. Viggiano et al. (2008) studied object recognition with animal photographs that were clear or blurred to make them harder to recognise. Observers relied more on their expectations and knowledge with the blurred photographs because information about object features or geons was less accessible.

EVALUATION

➕ The assumption that geon-like components are involved in object recognition is plausible and supported by much evidence.

➕ As predicted by recognition-by-components theory, concavities are of major importance in object recognition.

KEY TERM

Viewpoint-dependent perception: the notion that objects are easier to recognise from some viewpoints (especially typical ones) than from others.

○ Object recognition is often viewpoint-dependent (especially when identification requires difficult within-category discriminations) whereas the theory predicts it should be viewpoint-invariant.

○ Recognition-by-components theory de-emphasises the importance of top-down processes (e.g., expectations) in object recognition.

○ The notion that objects consist of invariant geons is too inflexible. As Hayward and Tarr (2005, p. 67) pointed out, "You can take almost any object, put a working light-bulb on the top, and call it a lamp."

Visual illusions

Visual perception is typically very accurate. If it were inaccurate, we would be in danger of falling over the edges of cliffs or being run over by cars when crossing the road. However, our visual perception is sometimes deficient. Consider **visual illusions**, which are generally two-dimensional drawings that most people see inaccurately. The Müller-Lyer illusion is the most famous one. The vertical line on the left seems longer than the vertical line on the right. In fact, they are the same length as can be shown with a ruler.

Expectations

How can we explain illusions such as the Müller-Lyer? Gregory (1970) argued that we treat two-dimensional figures as if they were three-dimensional. The figure on the left looks like the inside of a room whereas the one on the right is like the outside corner of a building. Thus, the outgoing fins represent lines approaching us whereas the ingoing fins stand for receding lines. Our *expectations* concerning what the figures would look like in three-dimensional space create the illusion effect (Redding & Vinson, 2010).

We can see the importance of expectations with the **Ames room illusion**, which involves a specially constructed room with a very peculiar shape. Of most importance, the rear wall is not at right angles to the adjoining walls. The fact that one end of the rear wall is much further from the viewer is disguised by making it much higher. The Ames room creates the same retinal image as a typical rectangular room, and our *expectation* that rooms are rectangular causes us to see the room as normal. This effect is so great that someone walking backwards and forwards in front of the rear wall seems to grow and shrink! It is unclear why observers ignore the reasonable expectation that people's heights do not change as they move around.

Glennerster et al. (2006) asked people to walk through a virtual-reality room as it expanded or contracted considerably. Their expectation that the room's size would remain the same caused them to be very inaccurate in their judgments of the sizes of objects in the room.

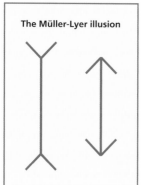

The Müller-Lyer illusion

The Müller-Lyer illusion

KEY TERMS

Visual illusions: drawings or other visual stimuli that are misperceived by nearly everyone.

Ames room illusion: the room looks like an ordinary room but actually has a very unusual shape; this causes distortions in the apparent heights of individuals standing in front of the rear wall.

What can we conclude? According to Glennerster (2015, p. 3), "We perceive a stable world if, when we move our head and eyes, the image we receive falls within the set of images that we were expecting." This makes us susceptible to visual illusions in studies such as the one by Glennerster et al. (2006).

Illusions due to artificiality?

Many visual illusions (e.g., Müller-Lyer) involve artificial figures, and you may be thinking they can be dismissed as tricks played by psychologists with nothing better to do. However, that argument does *not* account for all illusions. DeLucia and Hochberg (1991) showed the Müller-Lyer illusion with real three-dimensional objects. Three open books are placed in a line with the ones on the left and the right open to the right and the middle one open to the left. The spine of the middle book should be the same distance from the spines of each of the other books. In spite of this, the distance between the spines of the middle book and the one on the right appears longer.

What can the study of visual illusions tell us about how our visual system operates?

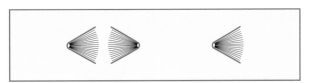

The spine of the middle book is closer to the spine of which other book? Now check your answer with a ruler.

Two perception systems

The existence of numerous visual illusions leaves us with an intriguing paradox – how has the human species survived if our visual perception is so error prone? Milner and Goodale (2008) provided an influential answer. They argued we have *two* visual systems. There is a vision-for-perception system used to identify objects (e.g., to decide whether we are confronted by a buffalo or a cat). We use this system when looking at visual illusions. There is also a vision-for-action system used for visually guided action. This system provides accurate information about our position with respect to objects. It is the system we use when avoiding a speeding car or rapidly grasping an object.

Suppose people were presented with three-dimensional versions of illusions such as the Müller-Lyer. The illusion should be present if they decided which line was longer because that would involve the vision-for-perception system. However, there should be a much smaller illusion if people were asked to point at the end of one of the figures, because that would involve the vision-for-action system. As predicted, a review of the relevant studies showed that the average illusion effect was four times greater when the vision-for-perception system was used than when the vision-for-action system was used (Bruno et al., 2008). Similar findings have been obtained with several other visual illusions (see Eysenck and Keane, 2015).

Milner and Goodale's ideas can be applied to the hollow-face illusion in which a realistic hollow mask looks like a normal face (visit the website: www.richardgregory.org/experiments/index.htm). Króliczak et al. (2006) placed a target (small magnet) on the hollow mask. When observers drew the target position (using the vision-for-perception system), there was a strong illusion –

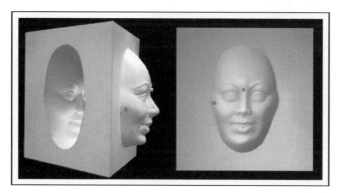

the target was seen as much closer than was actually the case. However, when observers made a fast flicking finger movement to the target (using the vision-for-action system), there was no illusory effect.

In sum, visual illusions are strongly influenced by our expectations concerning the world about us. However, this is mostly the case when we make judgments using the vision-for-perception system. When we point at visual figures using the vision-for-action system, there is little or no illusion effect, and our expectations are unimportant. The vision-for-action system allows us to avoid falling over cliffs even though the vision-for-perception system is fooled by visual illusions.

It is important to conclude with a note of caution. In practice, the two visual systems typically work together rather than separately, and most visual tasks require the use of both. Thus, visual processing is less neat and tidy than implied by Milner and Goodale (2008).

Change blindness

Have a look around you (go on!). You probably have a strong impression of seeing a vivid and detailed picture of the visual scene in front of your eyes. However, you may be deluding yourself. Suppose there was a unicycling clown wearing a vivid purple and yellow outfit, large shoes, and a bright red nose in front of you as you were walking along. Would you spot him? I imagine your answer is "Yes". However, Hyman et al. (2010) found only 51% of people walking on their own spotted the clown.

The study by Hyman et al. (2010) provided a demonstration of **inattentional blindness**, which is "the failure to notice an unexpected, but fully visible item when attention is diverted to other aspects of a display" (Jensen et al., 2011, p. 529). A closely related phenomenon is **change blindness**, which is "the surprising failure to detect a substantial visual change" (Jensen et al., p. 529).

Look at the pictures in the figure and try to spot the difference within each pair. Rensink et al. (1997) found observers took an average of 10.4 seconds to

KEY TERMS

Inattentional blindness: the failure to perceive the appearance of an unexpected object in the visual environment.

Change blindness: the failure to detect that a visual stimulus has moved, changed, or been replaced by another stimulus.

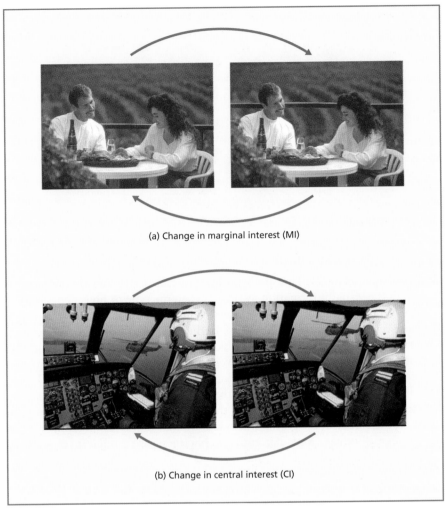

(a) Change in marginal interest (MI)

(b) Change in central interest (CI)

(a) The object that is changed (the railing) undergoes a shift in location comparable to that of the object that is changed (the helicopter) in (b). However, the change is much easier to see in (b) because the changed object is more important.

spot the difference between the first pair of pictures but only 2.6 seconds with the second pair. Why did this difference occur? The height of the railing is of *marginal* interest whereas the position of the helicopter is of *central* interest.

Hollingworth and Henderson (2002) studied the role of attention in change blindness. Observers looked at a visual scene (e.g., kitchen; living room) for several seconds, and it was assumed the object fixated at any given moment was being attended. Two kinds of changes could occur:

What is the difference between inattentional blindness and change blindness? Can you think of examples of both from your own life?

* *Type change*, in which an object was replaced by one from a different category (e.g., a plate replaced with a bowl).
* *Token change*, in which an object was replaced by one from the same category (e.g., a plate replaced by a different plate).

There were two main findings. First, changes were much more likely to be detected when the changed object had received attention (been fixated) before the change occurred. That supports the view that lack of attention plays an important role in producing change blindness.

Percentage of correct change detection as a function of form of change (type vs. token) and time of fixation (before vs. after change); also false alarm rate when there was no change.

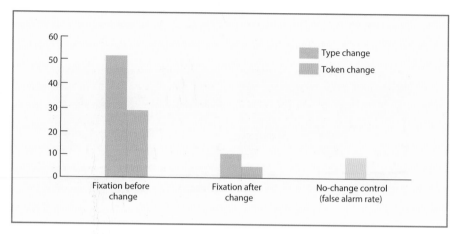

Second, change detection was much better when there was a change in the type of object rather than merely swapping one member of a category for another (token change). That finding occurred because there is a much larger change in the visual information available when the type of object changes.

An important factor in inattentional blindness is the *similarity* between an unexpected object and other objects in the visual environment. Simons and Chabris (1999) carried out a study in which a woman dressed in black as a gorilla strolled across a scene in which there were two teams, one dressed in white and the other in black. When observers counted the number of passes made by the team in white, only 42% of them saw the gorilla. In contrast, 83% of observers detected the gorilla when they counted the passes made by the team in black. In this case, the colour of the gorilla was similar to that of the task-relevant stimuli.

What factors could lead you to fail to notice a change in your visual environment?

Change blindness and inattentional blindness are similar because both involve a failure to detect a visual event occurring in plain sight and often depend on failures of attention. However, successful avoidance of change blindness involves more complex processes than avoidance of inattentional blindness. Jensen et al. (2011) argued that observers must engage successfully in five separate processes for change detection to occur:

1. Attention must be paid to the change location.
2. The pre-change visual stimulus at the change location must be encoded into memory.
3. The post-change visual stimulus at the change location must be encoded into memory.
4. The pre- and post-change representations must be compared.
5. The discrepancy between the pre- and post-change representations must be recognised at the conscious level.

IN THE REAL WORLD: movies and magic

Movie makers are very pleased we are susceptible to change blindness. The reason is that nearly all movies have unintended continuity mistakes when a scene has been shot more than once. For example, in the Bond movie *Spectre* (2015), a plane crashes into the back of a Range

Rover causing the plane's nose to crumple and a wheel to fall off. Shortly afterwards, the plane's nose is fine, and there is no problem with the landing gear!

Magicians also benefit from change blindness and inattentional blindness. It is often assumed magicians baffle us because the hand is quicker than the eye. In fact, most magic tricks involve **misdirection** – the magician manipulates the audience's attention away from some action crucial to the trick's success.

We can see misdirection causing inattentional blindness in the following trick (Kuhn & Findlay, 2010): (a) the magician picks up a lighter with his left hand; (b) he lights it; (c) and (d) he pretends to take the flame with his right hand; (e) he gradually moves his right hand away from the hand holding the lighter; (f) he reveals his right hand is empty while the lighter is dropped into his lap; (g) the magician directs his gaze to his left hand; (h) he reveals his left hand is also empty and the lighter has disappeared.

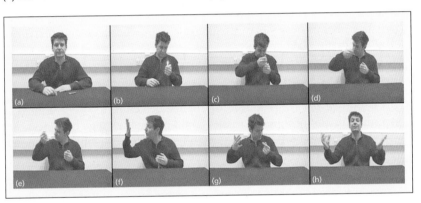

Misdirection was involved because those who missed the drop were mostly fixating further from the left hand than those who detected it when the lighter was dropped. However, 69% of those who detected the drop were fixating some distance away from the magician's left hand and so only detected the drop in peripheral vision. Thus, the lighter drop could be detected by overt attention (attention directed to the fixation point) or by covert attention (attention directed away from the fixation point).

Smith et al. (2012) studied change blindness. The magician passed a coin from one hand to the other and then dropped it on the table. The participants' task was to guess whether the coin would land with heads or tails facing up (see online at http://dx.doi.org/10.1068/p7092). The coin was switched (e.g., from a 50p to an old 10p). All participants fixated the coin the whole time it was visible, but 88% failed to detect the coin had changed! Thus, change blindness can occur even though the crucial object is fixated and so attention is not misdirected. The participants were fooled because they expected the coin to remain the same and because they failed to attend to coin features irrelevant to their task.

KEY TERM

Misdirection: a form of deception practised by magicians in which the audience's attention is focused on one object to distract its attention to another object.

> **Is change blindness a bad thing?**
>
> Phenomena such as inattentional blindness and change blindness apparently indicate that our visual system is inefficient. However, that is *not* the case. We generally expect the visual world to be relatively stable and unchanging, and this expectation is typically confirmed. The occasional loss of perceptual accuracy (e.g., with change blindness) is the small sacrifice we pay for perceptual stability (Fischer & Whitney, 2014).

EVALUATION

⊕ Change blindness and inattentional blindness are important phenomena occurring in everyday life (e.g., the movies; magic tricks).

⊕ Several factors increasing (or decreasing) the likelihood of change blindness occurring have been identified.

⊕ Attentional processes play a major role in producing change blindness and inattentional blindness.

⊖ Much remains to be discovered about precisely *how* attentional processes determine change blindness and change detection.

⊖ Five processes are required for change detection to occur and so a failure in any of these processes could produce change blindness. As yet, there has been little systematic research to distinguish among the various potential reasons for change blindness.

⊖ It is too often assumed that failure to report detecting a change in a scene means there has been little or no processing of the changed object. However, undetected changes often trigger brain activity, indicating that some processing of those changes has occurred (Fernandez-Duque et al., 2003).

Chapter summary

- According to the Gestaltists, observers typically perceive the simplest possible organization of the visual information available to them.
- The Gestaltists assumed that figure-ground segregation always occurs early in visual processing. This assumption is incorrect.
- The Gestaltists underestimated the importance of knowledge and experience in perceptual organization.
- Monocular cues to depth include linear perspective, texture gradient, interposition, shading, and motion parallax.
- The major binocular cue is stereopsis. There are two rather ineffective oculomotor cues: convergence and accommodation.
- Observers integrate information from different cues by assigning more weight to reliable cues. Such cues provide unambiguous information and/or information consistent with that provided by other cues.
- According to Biederman's recognition-by-components theory, object recognition involves identifying an object's basic shapes (known as geons).

- Biederman assumed that object recognition was viewpoint-invariant. However, it is actually viewpoint-dependent when object recognition is difficult.
- Biederman emphasised bottom-up processes and de-emphasised the roles of expectation and knowledge in object recognition.
- Many visual illusions occur when observers' expectations are mistaken.
- Some illusions reflect the artificiality of the visual displays presented to observers.
- Illusion effects are typically much greater when observers use the vision-for-perception system rather than the vision-for-action system.
- Most people greatly exaggerate their ability to detect visual changes in objects. In fact, most of us exhibit much change blindness.
- Change blindness is most commonly found when observers aren't expecting a change and when the object changed is of marginal interest.
- Change in an object is more likely to be detected when observers are attending to that object, especially when they are attending to the specific aspect of it that changes.

Further reading

- Eysenck, M.W., & Brysbaert, M. (2017). *Fundamentals of cognition* (3rd ed.). Oxford: Psychology Press. Chapter 2 of this textbook is devoted to topics in visual perception.
- Goldstein, E.B., & Brockmole, J. (2016). *Sensation and perception* (10th ed.). Belmont, CA: Wadsworth, Cengage Learning. Most major topics in visual perception are discussed in this textbook.
- Mather, G. (2016). *Foundations of sensation and perception* (3rd ed.). Abingdon, Oxon: Psychology Press. Major topics relating to visual perception are discussed in Chapters 10 and 11 of this excellent textbook.
- Peissig, J.J., & Tarr, M.J. (2007). Visual object recognition: Do we know more now than we did 20 years ago? *Annual Review of Psychology, 58*, 75–96. The authors provide a good overview of developments in our understanding of object recognition.

Essay questions

1. What are the strengths and limitations of the Gestalt approach to understanding perceptual organisation?
2. How do we achieve depth perception?
3. To what extent is object recognition viewpoint-invariant?
4. Why are we susceptible to visual illusions?
5. What role does attention play in inattentional blindness and change blindness?

Most people (including you?) find their memory for some things is very good but are very poor at remembering other things. Why do you think this is? How many different types of memory do you think we have? As we have discovered to our cost, it is very common to forget information (even important information). What are the main reasons that forgetting occurs?

It is really important for eyewitnesses to a crime to remember the details of what happened. However, their memories of the crime are often limited and inaccurate. Why is it that eyewitness testimony tends to be so poor?

Memory

22

How important is memory to us? Imagine what our lives would be like without it. We would not recognise anyone or anything as familiar. We would be unable to talk, read, or write because we would remember nothing about language. We would have no sense of sense because we would be unable to access information about our personal history. In sum, experience would have taught us absolutely nothing, and we would have the same lack of knowledge as a newborn infant.

Learning and memory are closely connected. Learning involves the accumulation of knowledge or skills and would be impossible in the absence of memory. In similar fashion, memory would not be possible in the absence of learning because we can only remember things previously learned.

Learning and memory involve three stages:

- *Encoding*: this is the process occurring during learning; it typically involves processing the meaning of the to-be-learned material.
- *Storage*: some of the encoded information is stored within long-term memory.
- *Retrieval*: information in long-term memory is accessed.

Are learning and memory different? If so, what are the differences?

Your ability to retrieve or remember stored information can be tested in several ways. You might remember someone you have met before by *recognising* their face as familiar or you might *recall* their name. It is perfectly possible (and embarrassing!) to recognise someone's face without being able to put a name to it.

Suppose you were asked to learn the following word list: *chair, table, leopard, watch, forest, mouth, garden, water*. Below are various ways you memory for this list could be tested:

- **Free recall**: this involves writing down all the words you remember in any order.
- **Cued recall**: this might involve being given the first few letters of each word (e.g., CHA —; TAB —) and producing the appropriate list words.

> **KEY TERMS**
>
> **Free recall:** a memory test in which words from a list can be produced in any order.
>
> **Cued recall:** a memory test in which cues or clues (e.g., first few letters of each list word) are given to assist memory.

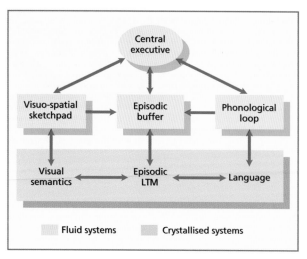

The Baddeley (2000) version of the multi-component working memory. Links to long-term memory have been specified and a new component, the episodic buffer, added. Fluid systems involve active processing whereas crystallised systems involve stored knowledge.

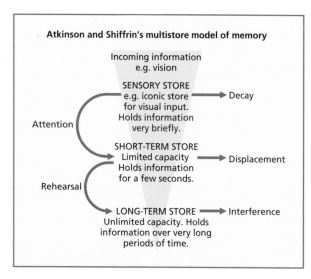

KEY TERMS

Recognition: a memory test in which previously presented information must be distinguished from information not previously presented.

Rehearsal: the verbal repetition of information (e.g., words), which typically increases our long-term memory for the rehearsed information.

- **Recognition:** this might involve being given the list words plus non-list words (e.g., *chair shelf elbow mouth frame table water photo tiger garden forest watch statue leopard robin ticket*) and selecting only the list words.

Short-term vs. long-term memory

There is a crucial distinction between short-term and long-term memory. Short-term memory is fragile and lasts for only a few seconds. It is used when we remember a phone number while dialling it or when listening to a conversation. Long-term memory is more durable. It is used when we recall the happiest time of our lives or when we ride a bicycle.

Multistore model

According to Atkinson and Shiffrin's (1968) multistore model, attended information is processed in a short-term memory store having very limited capacity. **Rehearsal** (saying the items over to ourselves silently) causes some of that information to proceed to the long-term store. The more you rehearse the list words, the better your long-term memory will be.

Findings

Convincing evidence that there are separate short-term and long-term memory stores comes from research on brain-damaged patients. Suppose there is only *one* memory system covering short-term and long-term memory. Patients with brain damage to this system would show poor short-term and long-term memory.

In contrast, suppose there are *two* memory systems. If these two systems are in different brain areas, some patients would have poor short-term memory but intact long-term memory. Other patients would have intact short-term memory but poor long-term memory.

Most brain-damaged patients with memory problems suffer from **amnesia**. These patients (discussed in detail later) have intact short-term memory, but their long-term memory is severely disrupted. They will re-read a newspaper without realising they read it a short time ago, and often fail to recognise someone they met recently.

A few patients show the opposite pattern. Shallice and Warrington (1974) studied a patient, KF, who had suffered brain damage following a motorcycle accident. He had very poor short-term memory but essentially intact long-term memory.

EVALUATION

➕ The multistore model has been very influential.

➕ There is convincing evidence for separate short-term and long-term memory systems.

➖ The role of rehearsal in producing long-term memory was exaggerated by Atkinson and Shiffrin (1968). Most of the information in your long-term memory was not rehearsed during learning.

➖ As is discussed next, the assumptions that we have a *single* short-term memory system and a *single* long-term memory system are gross oversimplifications.

Short-term memory

Short-term memory consists of the information of which we are consciously aware at any given moment. We can assess its capacity using **memory span** – the longest sequence of items (e.g., words; digits) that can be recalled immediately in the correct order. With memory span, the capacity of short-term memory is "seven, plus or minus two" (Miller, 1956).

It is important to distinguish between items and **chunks**, which are "groups of items that have been collected together and treated as a single unit" (Mathy & Feldman, 2012, p. 346). For example, *psychology* consists of 10 items but only one chunk. Mathy and Feldman (2012) presented information that could be encoded into chunks and found only three or four chunks could be recalled.

What is the approximate capacity of short-term memory?

Chen and Cowan (2009) argued that estimates of short-term memory capacity are sometimes inflated because of the use of rehearsal (repeating the items subvocally). They presented participants with chunks consisting of single words or pairs of words learned previously. Four chunks were recalled when rehearsal was possible, but this reduced to three in the absence of rehearsal.

Is short-term memory useful in everyday life? Textbook writers (including me earlier!) point out that it allows us to remember a telephone number for the few seconds taken to dial it. Of course, that is no longer relevant since we have most phone numbers stored in our mobile phones.

Working memory

Baddeley and Hitch (1974) provided a convincing answer to the question (i.e., "Is short-term memory useful in everyday life?"). Their central argument was

> **KEY TERMS**
>
> **Memory span:** maximum number of digits or other items repeated back in the correct order immediately after they have been presented.
>
> **Chunks:** stored units formed from integrating smaller pieces of information.

Alan Baddeley (on left) and Graham Hitch (on right)

that we generally use short-term memory when performing complex tasks. With such tasks, you need to carry out various processes to complete the task. It is often necessary to store information about the outcome of early processes briefly in short-term memory as you move on to later processes.

Suppose you were given the addition problem 13 + 18 + 24. You would probably add 13 and 18 and keep the answer (31) in short-term memory. You would then add 24 to 31 and produce the correct answer of 55.

Baddeley and Hitch (1974) argued we should replace the phrase "short-term memory" with "working memory". **Working memory** refers to a system that combines processing and short-term memory functions. Their crucial insight was that short-term memory is essential in the performance of numerous tasks (e.g., problems in mathematics) that are not explicitly memory tasks.

The working memory model put forward by Baddeley and Hitch (1974) has been revised several times since then. We will focus on the most recent version (Baddeley, 2012):

- **Central executive**: a limited capacity processing system acting as an attentional controller. It is the "boss" of the working memory system and can process information from any sensory modality (i.e., it is modality-free).
- **Phonological loop**: involved in the processing and brief storage of phonological (speech-based) information. For example, it is used to rehearse words on a short-term memory task.
- **Visuo-spatial sketchpad**: involved in the processing and brief storage of visual and spatial information; used when finding the route from one place to another or when watching TV. There is an important distinction between visual and spatial processing. For example, blind people often have good spatial processing without visual processing: Fortin et al. (2008) found blind people were better than sighted ones at finding their way through a human-size maze.
- **Episodic buffer**: This is a storage system holding information from the phonological loop, the visuo-spatial sketchpad, and long-term memory.

All four components of working memory can function fairly independently of the others. They all have limited capacity. You probably think the working memory model seems rather (or very!) complicated. However, the basic ideas are straightforward. When we carry out a task, we can make use of verbal processing (phonological loop), visual processing, or spatial processing (visuo-spatial sketchpad).

Performing the task successfully requires that we attend to relevant information and use verbal, visual, and spatial processes effectively (central executive). During task performance, we often need a general storage system combining and integrating information from the other components and from long-term memory (episodic buffer).

KEY TERMS

Working memory: a system that has separate components for rehearsal and for other processing activities (e.g., attention; visual processing).

Central executive: a modality-free, limited capacity, component of working memory.

Phonological loop: a component of working memory in which speech-based information is processed and stored and subvocal articulation occurs.

Visuo-spatial sketchpad: a component of working memory used to process visual and spatial information and to store this information briefly.

Episodic buffer: a component of working memory; it is essentially passive and briefly stores integrated information from the phonological loop, visuo-spatial sketchpad, and long-term memory.

Long-term memory

Atkinson and Shiffrin (1968) argued there is only one long-term memory system. However, that seems improbable when you consider the huge range of information stored in long-term memory: personal experiences, general knowledge, motor skills, language, and so on.

The most important distinction within long-term memory is between declarative and non-declarative memory. **Declarative memory** involves conscious recollection of events and facts – it refers to memories that can be "declared" or described and involves "knowing that" something is the case. Declarative memory is what you use when you remember someone's name when you see them, when you remember some fact in psychology, or when you remember how to find your friend's house.

In contrast, **non-declarative memory** does not involve conscious recollection. We typically obtain evidence of non-declarative memory by observing changes in behaviour. For example, we can see that someone has learned how to ride a bicycle by observing that they wobble less and have better control over it. However, they generally cannot put into words the skills they have learned.

How does amnesia affect procedural and declarative memory?

IN THE REAL WORLD: the famous case of Henry Molaison (HM)

Henry Molaison (known only as HM until his death in 2008) suffered from **amnesia**, a condition involving severely impaired long-term memory due to brain damage. He had an operation for epilepsy in 1953 that included removal of brain areas of central importance to long-term memory (the medial temporal lobes including the hippocampus). Corkin (1984, p. 255) reported many years later that HM "does not know where he lives, who cares for him, or where he ate his last meal." He recognised the faces of only two individuals (John Kennedy and Ronald Reagan), who became famous after the onset of his amnesia. Thus, his declarative memory was extremely poor.

In spite of his incredibly poor declarative memory, his non-declarative memory was generally good (Eichenbaum, 2015). For example, he performed well on various motor-learning tasks including the pursuit rotor (which involves manual tracking of a moving target). He also had essentially intact performance on short-term memory tasks. In sum, HM provided important evidence for two major distinctions: between short-term and long-term memory and between declarative and non-declarative memory.

The case of HM led to a marked increase in research on amnesia. Spiers et al. (2001) reviewed findings from 147 amnesic patients. All the patients had severely impaired declarative memory but *none* had impaired non-declarative memory. As mentioned earlier, Spiers et al. also found that none of these amnesic patients had impaired short-term memory. Thus, the basic findings on HM have been replicated numerous times.

KEY TERMS

Declarative memory: a long-term memory system concerned with personal experiences and general knowledge; it usually involves conscious recollection of information.

Non-declarative memory: a form of long-term memory that does not involve conscious recollection of information (e.g., motor skills)

Amnesia: a condition caused by brain damage in which patients have intact short-term memory but poor long-term memory.

Declarative memory

There are *three* main types of declarative memory: episodic memory, semantic memory, and autobiographical memory. We will consider them in turn.

Episodic memory

Episodic memory is used when we remember past events or episodes we have experienced (e.g., that we had cereal for breakfast; that we went to the movies yesterday. Most episodic memories fulfil the WWW criteria – they contain information about *what* happened, *where* it happened, and *when* it happened. One might imagine the episodic memory system resembles a video recorder providing us with accurate and detailed information about events. That is *not* the case. Episodic memory is rarely a literal reproduction of the past. Instead, it involves a *constructive* process that often produces errors.

Why is episodic memory prone to error? One reason is that we typically only want to remember the essence of an experience and so the precise details are of minor relevance. Another reason is that it would require an enormous amount of processing to produce a very accurate, semi-permanent record of all our experiences.

Semantic memory

Semantic memory is the memory system we use when remembering facts and information (e.g., the name of the current American President; the meaning of the word *psychology*). More generally, semantic memory consists of our knowledge of language and the world. Much of this knowledge is in the form of schemas (discussed later).

Semantic memory is less *vulnerable* to brain damage than episodic memory. I mentioned earlier that Spiers et al. (2001) reviewed 147 cases of patients with amnesia. Episodic memory was severely impaired in all cases, but semantic memory was often only slightly impaired.

In some cases of amnesia, semantic memory is intact. Vargha-Khadem et al. (1997) studied two patients (Beth and Jon) who had very poor episodic memory for the day's activities, television programs, and telephone conversations. However, Beth and Jon both attended ordinary schools, and their levels of speech and language development, literacy, and factual knowledge were normal.

Autobiographical memory

We use **autobiographical memory** when we remember personal experiences of importance in our lives. For example, we might think about our first boyfriend/girlfriend or the best holiday of our lives. Autobiographical memory resembles episodic memory but differs in that episodic memory tends to be concerned with relatively trivial experiences.

According to Conway and Pleydell-Pearce (2000, p. 266), "Autobiographical memories are primarily records of success or failure in goal attainment." An individual's goals depend in part on his/her personality. As a result, the autobiographical memories an individual regards as important should reflect his/her personality.

Woike et al. (1999) tested this hypothesis. They distinguished between two personality types. First, there is the agentic personality type focused on independence and achievement. Second, there is the communal personality type focused on interdependence and similarity to others.

> **KEY TERMS**
>
> **Episodic memory:** long-term memory for personal events.
>
> **Semantic memory:** long-term memory for general knowledge about the world, concepts, language, and so on.
>
> **Autobiographical memory:** memory across the lifespan for specific events involving the individual (especially those of personal significance).

Woike et al. (1999) asked participants to describe positive or negative personal experiences. Those with an agentic personality mostly recalled agentic autobiographical memories (e.g., involving success or failure). In contrast, those with a communal personality recalled communal memories (e.g., involving love, friendship, or betrayal of trust).

Non-declarative memory

The essence of non-declarative memory is that it does not involve conscious recollection but instead reveals itself through behaviour. There are two main forms of non-declarative memory: priming and skill learning. **Priming** is what happens when processing of a stimulus is easier because the same (or a similar) stimulus was presented previously. When children learn to read, they show priming as they recognise familiar words more and more easily.

Tulving and Schacter (1990) found that people found it easier to identify briefly presented words if they had been seen previously. This occurred even though the participants were unaware that their ability to perceive the flashed words had been influenced by the study list. This is an example of a priming effect.

What is involved in priming? Repeated presentation of a stimulus means it can be processed more *efficiently* using fewer resources. As a result, priming is often associated with reduced levels of brain activity (Poldrack & Gabrieli, 2001).

Skill learning is involved when we learn how to ride a bicycle or play a sport. There are several differences between priming and skill learning:

1. Priming often occurs rapidly whereas skill learning is typically slow and gradual (Knowlton & Foerde, 2008).
2. Priming involves learning tied to *specific* stimuli, whereas skill learning *generalises* to other stimuli. For example, it wouldn't be much use if you learned how to hit backhands at tennis very well, but could only do so provided the ball came towards you from a given direction at a given speed!

Hamann and Squire (1997) studied an amnesic patient, EP, who seemed to have no declarative memory. On a test of recognition memory, he was correct on only 52% of trials (chance = 50%) compared to 81% for healthy controls. However, his performance on priming tasks was as good as healthy controls.

Cavaco et al. (2004) used five tasks requiring skills similar to those needed in the real world. For example, there was a weaving task and a control stick task requiring movements similar to those involved in operating machinery. Amnesic patients showed comparable rates of learning to healthy individuals on all five skill-learning tasks in spite of having impaired declarative memory for the tasks assessed by recall and recognition tests. Such findings strengthen the notion that non-declarative memory is very different from declarative memory.

Summary and conclusions

The distinction between declarative and non-declarative memory has been very influential and productive. It has led to the identification of several important types of long-term memory including episodic memory, semantic memory, autobiographical memory, priming, and skill learning.

KEY TERMS

Priming: a form of non-declarative memory involving facilitated processing of (and response to) a target stimulus because the same or a related stimulus was presented previously.

Skill learning: a form of learning in which there is little or no conscious awareness of what has been learned.

It is becoming increasingly clear that the declarative vs. non-declarative distinction is oversimplified. Consider the assumption that amnesic patients have intact non-declarative memory. This is sometimes *not* the case when the task is relatively complex. Ryan et al. (2000) presented healthy individuals and amnesics with photographs of real-world scenes in a non-declarative task. Some scenes were presented twice with the positions of some objects altered on the second occasion. Healthy controls fixated the changed part of the scene and so showed implicit memory for the relations among the objects. In contrast, the amnesic patients did not fixate the changed part because they lacked non-declarative or implicit memory for the original scene. Thus, the memory difficulties of amnesic patients extend beyond declarative memory and include impaired non-declarative memory for relations among objects.

Categorical clustering is a useful tool for sorting and storing a mass of information. Imagine how difficult it would be to find anything in a library if books were organised by colour or size.

Organisation in memory

Human memory is generally highly organised, with well-organised information being better remembered than poorly organised information. The existence of organisation in memory can be shown very simply. A categorised word list is prepared consisting of words belong to different categories (e.g., four-footed animals; sports; flowers). The list is then presented in random order (e.g., tennis, cat, golf, tulip, horse, and so on) followed by a test of free recall (words are recalled in any order).

The words are not recalled in a random order. Instead, they are mostly recalled category by category. This is known as **categorical clustering**. It shows the to-be-remembered information is organised on the basis of knowledge stored in long-term memory.

Schema theory

We have seen that people use relevant knowledge to assist their learning and memory. Much of this knowledge is in the form of **schemas** (organised packets of knowledge stored in long-term memory). In a study on schemas, Bower et al. (1979) asked people to list 20 actions or events usually occurring in a restaurant. There was much agreement with respect to the restaurant schema – most people mentioned sitting down, looking at the menu, ordering, eating, paying the bill, and leaving the restaurant.

Schemas often enhance long-term memory. Read the following passage from Bransford and Johnson (1972, p. 722) and try to make sense of it:

The procedure is quite simple. First, you arrange items into different groups. Of course one pile may be sufficient depending on how much there is to do. If you have to go somewhere else due to lack of facilities, that is the next step; otherwise, you are pretty well set. It is important not to overdo things. That is, it is better to do too few things at once than too many. In

KEY TERMS

Categorical clustering: the tendency in free recall to produce words on a category-by-category basis.

Schemas: organised knowledge about the world, events, or people in long-term memory and used to guide action.

the short run this may not seem important, but complications from doing too much can easily arise . . .

I imagine you found it very hard to understand the passage. The reason is that you lacked the relevant schema. In fact, the passage title is "Washing clothes". Re-read the passage, and you should find it much easier to understand armed with that schematic information. Bransford and Johnson (1972) found that participants given the title before reading the passage recalled twice as much information as those not given the title.

Bartlett (1932) argued that our schematic knowledge can disrupt our long-term memory. He presented English students with stories from a different culture (North American Indian) to produce a *conflict* between the story and their prior knowledge.

Bartlett (1932) found people's schematic knowledge caused systematic distortions in their story memory. These distortions involved making the story conform to the readers' cultural expectations, a type of error Bartlett termed **rationalisation**. Such distortions are also found when eyewitnesses recall a crime they have witnessed (discussed later in this chapter).

Bartlett (1932) argued that memory for the precise information presented is forgotten over time, whereas memory for the underlying schemas is not. Thus, there should be more rationalisation errors (which depend on schematic knowledge) at longer retention intervals.

Sulin and Dooling (1974) obtained support for this prediction. The participants read a story about a ruthless dictator who caused the downfall of his country. In the story, he was called Adolf Hitler or Gerald Martin. Those participants told the story was about Hitler were much more likely to believe incorrectly they had read the sentence, "He hated the Jews particularly and so persecuted them." This rationalisation error was more common at a long than a short retention interval.

The research discussed so far indicates that schemas often lead to memory distortions. However, Steyvers and Hemmer (2012) argued schemas typically assist memory in the real world. They presented people with photographs of various scenes (e.g., kitchen; urban scene). Some objects in the scenes were highly consistent with the relevant schema (e.g., *car* and *building* for the urban scene) whereas others were less consistent (e.g., *shop* and *tree* for the urban scene).

What did Steyvers and Hemmer (2012) find when they asked the participants to recall all the objects? First, recall was much better for the most schema-consistent objects than for any of the others. Second, the false recall rate (i.e., mistakenly "recalling" an object that had not been presented) was much lower for the most schema-consistent objects than those less schema-consistent. In sum, the expectations generated by our schemas are mostly correct in the real world and so our long-term memory is enhanced by schematic knowledge.

KEY TERM

Rationalisation: In Bartlett's theory, the tendency in story recall to produce errors conforming to the rememberer's expectations based on their schemas.

EVALUATION

➕ Schematic knowledge of the world is used when we learn and remember.

➕ Schemas provide an organisational framework that often enhances long-term memory (especially in the real world).

⊕ Many errors and distortions in long-term memory are due to the influence of schematic information.

⊖ It is hard to assess how much information is contained in schemas.

⊖ The conditions determining *when* a given schema will be activated are unclear.

Forgetting

There is much forgetting over time – the rate of forgetting is generally fastest shortly after learning and decreases progressively after that. Many people believe they have a poor memory. Evidence that our memory for important information can be poor was reported by Brown et al. (2004): 31% of American students admitted to having forgotten passwords.

The rate of forgetting is generally fastest shortly after learning and decreases progressively after that. The German psychologist Hermann Ebbinghaus (1885/1913) found that forgetting of lists was most rapid over the first hour or so after learning.

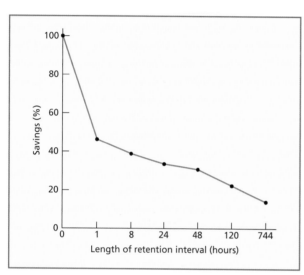

Forgetting over time as indexed by reduced savings during relearning. (0% savings would indicate total forgetting.) Data from Ebbinghaus (1885/1913).

It is generally assumed forgetting should be avoided. However, it is not useful to remember last term's schedule of classes or lectures or where your friends used to live. We need to *update* our memory of such information and forget what was previously the case. In addition, it would be counterproductive to remember all the information to which we are exposed. It is much more efficient to remember important information while forgetting trivial details (Norby, 2015).

There are many reasons why forgetting occurs. A simple (but neglected) explanation is decay, which is "forgetting due to a gradual loss of the substrate [underlying physical basis] of memory" (Hardt et al., 2013, p. 111). Hardt et al. argued we form numerous trivial memories during the course of each day and so a process is required to remove them. This is achieved by a physiological decay process that operates mostly during sleep. Other major theories of forgetting are discussed next.

Repression

Sigmund Freud claimed that much forgetting occurs as a result of **repression** (motivated forgetting of traumatic memories such as those relating to sexual abuse). Freud found that repressed memories were sometimes recalled during the course of treatment. However, Loftus and Davis (2006) argued that many so-called recovered memories are false memories (events and experiences that never happened) suggested by the therapist.

KEY TERM

Repression: a term used by Freud to refer to motivated forgetting of stressful or traumatic experiences.

Geraerts et al. (2007) divided adults reporting childhood sexual abuse into three groups:

1. those whose recovered memories were recalled *inside* therapy;
2. those who recovered memories were recalled *outside* therapy;
3. those who had had continuous memories of abuse.

Geraerts et al. (2007) found there was supporting evidence (e.g., the culprit had confessed) for 45% of patients with continuous memories, 37% of those who recalled memories outside therapy, and 0% for those recalling memories inside therapy. These findings suggest there are two types of recovered memories. First, many recalled inside therapy are false memories produced under the therapist's influence. Second, many recalled spontaneously outside therapy are genuine.

In sum, there is limited support for Freud's notion of repression. However, his approach to forgetting is limited because most forgetting does not relate to traumatic or other stressful events.

Interference

Two forms of interference cause much forgetting. First, there is **proactive interference** – our ability to remember what we are currently learning is interfered with by previous learning. Second, there is **retroactive interference** – what we are currently learning is interfered with by future learning.

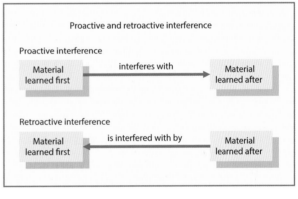

Proactive and retroactive interference are both greatest when two different responses have been associated with the same stimulus. Suppose you decide to keep your house key in a different location from the one you had used for a long time. The stimulus of wondering where your key is will probably lead you to start looking in the previous location rather than the current one – an example of proactive interference.

What causes proactive interference? There is *competition* between the correct and incorrect responses. Proactive interference is due much more to the strength of the incorrect response than the weakness of the correct response (Jacoby et al., 2001).

How can we reduce proactive interference? Bäuml and Kliegl (2013) argued it is important for people to minimise the extent to which they *retrieve* previously learned material. Participants learned three word lists and were then tested for their recall of the last list. Those instructed after the first two lists to forget them recalled 68% of the words in the final list. In contrast, only 41% of list-three words were recalled by those given no such instructions. Thus, proactive interference was greatly reduced when instructions restricted rememberers' retrieval to the relevant third list.

Retroactive interference occurs when later learning disrupts memory for previous learning. Isurin and McDonald (2001) argued that retroactive interference

KEY TERMS

Proactive interference: forgetting occurring when previous learning interferes with later learning and memory.

Retroactive interference: forgetting occurring when later learning disrupts memory for earlier learning.

explains why people forget some of their first language when acquiring a second one. Bilingual participants fluent in two languages were first presented with various pictures and the corresponding words in Russian or Hebrew. Some were then presented with the same pictures and the corresponding words in the other language. Finally, they were tested for recall of the words in the first language. There was substantial retroactive interference – recall of the first-language words became progressively worse the more learning trials with the second-language words.

Lustig et al. (2004) argued retroactive interference could occur because (1) the correct response is hard to retrieve or (2) the incorrect response is very strong. They found the second reason was more important.

Retroactive interference is generally greatest when the new learning resembles previous learning. However, there is some retroactive interference when people expend mental effort during the retention interval by performing a simple task (e.g., detecting tones) (Dewar et al., 2007). Thus, retroactive interference can occur in two ways:

1. expenditure of mental effort during the retention interval;
2. learning of material similar to the original learning material.

In sum, there is strong evidence for both proactive and retroactive interference. However, while interference theory explains why forgetting occurs, it does not explain why forgetting rate decreases over time. Interference can be reduced when people make use of various strategies (e.g., forget previous learning), but we do not know much about why and how strategies have these beneficial effects.

Cue-dependent forgetting: encoding specificity principle

Long-term memory is generally better when the information available at the time of retrieval matches (is the same as) that contained in the memory trace. This is the **encoding specificity principle** (Tulving, 1979). It follows there will be much forgetting if the information at retrieval fails to match that in the memory trace.

We can see the relevance of the encoding specificity principle in a study by Godden and Baddeley (1975). Divers listened to 40 words on the beach or under 10 feet of water. They then received a test of free recall in the same environment or the other one. Recall was much worse when the environment differed between test and learning than when it was the same.

The encoding specificity principle is very important. However, it has a few limitations (Nairne, 2015). First, it is too simple. Suppose you were asked the question, "What did you do six days ago?" It is improbable that you would simply compare the information contained in the question with stored memory traces – instead, you would probably use some problem-solving strategy to work out the answer.

Second, consider the following thought experiment (Nairne, 2002). Participants read aloud this word list: *write, right, rite, rite, write, right*. They then try to recall the word in the third position. We increase the overlap between the

KEY TERM

Encoding specificity principle: the notion that retrieval depends on the *overlap* between the information available at retrieval and the information within the memory trace.

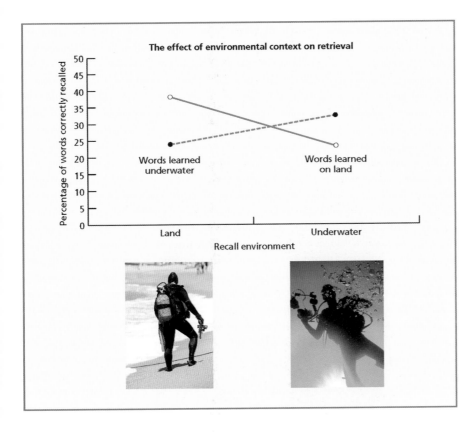

The effect of environmental context on retrieval

retrieval information and that contained in the relevant memory trace by providing them with the sound of the word in the third position. This would have no effect at all because the additional information provided by the sound totally fails to allow participants to *discriminate* the correct spelling of the word from the wrong ones.

Consolidation

Why does forgetting rate decrease over time? An influential answer is that it is due to **consolidation**, a long-lasting physiological process that fixes information in long-term memory. According to consolidation theory, recently formed memories still being consolidated are especially vulnerable to interference and forgetting.

Consolidation processes during sleep enhance long-term memory for important information (Oudiette & Paller, 2013). Previously formed memories have been cued during sleep by auditory or olfactory (smell-related) cues. Such cueing increases consolidation and improves subsequent long-term memory.

Amnesic patients who have suffered brain damage have poor long-term memory and often exhibit **retrograde amnesia** (Squire et al., 2015). This involves forgetting of information and events encountered prior to amnesia onset (especially information encountered shortly beforehand). Retrograde amnesia mostly affects memories that had not been fully consolidated at amnesia onset.

KEY TERMS

Consolidation: a physiological process involved in establishing long-term memories; this process lasts several hours or more.

Retrograde amnesia: forgetting by amnesic patients of information learned prior to the onset of amnesia.

Summary

Forgetting from long-term memory involves various physiological processes (e.g., consolidation; decay) and psychological processes (e.g., proactive interference; retroactive interference). A comprehensive account of forgetting would need to include the assumptions of all the theories considered here. Note, however, that consolidation theory provides the most detailed account of why the forgetting rate is initially rapid but then becomes much slower.

Everyday memory

The study of everyday memory is concerned with how we use memory in our everyday lives. A key issue is ecological validity (the extent to which laboratory findings apply to the real world).

The greatest difference between memory as traditionally studied and memory in everyday life relates to *motivation*. Laboratory participants are generally motivated to be as accurate as possible in their memory performance. In contrast, individuals in their daily lives are often motivated to entertain or impress their audience rather than to be totally accurate.

What we say about an event can distort our subsequent memory for it. In a study by Hellmann et al. (2011), participants saw a video of a pub brawl involving two men. They then described it to a student whom they were told believed person A was (or was not) responsible for what happened. The participants' retelling of the event reflected the student's biased views. Of most importance, when the participants were then told to recall the event accurately, their recall was systematically influenced by their earlier retelling of the event. This is an example of the **saying-is-believing effect** – tailoring a message about an event to suit a given audience distorts subsequent memory for that event.

Laboratory studies are generally more carefully controlled than studies in the real world, and so the findings are more reliable. We will consider laboratory research on **eyewitness testimony** (the evidence provided by the observer of a crime), which possesses a high level of ecological validity.

Eyewitness testimony

Suppose you are the only eyewitness to a serious crime in which someone is killed. Subsequently the person you identify as the murderer on a line-up is found guilty solely based on your evidence. Such cases raise the following question: is it safe to rely on eyewitness testimony?

The introduction of DNA tests has made it easier to answer this question. In the United States, over 200 falsely convicted individuals (mostly found guilty based on mistaken eyewitness identification) have been shown to be innocent by DNA tests.

Fragility of memory: misinformation effect

Loftus and Palmer (1974) showed people a film of a multiple-car accident. Afterwards, they answered various questions. Some were asked, "About how fast were the cars going when they smashed into each other?", whereas for other eyewitnesses the verb "hit" replaced "smashed into".

KEY TERMS

Saying-is-believing effect: inaccuracies in memory for an event caused by having previously described it to someone else to fit their biased perspective.

Eyewitness testimony: the evidence relating to a crime provided by someone who observed it being committed.

One week later, the eyewitnesses were asked whether they had seen any broken glass. Even though there was actually no broken glass, 32% of those previously asked about speed using the verb "smashed" said they saw broken glass. In contrast, only 14% of those asked using the verb "hit" said they saw broken glass. Thus, our memory is so fragile it can be distorted by changing *one* word in *one* question!

Loftus and Palmer (1974) findings illustrate the misinformation effect – systematic distortion of eyewitness memory for an event caused by the presentation of misleading information after the event. They focused on distortions for *minor* or peripheral details (e.g., presence of broken glass) rather than central or more important ones. This may have led them to underestimate the strength of the misinformation effect. Mahé et al. (2015) presented a clip about the murder of a politician from the movie "Z" and found the misinformation effect was larger for central details than for peripheral ones.

The existence of the misinformation effect helps to explain why lawyers in most countries are not allowed to ask leading questions implying the desired answer (e.g., "When did you stop beating your wife?"). Loftus and Zanni (1975) asked some eyewitnesses the leading question, "Did you see the broken headlight?" whereas others were asked the neutral question, "Did you see a broken headlight?" Even though there was no broken headlight, 10% more eyewitnesses asked the leading question said they had seen it.

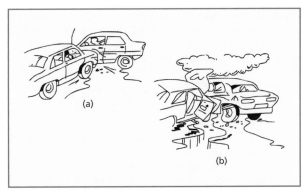

Loftus and Palmer (1974) found that assessment of speed of a videotaped car crash and recollection of whether there was broken glass present were affected by the verb used to ask the question. Use of the verbs "hit" and "smash" have different implications as shown in (a) and (b).

Remembering faces

Information about the culprit's face is often the most important information eyewitnesses may (or may not) remember. This face is typically unfamiliar, and it has been found unfamiliar faces are often much harder to recognise than familiar ones. Look at the figure and decide how many different individuals are shown. Produce your answer before reading on.

Jenkins et al. (2011) used a similar array of photos of unfamiliar faces. On average, participants believed 7½ different individuals were shown. The actual number for the array they used and the one in the figure is actually only two! When Jenkins et al. used an array of 20 photos of each of two celebrities, nearly all the participants correctly decided that only two different individuals were shown. The variability in different photos of the same person makes it hard to recognise unfamiliar faces. With familiar faces, in contrast, we possess much more relevant information, and this greatly simplifies face recognition.

Eyewitnesses are most likely to have problems with face recognition when the face is of someone of a different race: this is the **other-race effect**. This effect has been obtained in perception as well as memory. Megreya et al. (2011) presented Egyptian and British participants with a target face and an array of ten faces. Correct identifications of the target face when it was present in the array were 70% for same-race faces vs. 64% for other-race faces. When the target

Are the findings of laboratory studies on eyewitness testimony applicable to real-life crime scenarios?

KEY TERM

Other-race effect: the finding that recognition memory for same-race faces is more accurate than for other-race faces.

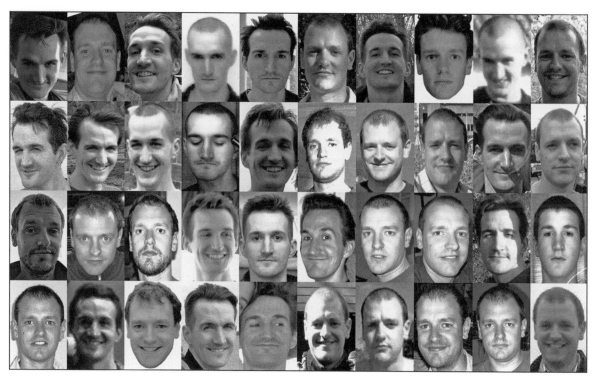

From Jenkins et al. (2011).

face was not present, there was mistaken identification of a non-target face 34% of the time with same-race faces vs. 47% with other-race faces.

Memory bias

Eyewitness testimony can be distorted by **confirmation bias**, i.e., event memory is influenced by what the eyewitness expected to see. This can happen because of the schemas (packets of knowledge; discussed earlier) we possess. Most people's bank-robbery schema includes information that robbers are typically male, wear dark clothes, and are in disguise (Tuckey & Brewer, 2003a). This schema leads us to form certain expectations. It can distort memory by causing eyewitnesses to reconstruct an event's details by including information from the bank-robbery schema even when it does not correspond to what they have observed (Tuckey & Brewer, 2003b).

Violence and anxiety

Much research indicates that anxiety and violence reduce the accuracy of eyewitness memory. Consider, for example, **weapon focus** – eyewitnesses' attention to the culprit's weapon reduces their memory for other information.

The obvious explanation for the weapon focus effect is that it is due to the threat posed by the weapon. However, there is an alternative explanation. People often attend to stimuli that are *unexpected* in the current situation (inconsistent with their situational schema), and this can impair their memory for other stimuli. As predicted, the weapon focus effect was greater when the

KEY TERMS

Confirmation bias: memory distortions caused by the influence of expectations concerning what is likely to have happened.

Weapon focus: the finding that eyewitnesses attend so much to the culprit's weapon that they ignore other details and have impaired memory for them.

presence of a weapon was very unexpected (e.g., a female criminal carrying a folding knife) (Pickel, 2009).

Fawcett et al. (2013) carried out a meta-analytic review (combining the findings from numerous studies) on weapon focus. There was evidence supporting both explanations discussed earlier. Thus, there was more evidence of weapon focus when the threat posed by the weapon was greater and when the presence of a weapon was unexpected. The findings were very similar regardless of whether they came from real-life crimes or laboratory studies.

Deffenbacher et al. (2004) combined the findings from several studies. Culprits' faces were identified 54% of the time in low anxiety or stress conditions compared to 42% for high anxiety or stress conditions. Thus, stress and anxiety generally impair eyewitness memory.

From laboratory to courtroom

Can we apply findings from laboratory studies to real-life crimes? There are certainly some important differences. Eyewitnesses are much more likely to be the victims of an attack in real life than in the laboratory, and their experiences are much more likely to be highly stressful. In addition, the evidence provided by eyewitnesses may be literally a matter of life or death in an American courtroom.

However, there are important similarities. Ihlebaek et al. (2003) used a staged robbery involving two robbers armed with handguns. In the live condition, eyewitnesses were ordered repeatedly to "Stay down". A video taken during the live condition was presented to eyewitnesses in the video condition. Participants in both conditions exaggerated the duration of the event and showed similar patterns in what was well and poorly remembered. However, eyewitness in the video condition recalled more information.

Tollestrup et al. (1994) analyzed police records concerning the identifications by eyewitnesses to crimes involving fraud and robbery. Factors important in laboratory studies (e.g., weapon focus; retention interval) were also important in real-life crimes.

In sum, artificial laboratory conditions typically do not distort the findings. If anything, the errors in eyewitness memory obtained under laboratory conditions *underestimate* memory deficiencies for real-life events. Overall, laboratory research provides evidence of genuine relevance to the legal system.

Chapter summary

- Learning and memory involve three successive stages: encoding, storage, and retrieval.
- Tests of long-term memory include free recall, cued recall, and recognition.
- There is a major distinction between short-term and long-term memory systems. According to the multistore model, rehearsal causes information to proceed from short-term to long-term memory.
- Amnesic patients have impaired long-term memory but intact short-term memory, whereas some other brain patients show the opposite pattern.

- It has been claimed that the capacity of short-term memory is seven chunks. However, when the contributions of long-term memory and rehearsal are removed, its capacity is only four chunks.
- The notion of a short-term store has been replaced with that of working memory, a system combining brief storage and processing.
- According to Baddeley's working memory model, working memory consists of four components: central executive, phonological loop, visuo-spatial sketchpad, and episodic buffer.
- Declarative memory involves conscious recollection of events and facts. Non-declarative memory does not involve conscious recollection and is often assessed by observing behaviour changes.
- The major types of declarative memory are episodic memory (for personal events), semantic memory (for remembering facts and information), and autobiographical memory (for important personal experiences).
- The major types of non-declarative memory are priming (enhanced stimulus processing with repetition) and skill learning (e.g., riding a bicycle).
- Human memory is generally highly organised (e.g., categorical clustering).
- Schematic knowledge often enhances long-term memory. However, it can cause memory distortions (especially with unfamiliar material and at long retention intervals).
- Forgetting is due to interference from what we learned previously (proactive interference) or what we learn during the retention interval (retroactive interference). It is also due to decay, repression, poor overlap between retrieval information and information in memory traces, and consolidation failures.
- In laboratory research, people are motivated to recall information as accurately as possible. In everyday life, in contrast, the emphasis is often on sounding impressive or being entertaining.
- Eyewitness memory is often distorted by information presented after the crime. It can also be inaccurate because it is hard to remember detailed information about unfamiliar faces.
- Eyewitnesses may be over-influenced by their expectations (confirmation bias) based on crime schemas. In addition, stress and anxiety can impair their memory.

Further reading

- Baddeley, A., Eysenck, M.W., & Anderson, M.C. (2015). *Memory* (2nd ed.). New York: Psychology Press. This textbook provides detailed coverage of the topics discussed in this chapter.

- Eysenck, M.W., & Brysbaert (2018). *Fundamentals of cognition* (3rd ed.). Abingdon, Oxford: Psychology Press. Chapters 4–6 of this textbook cover the topics discussed in this chapter in more detail.

- Frenda, S.J., Nichols, R.M., & Loftus, E.F. (2011). Current issues and advances in misinformation research. *Current Directions in Psychological Science, 20*, 20–23. Some of the main reasons why eyewitness memory is often distorted are discussed in this article.

- Yarmey, D. (2010). Eyewitness testimony. In J.M. Brown & E.A. Campbell (Eds.), *The Cambridge handbook of forensic psychology* (pp. 177–186). Cambridge: Cambridge University Press. This chapter provides a comprehensive account of the major factors influencing the accuracy or otherwise of eyewitness testimony.

Essay questions

1. Compare and contrast the concepts of "short-term memory" and "working memory".

2. Describe the various types of long-term memory and discuss evidence supporting their existence.

3. Describe *three* factors responsible for forgetting. Which is the most important and why?

4. Why is eyewitness memory often inaccurate in the laboratory? Can we generalise from laboratory findings to real-world settings?

You probably spend much of your time solving problems. Some are related to your studies, whereas others are concerned with your personal life and family. How useful is past experience when it comes to problem solving? Can it sometimes be a disadvantage?

Many people become real experts in their career or hobby. What are the secrets of being an expert? Is it simply a question of prolonged practice or is talent also very important?

Creativity is regarded as a very useful ability. Some people argue that scientific creativity involves special processes whereas others argue that it mostly depends on cognitive processes we use much of the time. What do you think?

Problem solving, expertise, and creativity

23

■ ■ ■ ■ ■ ■ ■ ■ ■ ■

This chapter is concerned with three related topics: problem solving, expertise, and creativity. We will start with problem solving.

Problem solving: introduction

Life presents us with many problems, although thankfully most are fairly trivial. What do we mean by problem solving? It involves the following (Goel, 2010, p. 613): "(1) there are two states of affairs; (2) the agent [problem solver] is in one state and wants to be in the other state; (3) it is not apparent to the agent how the gap between the two states is to be bridged; and (4) bridging the gap is a consciously guided multi-step process."

There are important differences among problems. **Well-defined problems** are ones in which *all* aspects of the problem are clearly specified, including the initial state, the range of possible moves or strategies, and the goal or solution. The goal is well-specified because it is clear when it has been reached (e.g., the centre of a maze). Chess is a well-defined (although very complex) problem – there is a standard initial state, the rules specify all legitimate rules, and the goal is to achieve checkmate.

In contrast, **ill-defined problems** are underspecified. Suppose you set yourself the goal of becoming happier. There are endless strategies you could adopt, and it is very hard to know ahead of time which would be most effective. Since happiness varies over time and is hard to define, how are you going to decide whether you have solved the problem of becoming happier?

Most everyday problems are ill-defined, but psychologists have focused mostly on well-defined problems. Why is this? Well-defined problems have a best strategy for their solution. This makes it easy for psychologists to identify clearly the errors and deficiencies in the strategies used by problem solvers.

Insight vs. non-insight problems

We have all found ourselves working slowly but surely through problems until we finally reach the solution – "grind-out-the-answer" problems. For example, solving a hard problem in multiplication involves several processing operations performed in the correct sequence.

KEY TERMS

Well-defined problems:
problems in which the initial state, the goal, and the methods available for solving them are clearly laid out.

Ill-defined problems:
problems that are imprecisely specified; for example, the initial state, goal state, and the methods available to solve the problem may be unclear.

Do you think most problems involve moving slowly towards the solution? If so, you are in for a rude shock! Many problems depend for their solution on **insight** or an "aha" experience involving a sudden transformation of the problem (see Box).

INSIGHT PROBLEM: the mutilated draughtboard

A draughtboard is initially covered by 32 oblong dominoes occupying two squares each. Then two squares are removed from diagonally opposite corners? Can the remaining 62 squares be filled by 31 dominoes? Think what your answer is before reading on.

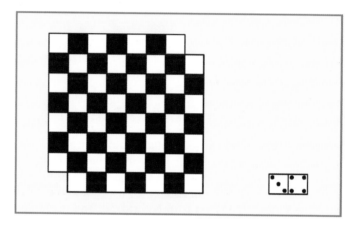

Most people start by mentally covering squares with dominoes. Alas, this strategy is not terribly effective: there are over 750,000 possible permutations of the dominoes! Since very few people solve the mutilated draughtboard problem without assistance, we will assume you are in that large majority (my apologies if you are not!). You may well rapidly solve the problem using insight if I tell you something you already know – each domino covers one white and one black square. Alternatively, note that the two removed squares *must* have the same colour. Thus, the 31 dominoes cannot cover the mutilated board.

Why do we find it hard to solve insight problems? Ohlsson (1992) pointed out that how we think about a problem (the problem representation) is often of great importance. Our initial problem representation is often misleading. Consider the following insight problem:

You have six matches and must put them together to form four triangles equal in length.

Most people's initial problem representation involves thinking of forming a two-dimensional structure with the matches rather than the three-dimensional pyramid required to solve the problem (see page 363).

KEY TERM

Insight: the experience of suddenly realising how to solve a problem based on looking at it in a different way.

Öllinger et al. (2014 developed Ohlsson's (1992) ideas. Prior knowledge and perceptual aspects of a problem lead to the formation of a problem representation. This is followed by a search process. If this search process is repeatedly unsuccessful, there is an impasse (block). A new problem representation is formed to try to overcome the impasse, followed by another search process.

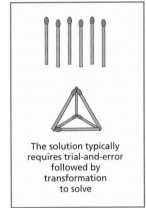

The solution typically requires trial-and-error followed by transformation to solve

Findings

Metcalfe and Wiebe (1987) obtained evidence indicating there are important differences between insight and non-insight problems. Participants reported a gradual increase in "warmth" (closeness to solution) during non-insight problems. This is expected since they involve a series of processes. In contrast, the warmth ratings during insight problems remained at the same level until *suddenly* increasing dramatically just before the solution was reached.

Brain-imaging findings have also revealed important differences in the processing of insight and non-insight problems. For example, Bowden et al. (2005) compared brain activity when problem solutions involved insight (i.e., sudden awareness) and when they did not. There were two key findings: (1) a part of the temporal lobe (towards the bottom of the cortex) was activated *only* when solutions involved insight; (2) this activation occurred one-third of a second before participants indicated they had achieved an insightful solution. According to Bowden et al., this brain area is vital to insight because it is involved in processing general semantic (meaning) relationships.

According to Öllinger et al.'s (2014) theory, an impasse or block occurs when individuals have formed a problem representation but have not yet become excessively attached to it. It follows that solution hints (facilitating switching problem representations) should be most valuable when given at the point of impasse rather than before or after. Moss et al. (2011) obtained support for that prediction.

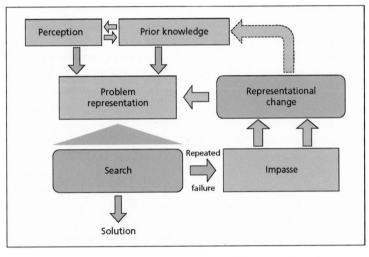

The dynamics of search, impasse, and representational change provide a coherent explanation of difficulty in the nine-dot problem. From Öllinger et al. (2014).

EVALUATION

➕ Insight problems differ from non-insight ones in suddenness of solution and in the involvement of specific brain areas.

➕ Solving insight problems typically involves a sudden replacing of an incorrect problem representation with the correct one.

🚫 The factors leading to changes in problem representations are not well understood.

🚫 It is oversimplified to argue that any given problem is solved using either special insight processes or "ordinary" cognitive processes. In fact, both types of processes are often used in combination to solve so-called insight problems (Weisberg, 2015).

Incubation

How can we facilitate insight? Wallas (1926) claimed that **incubation** (interrupting work on a problem for some time to focus on something else) was useful. This claim was supported by Sio and Ormerod (2009) in a review. They reported that incubation effects (generally fairly small) were obtained in 73% of studies. One reason why incubation is often helpful is because it allows people to *forget* misleading information that makes it hard for them to abandon their incorrect problem representation (Penaloza & Calvillo, 2012).

Past experience

What is the name of the tendency to think that objects can only be used for functions for which they have been used in the past?

Most people believe their ability to solve any given problem is improved after previous experience with similar problems. Indeed, an important reason adults solve most problems much faster than children is because of their much greater relevant past experience.

Research showing how past experience can benefit current problem solving is discussed shortly. Before that, we focus on evidence that past experience sometimes has *negative* effects.

Is past experience useful? No

Duncker (1945) studied **functional fixedness**, which is the tendency to think objects can only be used for a narrow range of functions for which they have been used in the past. He asked participants to mount a candle on a vertical screen. Various objects were spread around including a box full of nails and a book of matches.

The solution involves using the box as a platform. Only a few participants solved this problem because their past experience led them to regard the box as a container rather than a platform. Their performance was better when the box was empty rather than full of nails – the latter set-up emphasised the container-like quality of the box.

McCaffrey (2012) argued that people often ignore crucial but obscure features of objects because they focus on the typical functions of objects based on their shape, size, material of which they are made, and so on. This functional fixedness can be reduced by the following technique: (1) function-free descriptions of each part of an object are produced (e.g., a candle consists of a

KEY TERMS

Incubation: the notion that problems can sometimes be solved by putting them aside for a while.

Functional fixedness: an inflexible focus on the usual functions of an object in problem solving.

wick, wax, and string); (2) people decide whether each description implies a use. McCaffrey found that people given training in this technique solved 83% of problems (including Duncker's candle problem) compared to only 49% not receiving training.

Suppose you were given the following problem (Luchins, 1942). Jar A holds 28 quarts of water, Jar B 76 quarts, and Jar C 3 quarts (a quart is 2 pints). The task is to end up with exactly 25 quarts in one of the jars. The solution is easy. Jar A is filled, and then Jar C is filled from it, leaving 25 quarts in Jar A.

Luchins (1942) found 95% of participants who had previously been given similar problems solved it. More importantly, the success rate on this problem was only 36% for participants previously trained on problems all having the same complex three-jar solution. What is going on here? The participants in the latter condition developed a **mental set** or way of approaching the problems that led them to think rigidly.

We might expect experts given a problem in their area of expertise would be immune from the damaging effects of mental set. Sheridan and Reingold (2013) presented expert and novice chess players with a chess problem with one best move and another less good but familiar move. The key finding was that 47% of the experts and 47% of the novices showed the effects of mental set by choosing the familiar move even though it was not the best one.

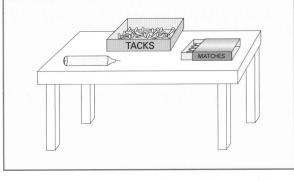

Some of the materials provided for participants instructed to mount a candle on a vertical wall in the study by Duncker (1945).

How can past experience both impair and promote problem solving?

Is past experience useful? Yes

In spite of this evidence that past experience can have negative effects on problem solving, the effects of past experience in everyday life are mostly positive. For example, we often make use of analogies or similarities between a current problem and those we have solved in the past. For example, the New Zealand physicist Ernest Rutherford used a solar system analogy to understand the structure of the atom. He argued electrons revolve around the nucleus in the same way that planets revolve around the sun.

Successful use of a previous problem to solve a current one requires the detection of *similarities* between the two problems. There are two main types of similarity:

1. *Superficial similarity*: solution-irrelevant details (e.g., specific objects) are common to both problems.
2. *Structural similarity*: causal relations among some of the main components are shared by both problems.

Gick and Holyoak (1980) wondered how likely it is that problem solvers would use a relevant analogy. They used a problem on which a patient with a malignant tumour can only be saved by a special kind of ray. A ray strong enough to destroy the tumor will also destroy the healthy tissue. However, a ray that does not harm healthy tissue is too weak to destroy the tumor.

> **KEY TERM**
>
> **Mental set:** a fixed or blinkered approach based on problem solutions that worked in the past that prevents people from thinking flexibly.

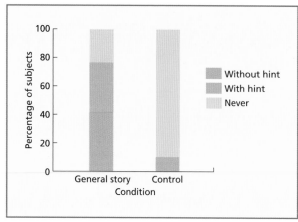

Some of the results from Gick and Holyoak (1980, Experiment 4) showing the percentage of subjects who solved the radiation problem when they were given an analogy (general-story condition) or were just asked to solve the problem (control condition). Note that just under half of the subjects in the general-story condition had to be given a hint to use the story analogue before they solved the problem.

Here is an analogy to help you to solve this problem. A general wants to capture a fortress. However, the roads leading to it are mined, making it too dangerous for the entire army to march along any one of them. The general divided his army into groups which marched along several different roads. Hopefully, this analogy helped you to solve the radiation problem – this involves having several weak rays all directed at the tumor.

Gick and Holyoak (1980) found 80% of participants solved the radiation problem when informed that the fortress story (which they encountered previously) was relevant. This dropped to 40% for participants who had encountered the fortress story earlier but were not informed of its relevance. Finally, only 10% of participants solved the radiation problem in the absence of the fortress story.

These findings indicate that having a relevant analogy stored in long-term memory is no guarantee it will be used. The main reason was that there were few superficial similarities between the two problems. People are much more likely to recall spontaneously a previous story superficially similar to the radiation problem (story about a surgeon using rays on a cancer) than one lacking superficial similarities (fortress story) (Keane, 1987).

We have seen that people focus on superficial rather than structural similarities between problems when *given* a relevant analogy beforehand. In everyday life, people generally *produce* their own analogies rather than being given them. Dunbar and Blanchette (2001) found with scientists generating hypotheses that the analogies they used involved structural rather than superficial similarities. Thus, we can focus on structural similarities between problems in certain circumstances.

How can we improve analogical problem solving? Monaghan et al. (2015) argued that sleep has been shown to have beneficial effects on long-term memory and information restructuring and so might plausibly enhance analogical problem solving. They presented participants with various source problems followed 12 hours later by target problems structurally related to the source problems. As predicted, sleep during the 12-hour interval enhanced performance on the target problems (51% vs. 36% for participants who did not sleep).

Problem-solving strategies

The publication in 1972 of a book entitled *Human Problem Solving* by Newell and Simon represented a landmark in research on problem solving. Their key insight was that our problem-solving strategies reflect our limited ability to process and store information. More specifically, Newell and Simon assumed we have very limited short-term memory capacity (see Chapter 22) and that complex information is typically serial (one process at a time). These assumptions were included in their General Problem Solver, a computer program designed to solve well-defined problems.

Define heuristic methods.

How do we cope with our limited processing capacity? Newell and Simon (1972) argued that we rely heavily on **heuristics,** or rules of thumb. Heuristics have the advantage that they do not require extensive information processing and so are easy to use. However, they have the disadvantage that they may not lead to problem solution.

Means-ends analysis

The most important heuristic identified by Newell and Simon (1972) was **means-ends analysis:**

- Note the difference between the current problem state and the goal state.
- Form a sub-goal to reduce the difference between the current and goal states.
- Select a mental operator that permits attainment of the sub-goal.

Means-ends analysis is generally very useful. However, Sweller and Levine (1982) found people used it even when it impaired performance. Participants were given the maze shown in the figure but most of it was not visible to them. Some could see the goal state (goal-information group) whereas others could not. Use of means-ends analysis requires knowledge of goal location of the goal, so only the goal-information group could have used that heuristic. However, means-ends analysis was not useful, because every move involved turning *away* from the goal. Participants in the goal-information group performed very poorly – only 10% solved the problem in 298 moves! In contrast, participants who could not see the goal solved the problem in only 38 moves on average. Thus, people use means-ends analysis even when this disrupts problem solving.

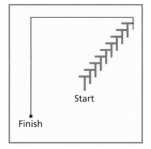

The maze used in the study by Sweller and Levine (1982).

Hill climbing

One of the simplest heuristics or rules of thumb is **hill climbing,** which involves changing the present state within the problem into one closer to the goal. It is called hill climbing because it resembles a climber whose strategy for reaching the highest mountain peak in the area is always to move upwards. It is a simpler strategy than means-ends analysis.

The hill-climbing heuristic involves a focus on *short-term* goals. As a result, it often fails to lead to problem solution (Robertson, 2001). A climber using the hill-climbing heuristic is likely to be trapped on top of a hill separated by several valleys from the highest peak.

Planning

Newell and Simon (1972) assumed most problem solvers engage in only limited planning because of short-term memory constraints. Patsenko and Altmann (2010) tested this assumption using the Tower of Hanoi task. Only one disc can be moved at a time, a larger disc cannot be placed on top of a smaller one, and the solution involves having all five discs on the last peg.

In one condition, Patsenko and Altmann (2010) added, deleted, or moved discs during participants' eye movements so they were not directly aware of any changes. If participants had been using plans, such changes should have had a very disruptive effect on performance. In fact, there was minimal disruption, suggesting

KEY TERMS

Heuristics: rules of thumb used to solve problems.

Means-ends analysis: an approach to problem solving based on reducing the difference between the current problem state and the solution.

Hill climbing: a simple heuristic used by problem solvers in which they focus on moves that will apparently put them closer to the goal or problem solution.

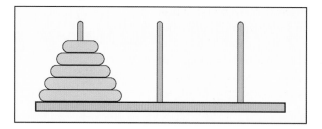

performance was determined by immediate perceptual and attentional processes. Thus, the next move was mostly triggered by the *current* state of the problem rather than by a pre-formed plan.

Delaney et al. (2004) used water-jar problems resembling those use by Luchins (1942; see earlier). Some participants were told to generate the complete solution before making any moves whereas others (controls) simply used their preferred strategy. The control participants showed little evidence of planning. However, those in the planning group engaged in much planning and solved the problem in far fewer moves than control participants. Thus, we have a greater ability to plan than is usually assumed. However, we often choose not to plan unless required to do so.

Summary

The strategies we use when solving problems take account of our limited processing and short-term memory capacities. Many of these strategies consist of heuristics or rules of thumb such as means-ends analysis and hill climbing. In spite of our limited processing capacity, most people can engage in a reasonable amount of planning. However, we often choose not to plan because planning is effortful and cognitively demanding.

Expertise

So far we have focused mainly on studies in which the time available for learning was short, the tasks were relatively limited, and prior specific knowledge was not required. In the real world, in contrast, individuals often spend several years acquiring knowledge and skills in a given area (e.g., psychology; law; medicine; journalism). As a result, they develop expertise, which involves a very high level of thinking and performance in a given area as a result of many years of practice.

We will start by discussing chess and medical expertise. After that, we focus on the roles played by practice and talent in acquiring expertise.

Chess expertise

There are various reasons researchers have focused on chess-playing expertise. First, we can measure chess players' level of skill very precisely based on their results against other players. Second, expert chess players develop cognitive skills (e.g., pattern recognition; selective search) useful in many other areas of expertise.

Why are some people much better than others at playing chess? The obvious answer is that they have devoted far more time to practice. Of particular importance, expert chess players have much more detailed information about chess positions stored in long-term memory than non-experts.

De Groot (1965) presented chess players with brief presentations of board positions. After removing the board, they reconstructed the positions. Chess masters recalled the positions much more accurately than less expert players

(91% vs. 43%, respectively). This finding was due to differences in stored chess positions rather than in memory ability – there were no group differences in remembering *random* board positions.

What is the precise nature of this chess-related information stored in long-term memory? Gobet (e.g., Gobet & Waters, 2003) provided an influential answer in his template theory, according to which (unsurprisingly) much of this information is in the form of templates. A **template** is an abstract schematic structure more general than an actual board position. Each template consists of a core (fixed information) plus slots (containing variable information about pieces and locations). According to template theory, chess positions are stored in three templates, each typically containing information relating to about 10 pieces, and their slots make templates flexible.

A key assumption of template theory is that outstanding chess players owe their excellence mostly to their superior template-based knowledge of chess rather than their use of slow, strategy-based processes. This template-based knowledge can be accessed rapidly and allows expert players to narrow down moves they need to consider. It follows that the performance of outstanding players should remain very high even when making their moves under considerable time pressure.

Findings

Support for the assumption that chess players possess very few templates was obtained by Gobet and Clarkson (2004). The number of templates possessed by chess players averaged out at about two regardless of playing strength. The maximum template size was 13–15 for masters compared to only about 6 for novices.

Support for the prediction that outstanding players can access much relevant knowledge very rapidly was reported by Burns (2004) in a study on blitz chess (the entire game must be completed within five minutes). Performance in blitz chess was strongly associated with performance in normal chess.

Moxley et al. (2012) gave experts and tournament players five minutes to select the best possible move on several problems. The players thought aloud while performing this task. The final move was generally much stronger than the first move mentioned for both experts and tournament players. These findings indicate that slow, strategy-based processes are very important in determining chess performance.

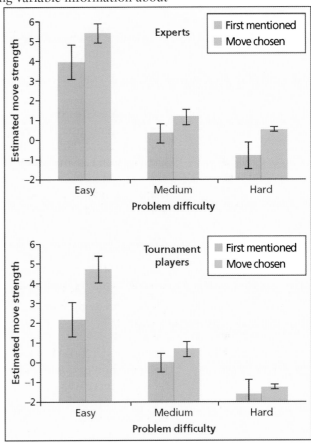

From Moxley et al. (2012).

KEY TERM

Template: as applied to chess, an abstract structure consisting of a mixture of fixed and variable information about chess pieces and positions.

EVALUATION

⊕ Much of the information chess players possess is in the form of a few, large templates.

⊕ Outstanding chess players possess much more knowledge of chess positions than non-experts, and this gives them a substantial advantage.

⊖ Slow, strategy-based processes are more important than assumed within template theory.

⊖ The precise nature of the information stored in long-term memory remains unclear.

Medical expertise

Expert radiologists typically make very rapid and accurate diagnoses based on X-ray evidence. How do their strategies differ from those of unskilled radiologists? We can answer that question with reference to the distinction between explicit and implicit reasoning (Engel, 2008). Explicit reasoning is slow, deliberate, and involves conscious awareness. In contrast, implicit reasoning is fast, automatic, and is not associated with conscious awareness. In essence, medical experts engage mainly in implicit reasoning whereas novices or unskilled radiologists rely mostly on explicit reasoning.

As we will see, this account is reasonably accurate but somewhat oversimplified. In fact, medical experts typically start with fast, automatic processes but generally cross-check their diagnoses with subsequent slow, deliberate processes (McLaughlin et al., 2008).

Findings

Kundel et al. (2007) tracked eye movements while skilled doctors examined difficult mammograms showing or not showing breast cancer. The average time to fixate a cancer was only 1.13 seconds and was typically less than 1 second for the most expert doctors. Overall, fast fixation on the cancer was an excellent predictor of accurate performance on the task.

Krupinski et al. (2013) showed in more detail the processes involved in the development of expertise among pathologists viewing breast biopsies over several years of training. The eye-tracking findings of one doctor are shown in the figure. There was a substantial reduction in the number of fixations per slide and less examination of non-diagnostic areas. Are the effects of expertise in other areas similar to those in medicine? Gegenfurtner et al. (2011) reported the answer is "Yes". Several differences between experts and non-experts were found in medicine, sport, and transportation:

1. Shorter fixations;
2. Faster first fixation on task-relevant information;
3. More fixations on task-relevant information;
4. Fewer fixations on task-irrelevant areas.

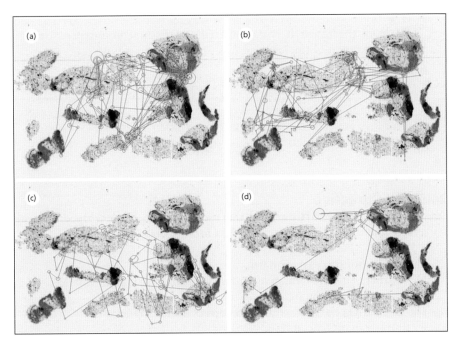

From Melo et al. (2012).

When photographs are presented for only 33 ms, observers can detect which type of animal has been presented on more than 90% of trials (Prass et al., 2013). This suggests that very rapid non-conscious processes are involved. Melo et al. (2012) wondered whether medical experts use similar processes to those we all use during ordinary visual perception. They found similarly fast times to diagnose lesions (diseases) in chest X-ray images and to name animals (1.33 vs. 1.23 seconds, respectively). Of most importance, diagnosing diseases and naming animals involved activation in very similar brain regions. In addition, there was greater activation in frontal regions while diagnosing lesions (diseases), suggesting that diagnosing is more cognitively demanding than naming animals.

How can we explain these findings? Melo et al. (2012) suggested medical experts engage in rapid pattern recognition: each slide is compared against stored patterns from the past. In other words, they use a predominantly *visual* strategy. The greater complexity of diagnosing diseases than naming animals means that, in addition, they need to engage in more detailed cognitive processing to perform the task.

EVALUATION

➕ There is much evidence that experts often use fast automatic processes where non-experts use slow deliberate processes.

➕ The fast automatic processes possessed by experts permit them to engage in rapid pattern recognition.

⊖ Most of the research has compared experts and non-experts and little is known of the learning processes producing expertise.

⊖ Little is known of how experts and non-experts combine fast and deliberate processes. For example, Kulatunga-Moruzi et al. (2011) found non-experts benefited from this combination when fast processes preceded deliberate ones but not when the processes occurred in the opposite order.

Deliberate practice

Ericsson and Towne (2010) argued that expertise can be developed through deliberate practice. **Deliberate practice** has four aspects:

1. The task is not too easy or hard.
2. The learner is give informative feedback about his/her performance.
3. The learner has adequate chances to repeat the task.
4. The learner has the opportunity to correct his/her errors.

According to Ericsson's theory, the development of expertise depends more on the amount of deliberate practice than simply on the number of hours devoted to practice. A second major prediction (and much more controversial) is that deliberate practice is *all* that is needed for expert performance. Thus, innate talent or ability is of little or no relevance to the development of expertise.

Findings

There is much support for the notion that expertise depends on substantial amounts of deliberate practice. Campitelli and Gobet (2011) found in a review of studies on chess-playing expertise that there was a moderately strongly correlation (above +.50) between total practice hours and chess skill. On average, players without international standing had devoted fewer than 10,000 hours to practice (slackers!). In contrast, international masters had devoted over 25,000 hours to practice.

Deliberate practice is also strongly correlated with expertise in many other areas. For example, Tuffiash et al. (2007) found that elite Scrabble players spent much more time than average players on deliberate practice. Overall, lifetime accumulated study of Scrabble was a good predictor of Scrabble-playing expertise.

Are you convinced expertise depends only on deliberate practice? I hope not! Studies on chess playing and music performance were re-analysed by Hambrick et al. (2014). Variations in deliberate practice accounted for only 34% of the variance in chess-playing performance and 30% of music performance. For example, Howard (2012) compared two groups who had played a similar number of games but who differed *fivefold* in the number of study hours. The two groups had comparable performance, suggesting the number of study hours is relatively unimportant.

KEY TERM

Deliberate practice: a form of practice in which the learner is provided with informative feedback and has the chance to correct his/her errors.

CASE STUDY: Magnus Carlsen

The Norwegian, Magnus Carlsen, was born on 30 November 1990. He became a grandmaster at chess at the amazingly young age of 13 and the world chess champion in November 2013 at the age of 22. In 2014, he was rated the strongest player in the history of chess. The difference between him and the second-best player (Levon Aronian) was almost as great as that between the 2nd and 14th best players. One of his greatest strengths is his "nettlesomeness", meaning that he is superb at making moves that pressurise opponents into making mistakes.

The reason for focusing on Magnus Carlsen is that he disproves the main assumptions of Ericsson's deliberate practice theory. First, he became a grandmaster after only 5 years of deliberate practice, although Ericsson claims that 10 years of deliberate practice are required to achieve outstanding levels of performance.

Second, according to Ericsson's theory, we would expect Magnus Carlsen to have accumulated more years of deliberate practice than other top chess players. In fact, however, when he became world champion, he had devoted 6½ years *fewer* to deliberate practice than the average of the next 10 best players in the world (Gobet & Ereku, 2014). Across the top 11 players in the world, the association between rating and number of years of practice was modestly negative. According to Ericsson's theory, it should have been strongly positive.

In sum, Magnus Carlsen provides dramatic support for the notions that deliberate practice on its own is insufficient for outstanding performance and that talent is also essential. Indeed, Carlsen's extraordinary talent has led to him being called "the Mozart of chess".

The fact that deliberate practice is positively related to expert performance does *not* necessarily mean the former causes the latter. For example, individuals with much talent are likely to enjoy early success, and this may motivate them to devote more time to deliberate practice than individuals with less talent. In other words, performance level may influence the amount of practice as well as the amount of practice influencing performance level. For example, there are probably very few individuals willing to devote thousands of hours to the practice of a skill when they totally lack any talent for it.

Dramatic evidence supporting this view was reported by Mosing et al. (2014) in a study on music practice and music ability in Swedish twins. Genetic factors played an important role in determining the hours of music practice – this probably occurred because individuals with more innate music talent practised more. Of importance, there was *no* difference in music ability between identical or monozygotic twins even when they differed in the amount of music practice they had had. Thus, the relationship between music practice and music ability depended much more on genetic factors than on the causal effects of practice on ability.

In sum, deliberate practice is necessary to produce high levels of expertise. However, it is not sufficient. Instead, talent sets a *ceiling* on what anyone can achieve, and the amount of deliberate practice they put in determines how close they come to realising their potential.

Creativity

What is **creativity**? It involves "the generation of ideas, insights, or problem solutions that are both novel and potentially useful" (Baas et al., 2008, p. 780). It seems reasonable to assume that highly creative individuals also tend to be highly intelligent. Silvia (2008) reviewed findings from several studies and found that overall there was a significant (but fairly small) positive relationship between intelligence and creativity. The relationship is modest because rather different kinds of thinking are involved. Unsurprisingly, individuals high in openness (a personality trait involving curiosity and imagination) are more likely than low scorers to be creative. Batey et al. (2010) found openness predicted creativity better than did intelligence.

Are originality and creativity easy or hard to measure?

It has often been claimed that people are more creative in certain mood states. Baas et al. (2008) addressed this issue in a review. Positive moods were associated with a slight increase in creativity whereas negative moods had no effect.

Scientific creativity

A popular view of scientific creativity is that a few "great" individuals (e.g., Newton; Einstein) are responsible for nearly all the major scientific achievements. The creative and intellectual abilities of these individuals allegedly stretch far beyond those of the mass of humanity (otherwise known as *us*). In essence, this view is "the belief that scientific discovery is the result of genius, inspiration, and sudden insight" (Trickett & Trafton, 2007, p. 868). As we will see, this view is largely incorrect.

Sternberg (1985) identified three processes involved in scientific discoveries:

1. *Selective encoding*: identifying what is crucially important from the available information. For example, Alexander Fleming noticed that bacteria close to a culture that had become mouldy were destroyed, and this led to the discovery of penicillin.
2. *Selective combination*: realising how the relevant pieces of information fit together. For example, Charles Darwin was aware of the relevant facts about natural selection before he combined them in his theory of evolution.
3. *Selective comparison*: relating information in the current problem to relevant information from another problem (problem solving by analogy). For example, Kekulé dreamt of a snake curling back on itself and catching its own tail. When he awoke, he realised this was an analogy for the molecular structure of benzene.

KEY TERM

Creativity: the ability to produce original, useful, and ingenious solutions to problems.

Klahr and Simon (2001) distinguished between two kinds of methods that might be used by creative scientists:

1. *Strong methods*: these methods are based on a very lengthy process of acquiring detailed knowledge in an area of science. Such methods are often sufficient to solve relatively simple scientific problems but are insufficient to permit creative scientific discoveries.
2. *Weak methods*: these methods are very general and can be applied to almost any scientific problem. Weak methods include means-ends analysis, hill climbing, and use of analogies.

Scientific creativity depends heavily on relatively simple weak methods. For example, Zelko et al. (2010) asked leading biomedical scientists in several countries to identify their research strategies. Every researcher had a main heuristic (rule of thumb) he/she used much of the time. The heuristics included the following: challenge conventional wisdom; adopt a planned, step-by-step approach; carry out numerous experiments on an unplanned or trial-and-error basis. Kulkarni and Simon (1988) found scientists made extensive use of the unusualness heuristic. This involves focusing on unusual or unexpected findings, which are then used to generate new hypotheses and experiments.

Another method used by scientists is "what if" reasoning in which they work out what would happen in imaginary circumstances. A famous example of such reasoning involves Albert Einstein. At the age of 16, he imagined himself riding a beam of light, which led indirectly to his theory of relativity.

Some theorists (e.g., Campbell, 1960; Simonton, 2011) have argued that aspects of the creative process do not use strong or weak methods. Campbell identified two major processes underlying creative achievements: (1) blind variation and (2) selective retention. In essence, scientists and others striving to make an important creative contribution start by generating a large number of ideas produced in an almost random manner. This initial process of blind variation is followed by systematic attempts to discriminate between valuable creative ideas and those that are relatively useless: selective retention. Zelko et al. (2010) found his elite scientists typically realised rapidly when they had made an important discovery.

It follows from this approach that even very successful creative individuals should produce numerous unworkable ideas. There is plentiful support for this prediction. Consider Thomas Edison, who was probably the most productive inventor of all time (e.g., he had over 1,000 American patents). One of his most famous quotes was the following: "I have not failed. I've just found 10,000 ways that won't work." In similar fashion, the very successful contemporary inventor, Sir James Dyson, admitted: "I spent years in my toolshed building thousands of prototypes of my bagless vacuum cleaner. Each one was a failure."

Simonton (2011) was generally supportive of Campbell's (1960) approach but admitted that the initial process was not entirely random. More specifically, the ideas generated by creative individuals are influenced by their expertise, the strategies they use, and by indirect associations from the knowledge they already possess. All these factors can bias the generation process away from the random and thus enhance the probability of a creative discovery.

EVALUATION

➕ The processes underlying scientific creativity and discovery are less mysterious than is sometimes assumed.

➕ Scientists striving for creative achievements often rely on the same weak methods and even almost random processes most of us use in our everyday lives.

➖ The role of scientists' huge relevant knowledge in leading to major scientific discoveries has been de-emphasised.

➖ The scientific creative process is somewhat more systematic and less random than argued by Campbell (1960) and, to a lesser extent, Simonton (2011). The ideas generated by scientists are generally pre-selected to some extent rather than being random.

Chapter summary

- Psychologists generally study well-defined problems, but most everyday problems are ill-defined.
- Solutions to insight problems often occur suddenly and relatively effortlessly. In contrast, solutions to non-insight or analytic problems emerge slowly and effortfully.
- Past experience can impair present problem solving through functional fixedness (focusing on only a few functions of objects) or mental set (rigid strategy).
- Past experience can enhance present problem solving when analogies are used. However, individuals often fail to detect the relevance of previous problems to the current one.
- The strategies we use to solve problems reflect our limited ability to process and store information.
- Means-ends analysis is a very common problem-solving strategy. It is designed to reduce the difference between the current and goal states.
- Problem solvers often engage in limited planning when less effortful heuristics are available but can engage in planning when required.
- Chess knowledge is stored in templates. Chess experts possess larger templates than non-experts and also make more effective use of slow, strategy-based processes.
- When diagnosing, experts use fast automatic processes more often than non-experts; this produces rapid pattern recognition. However, experts often cross-check their diagnoses with slow deliberate processes.
- Deliberate practice is necessary but not sufficient for expertise to develop. Natural ability or talent is also essential.
- Creativity involves the generation of ideas that are original and of potential value.

- Creativity is greater in individuals who are intelligent, high in openness, and in a positive mood.
- Creative scientists make extensive use of various heuristics or rules of thumb (e.g., the unusualness heuristic; "what if" reasoning).
- The scientific creative process is less random than implied by the hypothesis that blind variation and selective retention are involved.

Further reading

- Eysenck, M.W., & Brysbaert (2017). *Fundamentals of cognition* (3rd ed.). Abingdon, Oxford: Psychology Press. Chapter 10 of this textbook discusses problem solving and expertise in more detail than has been done here.

- Simonton, D.K. (2015). On praising convergent thinking: Creativity as blind variation and selective retention. *Creativity Research Journal, 27*, 262–270. Dean Keith Simonton discusses his thought-provoking theoretical ideas on scientific creativity.

- Ullén, F., Hambrick, D.Z., & Mosing, M.A. (2016). Rethinking expertise: A multifactorial gene-environment interaction model of expert performance. *Psychological Bulletin, 142*, 427–446. In this review, Fredrik Ullén and his colleagues show that expertise depends on genetic factors as well as deliberate practice.

- Weisberg, R.W. (2015). Toward an integrated theory of insight in problem solving. *Thinking & Reasoning, 21*, 5–39. Robert Weisberg provides a useful account of theory and research on insight problems.

- Zelko, H., Zammar, G.R., Ferreira, A.P.B., Phadtare, A., Shah, J., & Pietrobon, R. (2010). Selection mechanisms underlying high impact biomedical research: A qualitative analysis and causal model. *Public Library of Science One, 5*, e10535. This article provides insights into individual differences in the problem-solving strategies used by leading scientists.

Essay questions

1. How does past experience influence problem solving?

2. Discuss strategies used in problem solving. Why do problem solvers use these strategies?

3. To what extent can we explain the development of expertise in terms of deliberate practice?

4. Discuss the roles played by heuristics and "blind variation" in scientific creativity.

Part 6

Effective learning

Psychologists have discovered a considerable amount about the factors promoting effective learning. This knowledge is of great potential value to students who frequently find themselves needing to learn (and remember!) lots of information about any given topic. For example, it has been found that students who devote much of their revision time to trying to recall relevant course material typically perform better than other students on examinations.

Chapter 24 • Effective studying and learning

Ways in which research on learning and motivation can be used to enhance student examination performance are considered in detail.

You have almost certainly had to write essays and prepare for tests. Perhaps you have wondered why some students seem to find it much easier and less effortful than others to cope with these tests. A key part of the answer lies in good learning and study skills. What do you think are the key study skills required for successful academic performance? How do you think that students (including yourself!) could learn to improve their study skills?

Effective studying and learning

24

Students of psychology should find it easier than other students to develop good study skills and effective learning (at least in theory!). Psychological principles are of central importance to effective learning and remembering, and learning and memory are central areas within psychology (see Chapters 2 and 22). Study skills are also concerned with motivation and developing good work habits, and these fall squarely within the scope of psychology.

In this chapter, I will discuss several topics. First, I focus on factors determining the effectiveness of learning. My coverage is based on the levels-of-processing approach. Second, we will consider techniques designed to enhance people's ability to remember information over long periods of time.

Third, we will discuss an issue of central importance to students busy revising for a forthcoming exam. Should they devote their revision time to studying and restudying the material they need to remember or should they concentrate on trying to recall that material? Fourth, how can students motivate themselves?

Learning: levels of processing and beyond

What determines how well we remember information? Craik and Lockhart (1972) proposed a very influential answer in their levels-of-processing approach – they argued that what is crucial is how we *process* that information during learning. In essence, the greater the extent to which *meaning* is processed, the deeper the level of processing.

Craik and Lockhart's (1972) main theoretical assumptions were as follows:

- The level or depth of processing of a stimulus has a large effect on its memorability.
- Deeper levels of analysis produce more elaborate, longer lasting, and stronger memory traces than shallow levels of analysis (e.g., processing the sound of a word).

Numerous studies support these assumptions. Craik and Tulving (1975) compared recognition-memory performance as a function of the task performed at learning:

- *Shallow grapheme task*: Decide whether each word is in uppercase or lowercase letters.
- *Intermediate phoneme task*: Decide whether each word rhymes with a target word.
- *Deep semantic*: Decide whether each word fits a sentence containing a blank.

Depth of processing had impressive effects on memory performance – it was *three* times better following deep rather than shallow processing.

Elaboration

Craik and Tulving (1975) argued that *elaboration* of processing (the amount of processing of a given kind) is important as well as processing depth. They used the deep semantic task discussed earlier and varied elaboration by using simple sentence frames (e.g., "She cooked the _____" and complex ones (e.g., "The great bird swooped down and carried off the struggling _____"). Cued recall was twice as high for words accompanying complex sentences, showing that memory is better following more elaborate processing.

Distinctiveness

Another important factor in determining long-term memory is distinctiveness. **Distinctiveness** means that a memory trace differs from other memory traces (which are similar to each other) because it was processed differently at the time of learning. As Hunt (2013, p. 10) pointed out, distinctive processing can be defined as "the processing of difference in the context of similarity".

Suppose you tried to learn a list of 20 words. All the words are printed in black except for the tenth word which is bright red. You would probably guess that the word printed in red would be well remembered because it is distinctive or different from all the other list words. When experiments were done along these lines (von Restorff, 1933), there was indeed a higher probability that the distinctive word would be recalled than other non-distinctive ones. For obvious reasons, this became known as the **von Restorff effect**. See the Demonstration box for an alternative way of showing the beneficial effects of distinctiveness.

Why are distinctive memories so well remembered? Much forgetting is due to interference (see Chapter 22) – our long-term memory for information can be distorted (or interfered with) by other information learned beforehand or afterwards. That is especially so when the other information is very *similar* to what we are trying to remember. Distinctive memories are easy to remember because they are dissimilar to other memories and so less liable to interference (Eysenck, 1979).

KEY TERMS

Distinctiveness: memory traces that are distinct or different from other memory traces stored in long-term memory.

von Restorff effect: the finding that a to-be-remembered item that is distinctively different from other list items is especially likely to be remembered.

DEMONSTRATION: distinctiveness and long-term memory

Below is a list of 45 words (5 in each of 9 categories):

CHAIR	CAT	TANK
PIANO	ELEPHANT	KNIFE
CLOCK	GIRAFFE	POISON
TELPHONE	MOUSE	WHIP
CUSHION	TIGER	SCREWDRIVER
APPLE	BICYCLE	DRESS
GRAPEFRUIT	TRACTOR	MITTENS
COCONUT	TRAIN	SWEATER
PEACH	CART	SHOES
BLUEBERRY	SLED	PYJAMAS
CARROTS	MICHAEL	DONNA
LETTUCE	DANIEL	PAULA
ASPARAGUS	JOHN	BETH
ONION	RICHARD	SUSAN
POTATO	GEORGE	ANNE

Ask a friend of yours to consider the list words category by category. Their task is to write down one thing common to all five words within a category (Condition 1). After he/she has finished, present him/her with everything he/she has written down and ask them to recall as many list words as possible.

   Ask another friend to consider the list words category by category. Within each category, he/she should write beside each word one thing they know about that word that is not true of any other word in that category (Condition 2). After that, present him/her with what they have written down, and ask him/her to recall as many words as possible.

   This task is based on an experiment reported by Hunt and Smith (1996). They found recall was far higher in Condition 2 than Condition 1 (97% correct vs. 59%). The reason is that the instructions in Condition 2 led to much more distinctive or unique memory traces than those in Condition 1 because each word was processed differently from the others.

Limitations

So far I have emphasised the importance of what happens during learning. However, memory depends very much on the *relevance* of stored information to the requirements of the memory test. Consider a study by Morris et al. (1977). Participants answered semantic or shallow (rhyme) questions for lists of words. Memory was tested in one of two ways:

1. Standard recognition test on which participants selected list words and avoided non-list words.

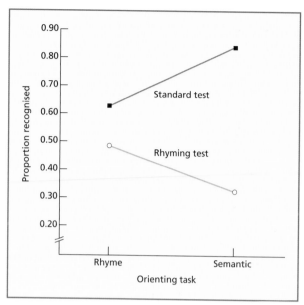

Mean proportion of words recognised as a function of orienting task (semantic or rhyme) and of the type of recognition task (standard or rhyming). Data are from Morris et al. (1977), and are from positive trials only.

2. Rhyming recognition test on which participants selected words that rhymed with list words; the words themselves had *not* been presented on the list. For example, if the word *fable* appeared on the test and *table* was a list word, participants should have selected it.

With the standard recognition test, there was the typical superiority of deep over shallow processing. More importantly, the *opposite* result was reported with the rhyme test, thus disproving the notion that deep processing always enhances long-term memory.

Morris et al. (1977) explained these findings in terms of **transfer-appropriate processing**. Whether what we have learned leads to good performance on a subsequent memory test depends on the *relevance* of that information (and its associated processing) to the memory test. For example, storing semantic information is irrelevant when the memory test requires the identification of words rhyming with list words. What is required for this kind of test is shallow rhyme information.

We turn now to another limitation of the levels-of-processing approach. The research discussed so far mainly involved explicit memory (conscious recollection). However, the effects of depth of processing are typically much less with implicit memory (memory not involving conscious recollection).

Challis et al. (1996) used various tests of explicit and implicit memory. One test of implicit memory was the word-fragment task. Participants were originally presented with a list of words (e.g., copper). Later they completed word fragments (e.g., c _ pp _ _) with the first word coming to mind. Implicit memory was assessed by the tendency to complete these word fragments with list words.

Challis et al.'s (1996) findings were clear-cut. There was a strong effect of processing depth on performance of all the explicit memory tests (e.g., recognition memory; free recall). In contrast, there was no effect of processing depth on the word-fragment task.

KEY TERM

Transfer-appropriate processing: the notion that long-term memory will be greatest when processing at the time of retrieval is very similar to processing at the time of learning.

EVALUATION

➕ "The levels-of-processing approach has been fruitful and generative, providing a powerful set of experimental techniques for exploring the phenomena of memory" (Roediger & Gallo, 2001, p. 44).

➕ The notion that long-term memory depends heavily on the extent to which meaning is processed at learning has been very influential.

➕ The levels-of-processing approach has led to the identification of elaboration and distinctiveness of processing as important factors in learning and memory.

- Craik and Lockhart (1972) underestimated the importance of the relationship between what has been learned and the nature of the retrieval environment.

- The relative importance of depth, elaboration, and distinctiveness in enhancing long-term memory has not been established.

- Processing depth is much less important for implicit than for explicit memory. As yet, the reasons for this difference remain unclear.

Mnemonics

Every self-help book designed to improve your memory provides numerous examples of effective techniques. Such techniques are often referred to as **mnemonics**. Here we will focus on a few of the most important mnemonics including an assessment of their strengths and limitations. Mnemonics vary in terms of whether they rely mostly on visual imagery or on verbal techniques. We will start with mnemonics based on visual imagery and then consider those involving verbal strategies.

Visual imagery techniques

One of the best-known visual imagery technique is the **method of loci**. What happens is that the to-be-remembered items are associated with well-known locations (e.g., places along a walk) (see Demonstration box).

DEMONSTRATION: method of loci

Think of 10 locations in your home, choosing them so the sequence of moving from one to the next is obvious; for example, from front door to entrance hall to kitchen to bedroom. Check that you can imagine moving through your 10 locations in a consistent order without difficulty.

Now think of 10 items and imagine them in those locations. If your first item is a *pipe*, you might imagine it poking out of the letterbox in your front door with great clouds of smoke billowing into the street. If the second item is a *cabbage*, you might imagine your hall obstructed by an enormous cabbage, and so on. When it comes to recall, walk mentally the route around your house.

Now try to create similarly striking images associating your 10 chosen locations with the words below:

| shirt | eagle | paperclip | rose | camera |
| mushroom | crocodile | handkerchief | sausage | mayor |

The same set of locations can be used repeatedly as long as only the most recent item in a given location is remembered.

Try to recall the 10 items listed two paragraphs ago in the correct order. No, don't look! Rely on the images you created.

KEY TERMS

Mnemonics: these consist of numerous methods or systems used by learners to enhance their long-term memory for information.

Method of loci: a memory technique in which to-be-remembered items are associated with locations well-known to the learner.

There is convincing evidence that the method of loci is very effective (Worthen & Hunt, 2011). It is somewhat more effective when learners use self-generated loci or locations rather than those suggested by others (Moè & De Beni, 2004). This difference occurs because the images formed with self-generated loci are more specific and detailed.

Suppose you wanted to learn several different lists of words using the method of loci. If you use the same locations with each list, it would seem likely there would be proactive interference (previous learning disrupting the learning and memory of subsequent lists; see Chapter 22). In fact, however, there is little proactive interference provided the words on successive lists are dissimilar (Massen & Vaterrodt-Plünnecke, 2006).

It has often been argued that the method of loci is of limited value when individuals learn information in the real world. Contrary evidence was reported by Moè and De Beni (2005). Students were presented with texts while using the method of loci or engaging in verbal rehearsal. When they listened to the texts, subsequent memory was much better when they used the method of loci. When they read the texts, however, there was no beneficial effect on memory of using the method of loci. The method of loci was ineffective with written presentation because the visual nature of the presentation *interfered* with the use of visual imagery associated with the method of loci.

Pegword method

The **pegword method** resembles the method of loci in that it relies on visual imagery and allows you to remember sequences of 10 unrelated items. First, you memorise 10 pegwords. As each pegword rhymes with a number from one to ten, this is relatively easy. Try it for yourself:

> One = *bun*; Two = *shoe*; Three = *tree*; Four = *door*; Five = *hive*; Six = *sticks*; Seven = *heaven*; Eight = *gate*; Nine = *wine*; Ten = *hen*

Having mastered this, you are ready to memorise 10 unrelated words. Suppose these are as follows: *battleship, pig, chair, sheep, castle, rug, grass, beach, milkmaid, binoculars*. Take the first pegword (bun) and form an image of a bun interacting with battleship (e.g., a battleship sailing into an enormous floating bun). Now take the second pegword (shoe) and imagine it interacting with pig (e.g., a large shoe with a pig sitting in it). Work through the rest of the items forming a suitable interactive image in each case.

The pegword technique is very effective. Indeed, it is as effective as the method of loci (Wang & Thomas, 2000). This is unsurprising given that both techniques produce distinctive memory traces via elaborate processing and serial organisation of the material with the locations or pegwords providing a well-learned retrieval structure.

What are the limitations of the pegword method?

1. It requires much training to have reliable and rapid access to the pegwords.
2. It is harder to use the method with abstract material because it is not easy to form interactive images involving abstract concepts such as *morality* or *insincerity*.
3. There are doubts about its applicability to everyday life since we rarely need to remember a sequence of unrelated items.

> **KEY TERM**
>
> **Pegword method:** a memory technique in which to-be-remembered items are associated with pegwords (words rhyming with numbers).

Remembering names

Most people have problems remembering names (I know I do!). When being introduced to someone new, we tend to look at them and make whatever initial remarks are appropriate. As a result, their name "goes in one ear and out the other."

One way of remembering people's names is based on a visual imagery mnemonic. You start by searching for an imageable substitute for the person's name (e.g., Eysenck becomes "ice sink"). Then some prominent feature of the person's face is selected, and the image is linked with that feature. For example, the nose might be regarded as a tap over the sink. Brief training in this method improved recall of names to faces by almost 80% under laboratory conditions (Morris et al., 1978). This finding is consistent with much evidence that long-term memory is better for information previously processed in a distinctive fashion (Eysenck, 1979).

The imagery mnemonic for learning names works well in the peace and quiet of the laboratory. In real-life social situations, however, it may be hard to form good imagery mnemonics. Morris et al. (2005) invited university students to attend a party having received instructions about learning the other students' names. One group was trained to use the imagery mnemonic. A second group tried to retrieve the name at increasing intervals after first hearing them (expanded retrieval practice). There was also a control group simply told to learn people's names.

Between 24 and 72 hours after the party, the students were shown photographs of the students who had been at the party and wrote their names underneath. Students in the expanded retrieval practice condition recalled 50% more names than those in the control group. The imagery mnemonic was even less effective than no specific memorising strategy. Thus, it is important to combine use of the visual imagery mnemonic with repeated attempts to recall the name.

Verbal techniques

There are several verbal techniques for improving memory (see Baddeley et al., 2015). One of the most effective of such techniques is the **story method**. It is used to remember a series of unrelated words in the correct order by linking them together within the context of a story. Note that it often involves using visual imagery as well as producing sentences. Here is how the story method could be applied to the 10 words used to illustrate the pegword technique:

> In the kitchen of the *battleship*, there was a *pig* that sat in a *chair*. There was also a *sheep* that had previously lived in a *castle*. In port, the sailors took a *rug* and sat on the *grass* close to the *beach*. While there, they saw a *milkmaid* watching them through her *binoculars*.

Several studies have found that the story method greatly increases long-term memory (Worthen & Hunt, 2011). For example, Bower and Clark (1969) found that use of the story method produced a 93% recall of words from 12 lists compared to only 13% in the control condition – a massive *sevenfold* advantage for the story method! However, the method is limited in that it requires fairly extensive training – it took me a few minutes to form the story given earlier! Another limitation is that you generally have to work your way through the list to find a given item (e.g., the seventh one).

KEY TERM

Story method: a technique for improving memory in which a story is generated that includes all of the to-be-remembered words or other items in the correct order.

IN THE REAL WORLD: Shereshevskii

The Russian, Solomon Shereshevskii (often referred to as S.), probably had the most astonishing memory powers of all time. His memory powers were first discovered when he was a journalist. His editor was concerned that S. never took notes, even when being given complex briefing instructions. S. convinced the editor he did not need to because he immediately committed everything to memory. S. was later studied by the Russian psychologist Luria.

Luria discovered there was practically no limit to the amount of information S. could remember – lists of over 100 digits, long strings of nonsense syllables, poetry in unknown languages (e.g., stanzas from Dante's *Inferno*), complex figures, and elaborate scientific formulae. According to Luria (1968), "He could repeat such material back perfectly, even in reverse order, and even years later!"

What was Shereshevskii's secret? The main one was that he had an amazing capacity for **synaesthesia**, the tendency for an experience in one sense modality to evoke experiences in one or more other sense modalities. For example, when presented with a tone, he said, "It looks like fireworks tinged with a pink-red hue. The strip of colour . . . has an ugly taste – rather like that of briny pickle." S. was also extremely skilled at creating vivid visual images. For example, he remembered the number "87" by imagining a stout woman cosying up to a man twirling his moustache. Finally, he used the method of loci (using locations to remember information in the correct order).

Do you envy S.'s memory powers? Ironically, his memory was so good it disrupted his everyday life! For example, this was his experience when trying to make sense of a prose passage: "Each word calls up images, they collide with one another, and the result is chaos." His acute awareness of details meant that he sometimes failed to recognise someone he knew if, for example, their facial colouring had altered because they had been on holiday. These limitations of his memory meant that he worked at dozens of jobs until finally developing a stage act as a memory man.

Why do mnemonic techniques work?

Why are techniques such as the method of loci, the pegword method, and the story method so effective? Ericsson (1988) argued that very high memory performance depends on three principles:

KEY TERM

Synaesthesia: the capacity to have an experience in one sense modality when a different modality is stimulated (e.g., a sound triggers visual imagery).

1. *Encoding principle*: The information should be processed meaningfully, relating it to pre-existing knowledge. This is clearly the case when use is made of known locations (method of loci) or the number sequence (pegword method).
2. *Retrieval structure principle*: Cues should be stored with the to-be-remembered information to assist subsequent retrieval. A connected series of locations or the number sequence provides an immediately accessible retrieval structure.

3. *Speed-up principle*: Extensive practice allows the processes involved in encoding and retrieval to function faster and more efficiently.

We can see these three principles at work in a study by Ericsson and Chase (1982) on SF, who practised the digit span task for one hour a day for two years. The digit span (the number of random digits that can be repeated back immediately in the correct order) is typically about 7 items. SF eventually attained a span of 80 items! He reached a span of 18 items by using his extensive knowledge of running times (encoding and retrieval principles). For example, "3594" was Bannister's time for the first sub-four-minute mile and so would be stored as a single unit).

We have seen that extensive practice is of vital importance in making mnemonic techniques effective. However, extensive practice on its own is not always sufficient if it does not allow us to form an effective retrieval structure (the second principle). For example, Kalakoski and Saariluoma (2001) asked Helsinki taxi drivers and students to recall lists of 15 Helsinki street names in the order presented. Unsurprisingly, the taxi drivers greatly outperformed the students when the streets formed a continuous route through the city because they could easily form a retrieval structure. However, their advantage disappeared when non-adjacent street names taken from all over Helsinki were presented in a random order. In this condition, the taxi drivers' special knowledge did not allow them to form an effective retrieval structure.

Learning by remembering

Answer this question taken from research by Karpicke et al. (2009):

> Imagine you are reading a textbook for an upcoming exam. After you have read the chapter one time, would you rather:
>
> A: Go back and restudy either the entire chapter or certain parts of the chapter.
> B: Try to recall material from the chapter (without the possibility of restudying the material)
> C: Use some other study technique.

Karpicke et al. (2009) found 57% of their students gave answer A, 21% gave answer C, and only 18% gave answer B. Of interest, the least frequent answer (B) is actually the correct one in terms of effectiveness in promoting good long-term memory!

Findings

The notion that long-term retention for material that needs to be learned is better when memory is tested during the time of learning rather than simply restudied is known as the **testing effect**. Rowland (2014) reviewed research on the testing effect. He found convincing evidence for its existence, with 81% of studies reporting positive findings. Most studies have used relatively simple learning material, but Karpicke and Aue (2015) found in a review that the testing effect is also present when the learning material is complex.

> **KEY TERM**
>
> **Testing effect:** the finding that long-term memory is enhanced when some of the learning period is devoted to retrieving the to-be-remembered information

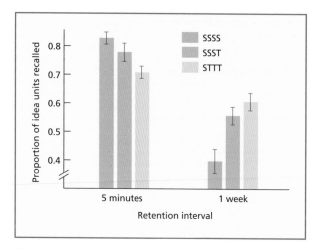

Memory performance as a function of learning conditions (S, study; T, test) and retention interval (5 min vs. 1 week).

Roediger and Karpicke (2006) carried out a thorough study on the testing effect. Students read a prose passage covering a general scientific topic and memorised it in one of three conditions:

1. *Repeated study*: The passage was read four times and there was no test.
2. *Single test*: The passage was read three times and then students recalled as much as possible from it.
3. *Repeated test*: The passage was read once and then students recalled as much as possible on three occasions. Finally, memory for the passage was tested after five minutes or one week.

The findings are shown in the figure. Repeated study was the most effective strategy when the final test was given five minutes after learning. However, there was a dramatic reversal in the findings when the final test occurred after one week. There was a very strong testing effect – average recall was 50% higher in the repeated test condition than the repeated study condition! That could easily make the difference between doing very well on an examination and failing it.

Students in the repeated study condition predicted they would recall more of the prose passage than did those in the repeated test condition. This helps to explain why many students mistakenly devote little or no time to testing themselves when preparing themselves for an examination.

Dunlosky et al. (2013) reviewed 10 learning techniques used by students preparing for examinations. The testing effect emerged as the most useful technique. Several other techniques were moderately useful. They included elaborative interrogation (generating explanations for stated facts), self-explanation (explaining how new information is related to known information), and interleaved practice (studying different kinds of material within a single study session).

Explanations

What factors explain the testing effect? First, learners experience failures of retrieval during testing, and these failures encourage them to find more effective ways of remembering the material (Pyc & Rawson, 2012). For example, learners may engage in more elaborate processing of the meaning of the learning material.

Second, testing often involves more effortful processing than restudying. Several brain regions associated with language processing are more active during testing than restudying (van den Broek et al., 2013). Rowland (2014) compared studies in which retrieval at initial testing was moderately effortful (i.e., it involved recall) or less effortful (i.e., it involved recognition memory). The testing effect was stronger when retrieval was more effortful. It remains somewhat unclear why effortful retrieval is so beneficial.

Third, it seems likely the positive effects of testing during learning would be greater for items that are successfully retrieved than for those not retrieved. If so, the testing effect should be greater when a high proportion of items is retrieved during learning than when only a small proportion is retrieved. Evidence supporting that prediction was discussed by Rowland (2014).

EVALUATION

➕ Numerous studies have found testing is more effective than restudying in promoting long-term memory, and this is the case for complex as well as simple learning materials.

➕ The testing effect was found to be the most effective of 10 major learning techniques (Dunlosky et al., 2013).

➖ As Rowland (2014, p. 1453) concluded, "The underlying mechanisms that produce the [testing] effect remain elusive."

➖ It remains unclear which of the several proposed explanations of the testing effect provides the best account.

➖ It is probable that the testing effect depends on several memory mechanisms. However, the relative importance of these mechanisms and how they interact or combine have not been established.

Motivation

Many (or even most) students find it hard to find the necessary motivation when having to learn and remember large amounts of information for an examination. There are more theories of motivation than you can shake a stick at. However, two of the most useful ones are goal-setting theory and the theory of implementation intentions, both of which are discussed below.

Goal-setting theory

The key assumption of goal-setting theory (Latham & Locke, 2007) is that *conscious goals* have a major impact on individuals' motivation and behaviour. More specifically, the harder the goals we set ourselves, the better our performance is likely to be. Sitzmann and Ely (2011) reviewed the evidence and found convincing support that learning and performance are strongly influenced by goal level. Why is that the case? The main reason is that individuals are more motivated and try harder when difficult goals are set.

The goals you set for yourself should be specific and clear as well as hard – make sure to avoid very vague goals such as simply "doing well". Latham (2003, p. 309) summarised some of the key points of goal-setting theory: the goal should be "specific, measurable, attainable, relevant, and have a time-frame (SMART)".

There is little point in setting for yourself the goal of obtaining an excellent examination result if you don't *commit* yourself fully to that goal. According to goal-setting theory, high performance occurs only when goal difficulty and goal commitment are both high. Goal commitment is especially important when goals are difficult because such goals require high levels of effort and are associated with a smaller chance of success than easy goals.

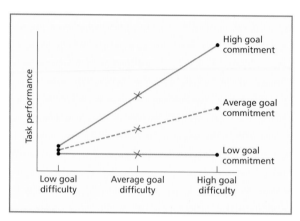

The effects of goal difficulty and goal commitment on task performance according to Locke's goal-setting theory.

Findings

Klein et al. (1999) reviewed numerous studies on the effects of goal setting and goal commitment on task performance. The pattern of the findings was as predicted from goal-setting theory. Higher levels of goal commitment were associated with higher levels of performance, especially when goal difficulty was high.

Various factors influenced the level of goal commitment. Two key ones were attractiveness of goal attainment and expectancy of goal attainment provided the individual applied reasonable effort. Other factors producing high goal commitment were having high ability, being personally involved in goal setting, and receiving performance feedback.

Most research on goal setting is limited because it involves performance of a single task over a short period of time in the absence of distractions. In the real world, in contrast, workers often set long-term performance targets, and they are exposed to numerous distractions (e.g., numerous e-mails). These differences may be important. Yearta et al. (1995) studied scientists and professional staff working for a multi-national company. Their work performance was negatively related to goal difficulty – this is diametrically opposite to the prediction from goal-setting theory.

Masuda et al. (2015) pointed out that most research is also limited in that it involves setting a single goal. In the real world, people often have various learning and performance goals at the same time. Masuda et al. asked their participants to perform various arithmetic tasks using Excel software. The key finding was that task performance was best when total goal difficulty was intermediate and was lower when total goal difficulty was either low or high. Why was performance lower with high than with intermediate goal difficulty? Being assigned several hard goals reduced people's self-efficacy (the belief that one can achieve one's goal or goals) and thus probably reduced motivation and commitment.

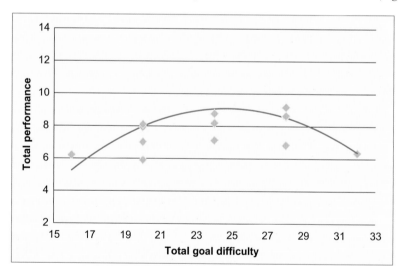

The effects of simultaneous learning and performance goals on performance. From Masuda et al. (2015).

EVALUATION

⊕ Performance is generally best when individuals set themselves hard goals accompanied by high goal commitment.

⊕ The most effective goals are specific, measurable, attainable, relevant, and have a time frame.

⊖ Most laboratory studies are artificial in that participants perform a single task for a relatively short period of time.

⊖ Beneficial effects of setting hard goals are sometimes not found when complex tasks are performed over long periods of time in the presence of distraction or when people are assigned several hard goals at the same time.

Implementation intentions

How can students move from goal setting to goal attainment in a world of complications and distractions? Gollwitzer (2014, p. 306) has focused on this issue. He defined his key concept of **implementation intentions** as follows: "'If situation Y is encountered, then I will perform the goal-directed response Z!' Thus, implementation intentions define exactly when, where, and how one wants to act toward realizing one's goals".

We can see the importance of implementation intentions by considering a student called Natalie who has the goal of spending four hours every Saturday revising for an exam. However, Natalie normally chats for several hours a day with her friends and also likes to watch television.

How can Natalie ensure her revision gets done? This is where implementation intentions come in. Here are two possible ones: "When one of my friends knocks on the door, I will tell her I'll see her at Costa's at 8 o'clock"; "If there is something interesting on television, I'll video it to watch later".

Relevant evidence was reported by Gollwitzer and Brandstätter (1997). Participants had the goal of writing a report on how they spent Christmas Eve within the subsequent two days. Half formed implementation intentions by indicating *when* and *where* they would write the report. The report was written within the time limit by 75% of those forming implementation intentions but by only 33% of those who did not.

Why are implementation intentions so effective? Our everyday behaviour is strongly influenced by habit – in any given situation, we tend to behave as we have done in the past. Gollwitzer (2014) argued that implementation intentions create "instant habits" that compete successfully with these habitual responses. Our habits are reliably triggered by relevant cues providing information about *when* and/or *where* certain actions occur. Similarly, implementation intentions specify when and where we will initiate behaviour to attain our goal.

One prediction from this viewpoint is that implementation intentions compete successfully with previously acquired habitual responses because they can be accessed as rapidly as those habitual responses. Adriaanse et al. (2011a)

KEY TERM

Implementation intentions: action plans designed to achieve some goal (e.g., writing an essay) based on specific information concerning where, when, and how the goal will be achieved.

reported evidence supporting that prediction. If implementation intentions are like "instant habits", there should be little activation in brain areas (e.g., dorsolateral prefrontal cortex) involved in effortful action control when such intentions are used. Supporting evidence has been obtained in several studies (Wieber et al., 2015).

Implementation intentions do not invariably enhance performance. Powers et al. (2005) found that implementation intentions had *negative* effects on performance in individuals high in perfectionism. In these individuals, implementation intentions led to excessive self-criticism, and this impaired performance.

Chapter summary

- Long-term memory depends on the depth of processing at the time of learning. It also depends on elaboration of processing and distinctiveness.
- Long-term memory also depends on the relevance of stored information to the requirements of the memory test.
- The method of loci is effective with word lists and lecture-style presentations. However, it is ineffective with written texts because visual material interferes with visual imagery.
- The pegword technique is useful when learning lists of unrelated words, but there are doubts about its applicability to everyday life.
- The story method is an effective way of learning lists of unrelated words.
- Successful mnemonic techniques involve meaningful encoding, an effective retrieval structure, and extensive practice.
- Long-term memory is generally much better when revision time is mostly devoted to recalling the material rather than to further study. This is known as the testing effect.
- The testing effect occurs in part because testing generally involves more effortful processing than restudying. In addition, testing during learning that involves effortful retrieval is associated with a stronger testing effect than when retrieval involves little effort.
- The memory mechanisms underlying the testing effect have not been clearly identified.
- According to goal-setting theory, the harder the goals we set ourselves, the higher the level of performance. This is especially the case when goal commitment is high.
- Implementation intentions (sometimes described as "instant habits") increase the probability of carrying out the actions required to attain a goal (e.g., exam success).

Further reading

- Baddeley, A., Eysenck, M.W., & Anderson, M.C. (2015). *Memory* (2nd ed.). Hove: Psychology Press. Chapter 17 in this introductory textbook contains full coverage of the main ways in which memory can be improved.

- Dunlosky, J., Rawson, K.A., Marsh, E.J., Nathan, M.J., & Willingham, D.T. (2013). Improving students' learning with effective learning techniques: Promising directions from cognitive and educational psychology. *Psychological Science in the Public Interest*, *14*, 4–58. John Dunlosky and his colleagues discuss (and assess) the effectiveness of several techniques designed to enhance learning and memory.

- Rowland, C.A. (2014). The effect of testing versus restudy on retention: A meta-analytic review of the testing effect. *Psychological Bulletin*, *140*, 1432–1463. The research literature on the testing effect is reviewed, and major theories of this effect are discussed.

- Wieber, F., Thürmer, J.L., & Gollwitzer, P.M. (2015). Promoting the translation of intentions by implementation intentions: Behavioural effects and physiological correlates. *Frontiers in Human Neuroscience*, *9* (Article 395). Peter Gollwitzer and his colleagues review theory and research on implementation intentions.

- Worthen, J.B., & Hunt, R.R. (2011). *Mnemonology: Mnemonics for the 21st century*. Hove: Psychology Press. In this book, the authors provide a comprehensive and authoritative account of the best-known and most effective memory techniques.

Essay questions

1. Describe the levels-of-processing approach to memory. What are its strengths and limitations?

2. Discuss the main mnemonic techniques. How effective are they likely to be in real-life situations?

3. Discuss research on the testing effect and consider possible explanations for this effect.

4. Discuss (and evaluate) ways of motivating students who need to learn and remember large amounts of information for a forthcoming examination.

Glossary

accommodation: in Piaget's theory, changes in an individual's cognitive organisation designed to deal more effectively with the environment.

actor–observer bias: others' actions tend to be attributed to internal dispositions, whereas our own actions are attributed to the current situation.

adaptations: inherited mechanisms that evolved to solve problems encountered in our ancestral past.

adjustment phase: this is the second period after divorce; it follows the **crisis phase** and is marked by less emotional distress than that phase.

adrenaline: a hormone producing increased arousal within the sympathetic nervous system.

adrenocorticotrophic hormone (ACTH): a hormone that leads to the release of the stress hormone cortisol.

agentic state: feeling controlled by an authority figure and therefore lacking a sense of personal responsibility.

aggression: forms of behaviour deliberately intended to harm or injure someone else.

altruism: a form of **prosocial behaviour** that is generally costly to the altruistic person, and which is motivated by the desire to help someone else.

Ames room illusion: the room looks like an ordinary room but actually has a very unusual shape; this causes distortions in the apparent heights of individuals standing in front of the rear wall.

amnesia: a condition caused by brain damage in which patients have intact short-term memory but poor long-term memory.

amygdala: a small, almond-shaped part of the brain buried deep within the temporal lobe; it is associated with several emotional states (e.g., fear).

androgen: male sex hormones (e.g., testosterone) typically produced in much greater quantity by males than by females.

androgyny: used to describe an individual who possesses a mixture or combination of masculine and feminine characteristics.

assimilation: in Piaget's theory, dealing with new environmental situations by using existing cognitive organisation.

attachment: a powerful emotional relationship between two people (e.g., mother and child).

attributions: our inferences concerning the causes of patterns of behaviour in other people and in ourselves.

authoritarian personality: a type of personality consisting of intolerance of ambiguity, hostility towards other groups, rigid beliefs, and submissiveness towards authority figures.

autism: a severe disorder involving very poor communication skills, deficient social and language development, and repetitive behaviour.

autobiographical memory: memory across the lifespan for events involving the individual (especially those of personal significance).

autonomic nervous system: the part of the **peripheral nervous system** that controls the involuntary movement of non-skeletal muscles; it is divided into the **sympathetic nervous system** and the **parasympathetic nervous system**.

avoidance learning: a form of operant conditioning in which an appropriate avoidance response prevents presentation of an unpleasant or aversive stimulus.

avoidant attachment: an insecure attachment of an infant to its mother, combined with an avoidance of contact with her when she returns after an absence.

behaviourism: an approach to psychology started in the United States by John Watson, according to which psychologists should focus on observable stimuli and responses and learning can be accounted for in terms of conditioning principles.

binocular cues: depth cues requiring the use of both eyes.

blocking effect: the absence of a **conditioned response** to a **conditioned stimulus** if another **conditioned stimulus** already predicts the onset of the **unconditioned stimulus**.

bogus pipeline: a sham lie detector used to elicit honest answers when individuals complete personality questionnaires.

burnout: long-term emotional exhaustion, depersonalisation, and lack of personal achievement triggered by excessive work demands.

bystander effect: the finding that a victim is less likely to be helped as the number of bystanders increases.

bystander intervention: an area of research focusing on the reasons why bystanders to a crime or incident decide whether to help the victim.

CAPTCHAs: Completely Automated Public Turing tests to tell Computers and Humans

Apart involve identifying distorted visual stimuli; they are typically very hard for machines to solve but relatively easy for humans.

case study: the intensive study of one or two individuals.

categorical classification: an all-or-none approach to diagnosis in which each mental disorder is regarded as a category applicable or not applicable to any given patient.

categorical clustering: the tendency in free recall to produce words on a category-by-category basis.

central coherence: the ability to interpret information taking account of the context; being able to "see the big picture".

central executive: a modality-free, limited-capacity component of working memory.

central nervous system: the brain and spinal cord; it is protected by bone and cerebrospinal fluid.

centration: in Piaget's theory, the tendency of young children to attend to only part of the information available in a given situation.

cerebral cortex: the outer layer of the **cerebrum**; it is involved in perception, learning, memory, thinking, and language.

cerebrum: a part of the forebrain crucially involved in thinking and language.

change blindness: the failure to detect that a visual stimulus has moved, changed, or been replaced by another stimulus.

child-directed speech: the short, simple, slowly spoken sentences used by mothers, fathers, or caregivers when talking to their young children; designed to be easy for children to understand.

chunks: stored units formed from integrating smaller pieces of information.

classical conditioning: a basic form of learning in which simple responses (e.g., salivation)

are associated with a new or **conditioned stimulus** (e.g., tone).

clinical method: an informal question-based approach used to assess children's understanding of problems.

coercive cycle: a pattern of behaviour within families in which aggression by one family member produces an aggressive response leading to an escalation in aggression.

cognitive appraisal: the individual's interpretation of the current situation; it helps to determine the nature and intensity of his/her emotional experience. It also helps the individual to decide whether he/she has the resources to cope with the situation.

cognitive neuropsychology: research on brain-damaged patients designed to increase our understanding of cognition in healthy individuals.

cognitive neuroscience: an approach designed to understand human cognition by combining information from behaviour and brain activity.

cognitive psychology: it is concerned with internal mental processes (e.g., attention; perception; learning; thinking) and how these processes influence our behaviour.

cognitive schema: organised information stored in long-term memory and used by individuals to form interpretations of themselves and the world in which they live.

cognitive triad: a depressed person's negative views of the self, the world, and the future.

collectivistic cultures: cultures (such as many in the Far East) in which the focus is on group solidarity rather than individual responsibility.

comorbidity: the simultaneous presence of two or more mental disorders in a given individual.

compliance: the influence of a majority on a minority based on its power; this influence is generally on public behaviour rather than private beliefs.

concordance rate: in twin studies, the probability that if one twin has a disorder, the other twin has the same disorder.

conditioned reflex: a new association between a **conditioned stimulus** and an **unconditioned stimulus** that produces a **conditioned response**.

conditioned response: a new response produced as a result of **classical conditioning**.

conditioned stimulus: a neutral stimulus paired with an **unconditioned stimulus** to produce **classical conditioning**.

confirmation bias: memory distortions caused by the influence of expectations concerning what is likely to have happened.

conformity: changes in attitudes or behaviour that occur in response to group pressure.

confounding variables: variables that are not of interest to the experimenter that are mistakenly manipulated along with the **independent variable**.

congenital adrenal hyperplasia: an inherited disorder of the adrenal gland causing the levels of male sex hormones in foetuses of both sexes to be unusually high.

conservation: In Piaget's theorising, the child's understanding that various aspects of an object may remain constant even though other aspects are transformed or changed considerably.

consolidation: a physiological process involved in establishing long-term memories; this process lasts several hours or more.

conventional morality: the second level of moral development in Kohlberg's theory; at this level, moral reasoning focuses on having the approval of others.

convergence: a depth cue provided by greater inward turning of the eyes when looking at a close object than one further away.

conversion: the influence of a minority on a majority based on convincing the majority that its views are correct; this influence is on private beliefs more than public behaviour.

coping flexibility: the ability to change one's coping strategies flexible depending on the nature of the current situation.

correlation: an association between two dependent variables or responses produced by participants.

counterbalancing: this is used with the repeated measures design; each condition is equally likely to be used first or second.

cortisol: the so-called "stress hormone" because elevated amounts are typically found in the bodies of highly stressed individuals.

creativity: the ability to produce original, useful, and ingenious solutions to problems

crisis phase: this is the first period following divorce; during this phase, the mother is less affectionate than usual.

critical period: according to the **maternal deprivation hypothesis**, a period early in life during which infants must form a strong attachment if their later development is to be satisfactory.

cross-cultural psychology: the systematic study of similarities in and differences among cultures around the world.

cross-sectional method: this method uses different groups (e.g., of different ages) which are all studied at the same time.

cued recall: a memory test in which cues or clues (e.g., first few letters of each list word) are given to assist memory.

cultural mindset: the beliefs and values that are active at any given time; individuals who

have extensive experience of two cultures have two cultural mindsets, with the one that influences thinking and behaviour being determined by the immediate social context.

cultural relativism: the notion we should view each culture from within that culture rather than the observer's own culture.

culture: the values, beliefs, and practices shared by members of a given society.

culture-bound syndromes: patterns of abnormal behaviour found in one or a small number of cultures.

decentration: In Piaget's theorizing, the ability to focus on several aspects of a problem at once and make coherent sense of them.

declarative memory: a long-term memory system concerned with personal experiences and general knowledge; it usually involves conscious recollection of information.

deindividuation: loss of a sense of personal identity; it can occur in a large group or crowd.

deliberate practice: a form of practice in which the learner is provided with informative feedback and has the chance to correct his/her errors.

demand characteristics: cues that are used by participants to try to guess the nature of the study or to work out what the experiment is about.

dependent variable: some aspect of the participants' behaviour that is measured in an experiment.

deprivation: the state of a child who has formed a close attachment to someone (e.g., its mother) but is later separated from that person; see **privation**.

deprivation-specific problems: problems (e.g., social deficits; interests that are intense but very limited) sometimes found following deprivation but uncommon following other kinds of childhood adversity.

diathesis-stress model: the notion that mental disorders are caused jointly by a diathesis (personal vulnerability) *and* a distressing event.

diffusion of responsibility: the larger the number of bystanders who observe what happens to a victim, the less the sense of personal responsibility to help experienced by each one.

direct tuition: one way of increasing a child's **gender identity** and **sex-typed behaviour** by being instructed by other people.

discrimination: negative actions of behaviour directed towards the members of some other group.

dispositional attribution: deciding that someone's behaviour is due to their personality rather than to the situation.

dissociative identity disorder: a mental disorder in which the patient has two or more separate personalities or identities, which alternate in controlling behaviour; there is also amnesia or forgetting of autobiographical information.

distinctiveness: memory traces that are distinct or different from other memory traces stored in long-term memory.

distraction: an emotion-regulation strategy in which attention is switched from emotional processing to neutral information.

dizygotic twins: twins derived from the fertilisation of two ova or eggs by two spermatozoa at approximately the same time; they share 50% of their genes and are also known as fraternal twins.

dysexecutive syndrome: a condition caused by brain damage (typically in the frontal lobes) in which there is severe impairment of complex cognitive functions (e.g., planning; decision making).

eclectic approach: the use of a range of different forms of treatment by therapists.

ecological validity: the extent to which research findings are applicable to everyday settings and generalise to other locations, times, and measures.

effortful control: a personality trait relating to the ability to suppress dominant responses (e.g., those involving rule-breaking behaviour).

egocentrism: an assumption made by young children that the ways other people see or think are the same as theirs; it is similar to being self-centred.

emotion-focused coping: a general strategy for dealing with stressful situations in which the individual attempts to reduce his/her negative emotional state.

emotion regulation: the management and control of emotional states by various processes (e.g., cognitive reappraisal; distraction).

emotional intelligence: an individual's level of sensitivity to one's own emotional needs and those of others; more related to personality than to intelligence.

empathy: the capacity to enter into another person's feelings and more generally to understand that person's perspective.

enactive experience: this involves the child learning which behaviours are expected of his/her gender within any given culture as a result of being rewarded or punished for behaving different ways.

encoding specificity principle: the notion that retrieval depends on the *overlap* between the information available at retrieval and the information within the memory trace.

episodic buffer: a component of working memory; it is essentially passive and briefly stores integrated information from the phonological loop, visuo-spatial sketchpad, and long-term memory.

episodic memory: long-term memory for personal events.

equilibration: in Piaget's theory, responding to cognitive conflicts by using the processes of **accommodation** and **assimilation** to return to a state of equilibrium.

equipotentiality: the notion that any response can be conditioned in any stimulus situation.

evolutionary psychology: an approach to psychology based on the assumption that much human behaviour can be understood on the basis of Darwin's theory of evolution.

expansions: utterances of adults that consist of fuller and more accurate versions of what a child has just said.

experimental hypothesis: prediction as to what will happen in a given experiment; it typically involves predicting the effects of a given **independent variable** on a **dependent variable** and is often theory-based.

experimental method: a method involving a generally high level of control over the experimental situation (especially the **independent variable**).

experimenter effect: the various ways in which the experimenter's expectations, personal characteristics, misrecordings of data, and so on can influence the findings of a study.

exposure therapy: a form of treatment in which clients are repeatedly exposed to stimuli or situations they fear greatly.

extinction: the elimination of a response when it is not followed by reward (**operant conditioning**) or by the **unconditioned stimulus** (classical conditioning).

extraversion: a personality **trait** reflecting individual differences in sociability and impulsiveness.

eyewitness testimony: the evidence relating to a crime provided by someone who observed it being committed.

factor analysis: a statistical technique used to find out the number and nature of the aspects of intelligence (or personality) measured by a test.

false consensus effect: the mistaken belief that most other people are similar to us in their opinions, behaviour, and personality.

false uniqueness bias: the mistaken belief that one's abilities and behaviour are superior to those of most other people.

field experiments: experiments carried out in real-world situations using the **experimental method**.

figure-ground segregation: perception of the visual scene as consisting of an object or figure standing out from a less distinct background.

Flynn effect: the progressive increase in **intelligence quotient (IQ)** in numerous countries over the past 50 or 60 years.

free recall: a memory test in which words from a list can be produced in any order.

functional fixedness: an inflexible focus on the usual functions of an object in problem solving.

functional magnetic resonance imaging (fMRI): a technique providing detailed and accurate information concerning activation in brain areas while a cognitive task is being performed.

fundamental attribution error: the tendency to think that the behaviour of other people is due more to their personality and less to the situation than is actually the case.

fundamental lexical hypothesis: the assumption that dictionaries contain words that refer to all of the most important personality **traits**.

gender identity: our awareness of being male or female; it depends to an important extent on social rather than biological factors.

gender identity disorder: distress associated with a conflict between biological gender and the gender with which an individual identifies.

gender-role stereotypes: culturally-determined expectations concerning jobs and activities thought suitable for males and females.

gender schemas: organised knowledge stored in long-term memory in the form of numerous beliefs about the forms of behaviour that are appropriate for each sex.

gender segregation: the tendency for young children from about 3 years to play mostly with same-sex peers.

gender similarities hypothesis: the notion that there are only small differences between males and females with respect to the great majority of psychological variables (e.g., abilities; personality).

gender-typed behaviour: behaviour conforming to that expected on the basis of any given culture's gender-role stereotypes.

geons: basic shapes or components combined in object recognition; an abbreviation for "geometric ions" proposed by Biederman.

grammatical morphemes: prepositions, prefixes, suffixes, and so on that help to indicate the grammatical structure of sentences.

group: in Piaget's theorising, the structure formed from the organisation of various related cognitive processes or operations.

group polarisation: the tendency of groups to produce fairly extreme decisions.

groupthink: group pressure to achieve general agreement in groups in which dissent is suppressed; it can lead to disastrous decisions.

hemispheric lateralisation: the notion that each hemisphere or half of the brain differs in its functioning to some extent even though both hemispheres coordinate their activities most of the time

hemispheric specialisation: each hemisphere or half of the brain carries out its own specific functions to some extent; however, the two hemispheres coordinate their activities most of the time.

heuristics: rules of thumb used to solve problems.

hill climbing: a simple heuristic used by problem solvers in which they focus on moves that will apparently put them closer to the goal or problem solution.

hindbrain: the "reptilian brain", concerned with breathing, digestion, swallowing, the fine control of balance, and the control of consciousness.

hindsight bias: the tendency to be wise after the event using the benefit of hindsight.

hostile expectation bias: the bias to expect aggression from others in ambiguous situations.

hydrocephalus: a condition known non-technically as "water on the brain" in which excessive cerebrospinal fluid crushes the cerebral cortex against the skull.

hypothalamus: a part of the forebrain involved in controlling body temperature, hunger, thirst, and sexual behaviour.

Hypotheses: predictions concerning the effects of some factor(s) on behaviour based on a given theory.

ill-defined problems: problems that are imprecisely specified; for example, the initial state, goal state, and the methods available to solve the problem may be unclear.

immune system: a system of biological structures and processes in the body that is involved in fighting disease.

implacable experimenter: the typical laboratory situation in which the experimenter's behaviour is uninfluenced by the participant's behaviour.

implementation intentions: action plans designed to achieve some goal (e.g., healthier eating) based on specific information concerning where, when, and how the goal will be achieved.

implicit personality theory: the tendency to believe (sometimes mistakenly) that someone who has a given personality trait will also have other, related traits.

inattentional blindness: the failure to perceive the appearance of an unexpected object in the visual environment.

inclusive fitness: the successful transmission of one's genes *directly* via reproduction and *indirectly* by helping genetically-related individuals.

incubation: the notion that problems can sometimes be solved by putting them aside for a while.

independent design: an experimental design in which each participant is included in only one group.

independent self: a type of **self-concept** in which the self is defined with respect to personal responsibility and achievement.

independent variable: some aspect of the experimental situation that the experimenter manipulates in order to test a given **experimental hypothesis**.

individualistic cultures: cultures (mainly in Western societies) in which the focus is on personal responsibility rather than group needs; see **collectivistic cultures**.

informational influence: one of the factors leading individuals to conform; it is based on the perceived superior knowledge or judgment of others.

ingroup bias: the tendency to view one's own group more favorably than other groups.

insight: the experience of suddenly realising how to solve a problem based on looking at it in a different way.

intelligence quotient (IQ): a measure of general intelligence; the average IQ is 100 and most people have IQs between 85 and 115.

interdependent self: a type of self-concept in which the self is defined with respect to one's relationships with others.

inter-observer reliability: the extent of agreement between two observers rating the behaviour of participants.

interposition: a depth cue in which a closer object partly hides another object further away.

interpretive bias: negatively biased or distorted interpretations of ambiguous stimuli and/or situations.

introspection: a careful examination and description of one's own conscious mental thoughts and states.

kin selection: helping genetically related relatives to enhance inclusive fitness.

law of Prägnanz: the notion that visual perception will tend to be organised as simply as possible.

law of reinforcement: the probability of a response being produced is increased if it is followed by reward but decreased if followed by punishment.

lexigrams: symbols used to represent words in studies on communication.

life events: these are major events (mostly have negative consequences) that create high levels of stress, often over a long period of time.

limbic system: a brain system consisting of the amygdala, the hippocampus, and septal areas, all of which are involved in emotional processing.

linear perspective: a strong impression of depth in a two-dimensional drawing created by lines converging on the horizon.

linguistic universals: features (e.g., preferred word orders; the distinction between nouns and verbs) found in the great majority of the world's languages.

longitudinal method: this is a method in which one group of participants is studied repeatedly over a relatively long period of time.

major depressive disorder: a common mental disorder characterised by depressed mood, tiredness, lack of interest and pleasure in activities, and feelings of worthlessness or excessive guilt.

matched participants design: an experimental design in which the participants in each of two groups are matched in terms of some relevant factor or factors (e.g., intelligence; sex).

maternal deprivation hypothesis: the notion that a breaking of the bond between child and mother during the first few years often has serious long-term effects.

means-ends analysis: an approach to problem solving based on reducing the difference between the current problem state and the solution.

means-ends relationship: the knowledge that behaving in a given way in a given situation will produce a certain outcome.

memory span: maximum number of digits or other items repeated back in the correct order immediately after they have been presented.

mental rotation: a task used to assess spatial ability, which involves imagining what would happen if the orientation of an object in space were altered.

mental set: a fixed or blinkered approach based on problem solutions that worked in the past that prevents people from thinking flexibly.

meta-analysis: an analysis in which the findings from many studies are combined statistically to obtain an overall picture.

method of loci: a memory technique in which to-be-remembered items are associated with locations well-known to the learner.

microgenetic method: an approach to studying children's changes in cognitive strategies by means of short-term longitudinal studies.

midbrain: the middle part of the brain; it is involved in vision, hearing, and the control of movement.

misdirection: a form of deception practised by magicians in which the audience's attention is focused on one object to distract its attention to another object.

mnemonics: these consist of numerous methods or systems used by learners to enhance their long-term memory for information.

monocular cues: cues to depth that only require the use of one eye.

monotropy hypothesis: Bowlby's notion that infants have an innate tendency to form special bonds with one person (generally the mother).

monozygotic twins: twins that are formed from the same fertilised ovum or egg that splits and leads to the development of two individuals sharing 100% of their genes; also known as identical twins.

moods: states resembling emotions, but generally longer lasting, less intense, and of unknown cause.

morality: A system of values that can be used to identify right and wrong ways of thinking and behaving.

morality of care: this is a form of morality in which the individual emphasises the importance of compassion and human well-being when deciding what is morally acceptable.

morality of justice: this is form of morality in which the individual emphasises the importance of laws and of moral principles when deciding what is morally acceptable.

moral self: an individual's self-perception of their moral values, internalisation of rules, guilt, empathy, and so on.

motion parallax: a depth cue provided by the movement of an object's image across the retina.

mutualistic collaboration: cooperation between two or more humans on a joint goal (e.g., survival) that is beneficial to all of them.

mutually responsive orientation: a mutually cooperative relationship between parent and child.

negative punishment: a form of operant conditioning in which the probability of a response being produced is reduced by following it with the removal of a positive reinforcer or reward.

negative reinforcers: unpleasant or aversive stimuli that serve to strengthen any responses that prevent these stimuli from being presented.

neuroticism: a personality **trait** reflecting individual differences in negative emotional experiences (e.g., anxiety; sadness).

non-declarative memory: a form of long-term memory that does not involve conscious recollection of information (e.g., motor skills)

noradrenaline: a hormone producing increased arousal within the sympathetic nervous system.

normative influence: one of the factors leading individuals to conform; it is based on people's desire to be liked and/or respected by others.

norms: standards or rules of behaviour that operate within a group or within society generally.

null hypothesis: prediction that the independent variable (manipulated by the experimenter) will have no effect on the dependent variable (some measure of behaviour).

object permanence: the belief that objects continue to exist even when they can't be seen.

observational learning: learning based on watching the behaviour of others and copying behaviour that is rewarded and not copying punished behaviour.

oculomotor cues: depth cues based on contractions of muscles around the eye.

operant conditioning: a form of learning in which an individual's responses are controlled by their consequences (reward or punishment).

opportunity sampling: selecting a **sample** of participants simply because they happen to be available.

other-race effect: the finding that recognition memory for same-race faces is more accurate than for other-race faces.

outgroup: a group to which the individual does not belong; such groups are often regarded negatively and with prejudice.

over-regularisation: this is a language error in which a grammatical rule is applied to situations in which it isn't relevant.

oxytocin: a hormone that promotes feelings of well-being by increasing sociability and reducing anxiety.

parasympathetic nervous system: the part of the **autonomic nervous system** that is involved in reducing arousal and conserving energy (e.g., by reducing heart rate).

peers: children of approximately the same age as a given child.

pegword method: a memory technique in which to-be-remembered items are associated with pegwords (words rhyming with numbers).

peripheral nervous system: it consists of all the nerve cells in the body not located within **the central nervous system**; it is divided into the **somatic nervous system** and the **autonomic nervous system.**

phobias: extreme fears of certain objects (e.g., snakes) or places (e.g., social situations) leading to avoidance of those objects or places.

phonological loop: a component of working memory in which speech-based information is processed and stored and subvocal articulation occurs.

phonology: the system of sounds within any given language.

population: a large collection of individuals from whom the **sample** used in a study is drawn.

positive punishment: a form of operant conditioning in which the probability of a response is reduced by following it with an unpleasant or aversive stimulus; sometimes known simply as punishment.

post-conventional morality: the third level of moral development in Kohlberg's theory; at this level, moral reasoning focuses on justice and the need for others to be treated in a respectful way.

posttraumatic stress disorder: a mental disorder triggered by a very distressing event and involving re-experiencing of the event, avoidance of stimuli associated with the event, and increased fear and arousal.

pragmatics: the rules involved in deciding how to make sure that what is said fits the situation.

pre-conventional morality: the first level of moral development in Kohlberg's theory; at this level, moral reasoning focuses on rewards and punishments for good and bad actions.

prejudice: attitudes and feelings (typically negative) about the members of some group solely on the basis of their membership of that group.

primacy effect: the finding that first impressions are more important than later ones in determining our opinion of others.

primary reinforcers: rewarding stimuli that are essential for survival (e.g., food; water).

priming: a form of non-declarative memory involving facilitated processing of (and response to) a target stimulus because the same or a related stimulus was presented previously.

privation: the state of a child who has never formed a close attachment with another person; see **deprivation.**

proactive aggression: forms of aggressive behaviour that are planned in advance to achieve some goal; this is cold-tempered aggression.

proactive interference: forgetting occurring when previous learning interferes with later learning and memory.

problem-focused coping: a general strategy for dealing with stressful situations in which attempts are made to act directly on the source of the stress.

productive language: this is language production that involves speaking or writing.

prosocial behaviour: behaviour that is positive (e.g., cooperative; affectionate) and that is designed to be of benefit to someone else.

psychoticism: a personality **trait** that reflects individual differences in hostility, coldness, and aggression.

quota sampling: selecting a **sample** from a **population** in such a way that those selected are similar to it in certain respects (e.g., proportion of females).

random sampling: selecting the individuals for a sample from a population using some random process.

randomisation: placing participants into groups on some random basis (e.g., coin tossing).

rationalisation: In Bartlett's theory, the tendency in story recall to produce errors conforming to the rememberer's expectations based on their schemas.

reactive aggression: this is aggressive behaviour that is triggered by the anger created by a perceived provocation; this is hot-tempered aggression.

reappraisal: an emotion-regulation strategy in which the emotional significance of an event is changed through additional cognitive processing.

recategorisation: merging the **ingroup** and **outgroup** to form a single large ingroup; it is designed to reduce **prejudice.**

receptive language: the comprehension or understanding of language (e.g., the speech of others).

reciprocal altruism: the nation that someone will show **altruism** in their behaviour towards someone else if they anticipate that person will respond altruistically.

recognition: a memory test in which previously presented information must be distinguished from information not previously presented.

recursion: turning simple sentences into longer and more complex ones by placing one or more additional clauses within them.

rehearsal: the verbal repetition of information (e.g., words), which typically increases our long-term memory for the rehearsed information.

reliability: the extent to which an intelligence (or other) test gives consistent findings on different occasions.

repeated measures design: an experimental design in which each participant appears in both groups.

replication: repeating the findings of a previous study using the same design and procedures.

representative sample: a **sample** of participants that is chosen to be typical or representative of the **population** from which it is drawn.

repression: a term used by Freud to refer to motivated forgetting of stressful or traumatic experiences.

resistant attachment: an insecure attachment of an infant to its mother combined with resistance of contact with her when she returns after an absence.

retroactive interference: forgetting occurring when later learning disrupts memory for earlier learning.

retrograde amnesia: forgetting by amnesic patients of information learned prior to the onset of amnesia.

reversibility: in Piaget's theory, the ability to undo mentally (reverse) some operation previously carried out (e.g., changing an object's shape).

safety behaviours: actions designed to reduce patients' level of anxiety and avoid catastrophes in social situations.

salient categorisation: the notion that someone needs to be regarded as typical or representative of a group if positive encounters with that individual are to lead to reduced prejudice towards the entire group.

sample: the participants actually used in a study drawn from some larger **population.**

saying-is-believing effect: inaccuracies in memory for an event caused by having previously described it to someone else to fit their biased perspective.

schemas: organised knowledge about the world, events, or people in long-term memory and used to guide action.

secondary reinforcers: stimuli that are rewarding because they have repeatedly been associated with **primary reinforcers;** examples are money are praise.

secure attachment: a strong and contented attachment of an infant to its mother, including when she returns after an absence.

selective placement: placing adopted children in homes resembling those of their biological parents in social and educational terms.

self-concept: the organised information about ourselves that we have stored away in long-term memory.

self-disclosure: revealing personal or private information about oneself to another person.

self-efficacy: according to Bandura, the beliefs about being able to perform some task so as to achieve certain goals.

self-esteem: the part of the **self-concept** concerned with the feelings (positive and negative) that an individual has about himself/herself.

self-regulation: according to Bandura, the notion that individuals learn to reward and punish themselves internally to regulate their own behaviour and achieve desired outcomes.

self-serving bias: the tendency to attribute your successes to your own efforts and ability, but to attribute your failures to task difficulty and bad luck; it is used to maintain self-esteem.

semantic dementia: a condition caused by brain damage in which the patient experiences considerable problems in accessing word meanings.

semantic memory: long-term memory for general knowledge about the world, concepts, language, and so on.

semantics: the meanings expressed by words and by sentences.

sex-typed behaviour: this is behaviour that conforms to that expected on the basis of any given culture's **sex-role stereotypes.**

shaping: a form of operant conditioning in which behaviour is changed slowly in the desired direction by requiring responses to become more and more like the wanted response in order for reward to be given.

situational attribution: deciding that someone's behaviour is due to the situation in which they find themselves rather than to their personality.

skill learning: a form of learning in which there is little or no conscious awareness of what has been learned.

social anxiety disorder: a disorder in which the individual has excessive fear of social situations and often avoids them; also known as social phobia.

social desirability bias: the tendency to provide socially desirable responses on personality questionnaires even when those responses are incorrect.

social identities: each of the groups with which we identify produces a social identity; our feelings about ourselves depend on how we feel about the groups with which we identify.

social influence: efforts by individuals or by groups to change the attitudes and/or behaviour of other people.

social norms: agreed standards of behaviour within a group (e.g., family; organisations).

social perception: the processes involved when one person perceives, evaluates, and forms an impression of someone else.

social phobia: a mental disorder in which the patient experiences very high levels of anxiety in social situations which often causes him/her to avoid such situations.

social power: the force that can be used by an individual to change the attitudes and/or behaviour of other people.

social roles: the parts we play as members of social groups based on certain expectations about the behaviour that is appropriate.

somatic nervous system: the part of the **peripheral nervous system** that controls the voluntary movements of skeletal muscles and hence the limbs.

somatosensation: several perceptual processes based on information received from the skin and body.

split-brain patients: individuals in whom the corpus callosum connecting the two halves of the brain has been severed; direct communication between the two hemispheres is not possible.

spontaneous recovery: the re-emergence of responses over time in **classical conditioning** after **extinction.**

standardised tests: tests that have been given to large representative samples, and on which an individual's ability (or personality) can be compared to that of other people.

stereopsis: a depth cue based on slight differences in the images on the retinas of the two eyes.

stereotype: an oversimplified generalisation (typically negative) concerning some group in society (e.g., the English; the Welsh).

story method: a technique for improving memory in which a story is generated that includes all of the to-be-remembered words or other items in the correct order.

sympathetic nervous system: the part of the **autonomic nervous system** that produces arousal and energy (e.g., via increased heart rate).

synaesthesia: the capacity to have an experience in one sense modality when a different modality is stimulated (e.g., a sound triggers visual imagery).

syntax: the grammatical rules that indicate the appropriate order of words within sentences.

technostress: the anxiety and stress caused by difficulties in coping with technological advances (especially in computing).

telegraphic period: the second stage of language development, during which children's speech is like a telegram in that much information is contained in two (or less often) three words.

telegraphic speech: children's early speech resembling a telegram in that much information is contained in two or (less often) three words.

template: as applied to chess, an abstract structure consisting of a mixture of fixed and variable information about chess pieces and positions.

testing effect: the finding that long-term memory is enhanced when some of the learning period is devoted to retrieving the to-be-remembered information

testosterone: a hormone present in much greater quantities in males than in females; it has been linked to aggressive and sexual behaviour.

texture gradient: a depth cue provided by the increased rate of change in texture density of a slanting object from the nearest part to the furthest part.

thalamus: a part of the forebrain involved in wakefulness and sleep.

theory of mind: the understanding by children and adults that other people may have different beliefs, emotions, and intentions than one's own.

third-party punishment: punishing someone else who has treated a third party unfairly even though it involves a personal sacrifice.

time-out technique: a form of negative punishment in which undesirable behaviour (e.g., aggression) is reduced by removing the individual from the situation in which he/she has been aggressive.

token economy: a form of therapy based on operant conditioning in which tokens are given to patients when they produce desirable behaviour; these tokens can then be exchanged for rewards

traits: aspects or dimensions of personality that exhibit individual differences and are moderately stable over time; they have direct and indirect influences on behaviour.

transfer-appropriate processing: the notion that long-term memory will be greatest when processing at the time of retrieval is very similar to processing at the time of learning.

Type A personality: a personality type characterised by impatience, competitiveness, time pressure, and hostility.

Type B personality: a personality type characterised by an easy-going approach to life and lacking the characteristics associated with Type A personality.

Type D personality: a type of personality that is characterised by high negative affectivity and social inhibition.

unconditioned reflex: a well-established association between an **unconditioned stimulus** and an **unconditioned response**.

unconditioned response: a well-established reaction (e.g., salivation) to a given **unconditioned stimulus** (e.g., food) in an **unconditioned reflex**.

unconditioned stimulus: a stimulus that produces a well-established **unconditioned response** in an **unconditioned reflex**.

validity: the extent to which an intelligence (or other) test measures what it is claimed to be measuring.

viewpoint-dependent perception: the notion that objects can be recognised more easily from some viewpoints or angles than from others.

viewpoint-invariant perception: the notion that it is equally easy to recognise objects from numerous different viewpoints.

visual illusions: drawings or other visual stimuli that are misperceived by nearly everyone.

visuo-spatial sketchpad: a component of working memory used to process visual and spatial information and to store this information briefly.

visual perception: the processing of visual information to see objects in the world.

von Restorff effect: the finding that a to-be-remembered item that is distinctively different from other list items is especially likely to be remembered.

weapon focus: the finding that eyewitnesses attend so much to the culprit's weapon that they ignore other details and have impaired memory for them.

weapons effect: an increase in aggressive behaviour produced by the sight of a weapon (e.g., gun).

well-defined problems: problems in which the initial state, the goal, and the methods available for solving them are clearly laid out.

working memory: a system that has separate components for rehearsal and for other processing activities (e.g., attention; visual processing).

zone of proximal development: in Vygotsky's theory, the gap between a child's current or actual problem-solving ability and his/her potential when provided with suitable guidance.

References

Abrams, D., Wetherall, M., Cochrane, S., Hogg, M.A., & Turner, J.C. (1990). Knowing what to think by knowing who you are: Self-categorization and the nature of norm formation, conformity and group polarization. *British Journal of Social Psychology*, 29, 97–119.

Adams, C.H., & Sherer, M. (1985). Sex-role orientation and psychological adjustment: Implications for the masculinity model. *Sex Roles*, 12, 1211–1218.

Adey, P.S. (1993). Accelerating the development of formal thinking in middle and high school students IV: Three years on after a two-year intervention. *Journal of Research in Science Teaching*, 30, 351–366.

Adorno, T.W., Frenkel-Brunswik, E., Levinson, D., & Sanford, R. (1950). *The authoritarian personality*. New York: Harper.

Adriaanse, M.A., Gollwitzer, P.M., De Ridder, D.T.D., de Wit, J.B.F., & Kroese, F.M. (2011a). Breaking habits with implementation intentions: A test of underlying processes. *Personality and Social Psychology Bulletin*, 37, 502–513.

Adriaanse, M.A., Kroese, F.M., Gillebaart, M., & De Ridder, D.T.D. (2014). Effortless inhibition: Habit mediates the relation between self-control and unhealthy snack consumption. *Frontiers in Psychology*, 5 (Article 444).

Adriaanse, M.A., Vinkers, C.D.W., De Ridder, D.T.D., Hox, J.J., & De Wit, J.B.F. (2011b). Do implementation intentions help to eat a healthy diet? A systematic review and meta-analysis of the empirical evidence. *Appetite*, 56, 183–193.

Aebli, H., Montada, L., & Schneider, U. (1968). *Über den Egozentrismus des Kindes. (Beyond Children's Egocentrism)*. Stuttgart: Ernst Klett Verlag.

Ainsworth, M.D.S., & Bell, S.M. (1970). Attachment, exploration and separation: Illustrated by the behavior of one-year-olds in a strange situation. *Child Development*, 41, 49–67.

Ainsworth, M.D.S., Blehat, M.C., Waters, E., & Wall, S. (1978). *Patterns of attachment: A psychological study of the strange situation*. Hillsdale, NJ: Lawrence Erlbaum Associates, Inc.

Aldao, A., Nolen-Hoeksema, S., & Schweizer, S. (2010). Emotion-regulation strategies across psychopathology: A meta-analytic review. *Clinical Psychology Review*, 30, 217–237.

Ali, S.S., Lifshitz, M., & Rae, A. (2014). Empirical neuroenchantment: From reading minds to thinking critically. *Frontiers in Human Neuroscience*, 8 (Article 257).

Allport, F.H. (1924). *Social psychology*. Boston: Houghton Mifflin.

Allport, G.W. (1954). *The nature of prejudice*. Reading, MA: Addison-Wesley.

Allport, G.W., & Odbert, H.S. (1936). Trait-names: A psycho-lexical study. *Psychological Monographs*, 47, 211.

Alnabulsi, H., & Drury, J. (2014). Social identification moderates the effect of crowd density on safety at the Hajj. *Proceedings of the National Academy of Sciences USA*, 111, 9091–9096.

Ambady, N., & Rosenthal, R. (1996). Experimenter effects. In A.S.R. Manstead & M. Hewstone (Eds.), *Blackwell encyclopedia of social psychology*. Oxford: Blackwell.

American Psychiatric Association: Diagnostic and Statistical Manual of Mental Disorders, Fifth Edition (2013). Arlington, VA: American Psychiatric Association.

Amodio, D.M. (2014). The neuroscience of prejudice and stereotyping. *Nature Reviews Neuroscience*, 15, 670–682.

Anderson, C.A., Benjamin, A.J., & Bartholow, B.D. (1998). Does the gun pull the trigger? Automatic priming effects of weapon pictures and weapon names. *Psychological Science*, 9, 308–314.

Anderson, C.A., & Bushman, B.J. (2002). Human aggression. *Annual Review of Psychology*, 53, 27–51.

Anderson, C.A., Ihori, N., Bushman, B.J., Rothstein, H.R., Shibuya, A., Swing, E.L. et al. (2010). Violent video game effects on aggression, empathy, and prosocial behavior in Eastern and Western countries: A meta-analytic review. *Psychological Bulletin*, 136, 151–173.

Anderson, J.L., Crawford, C.B., Nadeau, J., & Lindberg, T. (1992). Was the Duchess of Windsor right? A cross-cultural review of the socioecology of ideals of female body shape. *Ethology and Sociobiology*, 13, 197–227.

Andlin-Sobocki, P., Olesen, J., Wittchen, H.-U., & Jonsson, B. (2005). Cost of disorders of the brain in Europe. *European Journal of Neurology*, 12, 1–27.

Andlin-Sobocki, P., & Wittchen, H.-U. (2005). Cost of affective disorders in Europe. *European Journal of Neurology, 12*, 34–38.

Ang, S.C., Rodgers, J.L., & Wänström, L. (2010). The Flynn effect within subgroups in the US: Gender, race, income, education, and urbanization differences in the NLSY-children data. *Intelligence, 38*, 367–384.

Apperly, I.A., & Butterfill, S.A. (2009). Do humans have two systems to track beliefs and belief-like states? *Psychological Review, 116*, 953–970.

Archer, J., & Coyne, S.M. (2005). An integrated review of indirect, relational, and social aggression. *Personality and Social Psychology Review, 9*, 212–230.

Arnett, J. (2008). The neglected 95%: Why American psychology needs to become less American. *American Psychologist, 63*, 602–614.

Asch, S.E. (1946). Forming impressions of personality. *Journal of Abnormal and Social Psychology, 41*, 258–290.

Asch, S.E. (1951). Effects of group pressure on the modification and distortion of judgments. In H. Guetzkow (Ed.), *Groups, leadership and men* (pp. 177–190). Pittsburgh, PA: Carnegie.

Asch, S.E. (1956). Studies of independence and conformity: A minority of one against a unanimous majority. *Psychological Monographs, 70* (Whole No. 416), 1–70.

Atkins, J.E., Fiser, J., & Jacobs, R.A. (2001). Experience-dependent visual cue integration based on consistencies between visual and haptic percepts. *Vision Research, 41*, 449–461.

Atkinson, R.C., & Shiffrin, R.M. (1968). Human memory: A proposed system and its control processes. In K.W. Spence & J.T. Spence (Eds.), *The psychology of learning and motivation* (Vol. 2, pp. 89–105). London: Academic Press.

Atkinson, R.L., Atkinson, R.C., Smith, E.E., & Bem, D.J. (1993). *Introduction to psychology* (11th ed.). New York: Harcourt Brace College Publishers.

Baas, M., De Dreu, C.K.W., Carsten, K.W., & Nijstad, B.A. (2008). A meta-analysis of 25 years of mood-creativity research: Hedonic tone, activation, or regulatory focus? *Psychological Bulletin, 134*, 779–806.

Bachen, E., Cohen, S., & Marsland, A.L. (1997). Psychoimmunology. In A. Baum, S. Newman, J. Weinman, R. West, & C. McManus (Eds.), *Cambridge handbook of psychology, health, and medicine* (pp. 167–172). Cambridge, UK: Cambridge University Press.

Baddeley, A.D. (2007). *Working memory, thought, and action*. Oxford: Oxford University Press.

Baddeley, A.D. (2012). Working memory: Theories, models, and controversies. *Annual Review of Psychology, 63*, 1–29.

Baddeley, A.D., Eysenck, M.W., & Anderson, M.C. (2015). *Memory* (2nd ed.). Hove: Psychology Press.

Baddeley, A.D., & Hitch, G.J. (1974). Working memory. In G.H. Bower (Ed.), *Recent advances in learning and motivation* (Vol. 8, pp. 47–89). New York: Academic Press.

Bakker, A.B., Van der Zee, K.I., Lewig, K.A., & Dollard, M.F. (2006). The relationship between the Big Five personality factors and burnout: A study among volunteer counsellors. *Journal of Social Psychology, 146*, 31–50.

Balcetis, E., & Dunning, D. (2013). Considering the situation: Why people are better social psychologists than self-psychologists. *Self and Identity, 12*, 1–15.

Bandura, A. (1965). Influences of models' reinforcement contingencies on the acquisition of imitative responses. *Journal of Personality and Social Psychology, 1*, 589–593.

Bandura, A. (1977). *Social learning theory*. Englewood Cliffs, NJ: Prentice Hall.

Bandura, A. (1986). *Social foundations of thought and action: A social cognitive theory*. Englewood Cliffs, NJ: Prentice Hall.

Bandura, A., Ross, D., & Ross, S.A. (1963). Transmission of aggression through imitation of aggressive models. *Journal of Abnormal and Social Psychology, 66*, 3–11.

Banfield, J.C., & Dovidio, J.F. (2013). Whites' perceptions of discrimination against Blacks: The influence of common identity. *Journal of Experimental Social Psychology, 49*, 833–841.

Bannard, C., Klinger, J., & Tomasello, M. (2013). How selective are 3-year-olds in imitating novel linguistic material? *Developmental Psychology, 49*, 2344–2356.

Bannard, C., Lieven, E., & Tomasello, M. (2009). Modeling children's early grammatical knowledge. *Proceedings of the National Academy of Sciences of the United States of America, 106*, 17284–17289.

Baptista, M. (2012). On universal grammar, the bioprogram hypothesis and creole genesis. *Journal of Pidgin and Creole Languages, 27*, 351–376.

Barense, M.D., Ngo, L.H.T., & Peterson, M.A. (2012). Interactions of memory and perception in amnesia: The figure-ground perspective. *Cerebral Cortex, 22*, 2680–2691.

Barlow, F.K., Louis, W.R., & Terry, D.J. (2010). Minority report: Social identity, cognitions of rejection and intergroup anxiety predicting prejudice from one racially marginalised group towards another. *European Journal of Social Psychology, 40*, 805–818.

Baron, R. (2005). So right it's wrong: Groupthink and the ubiquitous nature of polarised group decision making. *Advances in Experimental Social Psychology, 37*, 219–253.

Bar-On, R. (1997). *The emotional intelligence inventory (EQ-i): Technical manual*. Toronto: Multi-Health Systems.

Bar-On, R. (2006). The Bar-On model of emotional-social intelligence (ESI). *Psicothema, 18*, 13–25.

Baronchelli, A., Chater, N., Pastor-Satorras, R., & Christiansen, M.H. (2012). The biological origin of linguistic diversity. *PLoS ONE, 7*(10), e48029.

Baron-Cohen, S., Leslie, A.M., & Frith, U. (1985). Does the autistic child have a "theory of mind"? *Cognition, 21*, 37–46.

Barrett, P.T., & Kline, P. (1982). An item and radial parcel analysis of the 16PF Questionnaire. *Personality and Individual Differences, 3*, 259–270.

Bartlett, F.C. (1932). *Remembering*. Cambridge: Cambridge University Press.

Bassoff, E.S., & Glass, G.V. (1982). The relationship between sex roles and mental health: A meta-analysis of twenty-six studies. *Counseling Psychologist, 10*, 105–112.

Bateson, M., Nettle, D., & Roberts, G. (2006). Cues of being watched enhance cooperation in a real-world setting. *Biological Letters, 2*, 412–414.

Batey, M., Chamorro-Premuzic, T., & Furnham, A. (2010). Individual differences in ideational behavior: Can the Big Five and psychometric intelligence predict creativity scores? *Creativity Research Journal, 22*, 90–97.

Batson, C.D., Cochrane, P.J., Biederman, M.F., Blosser, J.L., Ryan, M.J., & Vogt, B. (1978). Failure to help when in a hurry: Callousness or conflict? *Personality and Social Psychology Bulletin, 4*, 97–101.

Baumeister, R.F. (1998). The self. In D.T. Gilbert, S.T. Fiske, & G. Lindzey (Eds.), *The handbook of social psychology* (Vol. 1, 4th ed., pp. 680–740). New York: McGraw-Hill.

Baumeister, R.F. (2011). Self and identity: A brief overview of what they are, what they do, and how they work. *Annals of the New York Academy of Sciences, 1234*, 48–55.

Bäuml, K.-H., & Kliegl, O. (2013). The critical role of retrieval processes in release from proactive interference. *Journal of Memory and Language, 68*, 39–53.

Baxter, A.J., Scott, K.M., Ferrari, A.J., Norman, R.E., Vos, T., & Whiteford, H.A. (2014). Challenging the myth of an "epidemic" of common mental disorders: Trends in the global prevalence of anxiety and depression between 1990 and 2010. *Depression and Anxiety, 31*, 506–516.

Baynes, K., & Gazzaniga, M. (2000). Consciousness, introspection, and the split-brain: The two minds/one body problem. In M.S. Gazzaniga (Ed.), *The new cognitive neurosciences*. Oxford: Oxford University Press.

Beaman, A.L., Barnes, P.J., Klentz, B., & McQuirk, B. (1978). Increasing helping rates through information dissemination: Teaching pays. *Personality and Social Psychology Bulletin, 4*, 406–411.

Beck, A.T., & Dozois, D.J.A. (2011). Cognitive therapy: Current status and future directions. *Annual Reviews of Medicine, 62*, 397–409.

Becker, M., Vignoles, V.L., Owe, E., Easterbrook, M.J., Brown, R., Smith, P.B. et al. (2014). Cultural bases for self-evaluation: Seeing oneself positively in different cultural contexts. *Personality and Social Psychology Bulletin, 40*, 657–675.

Becofsky, K.M., Shook, R.P., Sui, X.M., Wilcox, S., Lavie, C.J., & Blair, S.N. (2015). Influence of the source of social support and size of social network on all-cause mortality. *Mayo Clinic Proceedings, 90*, 895–902.

Bègue, L., Bushman, B.J., Giancola, P.R., Subra, B., & Rosset, E. (2010). "There is no such thing as an accident", especially when people are drunk. *Personality and Social Psychology Bulletin, 36*, 1301–1304.

Bem, S.L. (1985). Androgyny and gender schema theory: A conceptual and empirical integration. In T.B. Snodegegger (Ed.), *Nebraska symposium on motivation: Psychology and gender* (pp. 179–226). Lincoln, NE: University of Nebraska Press.

Benigno, J.P., Byrd, D.L., McNamara, P.H., Berg, W.G., & Farrar, M.J. (2011). Talking through transitions: Microgenetic changes in preschoolers' private speech and executive functioning. *Child Language Teaching and Therapy, 27*, 269–285.

Berenbaum, S.A., & Beltz, A.M. (2011). Sexual differentiation of human behaviour: Effects of prenatal and pubertal organisational hormones. *Frontiers in Neuroendocrinology, 32*, 183–200.

Berger, A., & Krahé, B. (2013). Negative attributes are gendered too: Conceptualising and measuring positive and negative facets of sex-role identity. *European Journal of Social Psychology, 43*, 516–531.

Berger, S.E., Chin, B., Basra, S., & Kim, H. (2015). Step by step: A microgenetic study of the development of strategy choice in infancy. *British Journal of Developmental Psychology, 33*, 106–122.

Berk, L.E. (2013). *Child development* (9th ed.). New York: Pearson.

Berko, J. (1958). The child's learning of English morphology. *Word, 14*, 150–177.

Berkowitz, L. (1968). Impulse, aggression and the gun. *Psychology Today*, September, 18–22.

Berkowitz, L., & LePage, A. (1967). Weapons as aggression-eliciting stimuli. *Journal of Personality and Social Psychology*, 7, 202–207.

Berndt, T.J. (1979). Developmental changes in conformity to peers and parents. *Developmental Psychology*, 53, 1447–1460.

Berwick, R.C., Friederici, A.D., Chomsky, N., & Bolhuis, J.J. (2013). Evolution, brain, and the nature of language. *Trends in Cognitive Sciences*, 17, 89–98.

Bettencourt, B.A., & Miller, N. (1996). Gender differences in aggression as a function of provocation: A meta-analysis. *Psychological Bulletin*, 119, 422–447.

Beyerstein, B.L. (1999). Whence cometh the myth that we only use 10% of our brains? In S. Della Sala (Ed.), *Mind myths: Exploring popular assumptions about the mind and brain* (pp. 3–24). Chichester: Wiley.

Bhatt, R.S., & Quinn, P.C. (2011). How does learning impact development in infancy? The case of perceptual organisation. *Infancy*, 16, 2–38.

Bickerton, D. (1984). The language bioprogram hypo. *Behavioral and Brain Sciences*, 7, 173–221.

Biederman, I. (1987). Recognition-by-components: A theory of human image understanding. *Psychological Review*, 94, 115–147.

Bjornsson, A.S. (2011). Beyond the "psychological placebo": Specifying the nonspecific in psychotherapy. *Clinical Psychology: Science and Practice*, 18, 113–118.

Blandin, Y., & Proteau, L. (2000). On the cognitive basis of observational learning: Development of mechanisms for the detection and correction of errors. *Quarterly Journal of Experimental Psychology*, 53A, 846–867.

Bluck, S., & Alea, N. (2009). Thinking and talking about the past: Why remember? *Applied Cognitive Psychology*, 23, 1089–1104.

Boardman, J.D., Alexander, K.B., & Stallings, M.C. (2011). Stressful life events and depression among adolescent twin pairs. *Biodemography and Social Biology*, 57, 53–66.

Bohannon, J.N., & Warren-Leubecker, A. (1989). Theoretical approaches to language acquisition. In J. Berko-Gleason (Ed.), *The development of language* (2nd ed., pp. 167–225). Columbus, OH: Merrill.

Bohle, P., Quinlan, M., McNamara, M., Pitts, C., & Willaby, H. (2015). Health and well-being of older workers: Comparing their associations with effort-reward imbalance and pressure, disorganisation and regulatory failure. *Work & Stress*, 29, 114–127.

Bollich, K.L., Rogers, K.H., & Vazire, S. (2015). Knowing more than we can tell: People are aware of their biased self-perceptions. *Personality and Social Psychology Bulletin*, 41, 918–929.

Bond, M.H., & Smith, P.B. (1996a). Cross-cultural social and organizational psychology. *Annual Review of Psychology*, 47, 205–235.

Bond, R. (2005). Group size and conformity. *Group Processes and Intergroup Roles*, 6, 331–354.

Bond, R., & Smith, P.B. (1996b). Culture and conformity: A meta-analysis of studies using Asch's (1952b, 1956) line judgment task. *Psychological Bulletin*, 119, 111–137.

Bonta, B.D. (1997). Cooperation and competition in peaceful societies. *Psychological Bulletin*, 121, 299–320.

Booth, R.W., Sharma, D., & Leader, T.I. (2016). The age of anxiety? It depends where you look: Changes in STAI trait anxiety, 1970–2010. *Social Psychiatry and Psychiatric Epidemiology*, 51, 193–202.

Bordone, V., Scherbov, S., & Steiber, N. (2015). Smarter every day: The deceleration of population ageing in terms of cognition. *Intelligence*, 52, 90–96.

Boring, E.G. (1950). *A history of experimental psychology* (2nd ed.). Englewood Cliffs, NJ: Prentice-Hall.

Bouchard, T.J., Lykken, D.T., McGue, M., Segal, N.L., & Tellegen, A. (1990). Sources of human psychological differences: The Minnesota study of twins reared apart. *Science*, 250, 223–228.

Bowden, E.M., Jung-Beeman, M., Fleck, J., & Kounios, J. (2005). New approaches to demystifying insight. *Trends in Cognitive Sciences*, 9, 322–328.

Bower, G.H., Black, J.B., & Turner, T.J. (1979). Scripts in memory for text. *Cognitive Psychology*, 11, 177–220.

Bower, G.H., & Clark, M.C. (1969). Narrative stories as mediators for serial learning. *Psychonomic Science*, 14, 181–182.

Bowlby, J. (1951). *Maternal care and mental health*. Geneva: World Health Organisation.

Bowlby, J. (1969). *Attachment and love: Vol. 1: Attachment*. London: Hogarth.

Bowlby, J. (1988). *A secure base: Clinical applications of attachment theory*. London: Routledge.

Boxer, P., Groves, C.L., & Docherty, M. (2015). Video games do indeed influence children and adolescents' aggression, prosocial behaviour, and academic performance: A clearer reading of Ferguson. *Perspectives on Psychological Science*, 10, 671–673.

Brackett, M.A., Mayer, J.D., & Warner, R.M. (2004). Emotional intelligence and its relationship to everyday behavior. *Personality and Individual Differences*, 36, 1387–1402.

Bradbard, M.R., Martin, C.L., Endsley, R.C., & Halverson, C.F. (1986). Influence of sex stereotypes on children's exploration and memory: A competence versus performance distinction. *Developmental Psychology, 22*, 481–486.

Bradmetz, J. (1999). Precursors of formal thought: A longitudinal study. *British Journal of Developmental Psychology, 17*, 61–81.

Brannon, T.N., Markus, H.R., & Taylor, V.J. (2015). "Two souls, two thoughts", two self-schemas: Double consciousness can have positive academic consequences for African Americans. *Journal of Personality and Social Psychology, 108*, 586–609.

Bransford, J.D., & Johnson, M.K. (1972). Contextual prerequisites for understanding. *Journal of Verbal Learning and Verbal Behavior, 11*, 717–726.

Brehm, S.S., Kassin, S.M., & Fein, S. (1999). *Social psychology* (4th ed.). New York: Houghton Mifflin.

Breland, K., & Breland, M. (1961). The misbehaviour of organisms. *American Psychologist, 16*, 681–684.

Breslow, L., & Enstrom, J.E. (1980). Persistence of health habits and their relationship to mortality. *Preventive Medicine, 9*, 469–483.

British Psychological Society (2014). Code of ethics. www.bps.org.uk/sites/default/files/documents/code_of_ethics_and conduct.pdf.

Brody, G.H., & Shaffer, D.R. (1982). Contributions of parents and peers to children's moral socialization. *Developmental Review, 2*, 31–75.

Brody, L.R., & Hall, J.A. (2008). Gender and emotion in context. In M. Lewis, J.M. Haviland-Jones, & L. Feldman Barrett (Eds.), *Handbook of emotion* (3rd ed., pp. 395–408). New York: Guilford Press.

Brown, A.S., Bracken, E., Zoccoli, S., & Douglas, K. (2004). Generating and remembering passwords. *Applied Cognitive Psychology, 18*, 641–651.

Brown, G.W., & Harris, T.O. (1978). *Social origins of depression: A study of psychiatric disorder in women*. London: Tavistock.

Brownell, C.A., Iesue, S.S., Nichols, S.R., & Svetlova, M. (2013). Mine or yours? Development of sharing in toddlers in relation to ownership understanding. *Child Development, 84*, 906–920.

Bruno, N., Bernadis, P., & Gentilucci, M. (2008). Visually guided pointing, the Müller-Lyer illusion, and the functional interpretation of the dorsal-ventral split: Conclusions from 33 independent studies. *Neuroscience and Biobehavioral Reviews, 32*, 423–437.

Bryan, A.D., Webster, G.D., & Mahaffey, A.L. (2011). The big, the rich, and the powerful: Physical, financial, and social dimensions of dominance in mating and attraction. *Personality and Social Psychology Bulletin, 37*, 365–382.

Burger, J.M. (2011). Alive and well after all these years. *Psychologist, 24*, 654–657.

Burgess, R.L., & Wallin, P. (1953). Marital happiness of parents and their children's attitudes to them. *American Sociological Review, 18*, 424–431.

Burleson, B.R., & Kunkel, A. (2002). Parental and peer contributions to the emotional support skills of the child: From whom do children learn to express support? *Journal of Family Communication, 2*, 81–97.

Burns, B.D. (2004). The effects of speed on skilled chess performance. *Psychological Science, 15*, 442–447.

Bursztein, E., Bethard, S., Fabry, C., Mitvchel, J.C., & Jurafsky, D. (2010). How good at humans at solving CAPTCHAs? A large scale evaluation. *2010 Symposium on Security and Privacy*, 399–413.

Burt, C. (1915). The general and specific factors underlying the primary emotions. *Report to the British Association for the Advancement of Science, 69*, 45.

Burt, C. (1940). *Factors of the mind: An introduction to factor-analysis in psychology*. London: University of London Press.

Bushman, B.J., Baumeister, R.F., Thomaes, S., Ryu, E., Begeer, S., & West, S.G. (2009). Looking again, and harder, for a link between low self-esteem and aggression. *Journal of Personality, 77*, 427–446.

Buss, D.M. (1989). Sex differences in human mate preferences: Evolutionary hypotheses tested in 37 cultures. *Behavioral & Brain Sciences, 12*, 1–49.

Buss, D.M. (1995). Evolutionary psychology: A new paradigm for psychological science. *Psychological Inquiry, 6*, 1–30.

Buss, D.M. (2013). The science of human mating strategies: An historical perspective. *Psychological Inquiry, 24*, 171–177.

Bussey, K., & Bandura, A. (1999). Social cognitive theory of gender development and differentiation. *Psychological Review, 106*, 676–713.

Byrne, D. (1971). *The attraction paradigm*. New York: Academic Press.

Campbell, D.T. (1960). Blind variation and selective retention in creative thought as in other knowledge processes. *Psychological Review, 67*, 380–400.

Campbell, J.D., Krueger, J.I., & Vohs, K.D. (2005). Exploding the self-esteem myth. *Scientific American, 292*, 84–91.

Campbell, J.D., Schermer, J.A., Villani, V.C., Nguyen, B., Vickers, & Vernon, P.A. (2009). A behavioural genetic study of the dark triad of personality and moral development. *Twin Research and Human Genetics, 12*, 132–136.

Campitelli, G., & Gobet, F. (2011). Deliberate practice: Necessary but not sufficient. *Current Directions in Psychological Science, 20*, 280–285.

Capron, C., & Duyme, M. (1989). Assessment of effects of socio-economic status on IQ in a full cross-fostering study. *Nature, 340,* 552–554.

Card, N., & Little, T.D. (2006). Proactive and reactive aggression in childhood and adolescence: A meta-analysis of differential relations with psychosocial adjustment. *International Journal of Behavioral Development, 30,* 466–480.

Cardoso, C., Ellenbogen, M.A., Serravalle, L., & Linnen, A.-M. (2013). Stress-induced negative mood moderates the relation between oxytocin administration and trust: Evidence for the tend-and-befriend response to stress? *Psychoneuroendocrinology, 38,* 2800–2804.

Carpendale, J.I.M., Kettner, V.A., & Auder, K.N. (2015). On the nature of toddlers' helping: Helping or interest in others' activity? *Social Development, 24,* 357–366.

Carré, J.M., & Olmstead, N.A. (2015). Social neuroendocrinology of human aggression: Examining the role of competition-induced testosterone dynamics. *Neuroscience, 288,* 171–186.

Carroll, J.B. (1993). *Human cognitive abilities: A survey of factor analytic studies.* New York: Cambridge University Press.

Carver, C.S., & Connor-Smith, J. (2010). Personality and coping. *Annual Review of Psychology, 61,* 679–704.

Cattell, R.B. (1943). The description of personality: Basic traits resolved into clusters. *Journal of Abnormal and Social Psychology, 38,* 476–506.

Cattell, R.B. (1957). *Personality and motivation structure and measurement.* New York: World Book Company.

Cavaco, S., Anderson, S.W., Allen, J.S., Castro-Caldas, A., & Damasio, H. (2004). The scope of procedural memory in amnesia. *Brain, 127,* 1853–1867.

Challis, B.H., Velichkovsky, B.M., & Craik, F.I.M. (1996). Levels-of-processing effects on a variety of memory tasks: New findings and theoretical implications. *Consciousness and Cognition, 5,* 142–164.

Chen, Z., & Cowan, N. (2009). Core verbal working memory capacity: The limit in words retained without covert articulation. *Quarterly Journal of Experimental Psychology, 62,* 1420–1429.

Cheng, C. (2005). Processes underlying gender-role flexibility: Do androgynous individuals know more or know how to cope? *Journal of Personality, 73,* 645–674.

Cheng, C., Lau, H.-P.B., & Chan, M.-P.S. (2014). Coping flexibility and psychological adjustment to stressful life changes: A meta-analytic review. *Psychological Bulletin, 140,* 1582–1607.

Chertkoff, J.M., & Kushigian, R.H. (1999). *Don't panic: The psychology of emergency egress and ingress.* Westport, CT: Praeger.

Child, I.L. (1968). Personality in culture. In E.F. Borgatta & W.W. Lambert (Eds.), *Handbook of personality theory and research* (pp. 79–118). Chicago: Rand McNally.

Chomsky, N. (1957). *Knowledge of language: Its nature, origin, and use.* New York: Praeger.

Chomsky, N. (1965). *Aspects of the theory of syntax.* Cambridge, MA: MIT Press.

Chomsky, N. (1986). *Knowledge of language: Its nature, origin, and use.* New York: Praeger.

Choy, Y., Fyer, A.J., & Lipsitz, J.D. (2007). Treatment of specific phobia in adults. *Clinical Psychology Review, 27,* 266–286.

Christensen, W., & Michael, J. (2016). From two systems to a multi-systems architecture for mindreading. *New Ideas in Psychology, 40,* 48–64.

Christiansen, M.H., & Chater, N. (2015). The language faculty that wasn't: A usage-based account of natural language recursion. *Frontiers in Psychology, 6* (Article 1182), 1–18.

Cinnirella, M. (1998). Manipulating stereotype ratings tasks: Understanding questionnaire context effects on measures of attitudes, social identity and stereotypes. *Journal of Community and Applied Social Psychology, 8,* 345–362.

Cirillo, P., & Taleb, N.N. (2015). On the statistical properties and tail risk of violent conflicts. *Tail Risk Working Papers.* Cambridge, MA: National Bureau of Economic Research.

Clark, D.M., Ehlers, A., Hackmann, A., McManus, F., Fennell, M., Grey, N., Waddington, L., & Wild, J. (2006). Cognitive therapy versus exposure and applied relaxation in social phobia: A randomised controlled trial. *Journal of Consulting and Clinical Psychology, 74,* 568–578.

Clark, D.M., & Wells, A. (1995). A cognitive model of social phobia. In R.R.G. Heimberg, M. Liebowitz, D.A. Hope, & S. Scheier (Eds.), *Social phobia: Diagnosis, assessment and treatment* (pp. 69–93). New York: Guilford.

Cohen, A.B. (2015). Religion's profound influences on psychology: Morality, intergroup relations, self-construal, and enculturation. *Current Perspectives in Psychological Science, 24,* 77–82.

Cohen, S., & Williamson, G.M. (1991). Stress and infectious disease in humans. *Psychological Bulletin, 109,* 5–24.

Cohen-Kettenis, P.T., & van Goozen, S.H.M. (1997). Sex reassignment of adolescent transsexuals: A follow-up study. *Journal of American Child Adolescent Psychiatry, 36,* 263–271.

Colby, A., Kohlberg, L., Gibbs, J., & Lieberman, M. (1983). A longitudinal study of moral judgment. *Monographs of the Society for Research in Child Development*, 48(1–2, Serial No. 200), 1–124.

Collins, N.L., & Miller, L.C. (1994). Self-disclosure and liking: A meta-analytic review. *Psychological Bulletin*, 116, 457–475.

Colman, A.M. (2009). *A dictionary of psychology*. Oxford: Oxford University Press.

Colvin, C.R., Block, J., & Funder, D.C. (1995). Overly positive self-evaluations and personality: Negative implications for mental health. *Journal of Personality and Social Psychology*, 68, 1152–1162.

Colvin, M.K., & Gazzaniga, M.S. (2007). Split-brain cases. In M. Velmans & S, Schneider (Eds.), *The Blackwell companion to consciousness*. Oxford: Blackwell.

Comstock, G., & Paik, H. (1991). *Television and the American child*. San Diego: Academic Press.

Confer, J.C., Easton, J.A., Fleischman, D.S., Goetz, C.D., Lewis, D.M.G., Perilloux, C., & Buss, D.M. (2010). Evolutionary psychology: Controversies, questions, prospects, and limitations. *American Psychologist*, 65, 110–126.

Conway, M.A., & Pleydell-Pearce, C.W. (2000). The construction of autobiographical memories in the self-memory system. *Psychological Review*, 107, 262–288.

Cooley, C.H. (1902). *Human nature and the social order*. New York: Scribner.

Corkin, S. (1984). Lasting consequences of bilateral medial temporal lobectomy: Clinical course and experimental findings in HM. *Seminars in Neurology*, 4, 249–259.

Corr, P.J. (2010). The psychoticism-psychopathy continuum: A neuropsychological model of core deficits. *Personality and Individual Differences*, 48, 695–703.

Costa, P.T., & McCrae, R.R. (1992). *Revised NEO Personality Inventory (NEO-PI-R) and NEO Five Factor Inventory (NEO-FFI) professional manual*. Odessa, FL: Psychological Assessment Resources.

Coyne, S.M. (2016). Effects of viewing relational aggression on television on aggressive behaviour in adolescents: A three-year longitudinal study. *Developmental Psychology*, 52, 284–295.

Coyne, S.M., Archer, J., & Eslen, M. (2004). Cruel intentions on television and in real life: Can viewing indirect aggression increase viewers' subsequent indirect aggression? *Journal of Experimental Child Psychology*, 88, 234–253.

Craig, M.A., & Richeson, J.A. (2014). More diverse yet less tolerant? How the increasingly diverse racial landscape affects white Americans' racial attitudes. *Personality and Social Psychology Bulletin*, 40, 750–761.

Craik, F.I.M., & Lockhart, R.S. (1972). Levels of processing: A framework for memory research. *Journal of Verbal Learning and Verbal Behavior*, 11, 671–684.

Craik, F.I.M., & Tulving, E. (1975). Depth of processing and the retention of words in episodic memory. *Journal of Experimental Psychology: General*, 104, 268–294.

Cronbach, L. (1957). The two disciplines of scientific psychology. *American Psychologist*, 12, 671–684.

Cross, S.E., & Madsen, L. (1997). Models of the self: Self-construals and gender. *Psychological Bulletin*, 122, 5–37.

Cumberbatch, G. (1990). *Television advertising and sex role stereotyping: A content analysis*. Working Paper IV for the Broadcasting Standards Council. Communications Research Group, Aston University, Birmingham, UK.

Cunningham, M.R. (1986). Measuring the physical in physical attractiveness: Quasi-experiments on the sociobiology of female facial beauty. *Journal of Personality and Social Psychology*, 50, 925–935.

Cunningham, W.A., Preacher, K.J., & Banaji, M.R. (2001). Implicit attitudes measures: Consistency, stability, and convergent validity. *Psychological Science*, 12, 163–170.

Dalgleish, T., Hill, E., Golden, A.-M.J., Morant, N., & Dunn, B.D. (2011). The structure of past and future lives in depression. *Journal of Abnormal Psychology*, 120, 1–15.

Dalgleish, T., & Werner-Seidler, A. (2014). Disruptions in autobiographical memory processing in depression and the emergence of memory therapeutics. *Trends in Cognitive Sciences*, 18, 596–604.

Daniel, E., Madigan, S., & Jenkins, J. (2016). Paternal and maternal warmth and the development of prosociality among preschoolers. *Journal of Family Psychology*, 30, 114–124.

Darley, J.M., & Latané, B. (1968). Bystander intervention in emergencies: Diffusion of responsibility. *Journal of Personality and Social Psychology*, 8, 377–383.

Darwin, C. (1859). *The origin of species*. London: Macmillan.

Dasen, P.R. (1994). Culture and cognitive development from a Piagetian perspective. In W.J. Lonner & R. Malpass (Eds.), *Psychology and culture* (pp. 145–149). London: Allyn and Bacon.

David, B., & Turner, J.C. (1999). Studies in self-categorization and minority conversion: The in-group minority in intragroup and intergroup contexts. *British Journal of Social Psychology, 38,* 115–134.

Davidov, M., & Grusec, J.E. (2004). Untangling the links of parental responsiveness to distress and warmth to child outcomes. *Child Development, 77,* 44–58.

Davis, J.I., Senghas, A., Brandt, F., & Ochsner, K.N. (2010). The effects of BOTOX injections on emotional experience. *Emotion, 10,* 433–440.

De Boysson-Bardies, B., Sagart, L., & Durand, C. (1984). Discernible differences in the babbling of infants according to target language. *Journal of Child Language, 16,* 1–17.

De Groot, A.D. (1965). *Thought and choice in chess.* The Hague, Netherlands: Mouton.

De Long, K.A., Urbach, T.P., & Kutas, M. (2005). Probabilistic word pre-activation during language comprehension inferred from electrical brain activity. *Nature Neuroscience, 8,* 1117–1121.

de Oliviera, M.F., Pinto, F.C.G., Nishlkuni, K., Botelho, R.V., Lima, A.M., & Rotta, J.M. (2012). Revisiting hydrocephalus as a model to study brain resilience. *Frontiers in Human Neuroscience, 5* (Article 181), 1–11.

de Wied, M., Gispen-de-Wied, C., & van Boxtel, A. (2010). Empathy dysfunction in children and adolescents with disruptive behavior disorders. *European Journal of Pharmacology, 626,* 97–103.

De Wolff, M.S., & van IJzendoorn, M.H. (1997). Sensitivity and attachment: A meta-analysis on parental antecedents of infant attachment. *Child Development, 68,* 571–591.

Deady, D.K., North, N.T., Allan, D., Smith, M.J.L., & O'Carroll, R.E. (2010). Examining the effect of spinal cord injury on emotional awareness, expressivity and memory for emotional material. *Psychology, Health & Medicine, 15,* 406–419.

Declercq, M., & Houwer, J. (2011). Evidence against an occasion-setting account of avoidance learning. *Learning and Motivation, 42,* 46–52.

Deffenbacher, K.A., Bornstein, B.H., Penroad, S.D., & McGorty, E.K. (2004). A meta-analytic review of the effects of high stress on eyewitness memory. *Law and Human Behavior, 28,* 687–706.

Delaney, P.F., Ericsson, K.A., & Knowles, M.E. (2004). Immediate and sustained effects of planning in a problem-solving task. *Journal of Experimental Psychology: Learning, Memory, and Cognition, 30,* 1219–1234.

DeLongis, A., Folkman, S., & Lazarus, R.S. (1988). The impact of daily hassles, uplifts and major life events on health status. *Health Psychology, 1,* 119–136.

DeLucia, P.R., & Hochberg, J. (1991). Geometrical illusions in solid objects under ordinary viewing conditions. *Perception & Psychophysics, 50,* 547–554.

Denollet, J. (2005). DS14: Standard assessment of negative affectivity, social inhibition, and Type D personality. *Psychosomatic Medicine, 67,* 89–97.

Derakshan, N., & Eysenck, M.W. (1999). Are repressors self-deceivers or other-deceivers? *Cognition and Emotion, 13,* 1–17.

DeRubeis, R.J., Hollon, S.D., Amsterdam, J.D., Shelton, R.C., Young, P.R., Salomon, R.M. et al. (2005). Cognitive therapy vs. medications in the treatment of moderate to severe depression. *Archives of General Psychiatry, 62,* 409–416.

Deutsch, M., & Gerard, H.B. (1955). A study of normative and informational influence upon individual judgement. *Journal of Abnormal and Social Psychology, 51,* 629–636.

Dewar, M.T., Cowan, N., & Della Sala, S. (2007). Forgetting due to retroactive interference: A fusion of Müller and Pilzecker's (1900) early insights into everyday forgetting and recent research on retrograde amnesia. *Cortex, 43,* 616–634.

Dezecache, G. (2015). Human collective reactions to threat. *Wiley Interdisciplinary Reviews-Cognitive Science, 6,* 209–219.

Dhont, K., Roets, A., & Van Hiel, A. (2011). Opening closed minds: The combined effects of intergroup contact and need for closure on prejudice. *Personality and Social Psychology Bulletin, 37,* 514–528.

Diagnostic and Statistical Manual of Mental Disorders (DSM-5) (2013). New York: American Psychiatric Association.

Dickens, W.T., & Flynn, J.R. (2001). Heritability estimates versus large environmental effects: The IQ paradox resolved. *Psychological Review, 108,* 346–369.

Dickerson, S.S., & Kemeny, M.E. (2004). Acute stressors and cortisol responses: A theoretical integration and synthesis of laboratory research. *Psychological Bulletin, 130,* 355–391.

Dickinson, A., & Dawson, G.R. (1987). The role of the instrumental contingency in the motivational control of performance. *Quarterly Journal of Experimental Psychology, 39,* 78–94.

Diener, E., & Crandall, R. (1978). *Ethics in social and behavioural research.* Chicago: University of Chicago Press.

Dill, K.E., & Thill, K.P. (2007). Video game characters and the socialisation of gender roles: Young people's perceptions mirror sexist media depictions. *Sex Roles, 57,* 851–864.

Dion, K.K., Berscheid, E., & Walster, E. (1972). What is beautiful is good. *Journal of Personality and Social Psychology, 24,* 285–290.

Dionne, G., Dale, P.S., Boivin, M., & Plomin, R. (2003). Genetic evidence for bidirectional effects of early lexical and grammatical development. *Child Development, 74,* 394–412.

Dishion, T.J., & Owen, L.D. (2002). A longitudinal analysis of friendships and substance use: Bidirectional influence from adolescence to adulthood. *Developmental Psychology, 38,* 480–491.

Dishion, T.J., Véronneau, M.-H., & Myers, M.W. (2010). Cascading peer dynamics underlying the progression from problem behavior to violence in early to late adolescence. *Development and Psychopathology, 22,* 603–619.

Dollard, J., Doob, L.W., Miller, N.E., Mowrer, O.H., & Sears, R.R. (1939). *Frustration and aggression.* New Haven, CT: Yale University Press.

Domini, F., Shah, R., & Caudek, C. (2011). Do we perceive a flattened world on the monitor screen? *Acta Psychologica, 138,* 359–366.

Domjan, M. (2005). Pavlovian conditioning: A functional perspective. *Annual Review of Psychology, 56,* 179–206.

Dorahy, M.J., Brand, B.L., Şar, V., Krüger, C., Stavropoulos, P., Martinez-Taboas, A. et al. (2014). Dissociative identity disorder: An empirical overview. *Australian & New Zealand Journal of Psychiatry, 48,* 402–417.

Dovidio, J.F., Brigham, J.C., Johnson, B.T., & Gaertner, S. (1996). Stereotyping, prejudice, and discrimination: Another look. In C.N. Macrae, C. Stanger, & M. Hewstone (Eds.), *Stereotypes and stereotyping* (pp. 276–319). Guilford Press: New York.

Dovidio, J.F., Gaertner, S.L., & Saguy, T. (2015). Colour-blindness and commonality: Included but invisible? *American Behavioral Scientist, 59,* 1518–1538.

Dovidio, J.F., Gaertner, S.L., Shnabel, N., Saguy, T., & Johnson, J.D. (2010). Recategorisation and prosocial behaviour: Common identity and a dual identity. In S. Stürmer & M. Snyder (Eds.), *The psychology of prosocial behaviour* (pp. 191–208). Malden, MA: Wiley-Blackwell.

Dovidio, J.F., ten Vergert, M., Stewart, T.L., Gaertner, S.L., Johnson, J.D., Esses, V.M. et al. (2004). Perspective and prejudice: Antecedents and mediating mechanisms. *Personality and Social Psychology Bulletin, 30,* 1537–1549.

Drury, J., Cocking, C., & Reicher, S. (2009). Everyone for themselves? A comparative study of crowd solidarity among emergency survivors. *British Journal of Social Psychology, 48,* 487–506.

Drury, J., & Reicher, S.D. (2010). Crowd control. *Scientific American Mind, 21,* 58–65.

Dunbar, K., & Blanchette, I. (2001). The in vivo/in vitro approach to cognition: The case of analogy. *Trends in Cognitive Sciences, 5,* 334–339.

Duncker, K. (1945). On problem solving. *Psychological Monographs, 58* (Whole No. 270), 1–113.

Dunlosky, J., Rawson, K.A., Marsh, E.J., Nathan, M.J., & Willingham, D.T. (2013). Improving students' learning with effective learning techniques: Promising directions from cognitive and educational psychology. *Psychological Science in the Public Interest, 14,* 4–58.

Durisko, Z., Mulsant, B.H., & Andrews, P.W. (2015). An adaptationist perspective on the aetiology of depression. *Journal of Affective Disorders, 172,* 315–323.

Eastwick, P.W., Luchies, L.B., Finkel, E.J., & Hunt, L.L. (2014). The predictive validity of ideal partner preferences: A review and meta-analysis. *Psychological Bulletin, 140,* 623–665.

Ebbinghaus, H. (1885/1913). *Über das Gedächtnis* (Leipzig: Dunker). Translated by H. Ruyer & C.E. Bussenius. New York: Teacher College, Columbia University.

Eftekhari, A., Ruzek, J.I., Crowley, J.J., Rosen, C.S., Greenbaum, M.A., & Karlin, B.E. (2013). Effectiveness of a national implementation of prolonged exposure therapy in veterans affairs care. *JAMA Psychiatry, 70,* 949–955.

Egan, S.K., & Perry, D.G. (2001). Gender identity: A multidimensional analysis with implications for psychosocial adjustment. *Developmental Psychology, 8,* 25–37.

Eichenbaum, H. (2015). Amnesia: Revisiting Scoville and Milner's (1957) research on HM and other patients. In M.W. Eysenck & D. Groome (Eds.), *Classic studies in cognitive psychology* (pp. 71–85). London: Sage.

Ein-Dor, T. (2015). Attachment dispositions and human defensive behaviour. *Personality and Individual Differences, 81,* 112–116.

Ekman, P., Friesen, W.V., & Ellsworth, P. (1972). *Emotion in the human face: Guidelines for research and an integration of findings.* New York: Pergamon.

Ekman, P., Friesen, W.V., O'Sullivan, M., Chan, A., Diacoyanni-Tarlatzis, I., Heider, K. et al. (1987). Universals and cultural differences in the judgments of facial expressions of emotion. *Journal of Personality and Social Psychology, 53,* 712–717.

Elder, J.H., & Goldberg, R.M. (2002). Ecological statistics of Gestalt laws for the perceptual organization of contours. *Journal of Vision, 2,* 324–353.

Else-Quest, N.M., Hyde, J.S., Goldsmith, H.H., & Van Hulle, C.A. (2006). Gender differences in temperament: A meta-analysis. *Psychological Bulletin, 132*, 33–72.

Else-Quest, N.M., Hyde, J.S., & Linn, M.C. (2010). Cross-national patterns of gender differences in mathematics: A meta-analysis. *Psychological Bulletin, 136*, 103–127.

Ember, M. (1981). *Statistical evidence for an ecological explanation of warfare.* Paper presented at the 10th annual meeting of the Society for Cross-Cultural Research, Syracuse, NY.

Engel, P.J.H. (2008). Tacit knowledge and visual expertise in medical diagnostic reasoning: Implications for medical education. *Medical Teacher, 30*, e184–e188.

English, T., & Chen, S. (2007). Culture and self-concept stability: Consistency across and within contexts among Asian Americans and European Americans. *Journal of Personality and Social Psychology, 93*, 478–490.

English, T., & Chen, S. (2011). Self-concept consistency and culture: The differential impact of two forms of consistency. *Personality and Social Psychology Bulletin, 37*, 838–849.

Erb, H.-P., Bohner, G., Rank, S., & Einwiller, S. (2002). Processing minority and majority communications: The role of conflict with prior attitudes. *Personality and Social Psychology Bulletin, 28*, 1172–1182.

Erbas, Y., Coulemans, E., Koval, P., & Kuppens, P. (2015). The role of valence focus and appraisal overlap in emotion differentiation. *Emotion, 15*, 373–382.

Erel, O., Oberman, Y., & Yirmiya, N. (2000). Maternal versus nonmaternal care and seven domains of children's development. *Psychological Bulletin, 126*, 727–747.

Ericsson, K.A. (1988). Analysis of memory performance in terms of memory skill. In R.J. Sternberg (Ed.), *Advances in the psychology of human intelligence* (Vol. 4, pp. 137–179). Hillsdale, NJ: Lawrence Erlbaum Associates.

Ericsson, K.A., & Chase, W.G. (1982). Exceptional memory. *American Scientist, 70*, 607–615.

Ericsson, K.A., & Towne, T.J. (2010). Expertise. *Wiley International Reviews: Cognitive Science, 1*, 404–416.

Er-rafiy, A., & Brauer, M. (2013). Modifying perceived variability: Four laboratory and field experiments show the effectiveness of a ready-to-be-used prejudice intervention. *Journal of Applied Social Psychology, 43*, 840–853.

Evans, N., & Levinson, S.C. (2009). The myth of language universals: Language diversity and its importance for cognitive science. *Behavioral and Brain Sciences, 32*, 429–448.

Everett, D.L. (2005). Cultural constraints on grammar and cognition in Piraha. *Current Anthropology, 46*, 621–646.

Eysenck, H.J., & Eysenck, S.B.G. (1975). *Manual of the Eysenck personality questionnaire.* London: Hodder and Stoughton.

Eysenck, M.W. (1979). Depth, elaboration, and distinctiveness. In L.S. Cermak & F.I.M. Craik (Eds.), *Levels of processing in human memory* (pp. 89–118). Hillsdale, NJ: Lawrence Erlbaum Associates Inc.

Eysenck, M.W. (1992). *Anxiety: The cognitive perspective.* Hove, UK: Psychology Press.

Eysenck, M.W. (2015). *AQA psychology: AS and a-level year 1* (6th ed.). Hove, UK: Psychology Press.

Eysenck, M.W. (2016). Hans Eysenck: A research evaluation. *Personality and Individual Differences, 103*, 209–219.

Eysenck, M.W., Derakshan, N., Santos, R., & Calvo, M.G. (2007). Anxiety and cognitive performance: Attentional control theory. *Emotion, 7*, 336–353.

Eysenck, M.W., & Keane, M.T. (2015). *Cognitive psychology: A student's handbook* (7th ed.). Hove: Psychology Press.

Fagot, B.I., & Leinbach, M.D. (1989). The young child's gender schema: Environmental input, internal organisation. *Child Development, 60*, 663–672.

Fales, M.R., Frederick, D.A., Garcia, J.R., Gildersleeve, K.A., Haselton, M.G., & Fisher, H.E. (2016). Mating markets and bargaining hands: Mate preferences for attractiveness and resources in two national U.S. studies. *Personality and Individual Differences, 88*, 78–87.

Fawcett, J.M., Russell, E.J., Peace, K.A., & Christie, J. (2013). Of guns and geese: A meta-analytic review of the "weapon focus" literature. *Psychology, Crime & Law, 19*, 35–66.

Fehr, E., & Fischbacher, U. (2003). The nature of human altruism. *Nature, 425*, 785–791.

Fehr, E., & Fischbacher, U. (2004). Third-party punishment and social norms. *Evolution and Human Behavior, 25*, 63–87.

Fellner, C.H., & Marshall, J.R. (1981). Kidney donors revisited. In J.P. Rushton & R.M. Sorrentino (Eds.), *Altruism and helping behavior* (pp. 351–365). Hillsdale, NJ: Lawrence Erlbaum Associates Inc.

Fenson, L., Dale, P., Reznick, J., Bates, E., Thal, D., & Pethick, S. (1994). Variability in early communicative development. *Monographs of the Society for Research in Child Development, 59* (5, Serial No. 242), 1–97.

Fenstermacher, S.K., & Saudino, K.J. (2007). Toddler see, toddler do? Genetic and environmental influences on laboratory-assessed elicited imitation. *Behavior Genetics, 37*, 639–647.

Ferguson, C.J. (2015). Do angry birds make for angry children? A meta-analysis of video game influences on children's and adolescents' aggression, mental health, prosocial behaviour, and academic performance. *Perspectives on Psychological Science, 10*, 646–666.

Ferguson, C.J., & Dyck, D. (2012). Paradigm change in aggression research: The time has come to retire the general aggression model. *Aggression and Violent Behavior, 17*, 220–228.

Fernandez-Duque, D., Grossi, G., Thornton, I.M., & Neville, H.J. (2003). Representations of change: Separate electrophysiological marks of attention, awareness, and implicit processing. *Journal of Cognitive Neuroscience, 15*, 491–507.

Fijneman, Y.A., Willemsen, M.E., & Poortinga, Y.H. (1996). Individualism-collectivism: An empirical study of a conceptual issue. *Journal of Cross-Cultural Psychology, 27*, 381–402.

Filindra, A., & Pearson-Merkowitz, S. (2013). Together in good times and bad? How economic triggers condition the effects of intergroup threat. *Social Science Quarterly, 94*, 1328–1345.

Finkel, E.J., Norton, M.I., Reis, H.T., Ariely, D., Caprariello, P.A., Eastwick, P.A. et al. (2015). When does familiarity promote versus undermine interpersonal attraction? A proposed integrative model from erstwhile adversaries. *Perspectives on Psychological Science, 10*, 3–19.

Fischer, J., & Whitney, D. (2014). Serial dependence in visual perception. *Nature Neuroscience, 17*, 738–746.

Fischer, P., Krueger, J., Greitemeyer, T., Vogrincic, C., Kastenmüller, A., Frey, D. et al. (2011). The bystander effect: A meta-analytic review on bystander intervention in dangerous and non-dangerous emergencies. *Psychological Bulletin, 137*, 517–537.

Fiske, A.P. (2002). Using individualism and collectivism to compare cultures: A critique of the validity and measurement of the constructs: Comments on Oyserman et al. (2002). *Psychological Bulletin, 128*, 78–88.

Fiske, S.T. (2002). What we know now about bias and intergroup conflict, the problem of the century. *Current Directions in Psychological Science, 11*, 123–128.

Fiske, S.T., Cuddy, A.J.C., & Glick, P. (2007). Universal dimensions of social cognition: Warmth and competence. *Trends in Cognitive Sciences, 11*, 77–83.

Fleeson, W., & Gallagher, W. (2009). The implications of Big Five standing for the distribution of trait manifestation in behavior: Fifteen experience-sampling studies and a meta-analysis. *Journal of Personality and Social Psychology, 97*, 1097–1114.

Flett, G.L., Krames, L., & Vredenburg, K. (2009). Personality traits in clinical depression and remitted depression: An analysis of instrumental-agentic and expressive-communal traits. *Current Psychology, 28*, 240–248.

Flynn, J.R. (1987). Massive IQ gains in 14 nations – What IQ really measures. *Psychological Bulletin, 101*, 171–191.

Foels, R., & Tomcho, T.J. (2009). Gender differences in interdependent self-construals: It's not the type of group, it's the way you see it. *Self and Identity, 8*, 396–417.

Ford, M.R., & Widiger, T.A. (1989). Sex bias in the diagnosis of histrionic and antisocial personality disorders. *Journal of Consulting and Clinical Psychology, 57*, 301–305.

Forsythe, C.J., & Compas, B.E. (1987). Interactions of cognitive appraisals of stressful events and coping: Testing the goodness-of-fit hypothesis. *Cognitive Therapy and Research, 11*, 473–485.

Fortin, M., Haggerty, J., Almirall, J., Bouhali, T., Sasseville, M., & Lemieux, M. (2014). Lifestyle factors and multimorbidity: A cross-sectional study. *BMC Public Health, 14*, (Article 686), 1–8.

Fortin, M., Voss, P., Lord, C., Lassande, M., Pruessner, J., Saint-Arnour, D., Rainville, C. et al. (2008). Wayfinding in the blind: Large hippocampal volume and supranormal spatial navigation. *Brain, 131*, 2995–3005.

Fraley, R.C., & Spieker, S.J. (2003). Are infant attachment patterns continuously or categorically distributed? A taxometric analysis of Strange Situation behaviour. *Developmental Psychology, 39*, 387–404.

Frances, A. (2012). DSM-5 is a guide, not a bible: Simply ignore its 10 worst changes. *Huffington Post*, 3 December. www.huffingtonpost.com/allen-frances/dsm-5_b_2227626.html.

Franz, C., Weinberger, J., Kremen, W., & Jacobs, R. (1996). *Childhood antecedents of dysphoria in adults: A 36-year longitudinal study*. Unpublished manuscript, Williamstown, MA: Williams College.

Friesdorf, R., Conway, P., & Gawronski, B. (2015). Gender differences in responses to moral dilemmas: A process dissociation analysis. *Personality and Social Psychology Bulletin, 41*, 696–713.

Frigerio, A., Ceppi, E., Rusconi, M., Giorda, R., Raggi, M.E., & Fearon, P. (2009). The role played by the interaction between genetic factors and attachment in the stress response. *Journal of Child Psychology and Psychiatry, 50*(12), 1513–1522.

Fuglseth, A.M., & Sorebo, O. (2014). The effects of technostress within the context of employee use of ICT. *Computers in Human Behavior, 40*, 161–170.

Fumagalli, M., Vergari, M., Pasqualetti, P., Marceglia, S., Mameli, F., Ferrucci, R. et al. (2010). Brain switches utilitarian behaviour: Does gender make the difference? *Public Library of Science One*, 25 January; 5(1), e8865.

Furnham, A. (1981). Personality and activity preference. *British Journal of Social and Clinical Psychology, 20*, 57–68.

Furnham, A. (1988). *Lay theories: Everyday understanding of problems in the social sciences.* Oxford, UK: Pergamon.

Futrell, R., Stearns, L., Everett, D.L., Piantadosi, S.T., & Gibson, E. (2016). A corpus investigation of syntactic embedding in Pirahã. *PLoS ONE, 11*(3), e0145289. doi: 10.1371/journal.pone.0145289.

Gaab, J., Blatter, N., Menzi, T., Pabst, B., Stoyer, S., & Ehlert, U. (2003). Randomized controlled evaluation of the effects of cognitive-behavioural stress management on cortisol responses to acute stress in healthy subjects. *Psychoneuroendocrinology, 28*, 767–779.

Gaertner, S.L., & Dovidio, J.F. (2012). Reducing intergroup bias: The common ingroup identity model. In P.A.M. Van Lange, A.W. Kruglanski, & E.T. Higgins (Eds.), *Handbook of theories of social psychology* (Vol. 2, pp. 439–457). Thousand Oaks, CA: Sage.

Gaffan, E.A., Hansel, M.C., & Smith, L.E. (1983). Does reward depletion influence spatial memory performance? *Learning and Motivation, 14*, 58–74.

Gaillard, R., Dehaene, S., Adam, C., Clémenceau, S., Hasboun, D., Baulac, M. et al. (2009). Converging intracranial markers of conscious access. *PLoS Biology, 7*, e1000061.

Galton, F. (1869). *Hereditary genius.* London: Macmillan.

Galton, F. (1876). Théorie de l'hérédité. *La Revue Scientifique, 10*, 198–205.

Garcia, J., Ervin, F.R., & Koelling, R. (1966). Learning with prolonged delay of reinforcement. *Psychonomic Science, 5*, 121–122.

Gardner, H. (1983). *Frames of mind: The theory of multiple intelligences.* New York: Basic Books.

Gardner, H. (1993). *Creating minds: The theory of creativity as seen through Freud, Einstein, Picasso, Stravinsky, Eliot, Graham, and Gandhi.* New York: Basic Books.

Gardner, H., Kornhaber, M.L., & Wake, W.K. (1996). *Intelligence: Multiple perspectives.* Orlando, FL: Harcourt Brace.

Gardner, R.A., & Gardner, B.T. (1969). Teaching sign language to a chimpanzee. *Science, 165*, 664–672.

Gawronski, B. (2004). Theory-based bias correction in dispositional inference: The fundamental attribution error is dead, long live the correspondence bias. *European Review of Social Psychology, 15*, 183–217.

Gazzaniga, M.S. (2013). Shifting gears: Seeking new approaches for mind/brain mechanisms. *Annual Review of Psychology, 64*, 1–20.

Gazzaniga, M.S., Ivry, R.B., & Mangan, G.R. (2008). *Cognitive neuroscience: The biology of the mind* (3rd ed.). New York: W.W. Norton.

Gebauer, J.E., Sedikides, C., Wagner, J., Bleidorn, W., Rentfrow, P.J., & Potterm, J. (2015). Cultural norm fulfilment, interpersonal belonging, or getting ahead? A large-scale cross-cultural test of three perspectives on the function of self-esteem. *Journal of Personality and Social Psychology, 109*, 528–548.

Gegenfurtner, A., Lehtinen, E., & Säljö, R. (2011). Expertise differences in the comprehension of visualisations: A meta-analysis of eye-tracking research in professional domains. *Educational Psychology Review, 23*, 523–552.

Geher, G. (2004). *Measuring emotional intelligence: Common ground and controversy.* New York: Nova Science Publishing.

Gentile, D.A., Anderson, C.A., Yukawa, S., Ihori, N., Saleem, M., Ming, L.K. et al. (2009). The effects of prosocial video games on prosocial behaviors: International evidence from correlational, longitudinal, and experimental studies. *Personality and Social Psychology Bulletin, 35*, 752–763.

Genty, E., Neumann, C., & Zuberbühler, K. (2015). Bonobos modify communication signals according to recipient familiarity. *Scientific Reports, 5*(16442), 1–10.

Geraerts, E., Schooler, J.W., Merckelbach, H., Jelicic, M., Hunter, B.J.A., & Ambadar Z. (2007). Corroborating continuous and discontinuous memories of childhood sexual abuse. *Psychological Science, 18*, 564–568.

Gergely, G., Bekkering, H., & Kiraly, I. (2002). Rational imitation in preverbal infants. *Nature, 415*, 755.

Gershoff, E.T. (2002). Corporal punishment by parents and associated child behaviours and experiences: A meta-analytic and theoretical review. *Psychological Bulletin, 128*, 539–579.

Gershoff, E.T., Grogan-Kaylor, A., Lansford, J.E., Chang, L., Zelli, A., Deater-Deckard, K. et al. (2010). Parent discipline practices in an international sample: Associations with child behaviors and moderation by perceived normativeness. *Child Development, 81*, 487–502.

Gick, M.L., & Holyoak, K.J. (1980). Analogical problem solving. *Cognitive Psychology, 12*, 306–355.

Gilligan, C. (1977). In a different voice: Women's conception of the self and morality. *Harvard Educational Review, 47*, 481–517.

Gilligan, C. (1982). *In a different voice: Psychological theory and women's development.* Cambridge, MA: Harvard University Press.

Glennerster, A. (2015). Visual stability: What is the problem? *Frontiers in Psychology*, 6 (Article 958), 1–3.

Glennerster, A., Tscheang, L., Gilson, S.J., Fitzgibbon, A.W., & Parker, A.J. (2006). Humans ignore motion and stereo cues in favor of a fictional stable world. *Current Biology*, 16, 428–432.

Gobet, F., & Clarkson, G. (2004). Chunks in expert memory: Evidence for the magical number four . . . or is it two? *Memory*, 12, 732–747.

Gobet, F., & Ereku, M.H. (2014). Checkmate to deliberate practice: The case of Magnus Carlsen. *Frontiers in Psychology*, 5 (Article 878), 1–3.

Gobet, F., & Waters, A.J. (2003). The role of constraints in expert memory. *Journal of Experimental Psychology: Learning, Memory, & Cognition*, 29, 1082–1094.

Godden, D.R., & Baddeley, A.D. (1975). Context dependent memory in two natural environments: On land and under water. *British Journal of Psychology*, 66, 325–331.

Goel, V. (2010). Neural basis of thinking: Laboratory problems versus real-world problems. *Wiley Interdisciplinary Reviews – Cognitive Science*, 1, 613–621.

Gogate, L.J., & Hollich, G. (2010). Invariance detection within an interactive system: A perceptual gateway to language development. *Psychological Review*, 117, 496–516.

Goldberg, L.R. (1990). An alternative "description of personality": The Big-Five factor structure. *Journal of Personality and Social Psychology*, 59, 1216–1229.

Goldfarb, W. (1947). Variations in adolescent adjustment of institutionally reared children. *American Journal of Orthopsychiatry*, 17, 499–557.

Gollwitzer, P.M. (2014). Weakness of the will: Is a quick fix possible? *Motivation and Emotion*, 38, 305–322.

Gollwitzer, P.M., & Brandstätter, V. (1997). Implementation intentions and effective goal pursuit. *Journal of Personality and Social Psychology*, 73, 186–199.

Golombok, S., & Hines, M. (2002). Sex differences in social behavior. In P.K. Smith & C.H. Hart (Eds.), *Blackwell handbook of childhood social development* (pp. 117–136). Oxford, UK: Blackwell.

Goode, E. (1996). Gender and courtship entitlement: Responses to personal ads. *Sex Roles*, 34, 141–169.

Goodwin, G.P., Piazza, J., & Rozin, P. (2014). Moral character predominates in person perception and evaluation. *Journal of Personality and Social Psychology*, 106, 148–168.

Gosling, S.D., & John, O.P. (1999). Personality dimensions in non-human animals: A cross-species review. *Current Directions in Psychological Science*, 8, 69–75.

Gottesman, I.I. (1991). *Schizophrenia genesis: The origins of madness*. New York: W.H. Freeman.

Grande, G., Romppel, M., & Barth, J. (2012). Association between Type D personality and prognosis with cardiovascular diseases: A systematic review and meta-analysis. *Annals of Behavioral Medicine*, 43, 299–310.

Gray, J. (1992). *Men are from Mars, women are from Venus*. New York: HarperCollins.

Gray, J.A. (1981). A critique of Eysenck's theory of personality. In H.J. Eysenck (Ed.), *A model for personality* (pp. 248–276). Berlin: Springer-Verlag.

Greene, J.D. (2007). Why are VMPFC patients more utilitarian? A dual-process theory of moral judgement explains. *Trends in Cognitive Sciences*, 11, 322–323.

Greenberg, J.H. (1963). Some universals of grammar with particular reference to the order of meaningful elements. In J.H. Greenberg (Ed.), *Universals of language* (pp. 73–113). Cambridge, MA: MIT Press.

Greenwald, A.G., Banaji, M.R., & Nosek, B.A. (2015). Statistically small effects of the Implicit Association Test can have societally large effects. *Journal of Personality and Social Psychology*, 108, 553–561.

Gregory, R.L. (1970). *The intelligent eye*. New York: McGraw-Hill.

Greitemeyer, T., & Mügge, D.O. (2014). Video games do affect social outcomes: A meta-analytic review of the effects of violent and prosocial video game play. *Personality and Social Psychology Bulletin*, 40, 578–589.

Griffin, A.M., & Langlois, J.H. (2006). Stereotype directionality and attractiveness stereotyping: Is beauty good or is ugly bad? *Social Cognition*, 24, 187–206.

Grilli, M.D., & Verfaellie, M. (2015). Supporting the self-concept with memory: Insight from amnesia. *Social Cognitive and Affective Neuroscience*, 10, 1684–1692.

Groh, A.M., Roisman, G.I., van IJzendoorn, M.H., Bakermans-Kranenburg, M.J., & Fearon, R.P. (2015). The significance of insecure and disorganised attachment for children's internalising symptoms: A meta-analytic study. *Child Development*, 83, 591–610.

Gross, J.J., & Thompson, R.A. (2007). Emotion regulation: Conceptual foundations. In J.J. Gross (Ed.), *Handbook of emotion regulation*. New York, NY: Guilford Press.

Gross, R. (1996). *Psychology: The science of mind and behavior* (3rd ed.). London: Hodder & Stoughton.

Grossman, K., Grossman, K.E., Spangler, S., Suess, G., & Uzner, L. (1985). Maternal sensitivity and newborn responses as related to quality of attachment in Northern Germany. In J. Bretherton & E. Waters (Eds.), Growing points of attachment theory. *Monographs of the Society for Research in Child Development, 50*(209), 233–256.

Gudykunst, W.B., Gao, G., & Franklyn-Stokes, A. (1996). Self-monitoring and concern for social appropriateness in China and England. In J. Pandey, D. Sinha, & D.P.S. Bhawk (Eds.), *Asian contributions to cross-cultural psychology* (pp. 255–267). New Delhi: Sage.

Gueguen, N., Meineri, S., & Charles-Sire, V. (2010). Improving medication adherence by using practitioner nonverbal techniques: A field experiment on the effect of touch. *Journal of Behavioral Medicine, 33*, 466–473.

Guo, W., Xue, J.-M., Shao, D., Long, Z.T., & Cao, F.L. (2015). Effect of the interplay between trauma severity and trait neuroticism on posttraumatic stress disorder symptoms among adolescents exposed to a pipeline explosion. *PloS ONE, 10*(3), e0120493. doi: 10.137/journal.pone0120493.

Gupta, S. (2015). Why it pays to quit. *Nature, 522*, S58–S59.

Habermas, T., & de Silveira, C. (2008). The development of global coherence in life narratives across adolescence: Temporal, causal, and thematic aspects. *Developmental Psychology, 44*, 707–721.

Hackman, J., Danvers, A., & Hruschka, D.J. (2015). Closeness is enough for friends, but not mates or kin: Mate and kinship premiums in India and U.S. *Evolution and Human Behavior, 36*, 137–145.

Hackmann, A., Clark, D.M., & McManus, F. (2000). Recurrent images and early memories in social phobia. *Behaviour Research and Therapy, 38*, 601–610.

Hahn, A., Banchefsky, S., Park, B., & Judd, C.M. (2015). Measuring intergroup ideologies: Positive and negative aspects of emphasising versus looking beyond group differences. *Personality and Social Psychology Bulletin, 41*, 1646–1664.

Halim, M.L., & Lindner, N.C. (2013). Gender self-socialisation in early childhood. In R.E. Tremblay, M. Boivin, & R. De V. (Eds.), *Encylopaedia on early childhood development and strategic knowledge cluster on early child development* (pp. 1–6). Montreal, Canada: Centre of Excellence for Early Childhood Development.

Halim, M.L., Ruble, D.N., Tamis-LeMonda, C.S., Zosuls, K.M., Lurye, L.E., & Greulich, F.K. (2014). Pink frilly dresses and the avoidance of all things "girly": Children's appearance rigidity and cognitive theories of gender development. *Developmental Psychology, 50*, 1091–1101.

Hall, J.A., & Schmid Mast, M. (2008). Are women always more interpersonally sensitive than men? Impact of goals and content domain. *Personality and Social Psychology Bulletin, 34*, 144–155.

Hall, J.E., Sammons, P., Sylva, K., Melhuish, E., Taggart, B., Siraj-Blatchford, I., & Smees, R. (2010). Measuring the combined risk to young children's cognitive development: An alternative to cumulating indices. *British Journal of Developmental Psychology, 28*, 219–238.

Hallers-Haalboom, E.T., Mesman, J., Groeneveld, M.G., Endendijk, J.J., van Berkel, S.R., van der Pol, L.D. et al. (2014). Mothers, fathers, sons and daughters: Parental sensitivity in families with two children. *Journal of Family Psychology, 28*, 138–147.

Halpern, S.D., French, B., Small, D.S., Saulsgiver, K., Harhay, M.O., Audrain-McGovern, J. et al. (2015). Randomised trial of four financial-incentive programmes for smoking cessation. *New England Journal of Medicine, 372*, 2108–2117.

Hamann, S.B., & Squire, L.R. (1997). Intact perceptual memory in the absence of conscious memory. *Behavioral Neuroscience, 111*, 850–854.

Hambrick, D.Z., Oswald, F.L., Altmann, E.M., Meinz, E.J., Gobet, F., & Campitelli, G. (2014). Deliberate practice: Is that all it takes to become an expert? *Intelligence, 45*, 34–45.

Hamlin, J.K. (2015). The infantile origins of our moral brains. In J. Decety & T. Wheatley (Eds.), *The moral brain: A multidisciplinary perspective* (pp. 105–122). Oxford: Oxford University Press, New York.

Haney, C., Banks, C., & Zimbardo, P. (1973). Study of prisoners and guards in a simulated prison. *Naval Research Reviews, 26*, 1–17.

Haney, C., & Zimbardo, P.G. (2009). Persistent dispositionalism in interactionist clothing: Fundamental attribution error in explaining prison abuse. *Personality and Social Psychology Bulletin, 35*, 807–814.

Hanish, L.D., & Fabes, R.A. (2014). Peer socialization of gender in young boys and girls. In R.E. Tremblay, M. Boivin, & R. De V. Peters (Eds.), *Encylopaedia on early childhood development* (pp. 1–4). Montreal, Quebec: Centre of Excellence for Early Childhood Development and Strategic Knowledge Cluster on Early Child Development.

Hardt, O., Einarsson, E.O., & Nader, K. (2010). A bridge over troubled water: Reconsolidation as a link between cognitive and neuroscientific memory research traditions. *Annual Review of Psychology, 61*, 141–167.

Hardt, O., Nader, K., & Nadel, L. (2013). Decay happens: The role of active forgetting in memory. *Trends in Cognitive Sciences, 17,* 111–120.

Hare, O.A., Wetherell, M.A., & Smith, M.A. (2013). State anxiety and cortisol reactivity to skydiving in novice versus experienced skydivers. *Physiology & Behavior, 118,* 40–44.

Harley, T.A. (2013). *The psychology of language: From data to theory* (4th ed.). Hove, UK: Psychology Press.

Harrison, L.J., & Ungerer, J.A. (2002). Maternal employment and infant-mother attachment security at 12 months. *Developmental Psychology, 38,* 758–773.

Hasan, Y., Bègue, L., & Bushman, B.J. (2012). Viewing the world through "blood-red tinted glasses": The hostile expectation bias mediates the link between violent video game exposure and aggression. *Journal of Experimental Social Psychology, 48,* 953–956.

Haslam, S.A., & Reicher, S.D. (2012). Contesting the "nature" of conformity: What Milgram and Zimbardo's studies really show. *PLoS Biology, 10*(11), e1001426.

Haslam, S.A., Reicher, S.D., Millard, K., & McDonald, R. (2015). "Happy to have been of service": The Yale archive as a window into the engaged followership of participants in Milgram's "obedience" experiments. *British Journal of Social Psychology, 54,* 55–83.

Haslam, S.A., Ryan, M.K., Postmes, T., Spears, R., Jetten, J., & Webley, P. (2006). Sticking to your guns: Social identity as a basis for the maintenance of commitment to faltering organisational projects. *Journal of Organizational Behavior, 27,* 607–628.

Hatemi, P.K., Medland, S.E., Klemmensen, R., Oskarsson, S., Littvay, L., Dawes, C.T. et al. (2014). Genetic influences on political ideologies: Twin analyses of 19 measures of political ideologies from five democracies and genome-wide findings from three populations. *Behavior Genetics, 44,* 282–294.

Hayward, W.G., & Tarr, M.J. (2005). Visual perception II: High-level vision. In K. Lamberts & R.L. Goldstone (Eds.), *The handbook of cognition* (pp. 48–70). London: Sage.

Heider, F. (1958). *The psychology of interpersonal relations.* New York: Wiley.

Heine, S.J., & Buchtel, E.E. (2009). Personality: The universal and the culturally specific. *Annual Review of Psychology, 60,* 369–394.

Heine, S.J., Foster, J.A.B., & Spina, J.-A. (2009). Do birds of a feather flock together? Cultural variation in the similarity-attraction effect. *Asian Journal of Social Psychology, 12,* 247–258.

Heine, S.J., & Hamamura, T. (2007). In search of East Asian self-enhancement. *Personality and Social Psychology Review, 11,* 4–27.

Heine, S.J., Lehman, D.R., Markus, H.R., & Kitayama, S. (1999). Is there a universal need for positive self-regard? *Psychological Review, 106,* 766–794.

Hellmann, J.H., Echterhoff, G., Kopietz, R., Niemeier, S., & Memon, A. (2011). Talking about visually perceived events: Communication effects on eyewitness memory. *European Journal of Social Psychology, 41,* 658–671.

Henrich, J., McElreath, R., Barr, A., Ensminger, J., Barrett, C., Bolyanatz, A. et al. (2006). Costly punishment across human societies. *Science, 312,* 1767–1770.

Henrich, J., Heine, S.J., & Norenzayan, A. (2010). The weirdest people in the world. *Behavioral and Brain Sciences, 33,* 61–83.

Hervé, P.-Y., Zago, L., Petit, L., Mazoyer, B., & Tzourio-Mazoyer, N. (2013). Revisiting human hemispheric specialisation with neuroimaging. *Trends in Cognitive Sciences, 17,* 69–80.

Hetherington, E.M., Cox, M., & Cox, R. (1982). Effects of divorce on parents and children. In M.E. Lamb (Ed.), *Nontraditional families* (pp. 233–288). Hillsdale, NJ: Lawrence Erlbaum Associates Inc.

Hetherington, E.M., & Kelly, J. (2002). *For better or worse: Divorce reconsidered.* New York: W.W. Norton.

Heylens, G., De Cuypere, G., Zucker, K.J., Schelfaut, C., Elaut, E., Bossche, H.V. et al. (2012). Gender identity disorder in twins: A review of the case report literature. *Journal of Sexual Medicine, 9,* 751–757.

Hines, M., Constantinescu, M., & Spencer, D. (2015). Early androgen exposure and human gender development. *Biology of Sex Differences, 6,* 1–10.

Hitsch, G.J., Hotaçsu, A., & Ariely, D. (2010). What makes you click? Mate preferences in online dating. *Quantitative Marketing and Economics, 8,* 393–427.

Hockett, C.F. (1960). The origin of speech. *Scientific American, 203,* 89–96.

Hockey, G.R.J., Gray, M.M., & Davies, S. (1972). Forgetting as a function of sleep at different times of day. *Quarterly Journal of Experimental Psychology, 24,* 386–393.

Hodges, B.H. (2014). Rethinking conformity and imitation: Divergence, convergence, and social understanding. *Frontiers in Psychology, 5* (Article 726), 1–11.

Hodges, J., & Tizard, B. (1989). Social and family relationships of ex-institutional adolescents. *Journal of Child Psychology and Psychiatry, 30,* 53–75.

Hoffman, C., Lau, I., & Johnson, D.R. (1986). The linguistic relatively of person cognition. *Journal of Personality and Social Psychology, 51,* 1097–1105.

Hoffman, M.L. (1970). Moral development. In P.H. Mussen (Ed.), *Carmichael's manual of child psychology* (Vol. 2, pp. 52–86). New York: Wiley.

Hoffman, M.L. (2000). *Empathy and moral development: Implications for caring and justice.* Cambridge, UK: Cambridge University Press.

Hofling, K.C., Brotzman, E., Dalrymple, S., Graves, N., & Pierce, C.M. (1966). An experimental study in the nurse – physician relationship. *Journal of Nervous and Mental Disorders, 143,* 171–180.

Hogg, M.A., & Vaughan, G.M. (2005). *Social psychology* (4th ed.). Harlow: Prentice-Hall.

Hogg, M.A., Turner, J.C., & Davidson, B. (1990). Polarised norms and social frames of reference: A test of the self-categorisation theory of group polarisation. *Basic and Applied Social Psychology, 11,* 77–100.

Hollingworth, A., & Henderson, J.M. (2002). Accurate visual memory for previously attended objects in natural scenes. *Journal of Experimental Psychology: Human Perception & Performance, 28,* 113–136.

Hollis, K.L., Pharr, V.L., Dumas, M.J., Britton, G.B., & Field, J. (1997). Classical conditioning provides paternity advantage for territorial male blue gouramis (Trichogaster trichopterus). *Journal of Comparative Psychology, 111,* 219–225.

Hollon, S.D., DeRubeis, R.J., Shelton, R.C., Amsterdam, J.D., Salomon, R.M., O'Reardon, J.P. et al. (2005). Prevention of relapse following cognitive therapy vs. medications in moderate to severe depression. *Archives of General Psychiatry, 62,* 417–422.

Holmes, T.H., & Rahe, R.H. (1967). The social readjustment rating scale. *Journal of Psychosomatic Research, 11,* 213–218.

Hong, Y.Y., Morris, M.W., Chiu, C.Y., & Benet-Martinez, V. (2000). Multicultural minds: A dynamic constructionist approach to culture and cognition. *American Psychologist, 55,* 709–720.

Hortensius, R., & de Gelder, B. (2014). The neural basis of the bystander effect: The influence of group size on neural activity when witnessing an emergency. *NeuroImage, 93,* 53–58.

Howard, R.W. (2012). Longitudinal effects of different types of practice on the development of chess expertise. *Applied Cognitive Psychology, 26,* 359–369.

Howe, C.M.L., & Courage, M.L. (1997). The emergence and early development of autobiographical memory. *Psychological Review, 104,* 499–523.

Howe, C.M.L., Courage, M.L., & Edison, S.C. (2003). When autobiographical memory begins. *Developmental Review, 23,* 471–494.

Huesmann, L.R., Moise-Titus, J., Podolski, C.L., & Eron, L.D. (2003). Longitudinal relations between children's exposure to TV violence and their aggressive and violent behaviour in young adulthood: 1977–1992. *Developmental Psychology, 39,* 201–221.

Hughes, M. (1975). *Egocentrism in preschool children.* Unpublished PhD thesis, University of Edinburgh, UK.

Hunt, L.L., Eastwick, P.W., & Finkel, E.J. (2015). Levelling the playing field: Longer acquaintance predicts reduced assortative mating on attractiveness. *Psychological Science, 26,* 1046–1053.

Hunt, R.R. (2013). Precision in memory through distinctive processing. *Current Directions in Psychological Science, 22,* 10–15.

Hunt, R.R., & Smith, R.E. (1996). Accessing the particular from the general: The power of distinctiveness in the context of organization. *Memory & Cognition, 24,* 217–225.

Hunter, J.E. (1986). Cognitive ability, cognitive aptitudes, job knowledge, and job performance. *Journal of Vocational Behavior, 29,* 340–362.

Hupp, J.M., Smith, J.L., Coleman, J.M., & Brunell, A.B. (2010). That's a boy's toy: Gender-typed knowledge in toddlers as a function of mother's marital status. *Journal of Genetic Psychology, 171,* 389–401.

Huston, A.C., Bobbitt, K.C., & Bentley, A. (2015). Time spent in child care: How and why does it affect social development? *Developmental Psychology, 51,* 621–634.

Huston, T.L., Ruggiero, M., Conner, R., & Geis, G. (1981). Bystander intervention into crime: A study based on naturally occurring episodes. *Social Psychology Quarterly, 44,* 14–23.

Hwang, M.H., Choi, H.C., Lee, A., Culver, J.D., & Hutchison, B. (2016). The relationship between self-efficacy and academic achievement: A 5-year panel analysis. *Asia-Pacific Educational Research, 25,* 89–98.

Hyde, J.S. (2005). The gender similarities hypothesis. *American Psychologist, 60,* 581–592.

Hyman, I., Boss, S., Wise, B., McKenzie, K., & Caggiano, J. (2010). Did you see the unicycling clown? Inattentional blindness while walking and talking on a cell phone. *Applied Cognitive Psychology, 24,* 597–607.

Ibarra-Rouillard, M.S., & Kuiper, N.A. (2011). Social support and social negativity findings in depression: Perceived responsiveness to basic psychological needs. *Clinical Psychology Review, 31,* 342–352.

Ihlebaek, C., Love, T., Eilertsen, D.E., & Magnussen, S. (2003). Memory for a staged criminal event witnessed live and on video. *Memory, 11,* 310–327.

Imperato-McGinley, J., Guerro, L., Gautier, T., & Peterson, R.E. (1974). Steroid 5-reductase deficiency in man: An inherited form of male pseudohermaphroditism. *Science, 186,* 213–216.

Ingalhalikar, M., Smith, A., Parker, D., Satterthwaite, T.D., Elliott, M.A., Ruparel, K. et al. (2014). Sex differences in the structural connectome of the human brain. *Proceedings of the National Academy of Sciences, 111,* 823–828.

Isenberg, D.J. (1986). Group polarization: A critical review and meta-analysis. *Journal of Personality and Social Psychology, 48,* 1413–1426.

Isurin, L., & McDonald, J.L. (2001). Retroactive interference from translation equivalents: Implications for first language forgetting. *Memory & Cognition, 29,* 312–319.

Jacobs, R.A. (2002). What determines visual cue reliability? *Trends in Cognitive Sciences, 6,* 345–350.

Jacoby, L.L., Debner, J.A., & Hay, J.F. (2001). Proactive interference, accessibility bias, and process dissociations: Valid subjective reports of memory. *Journal of Experimental Psychology: Learning, Memory, & Cognition, 27,* 686–700.

Jaffee, S., & Hyde, J.S. (2000). Gender differences in moral orientation: A meta-analysis. *Psychological Bulletin, 126,* 703–726.

James, W. (1890). *Principles of psychology.* New York: Holt.

Janis, I.L. (1982). *Groupthink* (2nd ed.). Boston: Houghton Mifflin.

Jenkins, J.G., & Dallenbach, K.M. (1924). Oblivescence during sleep and waking. *American Journal of Psychology, 35,* 605–612.

Jenkins, R., White, D., van Montfort, X., & Burton, A.M. (2011). Variability in photos of the same face. *Cognition, 121,* 313–323.

Jensen, M.S., Yao, R., Street, W.N., & Simons, D.J. (2011). Change blindness and inattentional blindness. *Wiley Interdisciplinary Reviews: Cognitive Science, 2,* 529–546.

Joel, D., Berman, Z., Tavor, I., Wexler, N., Gaber, O., Stein, Y. et al. (2015). Sex beyond the genitalia: The human brain mosaic. *Proceedings of the National Academy of Sciences of the United States of America, 112,* 15468–15473.

John, O.P., Naumann, L.P., & Soto, C.J. (2008). Paradigm shift in the integrative Big Five taxonomy: History, measurement, and conceptual issues. In O.P. John, R.W. Robins, & L.A. Pervin (Eds.), *Handbook of personality: Theory and research* (3rd ed., pp. 114–158). New York: Guilford Press.

Johnson, J.G., & Sherman, M.F. (1997). Daily hassles mediate the relationship between major life events and psychiatric symptomatology: Longitudinal findings from an adolescent sample. *Journal of Social and Clinical Psychology, 37,* 1532–1538.

Jones, P.E. (1981). The formative years and the great discoveries 1856–1900. *The life and work of Sigmund Freud* (Vol. 1). New York: Basic Books.

Jones, P.E. (2007). From "external speech" to "inner speech" in Vygotsky: A critical appraisal and fresh perspectives. *Language & Communication, 29,* 166–181.

Joseph, D.L., Jin, J., Newman, D.A., & O'Boyle, E.H. (2015). Why does self-reported emotional intelligence predict job performance? A meta-analytic investigation of mixed EI. *Journal of Applied Psychology, 100,* 298–342.

Joseph, D.L., & Newman, D.A. (2010). Emotional intelligence: An integrative meta-analysis and cascading model. *Journal of Applied Psychology, 95,* 54–78.

Judge, T.A., Jackson, C.L., Shaw, J.C., Scott, B.A., & Rich, B.L. (2007). Self-efficacy and work-related performance: The integral role of individual differences. *Journal of Applied Psychology, 92,* 107–127.

Kaat, A.J., Farmer, C.A., Gadow, K.D., Findling, R.L., Bukstein, O.G., Arnold, L.E. et al. (2015). Factor validity of a proactive and reactive aggression rating scale. *Journal of Child and Family Studies, 24,* 2734–2744.

Kagan, J. (1984). *The nature of the child.* New York: Basic Books.

Kalakoski, V., & Saariluoma, P. (2001). Taxi drivers' exceptional memory of street names. *Memory & Cognition, 29,* 634–638.

Kalat, J.W. (1998). *Biological psychology* (6th ed.). Pacific Grove, CA: Brooks/Cole.

Kamin, L.J. (1969). Predictability, surprise, attention and conditioning. In R. Campbell & R. Church (Eds.), *Punishment and aversive behavior* (pp. 279–296). New York: Appleton-Century-Crofts.

Kandel, D. (1973). Adolescent marijuana use: Role of parents and peers. *Science, 181,* 1067–1070.

Kanizsa, G. (1976). Subjective contours. *Scientific American, 234,* 48–52.

Karpicke, J.D., & Aue, W.R. (2015). The testing effect is alive and well with complex materials. *Educational Psychology Review, 27,* 317–326.

Karpicke, J.D., Butler, A.C., & Roediger, H.L. (2009). Metacognitive strategies in student learning: Do students practice retrieval when they study on their own? *Memory, 17,* 471–479.

Kasser, T. (2016). Materialistic values and goals. *Annual Review of Psychology, 67,* 489–514.

Kato, T. (2015). Testing of the coping flexibility hypothesis based on the dual-process theory: Relationships between coping flexibility and depressive symptoms. *Psychiatry Research, 230,* 137–142.

Kaufman, S.B. (2013). Gorillas agree: Human frontal cortex is nothing special. *Scientific American*, 16 May, 1–4.

Keane, M. (1987). On retrieving analogs when solving problems. *Quarterly Journal of Experimental Psychology*, 39A, 29–41.

Kendler, K.S., & Baker, J.H. (2007). Genetic influences on measures of the environment: A systematic review. *Psychological Medicine*, 37, 615–626.

Kendler, K.S., Kuhn, J., & Prescott, C.A. (2004). The interrelationship of neuroticism, sex, and stressful life events in the prediction of episodes of major depression. *American Journal of Psychiatry*, 161, 631–636.

Kendler, K.S., Maes, H.H., Lönn, S.L., Morris, N.A., Lichtenstein, P., Sundquist, J. et al. (2015). *Psychological Medicine*, 45, 2253–2262.

Kenrick, D.T., & Keefe, R.C. (1992). Age preferences in mates reflect sex-differences in reproductive strategies. *Behavioral and Brain Sciences*, 15, 75–133.

Keogh, E., Bond, F.W., & Flaxman, P.E. (2006). Improving academic performance and mental health through a stress management intervention: Outcomes and mediators of change. *Behaviour Research and Therapy*, 44, 339–357.

Kernis, M.H. (2003). Toward a conceptualization of optimal self-esteem. *Psychological Inquiry*, 14, 1–26.

Kesselring, T., & Müller, U. (2011). The concept of egocentrism in the context of Piaget's theory. *New Ideas in Psychology*, 29, 327–345.

Király, I., Csibra, G., & Gergely, G. (2013). Beyond rational imitation: Learning arbitrary means actions from communicative demonstrations. *Journal of Experimental Child Psychology*, 116, 471–486.

Kirsch, J.A., & Lehman, B.J. (2015). Comparing visible and invisible social support: Non-evaluative support buffers cardiovascular responses to stress. *Stress & Health*, 31, 351–364.

Klahr, D., & Simon, H.A. (2001). What have psychologists (and others) found about the process of scientific discovery? *Current Directions in Psychological Science*, 10, 75–79.

Klein, H.J., Wesson, M.J., Hollenbeck, J.R., & Alge, B.J. (1999). Goal commitment and the goal-setting process: Conceptual clarification and empirical synthesis. *Journal of Applied Psychology*, 84, 885–896.

Klein, J., Frie, K.G., Blum, K., Siegrist, J., & von dem Knesebeck, O. (2010). Effort-reward imbalance, job strain and burnout among clinicians in surgery. *Psychotherapie Psychosomatik Medizinische Psychologie*, 60, 374–379.

Klein, N., Grossmann, I., Uskul, A.K., Kraus, A.A., & Epley, N. (2015). It pays to be nice, but not really nice: Asymmetric reputations from prosociality across 7 countries. *Judgment and Decision Making*, 10, 355–364.

Knafo, A., Israel, S., & Ebstein, R.P. (2011). Heritability of children's prosocial behavior and differential sensitivity to parenting by variation in the dopamine receptor D4 gene. *Development and Psychopathology*, 23, 53–67.

Knafo, A., & Plomin, R. (2008). Parental discipline and affection and children's prosocial behaviour: Genetic and environmental links. *Journal of Personality and Social Psychology*, 90, 147–164.

Knafo, A., Zahn-Waxler, C., Van Hulle, C., Robinson, J.L., & Rhee, S.H. (2008). The developmental origins of a disposition toward empathy: Genetic and environmental contributions. *Emotion*, 8, 737–752.

Knafo-Noam, A., Uzefovsky, F., Israel, S., Davidov, M., & Zahn-Waxler, C. (2015). The prosocial personality and its facets: Genetic and environmental architecture of mother-reported behaviour of 7-year-old twins. *Frontiers in Psychology*, 6 (Article 112), 1–9.

Knowlton, B.J., & Foerde, K. (2008). Neural representations of nondeclarative memories. *Current Directions in Psychological Science*, 17, 107–111.

Kochanska, G., Aksan, N., Prisco, T.R., & Adams, E.E. (2008). Mother-child and father-child mutually responsive orientation in the first 2 years and children's outcomes at preschool age: Mechanisms of influence. *Child Development*, 79, 30–44.

Kochanska, G., & Kim, S. (2014). A complex interplay among the parent-child relationship, effortful control, and internalised, rule-compatible conduct in young children: Evidence from two studies. *Developmental Psychology*, 50, 8–21.

Kochanska, G., Koenig, J.L., Barry, R.A., Kim, S., & Yoon, J.E. (2010). Children's conscience during toddler and preschool years, moral self, and a competent, adaptive developmental trajectory. *Developmental Psychology*, 46, 1320–1332.

Kohlberg, L. (1963). Development of children's orientations toward a moral order. *Vita Humana*, 6, 11–36.

Kohlberg, L. (1975). The cognitive-developmental approach to moral education. *Phi Delta Kappa*, June, 670–677.

Koluchová, J. (1976). The further development of twins after severe and prolonged deprivation: A second report. *Journal of Child Psychology and Psychiatry*, 50, 441–469.

Koole, S. (2009). The psychology of emotion regulation: An integrative review. *Cognition & Emotion*, 23, 4–41.

Kosslyn, S.M. (1994). *Image and brain: The resolution of the imagery debate.* Cambridge, MA: MIT Press.

Kosslyn, S.M., & Thompson, W.L. (2003). When is early visual cortex activated during visual mental imagery? *Psychological Bulletin, 129,* 723–746.

Kotov, R., Gamez, W., Schmidt, F., & Watson, D. (2010). Linking "big" personality traits to anxiety, depressive, and substance use disorders: A meta-analysis. *Psychological Bulletin, 136,* 768–821.

Kowalski, K. (2007). The development of social identity and intergroup attitudes in young children. In O.N. Saracho and B. Spodek (eds.), *Contemporary perspectives on social learning in early childhood education.* Charlotte, NC: Information Age Publishing Inc.

Krapohl, E., Rimfeld, K., Shakeshaft, N.G., Trzaskowski, M., McMillan, A., Pingault, J.-B. et al. (2014). The high heritability of educational achievement reflects many genetically influenced traits, not just intelligence. *Proceedings of the National Academy of Sciences, 111,* 15273–15278.

Krause, M.A. (2015). Evolutionary perspectives on learning: Conceptual and methodological issues in the study of adaptive specialisations. *Animal Cognition, 18,* 807–820.

Krebs, D.L., & Denton, K. (2005). Toward a more pragmatic approach to morality: A critical evaluation of Kohlberg's model. *Psychological Review, 112,* 629–649.

Krevans, J., & Gibbs, J.C. (1996). Parents' use of inductive discipline: Relations to children's empathy and prosocial behavior. *Child Development, 67,* 3263–3277.

Króliczak, G., Heard, P., Goodale, M.A., & Gregory, R.L. (2006). Dissociation of perception and action unmasked by the hollow-face illusion. *Brain Research, 1080,* 9–16.

Krueger, J., & Clement, R.W. (1994). The truly false consensus effect: An ineradicable and egocentric bias in social perception. *Journal of Personality and Social Psychology, 67,* 596–610.

Krull, D.S., Seger, C.R., & Silvera, D.H. (2008). Smile when you say that: Effects of willingness on dispositional inferences. *Journal of Experimental Social Psychology, 44,* 735–742.

Krupinski, E.A., Graham, A.R., & Weinstein, R.S. (2013). Characterising the development of visual search expertise in pathology residents viewing whole slide images. *Human Pathology, 44,* 357–364.

Kuhn, G., & Findlay, J.M. (2010). Misdirection, attention and awareness: Inattentional blindness reveals temporal relationship between eye movements and visual awareness. *Quarterly Journal of Experimental Psychology, 63,* 136–146.

Kulatunga-Moruzi, C., Brooks, L.R., & Norman, G.R. (2011). Teaching posttraining: Influencing diagnostic strategy with instructions at test. *Journal of Experimental Psychology: Applied, 17,* 195–209.

Kulkarni, D., & Simon, H.A. (1988). The processes of scientific discovery: The strategy of experimentation. *Cognitive Science, 12,* 139–175.

Kumsta, R., Kreppner, J., Kennedy, M., Knights, N., Rutter, M., & Sonuga-Barke, E. (2015). Psychological consequences of early global deprivation: An overview of findings from the English & Romanian Adoptees Study. *European Psychologist, 20,* 138–151.

Kundel, H.L., Nodine, C.F., Conant, E.F., & Weinstein, S.P. (2007). Holistic components of image perception in mammogram interpretation: Gaze tracking study. *Radiology, 242,* 396–402.

Kuper, H., Singha-Manoux, A., Siegrist, J., et al. (2002). When reciprocity fails: Effort-reward imbalance in relation to coronary heart disease and health functioning within the Whitehall II study. *Occupational and Environmental Medicine, 59,* 777–784.

Kuppens, P., van Mechelen, I., Smits, D.J.M., & de Boeck, P. (2003). The appraisal basis of anger: Specificity, necessity and sufficiency of components. *Emotion, 3,* 254–269.

Labrell, F., van Geert, P., Declercq, C., Baltazart, V., Caillies, S., Olivier, M. et al. (2014). "Speaking volumes": A longitudinal study of lexical and grammatical growth between 17 and 42 months. *First Language, 34,* 97–124.

La Freniere, P.J., Strayer, F.F., & Gauthier, R. (1984). The emergence of same-sex affiliative preferences among preschool peers: A developmental/ethological perspective. *Child Development, 55,* 1958–1965.

Langlois, J.H., Kalakanis, L., Rubenstein, A.J., Larson, A., Hallam, M., & Smoot, M. (2000). Maxims or myths of beauty? A meta-analysis and theoretical review. *Psychological Review, 126,* 390–423.

Lansford, J.E. (2009). Parental divorce and children's adjustment. *Perspectives on Psychological Science, 4,* 140–152.

Laposa, J.M., & Rector, N.A. (2014). Effects of videotaped feedback in group cognitive therapy for social anxiety disorder. *International Journal of Cognitive Therapy, 7,* 360–372.

Lapsley, D., & Carlo, G. (2014). Moral development at the crossroads: New trends and possible futures. *Developmental Psychology, 50,* 1–7.

Larson, J.R., Foster-Fishman, P.G., & Keys, C.B. (1994). Discussion of shared and unshared information in decision-making groups. *Journal of Personality and Social Psychology, 67,* 446–461.

Latham, G.P. (2003). Toward a boundaryless psychology. *Canadian Psychologist, 44,* 216–217.

Latham, G.P., & Locke, E.A. (2007). New developments in and directions for goal-setting research. *European Psychologist, 12,* 290–300.

Lazaridis, M. (2013). The emergence of a temporally extended self and factors that contribute to its development: From theoretical and empirical perspectives. *Monographs of the Society for Research in Child Development, 78,* 1–120.

Lazarus, R.S., & Folkman, S. (1984). *Stress, appraisal and coping.* New York: Springer.

Le, K., Donnellan, M.B., Spilman, S.K., Garcia, O.P., & Conger, R. (2014). Workers behaving badly: Associations between adolescents' reports of the Big Five and counterproductive work behaviours in adulthood. *Personality and Individual Differences, 61–62,* 7–12.

Leahey, T.H. (1992). The mythical revolutions of American psychology. *American Psychologist, 47,* 308–318.

Leaper, C. (2011). More similarities than differences in contemporary theories of social development? A plea for theory bridging. *Advances in Child Development and Behavior, 40,* 337–378.

Leaper, C. (2013). Parents' socialisation of gender in children. In R.E. Tremblay, M. Boivin, & R. De V. Peters (Eds.), *Encylopaedia on early childhood development* (pp. 1–6). Montreal, QC: Centre of Excellence for Early Childhood Development and Strategic Knowledge Cluster on Early Child Development.

Leary, M.R., & Baumeister, R.F. (2000). The nature and function of self-esteem: Sociometer theory. *Advances in Experimental Social Psychology, 32,* 1–62.

Leary, M.R., Haupt, A.L., Strausser, K.S., & Chokel, J.T. (1998). Calibrating the sociometer: The relationship between interpersonal appraisals and state self-esteem. *Journal of Personality and Social Psychology, 74,* 1290–1299.

Le Bon, G. (1895). *The crowd.* London: Ernest Benn.

Lee, S.W.S., Oyserman, D., & Bond, M.H. (2010). Am I doing better than you? That depends on whether you ask me in English or Chinese: Self-enhancement effects of language as a cultural mindset prime. *Journal of Experimental Social Psychology, 46,* 785–791.

Lee, W.E., Wadsworth, M.E.J., & Hotop, M. (2006). The protective role of trait anxiety: A longitudinal cohort study. *Psychological Medicine, 36,* 345–351.

Leek, E.C., Cristino, F., Conlan, L.I., Patterson, C., Rodriguez, E. et al. (2012). Eye movements during the recognition of three-dimensional objects: Preferential fixation of concave surface curvature minima. *Journal of Vision, 12* (Article 7), 1–16.

Lefkowitz, E.S., & Zeldow, P.B. (2006). Masculinity and femininity predict optimal mental health: A belated test of the androgyny hypothesis. *Journal of Personality Assessment, 87,* 95–101.

Leiter, M.P., Day, A., Oore, D.G., & Laschinger, H.K.S. (2012). Getting better and staying better: Assessing civility, incivility, distress, and job attitudes one year after a civility intervention. *Journal of Occupational Health Psychology, 17,* 425–434.

Lemmer, G., & Wagner, U. (2015). Can we really reduce ethnic prejudice outside the lab? A meta-analysis of direct and indirect contact interventions. *European Journal of Social Psychology, 45,* 152–168.

Lesar, T.S., Briceland, I., & Stein, D.S. (1997). Factors related to errors in medication prescribing. *Journal of the American Medical Association, 277,* 312–317.

Levenson, R.W. (1999). The intrapersonal functions of emotions. *Cognition & Emotion, 13,* 481–504.

Levenson, R.W. (2011). Basic emotion questions. *Emotion Review, 3,* 379–386.

Levine, M. (2002). *Walk on by?* Relational Justice Bulletin. Cambridge, UK: Relationships Foundation.

Levinger, G., & Snoek, J. D. (1972*). Attraction in relationship: A new look at interpersonal attraction.* Morristown, NJ: General Learning Press.

Lewinsohn, P.M., Joiner, T.E., & Rohde, P. (2001). Evaluation of cognitive diathesis-stress models in predicting major depressive disorder in adolescents. *Journal of Abnormal Psychology, 110,* 203–215.

Leyens, J.P., Camino, L., Parke, R.D., & Berkowitz, L. (1975). Effects of movie violence on aggression in a field setting as a function of group dominance and cohesion. *Journal of Personality and Social Psychology, 32,* 346–360.

Lieb, R., Wittchen, H.U., Hofler, M., Fuetsch, M., Stein, M.B., & Merikangas, K.R. (2000). Parental psychopathology, parenting styles, and the risk of social phobia in offspring: A prospective-longitudinal community study. *Archives of General Psychiatry, 57,* 859–866.

Lilienfeld, S.O., & Marino, L. (1995). Mental disorder as a Roschian concept: A critique of Wakefield's "harmful dysfunction" analysis. *Journal of Abnormal Psychology, 104,* 411–420.

Lindberg, S.M., Hyde, J.S., Petersen, J.L., & Linn, M.C. (2010). New trends in gender and mathematics performance: A meta-analysis. *Psychological Bulletin, 136,* 1123–1136.

Lindquist, K.A., Gendron, M., Barrett, L.F., & Dickerson, B.C. (2014). Emotion perception, but not affect perception, is impaired with semantic memory loss. *Emotion, 14*, 375–387.

Lisle, A.M. (2007). Assessing learning styles of adults with intellectual difficulties. *Journal of Intellectual Disabilities, 11*, 23–45.

Lo, C., Helwig, C.C., Chen, S.X., Ohashi, M.M., & Cheng, C.M. (2011). The psychology of strengths and weaknesses: Assessing self-enhancing and self-critical tendencies in Eastern and Western cultures. *Self and Identity, 10*, 203–212.

Lóchenhoff, C.E., Chan, W., McCrae, R.R., De Fruyt, F., Jussim, L., De Bolle, M. et al. (2014). Gender stereotypes of personality: Universal and accurate? *Journal of Cross-Cultural Psychology, 45*, 675–694.

Loehlin, J.C., & Nichols, R.C. (1976). *Heredity, environment and personality*. Austin, TX: University of Texas Press.

Loftus, E.F., & Davis, D. (2006). Recovered memories. *Annual Review of Clinical Psychology, 2*, 469–498.

Loftus, E.F., & Palmer, J.C. (1974). Reconstruction of automobile destruction: An example of the interaction between language and memory. *Journal of Verbal Learning and Verbal Behavior, 13*, 585–589.

Loftus, E.F., & Zanni, G. (1975). Eyewitness testimony: Influence of wording of a question. *Bulletin of the Psychonomic Society, 5*, 86–88.

Lopes, P.N., Brackett, M.A., Nezlek, J.B., Schutz, A., Sellin, I., & Salovey, P. (2004). Emotional intelligence and social interaction. *Personality and Social Psychology Bulletin, 30*, 1018–1034.

Lorber, J. (1981), Is your brain really necessary? *Nursing Mirror, 152*, 29–30.

Lourenço, O. (2012). Piaget and Vygotsky: Many resemblances, and a crucial difference. *New Ideas in Psychology, 30*, 281–295.

Love, J.M., Harrison, L., Sagi-Schwartz, A, van IJzendoorn, M.H., Ross, C., Ungerer, J.A. et al. (2003). Child care quality matters: How conclusions may vary with context. *Child Development, 74*, 1021–1033.

Lovell, P.G., Bloj, M., & Harris, J.M. (2012). Optimal integration of shading and binocular disparity for depth perception. *Journal of Vision, 12*, 1–18.

Lovibond, P.F. (2006). Fear and avoidance: An integrated expectancy model. In M.G. Craske, D. Hermans, & D. Vansteenwegen (Eds.), *Fear and learning: Basic science to clinical application* (pp. 117–132). Washington, DC: American Psychological Association.

Low, J., & Hollis, S. (2003). The eyes have it: Development of children's generative thinking. *International Journal of Behavioral Development, 27*, 97–108.

Lucas, T., Alexander, S., Firestone, I.J., & Baltes, B.B. (2006). Self-efficacy and independence from social influence: Discovery of an efficacy-difficulty effect. *Social Influence, 1*, 58–80.

Lucassen, N., Tharner, A., IJzendoorn, M.H., Bakermans-Kranenburg, M.J., Volling, B.L., Verhulst, F.C. et al. (2011). The association between paternal sensitivity and infant-father security: A meta-analysis of three decades of research. *Journal of Family Psychology, 25*, 986–992.

Luchins, A.S. (1942). Mechanization in problem solving: The effect of *Einstellung*. *Psychological Monographs, 54*, 248.

Luckow, A., Reifman, A., & McIntosh, D.N. (1998). *Gender differences in caring: A meta-analysis.* Poster presented at 106th annual convention of the American Psychological Association, San Francisco.

Luo, S., & Zhang, G. (2009). What leads to romantic attraction: Similarity, reciprocity, security, or beauty? Evidence from a speed-dating study. *Journal of Personality, 77*, 933–964.

Lundahl, B., Risser, H.J., & Lovejoy, M.C. (2006). A meta-analysis of parent training: Moderators and follow-up effects. *Clinical Psychology Review, 26*, 86–104.

Luria, A.R. (1968). *The mind of a mnemonist*. New York: Basic Books.

Lustig, C., Konkel, A., & Jacoby, L.L. (2004). Which route to recovery? Controlled retrieval and accessibility bias in retroactive interference. *Psychological Science, 15*, 729–735.

Lykken, D.T., & Tellegen, A. (1993). Is human mating adventitious or the result of lawful choice: A twin study of mate selection. *Journal of Personality and Social Psychology, 65*, 56–68.

Lyn, H., Greenfield, P.M., Savage-Rumbaugh, S., Gillespie-Lynch, K., & Hopkins, W.D. (2011). Nonhuman primates do declare! A comparison of declarative symbol and gesture use in two children, two bonobos and a chimpanzee. *Language & Communication, 31*, 63–74.

Lyn, H., Russell, J.L., Leavens, D.A., Bard, K.A., Boysen, S.T., Schaeffer, J.A. et al. (2014). Apes communicate about absent and displaced objects: Methodology matters. *Animal Cognition, 17*, 85–94.

MacDonald, G., & Leary, M.R. (2005). Why does social exclusion hurt? The relationship between social and physical pain. *Psychological Bulletin, 131*, 202–223.

Mackintosh, N.J. (1998). *IQ and human intelligence*. Oxford: Oxford University Press.

Magid, M., Finzi, E., Kruger, T.H.C., Robertson, H.T., Keeling, B.H., Jung, S. et al. (2015). Treating depression with botulinum toxin: A pooled analysis of randomised controlled trials. *Pharmacopsychiatry, 48,* 205–210.

Mahé, A., Corson, Y., Verrier, N., & Payoux, M. (2015). Misinformation effect and centrality. *Revue Européenne de Psychologie Appliquée, 65,* 155–162.

Main, M., Kaplan, N., & Cassidy, J. (1985). Security in infancy, childhood, and adulthood: A move to the level of representation. In I. Bretherton & E. Waters (Eds.), Growing points of attachment theory and research. *Monographs of the Society for Research in Child Development, 50*(1–2), 66–104.

Main, M., & Weston, D.R. (1981). The quality of the toddler's relationship to mother and to father: Related to conflict behavior and the readiness to establish new relationships. *Child Development, 52,* 932–940.

Mainous, A.G., Everett, C.J., Diaz, V.A., Player, M.S., Gebregziabher, M., & Smith, D.W. (2010). Life stress and atheriosclerosis: A pathway through unhealthy lifestyle. *International Journal of Psychiatry in Medicine, 40,* 147–161.

Malle, B.F. (2006). The actor-observer asymmetry in causal attribution: A (surprising) meta-analysis. *Psychological Bulletin, 132,* 895–919.

Malle, B.F., Knobe, J., & Nelson, S. (2007). Actor-observer asymmetries in behaviour explanations: New answers to an old question. *Journal of Personality and Social Psychology, 93,* 491–514.

Mann, L. (1981). The baiting crowd in episodes of threatened suicide. *Journal of Personality and Social Psychology, 41,* 703–709.

Manning, R., Levine, M., & Collins, A. (2007). The Kitty Genovese murder and the social psychology of helping: The parable of the 38 witnesses. *American Psychologist, 62,* 555–562.

Marcus, B., & Schulz, A. (2005). Who are the people reluctant to participate in research? Personality correlates of four different types of non-response as inferred from self-and observer ratings. *Journal of Personality, 73,* 969–984.

Marcus, D.K., O'Connell, D., Norris, A.L., & Sawaqdeh, A. (2014). Is the Dodo bird endangered in the 21st century? A meta-analysis of treatment comparison studies. *Clinical Psychology Review, 34,* 519–530.

Mares, M.L., & Woodard, E. (2005). Positive effects of television on children's social interactions: A meta-analysis. *Media Psychology, 7,* 301–322.

Mark, J. (2011). The menace within. *Stanford Alumni,* July–August, 1–6.

Mark, V. (1996). Conflicting communicative behaviour in a split-brain patient: Support for dual consciousness. In S. Hameroff, A. Kaszniak, & A. Scott (Eds.), *Toward a science of consciousness: The first Tucson discussions and debates* (pp. 189–196).

Markus, H.R., & Kitayama, S. (1991). Culture and the self: Implications for cognition, emotion and motivation. *Psychological Review, 98,* 224–253.

Marmot, M.G., Bosma, H., Hemingway, H., Brunner, E., & Stansfeld, S. (1997). Contribution of job control and other risk factors to social variations in coronary heart disease incidence. *Lancet, 350,* 235–239.

Marteinsdottir, I.M., Svensson, A., Svedberg, M., Anderberg, U.M., & Von Knorring, L. (2007). The role of life events in social phobia. *Nordic Journal of Psychology, 61,* 207–212.

Martin, C.L., & Halverson, C.F. (1987). The roles of cognition in sex role acquisition. In D.B. Carter (Ed.), *Current conceptions of sex roles and sex typing: Theory and research.* New York: Praeger.

Martin, C.L., Ruble, D.N. (2004). Children's search for gender cues: Cognitive perspectives on gender development. *Current Directions in Psychological Science, 13,* 67–70.

Martin, C.L., Wood, C.H., & Little, J.K. (1990). The development of gender stereotype components. *Child Development, 61,* 1891–1904.

Martin, R.A. (1989). Techniques for data acquisition and analysis in field investigations of stress. In R.W.J. Neufeld (Ed.), *Advances in the investigation of psychological stress.* New York: Wiley.

Martinez, C.S.M., Calbet, H.B., & Feigenbaum, P. (2011). Private and inner speech and the regulation of social speech communication. *Cognitive Development, 26,* 214–229.

Marzoli, D., Custodero, M., Pagliara, A., & Tommasi, L. (2013). Sun-induced frowning fosters aggressive feelings. *Cognition and Emotion, 27,* 1513–1521.

Maslach, C. (2011). Burnout and engagement in the workplace: New perspectives. *The European Health Psychologist, 13,* 44–47.

Maslach, C., & Jackson, S.E. (1981). The measurement of experienced burnout. *Journal of Occupational Behaviour, 2,* 99–113.

Maslach, C., Jackson, S.E., & Leiter, M.P. (1996). *Maslach Burnout Inventory manual* (3rd ed.). Palo Alto, CA: Consulting Psychologists Press.

Massen, C., & Vaterrodt-Plünnecke, B. (2006). The role of proactive interference in mnemonic techniques. *Memory, 14,* 89–96.

Masuda, A.D., Locke, E.A., & Williams, K.J. (2015). The effects of simultaneous learning and performance goals on performance: An inductive exploration. *Journal of Cognitive Psychology, 27,* 37–52.

Mathy, F., & Feldman, J. (2012). What's magic about magic numbers: Chunking and data compression in short-term memory. *Cognition, 122,* 346–362.

Matsumoto, D. (2009). Facial expression of emotion. In D. Sander & K.R. Scherer (Eds.), *The Oxford companion to emotion and the affective states* (pp. 175–176). Oxford: Oxford University Press.

Matt, G.E., & Navarro, A.M. (1997). What meta-analyses have and have not taught us about psychotherapy effects: A review and future directions. *Clinical Psychology Review, 17*, 1–32.

Matthews, D., Lieven, E., Theakston, A., & Tomasello, M. (2005). The role of frequency in the acquisition of English word order. *Cognitive Development, 20*, 121–136.

Matthews, K.A., Glass, D.C., Rosenman, R.H., & Bortner, R.W. (1977). Competitive drive, Pattern A, and coronary heart disease: A further analysis of some data from the Western Collaborative Group. *Journal of Chronic Diseases, 30*, 489–498.

Mayer, J.D., Salovey, P., Caruso, D.R., & Sitarenios, G. (2003). Measuring emotional intelligence with the MSCEIT V2.0. *Emotion, 3*, 97–105.

Mazureck, U., & van Hattem, J. (2006). Rewards for safe driving behaviour: Influence on following distance and speed. *Transportation Research Part F: Traffic Psychology and Behaviour, 12*, 99–106.

McCaffrey, T. (2012). Innovation relies on the obscure: A key to overcoming the classic problem of functional fixedness. *Psychological Science, 23*, 215–218.

McCartney, K., Harris, M.J., & Bernieri, F. (1990). Growing up and growing apart: A developmental meta-analysis of twin studies. *Psychological Bulletin, 107*, 226–237.

McCrae, R.R., & Costa, P.T. (1985). Updating Norman's "adequate taxonomy": Intelligence and personality dimensions in natural language and in questionnaires. *Journal of Personality and Social Psychology, 49*, 710–721.

McCrae, R.R., & Costa, P.T. (1990). *Personality in adulthood*. New York: Guilford Press.

McCrae, R.R., & Costa, P.T. (1997). Personality trait structure as a human universal. *American Psychologist, 52*, 509–516.

McDonnell, A.R. (2011). The multiple self-aspects framework: Self-concept representation and its implications. *Personality and Social Psychology Review, 15*, 3–27.

McGarrigle, J., & Donaldson, M. (1975). Conservation accidents. *Cognition, 3*, 341–350.

McGrew, K.S. (2009). CHC theory and the human cognitive abilities research: Standing on the shoulders of the giants of psychometric intelligence research. *Intelligence, 37*, 1–10.

McGuire, J. (2008). A review of effective interventions for reducing aggression and violence. *Philosophical Transactions of the Royal Society B, 363*, 2577–2597.

McEachrane, M. (2009). Emotion, meaning, and appraisal theory. *Theory & Psychology, 19*, 33–53.

McGuffin, P., & Rivera, M. (2015). The interaction between stress and genetic factors in the aetiopathogenesis of depression. *World Psychiatry, 14*, 161–163.

McLaughlin, K., Remy, M., & Schmidt, H.G. (2008). Is analytic information processing a feature of expertise in medicine? *Advances in Health Sciences Education, 13*, 123–128.

Megreya, A.M., White, D., & Burton, A.M. (2007). The other-race effect does not depend on memory: Evidence from a matching task. *Quarterly Journal of Experimental Psychology, 64*, 1473–1483.

Mehta, P.H., & Beer, J. (2010). Neural mechanisms of the testosterone-aggression relation: The role of orbitofrontal cortex. *Journal of Cognitive Neuroscience, 22*, 2357–2368.

Meichenbaum, D. (1985). *Stress inoculation training*. New York: Pergamon.

Melo, M., Scarpin, D.J., Amaro, E., Passos, R.B.D., Sato, J.R., Friston, K.J. et al. (2012). How doctors generate diagnostic hypotheses: A study of radiological diagnosis with functional magnetic resonance imaging. *PLoS ONE, 6*(12), e28752. doi: 10.1371/journal.pone.0028752.

Menges, R.J. (1973). Openness and honesty versus coercion and deception in psychological research. *American Psychologist, 28*, 1030–1034.

Metcalfe, J., & Wiebe, D. (1987). Intuition in insight and noninsight problem solving. *Memory & Cognition, 15*, 238–246.

Meyer, G.J., & Shack, J.R. (1989). Structural convergence of mood and personality: Evidence for old and new directions. *Journal of Personality and Social Psychology, 57*, 691–706.

Mezulis, A.H., Abramson, L.Y., Hyde, J.S., & Hankin, B.L. (2004). Is there a universal positivity bias in attributions? A meta-analytic review of individual, developmental, and cultural differences in the self-serving attributional bias. *Psychological Bulletin, 130*, 711–747.

Mickelson, K., Kessler, R.C., & Shaver, P. (1997). Adult attachment in a nationally representative sample. *Journal of Personality and Social Psychology, 73*, 1092–1106.

Miele, F. (2002). *Intelligence, race, and genetics: Conversations with Arthur R. Jensen*. Boulder, CO: Westview.

Milgram, S. (1974). *Obedience to authority*. New York: Doubleday.

Milivojevic, B. (2012). Object recognition can be viewpoint dependent or invariant: It's just a matter of time and task. *Frontiers in Computational Neuroscience*, 6 (Article 27), 1–3.

Miller, G.A. (1956). The magic number seven, plus or minus two: Some limits on our capacity for processing of information. *Psychological Review*, 63, 81–93.

Milner, A.D., & Goodale, M.A. (2008). Two visual systems re-viewed. *Neuropsychologia*, 46, 774–785.

Moè, A., & De Beni, R. (2004). Studying passages with the loci method: Are subject-generated more effective than experimenter-supplied loci pathways? *Journal of Mental Imagery*, 28, 75–86.

Moè, A., & De Beni, R. (2005). Stressing the efficiency of the loci method: Oral presentation and the subject-generation of the loci pathway with expository passages. *Applied Cognitive Psychology*, 19, 95–106.

Mols, F., & Denollet, J. (2010). Type D personality in the general population: A systematic review of health status, mechanisms of disease, and work-related problems. *Health and Quality of Life Outcomes*, 8 (Article 9), 1–10.

Monaghan, P., Sio, U.N., Lau, S.W., Woo, H.K., Linkenauger, S.A., & Ormerod, T.C. (2015). Sleep promotes analogical transfer in problem solving. *Cognition*, 143, 25–30.

Monasterio, E., Mei-Dan, O., Hackney, A.C., Lane, A.R., Zwir, I., Rozsa, S., & Cloninger, C.R. (2016). Stress reactivity and personality in extreme sport athletes: The psychobiology of BASE jumpers. *Physiology & Behavior, 167*, 289–297.

Montoya, R.M., Horton, R.S., & Kirchner, J. (2008). Is actual similarity necessary for attraction? A meta-analysis of actual and perceived similarity. *Journal of Social and Personal Relationships*, 25, 889–922.

Morgan, H., & Raffle, C. (1999). Does reducing safety behaviours improve treatment response in patients with social phobia? *Australian and New Zealand Journal of Psychiatry*, 33, 503–510.

Morris, C.D., Bransford, J.D., & Franks, J.J. (1977). Levels of processing versus transfer appropriate processing. *Journal of Verbal Learning and Verbal Behavior*, 16, 519–533.

Morris, P.E., Fritz, C.O., Jackson, L., Nichol, E., & Roberts, E. (2005). Strategies for learning proper names: Expanding retrieval practice, meaning and imagery. *Applied Cognitive Psychology*, 19, 779–798.

Morris, P.E., Jones, S., & Hampson, P. (1978). An imagery mnemonic for the learning of people's names. *British Journal of Psychology*, 69, 335–336.

Moscovici, S. (1980). Toward a theory of conversion behavior. In L. Berkowitz (Ed.), *Advances in experimental social psychology* (Vol. 13, pp. 209–239). New York: Academic Press.

Mosing, M.A., Madison, G., Pedersen, N.L., Kuja-Halkola, R., & Ullén, F. (2014). Practice does not make perfect: No causal effect of music practice on music ability. *Psychological Science*, 25, 1795–1803.

Moss, E. (1992). The socioaffective context of joint cognitive activity. In L.T. Winegar & J. Valsiner (Eds.), *Children's development within social context* (Vol. 2, pp. 117–155). Hillsdale, NJ: Lawrence Erlbaum Associates, Inc.

Moss, J., Kotovsky, K., & Cagan, J. (2011). The effect of incidental hints when problems are suspended before, during, or after an impasse. *Journal of Experimental Psychology: Learning, Memory, and Cognition, 37*, 140–148.

Mowrer, O.H. (1947). On the dual nature of learning: A reinterpretation of "conditioning" and "problem-solving". *Harvard Educational Review*, 17, 102–148.

Moxley, J.H., Ericsson, K.A., Charness, N., & Krampe, R.T. (2012). The role of intuition and deliberative thinking in experts' superior tactical decision-making. *Cognition*, 124, 72–78.

Mullen, B., Brown, R., & Smith, C. (1992). Ingroup bias as a function of salience, relevance, and status: An integration. *European Journal of Social Psychology*, 22, 103–122.

Myrtek, M. (2001). Meta-analyses of prospective studies on coronary heart disease, Type A personality, and hostility. *International Journal of Cardiology*, 79, 245–251.

Nairne, J.S. (2002). The myth of the encoding-retrieval match. *Memory*, 10, 389–395.

Nairne, J.S. (2015). Encoding and retrieval: Beyond Tulving and Thomson's (1973) encoding specificity. In M.W. Eysenck & D. Groome (Eds.), *Classic studies in cognitive psychology* (pp. 117–132). London: Sage.

National Institute of Child Health and Development (NICHD) Early Child Care Research Network (2003). Does quality of child care affect child outcomes at age 4½? *Developmental Psychology*, 39, 451–469.

Nauts, S., Langnet, O., Huijsmans, I., Vonk, R., & Wigboldus, D.H.J. (2014). Forming impressions of personality: A replication and review of Asch's (1946) evidence for a primacy-of-warmth effect in impression formation. *Social Psychology*, 45, 153–163.

Nedelec, J.L., & Beaver, K.M. (2014). Physical attractiveness as a phenotypic marker of health: An assessment using a nationally representative sample of American adults. *Evolution and Human Behavior*, 35, 456–463.

Nemeth, C., Mayseless, O., Sherman, J., & Brown, Y. (1990). Exposure to dissent and recall of information. *Journal of Personality and Social Psychology, 58,* 429–437.

Nesdale, D. (2013). Social acumen: Its role in constructing group identity and attitudes. In M. Banaji & S.A. Gelman (Eds.), *Navigating the social world: What infants, children, and other species can teach us* (pp. 323–326). Oxford: Oxford University Press.

Newell, A., & Simon, H.A. (1972). *Human problem solving.* Englewood Cliffs, NJ: Prentice Hall.

Newman, H.H., Freeman, F.N., & Holzinger, K.J. (1937). *Twins.* Chicago: University of Chicago Press.

Niedenthal, P.M. (2007). Embodying emotion. *Science, 316,* 1002–1005.

Norby, S. (2015). Why forget? On the adaptive value of memory loss. *Perspectives on Psychological Science, 10,* 551–578.

Norenzayan A., Choi, I., & Nisbett, R.E. (2002). Cultural similarities and differences in social inference: Evidence from behavioural predictions and lay theories of behaviour. *Personality and Social Psychology Bulletin, 28,* 109–120.

Norton, M.I., Frost, J.H., & Ariely, D. (2013). Less is often more, but not always: Additional evidence that familiarity breeds contempt and a call for future research. *Journal of Personality and Social Psychology, 105,* 921–923.

Nummenmaa, L., Glerean, E., Hari, R., & Hietanen, J.K. (2014). Bodily maps of emotions. *Proceedings of the National Academy of Sciences, 111,* 646–651.

Oakes, P.J., Haslam, S.A., & Turner, J.C. (1994). *Stereotyping and social reality.* Malden, MA: Blackwell.

O'Boyle, E.H., Humphrey, R.H., Pollack, J.M., Hawver, T.H., & Story, P.A. (2011). The relation between emotional intelligence and job performance: A meta-analysis. *Journal of Organizational Behavior, 32,* 788–818.

Ochs, E., & Schieffelin, B. (1995). The impact of language socialization on grammatical development. In P. Fletcher & B. MacWhinney (Eds.), *Handbook of child language* (pp. 73–94). Oxford: Blackwell.

O'Connor, T.G., Caspi, A., DeFries, J.C., & Plomin, R. (2003). Genotype-environment interaction in children's adjustment to parental separation. *Journal of Child Psychology and Psychiatry, 44,* 849–856.

O'Connor, T.G., & Croft, C.M. (2001). A twin study of attachment in pre-school children. *Child Development, 72,* 1501–1511.

O'Connor, T.G., Rutter, M., Beckett, C., Keaveney, L., Kreppner, J.M., and the English and Romanian Adoptees Study Team (2000). The effects of global severe privation on cognitive competence: Extension and longitudinal follow-up. *Child Development, 71,* 376–390.

Ohlsson, S. (1992). Information processing explanations of insight and related phenomena. In M.T. Keane & K.J. Gilhooly (Eds.), *Advances in the psychology of thinking* (pp. 1–43). London: Harvester Wheatsheaf.

Ojalehto, B.L., & Medin, D.L. (2015). Perspectives on culture and concepts. *Annual Review of Psychology, 66,* 249–275.

Öllinger, M., Jones, G., & Knoblich, G. (2014). The dynamics of search, impasse, and representational change provide a coherent explanation of difficulty in the nine-dot problem. *Psychological Research, 78,* 266–275.

Onishi, K.H., & Baillargeon, R. (2005). Do 15-month-old infants understand false beliefs? *Science, 308,* 255–258.

Orne, M.T. (1962). On the social psychology of the psychological experiment: With particular reference to demand characteristics and their implications. *American Psychologist, 17,* 776–783.

Oudiette, D., & Paller, K.A. (2013). Upgrading the sleeping brain with targeted memory reactivation. *Trends in Cognitive Sciences, 13,* 142–149.

Owusu-Bempah, P., & Hewitt, D. (1994). Racism and the psychological textbook. *The Psychologist, 7,* 163–166.

Padilla-Walker, L.M., Coyne, S.M., Collier, K.M., & Nielson, M.G. (2015). Longitudinal relations between prosocial television content and adolescents' prosocial and aggressive behaviour: The mediating role of empathic concern and self-regulation. *Developmental Psychology, 51,* 1317–1328.

Parke, R.D., & Slaby, R.G. (1983). The development of aggression. In P.H. Mussen (Ed.), *Handbook of child psychology* (Vol. 4, 4th ed., pp. 457–641). New York: Wiley.

Pass, J.A., Lindenberg, S.M., & Park, J.H. (2010). All you need is love: Is the sociometer especially sensitive to one's mating capacity? *European Journal of Social Psychology, 40,* 221–234.

Pasterski, M.E., Geffner, C., Brain, P., Hindmarsh, C., & Hines, M. (2005). Hormone-behavior associations in early infancy. *Hormones and Behavior, 56,* 498–502.

Pasupathi, M., & Wainryb, C. (2010). On telling the whole story: Facts and interpretations in autobiographical memory narratives from childhood through mid-adolescence. *Developmental Psychology, 46,* 735–746.

Patrick, R.B., & Gibbs, J.C. (2012). Inductive discipline, parental expression of disappointed expectations, and moral identity in adolescence. *Journal of Youth and Adolescence, 41,* 973–983.

Patsenko, E.G., & Altmann, E.M. (2010). How planful is routine behaviour? A selective-attention model of performance in the Tower of Hanoi. *Journal of Experimental Psychology: General, 139*, 95–116.

Patterson, G.R. (2002). The early development of coercive family process. In J.B. Reid, G.R. Patterson, & J. Snyder (eds), *Antisocial behaviour in children and adolescents: A developmental analysis and model for intervention*. Washington, DC: American Psychological Association.

Patterson, G.R., Reid, J.B., & Dishion, T.J. (1992). *Antisocial boys*. Eugene, OR: Castalia Press.

Paulhus, D.L. (2002). Socially desirable responding: The evolution of a construct. In H.I. Braun, D.N. Jackson, & D.E. Wiley (Eds.), *The role of constructs in psychological and educational measurement* (pp. 49–69). Mahwah, NJ: Erlbaum.

Paul-Savoie, E., Polvin, S., Daigle, K., Normand, E., Corbin, J.F., Gagnon, R. et al. (2011). A deficit in peripheral serotonin levels in major depressive disorder but not in chronic widespread pain. *Clinical Journal of Pain, 27*, 529–534.

Paunonen, S.V. (2003). Big Five factors of personality and replicated predictions of behavior. *Journal of Personality and Social Psychology, 84*, 411–424.

Paunonen, S.V., & Ashton, M.C. (2001). Big Five factors and facets and the prediction of behaviour. *Journal of Personality and Social Psychology, 81*, 524–539.

Paunonen, S.V., & O'Neill, T.A. (2010). Self-reports, peer ratings and construct validity. *European Journal of Personality, 24*, 189–206.

Pavlov, I.P. (1897). *The work of the digestive glands*. London: Griffin (translated 1902).

Payne, B.K. (2001). Prejudice and perception: The role of automatic and controlled processes in misperceiving a weapon. *Journal of Personality and Social Psychology, 81*, 181–192.

Pellicano, E. (2010). Individual differences in executive function and central coherence predict developmental changes in theory of mind in autism. *Developmental Psychology, 46*, 530–544.

Penaloza, A.A., & Calvillo, D.P. (2012). Incubation provides relief from artificial fixation in problem solving. *Creativity Research Journal, 24*, 338–344.

Penley, J.A., Tomaka, J., & Wiebe, J.S. (2002). The association of coping to physical and psychological health outcomes: A meta-analytic review. *Journal of Behavioral Medicine, 25*, 551–603.

Perry, G. (2014). The view from the boys. *Psychologist, 27*, 834–836.

Peterson, C., Slaughter, V., Moore, C., & Wellman, H.M. (2016). Peer social skills and theory of mind in children with autism, deafness, or typical development. *Developmental Psychology, 52*, 46–57.

Peterson, R.S., Owens, P.D., Tetlock, P.E., Fan, E.T., & Martorana, P. (1998). Group dynamics in top management teams: Groupthink, vigilance, and alternative models of organisational failure and success. *Organizational Behavior and Human Decision Processes, 73*, 272–305.

Pettigrew, T.F. (1958). Personality and sociocultural factors in intergroup attitudes: A cross-national comparison. *Journal of Conflict Resolution, 2*, 29–42.

Pettigrew, T.F., & Tropp, L.R. (2008). How does intergroup contact reduce prejudice? Meta-analytic tests of three mediators. *European Journal of Social Psychology, 38*, 922–934.

Pettigrew, T.F., & Tropp, L.R. (2011). *When groups meet: The dynamics of intergroup contact*. London: Psychology Press.

Pickel, K.L. (2009). The weapon focus effect on memory for female versus male perpetrators. *Memory, 17*, 664–678.

Pilgrim, D. (2007). The survival of psychiatric diagnosis. *Social Science and Medicine, 65*, 536–544.

Piliavin, I.M., Rodin, J., & Piliavin, J.A. (1969). Good samaritanism: An underground phenomenon? *Journal of Personality and Social Psychology, 13*, 289–299.

Piliavin, J.A., Dovidio, J.F., Gaertner, S.L., & Clark, R.D. (1981). *Emergency intervention*. New York: Academic Press.

Pinker, S. (1989). *Learnability and cognition*. Cambridge, MA: MIT Press.

Pinker, S. (2011). *The better angels of our nature: The decline of violence in history and its causes*. London: Allen Lane.

Pinquart, M., Feussner, C., & Ahnert, L. (2013). Meta-analytic evidence for stability in attachments from infancy to early adulthood. *Attachment & Human Development, 15*, 189–218.

Platow, M.J., & Hunter, J.A. (2014). Necessarily collectivistic. *The Psychologist, 27*, 838–841.

Plomin, R. (1990). The role of inheritance in behaviour. *Science, 248*, 183–188.

Plomin, R., & Daniels, D. (2011). Why are children in the same family so different from one another? *International Journal of Epidemiology, 40*, 563–582.

Plomin, R., & Deary, I.J. (2014). Genetics and intelligence differences: Five special findings. *Molecular Psychiatry, 20*, 98–108.

Pohl, R.F., & Hell, W. (1996). No reduction in hindsight bias after complete information and repeated testing. *Organizational Behavior and Human Decision Processes, 67*, 49–58.

Poldrack, R.A., & Gabrieli, J.D.E. (2001). Characterising the neural mechanisms of skill learning and repetition priming: Evidence from mirror reading. *Brain, 124*, 67–82.

Popper, K.R. (1968). *The logic of scientific discovery*. London: Hutchinson.

Postmes, T., & Spears, R. (1998). Deindividuation and anti-normative behavior: A meta-analysis. *Psychological Bulletin, 123*, 238–259.

Powers, T.A., Koestner, R., & Topciu, R.A. (2005). Implementation intentions, perfectionism, and goal progress: Perhaps the road to hell is paved with good intentions. *Personality and Social Psychology Bulletin, 31*, 902–912.

Prakash, S., & Mandal, P. (2014). Is the DSM-5 position on *dhat* syndrome justified? *Asian Journal of Psychology, 12*, 155–157.

Prass, M., Grimsen, C., König, M., & Fahle, M. (2013). Ultra-rapid object categorisation: Effect of level, animacy and context. *PLoS ONE, 8*(6), e68051.

Prot, S., Gentile, D.A., Anderson, C.A., Suzuki, K., Swing, E., Lim, K.M. et al. (2014). Long-term relations among prosocial-media use, empathy, and prosocial behaviour. *Psychological Science, 25*, 358–368.

Proulx, G., & Fahy, R.F. (2004). *Account analysis of WTC survivors*. Proceedings of the 3rd International Symposium on Human Behaviour in Fire, Belfast, UK, 1–3 September.

Pulsifer, M.B., Brandt, J., Salorio, C.F., Vining, E.P.G., Carson, B.S., & Freeman, J.M. (2004). The cognitive outcome of hemispherectomy in 71 children. *Epilepsia, 45*, 243–254.

Pyc, M.A., & Rawson, K.A. (2012). Why is test-restudy practice beneficial for memory? An evaluation of the mediator shift hypothesis. *Journal of Experimental Psychology: Learning, Memory, and Cognition, 38*, 737–746.

Rahe, R.H., & Arthur, R.J. (1977). Life-change patterns surrounding illness experience. In A. Monat & R.S. Lazarus (Eds.), *Stress and coping* (pp. 341–345). New York: Columbia University Press.

Rank, S.G., & Jacobsen, C.K. (1977). Hospital nurses' compliance with medication overdose order: A failure to replicate. *Journal of Health and Social Psychology, 18*, 188–193.

Redding, G.M., & Vinson, D.W. (2010). Virtual and drawing structures for the Müller-Lyer illusions. *Attention, Perception & Psychophysics, 72*, 1350–1366.

Reicher, S., & Haslam, S.A. (2006). Rethinking the psychology of tyranny: The BBC prison study. *British Journal of Social Psychology, 45*, 1–40.

Reicher, S., Haslam, S.A., & Smith, J.R. (2012). Working toward the experimenter: Reconceptualising obedience within the Milgram paradigm as identification-based followership. *Perspectives on Psychological Science, 7*, 315–324.

Reicher, S., Spears, R., & Postmes, T. (1995). A social identity model of deindividuation phenomena. In W. Stroebe & M. Hewstone (Eds.), *European review of social psychology* (Vol. 6, pp. 161–198). Chichester, UK: Wiley.

Reis, H.T., Maniaci, M.R., Capranello, P.A., Eastwick, P.W., & Finkel, E.J. (2011). Familiarity does indeed promote attraction in live interaction. *Journal of Personality and Social Psychology, 101*, 557–570.

Rensink, R.A., O'Regan, J.K., & Clark, J.J. (1997). To see or not to see: The need for attention to perceive changes in scenes. *Psychological Science, 8*, 245–277.

Reynolds, M.R., Scheiber, C., Hajovsky, D.B., Schwartz, B., & Kaufman, A.S. (2015). Gender differences in academic achievement: Is writing an exception to the gender similarities hypothesis? *Journal of Genetic Psychology, 176*, 211–234.

Richardson, K., & Norgate, S.H. (2015). Does IQ really predict job performance? *Applied Developmental Science, 19*, 153–169.

Robertson, S.I. (2001). *Problem solving*. Hove, UK: Psychology Press.

Robinson, J.L., Zahn-Waxler, C., & Emde, R.N. (1994). Patterns of development in early empathic behavior: Environmental and child constitutional influences. *Social Development, 3*, 125–145.

Rock, I., & Palmer, S. (1990). The legacy of Gestalt psychology. *Scientific American*, December, 48–61.

Roediger, H.L., & Gallo, D.A. (2001). Levels of processing: Some unanswered questions. In M. Naveh-Benjamin, M. Moscovitch, & H.L. Roediger (Eds.), *Perspectives on human memory and cognitive aging* (pp. 28–47). New York: Psychology Press.

Roediger, H.L., & Karpicke, J.D. (2006). Test-enhanced learning: Taking memory tests improves long-term retention. *Psychological Science, 17*, 249–255.

Roese, N.J., & Vohs, K.D. (2012). Hindsight bias. *Perspectives on Psychological Science, 7*, 411–426.

Roidl, E., Frehse, B., & Höger, R. (2014). Emotional states of drivers and the impact on speed, acceleration and traffic violations: A simulator study. *Accident Analysis and Prevention, 70*, 282–292.

Rolls, G. (2010). *Classic case studies in psychology* (2nd ed.). London: Hodder Education.

Rönnlund, M., Nyberg, L., Bäckman, L., & Nilsson, L.-G. (2005). Stability, growth, and decline in adult life span development of declarative memory: Cross-sectional and longitudinal data from a population-based study. *Psychology and Aging, 20*, 3–18.

Roos, P., Gelfand, M., Nau, D., & Carr, R. (2014). High strength-of-ties and low mobility enable the evolution of third-party punishment. *Proceedings of the Royal Society B, 281*(20132661), 1–7.

Rosenbaum, M.E. (1986). The repulsion hypothesis: On the non-development of relationships. *Journal of Personality and Social Psychology, 51*, 1156–1166.

Rosenberg, S., Nelson, C., & Vivekananthan, P.S. (1968). A multidimensional approach to the structure of personality impressions. *Journal of Personality and Social Psychology, 9*, 283–294.

Rosenman, R.H., Brand, R.J., Jenkins, C.D., Friedman, M., Straus, R., & Wurm, M. (1975). Coronary heart disease in the Western Collaborative Group Study: Final follow-up experience of 8½ years. *Journal of the American Medical Association, 22*, 872–877.

Rosenthal, R. (1966). *Experimenter effects in behavioral research.* New York: Appleton-Century-Crofts.

Rossen, E., & Kranzler, J.H. (2009). Incremental validity of the Mayer-Salovey-Caruso Emotional Intelligence Test Version 2.0 (MSCEIT) after controlling for personality and intelligence. *Journal of Research in Personality, 43*, 60–65.

Roth, A., & Fonagy, P., Parry, G., Target, M., & Woods, R. (2005). *What works for whom? A critical review of psychotherapy research* (2nd ed.). New York: Guilford Press.

Rothbaum, F., Pott, M., Azuma, H., & Wisz, J. (2000). The development of close relationships in Japan and the United States: Paths of symbiotic harmony and generative tension. *Child Development, 71*, 1121–1142.

Rowe, M.L. (2008). Child-directed speech: Relation to socioeconomic status, knowledge of child development and child vocabulary skill. *Journal of Child Language, 35*, 185–205.

Rowland, C.A. (2014). The effect of testing versus restudy on retention: A meta-analytic review of the testing effect. *Psychological Bulletin, 140*, 1432–1463.

Rubinstein, S., & Caballero, B. (2000). Is Miss America an undernourished role model? *Journal of the American Medical Association, 283*, 1569–1569.

Rush, A.J. (2009). The role of efficacy and effectiveness trials. *World Psychiatry, 8*, 48–49.

Rutter, M. (1970). *Education, health and behaviour.* Harlow, UK: Longmans.

Rutter, M. (1981). *Maternal deprivation reassessed* (2nd ed.). Harlow, UK: Penguin.

Rutter, M. (2013). Annual research review: Resilience-Clinical implications. *Journal of Child Psychology and Psychiatry, 54*, 474–487.

Rutter, M., & Solantaus, T. (2014). Translation gone awry: Differences between commonsense and science. *European Child and Adolescent Psychiatry, 23*, 247–255.

Rutter, M., Sonuga-Barke, E.J., & Castle, J. (2010). I. Investigating the impact of early institutional deprivation on development: Background and research strategy of the English and Romanian adoptees (ERA) study. *Monographs of the Society for Research in Child Development, 75*, 1–20.

Ryan, J.D., Althoff, R.R., Whitlow, S., & Cohen, N.J. (2000). Amnesia is a deficit in relational memory. *Psychological Science, 11*, 454–461.

Sagi, A., van IJzendoorn, M.H., & Koren-Karie, N. (1991). Primary appraisal of the strange situation: A cross-cultural analysis of the pre-separation episodes. *Developmental Psychology, 27*, 587–596.

Sagotsky, G., Wood-Schneider, M., & Konop, M. (1981). Learning to cooperate: Effects of modeling and direct instructions. *Child Development, 52*, 1037–1042.

Salter, J.E., Smith, S.D., & Ethans, K.D. (2013). Positive and negative affect in individuals with spinal cord injuries. *Spinal Cord, 51*, 252–256.

Salthouse, T.A. (2014). Why are there different age relations in cross-sectional and longitudinal comparisons of cognitive functioning? *Current Directions in Psychological Science, 23*, 252–256.

Samson, D., & Apperly, I.A. (2010). There is more to mind reading than having theory of mind concepts: New directions in theory of mind research. *Infant and Child Development, 19*, 443–454.

Saucier, G., Kenner, J., Iurino, K., Malham, P.B., Chen, Z., Thalmayer, A.G. et al. (2015). Cross-cultural differences in a global "Survey of World Views". *Journal of Cross-Cultural Psychology, 46*, 53–70.

Sauer, J.D., Drummond, A., & Nova, N. (2015). Violent video games: The effects of narrative context and reward structure on in-game and post-game aggression. *Journal of Experimental Psychology: Applied, 21*, 205–214.

Savage-Rumbaugh, E.S., McDonald, K., Sevcik, R.A., Hopkins, W.D., & Rupert, E. (1986). Spontaneous symbol acquisition and communicative use by pygmy chimpanzees (*Pan paniscus*). *Journal of Experimental Psychology: General, 115*, 211–235.

Savage-Rumbaugh, E.S., Murphy, J., Sevcik, R.A., Brakke, K.E., Williams, S.L., & Rumbaugh, D.M. (1993). Language comprehension in ape and child. *Monographs of the Society for Research in Child Development, 58*(3–4), 1–222.

Saville, P., & Blinkhorn, S. (1976). *Undergraduate personality by factored scores.* London: NFER Publishing Company.

Saxton, M. (1997). The contrast theory of negative input. *Journal of Child Language, 24*, 139–161.

Sbarra, D.A., Emery, R.E., Beam, C.R., & Ocker, B.L. (2013). Marital dissolution and major depression in midlife: A propensity score analysis. *Current Psychological Science, 2*, 249–257.

Sbarra, D.A., Law, R.W., & Portley, R.M. (2011). Divorce and death: A meta-analysis and research agenda for clinical, social, and health psychology. *Perspectives on Psychological Science, 5,* 454–474.

Scaini, S., Belotti, R., & Ogliari, A. (2014). Genetic and environmental contributions to social anxiety across different ages: A meta-analytic approach to twin data. *Journal of Anxiety Disorders, 28,* 650–656.

Schaefer, C., Lazarus, R.S., & Coyne, J.C. (1981). Health-related functions of social support. *Journal of Behavioral Medicine, 4,* 381–406.

Schaffer, H.R. (1996). *Social development.* Oxford, UK: Blackwell.

Schaffer, H.R., & Emerson, P.E. (1964). The development of social attachments in infancy. *Monographs of the Society for Research on Child Development,* (Whole No. 29), 1–77.

Scherer, K.R., & Ellsworth, P.C. (2009). Appraisal theories. In D. Sander & K.R. Scherer (Eds.), *The Oxford companion to emotion and the affective sciences* (pp. 45–49). Oxford: Oxford University Press.

Schieffelin, B.B. (1990). *The give and take of everyday life: Language socialization of Kaluli children.* Cambridge, UK: Cambridge University Press.

Schmidt, E.M.B., & Jankowski, P.J. (2014). Predictors of relational aggression and the moderating role of religiousness. *Journal of Aggression, Maltreatment & Trauma, 23,* 333–350.

Schmitt, D.P., Realo, A., Voracek, M., & Allik, J. (2008). Why can't a man be more like a woman? Sex differences in Big Five personality traits across 55 cultures. *Journal of Personality and Social Psychology, 94,* 168–182.

Schommer, N.C., Hellhammer, D.H., & Kirschbaum, C. (2003). Dissociation between reactivity of the hypothalamic-pituitary-adrenocortical axis and the sympathetic-adrenal-medullary system to repeated psychosocial stress. *Psychosomatic Medicine, 65,* 450–460.

Schonert-Reichl, K.A. (1999). Relations of peer acceptance, friendship adjustment, and social behaviour to moral reasoning during early adolescence. *Journal of Early Adolescence, 19,* 249–279.

Schonfeld, I.S., & Bianchi, R. (2016). Burnout and depression: Two entities or one? *Journal of Clinical Psychology, 72,* 22–37.

Schurz, M., & Perner, J. (2015). An evaluation of neurocognitive models of theory of mind. *Frontiers in Psychology, 6* (Article 1610), 1–9.

Schütz, H., & Six, B. (1996). How strong is the relationship between prejudice and discrimination? A meta-analytic answer. *International Journal of Intercultural Relations, 20,* 441–462.

Schweingruber, D., & Wohlstein, R.T. (2005). The madding crowd goes to school: Myths about crowds in introductory sociology textbooks. *Teaching Sociology, 33,* 136–153.

Segerstrom, S.C., & Miller, G.E. (2004). Psychological stress and the human immune system: A meta-analytic study of 30 years of inquiry. *Psychological Bulletin, 130,* 601–630.

Seligman, M.E.P. (1995). The effectiveness of psychotherapy: The consumer reports study. *American Psychologist, 50,* 965–974.

Senghas, A., Kita, S., & Özyürek, A. (2004). Children creating core properties of language: Evidence from an emerging sign language in Nicaragua. *Science, 305,* 1779–1782.

Sereno, S., Triberti, S., Villani, D., Cipresso, P., Gaggioli, A., & Riva, G. (2014). Toward a validation of cyber-interventions for stress disorders based on stress inoculation training: A systematic review. *Virtual Reality, 18,* 73–87.

Shackelford, T.K., Schmitt, D.P., & Buss, D.M. (2005). Universal dimensions of human mate preference. *Personality and Individual Differences, 39,* 447–458.

Shallice, T., & Warrington, E.K. (1974). The dissociation between long-term retention of meaningful sounds and verbal material. *Neuropsychologia, 12,* 553–555.

Shanks, D.R. (2010). Learning: From association to cognition. *Annual Review of Psychology, 61,* 273–301.

Shayer, M. (1999). Cognitive acceleration through science education II: Its effects and scope. *International Journal of Science Education, 21,* 465–485.

Shayer, M. (2003). Not just Piaget; not just Vygotsky, and certainly not Vygotsky as *alternative* to Piaget. *Learning and Instruction, 13,* 465–485.

Shayer, M., & Ginsburg, D. (2009). Thirty years on – a large anti-Flynn effect? (II): 13- and 14-year-olds: Piagetian tests of formal operations norms 1976–2006/7. *British Journal of Educational Psychology, 79,* 409–418.

Sheridan, H., & Reingold, E.M. (2013). The mechanisms and boundary conditions of the Einstellung effect in chess: Evidence from eye movements. *PloS ONE, 8*(10), e75796.

Sherif, M. (1966). *Group conflict and cooperation: Their social psychology.* London: Routledge & Kegan Paul.

Sherif, M., Harvey, O.J., White, B.J., Hood, W.R., & Sherif, C.W. (1961). *Intergroup conflict and cooperation: The robbers' cave experiment.* Norman, OK: University of Oklahoma.

Sherman, J.W., Stroessner, S.J., Conrey, F.R., & Azam, O.A. (2005). Prejudice and stereotype maintenance processes: Attention, attribution, and individuation. *Journal of Personality and Social Psychology, 89,* 607–622.

Shotland, R.L., & Straw, M.K. (1976). Bystander response to an assault: When a man attacks a woman. *Journal of Personality and Social Psychology, 34,* 990–999.

Sieber, J.E., & Stanley, B. (1988). Ethical and professional dimensions of socially sensitive research. *American Psychologist, 43,* 49–55.

Siegler, R.S. (2007). Cognitive variability. *Developmental Science, 10,* 104–109.

Siegler, R.S., & McGilly, K. (1989). Strategy choices in children's time-telling. In I. Levin & D. Zakay (Eds.), *Time and human cognition: A life-span perspective* (pp. 185–218). Amsterdam: Elsevier Science.

Siegler, R.S., & Munakata, Y. (1993). Beyond the immaculate transition: Advances in the understanding of change. *Society for Research in Child Development Newsletter, 36,* 10–13.

Siegler, R.S., & Svetina, M. (2002). A microgenetic/cross-sectional study of matrix completions: Comparing short-term and long-term change. *Child Development, 73,* 793–809.

Siegrist, J., & Rodel, A. (2006). Work stress and health risk behavior. *Scandinavian Journal of Work Environment, 32,* 473–481.

Silke, A. (2003). Deindividuation, anonymity, and violence: Findings from Northern Ireland. *Journal of Social Psychology, 143,* 493–499.

Silverman, K., DeFulio, A., & Sigurdsson, S.O. (2012). Maintenance of reinforcement to address the chronic nature of drug addiction. *Preventive Medicine, 55,* S46–S53.

Silverman, K., Robles, E., Mudric, T., Bigelow, G.E., & Stitzer, M.L. (2004). A randomized trial of long-term reinforcement of cocaine abstinence in methadone-maintained patients who inject drugs. *Journal of Consulting and Clinical Psychology, 72,* 839–854.

Silvia, P.J. (2008). Another look at creativity and intelligence: Exploring higher-order models and probable confounds. *Personality and Individual Differences, 44,* 1012–1021.

Simmons, V.N., Heckman, B.W., Fink, A.C., Small, B.J., & Brandon, T.H. (2013). Efficacy of an experiential, dissonance-based smoking intervention for college students delivered via the internet. *Journal of Consulting and Clinical Psychology, 81,* 810–820.

Simons, D.J., & Chabris, F. (1999). Gorillas in our midst: Sustained inattentional blindness for dynamic events. *Perception, 28,* 1059–1074.

Simonton, D.K. (2011). Creativity and discovery as blind variation and selective retention: Multiple-variant definition and blind-sighted integration. *Psychology of Aesthetics, Creativity and the Arts, 5,* 222–228.

Sio, U.N., & Ormerod, T.C. (2009). Does incubation enhance problem solving? A meta-analytic review. *Psychological Bulletin, 135,* 94–120.

Sitnick, S.L., Shaw, D.S., Gill, A., Dishion, T., Winter, C., Waller, R. et al. (2015). Parenting and the family check-up: Changes in observed parent-child interaction following early childhood intervention. *Journal of Clinical Child & Adolescent Psychology, 44,* 970–984.

Sitzmann, T., & Ely, K. (2011). A meta-analysis of self-regulated learning in work-related training and educational attainment: What we know and where we need to go. *Psychological Bulletin, 137,* 421–442.

Skinner, E.A., Edge, K., Altman, J., & Sherwood, H. (2003). Searching for the structure of coping: A review and critique of category systems for classifying ways of coping. *Psychological Bulletin, 129,* 216–269.

Skoe, E.E.A. (1998). The ethic of care: Issues in moral development. In E.A.A. Skoe & A.L. van der Lippe (Eds.), *Personality development in adolescence: A cross-national and life span perspective* (pp. 143–171). London: Routledge.

Slaby, R.G., & Crowley, C.G. (1977). Modification of cooperation and aggression through teacher attention to children's speech. *Journal of Experimental Child Psychology, 23,* 442–458.

Smith, C.A., & Kirby, L.D. (2001). Toward delivering on the promise of appraisal theory. In K.R. Scherer, A. Schorr, & T. Johnstone (Eds.), *Appraisal processes in emotion: Theory, methods, research* (pp. 121–138). New York: Oxford University Press.

Smith, E.R., & Mackie, D.M. (2000). *Social psychology* (2nd ed.). Philadelphia: Psychology Press.

Smith, J.D., Dishion, T.J., Shaw, D.S., Wilson, M.N., Winter, C.C., & Patterson, G.R. (2014). Coercive family process and early-onset conduct problems from age 2 to school entry. *Developmental Psychopathology, 26,* 917–932.

Smith, L.A., Roman, A., Dollard, M.F., Winefield, A.H., & Siegrist, J. (2005). Effort-reward imbalance at work: The effects of work stress on anger and cardiovascular disease symptoms in a community sample. *Stress and Health, 21,* 113–128.

Smith, P.B., & Bond, M.H. (1993). *Social psychology across cultures: Analysis and perspectives.* New York: Prentice-Hall.

Smith, R., & Lane, R.D. (2015). The neural basis of one's own conscious and unconscious emotional states. *Neuroscience and Biobehavioral Reviews, 57,* 1–29.

Smith, T.J., Lamont, P., & Henderson, J.M. (2012). The penny drops: Change blindness at fixation. *Perception, 41*, 49–492.

Smith, T.W., Marsden, P., Hout, M., & Kim, J. (2011). *General social surveys, 1972–2010.* Chicago, IL: National Opinion Research Center.

Snarey, J.R. (1985). Cross-cultural universality of social-moral development: A critical review of Kohlbergian research. *Psychological Bulletin, 97*, 202–232.

Solomon, R.L., & Wynne, L.C. (1953). Traumatic avoidance learning: Acquisition in normal dogs. *Psychological Monographs, 67* (Whole No. 354), 1–19.

Sorkin, A.R. (2009). *Too big to fail.* London: Penguin.

Spangler, G. (2013). Individual dispositions as precursors of differences in attachment quality: Why maternal sensitivity is nevertheless important. *Attachment & Human Development, 15*, 657–672.

Spangler, G., Johann, M., Ronai, Z., & Zimmermann, P. (2009). Genetic and environmental influence on attachment disorganization. *Journal of Child Psychology and Psychiatry, 50*, 952–961.

Spearman, C.E. (1904). General intelligence objectively determined and measured. *American Journal of Psychology, 15*, 201–292.

Spector, P.E., Dwyer, D.J., & Jex, S.M. (1988). Relation of job stressors to affective, health, and performance outcomes. A comparison of multiple data sources. *Journal of Applied Psychology, 73*, 11–19.

Sperry, R.W. (1968). Hemisphere deconnection and unity in conscious awareness. *American Psychologist, 23*, 723–733.

Spiers, H.J., Maguire, E.A., & Burgess, N. (2001). Hippocampal amnesia. *Neurocase, 7*, 357–382.

Spitz, R.A. (1945). Hospitalism: An inquiry into the genesis of psychiatric conditions in early childhood. *Psychoanalytic Study of the Child, 1*, 113–117.

Sprecher, S. (1998). Insider's perspectives on reasons for attraction to a close other. *Social Psychology Quarterly, 61*, 287–300.

Squire, L.R., Genzel, L., Wixted, J.T., & Morris, R.G. (2015). Memory consolidation. *Cold Spring Harbor Perspectives in Biology, 7*(8), a021766.

Stajkovic, A.D., & Luthans, F. (1998). Self-efficacy and work-related performance: A meta-analysis. *Psychological Bulletin, 124*, 240–261.

Stams, G.J.M., Juffer, F., & van Ijzendoorn, M.H. (2002). Maternal sensitivity, infant attachment, and temperament in early childhood predict adjustment in middle childhood: The case of adopted children and their biologically unrelated parents. *Developmental Psychology, 38*, 806–821.

Stein, J.A., Newcomb, M.D., & Bentler, P.M. (1992). The effect of agency and communality on self-esteem: Gender differences in longitudinal data. *Sex Roles, 26*, 465–481.

Stephen, I.D., Mahmut, M.K., Case, T.I., Fitness, J., & Stevenson, R.J. (2014). The uniquely predictive power of evolutionary approaches to mind and behaviour. *Frontiers in Psychology, 5* (Article 1372), 1–3.

Sternberg, R.J. (1985). *Beyond IQ: A triarchic theory of human intelligence.* Cambridge, UK: Cambridge University Press.

Sternberg, R.J. (2015a). Multiple intelligences in the new age of thinking. In S. Goldstein, D. Princiotta, & J.A. Naglieri (Eds.), *Handbook of intelligence: Evolutionary theory, historical perspective, and current concepts* (pp. 229–242). New York: Springer.

Sternberg, R.J. (2015b). Competence versus performance models of people and tests: A commentary on Richardson and Norgate. *Applied Developmental Science, 19*, 170–175.

Sternberg, R.J., & Kaufman, J.C. (1998). Human abilities. *Annual Review of Psychology, 49*, 479–502.

Stevens, S., Hynan, M.T., & Allen, M. (2000). A meta-analysis of common factor and specific treatment effects across the outcome domains of the phase model of psychotherapy. *Clinical Psychology: Science and Practice, 7*, 273–290.

Stewart, R. (1997). Evolution of the human brain. http://homepage.ac.com/binck/reports/bevolution/breport:html.

Stewart-Williams, S., & Thomas, A.G. (2013). The ape that thought it was a peacock: Does evolutionary psychology exaggerate human sex differences? *Psychological Inquiry, 24*, 137–168.

Steyvers, M., & Hemmer, P. (2012). Reconstruction from memory in naturalistic environments. In B.H. Ross (Ed.), *The Psychology of Learning and Motivation* (Vol. 56, pp. 126–144). New York: Academic Press.

Stieger, A.E., Allemand, M., Robinson, R.W., & Fend, H.A. (2014). Low and decreasing self-esteem during adolescence predict depression two decades later. *Journal of Personality and Social Psychology, 106*, 325–338.

Stone, A.A., Reed, B.R., & Neale, J.M. (1987). Changes in daily life event frequency precede episodes of physical symptoms. *Journal of Human Stress, 134*, 70–74.

Strack, F., Martin, L.L., & Stepper, S. (1988). Inhibiting and facilitating conditions of the human smile: A unobtrusive test of the facial feedback hypothesis. *Journal of Personality and Social Psychology, 54*, 768–777.

Strupp, H.H. (1996). The tripartite model and the consumer reports study. *American Psychologist, 51*, 1017–1024.

Sulin, R.A., & Dooling, D.J. (1974). Intrusion of a thematic idea in retention of prose. *Journal of Experimental Psychology, 103*, 255–262.

Svetlova, M., Nichols, S.R., & Brownell, C.A. (2010). Toddlers' prosocial behavior: From instrumental to empathic to altruistic helping. *Child Development, 81*, 1814–1827.

Swami, V. (2013). Cultural influences on body size ideals. *European Psychologist, 20*, 44–51.

Swami, V., Frederick, D.A., Aavik, T., Alcalay, L., Allik, J., Anderson, D. et al. (2010). Body weight ideals and body dissatisfaction in 26 countries across 10 world regions: Results of the International Body Project I. *Personality and Social Psychology Bulletin, 36*, 309–325.

Sweller, J., & Levine, M. (1982). Effects of goal specificity on means-ends analysis and learning. *Journal of Experimental Psychology: Learning, Memory, and Cognition, 8*, 463–474.

Swim, J.K., Aikin, K.J., Hall, W.S., & Hunter, B.A. (1995). Sexism and racism: Old-fashioned and modern prejudices. *Journal of Personality and Social Psychology, 68*, 199–214.

Szasz, T.S. (1960). *The myth of mental illness*. London: Paladin.

Szechtman, H., & Woody, E. (2004). Obsessive-compulsive disorder as a disturbance of security motivation. *Psychological Review, 111*, 111–127.

Tajfel, H., & Turner, J.C. (1979). *An integrative theory of intergroup conflict*. In W.G. Austin & S. Worchel (Eds.), *The social psychology of intergroup relations* (pp. 33–47). Monterey, CA: Brooks/Cole.

Talaska, C.A., Fiske, S.T., & Chaiken, S. (2008). Legitimating racial discrimination: Emotions, not beliefs, best predict discrimination in a meta-analysis. *Social Justice Research, 21*, 263–396.

Tanti, C., Stukas, A.A., Halloran, M.J., & Foddy, M. (2008). Tripartite self-concept change: Shifts in the individual, relational, and collective self in adolescence. *Self and Identity, 7*, 360–379.

Taylor, S.E., Cousino-Klein, L., Lewisz, B.P., Grunewald, T.L., & Updegraff, J.A. (2000). Behavioral response to stress in females: Tend and befriend, not fight-or-flight. *Psychological Review, 107*, 411–429.

Teper, R., Inzlicht, M., & Page-Gould, E. (2011). Are we more moral than we think? Exploring the role of affect in moral behavior and moral forecasting. *Psychological Science, 22*, 553–558.

Terracciano, A., Abdel-Khalek, A.M., Adamovova, L., Ahan, C.K., Ahan, H.-N., Alansari, B.M. et al. (2005). National character does not reflect mean personality trait levels in 49 cultures. *Science, 310*, 96–100.

Terrace, H.S., Pettito, L.A., Sanders, D.J., & Bever, T.G. (1979). On the grammatical capacities of apes. In K. Nelson (Ed.), *Children's language, Vol. 2*. New York: Gardner Press.

Tetlock, P.E., Peterson, R.S., McGuire, C., Chang, S., & Feld, P. (1992). Assessing political group dynamics: A test of the groupthink model. *Journal of Personality and Social Psychology, 63*, 403–425.

Thompson, A.E., & Voyer, D. (2014). Sex differences in the ability to recognise non-verbal displays of emotion: A meta-analysis. *Cognition & Emotion, 28*, 1164–1195.

Thompson, R.A. (2012). Whither the preconventional child? Toward a life-span moral development theory. *Child Development Perspectives, 6*, 423–429.

Tilker, H.A. (1970). Socially responsible behavior as a function of observer responsibility and victim feedback. *Journal of Personality and Social Psychology, 49*, 420–428.

Tindale, R.S., Smith, C.M., Dykema-Engblade, A., & Kluwe, K. (2012). Good and bad group performance: Same process – different outcomes. *Group Processes & Intergroup Relations, 15*, 603–618.

Toelch, U., & Dolan, R.J. (2015). Informational and normative influences in conformity from a neurocomputational perspective. *Trends in Cognitive Sciences, 19*, 579–589.

Tollestrup, P.A., Turtle, J.W., & Yuille, J.C. (1994). Actual victims and witnesses to robbery and fraud: An archival analysis. In D.F. Ross, J.D. Read, & M.P. Toglia (Eds.), *Adult eyewitness testimony: Current trends and developments* (pp. 144–160). New York: Wiley.

Tolman, E.C. (1948). Cognitive maps in rats and men. *Psychological Review, 55*, 189–208.

Tolman, E.C. (1959). Principles of purposive behaviour. In S. Koch (Ed.), *Psychology: A study of a science: Vol. 2. General systematic formulations, learning, and special processes* (pp. 92–157). New York: McGraw-Hill.

Tomasello, M. (2005). Beyond formalities: The case of language acquisition. *Linguistic Review, 22*, 183–197.

Tomasello, M., Melis, A.P., Tennie, C., Wyman, E., & Herrmann, E. (2012). Two key steps in the evolution of human cooperation: The interdependence hypothesis. *Current Anthropology, 53*, 673–692.

Trahan, L.H., Stuebing, K.K., Fletcher, J.M., & Hiscock, M. (2014). The Flynn effect: A meta-analysis. *Psychological Bulletin, 140*, 1332–1360.

Trautner, H.M., Ruble, D.N., Cyphers, L., Kirsten, B., Behrendt, R., & Hartmann, P. (2005). Rigidity and flexibility of gender stereotypes in childhood: Developmental or differential? *Infant and Child Development, 14*, 365–381.

Triandis, H.C., Carnevale, P., Gelfand, M., Robert, C., Wasti, A., Probst, T. et al. (2001). Culture, personality and deception in intercultural management negotiations. *International Journal of Cross-Cultural Management, 1,* 73–90.

Triandis, H.C., McCusker, C., & Hui, C.H. (1990). Multimethod probes of individualism and collectivism. *Journal of Personality and Social Psychology, 59,* 1006–1020.

Trickett, S.B., & Trafton, J.G. (2007). "What if . . .": The use of conceptual simulations in scientific reasoning. *Cognitive Science, 31,* 843–875.

Triesch, H., Ballard, D.H., & Jacobs, R.A. (2002). Fast temporal dynamics of visual cue integration. *Perception, 31,* 421–434.

Trivers, R.L. (1971). The evolution of reciprocal altruism. *Quarterly Review of Biology, 46,* 35–57.

Trujillo, L.T., Jankowitsch, J.M., & Langlois, J.H. (2014). Beauty is in the eye of the beholding: A neurophysiological test of the averageness theory of facial attractiveness. *Cognitive, Affective & Behavioral Neuroscience, 14,* 1061–1076.

Trzesniewski, K.H., Donnellan, M.B., Caspi, A., Moffitt, T.E., Robins, R.W., & Poultin, R. (2006). Adolescent low self-esteem is a risk factor for adult poor health, criminal behavior, and limited economic prospects. *Developmental Psychology, 42,* 381–390.

Tucker-Drob, E.M., Briley, D.A., & Harden, K.P. (2013). Genetic and environmental influences on cognition across development and context. *Current Directions in Psychological Science, 22,* 349–355.

Tuckey, M.R., & Brewer, N. (2003a). How schema affect eyewitness memory over repeated retrieval attempts. *Applied Cognitive Psychology, 7,* 785–800.

Tuckey, M.R., & Brewer, N. (2003b). The influence of schemas, stimulus ambiguity, and interview schedule on eyewitness memory over time. *Journal of Experimental Psychology: Applied, 9,* 101–118.

Tuffiash, M., Roring, R.W., & Ericsson, K.A. (2007). Expert performance in Scrabble: Implications for the study of the structure and acquisition of complex skills. *Journal of Experimental Psychology: Applied, 13,* 124–134.

Tulving, E. (1979). Relation between encoding specificity and levels of processing. In L.S. Cermak & F.I.M. Craik (Eds.), *Levels of processing in human memory* (pp. 405–428). Hillsdale, NJ: Lawrence Erlbaum Associates.

Tulving, E., & Schacter, D.L. (1990). Priming and human-memory systems. *Science, 247,* 301–306.

Turkheimer, E., Haley, A., Waldron, M., D'Onofrio, B., & Gottesman, I.I. (2003). Socio-economic status modifies heritability of IQ in young children. *Psychological Science, 14,* 623–628.

Turner, R.N., & Crisp, R.J. (2010). Explaining the relationship between ingroup identification and intergroup identification and intergroup bias following recategorisation: A self-regulation theory analysis. *Group Processes & Intergroup Relations, 13,* 251–261.

Turton, S., & Campbell, C. (2005). Tend and befriend versus fight or flight: Gender differences in behavioural response to stress among university students. *Journal of Applied Biobehavioral Research, 10,* 209–232.

Tuvblad, C., Raine, A., Zheng, M., & Baker, L.A. (2009). Genetic and environmental stability differs in reactive and proactive aggression. *Aggressive Behavior, 35,* 437–452.

Twenge, J.M. (2000). The age of anxiety? Birth cohort change in anxiety and neuroticism, 1952–1993. *Journal of Personality and Social Psychology, 70,* 1007–1021.

Twenge, J.M., Gentile, B., DeWall, C.N., Ma, D., Lacefield, K., & Schutz, D.R. (2010). Birth cohort increases in psychopathology among young Americans, 1938–2007: A cross-sectional meta-analysis of the MMPI. *Clinical Psychology Review, 30,* 145–154.

Tyerman, A., & Spencer, C. (1983). A critical test of the Sherifs' Robber's Cave experiment: Intergroup competition and cooperation between groups of well-acquainted individuals. *Small Group Behaviour, 14,* 515–531.

Tyrell, J.B., & Baxter, J.D. (1981). Glucocorticoid therapy. In P. Felig, J.D. Baxter, A.E. Broadus, & L.A. Frohman (Eds.), *Endocrinology and metabolism* (pp. 599–624). New York: McGraw-Hill.

Uchino, B.N. (2006). Social support and health: A review of psychological processes potentially underlying links to disease outcome. *Journal of Behavioral Medicine, 29,* 377–387.

Udry, J.R., & Chantala, K. (2004). Masculinity-femininity guides sexual union formation in adolescents. *Personality and Social Psychology Bulletin, 30,* 44–55.

Ullén, F., Hambrick, D.Z., & Mosing, M.A. (2016). Rethinking expertise: A multifactorial gene-environment interaction model of expert performance. *Psychological Bulletin, 142,* 427–446.

Űnal, B., Critchley, J.A., Fidan, D., & Capewell, S. (2005). Life years gained from modern cardiological treatments and population risk factor changes in England and Wales, 1981–2000. *American Journal of Public Health, 95,* 103–108.

Valentine, E.R. (1992). *Conceptual issues in psychology.* Hove: Psychology Press.

Valkenburg, P.M., Peter, J., & Walther, J.B. (2016). Media effects: Theory and research. *Annual Review of Psychology, 67,* 315–338.

Vancouver, J.B. (2012). Rhetorical reckoning: A response to Bandura. *Journal of Management, 38,* 465–474.

van den Broek, G.S.E., Takashima, A., Segers, E., Fernandez, G., & Verhoeven, L. (2013). Neural correlates of testing effects in vocabulary learning. *NeuroImage, 78,* 94–102.

van der Linden, D., te Nijenhuis, J., & Bakker, A.B. (2010). The general factor of personality: A meta-analysis of Big Five intercorrelations and a criterion-related validity study. *Journal of Research in Personality, 44,* 315–327.

van der Wal, R.A.B., Bucx, M.J.L., Hendriks, J.C.M., Scheffer, G.J., & Prins, J.B. (2016). Psychological distress, burnout and personality traits in Dutch anaesthesiologists: A survey. *European Journal of Anaesthesiology, 33,* 179–186.

van Houtem, C.M.H.H., Laine, M.L., Boomsma, D.I., Ligthart, L., van Wijk, A.J., & De Jongh, A. (2013). A review and meta-analysis of the heritability of specific phobia subtypes and corresponding fears. *Journal of Anxiety Disorders, 27,* 379–388.

Van IJzendoorn, M.H., & Kroonenberg, P.M. (1988). Cross-cultural patterns of attachment: A meta-analysis of the strange situation. *Child Development, 59,* 147–156.

Van Oudenhouven, J.P., Groenewoud, J.T., & Hewstone, M. (1996). Cooperation, ethnic salience and generalisation of inter-ethnic attitudes. *European Journal of Social Psychology, 26,* 649–662.

Vargha-Khadem, F., Gadian, D.G., Watkins, K.E., Connelly, A., Van Paesschen, W., & Mishkin, M. (1997). Differential effects of early hippocampal pathology on episodic and semantic memory. *Science, 277,* 376–380.

Vaughan, G.M., & Hogg, M.A. (2014). *Social psychology* (7th ed.). Frenchs Forest, NSW: Pearson Australia.

Vazire, S., & Carlson, E.N. (2011). Others sometimes know us better than we know ourselves. *Current Directions in Psychological Science, 20,* 104–108.

Venville, G., & Oliver, M. (2015). The impact of a cognitive acceleration programme in science on students in an academically selective high school. *Thinking Skills and Creativity, 15,* 48–60.

Verhulst B., & Hatemi P.K. (2013) Gene-environment interplay in twin models. *Political Analysis, 21,* 368–389.

Viggiano, M.P., Giovannelli, F., Borgheresi, A., Feurra, M., Berardi, N., Pizzorusso, T. et al. (2008). Disruption of the prefrontal cortex by rTMS produces a category-specific enhancement of the reaction times during visual object identification. *Neuropsychologia, 46,* 2725–2731.

Villegas de Posada, C., & Vargas-Trujillo, E. (2015). Moral reasoning and personal behaviour: A meta-analytic review. *Review of General Psychology, 19,* 408–424.

Viswesvaran, C., & Schmidt, F.L. (1992). A meta-analytic comparison of the effectiveness of smoking cessation methods. *Journal of Applied Psychology, 77,* 554–561.

Vögele, C., Ehlers, A., Meyer, A.H., Frank, M., Hahlweg, K., & Margraf, J. (2010). Cognitive mediation of clinical improvement after intensive exposure therapy of agoraphobia and social phobia. *Depression and Anxiety, 27,* 294–301.

von Restorff, H. (1933). Über die Wirkung von Brieichsbildungen im Spurenfeld. *Psychologische Forschung, 18,* 299–542.

Vukasović, T., & Bratko, D. (2015). Heritability of personality: A meta-analysis of behaviour genetic studies. *Psychological Bulletin, 141,* 769–785.

Waaktaar, T., & Torgersen, S. (2013). Self-efficacy is mainly genetic, not learned: A multiple-rater twin study on the causal structure of general self-efficacy in young people. *Twin Research and Human Genetics, 16,* 651–660.

Wachtel, P.L. (1973). Psychodynamics, behavior therapy and the implacable experimenter: An inquiry into the consistency of personality. *Journal of Abnormal Psychology, 82,* 324–334.

Wagemans, J., Feldman, J., Gepshtein, S., Kimchi, R., Poemerantz, J.R., & van der Helm, P.A. (2012). A century of Gestalt psychology in visual perception: II. Conceptual and theoretical foundations. *Psychological Bulletin, 138,* 1218–1252.

Walker, L.J., Pitts, R.C., Hennig, K.H., & Matsuba, M.K. (1995). Reasoning about morality and real-life moral problems. In M. Killen & D. Hart (Eds.), *Morality in everyday life: Developmental perspectives* (pp. 371–408). Cambridge, UK: Cambridge University Press.

Wallas, G. (1926). *The art of thought.* London: Cape.

Wallerstein, J.S. (1984). Children of divorce: Preliminary report of a ten-year follow-up of young children. *American Journal of Orthopsychiatry, 54,* 444–458.

Wang, A.Y., & Thomas, M.H. (2000). Looking for long-term mnemonic effects on serial recall: The legacy of Simonides. *American Journal of Psychology, 113,* 331–340.

Wang, K., Shu, Q., & Tu, Q. (2008). Technostress under different organizational environments: An empirical investigation. *Computers in Human Behavior, 24,* 3002–3013.

Ward, J. (2010). *The student's guide to cognitive neuroscience* (2nd ed.). Hove, UK: Psychology Press.

Warneken, F. (2015). Precocious prosociality: Why do young children help? *Child Development Perspectives, 9,* 1–6.

Wass, R., & Golding, C. (2014). Sharpening a tool for teaching: The zone of proximal development. *Teaching in Higher Education, 19,* 671–684.

Watson, D., & Clark, L.A. (1992). Affects separable and inseparable: On the hierarchical arrangement of the negative affects. *Journal of Personality and Social Psychology, 62,* 489–505.

Watson, D., & Clark, L.A. (1994). *The PANAS-X: Manual for the positive and negative affect schedule – expanded form.* Unpublished manuscript, University of Iowa, Iowa City.

Watson, D., & Pennebaker, J.W. (1989). Health complaints, stress, and distress: Exploring the central role of negative affectivity. *Psychological Review, 96,* 234–254.

Watson, J.B. (1913). Psychology as the behaviorist views it. *Psychological Review, 20,* 158–177.

Webb, T.L., Miles, E., & Sheeran, P. (2012). Dealing with feeling: A meta-analysis of the effectiveness of strategies derived from the process model of emotion regulation. *Psychological Bulletin, 138,* 775–808.

Weeks, D., & James, J. (1995). *Eccentrics: A study of sanity and strangeness.* New York: Villiard.

Weisgram, E.S., Fulcher, M., & Dinella, L.M. (2014). Pink gives girls permission: Exploring the roles of explicit gender labels and gender-typed colours on preschool children's toy preferences. *Journal of Applied Developmental Psychology, 35,* 401–409.

Wellman, H.M., Cross, D., & Watson, J. (2001). Meta-analysis of theory-of-mind development: The truth about false belief. *Child Development, 72,* 655–684.

Wells, A., & Papageorgiou, C. (1998). Social phobia: Effects of external attention on anxiety, negative beliefs, and perspective taking. *Behavior Therapy, 29,* 357–370.

West, T.V., Pearson, A.R., Dovidio, J.F., Shelton, J.N., & Trail, T. (2009). Superordinate identity and intergroup roommate friendship development. *Journal of Experimental Social Psychology, 45,* 1266–1272.

Westen, D. (1996). *Psychology: Mind, brain, and culture.* New York: Wiley.

Wheeler, L.R. (1942). A comparative study of the intelligence of East Tennessee mountain children. *Journal of Educational Psychology, 33,* 321–334.

White, F.A., Abu-Rayya, H.M., Bliuc, A.-M., & Faulkner, N. (2015a). Emotion expression and intergroup bias reduction between Muslims and Christians: Long-term Internet contact. *Computers in Human Behavior, 53,* 435–442.

White, F.A., Abu-Rayya, H.M., & Weitzel, C. (2014). Achieving twelve-months of intergroup bias reduction: The dual identity-electronic contact (DIEC) experiment. *International Journal of Intercultural Relations, 38,* 158–163.

White, F.A., Harvey, L.J., & Abu-Rayya, H.M. (2015b). Improving intergroup relations in the internet age: A critical review. *Review of General Psychology, 19,* 129–139.

White, J. (2005). *Howard Gardner: The myth of multiple intelligences.* London: Institute of Education.

Whiting, B.B., & Whiting, J.W.M. (1975). *Children of six cultures: A psychocultural analysis.* Cambridge, MA: Harvard University Press.

Wieber, F., Thürmer, J.L., & Gollwitzer, P.M. (2015). Promoting the translation of intentions by implementation intentions: Behavioural effects and physiological correlates. *Frontiers in Human Neuroscience, 9* (Article 395), 1–18.

Williams, J.E., & Best, D.L. (1990). *Sex and psyche: Gender and self viewed cross-culturally.* Newbury Park, CA: Sage.

Williams, T.M. (1986). Background and overview. In T.M. Williams (Ed.), *The impact of television: A natural experiment in three communities* (pp. 1–38). Orlando, FL: Academic Press.

Willoughby, T., Adachi, P.J.C., & Good, M. (2012). A longitudinal study of the association between violent video game play and aggression among adolescents. *Developmental Psychology, 48,* 1044–1057.

Wilson, S.J., Lipsey, M.W., & Derzon, J.H. (2003). The effects of school-based intervention programs on aggressive behavior: A meta-analysis. *Journal of Consulting and Clinical Psychology, 71,* 136–149.

Wimmer, H., & Perner, J. (1983). Beliefs about beliefs: Representation and the constraining function of wrong beliefs in young children's understanding of deception. *Cognition, 13,* 103–128.

Winkielman, P., Berridge, K.C., & Wilbarger, J.L. (2005). Unconscious affective reactions to masked happy versus angry faces influence consumption behaviour and judgments of value. *Personality and Social Psychology Bulletin, 31,* 121–135.

Woike, B., Gershkovich, I., Piorkowski, R., & Polo, M. (1999). The role of motives in the content and structure of autobiographical memory. *Journal of Personality and Social Psychology, 76,* 600–612.

Wojciszke, B., Bazinska, R., & Jaworski, M. (1998). On the dominance of moral categories in impression formation. *Personality and Social Psychology Bulletin, 24,* 1245–1257.

Wolsko, C.V., Park, B., Judd, C.M., & Wittenbrink, B. (2000). Framing interethnic ideology: Effects of multicultural and colour-blind perspectives on judgments of groups and individuals. *Journal of Personality and Social Psychology, 78,* 635–654.

Wood, D. (2015). Testing the lexical hypothesis: Are socially important traits more densely reflected in the English lexicon? *Journal of Personality and Social Psychology, 108,* 317–335.

Wood, W., & Eagly, A.H. (2002). A cross-cultural analysis of the behavior of women and men: Implications for the origins of sex differences. *Psychological Bulletin, 128,* 699–727.

Wood, W., Lundgren, S., Ouellette, J.A., Busceme, S., & Blackstone, T. (1994). Minority influence: A meta-analytic review of social influence processes. *Psychological Bulletin, 115,* 323–345.

Worthen, J.B., & Hunt, R.R. (2011). *Mnemonology: Mnemonics for the 21st century.* Hove: Psychology Press.

Wu, A.W., Folkman, S., McPhee, S.J., & Lo, B. (1993). How house officers cope with their mistakes. *Western Journal of Medicine, 159,* 565–569.

Ybarra, O. (2001). When first impressions don't last: The role of isolation and adaptation processes in the revision of evaluative impressions. *Social Cognition, 19,* 491–520.

Yearta, S.K., Maitlis, S., & Briner, R.B. (1995). An exploratory study of goal-setting in theory and practice – A motivational technique that works. *Journal of Occupational and Organizational Psychology, 68,* 237–252.

Yeung, K.-T., & Martin, J.L. (2003). The looking glass self: An empirical test and elaboration. *Social Forces, 81,* 843–879.

Young, S.D., Adelstein, B.D., & Ellis, S.R. (2007). Demand characteristics in assessing motion sickness in a virtual environment: Or does taking a motion sickness questionnaire make you sick? *IEEE Transactions on Visualization and Computer Graphics, 13,* 422–428.

Zahavi, S., & Asher, S.R. (1978). The effect of verbal instructions on preschool children's aggressive behaviour. *Journal of School Psychology, 16,* 146–153.

Zahn-Waxler, C., Radke-Yarrow, M., Wagner, E., & Chapman, M. (1992). Development of concern for others. *Developmental Psychology, 28,* 1038–1047.

Zakowski, S.G., Hall, M.H., Klein, L.C., & Baum, A. (2001). Appraised group, coping, and stress in a community sample: A test of the goodness-of-fit hypothesis. *Annals of Behavioral Medicine, 23,* 158–165.

Zeidner, M., Matthews, G., & Roberts, R.D. (2009). *What we know about emotional intelligence.* Cambridge, MA: MIT Press.

Zelko, H., Zammar, G.R., Ferreira, A.P.B., Phadtare, A., Shah, J., & Pietrobon, R. (2010). Selection mechanisms underlying high impact biomedical research – A qualitative analysis and causal model. *PLoS ONE, 5,* 10535.

Zell, E., Krizan, Z., & Teeter, S.R. (2015). Evaluating gender similarities and differences using metasynthesis. *American Psychologist, 70,* 10–20.

Zhu, Y.-S., & Imperato-McGinley, J. (2008). Male sexual differentiation disorder and 5a-reductase-2 deficiency. *Journal of the Global Library of Women's Medicine,* (ISSN: 1756–2228). doi: 10.3843/GLOWM.10350.

Zillmann, D., & Weaver, J.B. (1997). Psychoticism in the effect of prolonged exposure to gratuitous media violence: On the acceptance of violence as a preferred means of conflict resolution. *Personality and Individual Differences, 22,* 613–627.

Zimbardo, P.G. (1970). The human choice: Individuation, reason, and order versus deindividuation, impulse, and chaos. In W.J. Arnold & D. Levine (Eds.), *Nebraska symposium on motivation* (Vol. 17, pp. 237–307). Lincoln, NE: University of Nebraska Press.

Zimbardo, P.G. (2007). *The Lucifer effect: Understanding how good people turn evil.* New York: Random House.

Zimmermann, F.G.S., & Eimer, M. (2013). Face learning and the emergence of view-independent face recognition: An event-related brain potential study. *Neuropsychologia, 51,* 1320–1329.

Zosuls, K.M., Ruble, D.N., Tamis-LeMonda, C.S., Shrout, P.E., Bornstein, M.H., & Greulich, F.K. (2009). The acquisition of gender labels in infancy: Implications for gender-typed play. *Developmental Psychology, 45,* 688–701.

Zuriff, G.E. (2015). The gender similarities hypothesis is untestable as formulated. *American Psychologist, 70,* 663–664.

Index

11th September 2001 terror attacks 240

abnormality 309–10, 322, 323; and cultural factors 311; cultural relativism 311; culture-bound syndromes 311
abnormal psychology 1, 20, 22, 24, 25, 37, 307, 309–23
abuse 33, 187; physical 188, 300–1; sexual 188, 282, 350–1; substance 159, 160
addiction 30; alcohol 32, 37; behavioural 312; cocaine 32, 37; drug 34
adolescence 25, 123, 171, 174, 269, 294–5, 302, 305, 306, 317
adoption studies: and intelligence 267–9; and selective placement 267–8
adulthood 33, 62, 121, 294, 302
affect: negative 96, 102, 110, 112; positive 96, 102
affectivity: negative 83–4, 406
Africa 8, 214, 228
agentic state 234–5, 242, 397
aggression 33, 34, 35, 57, 61, 72, 98, 104–19, 164, 182, 190–1, 192, 195, 238, 284, 302, 397, 398, 401, 404, 406; and attachment 182; and child care 190–1, 192; and culture 106; definition 105; direct 105, 108, 117; and drinking 112; frustration-aggression hypothesis 106; and gender 104, 105, 114–15, 118, 164; general aggression model 110–13, 118; hostile expectation bias 112, 118, 401; indirect 105, 108, 112, 115, 117; and media violence 108–10, 118, 119; and narcissism 302; observational learning 107–8, 118; overt 105, 114–15, 118; physical 109, 115; proactive (instrumental) 105, 114, 117, 404; reactive (hostile) 105, 114, 117, 404; relational 105, 109, 112, 115, 117, 118; and self-esteem 302; and social learning 107–8; and social norms 106, 117; and testosterone 114–15,

118; and video games 110–13, 118, 119; and weapons effect 111, 406; see also causality issue
aggressive behaviour 33–4, 48–50, 105, 107–18, 167, 212, 217, 242, 311, 404, 406; and child-based interventions 116–18; coercive cycle 113–14, 116–17, 118; and crowds 239; and divorce 189; and family 113–14, 118; and Family Check-Up (FCU) intervention 117, 118; and genetic factors 113–15; and parent-based interventions 116–17; and personality 111–12; and video games 217; see also aggression; causality issue
agreeableness 82, 112, 159, 165, 174, 197, 215, 256–8, 286–7, 291
Allport, Floyd 21, 195, 203–4, 283
altruism/altruistic behaviour 60, 150, 211–18, 223, 225, 397, 404; altruistic helping 212; among children 215, 223; and competition 216; and cultural factors 216–17, 223, 225; and interdependence hypothesis 214; mutualistic collaboration 214, 215; parental influence 218; reciprocal 213–14, 215, 216, 404; and reputation 214, 215, 223; and third-party punishment 214–15, 223
American Sign Language 143
amnesia 6, 20, 50–1, 300, 327, 342–3, 345–8, 353, 357, 397, 399, 404; Henry Molaison case 345; retrograde 353, 404
androgyny 173, 174, 307; and mental health 173, 174; model 173
anger 4, 81, 92, 94, 95, 96, 98, 99, 105, 106–7, 115, 117–18, 195, 206, 404
antisocial behaviour 4, 156, 159, 182, 212, 239, 241; and attachment 182; see also crowd behaviour; selfishness
antisocial personality disorder 285, 309, 311
anxiety 9–10, 28, 34, 74–6, 78, 80–4, 92, 94, 101, 102, 112, 182, 197, 204, 206–7, 209, 257, 284, 289, 302, 305, 311, 313, 319–20,

356–7, 358, 403, 404, 405; and attachment 182; functions of 94, 102; and memory 356, 358; and self-esteem 302, 305
anxiety disorders 9–10, 28, 34, 76, 101, 102, 280, 302, 311, 316, 321–2; and emotions 101, 102; generalised 321; and life events 316–17; see also cognitive behavioural therapy; posttraumatic stress disorder (PTSD); social anxiety disorder (social phobia)
appearance: personal 244; physical 250
appraisal processes see cognitive appraisal
Arabic (language) 138
Aristotle 16
Asch, Solomon 22, 227–30, 242, 248–9; see also conformity behaviour
Asia 214, 228; East 298, 303
attachment 177–84, 188, 190–3, 397, 399, 404; avoidant 180–3, 190, 191, 397; and child care 178, 179, 190–1, 193; and culture 182–3, 191; dimensions of 181, 183, 193; disorganised and disoriented 181–2; insecure 180, 182, 190, 282, 397, 404; and maternal sensitivity hypothesis 181–2, 183, 191; and monotropy hypothesis 184, 191, 402; and parental death 184, 282; and parental divorce 179, 184, 282; and paternal sensitivity 181, 183, 282; peer 164; resistant 180–3, 190, 191, 404; secure 180, 183, 190, 191, 404; and separation protest 179; Strange Situation test 180–1, 182–3, 191; and temperament hypothesis 181–2; see also deprivation; privation
attentional process(es) 19, 27, 66, 94, 101–2, 116, 125–6, 129, 142, 221, 307, 319–20, 322, 334–9, 344, 368, 398, 402, 406; spatial 67; visual 67; see also change blindness
attraction 22, 177, 244–5, 253–9; and familiarity 254; and gender 255–7; and personality 257;

romantic 244, 245, 255–7, 259; and self-disclosure 254; and similarity 252–3; *see also* mating strategies; person perception; physical attractiveness
attributions 198, 245–7, 258, 397; actor-observer bias 246–7, 258, 397; dispositional (internal) 245–6, 247, 258, 399; fundamental attribution error 246–7, 258, 400; situational (external) 245–6, 247, 258; theory 258, 259
Australia 130, 299
Austria 216, 234
authority 5, 53, 177, 199, 207, 226, 227, 232–5, 238, 242, 243, 397; and agentic state theory 234–5, 242; and engaged followership 235, 242; figure(s) 199, 226, 232, 234, 397; in Nazi Germany 235; obedience to 227, 232; *see also* Milgram, Stanley
autism 132, 133–4, 135, 397

Bandura, Albert 34–6, 37, 107–8, 110, 166, 170, 281, 288–91, 404, 405; *see also* social cognitive approach
behaviourism 16, 17–19, 26, 37, 397; *see also* behaviourist approach; conditioning
behaviourist approach 12, 13, 19, 39
behaviour therapy 318, 320
Belgium 108
Binet, Alfred 264
biological approach 12, 13, 22–3, 57–9, 114, 115, 119, 166, 172, 175, 315; to gender development 166, 175
biological factors: and aggressive behaviour 108, 114–15; and gender 166, 170–2; and gender identity 163, 400; and personality 281
biological psychology 37, 57
biopsychology *see* biological psychology
Bowlby, John 184–5, 188, 191; monotropy hypothesis 184, 191, 402
brain 3, 20, 57, 58, 59, 60, 63, 65–71, 93, 102, 115; corpus callosum 68, 405; -damaged patients 19–20, 50, 66, 96, 342, 398; and gender 165; hemispheres 66, 67–9, 270; hemispheric lateralisation 67–8, 401; hemispheric specialisation

67, 72, 73, 401; hydrocephalus 269–70, 401; and intelligence 269–70; organisation of 57, 65–8, 72; size 59–60; visceral 284; visual processing 20, 66, 72, 325; *see also* brain activity; cerebral cortex; forebrain; hindbrain; midbrain; split-brain patients
brain activity 11, 20–1, 23, 37, 68–71, 284, 338, 347, 363, 371, 394, 398; and priming 347; and problem solving 363; *see also* functional magnetic resonance imaging (fMRI)
British Psychological Society (BPS) 51
burnout 81, 82–3, 90, 91, 397; Maslach Burnout Inventory 82
bystander effect/intervention 211, 219–23, 225, 397; arousal: cost-reward model 221–2, 223; diffusion of responsibility 219–20, 223, 399; Kitty Genovese 219

Canada 109
cancer 81, 366, 370
CAPTCHAs (Completely Automated Public Turing tests to tell Computers and Humans Apart) 325, 397
cardiovascular disease 81, 83
case studies 50–1, 54, 144, 311, 373, 398; Henry Molaison (HM) 50–1; Kanzi and Panbanisha 144–5; Little Hans 50; Magnus Carlsen 373
Cattell, Raymond 271, 281, 283–5, 291; *see also* trait approach
causality issue 88, 108–10, 157, 217–18
cerebral cortex 66–7, 72, 73, 269, 363, 398, 401; Broca's area 67; frontal lobe 60, 66–7, 72, 399; medial temporal lobe 345; motor centre 67; occipital lobe 66, 72; parietal lobe 66, 72; prefrontal cortex 66, 394; somatosensory centre 67; temporal lobe 66, 72, 284, 363, 397; Wernicke's area 67
change blindness 334–8, 339, 398; and inattentional blindness 334–8, 339, 401; and misdirection 337
childhood 4–5, 13, 21, 37, 43, 47, 62, 109, 121, 124, 148, 164, 171, 188, 208, 269, 281–2, 286, 291, 294–5, 300, 306, 312, 316, 317, 351, 399
China 34, 216, 279, 298, 312–14

Chinese (language) 138, 249, 286, 293, 303
Chomsky, Noam 21, 140–3, 146
classical conditioning 18, 19, 25–9, 37, 39, 316–17, 398, 400, 405; backward 27; blocking effect 27, 397; and discrimination 26–7; and extinction 27–9, 31, 33, 37, 400, 405; and generalisation 26–7; and spontaneous recovery 27, 405; *see also* reflex; responses; stimulus(i)
clinical method 124, 128, 398
clinical psychology 9
cognition(s) 19–20, 23, 70, 94, 100, 290, 310, 318, 398; meta- 130; social 188
cognitions (thoughts) 110–12, 217, 290
Cognitive Acceleration through Science Education (CASE) programme 130, 134
cognitive appraisal 99–100, 111, 398; primary 99; reappraisal 99, 100, 101, 102, 400; secondary 99; theory 99, 102
cognitive approach 12, 13, 20–1, 23, 33, 37, 39, 170, 307, 315; means-ends relationship 33; social 288–90
cognitive behavioural therapy 9–10, 13, 318–22
cognitive development 21, 121, 123–35, 150, 182, 190, 192; and attachment 182; central coherence 133–4, 398; centration 125, 126, 398; and child care 190, 192; cognitive conflict 123, 130, 230, 400; concrete operations stage 126–7, 134; conservation 125, 128, 398; cultural factors 125; decentration 126, 399; disequilibrium 123, 130; egocentrism 126, 128, 132, 400; formal operations stage 127–8, 134; object permanence 124, 128, 403; overlapping waves model 130–2, 135; preoperational stage 124–6, 134; reversibility 125, 127, 128, 404; sensori-motor stage 124, 134; zone of proximal development 128–9, 134, 406; *see also* language
cognitive map 19
cognitive neuropsychology 19–20, 398
cognitive neuroscience 20–1, 23, 37, 69–71, 398

cognitive organisation 123, 397; accommodation 123, 134, 397, 400; assimilation 123, 134, 397, 400; equilibration 123, 400; imitation 108, 123, 139, 166

cognitive processes 18, 22, 29, 37, 60, 69, 71, 98, 99, 101, 102, 108, 111, 118, 127, 131, 154–5, 168, 289, 290, 360, 364, 371, 401

cognitive psychology 19–20, 21, 71, 307, 398; see also cognitive approach

cognitive therapy 318–20

collectivism 7–8; see also culture(s)

comparative psychology 23

compulsions 60; see also obsessive-compulsive disorder (OCD)

conditioning 17, 25–35, 397; see also classical conditioning; operant conditioning

conformity behaviour 227–30, 232, 237, 242, 243; compliance 230, 242, 398; conversion 230, 242, 399; and cultural factors 228–9, 230; direct private influence 231; and dual-process theory 230–1; indirect private influence 231; informational influence 228–30, 242, 401; normative influence 228–30, 242, 403; public influence 231; see also groupthink

congenital adrenal hyperplasia 171–2, 398; and androgen 171, 398

conscientiousness 82, 159, 165, 174, 197, 257, 281, 286–7, 290, 291; and mental disorders 287

consciousness 65–6, 68–9, 72, 97, 401; social 8; see also split-brain patients

coping 82, 86–8, 91, 111, 173, 181, 263, 405; emotion-focused 87–8, 91, 400; flexibility 87–8, 91, 399; and goodness-of-fit hypothesis 87–8; problem-focused 87–8, 91, 404

correlational studies 49–50, 54

covariation: active 62, 72; passive 62, 72; reactive 62, 72

creativity 272, 307, 360–1, 374–7, 399; and expertise 375; and intelligence 374, 377; and mood states 374, 377; and openness 374, 377; scientific 360, 374–6, 377

cross-cultural psychology 7, 399

cross-sectional method 49, 54, 399

crowd behaviour 227, 239, 241, 243; and collective resilience 239; and deindividuation 239, 241,

242, 399; lynch mobs 239; rioting 239; social identity model 239, 240–1

cultural factors 4, 13, 125, 174; and gender 174; and personality 279–80; and prosocial behaviour 216–17, 223, 225; and self-concept 293, 297–8; and self-esteem 302–3

culture(s) 7; collectivistic 7, 13, 88, 216–17, 223, 228, 247, 258, 263, 279–80, 290, 293, 297–8, 300, 302–5, 398, 401; individualistic 7, 13, 88, 216–17, 223, 228, 247, 258, 263, 279–80, 290, 293, 297–8, 299, 300, 302–5, 401

cyberbullying 207

Darwin, Charles 22–3, 37, 59, 73, 213, 374, 400

decision making 19, 66, 87, 236–7, 263, 399

demand characteristics 46, 48, 399

dementia: semantic 96, 405

Denmark 216

depression 9–10, 33, 74, 76, 80, 83–4, 87, 90, 94, 98, 101, 102, 182, 257, 282, 295–6, 302, 305, 309, 311, 312, 315–16, 318–19, 322; and attachment 182; clinical 9, 76; and cognitive factors 315, 316; cognitive schema 315, 319, 322, 398; cognitive triad 315, 398; and emotions 101, 102; and genetic factors 315–16, 322; and life events 315–16, 317, 322; major depressive episode/disorder 80, 101, 302, 310–11, 312, 315–16, 317, 318–19, 321, 322, 323, 402; Memory Specificity Training (MEST) 297; method of loci 297; and self-concept 295–7, 305; and self-esteem 302, 305; and serotonin 319; serotonin reuptake inhibitors (SSRIs) 319; and work 191; see also cognitive behavioural therapy; drug therapy

deprivation 177, 184–8, 191, 193, 399, 404; deprivation-specific problems 188, 399; maternal deprivation hypothesis 184–5, 188, 399, 402

depth perception 327, 328–30, 339; accommodation 329, 338; binocular cues 328–9, 397; convergence 329, 338, 399; interposition 328, 338, 402; linear perspective 328, 338, 402; monocular (pictorial) cues 328,

338, 402; motion parallax 328, 329, 338, 403; oculomotor cues 328, 329, 403; shading 338; stereopsis 328–30, 338, 405; texture gradient 328, 329, 338, 406

developmental approach 12, 13, 25, 37

developmental psychology 17, 20, 21, 121

diabetes 11, 80

Diagnostic and Statistical Manual of Mental Disorders (DSM-5) 310, 311–12, 316, 322; categorical classification 310, 311, 322

discrimination 22, 177, 195–6, 198, 202–3, 205, 208–9, 399; anti-locution 195; avoidance 195; extermination 196; in Nazi Germany 195–6, 200, 235; physical attacks 196; racial 205; and recategorisation 205–9, 404; and social identity 202

disgust/contempt 94, 95, 96, 254

dissociative identity disorder 300–1, 305, 399; The Three Faces of Eve 300

divorce 61, 79–81, 178, 179, 184, 188–90, 192, 193, 282, 315, 397, 399; adjustment phase 189, 192, 397; and children's well-being 188–90, 193, 282; crisis phase 189, 192, 397, 399; and genetic factors 189–90, 192

"Dodo Bird verdict" 9, 320–1

Dominican Republic 171

drug therapy 318, 319, 322

dysexecutive syndrome 66, 399

East, the 8

Eastern society/culture 110, 305

ecological validity 21, 46, 48, 54, 354, 399

Edison, Thomas 375

Einstein, Albert 272, 374, 375; theory of relativity 375

Eliot, T.S. 272

emotion(s) 28, 57, 92–103, 132, 153, 165, 179, 197, 206, 208, 211, 217, 218, 273–4, 284, 290, 295, 301, 310, 313, 318, 402, 406; basic 95–6; and bodily state 97–8, 100; and Botox 98; complex 95; definition 93; differentiation 99; and facial expressions 95, 97, 98, 102; functions of 94–5, 102; and gender 94, 102; vs. moods 93; moral 153; negative 80, 84,

87, 92, 94, 96, 98, 101, 102, 165, 206, 284, 313, 400, 403; positive 96, 98, 101, 181, 197, 206; Positive and Negative Affect Schedule (PANAS-X) 95–6, 102; regulation 100–1, 102, 103; *see also* anger; cognitive appraisal; disgust/contempt; fear; happiness; James-Lange theory; sadness; surprise
emotional dependence 182
emotional development 178, 179, 184, 188; and attachment 182, 183; and child care 190, 192; and deprivation 184, 188; and privation 188
emotionality 25, 311
emotional processes 154–5
empathy 116, 118, 153, 156, 158, 204, 209, 211, 213, 218, 223, 274, 321, 400, 403; among children 212–13, 223; empathic helping 212; therapist 321
England 10, 187, 309; 7th July 2005 bombings 240; London 239–40
English (language) 138, 140, 249, 268, 286, 303, 330
environmental factors 18, 19, 36, 58, 61–3, 115, 158, 166, 172, 198, 212, 215, 219, 223, 262, 267–9, 275, 286, 288, 315; and gender 166, 168, 172; and intelligence 62–3, 266–9, 277; non-shared 61–2, 268–9; and personality 286, 288; and prejudice 198; and prosocial behaviour 212, 223; shared 61–2, 268–9; and social anxiety disorder 317
epilepsy 345
ethical issues 51–3, 54, 55
Europe 10, 228, 293
event-related potentials (ERPs) 69–70, 72
evolution, theory of 23, 59, 73, 213, 374, 400; inclusive fitness 213, 401, 402; interdependence hypothesis 214; kin selection 213–15, 402; mutualistic collaboration 214, 215, 403; and sexual attraction 255–6; survival of the fittest 23
evolutionary approach 60, 214, 215, 223, 255–7, 259
evolutionary psychology 23, 59–60, 72, 213, 255, 400; and adaptations 59; and altruism 213–15, 223, 225
executive functions 133–4, 135

experimental approach 37, 47, 131
experimental control 4, 47, 54
experimental design 44, 47, 50, 401, 402, 404; counterbalancing 45, 54, 399; independent 44, 47, 54, 401; matched participant 44, 47, 54, 402; repeated measures 44–5, 47, 54, 399, 404; *see also* demand characteristics; ecological validity; experimental method; experimenter effect; field experiments; implacable experimenter; laboratory experiments; order effects; randomisation; replication; standardised procedures; voluntary informed consent
experimental method 5, 21, 41–9, 54, 55, 124, 400; false-belief studies 133, 134, 154; microgenetic method 131–2, 135, 402
experimental psychology 17
experimenter effect 45, 46, 48, 54, 400
expertise 221, 360, 361, 365, 368–77; chess 361, 365, 368–70, 372–3, 376, 405; and creativity 375; and deliberate practice 372–4, 376, 377, 399; Magnus Carlsen 373; medical 368, 370; pattern recognition 368, 371, 376; and talent 46, 360, 368, 372–4, 376; template theory 369–70, 376, 405
exposure therapy 28–9, 37, 320, 400
externalising symptoms 182; and attachment 182; *see also* aggression; antisocial behaviour
extraversion 25, 82–3, 165, 174, 197, 252, 257, 274, 275, 280, 281, 284–7, 290, 291, 400; and mental disorders 287; and physical attractiveness 252; *see also* introversion
eyewitness testimony 340, 349, 354–7, 358, 359, 400; and anxiety 356–7, 358; confirmation bias 356, 358, 398; vs. DNA tests 354; face recognition 331, 355–6, 358; misinformation effect 354–5; other-race effect 355–6, 403; retention interval 349, 352, 357, 358; and stress 357, 358; and violence 356; weapon focus 356–7, 406
Eysenck, H.J. 25, 281, 284–5, 286, 291, 387; *see also* trait approach

factor theories 270–1, 275; Cattell-Horn-Carroll theory of intelligence 271; hierarchical theory 270–1, 275
Far East 7, 247, 292, 398
fear 25, 27–8, 34, 50, 72, 93–6, 164, 195, 201, 238, 253, 284, 313, 316–7, 320, 397, 400, 403, 405; functions of 94
femininity 173, 174; and mental health 173
field experiments 41, 45, 46–8, 54, 400
fight or flight 64, 77, 89, 90, 94
forebrain 65–7, 72, 398, 401, 406; amygdala 65, 284, 397, 402; cerebrum 65–6, 72, 398; hippocampus 65, 345, 402; hypothalamus 65, 72, 401; limbic system 65, 72, 402; thalamus 65, 72, 406; *see also* cerebral cortex
forgetting 300, 312, 340, 350–4, 358, 359, 382, 399, 404; consolidation 353–4, 358, 398; decay 350, 354, 358; interference 382; proactive interference 351–2, 354, 358, 386, 404; repression 350–1, 358, 404; retroactive interference 351–2, 354, 358, 404
French (language) 138
Freud, Sigmund 3, 9, 21, 23–4, 37, 50–1, 59, 62, 121, 212, 272, 281–2, 291, 308, 350–1, 404; *see also* psychoanalysis; psychosexual development
functional magnetic resonance imaging (fMRI) 20, 69–70, 72, 400

Galton, Sir Francis 24
Gandhi, Mahatma 7, 272
Gardner, Howard 271–3, 275, 277; *see also* multiple intelligences theory
gender 21, 35, 89, 94, 114–15, 121, 150, 154–5, 161, 163–75, 190, 197, 252, 255–8, 261, 268, 298–9, 302, 306, 311, 399, 400, 401; and aggression 114–15; androgyny model 173; bias 311; congruence model 173; development 21, 166–75; difference(s) 89, 94, 114–15, 154–6, 161, 197, 255–8, 298–9, 302, 306; equality 155; gender schema theory 168, 170; gender similarities hypothesis 164–5, 174, 175, 401; and *Guevedoces* 171, 172; identity 163–4, 166–72,

399, 400; identity disorder 172, 400; masculinity model 173; and media 167, 172; and morality 150, 154–6, 161; and parents 166–7, 170, 172; and peers 167, 170, 172; and personality 197; roles 35; -role stereotypes 163–4, 166, 401; schemas 168, 170, 401; segregation 164, 167, 401; stereotypes 167, 197, 311; -typed behaviour 163–4, 166–70, 401; and video games 167; *see also* androgyny; congenital adrenal hyperplasia; femininity; masculinity; self-socialisation theory; social cognitive theory
generosity 215–17
genetic factors 5, 19, 25, 36, 37, 57, 58, 59, 61–3, 72, 78, 113–15, 118, 148, 156, 158–60, 172, 181, 198–200, 208, 213, 218–19, 223, 266–9, 275, 281, 282, 284–6, 288, 290–1, 309, 315–17, 322, 373–4; and aggression 113–15, 118; and attachment 181–2; and depression 315–16, 322; and expertise 373–4; and gender 172; and intelligence 62–3, 266–9, 275, 277, 278; and mental disorders 309, 317; and moral development 148, 158, 160; and personality 159, 198–200, 278, 281, 282, 284–8, 290–1; and prejudice 208; and prosocial behaviour 213–14, 218–19, 223; and social anxiety disorder 317, 322
genetics *see* genetic factors
German (language) 286
Germany 234
Gilligan, Carol 154–6, 160
Graham, Martha 272
Greece 95, 298
group decision making 236; and social comparison 236, 242; *see also* group membership; group polarisation
group membership 7, 195, 201, 202, 204–9, 226, 279, 295, 298, 301; common ingroup identity model 205; dual identity 205, 207, 208; dual-identity recategorisation 206–7; ingroup bias 202, 209, 401; ingroups 198, 202, 205–6, 220, 231, 236; intergroup contact theory 203–4, 209; outgroups 198, 202, 204–5, 208, 209, 220, 231, 236; realistic conflict theory 200–1, 208; and recategorisation 205–6, 208, 209; and salient

categorisation 204–5, 207, 209; *see also* conformity behaviour; group decision making; group polarisation; groupthink; multiculturalism; prejudice
group polarisation 227, 236, 242, 401
groupthink 227, 236–7, 242, 401; causes of 236–7
guilt 94, 95, 148, 149, 153, 158, 222, 310, 402, 403

habits 11, 79, 88, 381, 393–4
happiness 92, 93, 95, 96, 98, 361
health psychology 9, 10
heart attack 80, 81, 222
heart disease 10, 11, 13, 83–4
Hebrew (language) 286, 352
heredity 18, 23, 24–5, 61–2, 162, 266–8, 277, 278; and intelligence 266–7, 277
hindbrain 65–6, 72, 401; cerebellum 66, 72; medulla 66, 72; pons 66, 72; reticular activating system 65–6
hindsight bias 6, 13, 401
histrionic personality disorder 311
Hitler, Adolf 7, 349
Holland 234
homosexuality 60
Hong Kong 303
hypertension 84
hypothalamic-pituitary-adrenocortical (HPA) axis 77, 78–9, 90; adrenocorticotrophic hormone (ACTH) 78–9; and cortisol 78–9, 86, 89, 90
hypothesis: experimental 41–2, 46, 54, 400, 401; null 42

ICD-10 (International Statistical Classification of Diseases and Related Health Problems) 310, 322
identity 157, 163–4, 166–72, 201–41, 242, 293, 295, 399, 400, 405; common 205, 208; common ingroup 205; common ingroup identity model 205; and deindividuation 239; dual 205–8; gender 163–4, 166–72, 399, 400; group 205, 208, 295; ingroup 202; moral 157; personal 239, 293, 399; shared 239, 241; social 168, 201–241, 242, 405; subgroup 206; *see also* dissociative identity disorder; gender; group membership; social identity theory/model

immune system 79, 84–5, 89, 90, 91, 401
implacable experimenter 46, 48, 401
implementation intentions 11, 391, 393–4, 401
India 34, 216; Indian subcontinent 311
individual differences' approach 12, 13, 17, 22–5, 37, 39; *see also* intelligence; personality
individualism 7–8; *see also* culture(s)
infancy 121, 123, 182, 269, 326
instinct: death 23; instinctive behaviour 31, 35; instinctive drift 31; life 23
intellectual development: and deprivation 184; and privation 187
intelligence 4, 5, 13, 17, 19, 21–5, 37, 43–4, 51, 61–3, 124, 127, 134, 164–5, 187, 244, 256, 257, 258, 261, 262–77, 280, 290, 310, 374, 400, 401, 402, 404, 406; and creativity 374, 377; cultural meanings of 263; and educational achievement 265; emotional 264, 266, 272, 273–6, 277, 400; and environmental factors 62–3, 266–9, 277; and gender 164–5; and genetic factors 62–3, 266–9, 275, 277; genius-based approach 273; interpersonal 263, 272; language ability 270, 271, 272; mathematics 165, 263, 270, 271, 272; mental rotation ability 164–5; numerical ability 266; and openness 374; spatial ability 164–5, 264, 266, 271, 272; verbal ability 164, 266; writing skills 165; *see also* factor theories; intelligence tests; IQ; multiple intelligences theory
intelligence tests 127, 262–6, 271, 272, 275, 277, 280; ability 273, 274–5, 276; American Stanford-Binet test 264; British Ability Scales 264; and cultural bias 266; Emotional Quotient Inventory (EQ-i) 274; Mayer-Salovey-Caruso Emotional Intelligence Test (MSCEIT) 274; reliability of 264, 266, 275; self-report 273–5, 276; validity of 264–5, 266, 275; Wechsler Intelligence Scale for Children 264
internalising symptoms 182; and attachment 182; *see also* anxiety; depression

Internet 11, 206, 207, 269
interpretive bias 84, 319, 322, 402
introspection 17–18, 37, 402;
  experimental 17
introversion 25, 284; *see also*
  extraversion
IQ 24, 127, 190, 262, 264–71, 274,
  275, 400, 401; Flynn effect 268,
  275, 400; tests 262
Italy 34, 234

James, William 18, 97–8, 102, 293;
  see also James-Lange theory
James-Lange theory 97–8, 102
Japan 95, 182, 279; Okinawa 216
Japanese (language) 286

Kenya 34, 216
kindness 256, 258
Kohlberg, Lawrence 150–4, 160,
  161, 398, 403
Kohlberg's cognitive-developmental
  theory 150–1, 161; conventional
  morality 151, 160, 398; post-
  conventional morality 151, 152,
  160, 403; pre-conventional
  morality 151, 152, 160, 403
Korean (language) 286

laboratory experiments 17, 41–3,
  46–8, 355, 357, 393
laboratory studies *see* laboratory
  experiments
Lange, Carl 97–8; *see also* James-
  Lange theory
language 19, 21, 65–8, 72, 96,
  121, 129, 132–47, 154, 206,
  249, 263, 268, 270–2, 282, 294,
  303, 330, 341, 345–6, 352, 382,
  388, 390, 397, 398, 402, 403,
  404, 405; and autism 134, 135,
  397; and bonobos 143–6, 147;
  child-directed speech 141–3,
  147, 398; comprehension and
  production 19, 138; definition
  137; development 21, 121,
  129, 132, 137–43, 147, 346,
  397, 405; egocentric speech
  129; grammar 137–44, 146,
  187; innate universal grammar
  140–1; inner speech 129, 134;
  inside-out theories 140–1,
  147; language bioprogramme
  hypothesis 140–1, 146; learning
  352; linguistic universals 140–2,
  146, 402; outside-in theories 140,
  142–3, 147; phonology 138, 403;
  pragmatics 138, 403; processing
  67, 68, 72, 390; productive 138,
146, 404; receptive 138, 146,
404; recursion 140, 141, 404;
semantics 138, 382, 405; syntax
138, 140, 405; telegraphic speech
138, 405; use of 65; vocabulary
139, 141, 144, 147, 263–4;
see also cerebral cortex
learning 6, 12, 16–19, 24–7, 29,
  34–7, 42–5, 65–6, 72, 107–8,
  110, 113, 118, 128–32, 134,
  142, 146, 148, 166–8, 174,
  179, 232, 235, 269, 272–3,
  281, 290, 326–7, 331, 341, 343,
  345, 347–9, 350–2, 357–8, 368,
  372, 379–84, 386–7, 389–92,
  394, 397, 398, 400, 403, 404,
  405, 406; auditory presentation
  272; avoidance 34; depth of
  processing 381, 382, 384, 394;
  direct tuition 166–7, 174, 399;
  and distinctive processing 382–4,
  394; effective 12, 128–9, 379,
  381; effectiveness of 381; and
  elaboration of processing 382–4,
  386, 394; enactive experience
  166–7, 174, 400; encoding 341,
  352, 357, 374, 389, 394, 400;
  and gender development 166–7,
  174; imitation 35, 108, 123, 139;
  and interference 351; kinesthetic
  presentation 272; and memory
  341, 343, 347, 358; multi-modal
  presentation 272; and object
  recognition 331; observational
  25, 29, 35–6, 37, 107–8, 118,
  166–7, 174, 403; physical practice
  35; retrieval 341, 352, 357; and
  schemas 348–9; of skills 347,
  358; storage 341, 357; testing
  effect 389–91, 394, 395, 405;
  visual presentation 272; *see also*
  forgetting; memory; object
  recognition; rewards
levels-of-processing approach
  381–4, 395
life events 62, 79–81, 87, 90, 315–17,
  322, 357, 402; controllable 316,
  317; and depression 315–16,
  317, 322; and mental disorders
  317; and social anxiety disorders
  316–17, 322; uncontrollable 316
longitudinal method/study 49, 54,
  152, 157, 217, 402
long-term memory 6, 20, 35, 48, 50,
  168, 315, 330, 331, 341–50, 352,
  353–4, 357–8, 359, 366, 368–70,
  382–5, 387, 389, 391, 397, 398,
  399, 400, 401, 402, 403, 404,
  405, 406; autobiographical
294–6, 300, 305, 346–7, 358,
397, 399; consolidation 353–4,
358, 398; cued recall 341, 357,
382, 399; declarative 345–8, 358,
399; depth of processing 381,
382, 384, 394; and distinctive
processing 382–5, 387, 394;
and elaboration of processing
382–5, 386, 394; episodic 48–9,
346, 347, 358, 400; episodic
buffer 344, 358, 400; free recall
341, 347, 348, 352, 357, 384,
398, 400; non-declarative 345,
347–8, 358, 403; and personality
346–7; priming 347, 358,
403; rationalisation 349, 404;
recognition 342, 347, 355, 357,
384, 389; rehearsal 342–4, 357–8,
386, 404; schemas 346, 348–50,
356, 358; semantic 48–9, 346,
347, 358; skill learning 347,
358; testing effect 389–91, 394,
395, 405; transfer-appropriate
processing 384, 406; von Restorff
effect 382, 406; *see also* amnesia

masculinity 173, 174; and mental
health 173, 174; model 173
mating strategies 23, 60, 255–8; and
gender 255, 258; online dating
256–7; personal ads 256; speed
dating 256–7
media 2, 104, 165, 167, 172; and
gender 167, 172; *see also* media
violence
media violence: and aggression
107–10, 118, 119
memories 3, 5, 99, 294, 296–7, 315,
340, 345–7, 350–1, 353, 382,
398; false 350–1; genuine 351;
recovered 350–1; repressed 350
memory 19, 43, 48–9, 65, 72,
99, 307, 340–59, 381–4;
categorical clustering 348, 358,
398; encoding 341, 352, 357,
374, 388–9, 394, 400; encoding
specificity principle 352, 400;
episodic 48–9, 346, 347, 358,
400; everyday 354; explicit
memory 384–5; false recall
349; fragility of 354–5; implicit
348, 384–5; and learning 341;
memory trace 352–3, 358, 381–3,
386, 399, 400; multistore model
342–3, 357; retrieval 341, 351–3,
357, 358, 384–90, 394, 400,
406; saying-is-believing effect
354, 404; speed-up principle
389; storage 341, 357; *see also*

amnesia; forgetting; levels-of-processing approach; long-term memory; mnemonics; short-term memory; working memory

mental disorders 3, 9–10, 13, 17, 21, 24, 25, 28, 76, 287, 307, 308–12, 317–18, 321–3, 398, 399; causes of 309, 312–14, 323; comorbidity 311, 398; and cultural factors 322; definition 310; diagnosing 309, 310–12; diathesis-stress model of 312, 313–14, 316, 317, 322, 399; and genetic factors 309, 312, 317; and life events 317; multi-dimensional models of 312, 316, 317; one-dimensional models of 312, 316; and personality 287; treatment of 309; *see also* anxiety disorders; depression; *Diagnostic and Statistical Manual of Mental Disorders* (DSM-5); phobia; therapy

mental illness(es) *see* mental disorders

method of loci: and depression 297; and mnemonics 385–6, 388, 394, 402

Mexico 216

midbrain 65, 72, 402; reticular activating system 65–6

Milgram, Stanley 5, 53, 232–5, 242

Minnesota Multiphasic Personality Inventory (MMPI) 76

mnemonics 385–9, 395, 402; expanded retrieval practice 387; method of loci 385–6, 388, 394, 402; names 387; pegword method 386–8, 394, 403; story method 387, 388, 394, 405; verbal techniques 385; visual imagery techniques 385

mood(s) 93, 95–6, 274, 280, 285, 298, 310–11, 319, 374, 377, 402; depressed 310–11, 402; vs. emotions 93; state 96, 285, 374, 377

moral development 21, 35, 121, 148–61, 398, 403; and effortful control 158, 160, 165, 399; and genetic factors 148, 158, 160; and moral self 158, 402; and mutually responsive orientation 157–8, 160, 403; and parents 156–8, 160, 161; and peers 159, 160; and personality 159, 160; theory of 150–1; *see also* Kohlberg's cognitive-developmental theory; moral emotions; theory of mind

moral emotions 153; *see also* empathy; guilt; shame; sympathy

morality 149–56, 159–61, 249, 386, 398, 402, 403; behavioural 149–50, 159; of care 154–6, 160, 402; cognitive (moral reasoning) 149–53, 154–6, 159, 160, 398, 403; conventional 151, 160, 398; emotional 149, 159; and gender 154–6, 160, 161; of justice 154–6, 160, 402; post-conventional 151, 160, 403; pre-conventional 151, 160, 403; *see also* moral development

moral judgment 8, 154; dual-process model of 154

moral values 121, 148, 156, 158, 159, 402

mortality 10, 83, 84, 85, 89, 90

Moscovici, Serge 230–2; *see also* conformity behaviour

motivation 6, 11, 30, 60, 75, 117, 128–9, 134, 141, 145, 146, 195, 198, 208, 236, 264, 289–90, 301, 354, 379, 381, 391–4, 395; goal-setting theory 391–3, 394; internal 128–9, 134; SMART goals 391, 393; theory of implementation intentions 11, 391, 393–4, 401

multiculturalism 205, 207–8, 209; and colour-blind approach 208, 209

multiple intelligences theory 271–2, 275, 277

National Institute of Child Health and Development (NICHD) 190

nature-nurture debate 23, 61, 72, 73, 162

nervous system 57, 62–5, 72, 77, 93, 96, 111, 397, 398, 403, 405; autonomic 63–4, 72, 77, 93, 111, 397, 403, 405; central 63–5, 72, 398, 403; parasympathetic 64–5, 72, 77, 397, 403; peripheral 63–5, 72, 397, 403, 405; somatic 63–4, 72, 403, 405; sympathetic 64–5, 72, 77, 397, 403, 405; *see also* brain; brain activity

neuroenchantment 70, 71

neuroticism 25, 80–1, 82–4, 90, 112, 165, 174, 197, 257, 274, 275, 284–7, 290, 291, 313–14, 403; and mental disorders 287, 313–14

New Guinea 142

New Zealand 365

normality 310; *see also* abnormality

norms 106, 200, 202, 208–9, 214–17, 239, 403, 405; cultural 200; distribution 214, 215; group 202, 208, 209, 239, 241, 242; mutual exchange 216; reciprocity 216; social 106, 117, 405; society's 214, 239

North America 214, 228

Northern Ireland 241; attacks in 241

Norway 155

Obama, Barack 18, 249

obesity 10, 11, 59

object recognition 326, 330–2, 338–9, 401; categorisation 331; and expectations 339; geons (geometric ions) 330–2, 338, 401; identification 331; and learning 331; recognition-by-components theory 330–2, 338; viewpoint-dependent perception 331–2, 339, 406; viewpoint-invariant perception 330–2, 339, 406

observational studies 48, 54; and inter-observer reliability 48, 54

obsessions 60; *see also* obsessive-compulsive disorder (OCD)

obsessive-compulsive disorder (OCD) 60

Oceania 214

oestrogen 89, 170; and gender 170

openness 197, 286–7, 291; and creativity 374, 377

operant conditioning18, 19, 25, 27, 29–37, 39, 397, 400, 403, 405, 406; and equipotentiality 31, 35, 400; and instinctive drift 31; and law of reinforcement 29, 402; and shaping 30, 405; *see also* learning; punishment; reinforcement; rewards; stimulus(i)

order effects 45, 54

panic disorder 321; *see also* cognitive behavioural therapy

Pavlov, Ivan 18, 26–8; *see also* conditioning; classical conditioning

perception *see* person perception; social perception; visual perception

perceptual organisation 325–7, 338, 339; figure-ground segregation 326–7, 338, 400; Gestaltists and 326–7, 338; Gestalt law of proximity 326–7; law of closure 326; law of good continuation

326–7; law of Prägnanz 326–7, 402; law of similarity 326
personality 4–6, 13, 17, 19, 22–5, 37, 43, 47, 61, 62, 76, 79–80, 82–4, 90, 104, 109, 111–12, 118, 158–60, 164–6, 175, 181, 191, 194, 197–201, 208, 215, 239, 243–50, 252–3, 257–9, 261, 264–5, 270, 273–6, 278–92, 297, 300, 303, 309, 311, 313, 321, 346–7, 374, 397, 399, 400, 401, 403, 404, 405, 406; agentic type 346–7; aggressive 4, 111–12, 118, 164; and attachment 181; authoritarian 199–200, 208, 397; Big Five personality factors 82–3, 281, 285–8, 291; central traits 248, 250; communal type 346–7; and cultural factors 279–80; and educational achievement 265; and emotional intelligence 264, 273; and environmental factors 286, 288; and F (Fascism) Scale 199, 200; and gender 164, 165–6, 175; and gender stereotypes 197; and genetic factors 159, 198–200, 278, 281, 282, 284–8, 290–1; implicit personality theory 248, 250, 258, 259, 401; and moral behaviour 159, 160; peripheral traits 248; and prejudice 194, 198–200, 208; and prosocial behaviour 215; psychoanalytical approach 282; and stress 83–4, 90; Type A 83–4, 90, 406; Type B 83, 406; Type D 84, 90, 406; unsociable 245; see also agreeableness; conscientiousness; extraversion; intellect; neuroticism; personality assessment; social cognitive approach; trait approach
personality assessment 280–1; bogus pipeline 280, 397; other-ratings 281, 283, 288, 297; questionnaires 280–1, 282, 286, 291; reliability 280–1, 290; self-reports 281, 283, 288, 297; and social desirability bias 280, 405; standardisation 280, 290; Twenty Statements Test 279, 298, 300; validity 280–1, 290
person perception 248–50, 258, 302; competence (intellectual desirability) 248–50, 258, 302; and implicit personality theory 248–50, 258, 259, 401; and moral character 249, 250, 258; and primacy effect 248, 249–50, 258,

403; warmth (social desirability) 86, 117, 167, 185, 197, 208, 212, 215, 223, 248–50, 258, 321, 363
Philippines 34, 216
phobia 28–9, 37, 316–17, 403, 405; and genetic factors 317; situational 317; social 28, 316, 405; see also exposure therapy; social anxiety disorder
physical attractiveness 245, 250–2, 255–8, 302; averageness 250; facial 250, 258; and gender 255–8, 302
Piaget, Jean 21, 37, 123–8, 130–2, 134, 135, 150, 212, 397, 398, 399, 400, 401, 404; see also cognitive development
Picasso, Pablo 272
Pinker, S. 106, 140
Plato 16
Portuguese (language) 286
posttraumatic stress disorder (PTSD) 28, 84, 313–14, 318, 403; see also exposure therapy
prejudice 22, 177, 194, 195–209, 403, 404; attitudinal 195; causes of 198, 200–1, 208, 209; and colour-blind approach 208; and common ingroup identity model 205; and dual-identity recategorisation 206–7; and electronic (E)-contact 206–7, 208; emotional 195; and genetic factors 208; and ignorance 203; ingroup bias 202, 209, 401; and ingroups 198, 202, 205–6; and intergroup contact 203–4, 209; modern racism 196, 208; and outgroups 198, 202, 204–5, 208, 209; and personality 194, 198–200, 208; racial 196, 200; and realistic conflict theory 200–1, 208; and recategorisation 205–9, 404; Robbers Cave study 200–1; and salient categorisation 204–5, 207, 209; salient recategorisation 404; and social identity 202; see also group membership; multiculturalism; stereotypes
Prisoner's Dilemma 8
privation 184–5, 187, 188, 191, 193, 399, 404; English & Romanian Adoptees Study 187–8; extreme 185–7; see also deprivation
problems: ill-defined 361, 376, 401; insight 361–4, 376; non-insight 361–3, 376; structural similarity 365–6; superficial similarity

365–6; Tower of Hanoi task 367; well-defined 361, 366, 376, 406
problem solving 19, 88, 101, 129, 132, 263, 275, 307, 360–8, 374, 376, 377, 400, 402; analogical 366, 374, 375, 376; functional fixedness 364, 376, 400; and heuristics (rules of thumb) 367–8, 375, 376, 377, 401; hill climbing 367–8, 375, 401; incubation 364, 401; means-ends analysis 367–8, 375, 376, 402; mental set 365, 376, 402; and past experience 364–6, 376, 377; planning 87, 367–8, 376, 399; problem representations 362–4
prosocial behaviour 22, 210–25, 397, 404; altruistic helping 212, 223; among children 211, 212–13, 215, 218, 223, 225; and cultural factors 216–17, 225; and emotional closeness 214, 215; empathic helping 212; environmental factors 212, 215, 219, 223; genetic factors 213–14, 218–19, 223; instrumental helping 212, 223; parental influence 218–19, 223; and personality 215; and television 217, 219, 223; and video games 217–18, 219, 223; see also altruism/altruistic behaviour; antisocial behaviour; bystander intervention; empathy
psychoanalysis 9, 23–4, 308, 321
psychodynamic approach 318
psychodynamic therapy 320–1; see also psychoanalysis
psychology: definition 3, 13
psychopathic behaviour 4, 309
psychosexual development 282, 291; and adult personality 282; anal stage 282; genital stage 282; latency stage 282; oral stage 282; phallic stage 282
psychotic disorders 285; see also psychoticism; schizophrenia
psychoticism 109, 284–5, 291, 404
punishment 29, 33–4, 37, 112, 151, 166, 167, 199, 214–15, 223, 284, 285, 402, 403, 406; law of reinforcement 402; negative 33–4, 37, 403, 406; positive 33–4, 37, 403; third-party 214–15, 223, 406

racism 196, 208; overt 208; modern 196; subtle 196, 208
randomisation 44, 404

reasoning 19, 125, 130, 136, 149–56, 159–60, 263, 275, 307, 370, 375, 377; abstract 263, 275; explicit 370; implicit 370; moral 149–53, 154–6, 159, 160, 398, 403; scientific 130; spatial 125; "what if" 375, 377

reflex 26–7, 398, 406; conditioned 26–7, 398; unconditioned 26, 406; see also stimulus(i)

reinforcement 29–33, 37, 116, 402; continuous 30–1; law of 29, 402; partial 30–1

reinforcers 29–34, 403; negative 33, 34, 37; positive 29–30, 32, 33, 403; primary 30, 403, 404; secondary 30, 404; see also rewards

relationships 22, 42, 76, 99, 105, 132, 170, 182, 185, 187, 189, 191, 213, 220, 253, 257–8, 263–4, 280, 282, 292, 293, 295, 298–9, 301, 305, 363, 402; awareness 257; family 185; interpersonal 76, 264, 295; mutuality 257; romantic 189, 253; semantic 363; social 263, 305; surface contact 257

replication: experimental 46, 404; genetic 213, 223

representative sample 43–4, 54, 265, 280, 404, 405; opportunity sampling 44, 403; quota sampling 44, 54, 404; random sampling 43–4, 54; time-sampling 48

responses 18, 19, 25–7, 29–30, 33, 35, 49, 90, 100, 108, 152, 155, 158, 229, 393, 397, 398, 399, 400, 403, 405; conditioned 26–7, 397, 398; dominant 158, 400; learned 26; reinforced 33; rewarded 35; unconditioned 26, 406; see also reflex

retina 324, 325, 327, 328–9, 332, 403, 405; two-dimensional image 324, 325, 327, 328

rewards 29–30, 32–5, 37, 81, 116–17, 151, 166, 167, 211, 221–3, 403, 406

"road rage" 4

Romania 187

Russia 18, 26, 123, 216, 309, 388

Russian (language) 352

Rutherford, Ernest 365

sadness 92, 94, 95, 96, 98, 206, 284, 403

schizophrenia 25, 285, 317, 318

self-concept 261, 292–306, 404; collective self 295, 305; and cultural factors 261, 293, 297–9, 300, 306; delayed self-recognition test 294, 305; and depression 295–7; development of 294–7; and gender 261, 298–9, 305, 306; independent self 298–9, 305, 401; individual self 295, 305; interdependent self 298–9, 305, 402; "looking-glass self" 293; mirror self-recognition test 294; multiple self-aspects framework (MSF) 300, 305; relational self 295, 300; self-descriptions 295; self-knowledge 297–8; social role self 300; unitary 300; see also dissociative identity disorder; memory; self-esteem

self-confidence 252, 302–3; see also self-esteem

self-esteem 190–1, 202, 253, 258, 297–9, 301–6, 404, 405; and anxiety 302, 305; and cultural factors 302–4; cultural mindset 303, 399; and depression 302, 305; false uniqueness bias 303, 400; fragile high 302; and gender 302; secure high 302; self-serving bias 302–3, 305, 405; and social dominance 304, 305; and social exclusion 301; sociometer theory 301–2

selfishness 210, 212, 214, 216–17; and third-party punishment 214–15

self-socialisation theory 168–9, 170, 174, 175; see also gender schema theory

sex 23, 44, 89, 110, 114–15; 121, 162–75, 198, 244, 253–6, 397, 398, 399, 401, 402, 405, 406; drive 23; hormones 89, 114–15, 170–2, 174, 397, 398, 406; -role stereotypes 163, 405; -typed behaviour 163, 166, 169, 399, 405; see also oestrogen; testosterone

sex drive 23; see also instinct

shame 95, 148, 153

short-term memory 20, 24, 342–5, 357–8, 359, 366–8, 397; chunks 343, 358, 398; memory span 343, 402; see also amnesia

Siegler, Robert 123, 128, 131–2, 135; see also cognitive development

similarity 222, 245, 252–3, 257–8, 286, 346; actual 252–3, 258; false

consensus effect 252–3, 258, 400; perceived 252–3, 258; and self-esteem 253, 258

Skinner, B. F. 29–30, 33, 34–5, 37, 39, 59, 88, 143; Skinner box 29, 33; see also operant conditioning

smoking 3, 10–11, 13, 32, 49–50, 84, 85, 290

social anxiety disorder (social phobia) 312, 316–22, 405; avoidance behaviour 320, 322; and environmental factors 317; and genetic factors 317, 322; interpretive bias 319, 322, 402; and life events 316–17, 322; and parental overprotectiveness 317, 322; and parental rejection 317, 322; safety behaviours 320, 322, 404; see also cognitive therapy; cognitive behavioural therapy; exposure therapy

social approach 12, 13, 177–259

social cognitive approach 288–91; self-efficacy 289–90, 392; self-regulation 290

social cognitive theory 166–8, 174, 175, 288, 291; see also social learning theory

social competence training 116; incompatible-response technique 116; time-out technique 33–4, 116, 406

social development 182–3; and attachment 182, 183; and child care 190, 192; and deprivation 184, 188; and privation 187

social facilitation 22

social factors 170–2, 200, 228, 317; and gender 170–2, 174; and prejudice 200

social identity theory/model 201–2, 239, 241

social influence 22, 53, 128, 134, 177, 227–43, 405; see also authority; conformity behaviour; crowd behaviour; group polarisation; groupthink; social power

social learning theory 107–8, 110, 166

social norms 106, 117, 405; see also norms

social perception 245–59, 405

social power 227, 232, 405

social psychology 17, 21–2, 37, 177, 228, 246

Social Readjustment Rating Scale 79; life events 79–81

social roles 237–9, 279, 292, 300, 405

somatosensation 67, 72, 405
South Africa 106, 200
Spain 234, 255
Spanish (language) 141
Spearman, Charles 24, 270
split-brain patients 68–9, 72, 405
standardised procedures 45, 46, 54
Stanford prison experiment 53, 237–9, 242, 243
stereotypes 163–7, 195–8, 203, 208, 209, 249, 311, 401, 405; "beauty-is-good" 251; changing 203–5; functions of 198, 209; gender 197; Implicit Association Test 197–8; intergroup contact theory 203–4, 209; national character 197; "unattractiveness-is-bad" 251; see also multiculturalism; prejudice
stimulus(i) 18, 19, 25–29, 30–1, 33–4, 37, 70, 99, 227, 316, 334, 336, 347, 351, 356, 358, 381, 397, 398, 400, 403, 406; aversive (unpleasant) 28, 29, 33–4, 37, 397, 403; conditioned 25–8, 316–17, 397, 398; neutral 26, 27, 37, 398; phobic 28; test 26; training 26; unconditioned 26–9, 34, 316–17, 397, 398, 400, 406; warning 34; see also positive reinforcers
Stravinsky, Igor 272
stress 57, 65, 74, 75–91, 179, 236, 274, 312–15, 322, 357, 358, 397, 402, 404, 405; causes of 79–83, 91; and coping strategies 87–8, 111, 173; definition 75; effects of 75; and illness 84–5; and immunity 84–5, 90, 91; and life events 62, 79–81, 85, 87, 89, 90, 315–16, 402; and memory 357, 358; and personality 83–4, 90; reducing 86–9; and social support 88–90, 91; stress inoculation training 86, 90; techno- 82, 90, 405; workplace 81, 82, 90; see also coping; hypothalamic-pituitary-adrenocortical (HPA) axis; sympathetic adrenal medullary (SAM) system
stressor 75–82, 85–7, 89–91
stroke 81
study skills 12, 380, 381; elaborative interrogation 390; interleaved practice 389; self-explanation 390; testing effect 389–91, 394, 395, 405
substance abuse 159, 160; see also abuse; addiction

suicide 60, 241
Sumatra 95
surprise 95, 96
survival value 37
sympathetic adrenal medullary (SAM) system 76–8, 90; adrenaline 76–8, 397; noradrenaline 77
sympathy 153
synaesthesia 388, 405

taste aversion 29, 37
television 40, 49, 108–10, 167, 217, 219, 223, 238, 346, 393; and aggression 108–10; and prosocial behaviour 217, 219, 223; see also media violence
tend-and-befriend 89, 90; and oxytocin 89
testosterone 406; and aggression 114–15, 118; and gender 170, 171, 397
Thailand 34
theory of mind 126, 132–5, 153–4, 406
therapy 9–10, 24, 32, 308, 310, 320–2, 323, 351; eclectic approach 321, 322; efficacy of 321; effectiveness of 321, 322, 323; see also behaviour therapy; cognitive behavioural therapy; cognitive therapy; drug therapy; exposure therapy; psychodynamic therapy
time-out technique 33–4, 116, 406
token economy 32, 34, 37, 406
trait anxiety 76, 284
trait approach 281, 282–9; Big Five model 281, 285–8, 291; Eysenck Personality Questionnaire (EPQ) 284; and fundamental lexical hypothesis 282–3, 286–8, 400; NEO-PI Five-Factor Inventory 286; Sixteen Personality Factor (16PF) test 283, 285, 291
transsexual(s) 115
Turkey 95, 216
twins: fraternal 24, 36, 61–2, 114, 159, 172, 181, 199, 213, 266–7, 275, 286, 315, 373–4, 399; identical 24, 36, 61–2, 114, 159, 172, 181, 199, 213, 266–7, 275, 286, 315, 317, 373–4, 402
twin studies 23, 24, 61–3, 72, 114–15, 159–60, 170, 172, 199, 218, 266–7, 315, 317, 398; and aggression 114–15;

and attachment 181; and authoritarian personality 199–200; and concordance rate 315, 398; and depression 315; and expertise 373–4; and gender 170, 172; and intelligence 24, 266–7, 268–9, 275; and moral development 159–60; and nature-nurture debate 61–3, 72; and personality 62, 286; and prosocial behaviour 218; and social anxiety disorder 317

United Kingdom 7, 10, 51, 76, 81, 106, 130, 183, 188, 216, 247, 279, 298
United States 7, 18, 76, 106, 114, 152, 183, 188, 196, 200, 216, 228, 239, 247, 279, 293, 298, 302, 354, 397; and altruistic behaviour 216

variable: confounding 43, 46, 54; controlled 43; dependent 42, 49, 54; independent 42–3, 54
video games 107, 110–13, 118, 119, 167, 217–18, 219, 223: and aggression 110–13, 118, 119; and aggressive behaviour 217; and gender 167; and prosocial behaviour 217–18, 219, 223
visual illusions 324, 332–4, 339, 406; Ames room illusion 332, 397; and expectations 332–4, 339; hollow-face illusion 334; Müller-Lyer illusion 332–4
visual perception 20, 230, 307, 324–39, 371, 402, 406; perceptual stability 338; vision-for-action system 333–4, 339; vision-for-perception system 333–4, 339; see also change blindness; depth perception; object recognition; perceptual organisation; visual illusions
visual processing 20, 325–6, 334, 338, 344, 406; brain and 20, 66, 72, 325
voluntary informed consent 47, 53
Vygotsky, Lev 123, 128–30, 134, 135, 406; see also cognitive development

Wales 10
Watson, John 18, 59, 96, 397; see also behaviourism

West, the 8; *see also* Western countries/culture/society/world

Western countries/culture/society/world 7, 8, 11, 13, 59, 87, 106, 108, 110, 163, 182, 188, 190, 196, 206, 210, 211, 252, 258, 263, 266, 268, 292, 302, 305, 401

Western, Educated, Industrialised, Rich, and Democratic (WEIRD) societies 7

working memory 343–4, 358, 359, 398, 400, 403, 406; central executive 344, 358, 398; episodic buffer 344, 358, 400; phonological loop 344, 358, 400, 403; visuo-spatial sketchpad 344, 358, 406

Wundt, Wilhelm 17–18

Zimbabwe 263

Zimbardo, Philip 53, 238–9, 241; *see also* crowd behaviour; Stanford prison experiment

Illustrations credits

Chapter 1
Page 7: Shutterstock.com. Page 9: © adoc-photos / Corbis. Page 11: Paul Maguire / Shutterstock.com.

Chapter 2
Page 31: Ingram Publishing/Thinkstock

Chapter 4
Page 67: Dorling Kindersley/Getty Images. Page 69: Shutterstock.com. Page 71: From Ali, Lifshitz & Raz (2014). Used by permission of the US National Library of Medicine.

Chapter 5
Page 78: From Hare et al., 2013. Used by permission of Elsevier. Page 80: From Sbarra et al., 2013. Used by permission of SAGE.

Chapter 6
Page 95 (left): Shutterstock.com. Page 95 (right): Bruce Yeung / Shutterstock.com. Page 97: From Nummenmaa, L., Glerean, E., Hari, R., & Hietanen, J.K. (2014). Page 100: From Winkielman, P., Berridge, K.C. & Wilbarger, J.L. (2005). Reprinted by permission of SAGE Publications. Page 101: From Gross, J.J. & Thompson, R.A. (2007). Used by permission of Guilford Press.

Chapter 7
Page 107: Reproduced by kind permission of Albert Bandura. Page 112: sundrawalex/Thinkstock.

Chapter 8
Page 123: © Farrell Grehan / Corbis. Page 124: Pinkcandy / Shutterstock.com.

Chapter 9
Page 138: Photo supplied by Professor Michael W. Eysenck. Page 139: Reproduced with permission from the International Linguistic Association. Page 145: Getty images.

Chapter 10
Page 158: From Kochanska and Kim (2014). © 2013 American Psychological Association (2014).

Chapter 11
Page 169 (left): Shutterstock.com. Page 169 (right): Shutterstock.com.

Chapter 12
Page 186: © Bernard Bisson / Sygma / Corbis via Getty Images. Page 189: paulaphoto / Shutterstock.com

Chapter 13
Page 196: © Bettmann / Corbis via Getty Images. Page 197: Image Source / Alamy. Page 207: From White et al. (2015). Reproduced with permission from APA.

Chapter 14
Page 213: Rene Jansa / Shutterstock.com. Page 219: Everett Collection Inc / Alamy. Page 221: Stock Foundry Images / Alamy.

Chapter 15
Page 233: From the film Obedience © 1968 by Stanley Milgram. Copyright © renewed 1991 by Alexandra Milgram and distributed by Penn State Media Sales. Permission granted by Alexandra Milgram. Page 240: iStock

Chapter 16
Page 246: Lisa F. Young / Shutterstock. Page 248: Fiske et al. (2007). Reproduced with permission from Elsevier. Page 251 (top left): © Rune Hellestad / Corbis. Page 251 (top right): courtyardpix / Shutterstock.com. Page 251 (bottom left): ZUMA Press, Inc. / Alamy. Page 251 (bottom right): tikona / Shutterstock.com. Page 256: sturti/iStock

Chapter 17
Page 269: From Tucker-Drob et al. (2013). Reproduced with permission from SAGE.

Chapter 19
Page 296: From Dalgleish and Werner-Seidler (2014). Reproduced with permission from Elsevier. Page 301: © Getty Images. Page 304: From Becker et al. (2014). Reproduced with permission from SAGE.

Chapter 20
Page 313: © Getty Images. Page 314: From Guo et al. (2015). Reproduced with permission from PLoS ONE.

Chapter 21
Page 328: Ale-ks/Thinkstock. Page 333: PETER ENDIG / AFP / Getty Images. Page 334: From Króliczak et al. (2006). Reprinted with permission of Elsevier. Page 335: From Rensink et al. (1997). Copyright © 1997 by SAGE. Reprinted by permission of SAGE Publications. Page 337: From Kuhn & Findlay (2010). Reprinted with permission of Taylor & Francis.

Chapter 22
Page 344: © Alan Baddeley and Graham Hitch. Page 348: Kristin Smith / Shutterstock.com. Page 356: From Jenkins et al. (2011). Reproduced with permission from Elsevier.

Chapter 23
Page 363: From Öllinger et al. (2014). Reproduced with permission from Springer. Page 369: From Moxley et al. (2012). Reproduced with permission from Elsevier. Page 371: From Melo et al. (2012). Reproduced with permission from PloS ONE.

Chapter 24
Page 390: From Roediger & Karpicke (2006). Copyright © Blackwell Publishing. Reproduced with permission. Page 392 (top): From Klein et al. (1999). Copyright © American Psychological Association. Reproduced with permission. Page 392 (bottom): From Masuda et al. (2015). Reproduced with permission from Taylor & Francis.

All cartoons by Sean Longcroft www.longcroft.net/ © Psychology Press.